DANIEL MARTIN VARISCO

Reading Orientalism

Said and the Unsaid

UNIVERSITY OF WASHINGTON PRESS

SEATTLE AND LONDON

This publication is supported in part by the Donald R. Ellegood International Publication Endowment.

University of Washington Press
PO Box 50096, Seattle, WA 98145
www.washington.edu/uwpress

Library of Congress Cataloging-in-Publication Data

Varisco, Daniel Martin.
Reading orientalism : said and the unsaid / Daniel Martin Varisco.
   p. cm. — (Publications on the Near East)
Includes bibliographical references and index.
ISBN-13: 978-0-295-98758-3 (hardback : alk. paper)
ISBN-10: 0-295-98758-8 (hardback : alk. paper)
ISBN-13: 978-0-295-98752-1 (pbk. : alk. paper)
ISBN 10: 0-295-98752-9 (pbk. : alk. paper)
1. Orientalism.   2. Said, Edward W. Orientalism.   3. Asia—Study and teaching.
4. Middle East—Study and Teaching.   5. East and West.   I. Title.
DS61.85.V37   2006
950—dc22   2007013795

Cover: Etienne Dinet, *The Snake Charmer* (detail), 1889. Oil on canvas, 176.5 × 180.4 cm. Collection of Art Gallery of New South Wales. Photo: Christopher Snee

For Jihan, caught but not trapped between multiple identities in a web not of his own devising.

The philosophers have only interpreted the world differently in various ways, the point is to change it.

—KARL MARX, *THESES ON FEUERBACH*

"The East is used up."

"It is not more used up than when Mahomet arose," said Tancred. "Weak and withering as may be the government of the Turks, it is not more feeble and enervated than that of the Greek empire and the Chosroes."

—BENJAMIN DISRAELI, *TANCRED*

Contents

Acknowledgments

"No man is an island, entire of itself," remarked John Donne in a phrase that has been haunting introductory English literature texts ever since. Neither is a book. This book evolved out of a nagging iconoclastic impulse to open the blinds of my comfortable closeting in Ivory Tower isolation. There is no viably efficient way to recall all who in some way inflected—and at times deflected—the various nuances in my perilously long narrative, but a list of the primary names is more than perfunctory in my mind. Many authors save the most thanks to last or to the recipient of the book's dedication. I prefer to up-end my beginning. One person, more than any other, has helped shape the existing contours of the ways I think, especially when I do so in an unreflexively male American manner. My wife, Najwa, colleague in the field as well as unflinching critic of virtually everything I write, has been the primary stimulus to not feel too comfortable with a particular point of view. She provides a necessary cudgel to batter my tendencies to be excessively "thick" in my description and thinly disguised in my frustration with canonized methodologies and solidified theories. The iconoclasm appears to be a rhetorical malady wired from birth.

Those who have read early drafts or responded to my queries extend across formal discipline boundaries. Among anthropologists I thank Tom Abowd, Jon Anderson, Steve Caton, Matthew Cook, Dale Eickelman, Sayed el Aswad, Andre Gingrich, Engseng Ho, Diane King, Chris Leonard, Herbert Lewis, Leif Manger, Chris Matthews, and Larry Michalak. I benefited from the comments of students in Caton's graduate anthropology seminar at Harvard and at lectures on Said at the University of London, University of Pennsylvania, and New York University. Historians, Arabists, and others include Jacques Berlinerblau, Magnus Bernhardsson, Richard Bulliet, François Charette, Fred Donner, Andrew Foster, McGuire Gibson, Peter Golden, David King, Kathy Kueny, George Makdisi, Jack Moore, Maggie Nassif, Sasha Naymarck, Laura Otis, Dagmar Riedel, Rex Smith, Marina Tolmacheva, Michel Tuchscherer, Bob Vitalis, and Patricia Welch. I thank a number of members of the Middle East Medievalist e-list and several colleagues who heard me out at Hofstra. Advice on translation clarification was gratefully received from Najwa Adra, Neil Donahue, Aykut Gürçaglar, Livnat Holtzman, Tad Krauze, and Giorgio Vercellin. With such significant help, I share the pragmatism of my friend and colleague Jacques Berlinerblau, whose Edward Said was Martin Bernal: "I do not expect to make many friends writing this volume, so let me hold on to the ones that I have now."[1] But neither do I wish to make enemies.

To the Reader

As an intellectual, I feel challenged by the theoretical inco-
herence; I feel driven to strive for an answer that, if it has not
yet attained universal validity, will at least have transcended
the evident limitations of the dichotomized past.

—WILFRED CANTWELL SMITH, *RELIGIOUS DIVERSITY*

And is it not further tribute to his triumph to see more clearly
what he was battling?

—MARÍA ROSA MENOCAL, *THE ARABIC ROLE
IN MEDIEVAL LITERARY HISTORY*[2]

You have before you two books about one book.

The one book is Edward Said's *Orientalism*, a copy of which should
preferably be read before and after you tackle my critical engagement with
this powerful text and the ongoing debate over it. More than a quarter-
century after its first publication, *Orientalism* remains a milestone in critical theory. Yet, as the years go by, it survives more as an essential source
to cite than as a polemical text in need of thorough and open-minded reading. I offer a commentary, not a new sacred text.

Of the two books here, the first is the narrative that provides a critique
of Said's Orientalism thesis. Many of the details of my argument have been
made before by a wide range of scholars, although not in one textual bundle. I add my own focus on Said's rhetoric as a persuasive device, despite
the manifest flaws in content and the important material left out of his work.
My book can be read the way you would read Said's original narrative, with
one major caveat: *Orientalism* is a forceful polemic that demands not to
be ignored, whereas *Reading Orientalism* is judicious satirical criticism
that suggests we move beyond the polemicized rhetoric of the binary
blame game.

More than any other individual scholar in recent history, Edward Said laid bare the discursive ideological undertones that have infested public and academic representation of an idealized "Orient." No one reading his *Orientalism* can fail to appreciate that much of the previous writing and lecturing about Muslims, Arabs, and stylized "Orientals" reveals more about those doing the writing than about real people in a geographical space east of Europe. The "Orient" as framed in *Orientalism* is indeed an imaginary; but so is the very Occidental (and certainly not accidental) frame that Said reduces to Orientalist discourse. Said's book stimulated a necessary and valuable debate among scholars who study the Middle East, Islam, and colonial history. Nearly three decades later, I suggest it is time to move beyond PhD cataloguing of what the West did to the East and self-unfulfilling political punditry about what real individuals in the East say they want to do to the West. Edward Said brought us a long way in this process, but the politics of polemics can only go so far, as he himself acknowledged in his later years. I prefer to reproach ongoing injustice across the colonial divide at the expense of verbose post-colonial indignation.

The second book is in the endnotes and bibliography, where all the references are mercifully archived. Here you will also find the asides and gratuitous rhetorical overkill that even the author finds too profligate for the narrative. By simply ignoring the superscripted numbers you may read the narrative for entertainment, freed of the need to verify the critical exegesis. The anal citational flow of endnotes in itself illustrates the vast number of books and articles that in one way or another draw on *Orientalism* as a text. The sheer bulk of references for a seminal book available in multiple translations is staggering. Although I could no more sample all texts on *Orientalism* than Said could examine the thousands of "Orientalist" texts published, I have tried to err on the side of redundancy.

Both of my books are intended as a reading against *Orientalism* but certainly not as a justification for past Orientalism, nor as a politicized dismissal of Edward Said, an impassioned advocate of human rights for all victims of past imperialism and present neo-colonial co-option. Said, the relentless critic, defined his intellectual role through worldly engagement with ideas that affect, and often disaffect, real people. No established theory was sacred, no argument innocent in a reality-checked world where Palestinians had their homes bulldozed, cluster bombs were dropped on Beirut suburbs, and Muslims were indiscriminately targeted as terrorists long before the fatal crashes into the Twin Towers. Among his many critics, some attacked the man and what he stood for rather than embracing the need for dialogue on critical issues that are usually in danger of being monologued to death. Those who mourn the passing of Edward Said feel diminished by the silencing of his unique voice, especially at a time when so many of the untruths he fought to expose still fuel media pundits and political operatives.

The mantra that defines the author of *Orientalism* is the speaking of truth to power. It would be absurd today to deny the pervasiveness of discursive power and ideology, particularly in Western representations of an assumed Orient. The problem, as I will argue, is that Edward Said often saw this process as unidirectional.[3] His numerous writings and interviews strongly suggest that he has the needed truth or at least the right kind of truth. In *Orientalism*, Said clothes his critical activity with the appealing moralism of a victim. He is not just an academic writing about abstract discourse, he is actively writing back against the tail of empire that "wogged" him. Caustic critique was wielded to perfection by Said, but generally with imperfection by those who attacked him. How then, in my own writing, can I avoid the time-dishonored homiletic of ad-hominizing? Is it the case, as W. J. T. Mitchell reflects, that any "guise of critical neutrality or objectivity" must drop away when dealing with Edward Said?[4] How can I, or anyone else in general agreement with the thrust of Said's overall argument, point out the flaws and fallacies in a specific text like *Orientalism* without unintended repercussions for the acceptance of those very parts agreed with?

Fortunately, I am not alone in this predicament. Among those agonizing in print over their critical differences with some of the writings of Edward Said is Aijaz Ahmad, who finally concludes: "Those of us who admire his courage and yet disagree with him on substantive issues also have to carry on our own critical pursuits."[5] Fred Halliday refers to Said as "a friend, a man of exemplary intellectual and political courage," and yet faults *Orientalism* for its many flaws.[6] Ali Behdad travels far and wide with Said's basic thesis, but departs from Said's "inadequate attention to the complexities of power relations between the orientalist and the Oriental."[7] Javed Majeed finds *Orientalism* "an indispensable starting point," but only if the shortcomings of Said's argument are "kept clearly in view."[8] Bobby Sayyid no doubt speaks for many ambivalent critics who acknowledge an intellectual debt to Said for opening up the horizons which permit a reasoned critique of Said.[9] In this vein many critics seek to "strengthen" rather than "jettison" what Said has done.[10] I count myself among this group.

Every "how" presupposes a "how not." I can think of several ways I do not want to read *Orientalism* today. First and foremost, I do not criticize the text because of who wrote it. One of the most egregious attacks on the character and work of Edward Said is Martin Kramer's loosely constructed *Ivory Towers on Sand*, in which *Orientalism* is blamed for unleashing a revolution that "has crippled Middle Eastern studies to this day," the operative day being September 11, 2001.[11] Kramer raids previous criticism of Said's thesis on Orientalism to discredit everything Said and an alleged coterie of "the lords of Middle East studies" have ever said or done. In a taunting and all too tawdry conspiracy scenario, the man who wrote *Orientalism* and *Covering Islam* is dismissed as a left-wing culprit who "delegitimized the genealogy of established scholarship,"[12] provided a "manifesto of affirmative action for Arab and Muslim scholars" that "established a negative predisposition toward American (and imported European) scholars,"[13] and fostered "the rise of antigovernment zealotry in Middle Eastern studies."[14] Said, in this scenario is indirectly—"a telling coincidence"—responsible for the Shi'ite bombing of the American University of Beirut (AUB) hospital, AUB President Malcolm Kerr's tragic assassination,[15] the taking of American hostages in Lebanon,[16] and even for foolhardily setting up Rushdie's death sentence![17] Indeed, for Kramer the real fault of Said and of the whole Middle East studies network that is said to worship the theoretical ground Said walks on is that "they" failed to anticipate militant "Islamism."

Ivory Towers on Sand is itself built on sand, much of which is kicked ungraciously into Said's face. For example, Kramer criticizes Said for failing to mention Iran in a book written and published before the Iranian revolution, and then his *Covering Islam*, devoted to that very revolution, is characterized as an attempt to "cover the gaping hole."[18] The Columbia professor who received a quintessential humanist training is lumpenproletariated with a generation of radicals "summarized in three words: resistance, revolution, liberation."[19] Said is branded by Kramer as the patron saint of "an entire generation of leftist scholars nurtured on radical commitments" without even a mention that Said berated the left, especially Marxist critics, left and right.[20] Blaming the Palestinian, however, is only prelude to Kramer's broader goal of degrading a large number of the Middle East scholarly cohort as co-whores in a Saidian conspiracy far more contrived than Said's polemical trashing of Orientalists. Kramer admits that even before *Orientalism* the old guard in Middle East studies failed to predict Palestinian resistance, the Lebanese civil war, the political rise of the right wing in Israel, and the collapse of the Shah, but then he turns around and says that everyone who followed Said also failed to predict current events involving Islam and the Middle East.[21] Kramer, showing off his narrowly focused political-scientism, seems to think that scholars who specialize in Islam and Middle Eastern history and culture live only to make political statements and to consult, or wish they could, for nefarious government agencies. His hindsight criticism fails to consider that perhaps all were blindsided. Kramer's unseemly screed would be laughable were it not for the favorable reception it received from the neocon clique that engineered the wars against Taliban Afghanistan and Saddam Hussein's Iraq.

Attacks on Edward Said from ardent supporters of Israel are to be expected, but Said also takes heat from fellow "Oriental" intellectuals in exile. A particularly vehement rejection of *Orientalism* comes from Kanan Makiya, an Iraqi whose *Republic of Fear*, a methodical critique of Saddam Hussein, gained notoriety after the first Gulf War. Makiya argues that Said's attack on Orientalism is "premised on the morally wrong idea that the West is to be blamed in the here-and-now for its long nefarious history of association with the Middle East. Thus it unwittingly deflected the real problems of the Middle East at the same time as it contributed more bitterness to the armory of young impressionable Arabs when there was already far too much of that around."[22] Said's alleged failure to address political alternatives is the primary cause of concern. "Real" Arabs disappear after the first page of *Orientalism*, Makiya points out, except for those Orientalized lackeys Said cites near the end of his narrative. Intellectuals such as Said, who generate ideas that do not offer an alternative, are as accountable for the moral collapse of progressive political action and the rise of dogmatic religionists as are the tyrants, Makiya concludes.[23]

Makiya's secular stance is paralleled by that of Ziauddin Sardar, a Muslim critic who questions the fundamental credentials of Said, a non-Muslim secular humanist, to speak on behalf of Islam. Sardar argues that in Said's world "there is no place for Islam or Muslims to exist by their own definition."[24] Sardar further insists that Said wants the native Muslim to be passive and mute because he does not want Muslims to represent themselves.[25] Indeed, Said's secular humanism is portrayed by Sardar as an echo of Salman Rushdie, thus uniting a novel polemic with a polemical novel. Sardar has read much of the major criticism of Said, but seems to reject *Orientalism* primarily because of Said's limited knowledge of previous resistance to Western bias, especially by Muslims. The bottom line is that "Said is certainly not raising any new questions; neither is he providing a critique more profound or more thorough than his predecessors."[26] Ben Jelloun, another Muslim critic of Said, observes that the average Muslim is no more fascinated by Said's secularism than Western secularists are by Islamic fundamentalism.[27] Said's "excessive familiarity with the most arcane and inaccessible philosophical and literary traditions of the West" makes him appear "unsettlingly unreliable to many non-Westernized Muslims," suggests Anouar Majid.[28] The author of the polemic *Orientalism* is himself polemicized from all sides.

It is time that the issues raised in *Orientalism* move beyond a referendum on Edward Said. My aim here is to move, even if only to nudge, the debate beyond polemical stalemate, at least in scholarly venues. Dogma of any sort and from any direction deserves to be challenged and aired out in lively discussion, but there is no single kind of truth that effectively speaks to worldly power. I declare my own operational truths from the start. Truth with a capital T does not exist for anyone. Facts do not speak for themselves, and I doubt that most credible scholars of the recent past ever assumed that they did. Yes, the Orient was imagined by the West. Logically, the West has also imagined itself in the process. The real Orient has also created imaginaries subsumed under its discourse on the West, just as it (rather, many of its many constituent parts) defines itself against an imperially minded history of recent commercial conquest and political contest. We need to think outside the binary that binds us to us-versus-them-ism.

One book does not define a man; nor should its faults take away from his justly deserved stature as a literary and cultural critic. Edward Said's identity as a Palestinian Arab-American permeates his written work just as it guided his political activism. *Orientalism* was only the opening salvo in a sequence of controversial critical essays and books by a prolific public intellectual. It is clear that Said's persuasive support for Palestinian rights led to his being branded unfavorably and unfairly a "professor of terror." I intend to show why I think Said is at times prone to error, but I categorically reject the politically motivated ad hominem diatribe that ridicules Said because of where he was born, how he chooses to align himself politically, and how many pebbles he once tossed unphotogenically at a border fence inside Lebanese territory. His unflinching support of humanism in the academic minefields of nihilistic unconstructivism is to be admired. His courageous stand against widespread anti-Arab bias in the United States is to be commended.[29]

I happen to agree with most of Said's political positions on the real Orient. I do not wish to add fuel to the polemical fire just because it is easy or past time to do so. Nor do I see myself as a critico-commander launching "an exchange of blind charges and counter charges."[30] As Mustapha Marrouchi warns, much of Said's wide-ranging corpus can be "the fodder for countless deconstruction."[31] And as Bryan Turner predicts, "with a canvas so broad and diverse, there is much with which to disagree and question."[32] But I can no more return to *Orientalism* in time and innocence than I can undo the aging that accompanies all growth. The key point here is neither Said's politics nor his intellectual legacy, but what to do with *Orientalism* as a polemical text that is not about to quietly disappear from bookstores and academic reading lists.

Reading Orientalism

Said and the Unsaid

Introduction

I

> Facing an awesome mountain of detail, the critic's mind becomes a confident David going straight for the vulnerable spot on Goliath's forehead. The critic cuts out a patch in the detail as a way of constraining the vast body of which it is a part, and then he focuses exclusively on that patch. Emotionally he asserts his mind's undoubted sway over what seems to be a totally resisting mass of detail; morally he demonstrates his right to control it because he has a victorious tool, proven in the encounter.
>
> —EDWARD SAID, *BEGINNINGS: INTENTION AND METHOD*[1]

Goliath, for the critic Edward Said, was Orientalism, the first target of his successive critiques of Western discourse about the Orient, Islam, and Palestinians. By most accounts the rhetorical barbs in his *Orientalism* brought the giant down to earth, knocked the wind out of a passing generation of academically enshrined windbags, and inaugurated a new intellectual integrity for writ[h]ing against empire. As Gyan Prakash politely phrases it, "*Orientalism* came as a breath of fresh air to many, but it also left others gasping for breath."[2] For all its innovative force and in spite of its acknowledged flaws, this single volume has been the subject of more debate and citation than any other text in and about the broad field once proudly ignored as Oriental studies. In an address to the Society for Asian Studies, Wendy Doniger reflected that Said's book "changed our way of thinking forever."[3] Those who have lauded the audacity of Said, a Western-educated Arab-American taking on the established Euro-American elite, still sing his praises; those who felt the blows have yet to put the ghost of their perceived free fall to rest. Said, however, has long since taken his place in the post-colonial canon of critical acclaim.

Because *Orientalism* has been so widely read, it has generated a great deal of force in the breaking of intellectual winds over late-twentieth-century postmodern theoretical drift. It should go without saying that *Orientalism* is one of the most oft-quoted texts across the various disciplines engaged in studying the Middle East or Islam—a.k.a. the Orient in the Saidian sense.[4] Reviews, journal articles, book chapters, books, conference papers, debate forums, guest lectures, newspaper columns, interviews on radio and television, documentaries, websites: for more than two decades Edward Said was visible as America's intellectual everyman. Entire symposia have been devoted to *Orientalism*'s claims, including an emotional public duel between Edward Said and historian Bernard Lewis, both with seconds, at the annual convention of the Middle East Studies Association (MESA) in 1986. Witnessed by some 3,000 people, including me, this event lived up to its billing by some unknown wit as the "shoot-out at the MESA corral."[5] A year later Said was invited to participate in a panel on his work at the annual meeting of the American Anthropological Association, my disciplinary home base.[6] Said's ascension to the top of his art was established with his election as President of the Modern Language Association of America in 1998, the same year he received an honorary award from MESA. In 1999 he became the first recipient of the Dutch Spinoza Prize in honor of his independent secular scholarship. In 2001 he was granted a lifetime achievement award by the Lannan Foundation. Indeed, the decade of the 1990s witnessed a virtual cottage industry of literary and post-colonial studies devoted to what can justifiably be classified as a new genre of Saidiana.[7]

There are texts that recede into oblivion and there are texts that are more than *texts*; *Orientalism* is decidedly one of the latter, serving as a pretentious pretext for much of critical literary and post-colonial studies in the past two decades. Said contributed a needed corrective at a time when establishment discourse-as-usual was being challenged in American intellectual circles. As a newly elited member of the academy, he wrote toe-to-toe—even as some took his snub for a stub—with those of the old guard who had made a career over and out of his natal East. Endnote for endnote, citation for citation, *Orientalism* initiated a blistering counter to the blunder and bluster of the establishment canon. More than any other critique, this one made analytical innocence impossible.[8] "After Said," notes

Thomas Greene in an early review, "it will be harder for scholars in even the most recondite disciplines to blind themselves to the political implications of their working principles."[9] "A tornado of protest was aroused," asserts Magdi Wahba, "and the discourse of academic orientalism was never to be the same again, even after the dust had settled."[10] The renowned French scholar Maxime Rodinson describes the book's "great merit" as shaking the "self-satisfaction of many Orientalists," a welcome appeal to stop seeing their ideas as "a natural, unprejudiced conclusion of the facts, studied without any presupposition."[11] Mustafa Marrouchi magnifies the metaphor to a "stone thrown through the window glass of the West."[12] This was a book that had to be written. We can hardly condemn the author for writing it.

The story that had to be told was that of a generic Western complicity throughout at least two centuries of virtually unimpeded imperial ambition and colonial expansion in all directions. By the 1970s most of Europe's remaining colonies had been freed in name, although not necessarily in realpolitik: In the cold spell of a post–World War II climate that sharpened a global opposition between Capitalist West and Communist East, the United States had become by stealth and wealth the neo-colonial superpower that needed to be told a range of disturbing truths. Edward Said was not the first theoretical other to say how destructive colonialism had been. But his was the first authorizingly Western academic voice to advocate convincingly "the idea that colonialism operated not only as a form of military rule but also simultaneously as a *discourse* of domination," as Robert Young phrases it.[13] Said targeted the obsequious objectivity of much academic scholarship, the smug above-it-all-ness of expertise in one particularly innocent-looking field of study. In biblical terms, this Columbia University humanities professor strode in through the front door of the guild, knocked over the props of positivist indifference, and screamed at the mentality-changers, "Get out of my forefathers' house!"

Said pens a portrait of despotic Orientalism, the malformed creation of Western romantics, masochistic explorers, ardent imperialists, and text-driven university dons. It is necessary to stress that in many ways Said hardly scratched the surface of the vast sewerage of racist and ethnocentrist writing, art, and cinema that for so long has severed an imaginary East from the dominating West.[14] There is probably no epithet that has not been hurled with hypercritical aforethought at Orientals. From "rock ape" to "wog," generations of visibly non-Western men and women have been despised, debased, and dehumanized. In particular, almost anything that Muslims would consider holy has at one time or another been profaned by Western writers. Perhaps the frustrated worldwide Muslim anger at Salman Rushdie's *The Satanic Verses* was emetic justice for centuries of vicious and malicious verbal abuse from the West, where this controversial best seller incubated. Most significantly, unjust and atrocity-burdened wars were waged and callous crimes committed with virtual impunity on "real" Orientals. I do not fault *Orientalism* for being too hard on the checkered history of European imperialist [wreck]resentation and colonialist penetration into the Near, Middle, and Far[thest] parts of the East.[15] I offer my critique as a corrective to the factual errors and polemical airs of *Orientalism*, not as a defense of Orientalism in any of the demonstrable ways it—whatever *it* was or is—played a discursive role in the sins of Western history.

"The basic trouble," comments historian Richard Bayly Winder, "is that *Orientalism* is a polemic, in a good cause, but a polemic."[16] Critics from across disciplines have found the text to be "written in anger,"[17] whether out of "unrelieved vehemence"[18] or euphemistically in a "provocative *J'accuse!* tone."[19] Said argues that his entry into the subject was out of conviction as a disheartened Arab Palestinian in the West. To the extent that Orientalist discourse obliterates him as a human being, exposing the "nexus of knowledge and power creating 'the Oriental'" is not for him "an exclusively academic matter."[20] In the process of writing against the grain of scholarly discourse, Said does not abide by the rules of gentleman[dated] disagreement. Anthropologist Akbar Ahmed laments that Said's "ritual slaying of the elders," including Bernard Lewis, became "too noisy and too bloody."[21] It is one thing to stick a knife in the heart of Orientalist bias, but quite another to twist it around and bloody the whole establishment in a fit of intellectualized rage.

Said the maverick activist begs to be polemicized from the start.[22] His style of choice is emblematic in the harbinger epigraphs chosen for *Orientalism*'s opening. The first is Karl Marx's "They cannot represent themselves; they must be represented." The second is Benjamin Disraeli's laconic "The East is a career." In a Jungian sense both statements serve as descriptive of the author's own agenda. Beginning with Disraeli's quote, those who made the East a career launched Said's career. If Disraeli's East could become "something bright young Westerners would find to be an all-consuming passion,"[23] how true it could be that representing the phenomenon of Orientalism soon became Said's own all-consuming passion. His *Orientalism* encouraged a publication-driven growth industry for a variety of newly activated intellectual perspectives fed up with the conservative political realities of the West's impishly imperial ethos. But why must it be assumed that real Orientals had previously been incapable of representing themselves, even if not in Marx's original political sense?

As a scholar, Edward Said has a tenaciously textual attitude, despite grave misgivings about the canon-conscious limitations of his chosen field of literary criticism. He has hardly been shy about this.[24] As a literary critic, Said takes as his starting point for opposing the hege-moniker of imperialist culture the explanation of human intention through texts. He rightfully scorns fellow critics who stop short at reading and writing, but he paradoxically avoids those disciplines that start by actually studying human behavior. The critical theory of anthropologists, sociologists, and psychologists appears in *Orientalism* only as textually deficient. Sociologist Bryan Turner responds to the Saidian focus on textualism by calling it "a vicious solipsism in which there can be no distinction between fictional writing and social reality."[25] Discourse, in the textualized sense conventionalized via Michel Foucault, replaces the pan-human experience of social practice. It is as though Said is unable to imagine human interaction in a world not dominated by texts, which explains in part why he privileges the tools he uses in understanding literary texts for explaining cultural behavior in any context.

As a text, *Orientalism* has been colonized in so many ways by so many commentators that it is impossible to step back to its point of public origin. There can be no single meta-reading of this text. "For in all sorts of ways," writes Said in his 1994 afterword, "*Orientalism* now seems to me a collective book that I think supersedes me as its author more than I could have expected when I wrote it"[26] As anthropologist Nicholas Thomas cautions, "The *Orientalism* often argued about may thus be rather different from the book that Said wrote."[27] Negative critics tend to read it contrapuntally, focusing on what is excluded and not directly articulated in this history of Orientalist discourse. The most positive readings tend to expand Said's tentative ideas to gospel truisms that serve as rallying cries for all sorts of writing back at the establishment. For example, who wrote "The panoptic eye of the imperialist, masquerading as ethnographer or Orientalist, asserts the hegemony of the dominant culture by the right it assumes of positioning the other in a field of sight that is also and always a field of power"?[28] Not Said, as it happens, but it certainly sounds like the epitome of Said's epistemic rendering of Orientalist discourse. The mantra that Western imperialists hegemonically dominate the other easily becomes the lowest common terminator of Said's more humanistically nuanced rhetoric. Thus, the road back to *Orientalism* is mined with a range of readings that guarantee it will be a bumpy ride.

Rereading Said's original text would lack relevance were it not to be read through its many readers. Who were the originally intended readers? In an interview given while he was writing the book, Said suggested several audiences:

"I am an Oriental writing back at the Orientalists, who for
so long have thrived upon our silence. I am also writing
to them, as it were, by dismantling the structure of their
discipline, showing its metahistorical, institutional, anti-
empirical, and ideological biases. Finally, I feel myself to
be writing for compatriots and colleagues about matters
of common concern."[29]

Explicit in this remark is a distinction between the Orientalists who must
be written back to in order to break the silence and those readers whom
Said pragmatically saw as potentially more sympathetic—in the main, the
"literary colleagues" he engaged with professionally.[30] It would be foolish
to assume that Said, the worldly author, had only a narrow audience in
mind; this is clearly a net cast for the "general reader," despite the dense
prose and large number of endnotes.[31] Yet the author had reason to suspect that those who most needed to heed the message, the overt and shadow
targets of his polemic, would reject his thesis. Said implies that he was not
writing to convince members of the guild as a "*principal* intended audience"
but rather "to make other humanists aware of one field's particular procedures and genealogy."[32] In this respect, the intent is spun as setting the
record straight rather than as trying to evangelize the errant. The historical record of what Said labels "Orientalism" was certainly not set straight
in *Orientalism* by established historiographic measures. Said's selective,
idiosyncratic, and polemical contextualization of Orientalist discourse
distorts individuals, institutions, and events. Said wrote back in fury, a
scorched-earth form of literary criticism. There is a need to sift through the
ashes. Fortunately, many of the errant saw the light, despite the rhetorical damage.

A common misperception in most general readings of *Orientalism* is
the assumption that the nemesis for Said is the old-fashioned academic
Orientalist who interprets the reality of Orientals through fancifully biased
images derived from texts. Such Orientalists, Said asserts in the afterword
to his second edition, were "not unexpectedly, the most exercised and
vociferous in responding to my book." Yet, scholars and students firmly
enshrined in the field once styled Oriental studies have in the main
accepted Said's exposure of the biases and methodological dogmatics that
for so long had dominated academic and popular treatment of most things
Oriental. Despite the flaws in presenting his thesis, Said's stated hope that
his book "stimulates a new kind of dealing with the Orient," accomplished
just that.[33] Orientalists, in that broad Saidian sense that includes virtually
anyone who studies the Orient, became a necessary audience and have

remained so to this day. The main resistance to Said has come from the modern-day American Middle East expert who creates or justifies policy towards the Arabs and "terrorism," most notably over the issue of Palestinian rights. Oriental history, as told and retold by historian Bernard Lewis, would not be of interest for Said were it not for this prominent scholar's "pro-Zionism, anti-Arab nationalism, and strident cold Warriorism."[34] Thus, the most virulent critics of Said have not been students of Oriental history and languages—the ubiquitous Lewis notwithstanding—but political scientists and protagonists in present-day Arab-Israeli politics.[35] It is no accident that the longest chapter in Said's narrative is "Orientalism Now."

There are complex reasons for the continuing resonance of this single book. Literary and post-colonial studies focused on *Orientalism* as a kind of touchstone, at times a launch pad for legitimizing their own posturing against a colonialism that wavers between neo- and post-. If you read widely in critical texts and literary journals of the last two decades, you will encounter a biblio[porno]graphic form of citational involution at work.[36] Citing Said almost became a kind of initiatory *bismillah* in literary texts about colonial discourse. In pyramid schematics Said was soon joined by Homi Bhabha and Gayatri Spivak in a kind of post-colonial trinity, three elevated subalterns on the vanguard of a newly posted and critically lit movement.[37] These founders found themselves delivering papers at the same conferences, writing about and to each other, seeing their seminal writings recirculated in college readers,[38] commenting on each other and common enemies, even providing blurbs for each other's book jackets.[39] As Henry Louis Gates wryly observes, the chain of transmitters can be reduced to "Spivak's critique of Parry's critique of JanMohamed's critique of Bhabha's critique of Said's critique of colonial discourse."[40] Worldliness and wordiness without end.

Is *Orientalism* the text that launched post-colonial studies?[41] Many scholars assume so, citing *Orientalism* as "one of the key sources, if not the key source, of inspiration for much later work by others in the fields of literary, critical and cultural theory, especially in post colonial studies,"[42] "the catalyst and reference point for postcolonialism,"[43] or simply "the essential book of post-colonial theory."[44] Ali Behdad applauds Said as the "founder of postcolonial discursivity" in a Foucauldian sense.[45] Despite other approaches drawing on the two most prominent postmodern Jacques—Lacan and Derrida—Said is said by Aijaz Ahmad to be the "central figure" influencing the study of post-coloniality in literary studies.[46] At one extreme are those post-colonials who claim that the impact of *Orientalism* cannot be exaggerated.[47] At the other it is argued that the text's basic failure to see beyond the Orient keeps it from serving as the "theoretical charter" for colonial cultural studies.[48] To regard this one text as the beginning would be to overlook a variety of earlier critics, such as Chinua Achebe and Frantz Fanon, from the assumed post-colonial world.[49] Ironically, Said himself thought that the word "post-colonialism" is a misnomer, because neo-colonialism is ongoing.[50]

In any event, Gyan Prakash is certainly on target in noting that *Orientalism* "opened the floodgate of postcolonial criticism."[51] The metaphor is poignant. As Mark Crinson contends, "Other recent works in what is now called post-colonial theory have sometimes tended to apply Said's methods wantonly as a fixed set of responses to far-flung and very disparate colonial situations or to essentialize the participants in what sometimes appears to be a colonial psychodrama."[52] *Orientalism* as a text has come to serve as far more than a look at one discursive field and an exposé of one geographical imaginary. For the foreseeable future it will continue to be read for at least two simple reasons: because it is well established as seminal, and because it *can* be read in so many different languages. Why was this book so widely read and so passionately read into? Certainly it is not due to overt readability; Saidian prose is not for the speed reader or literary novice. As one of the book's earliest reviewers complained, "underneath the self-posturing verbiage there is an acute analytical mind at work, but the book, unfortunately, is almost impossible to read."[53] *Orientalism* is thus the kind of narrative that is so over-articulate by design that it risks being dismissed as ultimately [dis]articulated and out of joint. At the same time it was Said's eloquent "reach of erudition" that was so fresh and innovative.[54] His verbal indignation, for the most part latent in his rhetoric, was manifest through bon mot rather than mala fide. Paradoxically, this is a text that engages even the reader it enrages.

I find it remarkable that despite hundreds of references that discuss *Orientalism* in some way, there has yet to be a systematic survey or summation of what has been said about it across the board.[55] There has been a continuous stream of dispersed commentary from such eminently [ex]citable critics as Aijaz Ahmad, Homi Bhabha, James Clifford, Henry Louis Gates, and Gayatri Spivak, but most of these are fellow literary scholars rather than individuals trained in what Said would label a discipline dominated by Orientalist discourse.[56] For many contemporary readers, Said's definition of Orientalism has become *the* definition, the authorized version for the euphemistically titled counter-establishment. Accepting Said's accounting for Orientalism has become, as J. J. Clarke notes, "almost a fashionable orthodoxy amongst scholars."[57] For Moustapha Marrouchi, *Orientalism* "is sure to remain part of the canon of modern Third World literature so long as it requires a canon."[58] The ultimate test of its sustainability, that is, canonicity, is that much of the thoughtful critique of the text has been forgotten, summarily brushed aside, or conveniently ignored.

Orientalism has indeed passed the critical lit-mus test. In a recent didactive compendium, *Key Concepts in Post-Colonial Studies*, the entry for "Orientalism" is simply a paraphrase of Said's thesis with no acknowledgment of any critique.[59] Post-colonial writers and cultural critics routinely begin long-winding, and generally long-winded, statements with "Edward Said established some time ago . . . "[60] It is apparently enough for some that Edward Said said it, wrote it, and therefore established it. Ironically, as Saree Makdisi observes, what Said proposed as "a provocation and an intervention, a beginning," has now become an "ending," something so proven that "it requires little further effort."[61] I suggest that returning to Said's proofs is well worth the effort.

II

> Since those early responses, a vast, interdisciplinary palimpset has mushroomed around the book; one could go so far as to argue that, for good or ill, *Orientalism* has given rise to an entirely new discourse—one which goes far beyond what is known as postcolonial theory.
>
> —ABDIRAHMAN HUSSEIN, *EDWARD SAID: CRITICISM AND SOCIETY*

Orientalism first appeared in 1978 as a high-end, mass-market offering of Pantheon Books, a division of the major publish-for-profit conglomerate Random House. At last count, translations have appeared in some thirty-six languages, including Arabic, Catalan, Chinese, French, German, Greek, Hebrew, Italian, Japanese, Norwegian, Persian, Polish, Portuguese, Russian, Serbo-Croatian, Spanish, Swedish, Turkish, and Vietnamese.[62] Although this is nowhere near the mounting universality of missionaried rendering of the *Gospel of John* into rapidly disappearing native tongues, this single book of literary criticism is available in its entirety in almost as many languages as is Darwin's *On the Origin of Species*. Regardless of those copies bought only to sit unread on dusty shelves, the potential readership alone separates *Orientalism* from any other critical text written in any language in the latter part of the last century. Barring a similar distribution of any systematic critique, including my own, the arguments made by Said will continue to be taken as a kind of traveling, godfatherly truth and be adapted to attack new kinds of Orientalisms wherever those Orients can be imagined.

In preparing this critique I have looked at commentary on Said's *Ori-*

entalism from "guilded" practitioners of anthropology, American studies, Arabic studies, archaeology, art history, biblical studies, economics, cultural studies, English literature, film studies, gender studies, geography, intellectual history, literary criticism, medieval history, philosophy, political science, religious studies, psychology, sociology, *et disciplinalia*.[63] The various orientations of these critics, pro and con, find representation in activists, anarchists, feminists, evangelicals, Foucauldians and anti-Foucauldians, ghost writers, Islamists, journalists, Marxists, positivists, post-colonialists and postcolonialists, postmodernists and subalterns. In the humanities and social sciences it might be easier to list the kinds of scholars who have not read, or at least not heard of, Edward Said's *Orientalism*. Yet while it is true that *Orientalism* is available in many languages and is frequently cited in academic circles around the globe, there has been little direct application of Said's specific methods without major caveats.[64]

Among the accrued accolades and acerbic accusations in hundreds of articles and books commenting on *Orientalism*, there is wide variation in what readers think Said is saying as well as in what they would rather have him say. One of the most operative words in my reading through reviews and commentaries is how "provocative" *Orientalism* is.[65] Insofar as "provocateur" connotes an activist role that Said relished in print and interview, it is perhaps the best common denominator for all his diverse critics as well. In its adjectival form, *provocative* captures the spirit of Said's carefully crafted rhetoric. This is a book that is intentionally annoying, a polemic that is powerful precisely because it so irritates the reader, an argument that must provoke a response of some kind. Whether you find *Orientalism* unrelenting, unfair, or simply quite unreadable, there is no escaping the fact that this book stimulated the unraveling of overt misrepresentation of the Orient.

Review and commentary phrases tease out with tabloid precision what this book has been capable of meaning. We can start with the poignant tributes in the book's original paperback packaging: "powerful and disturbing," "a stimulating, elegant yet pugnacious essay," "an important book."[66] With the commercial positioning of op-ed-page relativism, such blurbs are inviting regardless of whether you agree or disagree with what Said is saying. Consider your own reaction, whether or not you have read *Orientalism* recently or at all, to the following out-of-context text bites from reviews and commentaries: "ambitious,"[67] "angry,"[68] "audacious,"[69] "bold message,"[70] "bombshell,"[71] "breakthrough,"[72] "brilliant,"[73] "broadside,"[74] "celebrated,"[75] "challenging and troubling,"[76] "critical, though necessarily redundant, inventory of clichés,"[77] "dazzling attack,"[78] "deconstructive reflection,"[79] "deeply flawed and deeply disturbing,"[80] "une diatribe violente,"[81] "dyslogistic signifier,"[82] "empowering,"[83] "enabling,"[84] "enormously intellectually challenging,"[85] "erudite, yet somewhat belabored,"[86] "exemplary model of worldly criticism,"[87] "grand fracas,"[88] "grands récits,"[89] "groundbreaking,"[90] "harsh interpretation,"[91] "high scholarship,"[92] "important,"[93] "influential,"[94] "interesting if debatable thesis,"[95] "jeremiad,"[96] "justly famous study,"[97] "landmark work,"[98] "lasting theoretical imprint,"[99] "magisterial,"[100] "masterful,"[101] "meditation,"[102] "milestone text,"[103] "monumental,"[104] "pathbreaking,"[105] "phenomenology,"[106] "pioneering,"[107] "political fiction that is at the same time an act of scholarly violence,"[108] "powerful critique,"[109] "prescient,"[110] "pugnacious yet elegant,"[111] "revelatory,"[112] "scathing,"[113] "seminal critique,"[114] "semiotic of 'Orientalist' power,"[115] "sprawling and obsessive,"[116] "stimulating,"[117] "superficial and politically motivated,"[118] "sweeping and passionate indictment,"[119] "totemic,"[120] "tour de force,"[121] and "watershed."[122] The adjectives are sometimes both compounded and confounded, as in Jeffrey Myers's schizo-comment that Said's book "is learned, elegantly written, fascinating, angry, provocative; but it is also formless, repetitive, irritating, muddled, and wrongheaded."[123] It is, in perilously Pauline terms, a text that can "please all men in all things," or at least displease.[124]

At times it is hard to tell if a reviewer is admiring or envious, seriously pulling punches or facetiously pulling our legs. Was a book that "jolted academe and reverberated through the social sciences and humanities"[125] enlightening, or a damaging lightning strike? Is the "enormous impact"[126] more that of a crashing meteor or that of a cure for cancer? Should the emphasis in a "succès de scandale"[127] be on the success or the scandal? Indeed, is it politically and desirably correct for a non-Sicilian critic to be known as the "godfather of post-colonial literature"?[128] And what un-secular irony comes from David Gordon's offhand remark that *Orientalism* is "a work that in certain circles has been almost Koranic in its prestige"?[129]

After reviewing the reviews of *Orientalism* it is not surprising that Said later noted that his book "almost in a Borgesian way, has become several different books."[130] Some critics realized that there was more than one text from the start. "Inside this prolix and ill-considered book," suggests Mahmoud Manzalaoui, "there is a slimmer and genuinely excellent one trying to get out."[131] Manzalaoui was not making the banal observation that a critic invariably sees a different book than does the author; in this case the polemics marred the author's rightful passion. There are clearly many possible and now entrenched readings of the original text, which remains unrevised. Throughout the early reviews and continuous commentary I sense a critical double vision, as though Said had created the literary equivalent of an optical illusion in which one person admires a beautiful Victorian woman and another sees a human skull. This is perhaps not unusual for an author who uses his impeccable establishment credentials to unsettle that very establishment.

Regardless of what Said said, the fact that he was able to say it and reach a wide audience served as a model for many up-and-raising voices in the narrow confines and ivy[stone]walled halls of academe. For more than two decades, many English-writing scholars have included testimonials about the stimulus of Said's *Orientalism* in their own texts even when there was cause for disagreement, however muted. As Robert Young suggests, *Orientalism* "enabled those from minorities, whether categorized as racial, sexual, social, or economic, to stake their critical work in relation to their own political positioning rather than feel obliged to assume the transcendent values of the dominant discourse of criticism."[132] Said's "pioneering oeuvre" provided Homi Bhabha with "a critical terrain and an intellectual project."[133] *Orientalism* is idolized by Gayatri Spivak as having "blossomed into a garden where the marginal can speak and be spoken."[134] One admirer goes so far as to credit Said's critical analysis of colonialist rhetoric as "foundational for **multiculturalism** in the United States."[135] Partha Chatterjee discovered that *Orientalism* "talked of things I felt I had known all along but had never found the language to formulate with clarity."[136] From similar subaltern space, Fakrul Alam confides that Said's text "taught me the inadequacy of my own commitment to criticism and the insufficiency of my stance as a post-colonial intellectual."[137] Even some medievalists were taken with Said's book; Kathleen Biddick recalls

> the exhilaration of first encounter in the early 1980's, when a colleague chose it for our reading group. *Orientalism* exposed different cultural and institutional ways in which Europeans fabricated objects of study by assigning and hierarchizing boundaries between East and West and unmasked "Europe" as a "theatrical stage whose audience, manager, and actors are for Europe" (p. 71). Its critique of imaginary racialized geographies hooked me.[138]

The intensity of the [sub]alternate panning and praising of this text leads Gyan Prakash to characterize *Orientalism* as iconoclastic, seditious, and subversive, breathing insurgency. "Said's transgression of disciplinary boundaries to force the recognition of Orientalism as a discipline of power," argues Prakash, "has become a model for navigating between literature, history, philosophy, and anthropology, and has gone on to inspire studies in such new fields as cultural, feminist, and postcolonial studies."[139]

But what kind of model? Much of Said's polemic is navi-negating, passing by but never really landing squarely in specific disciplines other than his own.[140] When does the novelty of violating disciplinary borders, challenging authorial intentions and discursive regimes, and producing a profound uncertainty about all methodological rules wear off? "Reading it sympathetically though interrogating it rigorously," Prakash continues, "scholars find *Orientalism* a rich resource for asking fundamental questions about the relationship between discipline and desire, history and fantasy, discourse and its enunciation."[141] But why only for the asking of questions, unless *Orientalism* has little to offer in the way of practical solutions?

Orientalism has the remarkable star quality of a seminal book that many of its readers have probably not read all the way through. Said's short and poignant introduction is required reading in graduate courses across several disciplines, but how many of those inspired or turned off by this excerpt actually read the book cover to cover, including endnotes? Graham Huggan observes that "one of the most interesting aspects of the continuing saga of (not) reading *Orientalism* has been a tendency to bypass the text, either in the interests of declaring a political allegiance or in the more disguised attempt to make the book symptomatic for the entirety of its author's work."[142] Most of the early reviews focused on those parts of the book the reviewer knew something about. Only a few of these reviewers took time to actually read the sources cited, and at times misquoted, by Said. Consider the irony that one of the paramount examples of twentieth century literary criticism is so rarely read as a whole text.

One of the more consistent critical refrains about *Orientalism* is that its author is frequently inconsistent, both in theory and execution. In an early review Robert Irwin characterizes the text as "full of ambiguity and self-contradiction," so much so that he gets "hopelessly lost" trying to sort through the different styles of Orientalist discourse.[143] Ulrike Freitag refers to Said's "sometimes contradictory and often less than systematic and methodologically rigorous approach."[144] Said's response to critics is that he wrote a "partisan book" rather than a "theoretical machine," as though this is a meaningful pairing.[145] James Brown disputes Said's belated self-servism that *Orientalism* was designed to be inconsistent, since the book articulates no "rationale for such theoretical inconsistency."[146] As John Whalen-Bridge concludes, "To believe that he created theoretical inconsistency . . . is asking a great deal from the reader."[147] One of the major inconsistencies is Said's ambiguous fence-straddling between old-style humanism and post-structuralist criticism. Grewgious, for example, first chides Said for a "theoretical inconsistency" that produces confusion, but then concludes that "Said's recalcitrant humanism is very much *Oriental-*

ism's value."[148] This is echoed by Gyan Prakash, who claims "But even as *Orientalism* embraces the straitjacket of humanism, its restless energy and sheer inventiveness offers [*sic*] stunning insights."[149] In all of this the definition of humanism is blurred beyond recognition. Ashcroft and Ahluwalia aver that Said is not an out-of-fashion humanist: "Thus, Said's humanism is not Enlightenment so much as oppositional, not homogenising so much as liberational, not theoretical so much as 'worldly.'"[150] Have these modern philosophers not read their Hume?

Said has no qualms about being a secular humanist, adding that "there is nothing I disagree with in the broad, humanistic tradition."[151] Said's "secular divination," as W. J. T. Mitchell styles it, assumes that religion is always the enemy of criticism, because it "furnishes us with systems of authority and with canons of order whose regular effect is either to compel subservience or to gain adherents."[152] Drawing on Giambattista Vico as an enlightened liberator from a "priest-ridden age," Said faces a quandary in discussing the rampant distortions of Islam in his own age. "For Europe," observes Said, "Islam was a lasting trauma."[153] That trauma was less the religion of, or even the vast majority of, Muslims in the world, than the military incursions that threatened European politics and trade interests. Said has positioned himself as sharing in Islam, the culture, even though he was raised as a Protestant Christian.[154] As a secular critic he has no problem defending the religion from outright distortion, especially from media coverage.[155] Conservative and militant Muslims might praise Said for exposing Western bias, but even progressive Muslims must wonder why Said is so insistent on not saying something about what Islam actually is for Muslims. It does not help matters that *Culture and Imperialism* lumps the term *Islam* as a troublesome "essence" along with *négritude*, Irishness, or Catholicism.[156] But Said refuses to acknowledge what Islam might be beyond such an essence.[157] Perhaps it should not be surprising that a secularized Christian Arab who never experienced Islam from the inside and did not take the time to penetrate it with resolve from the outside should have little to say about the religion; this is perhaps the fate of the "secular border intellectual."[158]

Most early reviewers recognized that *Orientalism* was no ordinary academic book. Daniel O'Hara praised Said's analyses of Orientalism as "unequalled by anything else in contemporary criticism" at the time.[159] David Kopf included Said's text in the same genre as Nehru's *The Discovery of India*, Nirad Chaudhuri's *Autobiography of an Unknown Indian*, Simone de Beauvoir's *The Second Sex*, and Eldridge Cleaver's *Soul on Ice*.[160] This is a somewhat strange bed for a pervasively pedantic review of an academic field most people thought dull and boring to the extreme. Certainly the birth pangs of post-colonial India, the feminist revolution, and civil rights were powerful issues of the day, so perhaps Kopf's comparison is not so much about the content of the narrative as the type of polemical issue it forced. Scholars in a variety of fields were inspired by Said's salvo against an entrenched establishment. There have been calls and sporadic attempts to "do a Said" in African-American studies,[161] American studies,[162] Andean-ism,[163] Japanese studies,[164] Italy's "southern question,"[165] pre-Alexandrian Greek texts,[166] and analysis of missionary narratives.[167] Anthropologist Michael Herzfeld coins "Mediterraneanism" in conscious imitation of Said's Orientalism.[168] *Orientalism* even inspired an "ismic" deconstruction of Anglosaxonism[169] and Celticism.[170] But beyond the calls and frequent citations, few smoking polemics have done it Said's way.

In an ironic, self-unfulfilling sense, Said's exposé of Western Orientalism has received limited attention in the real Orient. Said wrote as a self-proclaimed Oriental writing back—by representing back—for those who he assumed had not been able to represent themselves. A decade after the original publication of *Orientalism*, Magdi Wahba found it strange "how little response there is to be found in Arabic to the theses set forth by Said," even though an Arabic translation had been available since 1981.[171] The relatively few Arabic scholars who did respond in print were largely unheard from in English writings, except in secondary comments about their criticism.[172] Said was genuinely disturbed, as he confided in the afterward to *Orientalism*'s second edition, that his book had not made a difference in the Arab world; the Orient's representative, in this case, had been rejected as being too Eurocentric.[173] This indifference to Said's book may be due in part to its failure to engage with anything actually written in Arabic. Consider that one of the few Arabic phrases used in *Orientalism* is one actually composed by the French savant Silvestre de Sacy.[174] How exactly does a Western-educated scholar of Arab origin convince people whose language he does not bother to consult in the process of representing them?[175]

All texts have meaningful contexts, despite what impatient critics often assume about texts they do not like. In some ways it is significant simply to note that *Orientalism* appeared at the end of the 1970s. It rose out of almost two decades of political activism in the United States: activism for civil rights and feminism, Native American resistance, protest against the Vietnam War, and general student unrest—including at Columbia University, where Said was comfortably positioned teaching the canon. With an eager audience reeling from the rightward shift of Reagan and Thatcher, Said rode the crest of a wave of intellectual criticism challenging the project of positivist science and exposing a lack of morally conscious progress in modernism. Marx, Freud, and even Weber were still being invoked, but metaphysics had experienced an existential twist in which Nietzsche eroded Descartes.[176] In the study of history, Toynbeean tomes had been thoroughly trashed by Hayden White's wit; geography had just begun to locate its imperial baggage.[177] In my own discipline of anthropology, the short tryst with Lévi-Strauss was becoming a structure built on sand, blown over by a Geertzian interpretive wink. The nouvelle intellectual cuisine now consisted of Theodor Adorno, Roland Barthes, Pierre Bourdieu, Paul de Man, Jacques Derrida, Michel Foucault, Jurgen Habermas, François Lyotard, Paul Ricoeur, and Raymond Williams.[178] Of course, the inevitable and hard-to-digest pace of culture change in the real world soon makes passé even the freshest nouveau philosophical pâte.

The visibility of *Orientalism* as a text that defends Arabs and Muslims in a high cultural mode was heightened by the coincidence of contemporaneous politics in the Middle East. As Yvonne Haddad observes, the year 1979 "can be seen as a kind of watershed, a point of departure for the dramatic rise in interest in the religion of Islam."[179] Muslims dominated the international news in the 1970s, starting with the separation of Pakistan and Bangladesh. In 1973, the Ramadan War showed that an Arab state could make military gains against Israel, at least in principle, before the superpowers stepped in. This was the same year the oil embargo led to lines of Western awareness that economic oil pressure was also a force to be reckoned with. The middle of the decade saw the outbreak of civil war in Lebanon. In 1977, General Zia ul-Haqq came to power in Pakistan and promoted Islamization, followed, before the decade had ended, by the jihad in Afghanistan against the Soviets and by the 1979 Islamic Revolution in Iran. Even Mecca was not immune to "terrorism," as a radical group tried to seize the holy sanctuary during the annual pilgrimage. In 1980, Hizbollah was founded in Lebanon and Islamic Jihad in Palestine. "The tenebrific clouds hitherto obscuring Muslim endeavour began to shift," remarks Akbar Ahmed, "and Muslims felt a sense of jubilation."[180] Clearly, *Orientalism* arrived at a time when the real Orient was no moot point. Just as clearly, it appeared alongside an emergent political resistance to Western policy in the region.[181]

Said's magnum opus thus appears at a nodal point of preponderance not just of movements and ideas, but in the world of print.[182] Establishment thinking, of the kind Said was criticizing, was the target of a range of scholars. In history, for example, Hayden White published *Tropics of Discourse*, returning the study of history to the problems of language—tropes and discourse.[183] White, like Said, was taken—for a short ride—with the historical imagination of Vico and the metaphysical counter-musing of Foucault. Another historian, Lawrence Stone, published "The Revival of Narrative: Reflections on a New Old History," a seminal survey that questioned the elusive faith that historians had in arriving at a coherent scientific explanation of historical change.[184] There was clearly much "disarray of the discipline" among historians, although, as Oscar Handlin put it at the time in his *Truth in History*, this was due as much to a decline in rigor and craftsmanship as to faulty theoretical ground.[185] Among those who sided with Handlin was Bernard Lewis, who found a pronounced lack of vigor in the study of Middle Eastern history.[186]

Appearing across the Atlantic at the same time was Bryan Turner's *Marx and the End of Orientalism*. In his text Turner also criticizes Middle East studies as "riddled by ideological and conceptual difficulties."[187] Referring to an Orientalism based on a biased epistemology, Turner attacks the perverse essentialism that Islam is flawed from the start. As a Weber-authorized syndrome, Orientalism is said to establish a "dichotomous ideal type of Western society whose inner essence unfolds in a dynamic progress towards democratic industrialism, and Islamic society which is either timelessly stagnant or declines from its inception."[188] Turner also takes Orientalists to task for burying themselves in philological matters at the expense of critical theory. Turner addresses limitations in Orientalist thinking that he himself had succumbed to; thus, his work becomes "in large measure a work of personal de-colonization."[189] Turner, like Said, was seeking an end to the wrong kind of Orientalism, but he also specifically argues for "something more than the valid but indecisive notion" that it was "a justification for colonialism."[190]

The intellectual climate in which *Orientalism* emerged was, in a word, "after." It came after the author had articulated the failures of structuralism and partly embraced Foucault in his *Beginnings* (1975). It also came after an acrimonious public debate with Bernard Lewis in the book review section of the *New York Times*. The positivist glow of modernism had dimmed to the point of virtual nonexistence in literary studies. The dismantling of real-life colonies into coveys of wannabe nation-states pulled this way and that by global economic strings implied a post-colonial condition, akin to the recovery time after major surgery. When *Orientalism* came into print, the world of its readers was literally at the post.[191] Those who had been left outside waiting at the margins were hungry for something. Even those within the ranks of Oriental studies were after new approaches to the study of a region that was front and center on the evening news.

III

> In the absence of a precise critique of orientalist scholarship
> firmly rooted in historical sources and documentary evidence,

Revisiting classic texts became à la mode across disciplines in the post-modern finale of the last century. There are many ways to follow in the wake of Said's disorienting text. Timewise, I follow a backward and, I hope, [hind]insightful look at a text that has aged, like all polemics. Sufficient words have passed over and around *Orientalism* to allow a more dispassionate retrospective than was the case when it first appeared. I offer here a critique of *Orientalism* enabled by what is missing from Said's text—what Said largely left unsaid. I do not wish to write an exhaustive history of the multiple discourses culpable of being labeled "Orientalist" any more than Said did, but neither do I think it useful to write them off, as happens with Said's polemical excess. My goal is to take those paths that will allow me to reach a clearing beyond our continued binary vision. I therefore offer an exegetical excursion through the phenomenon of *Orientalism*; it will be a broad sweep, and at times it will not be innocent.

The reviews at the time of the book's publication were mixed, ranging from jubilation, for a welcome pro-Arab polemical defense, to the gut reactions of those who bore the annoying pricks of Saidian épée.[192] Admirers of *Orientalism* have offered a number of alternatives to the limitations of Said's own analytical frame. Depending on which critic you read, Said should have used Foucault in a truly Foucauldian way, or he should have read more Marx and less Foucault, or left Marx well enough alone, fostered a more Freudian fetish for stereotypes,[193] done more with Derrida,[194] grappled with Gadamer,[195] or at least let Bakhtin in through the back door.[196] Arnold Krupat, for example, would turn Said's critical stance on end with an ethno-criticism that is "concerned with differences rather than oppositions, and so seeks to replace oppositional with dialogical models."[197] Saree Makdisi offers "an extensive elaboration" of Said's central thesis, agreeing that Europeans not only invented the Orient, but continually reinvented it.[198] Jayant Lele discusses "ways in which his analysis needs to be enriched."[199] Mrinalini Sinha draws inspiration from Said's work but goes on to "re-think" his critique from "a historical materialist perspective."[200] Nicholas Thomas suggests that attention be shifted from discourse to specific colonial projects.[201] John McGowan offers ideas on how Said can save himself by accepting a "full-scale relativism accompanied by universal tolerance."[202] The list goes on and on. There is indeed a large amount of Saidism without Said, following the spirit rather than the methodological letter of his thesis.[203]

Detractors of *Orientalism*, which is now frozen in unrevised form, come in several varieties. There are those who are reluctant to criticize Said because they are in general agreement with much of what he says about negative stereotypes of the Orient and Islam. Historian Roger Owen, for example, acknowledges that he encouraged the non-Orientalist Said to write his book. Although he praised Said's courageous exposé of Orientalist bias, Owen is clearly uncomfortable with Said's application of Foucault and disappointed by what is left out in the polemic.[204] Even admitted, though not necessarily committed, admirers of Said, such as Aijaz Ahmad, still find his book "deeply flawed."[205] Most critics point to flaws in Said's representation, yet agree that the Orientalist bias he reveals needs to be recognized and rejected. Given Said's hatchet treatment of established scholars, there are probably some who have been reluctant to return equally polemical fire. Then there are those who simply do not like the man or his ideas. Historian Bernard Lewis comes to mind, but few could be harsher than Simon Leys, who dismisses the work as "three hundred pages of twisted, obscure, incoherent, ill-informed, and badly written diatribe."[206] For these caustic critics, Said's text is a calumny so callous it might better be called *Orientalschism*.

Panning much of what Said passionately argues for in *Orientalism* must inevitably involve a destructive rhetoric, even if pains are taken to avoid maliciousness.[207] As a text about texts, Said's rhetoric should be taken seriously. How Said persuades is as important, perhaps more so as time goes by, as what exactly he says. Ironically, few commentaries on this literary critic focus on his rhetorical style or apply the classical logic of rhetoric as a humanistic art to *Orientalism* as a whole. One power inherent in the book's rhetorical force is the continuing relevance of key words woven from the intellectual maelstrom of the 1970s into jousting, even if not judicious, academic prose. Alongside the categorical sense of discourse, the terms that have most resonated in post-*Orientalism* criticism are very much truth-to-power words: knowledge, power, imperialism, colonialism, hegemony, other, reality, representation, truth itself. Whether Said got it right or got it wrong, he got into the critical rhythm just as continental philosophy and social conscience were awakening to what was clearly not the envisioned brave new world.

Why devote an entire book to critiquing another book? Is that not what mercifully short and obscure reviews are for? Why bother to criticize a book written more than two and a half decades ago when the debate and the author have moved far beyond the initial demand for such a book in the first place? I could follow the pragmatic advice of Robert Adams, who suggests that "critical systems inevitably become obsolete without formal refutation" simply because critics change.[208] Although I would agree that *Orientalism* will eventually reach obsolescence, the rhetorical and methodological tropes in the text will no doubt continue to be relevant as long as there are texts to critique. Fred Halliday has insisted that the ongoing debate over *Orientalism* "is by no means burnt out."[209] But why should I be adding flames to the ongoing, even if shifting, polemical fire rather than just letting it burn out? I am, after all, an anthropologist, theoretically more at home in villages than in libraries, and clearly interloping as a literary critic.[210] When I first read Said's *Orientalism*, having just returned from ethnographic fieldwork in rural Yemen, I was mesmerized by his persuasive style. Othering as an intellectual exercise of power: this was an issue someone had to drag out of the closet. It was the general thrust, the vivid examples of stereotyping, that I recall most attracting me. At the time I was youthfully unaware that a number of points I thought devastatingly new were being reshaped by Said rather than invented. As an intellectual child of the American 1970s, I was in a poor position to judge such a verbal shakedown of the stodgy crowd that claimed the Orient as sacrosanct academic turf. But I grew up fast in the field. The Yemeni men and women I met during ethnographic fieldwork certainly belied the stereotypes spun in Orientalist and popular fantasies. *Orientalism* fascinated me; I, too, was a victim of *National Geographic* exoticism. But I was never quite satisfied by all that Said left out: the level of self-critique—or at least overt dissatisfaction— among students like myself, and a fair number of my professors.[211]

A major reason I want to return to *Orientalism* is the importance of placing what Said labeled "Orientalism" in a more soundly recovered historical context. Although I do not agree fully with Thierry Hentsch's avowal that Said's book is "the corridor through which all examination and discussion of Orientalism must pass,"[212] Said's tunnel criti-vision is still the obvious place to start. There is always a critical need for retooling approaches to academic discourses, but mere importation of tools designed for literary analysis to [mis]treat established historical and social analyses will not do the trick. Said's amateurish and ahistorical essentializing of an Orientalism-as-textualized discourse from Aeschylus to Bernard Lewis has polemical force, but only at the expense of methodological precision and rhetorical consistency. Said's intellectual acumen is not the issue, but being well read does not guarantee reading well; nor does how well he writes ensure credibility for what he writes. As Alain Roussillon rightly notes, "la 'réfutation de l'orientalisme' peut ne pas être la garantie automatique d'une libération de la pensée."[213] I write to move beyond the discursive bashing from which *Orientalism* has failed to liberate scholarly study of the real Orient.

Criticism, however defined, is inevitably conducted in an attack mode, offensive in more than one sense. This is the power of *Orientalism*, and no critique of the text could afford to do otherwise. But not all counter-critiques need be dismissed as equally polemical, a term usually reserved for what is being criticized. I have endeavored to be comprehensive, sampling the range of reviews and commentaries from all sides. My aim is not just to survey what has been said, but to frame the debate over the text by continually returning to Said's narrative and to the sources that inform it. In the process, I have reread most of the works cited by Said, including those that are only listed to be dismissed. I take to heart Nicholas Thomas's comment that much of the debate has been either hypercritical or uncritical.[214] But I do not subscribe to the absurd dismissal of Said's critics as "calumniating legions" of "conformists, sycophants, and pseudointellectuals inside and outside academia."[215] I propose to tackle the subject by tickling your fancied views and subverting the polemical stalemate. [216]

My approach here is to shed light through a less seriously used prism: the highly suspect yet much regaled dis-course of satire, often [es]chewed as fool's food for critical thought.[217] I adopt the optimistic view of Horace, who reminds us that the satirist, though he laughs, tells the truth.[218] Such a truth would seem to be the right kind to speak back to someone who insists on speaking truth to power. So much impassioned appraisal of *Orientalism* has been made that a decidedly more lighthearted approach is called for, if only for the sake of novelty.[219] "Satire," muses Richard Posner, "is the public-intellectual genre par excellence."[220] Unfortunately, this legalistic chronicler of modern American intellectualism undermines the critical role of satire by defining it as "a literary rather than an academic genre." Where then does that leave satire as a serious form of cultural criticism? Parody, I suggest, has the potential to create a parity between the textual attitudes of critic and criticized. In a study of nineteenth-century Orientalist painting, Carol Ockman argues that parody allowed the artist "to usurp dominant imagery, to steal its meaning, and to make use of that very imagery to better expose its underlying implications."[221] I view this as an alternative iconclasm to the polemics of blame, which *Orientalism* paradigmatically politicizes.

The major in-printed fault of *Orientalism*'s prose is the systemic literary blindness to the subversive power inherent in satire. Ironically, Said's own gloss on how best to understand what he calls a "textual attitude" refers to a way of writing about or approaching reality by satirists such as Voltaire in *Candide* and Cervantes in *Don Quixote*.[222] *Orientalism*, of course, is a candid expression and it can be quite quixotic at times. Unfortunately, satirical representations of common stereotypes about the Orient, as brilliantly articulated in Mark Twain's *The Innocents Abroad*, are totally ignored in Said's narrative. Why would a literary critic who has certainly read his fair share of canonical satires so minimize the role of satirical and theatrical farce as a form of cultural critique capable of subverting Orientalist discourse?[223] Such satires continue to be read, while most of the Orientalist texts he criticizes have long since been relegated to footnotes.

Candide, published four decades before Napoleon invaded Egypt, can serve as an antidote to the moralistic [ad]vice of *Orientalism*. The gentle youth Candide begins his philosophical angst in European Westphalia, and ends up with a post-Inquisitional disposition in the Eastern splendor of Constantinople. Upon discovering by the conceit of his britches that the wretched conditions of all humanity at the time could neither be panned nor glossed as "the best of all possible worlds," he finds an honest man— more significantly, an "honest Turk." Candide, accompanied by his philosophical mentor, Dr. Pangloss, asks the Turk for information about a certain religious official who was strangled by the Ottoman sultan. The simple Muslim farmer responds that he does not trouble his head about politics in Constantinople, but contents himself with just selling the fruits of his garden. Voltaire then portrays his imagined Turkish family as an ideal to be emulated rather than a surrogate to be denigrated.

> Having said these words, he [the Turk] invited the strangers into his house; his two sons and two daughters presented them with several sorts of sherbet, which they made themselves, with Kaimak enriched with the candied peel of citrons, with oranges, lemons, pineapples, pistachio-nuts, and Mocha coffee unadulterated with the bad coffee of Batavia or the American islands. After which the two daughters of the honest Mussulman perfumed the strangers' beards.[224]

Voltaire does not valorize the contrast between a superior West and inferior East, but between modest, hardworking, and hospitable men, such as the honest Turk, and all tyrants, whether Ahmet III of the Ottomans or the supposedly civilized Prince Charles of England.

Critics of *Orientalism* cover both the author and his ideas, but only a few have ventured to un-cover the colorful entry point to the physical text. I refer here to the 1979 paperback version with its enticing cover illustration that begs to be touched upon. This is a portion of Jean-Léon Gérôme's 1880s *Le charmeur des serpentes* (The Snake Charmer), which oddly enough is not discussed in the text; the astute reader is left guessing whether this seductively symbolic packaging is of the author's or publisher's choosing.[225] In fact, Said chose the image after seeing the painting on display in the Sterling and Francine Clark Art Institute in Williamstown, Massachusetts, near Northfield Academy where he attended prep school. The painting highlights a naked white youth, with prominent symmetrical buttocks toward the viewer, holding aloft the head of a large snake as the body of the reptile twists around the upper torso of the unclad lad. To the right is an old man playing a flute to soothe the beast, while its empty basket-home shares the kilim on which the boy stands. Directly in front, staring voyeuristically at private-parts level, is an aged, green-turbaned, white-bearded "Arab" sitting with feet outstretched and curved sword propped against his side. To either side is a mix of black and light-skinned retainers, some with quizzical looks. But is the barely perceptible excitement on the faces of these imagined Orientals more for the naked boy or the relaxed snake? It is left to our imagination, of course, as we are forced to focus our voyeurism mainly on the men pictured, once we get past those glistening buttocks. Nor can we know, except from the observers' mirrored, veiled expressions, the state of excitement of the boy himself. This suggestive scene, a counterpoint to the direct gaze on the female form in Orientalist odalisque renditions, is enshrined in an ornate palace of a bygone era with Quranic-style calligraphy along the top of the back wall.

Torn out of context, devoid of any textual integration, the reader of *Orientalism* begins with the only image available. Why *The Snake Charmer*? Not given a reason to agree or disagree with, each reader must become an instant art critic. I am struck right away by the stark contrast of the architecture of spirituality framing a quintessentially erotic act. Were this a mosque, I would expect the boy to be praying; after all, his feet are placed on the appropriate part of the rug for prayer. But instead he stands exposed, lifting up a snake as though making an offering, under the gaze of his masters or at least those who pay for the act. Instead of a neat line of devout men in prayer, I see a motley mass of over-clothed misfits and an obvious figure of bearded authority. The fixed gaze on the boy's private parts suggests pedophilia, just as contemporaneous depictions of the harem beauty eroticize the feminine form. Decadence and a hollow faith: these are the feelings evoked by my uninformed before-reading viewing of this cover of *Orientalism*. The stark thesis of *Orientalism* can so easily be replicated in this one image.[226]

Further reflection on the exotica of the scene brings familiar symbols into focus. I wonder why the emphasis is on a snake. My own Christian genesis easily absorbs such a familiar, garden-variety icon. The snake is temptation, the kind that leads to a perversion in which a naked boy apparently feels no shame and connives with the Devil for an entertainment complete with a pre-Freudian flute. The right kind of Christians, being civilized, do not play with snakes, nor do they let such dangerous creatures out of their box. Good Christians do not show off their genitals, especially to dirty old men. Gérôme, as a French Catholic, most likely knew this when he applied his studio-inspired brush to canvas. If this is how the Western artist depicts Oriental life, I have little choice but to open the book with disgust at Orientalists before I read a word.

But the cover of *Orientalism*, like Said's argument itself, only tells half of the story. There are other snake charmers in the history of this discourse. I can only imagine how different my reaction to Said's text would be if instead of Gérôme's homoerotic image the publisher had chosen Etienne Dinet's equally serpentine *Le charmeur de vipères* (1889). This was painted less than a decade later and by a lesser known European artist, and it is hard to imagine a greater contrast. Dinet celebrates the nuance of light in North Africa; Gérôme focuses on the inner darkness, artistically and thematically. Where Gérôme chooses a naked boy fully exposed to an old sheikh, Dinet portrays the snake charmer as an independent old man out in public and looking back directly at the viewer. Around him are not sullen voyeurs sitting in a blue-cold hall, but everyday men, women, and children gawking—as might be the case in a modern art museum—at an entertainer with one snake draped non-threateningly over his balding head and the other hanging limp in his firm right hand. For Gérôme, the boy is dwarfed and engulfed by a large boa; for Dinet, the small brown snakes are the harmless props of a popular prankster.

Gérôme's painting fits Said's sense of cultural imperialism like a glove; the charm in their shared image of Orientalism is one dirtied by a colonial presence that dehumanizes both the charmer and the charmed. Here is the "iconic distillation of the Western's notion of the Oriental" in one canvas.[227] Contrapuntally, this particular cover image leaves out women, even the fictionalized kind, thus presaging their absence in Said's text.[228] Artist Dinet would have been an uncomfortable fit, a reminder that not all Westerners approaching the Orient were Burtonesque voyeurs, Flaubertian dilettantes, or Disraelian careerists. Unlike Gérôme, Dinet combined his compassion with a recognition of the humanity of those he painted. He became fluent in Arabic, chose to live his life in an Algerian oasis, and eventually converted to Islam. Here was an "Orientalist" who was both "profoundly sympathetic" and had an "'inside' knowledge of a local culture."[229] What a difference a picture makes.

Covers continue to illustrate the fundamental problem in the canonization of *Orientalism* as a text so intent on telling truth to power that the flawed content can be forgiven. The British Penguin edition of 2003 captures the continuing uncritical reception of the book. The image chosen is a meticulously detailed 1840 Orientalist scene by the French artist Emile-Jean-Horace Vernet. There is no ambiguity about sexual domination here. A dark-skinned Bedouin-looking man in robes bends close to stare lustfully at a white-skinned beauty, a half-inclined odalisque coquette on a rock, with her left thigh and right breast exposed to the light through the opening folds of alluring white dress. She holds a wisp of her light linen veil over her mouth as though to pretend demurral, but the viewer has little doubt about what or even who will come next. In artistic overthrill, the camel goad of the desert rider is pointed directly at the woman's pubic zone. The camel, fully saddled and chewing contentedly, stands behind as both screen and witness. The Orientalist male imagines and penetrates the weak and feminized object of his imperial greed; this is how *Orientalism* is meant to be read.

But the picture chosen by Penguin has a history that interrupts the discourse. At first the overlay with Said's thesis would seem a perfect match; the French artist Vernet specialized in military battles and generals, including Napoleon. An Arab-looking man is about to force himself on a vulnerable but alluring woman not protected inside a harem; this is how Orientalist thinking would expect both idealized characters to behave. Or it could be read as the Western Orientalist gaze stripping the woman of her honor and controlling her fate as she lies mute; this is Said's basic thesis. To be sure, Vernet exploited Oriental imagery, but this particular scene is obscenely biblical. It draws on the sad fate of Judah, the great patriarch Jacob's eldest son, about to be enticed into providing an heir for his widowed daughter-in-law Tamar, whom he does not recognize.[230] It is tale of incest, a lot like Lot with his daughters in his cave, at the core of Judeo-Christian sacred history. Between Tamar's opening thighs there is a direct line to the future King David of Israel, and ultimately the Messiah Christ. The story behind the scene is not as obvious as our first viewing suggests.

Going beyond the cover, I invite you to reread Said's seminal text before investing time in the analysis that follows. In chapter 1, I introduce the phenomenon of *Orientalism*, leading to an emphasis on the ways in which Orientalism has been defined and redefined as an object of study, followed by an etymological excavation of the imagined "Orient" and a close look at the growth of institutional Orientalism in Europe. Chapter 2 surveys the critical reaction to Said's Orientalism thesis, covering the faults in his historical hindsight. The focus is not just on what Said said, but on the absent self-critique of Orientalist authors and the self-representation of Orientals capable of representing themselves. I also turn to literary texts in order to refocus the blurring of textual genres in *Orientalism*. The essence of Said's essentializing thesis is engaged in chapter 3. How does Said as an intentional author present representation? What is the theory behind the polemical madness? Why is Said himself impossible to separate from his text? And how, at least for the sake of argument, can a real Orient ever stand out in the mire of binary thinking that opposes East and West?

1

Orienting *Orientalism*

Orientalism is not merely associated with one country, race or era. It is a complex idea made up of history and scenery, suffused with imagination and irradiate with revelation.

—*Knickerbocker Magazine*, 1853

Critically and philosophically regarded, it is a catchall in which we have assembled a massive disarray of motifs and themes, images and symbols from poetry reflecting imaginative and speculative excursions across the cloudy boundaries between East and West.

—James Beard, "Critical Problems in the Orientalism of Western Poetry"

I "One That Cannot Now Be Rewritten"

As a set of beliefs and as a method of analysis, Orientalism cannot develop. Indeed, it is the doctrinal antithesis of development.
—EDWARD SAID, "ORIENTALISM AND THE OCTOBER WAR"

Any European or American representation of Islam and the geographic space that claims it is often called a kind of "Orientalism." Centuries of contact on all levels between Christian Europe and its Islamic East have generated a long and varied historical trajectory of textual discourse. The East was a concern for the West on virtually every level: material, political, aesthetic, and spiritual. It was, after all, in the Holy Land where Adam fell from grace, Noah and his family disembarked, Abraham journeyed by faith, Moses brought down the Ten Commandments, and Jesus wept. Pilgrims, merchants, soldiers, and tourists came, saw, and occasionally conquered, more often in print than in reality. The geography of these Bible Lands was a sacred one that crisscrossed the boundaries of European and American imagination. New Jerusalems, even new Cairos as far afield as Illinois, plotted and dotted the growth of Western frontiers. The much appropriated Orient, as Said and so many others remind us, was "almost" a European invention.[1]

To the extent that the Orient and Islam have been invented, abused, and abjured in the West, any analysis of the rhetoric of representation must address the wide-ranging but not-quite-satisfying debate over Orientalist discourse that in a parallel way is "almost" an invention of Edward Said.[2] His *Orientalism* addresses and then dresses down the ghosts of Orientalism still haunting his world in the late 1970s. Only a century ago the scholar identified as an Orientalist or expert in Oriental studies would be held in high esteem, even among many of the Orientals who formed the object of that expertise. By the time Edward Said rudely exposed the academically sterile skeletons undergirding Orientalism's panoptic perch, it was becoming clear across a wide simulacrum of academic disciplines, and certainly from Oriental intellectuals themselves, that the presumption of disinterested objectivity among Orientalist scholars had to go the way of the camel. Whether Said was the crucial assassin or simply helped nail the coffin shut, the Orientalism he descried is dead but neither fully buried nor redeemed.

Whether it be more because of what Said has said, or because of what others said before Said said it, or simply because by now enough has been said and done, the term "Orientalism" has effectively been terminated in twenty-first century American academic discourse. Since the early 1970s, most departments and programs in Oriental studies have been renamed and revamped as area programs in Middle Eastern or Asian studies.[3] Andre Raymond suggests that the end of classical Orientalism occurred in 1957 with the publication of Gibb and Bowen's *Islamic Society and the West*, "the last great endeavour of European Orientalists."[4] Starting in the 1960s, prominent established scholars and indigenous Middle Eastern historians were calling for an open-ended academic approach to the Orient that no longer focused on one large part of the globe as unique and homogenous.[5] In 1973, on the hundredth anniversary of the First International Congress of Orientalists, the academicians most identifiable as Orientalists met in Paris and voted to abandon the label altogether.[6]

The study of languages and literatures under the rubric of Orientalism had become handicapped by its ghettoization outside of advances in disciplines concerned with history and the social sciences. Contrary to Said's assumption, this had become a no-longer-academic problem. The influential French Arabists Claude Cahen and Charles Pellat wrote in 1973 that the failure to study Islam in terms of new ideas in linguistics, history, and the social sciences had become a serious handicap.[7] "The Orientalists," lamented Morroe Berger earlier, in his popular 1964 paperback *The Arab World Today*, "have been absorbed in detailed philological and literary analysis."[8] As early as 1954, Bernard Lewis coined the gibe that in the West the history of the Arabs has chiefly been written by historians who knew no Arabic and by Arabists who knew no history.[9] Nor was such an idea only born in the 1950s. In his 1919 presidential address to the American Oriental Society, James Henry Breasted admitted: "The heavy burden of recovering and mastering the lost oriental languages has made us orientalists chiefly philologists and verbalists, equipped to utilize written documents, and a little perplexed and bewildered in the presence of other kinds of evidence."[10] By the time of Said's writing it was not only the term that had outlived its usefulness among scholars, but also the notion that contexts of whole cultures could be encycled pedantically from exotic texts alone. The Goliath Orientalism that Said felled with slinging and stinging criticism was at the time of his writing a rather doddering gladiator, and the Gotham of the historically instituted guild was already in ruins.

DOWN ORIENTALIST MEMORY LANE

> At once the most remarkable description of a people ever written, and one that cannot now be rewritten, it will always live in the literature of England.
>
> —EDWARD STANLEY POOLE, "EDITOR'S PREFACE"
> TO EDWARD LANE'S *AN ACCOUNT OF THE MANNERS
> AND CUSTOMS OF THE MODERN EGYPTIANS*

The need now is for a reorientation to the context that enabled *Orientalism* to blockbust the Academy. Before examining what Said says Orientalism was, it is interesting to look at a textual example of what made Orientalism necessary. What better text to begin with than Victorian scholar Edward Lane's *An Account of the Manners and Customs of the Modern Egyptians*. First published in 1836, this soon became a descriptive *tour de force* in defining the Oriental Muslim as the "other" for a literate Western audience, at least those who read English. Invigorated by a reprint edition that is both affordable and still available in many bookstores, this hefty tome keeps on presenting what the modern editor calls "the warp and woof of the rich tapestry of Islam before the fabric was rent by corruptions and self-corruptions that came with Western influence."[11] Here was the mild-mannered master of Arabic who donned Arab robes, masqueraded as Muslim savant Mansur Effendi, sailed up and down the Nile, visited the hashish dens, and even lived for a spell in the uncomfortable shade of abandoned tombs. God alone knows how gentleman Lane fleshed out the intimate details of harem life. But his own life certainly took a turn to the interior. In the forty years after releasing his acclaimed narrative he plodded on in bookish fashion to expurgatively translate the monumental *Arabian Nights* and half-complete what is still *the* Arabic-English lexicon, mercifully available in reprint.

As a poster child for Orientalist Extraordinaire, Edward Lane shares discursive space with fellow would-be pilgrims Sir Richard Burton and the surly Charles Doughty, even if Lane's prose has proven to be somewhat more prosaic than that of his literary bedfellows. There is enough exotica—raw, classified, and sometimes sensual—to delight readers even today. Consider Lane's erudite unveiling of the Egyptian harem in the chatty Anglo-prose so characteristic of Victorian travelers. In particular, the rhetoric is telling in spelling out details on female slaves:

> I should here mention, that the slaves who are termed "Abyssinians" are, with few exceptions, not from the country properly called Abyssinia, but from the neighboring territories of the Gallas. Most of them are handsome. The average price of one of these girls is from ten to fifteen pounds sterling, if moderately handsome; but this is only about half the sum that used to be given for one a few years ago. They are much esteemed by the voluptuaries of Egypt; but are of delicate constitution: many of them die, in this country, of consumption.[12]

Now we can guess one reason why so many young English gentlemen would buy a copy of this book and perhaps read a passage or two over port and between cigars after an evening repast. Imagine, and that is precisely what the value of such prose affords, being able to buy a handsome girl who would be your esteemable slave and do whatever you wanted. What is lost in the gloss, of course, is the humanity. These girls were sold as slaves, ripped from their families and often dying from disease if not first from abuse. That these were not English girls, at least of a certain class, and that they were in a Muslim country unspoiled and therefore uncivilized by Western values allowed the rhetoric to deliver without compelling a moral response from the reader. After all, Lane could be seen as simply describing static Oriental life as it was, so that Britain could patronizingly change it.

Not surprisingly, given the revenues already accumulated, the editor of the 1860 edition of Lane's work prophesied: "Scholars will ever regard it as most fortunate that Mr. Lane seized this opportunity, and described so remarkably a people while yet they were unchanged."[13] As late as 1963, at least one prominent critic of English-speaking Orientalists also praised Lane as one of the few "disinterested" scholars not out to convert Muslims.[14] One critic who does not share this editorial stance is Edward Said, who chooses the earlier Edwardian tome as a paragon of the evolving intellectual orientation for studying the so-called "Oriental" that served the political interests of Western imperialism in exoticizing both the Orient and Islam. "If we read Lane's *Modern Egyptians*, not as a source of Oriental lore, but as a work directed towards the growing organization of academic Orientalism," insists Said, "we will find it illuminating." [15] Said sets out to illuminate the dark motives lurking in the ivory tower that canonized texts backwards and forwards of Lane and his cohort. The Englishman's presence as the intelligent observer who lived *their* life as a kind of descriptive ethnographer gave the book an aura of objectivity that for Said invalidates what is being said. For Said, Lane almost literally disemboweled the Egyptians for scholarly exposition.

Edward Lane's discussion of Egyptians was no longer modern by the time Edward Said read it. Although the book is acknowledged by modern literary critics as one of those "great Orientalist works of genuine scholarship," Said nonetheless trashes it as coming out of "the same impulse" as racist tracts and pornographic novels.[16] The problem is that Said reads Lane contemptuously rather than carefully, failing to appreciate the critical assessment Lane made in the 1830s of earlier stereotypical accounts of life in Egypt.[17] I find it hard to fault Lane's lengthy description of Islam, which is notably devoid of sarcasm or Christian bigotry. Unlike most pilgrims and travelers who have left us journalistic and impressionistic memoirs, Lane lived in Cairo, became fluent in Arabic and sought to document the life around him by talking to the most knowledgeable Muslim scholars there. Unlike Edward Said, Lane revised his second edition after receiving criticism from others and finding materials he had forgotten at first writing. As John Rodenbeck concludes, after a detailed examination of *Orientalism*'s literary damning of Lane, Said's "persistent misconstruction and misquotation of Lane's words are so clearly willful that they suggest precisely the 'bad faith' of which he accuses Lane."[18]

Lane's primary sin appears to be in his attempt to learn about Islam without becoming a true Muslim. "Thus while one portion of Lane's identity floats easily in the unsuspecting Muslim sea," argues Said, "a submerged part retains its secret European power, to comment on, acquire, possess everything around it."[19] As a "counterfeit believer" and "privileged European" Edward Lane is delegitimized by Edward Said as "the very essence of bad faith." But whose battle is the secular literary critic fighting here? Lane's main informant and closest friend was a Muslim who probably knew if Lane was sincere or not, yet apparently did not condemn him.[20] Why does Lane's ruse matter so much to Said, who likewise does not accept Islam as the revealed religion? If Lane in Egypt is indeed a privileged European, this is due in part to the desire of the Egyptian leader Muhammad Ali to emulate Western ways. The British did not control Egypt directly at the time, and Lane cautiously adopted the dress of an educated Turk rather than that of a Brit. Orientalist scholars should be criticized for not trying to understand the real Orient on its own terms, but why deride Lane, who provided what arguably was at the time the most detailed and sympathetic description of everyday life for any culture of the region?[21]

A Life More than What Is Written

> Indeed, anywhere that intellectuals with a progressive or internationalist outlook gather on this planet, there is an awareness and appreciation of the indispensable contributions that Said has made to the life of free and independent inquiry, and beyond this, to a whole style and method of thought that takes ideas and culture seriously as crucially linked to structures of opposition and processes of emancipation.
>
> —Richard Falk, "Empowering Inquiry"

Said's *Orientalism* rivals Lane's *An Account of the Manners and Customs of the Modern Egyptians* as one of the most influential books about the Orient ever written. I say "influential" not strictly as praise, but in recognition of its having stimulated a necessary debate in English-speaking academe that has hardly abated. *Orientalism* is a distinctly controversial book with a unique author. Said as the individual author defies theoretical pigeonholing. Like a bird darting in and out of a host of isms in which he cannot truly feel at home, he chose to sing from a lonely, self-imposed perch of exile. His voice is much admired for its intricacy and shrill trills, for words with worldly import; he remains the consummate critic, somehow refined and raw at the same time. He is a postmodern, not for the sake of the label, but to find a way to be modern and yet not be trapped into denying the essential humanism he admires in the philosophy and music of his adopted West.[22] By choice, and partly by luck, he is not a Marxist, not a structuralist; he is most definitely not a feminist. But, for all his railing against the academic establishment, his club membership is what allows his critical voice to be heard even if he is a feuilletonist in spite of himself. Stubbornly humanist scholar vs. political activist, teacher and mentor vs. polemicist, Said's paradoxical passions can be misconstrued as schizophrenic. Perhaps we should accept that, when all is said and done, Said's voice is perpetually in an act of beginning.[23]

From the start the reactions to *Orientalism*, ranging from the ad hoc to the ad hominem, read into Said the critic as well and as poorly as into what the critic was saying. Said's origins and political activism as an Arab-American intellectual can hardly be left out of analysis. Born an Arab in

Palestine in 1935, he was named for Edward, Prince of Wales, even as his father changed his own name from Wadie to William. In this mandated yet unmeltable monotheistic block of Christian Orthodox, Roman Catholics, Muslims, and Jews, young Edward was born into—irony of ironies—an Anglican household. The emergent Palestinian diaspora generated by the postwar creation of Israel in 1948 affected his family, who earlier had moved to Cairo for business purposes. Egypt was the center of his early childhood and schooling; English may have been his first language.[24] The United States became his home when he was a teenager. A family photograph in his auto-biography, *Out of Place*, shows him standing, hands in pockets, in front of a Howard Johnson in Jamaica, New York, in March 1951.[25] Said went on to study at two of the top Ivy League schools, Princeton and Harvard, and then to an accomplished career in literature at Columbia University, where he became University Professor of English and Comparative Literature.

The continued ironies of his life trajectory as both scholar and politi-cal activist abound. By his own admission, he grew up in the literal Orient, at least the littoral Mediterranean portion, "in a pre-political way in which all the political realities of the present nevertheless are somehow there in a figured or implicit form, held in suspension."[26] As he explains by way of an abstract example, the young Said saw Egypt's President Nasser as a hero of Arab nationalism, openly defying Western imperialism, yet Said later admits failing to realize the reality of the tension such heroics created in Egyptian society.[27] The Six-Day War was the major stimulus to Said's activist concern over the plight of Palestine.[28] Out of this political trauma he became an Arab activist; the Israeli army on the road to Jerusalem mirrored the previously apolitical Said on his personal road to Damascus.[29] His role in writing about Palestinian suffering and dreams led to his eventual partic-ipation, however limited, in the Palestine National Congress. His ringing insistence on Palestinian rights brought harsh diatribes and even death threats to his office door. He resolutely defended Islam against rabid stereo-types in the media, yet he was not Muslim, nor did he hold back his anger at the Iranian *fatwa* bounty put on Salman Rushdie's literary head. As an Arab, Said positioned himself as part of the "Islamicate" in a politicized cultural sense, a sort of ethnicized Muslim by default.[30] As a Palestinian awakened to Zionist denial of his native Palestine, Said took as his mimetic model Erich Auerbach, a Jewish refugee from Nazi Europe seeking the rel-ative safety of Istanbul, a less war-torn Islamic haven.

The story of Edward Said's life, like the intellectual colonial history he so eloquently engages, is a microcosm of paradox. His intellectual stance as an advocate of secular criticism from the humanities prevents him from advocating an intellectual position that is not oppositional. "Perhaps," muses Mustapha Marrouchi, "it is precisely his intellectual as well as political incorrectness that intrigues us; perhaps—as scholars of his life along with his art—we are bemused, even bewitched, by the ways he does not fit into our current systems of thought."[31] But not fitting into his own episteme does not prevent Said's being placed in a pantheon of intellectual icons, a stature enhanced by peer praise. Nobel laureate Nadine Gordimer views him as "one of the truly important intellectuals of our century."[32] If a paean of pièce-de-résistance dimensions is needed to sum up the author as larger than textual life, consider the following praise for a man bent on toppling the intellectual props of Western imperialism in his distant, native land: "Highly cultured, steeped in European classical music (he is an accomplished if these days strictly amateur pianist), well-travelled and at home in Cairo, Paris, London, and New York alike, he incarnates the very ideal of the cosmopolitan intellectual that remains so central to the humanities' self-image today."[33]

When Edward Said passed away in September 2003, after a sustained illness, there was an outpouring of admiration for the man and his work.[34] The resonance of his political advocacy and his visibility as an Arab-American in a profoundly biased media made Said a lightning rod in the debate over academic objectivity about the real Orient and Islam. "The Palestinians will never know a greater polemical champion," wrote Alexander Cockburn in his eulogy for a comrade in arms struggling against intolerance and political terrorism.[35] Indeed, despite the prodigious published output of Said as literary and cultural critic, it is his unabashed Palestinian identity that is most likely to mark his legacy. When the words from his admirers and critics have finally subsided, the most important tribute may be that of Said's close friend Daniel Barenboim, the Israeli conductor, who mourned "The Israelis have lost an adversary—but a fair and human one. And I have lost a soul mate."[36] Said's lifelong love of Western classical music serves as the counterpoint for the polemical fervor infusing *Orientalism*. The joint creation by Said and Barenboim of an orchestra for young Israeli and Arab musicians is a worthy worldly memorial to a man who achieved extraordinary success and still felt out of place.

"No twentieth-century intellectual has been the subject of such a large body of criticism in a wide array of disciplines over the past several years as Edward Said," observes Andrew Rubin.[37] The author of *Orientalism* will no doubt be written about, and rewritten up in the process, as long as the issues he raised continue to resonate, but the text itself is one that will never be rewritten. The achievement of seminal status, top seed among the prime and at times establishment movers in literary circles, forgoes the urgency for textual revision. For more than two decades Said felt no need to revise his book, a task he sometimes dismissed citing lack of time.[38] The emphasis in his reconsiderations of Orientalism was on explaining to readers why his critics had it all wrong. In retrospect, *Orientalism*, like Darwin's *On the Origin of Species*, speaks the kind of truth to power that does not depend on getting everything right. Given its position as a book that readers usually want to agree with but few actually have sufficient background knowledge to judge thoroughly, it would almost be perverse to suggest that it be revised. Would Conrad's *Heart of Darkness* beat louder if its faults were smoothed out in Time-Life consensus? Could *Huckleberry Finn* survive expurgatory editing for the sake of a current political correctness it arguably helped foster? And if someone did try to revise *Orientalism* and satisfy the many critics, what would happen to the three dozen or so existing translations?

Orientalism need not be rewritten. As a polemic it has served its purpose in stimulating an ongoing debate over the ways in which representation is never just a description of manners and customs, modern or otherwise. For a generation of scholars it has remained a book that must be read. But it is also a book with manifest flaws that need to be acknowledged and corrected to prevent it from becoming the kind of sacred text Said defined as problematically Orientalist. Were this not so, I would not have written this critique.

II   Defin[ess]ing Orientalism

> It will be clear to the reader (and will become clearer still
> throughout the many pages that follow) that by Orientalism I
> mean several things, all of them, in my opinion, interdependent.
> —EDWARD SAID, *ORIENTALISM*[39]

> To me this methodology is not good enough, because we are
> never quite sure in which sense at any one time Orientalism
> is being attacked; even conceding interdependence, which does
> not amount to identity, we must avoid ambiguity.
> —NORMAN DANIEL, "EDWARD SAID AND THE ORIENTALISTS"

If the Orient was "almost a European invention," it was at the same time a politicized representation that served the vested interests of imperial ambition and served up the colonized as the *they* who cannot represent themselves.[40] The literary Orient and the literal penetration of it were fused by Said into a latent, although blatantly lasting, discourse that he saw as manifest in canonized novels as well as in the fire of His or Her Majesty's noxious cannon balls or Gustave Flaubert's less imperially bent but well jostled balling of real-life odalisques. Orientalists, previously ignored as the conservators of texts, were now accused of being the producers not merely of texts but of a textual stance, a pervasive style, a self-authorizing of the Orient as other. From his own intellectual genealogy—one that stretches vicariously from Vico via Auerbach, Gramsci, and Williams to a flirtation with Foucault—Said spoke back to those who had not yet accepted the mega-truth that all knowledge is power. The mantra is tersely put by William Hart: "Western thought is in the grips of a metaphysics which makes an array of invidious distinctions between a decadent East and enlightened West, and underwrites ideological and military domination of the East by the West."[41] But to deconstruct Orientalism, it first had to be defined.

As a scholarly endeavor, Orientalism had been narrowly and naively viewed as a tradition of "techniques for identifying, editing and interpreting written texts," as Albert Hourani phrases it, from that philological amalgam labeled Semitic and Oriental languages.[42] Consider the definition offered by another real Oriental, Abdülhak Adnan-Adivar, in his introduction to the 1939 Turkish edition of the *Encyclopaedia of Islam*: "an organic whole which is composed of the knowledge derived from the original sources concerning the language, religion, culture, history, geography, ethnography, literature and arts of the Orient."[43] Reflecting on graduate training in the 1950s, Jacob Lassner captures the essence of pre-Saidian Oriental Studies:

> Their training, still heavily dependent on nineteenth-century models, featured a positivist outlook, a strong emphasis on philology, control of original sources, and a broad familiarity with several different cultures spanning the ancient, the medieval, and, in some cases, even the modern Near East. The focus was on the world of the ruling institution and a sophisticated literary milieu loosely defined as "high culture."[44]

In a word, Orientalists were being trained to participate in what Matthew Arnold, Said's favored modeler of the culture concept, would have called the "best of the best," the kind of sweetened culture that countered the impending anarchy of the irrational illiterati.[45] Few language specialists and historians are still being nurtured on this premise, although the critical lack of students and specialists with appropriate language skills has long been a recurring theme in state-of-the-art assessments.[46]

THE DEFINITION REVISITED

> Strictly speaking, Orientalism is a field of learned study.
>
> —EDWARD SAID, *ORIENTALISM*

It should be clear to the reader that by "Orientalism" I think Said means several things, all of them interpolated. I begin by laying out Said's argument from a close reading of *Orientalism* and of an embryonic positioning that appeared two years earlier in a *New York Times* book review. In the book, Said starts with three working definitions for "Orientalism."[47] The first, by virtue of its being "most readily accepted," is seemingly academic: "Anyone who teaches, writes about, or researches the Orient—and this applies whether the person is an anthropologist, sociologist, historian, or philologist—either in its specific or its general aspects, is an Orientalist, and what he or she does is Orientalism."[48] The gist here is that Orientalism is what Orientalists do and that whatever Orientalists do is Orientalism. What makes this a strictly "academic" exercise is that such a tautology provides the critic virtually unlimited ground for maneuvering among a wide variety of texts no one previously would have grouped together. Said immediately suggests that such a "vague and general" label was, at the time of his writing, no longer popular, having been progressively neutralized into "area studies."[49] Orientalism, however, is assumed to live on "through its doctrines and theses about the Orient and the Oriental."

Said broadens the preexisting sense of Orientalism beyond the philological and area studies that this general term had previously embraced. The formal fields that made up Oriental studies in the 1970s are passed over in the process. Orientalists were part of an academic domain that had a historical bias. In Ancient Near Eastern studies, archaeologists and linguists attempted to resurrect long-dead languages such as Ancient Egyptian (from hieroglyphics), Sumerian, Akkadian, Ugaritic, and Assyrian. Even here an Egyptologist would be distinguished from an Assyriologist. "Semitic studies" still served to define scholars of biblical Hebrew and ancient Israel, with British practice stubbornly including Aramaic and Arabic. Judaic studies covered research on the history of Judaism through the present. Arabic studies, Iranian studies, and Central Asian studies bordered each other on a quasi-geographical plain. Indology reigned over Indian studies, perhaps to avoid confusion with Columbus's New World error which paved the way for American Indians; fortunately, Indianology never evolved. Sinology and Chinese studies could both fit under the broader umbrella of Far East studies.[50] As historian Richard Bulliet notes, Orientalism was about languages and texts, not the various "reportage" of travelers, novelists, and poets.[51] Post-Said, the notion of Orientalism seems to have been liberated from any pretense of studying real parts of the historical Orient.

Inherent in this first redefinition are two weak assumptions. The first is that you can be an Orientalist and not know it; indeed, such a definition assumes there is no way to teach, write, or do research on the Orient without being an Orientalist. As stated, even an expert in literary-cum-cultural criticism such as Roland Barthes should fall under the rubric, although this is clearly not what Said would argue in more, or perhaps less, judiciously crafted prose. This blanket bundling of scholars and writers of many genres is not a supposition to be accepted at face value.[52] Second, as numerous critics have pointed out, Said's highly selective sample of "dogmatic" Orientalists ignores scholars who not only were skeptical of earlier dogmatism, but also were working more objectively to counter and refute stereotypes. It is easy to target a biased nineteenth-century racial apologist such as Comte de Gobineau, but what of seminal figures like Ignaz Goldziher, whose pioneering scholarship is still respected and consulted?[53] The Egyptian scholar Muhammad Amin Fikri Bey met Goldziher at the eighth International Congress of Orientalists in Stockholm and honored him with the title of al-Azhari because of Goldziher's earlier study at that Islamic university. Most blatantly, Said was either unaware of or willfully ignored the scholarly output of quite respectable "Arab" or "Muslim" Orientalists such as Ihsan Abbas, G. C. Anawati, Mohammed Arkoun, Aziz Atiyeh, Abd al-Aziz al-Duri, Philip Hitti, Albert Hourani, George Makdisi, Muhsin Mahdi, Said Nafisi, Seyyed Hossein Nasr, Fazlur Rahman, Hisham Sharabi, and Farhat Ziadeh;[54] nor does he see any agency among Arab and Muslim intellectuals not in exile in the West.[55] I can think of few anthropologists—the first discipline singled out in Said's definition—who thought of themselves as "Orientalists" or who were even fluent in the discourse taught in Oriental Studies departments; this includes major Muslim anthropologists such as Akbar Ahmed, Talal Asad, and Abdul Hamid El Zein.[56] Certainly none of these anthropologists, who all pursued ethnographic fieldwork in Muslim communities, would have subscribed to the biased philological assumption that abstractions from classical texts "are always preferable to direct evidence drawn from modern Oriental realities."[57]

Political scientist Malcolm Kerr chides Said for ignoring a large number of credible European Orientalist writers, including Snouck Hurgronje, Becker, Nöldeke, Wellhausen, Gabrieli, Levi Della Vida, Schacht, Rosenthal, Goitein, Arberry, Watt, Coulson, Gellner, Evans-Pritchard, Cahen, Brunschwig, Le Tourneau, Laoust, Gardet, Rodinson, Miquel, and Berque, "which is rather a lot."[58] "Surely as a group," concludes Kerr, "they have exerted as much intellectual influence as Said's select roster of ogres, and surely they have not been altogether brainwashed by the tradition."[59] Anthropologist Akbar Ahmed lists a number of "post-orientalist" Western scholars who allow the native voice to speak and who suggest little evidence of cultural superiority. These include Lois Beck, William Chittick, Hastings Donnan, Ross Dunn, John Esposito, Michael Fischer, Michael Gilsenan, Barbara Metcalf, Henry Munson Jr., Francis Robinson, André Singer, Pnina Werbner, and Theodore Wright Jr.[60] Said retorts with the self-serving complaint that he does not need to catalogue "every Orientalist who ever lived."[61] No one is asking that. The issue is why he selects only those scholars who seem to have demonstrable racist and ethnocentrist bias.

A second problem emerges in linking membership in the proposed class of Orientalists to doctrines and theses associated in general with being an Orientalist. The boundary between scholars who critically study an Oriental language and mere devotees of the Orient does not exist in Said's textual homogenization. For example, in labeling modern American political scientists Orientalists, Said admits that his use of the word is "anomalous," because they do not call themselves that.[62] The beauty of this rhetorical ploy is that being an Orientalist is in the eyes of the beholder; Said, in this case, is the one beholding. Thus, he can target a wretched excuse for scholarship like Sania Hamady's *Temperament and Character of the Arabs* as indicative of Orientalist scholarship simply because it was written about the Orient. By the same token, a piece of uninformed and irreducibly nonscholarly speculation like Erich von Däniken's wildly popular *Chariots of the Gods* should qualify, as it includes a number of archaeological and mythological tidbits about the Orient, such as a modern battery allegedly found in ancient Babylon.[63] Anything written about the Orient becomes relevant for understanding Orientalism as an academic discourse; this is the pernicious orientation of *Orientalism*. If there is one rotten text in the barrel, then the whole lot must be contaminated by a routinizing textual attitude. The result is definition by quarantine. Behind the smokescreen of a "readily accepted" working definition, Said assumes what needs to be proven, the common fallacy of a circular argument.[64]

The imprecise stretching of "Orientalist" to include virtually anyone who has anything to say about the Orient is hard even for Said to maintain. His admiration for Raymond Schwab, a French historian who wrote a survey on the growth of professional Orientalism in Europe, is a case in point: "So profound and beneficent is Schwab's view of the Orient that one is doubtless more accurate in describing him as an orienteur than as an orientaliste, a man more interested in a generous awareness than in detached classification."[65] Schwab is recognized as pursuing a "criticism of sympathetic cast," and documents, like Said, the "condescending veneration" and "saddening impoverishment" of modern Orientalism.[66] Schwab wrote about the Orient, so how does this Orientalist-by-default escape the hegemonic discourse that affects other scholars?

Nasrin Rahimieh, among others, finds a major methodological weakness in Said's claim that writers cannot escape the misrepresentations inherent in Orientalism.[67] Take the case of Louis Massignon, an admired French scholar who figures prominently in *Orientalism*. If "Massignon's presence in Orientalism was a constant challenge to his colleagues,"[68] and if he was "willing to cross disciplinary and traditional boundaries in order to penetrate to the human heart of any text,"[69] what exactly was his sin? Said goes to great lengths to praise Massignon's lack of hostility to Islam and political activism on the part of Palestinians, yet in his uncritically oppositional mode Said then falls back on his prior and unprovable assumption that not even a scholar of Massignon's stature "can resist the pressure on him of his nation or of the scholarly tradition in which he works."[70] In Massignon's case, he is accused of not outgrowing the racial categories of his generation, of positing an essential difference for the Orient even as he so well represented it as "the rarest-veined unraveler of Islamic civilization the West has produced."[71] But Said does not prove his point here by pinpointing wilful misrepresentations, as he so emphatically tries to do with Gibb or Lewis. In the end, an "exceptional genius" like Massignon cannot escape the latent will to dominate in the "universe of discourse"[72] simply because all Orientalist "truth" is by Saidian definition "representation" embedded in the cultural and institutional context of the scholar.

So is Massignon a culturally discoursed robot or a thinking author? Said is well aware that Foucault would opt for the former: "Yet unlike Michel Foucault, to whose work I am greatly indebted," Said admits, "I do believe in the determining imprint of individual authors upon the otherwise anonymous collective body of texts constituting a discursive formation like Orientalism."[73] Said proposes, contra Foucault, to "employ close textual readings whose goal is to reveal the dialectic between individual text or writer and the complex collective formation to which his work is a contribution."[74] Yet in the case of Massignon it is not Said's reading of texts that reveals a dialectic but his underlying assumption about the discursive dominance of Orientalism that conceals agency. James Clifford refers to this un-Foucauldian maneuver as sidetracking "by humanist fables of authenticity,"[75] but I think it might also be described as a de-tracting through de-humanizing the individual from his or her ability to negotiate within a cultural context. To blame Massignon for not knowing what we now accept as a better and certainly bitter "truth" should not negate the extent to which this particular Orientalist was able in his time to critique Orientalist stereotypes for their individually determinable "untruth." Mohammed Sharafuddin, in critiquing Said, suggests we "rethink the context and purpose of a given text and what it aims to achieve in its audience before we condemn its author as a partaker of his age's ignorance and blindness."[76]

Said is forced to flip-flop on who is a good Orientalist and who is bad. The historian R. W. Southern is praised for "brilliantly," "elegantly," and "superbly" showing that Europeans had a "complex ignorance" of Islam.[77] Said is right to commend Southern, whose 1962 book sought to correct stereotypes about Islam and suggested that this would be a struggle, especially "against the conservatism of established academic routine."[78] Similarly, Said mentions Norman Daniel's "admirable" study of Western attitudes to Islam, even finding "remarkable implications" for his analysis of Orientalism.[79] Yet by Said's broad definition, Southern and Daniel are guild members of Orientalism. These scholars do not fit the paradigm: "what the Orientalist does is to confirm the Orient in the readers' eyes; he neither tries nor wants to unsettle already firm convictions."[80] It is this very aim of unsettling firmly ignorant convictions that compels Southern and Daniel to write their books. "Of itself, in itself, as a set of beliefs, as a method of analysis, Orientalism cannot develop," claims Said.[81] If Southern and Daniel, as well as Schwab and Massignon, are exceptions, why does Said's polemicized rhetoric leave no room for such individual positivities?

Orientalism must exist for Said as a cancerous whole as long as certain doctrines, suspect because of their origins in an imperialist colonial context, are still around. In this scenario, the gross stereotypes inherent in racist, ethnocentric, and sexist renderings of the Orient can not be eradicated; they flourish among the worst offenders and inevitably debilitate the work of would-be sympathizers. Said insists that Orientalists have been incapable of being self-critical or moving beyond the limitations of earlier doctrines, attitudes, and dogmas. In this case the tales of Orientalist discourse wag the dog. Such reductionism prompts Samir Amin to rectify Said's generic fallacy:

> Orientalism is not the sum of the works of Western specialists and scholars who have studied non-European societies: this clarification is necessary to avoid misunderstandings and quarrels. This term refers to the ideological construction of a mythical "Orient," whose characteristics are treated as immutable traits defined in simple opposition to the characteristics of the "Occidental" world.[82]

Rhetorically, Said's first definition is a case of original synecdoche in which the sum of Orientalist thought is inflated to cover virtually anything ever imagined about an Orient.

The second sense of Orientalism proposed by Said is a general, but more straightforward, reduction of Orientalism to "an ontological and episte-mological distinction made between 'the Orient' and (most of the time) 'the Occident.'" The epistemological dimension is self-evident; such a division had been widely used for centuries as a cultural overlay on geographical space. Examples of such othering abound in Said's book. Greek playwrights, medieval Christian monks, and vulgar Italian poets set the stage for an Enlightenment rendering of the world where the bulk of the light shone out of Europe toward allegedly darker climes. The classic case for the binary bondage of an East inferior to the West can be found in a book that has been a primary source in Western libraries for more than half a century. I refer to Edith Hamilton's acclaimed *The Greek Way*, in which "it is the spirit of the East that never changes" and India is dismissed as a space where "the idea of truth became completely separated from outside fact."[83] This is classicist snobbery at its zenith, but please note that Edith Hamilton was no Orientalist.

This radical distinction between East and West is labeled by Said as both ontological and epistemological, an odd philosophical pairing for a literary critic intent on challenging the assumptions of texts. As a way of knowing, the construction of an Orient calls for an epistemology in need of a hermeneutic, not a literary metaphysic. The interpretive frame for the Orient as knowledge leads to Said's rendering of Orientalism as discourse in the Foucauldian sense, a knowledge that empowers its maker through the subterfuge of ordering reality. But in what sense can an ordinary linguistic binary ordering be labeled ontological? Said is content to assert that there is no disagreement among modern studies of culture and imperialism on the "fundamental ontological distinction between the West and the rest of the world." If the Orient is an invention, how much more so is the post-*Orientalism* reification of *rest* to ontological status? With apologies to Ernst Haeckel, ontology is not recapitulated by phylogeny.

Said builds on a compelling linguistic metaphor: how can we imagine an east without a west, an up not paired with a down, a self with no other? Such a seemingly semiotic yet disappointingly semantic rationale is contorted from historical context. From the standpoint of Europe there is indeed peopled land to its east. Such a spatial ordering in and of itself is innocuous as a label. For someone in the region defined as east of Europe, there would inevitably be an equivalent response to the west that defines it as east. Platonic idealism aside, east or west arise out of the geography that allows us to conceive of directions as orientations. The distinction between east and west is in its origins relational, not essential. The philosophical concern with being and existence, whether in a Western or Eastern sense here, plays no role in Said's critical assessment. In the realm of representations, the only realm that Said wishes to address in his book, ontology becomes as irrelevant as theology. Even so, as Johannes Fabian comments on a different author in a different context, "ontology does not get us through the day."[84] The point is that alterity is an epistemological problem before it becomes an ontological issue.

For Said, the East-West distinction must exist prior to all else. It is the fundamental starting point for a "large mass of writers" that includes poets as well as economists and imperial administrators. To assume, with little subsequent attention to proof, that a poet and an economist could meaningfully share such a starting point seems out of place for a literary critic of Said's training and expertise. The implication is that those who write about the Orient must be motivated by the absolute distinction between themselves and the Orient. This parallels, in error, Said's earlier insistence that anyone who writes about the Orient is ipso facto an Orientalist. Thus, all individual, cultural, class, gender, and a myriad of cross-cutting influences are rendered mute by the alleged ontological primacy of Occident vs. Orient. This is tantamount to asserting that any Christian theologian writing about his religion must be molded immutably by the textualized opposition of God and Devil or Heaven and Hell. That such binary oppositions exist, that they can bedevil writers of all shades, is easily established and hardly a novel insight. Perhaps Said wishes to replicate the intellectually stimulating and historically unsatisfying Hellenism/Hebraism dyad of Victorian critic Matthew Arnold.[85] How impotent the human imagination and how feeble the creative impulse if the authors of texts are condemned to be unwitting slaves to the hege-mono-homogenized texts of their fathers.

By subsuming all potential individual and cultural difference into the interplay of Orientalists' West as ego contra Orientalists' Orient as alter ego, Said implies that only one *other* is significant. This reductionist rendering of cross-cultural interaction, imaginative or otherwise, is in itself ideological. Having assumed that there is no meaningful difference in how various European nationalities view the sum total of others, Said is freed to range in a general near-easterly direction and to fire shots at the nearest ships on the horizon; the true colors of their flags can not save them. There are, however, several others imaginable. Ter Ellingson, for example, refers to a tripartite contrast among European, Oriental, and Savage in the construction of European identity after the Renaissance.[86] The colonial other that became the United States hardly evolved along the imagined East/West divide that Said attributes to contemporary political scientists. Oleg Grabar says it well for the American context of Orientalism: "The complexity of modern American culture is such that there are many 'others' in its psychological makeup and that the 'others' of some are the 'us' of others. And it is in fact difficult to argue today for a single or even for a prevalent vision or myth about the past or about the rest of the world."[87]

The Orient for Said is the West's major significant other, even though it is never quite clear where the West begins and ends. "It could be a form of paranoia on my part," admits Said, "but it does seem to me that the Orientalism I was speaking of contains a unique set of attitudes, a kind of virulence and persistence that I haven't seen elsewhere."[88] Setting aside whether or not this implies something especially alluring about the Orient in Europe's colonial expansion, Said can be criticized along Derridian lines for embracing the very dichotomy he wishes to attack. A central problem with flawed Orientalist renderings of an essentialized East is the privileging of sameness over difference. Said's rhetorical representation of Orientalism as a unified discourse buys into the very logic it opposes. By building his counter-argument on the same fundamental distinction between two essentialized abstractions, Said does little more than replace one flawed scheme with another. As Catherine Gimelli Martin argues, Said's East–West binary does not provide a critique of the Western epistemology that creates Orientalist discourse, but succumbs to "a repetition of its own inherent dichotomies."[89] Neither the Orient as envisioned nor Orientalism as envenomed can adequately represent the reality that Said and his readers care about.

My objection raised here is anticipated but deftly deflected by Said himself, who promises to speak later of "methodological problems one encounters in so broadly construed a 'field' as this."[90] As an author choosing pronouns, Said positions himself at the start of his introduction as an "I" who continually calls out against Orientalism. The "I" is reiterated and reinforced by "in my opinion" as he starts to define Orientalism. Here the "I" reveals the narrator's intent to deal later with methodological problems. Yet the "I" who is willing to challenge an entire range of scholars absents itself from the problems that "one" encounters along the way. Unwilling to engage the reader in dialogue as a *you* with a potential counter-voice, the author leaves it to the undirected and anonymous "one" to encounter any difficulty with the definitions being articulated. The "I" comes back quickly in the narrative in order to come to a third meaning of Orientalism, to find Foucault useful, to be content, to believe, to examine—all text-framed assertions of the narrator's total power. In Said's introduction, the "one" only returns rhetorically to state qualifications of his definitions. Finally the "one" and the "I" cross paths in a rhetorical ploy, intended or not, that mutes criticism:

One ought never to assume that the structure of Orientalism is nothing more than a structure of lies or of myths which, were the truth about them to be told, would simply blow away. I myself believe that Orientalism is more particularly valuable as a sign of European-Atlantic power over the Orient than it is as a veridic discourse about the Orient.[91]

A critical inquisition of Said's rhetoric is revealing here, as there is more to an author than what meets the "I." The authorial "I" of Said is one of demonstration in the polyvocal—or shall I say polyscriptal—sense of the author function, as Foucault suggests in his "What Is an Author?" essay.[92] This need not be the individual Edward Said, even though he emphasizes the *myself* truth of his reasons for writing about Orientalism. The narrated ego is altered to include anyone who would accept what is already remonstrated and about to be demonstrated. Yet, in this passage there is a pronoun shift that could be called author dysfunction. The "I" of Said proposes, while an indeterminate and therefore unempowered "one" is the one prone to skepticism and gullibility. In the narrative flow of *Orientalism*'s introduction this ambiguous "one" reappears to ask itself a brief question and then disappears from textual presence to be firmly replaced by the dominating "I" of Said himself. The "one" as foil is no match for the claims of the author. It serves as an illusion of dialogue that only perpetuates the force of Said's demonstrative monologuery.[93]

Critics of Said's threefold rendering of Orientalism frequently point to his inconsistencies, but less attention has been paid to the passionate devotion he shows for the persuasive power of absolute dualisms. Scott Nygren rightly chides Said for assuming that "these already formed a magical polarity rather than a juxtaposition of different social and cultural constructs."[94] I am reminded of Durkheim's enormously influential, yet practically flawed, reduction of religion to an absolute demarcation between sacred and profane. As with Said, Durkheim's problem comes from clothing an epistemological device in ontological status. Durkheim insists, to the point of theologizing sociology, that the absoluteness in the distinction between sacred and profane is what makes religion so pervasive and powerful.[95] One can find—even I can find—ready-made examples of sacred and profane, from totemic taboos to the Eucharist. But so reducing the religious says more about the binary penchant of human classification through language than it does about the distinctive characteristics of religious beliefs and behavior. Durkheim, like Said, accepted the terms of the very position he set out to dislodge: that there is no effective counter and no turning back from that which becomes "sacred." Whether or not this distinction is formally said to be absolute, human fear and existential dilemma suggest that it often is not. To stress the absolute distinction is to sidestep, not resolve, the paradox inherent in the opposition. If this can be said about religious ideology, certainly we should examine the same problematic in as politically charged a discourse as Said's Orientalism thesis.

Said might have evaded this foundational essentialization of East and West had he stayed with his earlier gloss of this distinction as dogma rather than discourse. In introducing the first of his proposed "primary dogmas of Orientalism" as "the absolute and systematic difference between the West (which is rational, developed, humane, superior) and the Orient (which is aberrant, undeveloped, inferior),"[96] he cites a stereotype that at the time of his writing would have been similarly rejected by the vast majority of those he lumps together as Orientalists. But at least a dogma, unlike Foucauldian discourse, can be doggedly attacked and overturned. As Kwame Anthony Appiah has wryly noted, this binarism of self and other "is the last of the shibboleths of the modernizers that we must learn to live without."[97] Unfortunately, much of the debate following Orientalism has been "locked into the categories of colonizer vs. colonized, East vs. West, Islam vs. Christendom, Western Self vs. Native Other in ways that keep our gaze fixed upon the discursive hegemony of the West."[98]

In *Orientalism*, Said does not consider alternative approaches to Eurocentric assumptions about alleged ontologically induced binaries. The African scholar Léopold Senghor, for example, deplores the Western approach as "essentially static, objective, dichotomic; it is, in fact, dualistic, in that it makes an absolute distinction between body and soul, matter and spirit."[99] For Senghor and others, there is an "African" approach that "conceives the world, beyond the diversity of its forms, as a fundamentally mobile, yet unique, reality that seeks synthesis." In *Culture and Imperialism*, Said reduces Senghor's *négritude* to one of those chauvinism-prone "nativist and radical nationalisms" alongside Islamic fundamentalism and Arabism.[100] To adopt *négritude*, Said argues, it is necessary to accept "the consequences of imperialism, the racial, religious, and political divisions imposed by imperialism itself."[101] But surely, this is the very problem with Said's thesis. Rather than offering an alternative synthesis to binary thinking, Said's polemic rides the oppositional wave of antithesis.

This insistence on an ontological distinction between East and West as a defining element of Orientalism fails to build on previous critiques leveled by a number of scholars who would per force be dismissed as biased Orientalists. Said was apparently unaware of the most thorough study of the intellectual roots for the "myth" of East vs. West: Kurt Goldammer's

Der Mythus von Ost und West: Eine kultur- und religionsgeschichtliche Betrachtung (1962). Goldammer targets the tendency in the literature to ignore factual differences and posit a false uniformity, to reduce the East to a racial question, and to portray the East falsely as a mirror of the West. "The entire phenomenon," concludes Goldammer, "belongs to a large number of pre-conceived opinions and dogmatic definitions with which we live and under which we suffer, that imbue our daily life and knowledge, and which do not disgust us even after a generation of use."[102] Other criticisms of such an East–West binary were available, even in English. A decade before *Orientalism* appeared, John Steadman wrote, "Many a writer on Asia treats the Orient as though it were a single entity (which it is not)—and thus postulates a unity that has no real existence outside his own imagination."[103] Arguing that there was "no objective basis for the dichotomy of East and West," Steadman studies the "myth" of Asia as "the anatomy of an illusion, the dissection of an eidolon."[104] Writing at almost the same time, Stephan Hay goes so far as to say that the "idea of 'the East' is now all but extinct."[105] The binary was already under indictment by scholars within, as well as without, the very guild Said thinks incapable of such self-critique. The reflective self-criticism in *Orientalism*, as Azim Nanji argues, "was by no means the first of its kind."[106] Yet Said writes as if he were the first to see through the myth.

To add to this geographical disorientation, Said forgets that Europe equally misrepresented its own West. For British imperialism in particular, Said fails to make a case that the notion of Orient was unique in the mapping of an empire upon which the sun never set. Such an argument might be made, but only after comparative historical research on the full range of British expansion.[107] Consider the Irish, who were barbarized within Christendom.[108] Fynes Moryson, secretary to Lord Mountjoy in 1615, had traveled to North Africa and the Middle East, thus making him a potential Orientalist in Said's eyes. Yet, it was not the Orient that he scorned, but the unruly Irish as "more barbarous and more brutish in their costomes and demeanures then in any other parte of the world that is knowne."[109] Ireland would fit well in Said's geographically imagined Orient, except for the fact it was an other within Europe and lies due west of London. Similarly, English travellers to the Bosphorus often tarred modern Greek Orthodox "with the same brush" as they did the Turks.[110] Then there is northern Europe's "southern question," a legacy of prejudice within the West.[111] By treating the West as the homogenized geographical space of Orientalists, Said avoids having to look at the implications of localized East–West differences within European history.

With the East–West fault line first defined as a generic given, Said is able to avoid the all-too-real post–World War II political map of the West as the Free World vs. the East as a communist bloc under Soviet and Chinese influence. Said consistently approaches European and American foreign policy as specifically directed against an Oriental other rather than caught up in ideological alliances fueled by recent history. World War II served as a major transition in modern Orientalism, leading to a shift from European to American political dominance and to the eventual politicization of Arabs in the American consciousness.[112] Ironically, the world war itself did much to dispel the old notion of "Orient" as the playpen for Western imperialists. The Japanese sided with the Germans; the Chinese were forced into the arms of the British, Americans, and Russians.[113] As the Cold War started to warm up, the epoch of East-as-a-career imperialism was superseded. By implying that an unbroken line linked Napoleon's entry into Cairo with the Israeli occupation of Palestine, Said ignores the complexities of the intervening history. East Block–West Block politics surveyed over the Berlin Wall is a far cry from Raj India spread before Kipling's colonial veranda.

Thus, the conflict in *Orientalism* is binarily escalated by indiscriminately opposing linguistic bundles. The pairs of East and West, Orient and Occident, Asia and Europe, Islam and Christianity are used by Said interchangeably.[114] Orient dominates as the rhetorical counterpart of West; Said only occasionally resorts to the pedantically distanced Occident apart from other scholars' book titles. Such a shift is common and trivial, a matter of direction no matter what the romantic origin. But much of the time Orient takes its place in opposition to Europe, in which case an area only bounded by the limits of imagination plays off against a continent. The bulk of Said's focus is on the Near or Middle East, which is idiosyncratically labeled the "Near Orient" in *Orientalism*'s index, with occasional jumps to British India.[115] As D. K. Fieldhouse notes, this is problematic beyond the constrictive geography, for the British administrators and Orientalists in India were more aware of local culture than most of their peers in the Near East.[116] China and Japan appear on the first page of *Orientalism*, but only to be dismissed as an American penchant for limiting the term to the Far East. Because Said's analysis virtually excludes Orientals who are not Arabs or Muslims, a large part of Asia is effectively subsumed under the category but not subjected to analysis. As a result, Said shows, in the words of H. D. Harootunian, "an astonishing indifference to the rest of the colonial world."[117]

It is the third meaning of Orientalism that fully engages the critical acumen of Said and most excites and incites his readers. The two generalized senses of Orientalism as whatever Orientalists do and what they always do to an othered Orient are situated "historically and materially" in the colonial expansion of Britain and France over the past two centuries. Orientalism is now fully exposed "as a Western style for dominating, restructuring, and having authority over the Orient."[118] Style is, of course, too light a term for the politically charged sense of hegemonic discourse that Said conjures out of Foucault and Gramsci. Aijaz Ahmad observes that Said suggests mainly what this style is "not," so that we are told it is not what colonialist ideology says it is; pinpointing what Said means is largely left to our own imagination.[119] Said argues that a fundamental corollary of Orientalism's stylistic production of the Orient is its representational function as "a sort of surrogate and underground self" to imperial Europe. Has there ever been an imperialist colonizer for whom its colonies did not serve as "a sort of surrogate"?

Rather than parse out the principles by which an overarching ideology engineered historical interaction, Said performs a post hoc sleight of hand. Orientalism as a specific and absolute discourse must exist. How else can "one" possibly "understand the enormously systematic discipline by which European culture was able to manage, and even produce, the Orient politically, sociologically, militarily, ideologically, scientifically, and imaginatively during the post-Enlightenment period"?[120] The argument is that such an obvious historical overmatch in all its colonial strength requires an all-powerful discourse. This a priori validation of discourse, fueled consciously by Said's own passionate understanding of the damage done to the real Orient, allows him to avoid historiographic method, the rigorous kind of analysis that he admits not having the expertise to do.[121]

There is ground for more than philosophical disputation when we are asked to deal with specific writers from specific countries writing specific texts. The bulk of *Orientalism* is exactly this: hindsight criticism of selected paradigmatic Orientalist texts. But rather than engage in an empirical investigation to induce a characterization of Orientalism as a limited or limiting discourse, Said proposes "a different methodological alternative." This comes down to the "historical generalizations" he makes in first defining the concept. Although his numerous introductory generalizations are eventually discussed "in more analytic detail" in his narrative, it is with the narrowly focused lens of a literary critic rather than the methodological tools of a trained historian. "The result," concludes Leonard Binder "is a rather well-worn restatement of the concept of ideology linked closely to the idea of the sociology of knowledge, applied to imperialist politics, and pursued by the methods of textual criticism which here seem to have granted a license to assemble only the exemplary evidence which supports the writer's theme, without defining the field of evidence in advance."[122]

Said reads over the discourse he labels as Orientalism, but his chosen texts are contested outside of their cultural context. We read about Napoleon in Egypt and about the French travelers who benefited from this short-lived imperialist incursion, but the voices of Egyptians are missing. Indigenous voices, representing themselves, can be found through rigorous historical investigation. Said simply assumes them to be as mute as the decaying mummies that some Europeans wanted to ship back to their national museums.

Have the European powers been such a juggernaut over the last few centuries that the entire Orient lay prone, like a lounging odalisque, for a penetration that struck with impunity at the very core ability of peoples in the region to define themselves? The assertion of an absolute hegemonic muting of indigenous response should not go unchallenged. Non-exilic voices were raised in protest and defiance in Arabic, Persian, Turkish, and even the colonizers' languages.[123] None of the real Orientals representing themselves in the face of overt othering are consulted in Said's text. The lone reference to al-Jabarti, who chronicled Napoleon's invasion, focuses inexplicably on how this Arab scholar was impressed by the French scholars.[124] Is this shortcoming a result of the damage that the presence of such counterhegemonic discourse might imply for his own assumptions, or is it simply the naive error of a scholar with amateur status outside his specialty? Ironically, Said's presence as an authoritative critic of Orientalism "is enabled by the Orient's effective absence."[125] The force of Said's argument persuades in large part because the real Orient is "all absence."

The further assumptions implied in Said's third definition pose more problems. European cultures, of which America becomes an extension by default, are said to have both managed and produced the Orient. With no specification of what qualifies as either managing or producing, we are left only with the obvious historical fact that Britain and France managed to gain a colonial foothold in parts of the region. From a strict political view it would be nonsensical to speak of the actual history over the past few centuries as well managed. Up until the end of the Ottoman empire, it can hardly be said that this region was controlled on puppet strings by European powers. British and French encroachment was at the margins, as befit empires built on naval superiority. Both imperial powers were adept at negotiating with indigenous leaders in order to further the economic interests of empire without always having to suffer the bruises of direct colonial control. If Britain managed an empire on which the sun never set, it must also be noted that not all natives, intellectual or otherwise, foreswore their own place under that sun. There was virtually no on-the-ground management of most people in the Middle East, China, Japan, or large chunks of India. Islam, far from being replaced or even dented by Christianity, despite the collusion of missionary and military interests, spread dramatically in Asia and Africa during this same period of European colonial expansion.[126] The fact that all these colonies were dismantled after World War II is a sign of the ultimate failure of imperialist Orientalist discourse in empire-molding.

As Said suggests, the meaning of Orientalism becomes clearer in the title of the first part of his final chapter: "Latent and Manifest Orientalism." The clearest representation of this dual nature of Orientalism stands out in the following key passage:

> The distinction I am making is really between an almost unconscious (and certainly an untouchable) positivity, which I shall call latent Orientalism, and the various stated views about Oriental society, languages, history, sociology, and so forth, which I shall call manifest Orientalism. Whatever change occurs in knowledge of the Orient is found almost exclusively in manifest Orientalism; the unanimity, stability, and durability of latent Orientalism are more or less constant.[127]

Before teasing out the meaning of this passage, it is important to look at Said's rhetorical style. Beyond the working definitions outlined at the start, this distinction here is what he "really" means, the heart of the matter. Notice how this passage sidesteps a totalizing sense by qualifying "unconscious" with "almost," "found" with "almost exclusively," and "unanimity, stability, and durability" with "more or less." This trope of the adverbial caveat dangled like catnip before the reader allows Said to speak in round numbers, so to speak, rather than giving what might be called a statistical, and thus potentially falsifiable, sense to his argument. As a result, any exceptions pointed out by a critic are pre-mitigated. The caveats appear to flow from cautious scholarship, but the latent intent is that of a polemicist.

LATENT IN THE MANIFEST

> So far as anyone wishing to make a statement of any consequence about the Orient was concerned, latent Orientalism supplied him with an enunciative capacity that could be used, or rather mobilized, and turned into sensible discourse for the concrete occasion at hand.
>
> —EDWARD SAID, *ORIENTALISM*

My critique of this tripartate definition of Orientalism is necessarily incomplete, and would clearly remain unconvincing to Said himself for a very simple reason. The "three things" that Said means by Orientalism are the manifest part of his argument. They point to Said's reluctance to define the concept in a definitive way that could then be challenged for being too narrow, inconsistent, or idiosyncratic. By offering the reader three interdependent ways of approaching Orientalism, he avoids having a central defining element that can be dismissed up front. To argue against any one of these only whittles away at the connotations; it does not get to the heart of the matter. Thus, when Aijaz Ahmad argues that Said's three definitions are "mutually incompatible," he glosses a crucial and far more critical point.[128] It does not really matter whether Said's variant readings are incompatible to the reader, for each contains at least a grain of truth. These are the working and negotiated word-meanings Said employs to serve the presentation of his argument. Faulting his rhetoric, although certainly a valid form of criticism, does not negate Said's argument as such. Situating his polemical rhetoric in historical context allows readers to rescue it from itself.

Unlike his use of Foucault's discourse and Gramsci's hegemony, Said's borrowing of "manifest" and "latent" is not itself made manifest in *Orientalism*. These terms are laden with meaning in the pyschoanalytic interpretation of dreams, especially in Lacan's reworking of Freudian theory.[129] But is Said setting up a philosophical or a psychoanalytic other? With "manifest" Said refers to those parts of Orientalist discourse that can be negotiated, viewed differently, or even debated. The manifest comprises the material elements of Orientalism: texts, authors, guilds, the apparatus of academic disciplines, professional societies, the publishing industry, colonial administrative structure, and the like. Said draws examples from these material elements, especially texts, but his whole point is that nothing manifest makes sense without grounding the whole complex in the "positivity" that ultimately defines it as hegemonic discourse. In Said's own conceptual sense, the latent is what makes an otherwise dull and academic system worldly, what links it to the real world where people are abused and killed, not just thought to be inferior.

It is relevant that Said only uses "manifest" and "latent" in an adjectival sense; each describes an aspect of Orientalism without having to give that aspect a form or name of its own. It is easy to provide multiple examples of the manifest, because in a real sense it is only the manifest that can be documented. The latent can be elicited only by reading between the lines, but Said has a tendency to choose lines of such seemingly singular meaning that they override an alternate, even a nuanced, reading. What could be more damning than quoting Flaubert's crass reduction of the Oriental woman to a sex object: "The oriental woman is no more than a machine: she makes no distinction between one man and another man."[130] The manifest reading of such an isolated musing shocks the reader into thinking there is no need to probe the context and intent of the author. But is this how Flaubert sees *the* Oriental woman, certain types of Oriental women, or all Oriental women, or is it the result of an experience with a particular Oriental woman? Is this the way Flaubert desired to look at Oriental women before he went to the Orient? Is Flaubert expressing his rock-hard feelings here, or is he trying to impress the intended reader? Manifest readings, as Said so often demonstrates, always have hidden possibilities, yet the questions I raise are unexamined by Said. Said represents Flaubert just as surely as Flaubert "spoke for and represented her."[131]

What exactly does Said say was latent in Orientalism? His examples are primarily "latent and unchanging characteristics" that get presented as "dogmas." The specific characteristics he mentions fall into three broad categories: racist, ethnocentric, and sexist. Orientalist texts are said to reflect racial characteristics assumed to be inherent or natural—what passed for biological at the time. Thus, the essentializing of Orientals as exuding inferiority and being degenerate accentuated a racist contrast to "white" Europeans. Because they were born—say as Arab or Indian—with innately inferior racial characteristics, they were subjectable to more refined European control. This line of reasoning had long been directed at African slaves. A second set of characteristics overlaps with the racial but refers more to cultural failings, such as religious and social customs. It was European ethnocentrism that labeled Orientals as being backward and uncivilized, having supine malleability—which appears to mean lacking moral stamina—and appearing eccentric or exotic. The third variety of traits centers on a dual sense of sexism. On the one hand, the Orient is exploitable because of its feminine penetrability; the masculine master can rape, in the extreme sense, the feminine subject at will because he has both the power and the will to do so. Moreover, manifest Orientalists—the ones writing texts and making policy—were almost exclusively men writing for men.[132] Said rightly notes that Western society lumps together its own "delinquents, insane, women, and poor" as the "lamentably alien elements" that best model the Orient. If this is true, the latent tendencies must transcend rather than define a specifically Orientalist discourse.

Finding examples of latent Orientalism is complicated precisely because it is hidden or disguised, assumed to be real but only seen in its manifest effects. The words Said chooses to give linguistic form to such a definitively abstract concept are notably vague. Latent Orientalism is described as "an almost unconscious (and certainly an untouchable) positivity," "group of ideas," "widely diffused notions," "Orientalist consensus," "far more intimate and proprietary attitude," "Western handling," "commonly held view," "cumulative vision," and "enunciative capacity."[133] Nothing here is readily observable or concrete; the terminology refers to ideas and the generation of meaning. To the extent that Said discovers a smoking gun, all he really provides is smoke. I do not deny the existence of such biased smoke, nor the smokescreens often created to avoid dealing with such prejudice, but the gun must be palpable, and it should be more than the literary dueling of East and West. Indeed, Said argues that it is all too easy to ignore the latent because the underlying meaning is not apparent. His analysis proposes a hermeneutic unveiling of what informs and compels the manifest structure of Orientalism. What results is Orientalist discourse as hermetically sealed with an authoritative, monoglot voice. Caveats aside, manifest Orientalism was "built upon the prestigious authority of the pioneering scholars, travelers, and poets, whose cumulative vision had shaped a quintessential Orient; the doctrinal—or doxological—manifestation of such an Orient is what I have been calling here latent Orientalism."[134] Said's rhetoric stresses what might best be called a metaphysic by metaphor: that which is hidden is described as acting the way it would have to act if it were manifest.

The underlying insistence on discursive homogeneity overrides manifest differences in Orientalist discourse. Terms like "latent" and "hegemonic" stem from Said's own description, but his examples suggest that what is hidden and more powerful than individual intention is also superorganic in the sociological sense of transcending individual organisms or Orientalist authors. Such latent discourse becomes homogenizing when it blends all manifest differences into a pervasive mode of cultural domination. My quarrel is not with Said's contention that there is more to the manifest aspects of Orientalism than meets the eye. The history of academic Orientalism is as skeleton-prone as literary criticism, for example, because real authors inevitably write from an ethnocentric perch. What I fail to find, other than Said's categorical insistence that he can see through to the latent, is a mechanism that goes beyond metaphor.[135] Issues of racism, ethnocentrism, and sexism not only are factors in European representation of the Orient, but also are relevant for all known human interaction involving others.[136] The Egyptian critic Radwan al-Sayyid observes that the problems latent in imperialism afflict both East and West.[137] The mechanism that Said unrepentantly refuses to invoke is one that would link discourse to the biological givens of being human or the economic drives that everywhere shape human behavior. To do so would negate the imposed uniqueness of an ontological East/West divide.

Said further muddies his argument by enticing the reader to accept his rhetorical trope of using the term "Orient" to mean quite different things without clarifying each usage. The first "Orient" posed is "almost a European invention," a place to be thought about in fanciful terms. Such an Orient was, at the time of Said's writing soon after the start of the Lebanese civil war, "disappearing; in a sense it had happened, its time was over."[138] Immediately Said clarifies this as a "European representation of the Orient." The second "Orient" is that of the "Orientals themselves," real people who live and suffer there. The real Orient is one in which bombs drop, people are deprived of their rights, where the West buys its oil. The real Orient is what biased Orientalism has systematically and pathologically failed to truthfully represent.[139] Indeed it is the very existence of this second Orient, despite the damage done by the first, that propelled Said as an Arab Palestinian in the West to write his book.

Consider *Orientalism*'s seminal second paragraph, in which the word "Orient" appears nine times, not to mention its multiple it-ing and one adjectival variation. There are clearly several Orients at work here: "the" Orient, "this" Orient, and "that" Orient. There are two Orients as generally understood by Americans, a Far-ther East and a Near or Middle East, both with material consequences. The following passage stands out:

> The Orient is not only adjacent to Europe; it is also the place of Europe's greatest and richest and oldest colonies, the source of its civilizations and languages, its cultural contestant, and one of its deepest and most recurring images of the Other. In addition, the Orient has helped to define Europe (or the West) as its contrasting image, idea, personality, experience. Yet none of this Orient is merely imaginative. The Orient is an integral part of European material civilization and culture.[140]

Here we find the Orient as a geographic space adjacent to Europe, a colonial space carved out by colonialist intrusion, a place from which cultural and linguistic traits diffused, a competing cultural tradition and an image by which the West can define itself. Some of this Orient is imagined, to be sure, but there is a material—hence quite real—aspect of Orient in evidence. The Orient, similar to Said's definition of Orientalism, is thus many different things.

The first part of *Orientalism*'s introduction consistently (mis)pairs

Europe or America with the Orient.[141] To say the Orient is next to Europe is an apples-and-oranges fallacy. For most readers, Europe would denote a specifically bordered political space; the geographical coordinates of Orient are relational. "Orient" pairs with "Occident," and "East" with "West," but "Europe" demands "Asia." Said rarely resorts to the use of "West" in his argument. On the first page we are served parenthetical notice that the Orient helped to define Europe "(or the West)," which is soon followed by the East/West distinction in the second proposed meaning of Orientalism. But apart from a few introductory passages, it is overwhelmingly Europe that Said links to the Orient and fixes as the historical locus of Orientalism. As a result, whether intended or not, sheer repetition enforces the notion that a very recognizable and challengeable entity called "Europe" or "America" is equivalent for the purpose of argument to a vague and imagined invention labeled "Orient." The very notion of Europe should be treated as an invention, as many scholars have shown, but nowhere in *Orientalism* does Said follow this tack. The existence of Europe and America is never in doubt, because it is their disturbingly real complicity that Said seeks to indict. The reader is semantically set up to be sympathetic to his critical agenda from the start.

Setting aside lexical [dis]cohesion in the single passage quoted above, it is important to look at the content. What kinds of things are we being told about this multiply signified Orient? The spin on European colonialism is that Europe's greatest, richest, and oldest colonies were in the Orient. This is an astoundingly Orientocentric claim. Chronologically and in terms of the exploitation of resources, the colonies that initially sustained the imperialism and trade ambitions of Spain, France, and England surely lay in the opposite direction. The age of exploration and colonialism that seethed in the sixteenth century was in fact global, including the opening up of what seemed like new worlds. Asia, by its sheer bulk and uncharted boundaries, became an obvious but difficult target, although the greatest inroads were made far beyond Said's narrowed Near Orient. The observation by Said that the Orient was the source of European civilizations and languages is probably better explained by Said's sense of nostalgia than his attraction to some discredited diffusionist idea about civilization originating in Egypt or the lost tribes peopling Ireland. Why call myth, even of biblical proportions, the "source," unless actual history simply does not matter? Nor should we pass by the claim that an almost invented Orient was a "cultural contestant" for Europe. Certainly there was cultural borrowing, from lutes to tulips, but the contests most trumpeted in historical records were economic and political.

Another way of reading through Said's definitional rhetoric is provided by Sadiq Jalal al-'Azm's perceptive distinction between those aspects of Said's analysis about "Institutional Orientalism" and the more specifically targeted "Cultural-Academic Orientalism" that bears the brunt of the polemic.[142] The first type encompasses the institutions, the body of theory and practice, the ideological superstructure, and the vital interests of commercial, economic, and strategic dimensions. As such, this could as equally be an institutional "Occidentalism" if the subject were colonization of the New World west of Europe. Al-'Azm coins the term "Ontological Orientalism" for the "ahistorical, anti-human, and even anti-historical 'Orientalist' doctrine" that Said rightly exposes.[143] To the extent that Said sets out to deflate the disciplinal hubris of scientific detachment, objectivity, and independence from political bias, al-'Azm and most readers would concur. The issue here is not that Said was wrong in targeting prejudice, but rather that he applies slippery methods in folding back the literary productions of academic Orientalism into the broad and complex discourse of European imperial and cultural expansion. The manifest result of Said's polemical excess might as well be an "Orientalism in reverse,"[144] "occidentalism by detour,"[145] or even "reverse-Eurocentrism."[146]

III   Verbalizing an Orient

> In its connotations perhaps no single word has been so loaded
> with emotion, even passion, as has the term "Orient."
>
> —RAYMOND SCHWAB, *THE ORIENTAL RENAISSANCE*

"East is east, and west is west, and never the twain shall meet." I remember this white-man-ly burdened ditty as coming from my grandmother at a time when my knowledge of east and west centered on which side of the house her porch faced.[147] Through sheer geographic accident, the very notion of an orient or an east stems ultimately from historical exigencies. When Europe as ground zero for the invention of Orientalism began representing Orientals, it was the self-proclaimed center of a rather flat and closed-minded view of the world. For those who start intellectual history with the Greeks, the idea of an East has often been elicited, à la Said, out of Homer's *Iliad* and Aeschylus's *The Persians*, two texts assigned as required reading in the formal schooling of earlier Orientalists. "Europe is powerful and articulate; Asia is defeated and distant," Said concludes in his reading of Aeschylus.[148] But Aeschylus is not concerned with a generic Oriental; his literary nemesis is the historically significant Asiatic Persians led by Xerxes against Athens. There is no European imagination in this play, only the hubris of a Greek praising the gods for the prowess of his own civilization's warriors. In expanding the notion of a specific cultural group to later generic usage, Said conveniently overlooks the fact that this Greek portrays the Persians sympathetically, recalling their past glories.[149] "Certainly Homer, Euripides, Dante, St. Thomas, and all other authorities that one may care to mention," cautions Sadiq Jalal al-ʿAzm, "held the more or less standard distorted views prevalent in their milieux about other cultures and peoples."[150] Real-time enemies are always ripe for imagining.

Nowhere in *Orientalism* does Said discuss the etymology of the term "Orient," although the evolution of its use in Greek, Latin, and the Romance languages had been thoroughly documented at that point. The reader is reminded that "Orient" is one of those commonly sensed truths conjured by Herodotus and his ilk.[151] If indeed Europeans over time created a false idea of Orient, then it is useful to examine what the term originally meant to the Greeks themselves. The classical origin of the term "orient" points to an astronomical role: to speak of the orient is to designate where the sun rises or mark a nodal point for coordinating the stars.[152] The Greeks used "orient" for the direction of the rising sun rather than for a space, real or imagined, for some surrogate other. Following the Greeks, Roman administrators spoke of an oriens-occidens orientation, but not in the later Christendom[inated] sense of a civilizational clash with divinely fired proportions. It is highly dubious that a notion of Orient captured a meaningful geopolitical reality for the phalanxes of Alexander or the legions of Pompey. As Madeleine Dobie warns, "When we examine the historical record, it is clearly important to look for historical breaks as well as patterns of continuity, for we otherwise risk transforming an historically limited relationship of inequality into a quasi-ontological affirmation of the differences between two opposing cultures."[153] In this regard, it is significant to note that the motto *Ex Oriente Lux*, not to be taken lightly in framing a modern sense of the East as a spiritual homeland, is itself a modern turn of phrase.[154]

In writing his history, Herodotus described the customs of numerous peoples outside Greece, but those toward the rising sun as he saw it were geographically Asiatic (*Asiatikos*) rather than oriental. Of the many groups to be encountered, it was the Persians who invaded Greece and thus took pragmatic oriental precedence for this Greek intellectual.[155] The relevant term used in classical Greek to define and at times denigrate the collective non-Greek other is *barbaros*, from which European languages derived the highly pejorative sense of barbarian and by which the indigenous North Africans were later grouped by outsider logic as Berbers. The origin of *barbaros* is a philological trope, generally accepted as a reference to anyone who could not speak Greek and thus produced sounds that came across as nonsense, a kind of barbarbarbarbaristic stuttering.[156] This had not been an important designation in Homer's day, when the Trojans inhabited a joint Grecocentric sphere, even though modern-day geography would locate them in what Said at times labels the Near Orient. Usage of *barbaros* coincided with the sense of a unified Greek people or Hellenes, their joint koine-ing emerging from the invasion of real Persians. As historian James Romm explains, "once Greeks had faced foreigners in a life-or-death struggle and soundly defeated them, they began to speak of *barbaroi* as peoples naturally or culturally inferior to themselves, not simply 'non-Greek-speakers' but 'barbarians' as well."[157] Someone did not have to be from some imagined space called an Orient to be a barbarian. The divide was not according to fixed geographical directions but concentric ones; Greece was the ethno-concentric focal point for everything, and all others spiraled out as barbarians.[158]

To accuse Greek writers, even playwrights, of Eurocentrism is perhaps the ultimate Eurocentric assumption. Although Said is correct, and hardly original, in describing a later discursive milieu in which Europe "articulates the Orient," the fault line does not commence in Greek texts.[159] To the Greeks there was nothing intrinsic about Orientals that made them more barbarian than Picts or Celts—or even Etruscans. Indeed, it is not probative to assume that the Greeks thought of themselves as "European." Aristotle, in what we can assume was a rhetorically correct *Politics*, argues that Greeks are neither European nor Asian and thus have an intermediate character of being "both high-spirited and intelligent."[160] As Franco Cardini argues, the creation of Europe in the modern sense was very much a product of interaction with Islamic history: "Repeated Muslim aggression against Europe between the seventh to eighth and the tenth centuries, then between the fourteenth and the eighteenth centuries, whether it was successful or was simply viewed as successful by the Europeans, was a 'violent midwife' to Europe."[161] To argue that the East–West divide is endemic in "Western" civilization is to collapse historical evolution into the methodological anarchy of ahistorical synecdochism.[162]

Said looks at the post-Enlightenment, imperialist "West" of Europe and America and uncritically reflects this back through history to mythic origin in ancient Greece. Greece cannot stand for what was to later evolve as Europe anymore than the cultures on the continent we now call Europe owe all to Greek civilization. What Edith Hamilton says about Herodotus is not, after all, what Herodotus said. Neither do the Persians crossing the Adriatic Sea prefigure an Orient to be succeeded by Arabs, Mongols, and Ottomans. As there was no full-blown Orient in the Greek psyche, there could hardly be the subversive ontological fetus of hegemonic Orientalism.[163] The European discourse that invented the Orient just as surely invented itself, as Said argues. In a literally negative world with enemies to the west, north, or south, the issue would be—but for the grace of context—Occidentalism, Borealism, or Australism.

> A riot of color; sumptuous and savage ferocity; harems and
> seraglios; heads chopped off and women thrown in sacks into
> the Bosphorus; feluccas and brigantines flying the Crescent
> banner; roundness of azure domes and soaring whiteness of
> minarets; viziers, odalisques, and eunuchs; cooling springs
> beneath the palms; giaours with their throats slit; captive
> women subjected to the victor's ravenous lust.
>
> —MAXIME RODINSON, "THE WESTERN IMAGE
> AND WESTERN STUDIES OF ISLAM"

The term "Orient" as a marker of geographical space can be looked at in
several ways. One is a relational sense of everything to the east of "us."
In the medieval flat-earth scenario, the de facto—even if not factual—
boundary would have been that point where ships run out of ocean, or
camel caravans out of terra firma, and drop off into the abyss. After Columbus and Magellan, a circular argument was needed, one that could define
a Greenwich mean space not only for West going East but also for that East
coming back to the West. The new boundaries were skewed by European
expansion, as the New World became the frontier of the West, and the somewhat pacific regions where Orientals still ruled were pushed farther east
to China and Japan. That such an East–West model soon lost practical value
is underscored by the paradox specific to mid-Pacific islanders. When Captain Bligh and his semi-mutinous crew, for example, dropped anchor in
Tahiti, were they in the East or the West; or was it simply a primitive and
as yet uncolonized paradise where such a distinction did not matter?

The Orient begins with *Genesis* and hardly ends at *Revelation*. Bibliolatry preceded Orientalism in any of the forms represented by Edward
Said. In early Christianity, east was held in far higher regard symbolically
than west. East was the specific direction of the original paradise, whence
the Wise Men came following a star (Matthew 2:1), and where a risen Jesus
will one pre-judgment day come to usher in a new world (Matthew 24:27).
According to the early church fathers, east was light and west was dark;
east breathed life and west spelled death.[164] In the first thousand years of
the faith, almost half of that time saw its sacred sites in the hands of the
newer and rival religion of Islam. Even so, the commercial potential of the
pilgrim's purse usually won out over the occasional zealous fanaticism of
imams and emirs. Droves of Christian monks and lay people had visited
Jerusalem in full expectation that at any moment the apocalyptic scenario
would alter whatever the ephemeral political powers of the day tried to

do. Indeed, it may be the combined disappointment of having passed the millennium of Christ's birth and seeing the Holy Land still in the hands of "infidels" that led to the eventual success of Pope Urban's 1095 CE appeal for what we now dub the First Crusade.[165]

A third set of meanings flows from the idea of east as a metaphor. As Iain Higgins argues, for the medieval Europeans "east was the direction of return, restoration and old beginnings: in short, of origins."[166] Western Christians had good reason to orient themselves to an essential Orient as the origin of their faith. In German romanticism, exemplified by Johann Gottfried Herder and Friedrich Schlegel, the Orient became the source of original wisdom, the spiritual light for an enlightened Western philosophy darkened by too much *Aufklärung* and the soot of nascent industrial capitalism.[167] A radical critique of the European present came to be framed by "a spiritual return to a superior past, to its own forgotten origins."[168] Schlegel focused on India as the post-premodern origin myth of his day, replacing the biblical mode: "Ici (en Inde) se trouve la source de toutes les langues, de toutes les pensées et de toute l'histoire de l'esprit humain; tout, sans exception, est originaire (stammt) de l'Inde."[169] Indeed, the idea of Orient became synonymous with spirituality, the opportunity for a synthesis of universal religion. In a mystical way the Orient was all or it was nothing. The romantic Orient was soon reinvented as an exotic other, as Schwab eloquently phrases it, "an entire Orient of sofas and erotic and satiric masques that only too often encouraged literary history to frolic in shabby exoticism."[170] Such an Orient was only limited by the imagination. This is the Orient Said revel[ation]s in.

What became by colonial fiat the borders of the Orient? If a view from the sea is taken, the easternmost Mediterranean coast began at the Levant, a French synonym for Orient. But then what was to be done with North Africa? Is Morocco part of the East, even for a near-sighted European? Apparently it was not for Flaubert, a key figure in the Orientalist line-up.[171] Historian Jean Sauvaget resorts to calling northwest Africa, Sicily, and Spain "the Muslim West."[172] In so doing, Sauvaget recognizes that this is precisely how Muslims have always viewed the region, Morocco being derived from the Arabic "Maghrib" in reference to the setting sun and by extension the west as such. Ironically, the Arabic term follows a similarly ethnocentric linguistic ecliptic to the Western use of "Orient," except that the verbal rendering of the setting sun is related to strangeness and exotica. Indeed the difference between someone who is Westernized (*mustaghrib*) and someone who is strange or bizarre (*mustaghrab*) does not even show up in normal vowel-less Arabic print.

The perspective from land is a bit more complicated, in large part because of the Ottoman Turkish legacy. If the Bosphorus is in any sense a dividing line between continents, Turkey—the Anatolian land of the rising sun for Greeks—is both East and West. Russia would also seem to have a schizophrenic geography, even before being blocked into the East as the Soviet Union. At what point does European-looking Russia fade into the Eastern steppe? This was a quandary for the author Josef Washington Hall, who in a 1929 book on six great personalities of the "New East" placed Josef Stalin—"an Asiatic from across the Caucasus"—between chapters on Mustapha Kemal and Mahatma Gandhi.[173] Should we not include the Balkans in the West, given how the rest of Europe has generally (mis)treated them? As Europe's "resident alien" and "inside other," argues K. E. Fleming, the Balkans do not fit comfortably into Said's East–West dyad, nor were they the direct target of Western imperialism; there has not even been an academic establishment for their study.[174] Until recently most Europeans have balked at inventing an academically approved Balkanism.

The dividing ablunder of the East as Near and Far was sufficient in the age of colonial expansion and early archaeological exploitation. By the twentieth century it was no longer possible to think of a single Orient stretching from the western shores of the Mediterranean to the eastern isles of Japan. In 1902 this was redrawn by Alfred Thayer Mahan, an American naval historian who suggested that "Middle East" be carved out for the British space between Arabia and India; its usage was fixed soon after, when Lord Curzon applied it in the British House of Lords.[175] After World War II, with good and bad guys on both sides of the continental divides, the concept of Orient began to elide with that of the Third World in general. In describing the major constituents of the Orient as a culture area, Anouar Abdel Malek starts with the circles of Chinese civilization and the civilizational-cultural circle of Islam—near and far redefined—but then adds those parts of Latin America with direct links to Africa, such as Brazil and the Caribbean, and sub-Sahara in Africa.[176] In the globalizing of the undeveloped world, cultural heroes of the old Orient, such as Nehru and Nasser, became spokesmen for the non-aligned part of the world that was more appropriately just non-West and shifting south.

As the land where history began, the Orient attracted the rapt attention of Enlightenment historians and philosophers. Hegel, for example, begins his philosophical treatment of history with the "Oriental World."[177] For this he looks back at his Christian roots to the part of the world that first elaborated distinct and recognizable principles of ethics and morality. Relevant to Said's thesis is Hegel's view of the Orient as unable to evolve an acceptance of individual freedom, which becomes the culminating consciousness of Western civilization. Not surprisingly, Hegel was highly critical of the German romanticists, who in turn thought little of his model of Oriental history.[178] Hegel's philosophical speculation had an enormous influence on subsequent intellectual currents in European academics. It may be one of the main reasons Oriental studies was marginalized in the European curriculum.[179] But Hegel similarly dismissed the "New World" of America as "physically and spiritually impotent," showing that the idea of an inferior other was not confined to the Orient.[180]

The limitations of historical knowledge about the East are evident when the father of dialectics proposes a fourfold division of Asia by major river-based regimes, yet summarily rejects Siberia and Upper Asia as "unhistorical." Hegel's idealization of Oriental history serves mainly to accentuate the superiority of Greek thought, the avatar of his own intellectual tradition. All of this is spread on a philosophical plain; there was little sense of political difference that would justify imperialist incursion in his time. There was no viable Germanic imperial ambition in the real Orient to be legitimized. Hegel viewed the absence of a "German" empire as a source of moral pride.[181] The dividing line between East and West, a process initiated historically in the Orient, is for Hegel and so many others the abstraction of spirit from material, the realization of God as other than nature. This abstraction of the Orient or Islam as a kind of civilization had come under attack from within the cadre of Orientalists in the decade in which *Orientalism* appeared.[182] However, Hichem Djait still praises Hegel as providing "the most perceptive account by a European up till that time," about Islam, an account said to contravene the attribution of barbarism and caprice.[183] It would seem that the Orient was not seamless, even to the master of European intellectual history.

THE NEAREST ORIENTALS

> Let me tell you 'bout Ahab The Arab
> The Sheik of the burning sand
> He had emeralds and rubies just dripping off 'a him
> And a ring on every finger of his hands.
> He wore a big ol' turban wrapped around his head
> And a scimitar by his side
> And every evening about midnight
> He'd jump on his camel named Clyde . . . and ride.
>
> —RAY STEVENS, "AHAB THE ARAB"[184]

The Orient was the ancestral home of the Oriental, a tautological spectre that haunts the entire narrative of *Orientalism*. Anything about the Orient is assumed to be Oriental, including its inhabitants, both real and imagined. Said implies that in real time there could be no composite Oriental apart from the generic inferior other. But then the visage with a hooked nose and slanted eyes must share discursive space with those one-footed medieval monsters Columbus thought he might encounter on his voyage west to find the East. The Orient, from the start, was not just home base to the Oriental. For the speakers of various European languages over the course of more than two millennia, the flesh-and-blood inhabitants to the east included Arabs, Armenians, Asiatics, Bedouins, Chinamen, Copts, Hindoos, Indians, Ishmaelites, Jews, Mahometans, Nestorians, Persians, Saracens, Semites, Turks, Zoroastrians, and on and on *ad nominen*. As Europeans were forced to deal with cultural diversity, at least in what tends to be dismissed as the Dark Ages following the fall of the Roman Empire, it was hard to escape a biblical set of readily begotten names for just about anyone to be encountered or imagined. Surely, as holy writ would have it, all are descended from Adam and Eve, with a second common stock spreading out after the Deluge from Noah's three sons: Shem, Ham, and Japheth.[185] Shem, patriarch of the Semites, fits logically as the shared ancestor of Jews and Muslims alike. Self-invoked ethnic labels such as Arab, Bedouin, Persian, and Turk were not unknown in European languages and appear quite early, but for a considerable stretch of European imaginative time these people were perceived almost entirely as remnants of the biblical table of nations.

In developing Christendom, for the most part, the Muslims to the east and in its own midst were a toss-up—and potential toss-out—between heathen infidels and heretic apostates. In the biblicist rendering of antiquity as a postdiluvian family of nations, the Muslim Arabs came from the same loins as the Hebrews, both scions of father Abraham. This made the Arab a semantic Semite, even if anti-Semitism came to be the accepted term in Western usage for the Isaac branch rather than the outcast Ishmael. In academic circles before the nineteenth century, an Oriental was a semantic sibling of a "Semite," a term coined by a German scholar two decades before Napoleon invaded Egypt.[186] Arabic came to be considered a Semitic language; indeed the very idea of a Semitic language covered the sense of "Oriental" language until the end of the eighteenth century. Then along came Sanskrit and spread the ur-consciousness of Orient further east.[187] Marco Polo was followed by Jesuit fathers who sought knowledge about others eastward even unto China. But the significant other in *Orientalism* is the shared secret of Semitism. So powerful is the linkage of Semite and Arab that the latest *Oxford English Dictionary* still anachronistically defines an Arab as "One of the Semitic race inhabiting Saudi Arabia and neighboring countries." That race, unbeknownst to the modern editors, is now over. An Oriental by any other name, it should be stressed, may not be the same.[188]

The term "Arab" has long had a wide and imprecise usage. There were linguistic Arab nomads as early as the ninth century BCE, when they rode camels against an Assyrian king at the revolutionary Battle of Qarqar. But modern usage harks back to the people inhabiting the Arabian Peninsula (*jazirat al-'Arab* in Arabic). The *OED* has that part right. In Arabic usage, there are several ways of being an Arab. An Arab can be someone who speaks Arabic as a native tongue, an inhabitant of the Arabian Peninsula, or a descendant of ancestral Arabs, who are largely the stuff of legend. According to Arabic sources, the two major founders of legendary Arab tribes were Qahtan, for the so-called Southern Arabs or self-styled "true" Arabs, and 'Adnan, progenitor of the Northern Arabs from which the Prophet Muhammad himself claimed descent.[189] When Qahtan is linked with the biblical Joktan, a descendant of Shem, and 'Adnan is hooked up to a line leading back to Abraham through Ishmael, the Semitic ethnicity of the Arab is locally fixed, at times even fixated. In nineteenth-century writing with a scriptural fetish, Arabs were, as often as not, simply referred to as bloody Ishmaelites.[190]

"Arab" has become the ethnic term of choice for many people from Morocco to Iraq. Unfortunately, it can be stretched ludicrously, as in the mindless appellation of Raphael Patai's book *The Arab Mind*. In popular Western imagination "Arab" becomes anyone who lives in the Near or Middle East and is a Muslim; neither assumption—like the Arabian desert itself—holds much water in reality. There is no viable Arabdom to counter Christendom, although the former term survives in the dictionary.[191] Scholars are also guilty in speaking of Arab history when it is really the history of Islamic dynasties that is at stake. Historian Marshall Hodgson noted as long ago as 1960 that the tendency to elide Arab and Muslim "is as unfair to Christian and Jewish Arabs as to the overwhelming majority of non-Arab Muslims."[192] Indeed, the etymological history of the term "Arab" needs a thorough purging of the multitude of ways it has been used, misused, and abused. It is by no means certain that the people living in Arabia at the time of Muhammad thought of themselves meaningfully as Arab. Given the numerous "crude nationalist interpretations" about Arabs, historian Fred Donner suggests that we reserve "Arabian" for the geographical region of the peninsula, "Arabic" for the language, and "Muslim" for matters pertaining to the specific religion of Islam.[193]

It is somewhat easier to survey more recent ethno-slandering slang, especially stereotyped terms encoded in literary texts and vulgar usage. Take "Arab," for instance. Although most writers have applied it in a cultural sense, ethnic disdain helped foster such usages as "street Arabs" for turn-of-the-nineteenth-century homeless waifs on the streets of lower Manhattan.[194] Oldies radio stations still manage to slip in "Ahab the Arab." Similarly, the Anglicized "Bedouin," via French pronunciation of an Arabic term denoting a desert dweller (*badawi*), was not reserved exclusively for the pastoral reincarnation of Abraham's kindred, but was also extended in European linguistic usage to gypsies and other nomadic societal "low life."[195] There are also local derogations, such as the British slang of "wog." As with many offensive epithets, the origin of "wog" is difficult to pinpoint; perhaps it is simply the clever acronym for a "Western Orientalized Gentleman."[196] This term came into prominence during World War II, as reflected in humorist Spike Milligan's self-deprecatory satire of life in the North African campaign:

> A stark white sign with the red letters BEJA, no admission, TYPHUS.
> "I wonder what Typhus is like," said Edgington.
> "Typhus is an Arab village," I said.
> "Then wot's Beja?"
> "Beja is a disease that has struck down the people of Typhus."
> "You notice that the Wogs don't have these diseases until we arrive." We drove along in silence.[197]

The term "Turk" is another of those epithetical ethnic designations that forcefully bears the mark of embedded ethnocentrism. The replacement of some variant of "Muslim" with "Turk" in Western polemic began with the Ottoman victories over much of the Islamic Middle East by the early sixteenth century, although both terms continued to be used interchangeably.[198] Ahmad bin Qasim, a seventeenth-century Arab visitor to Spain, observed that "the *ifranj* do not describe a Muslim except as a Turk."[199] This was an ethnocentrically balanced etymological payback, since Arab historians had long used "Franj" (derived from "Frank" for the French) for all the crusading Christians who came east.[200] In Elizabethan England, the image of a Turk's head was used as an archery target, the butt of the joke here being "shooting at the butt."[201] To "turn Turk" primarily meant to convert to Islam. From at least 1583, "Turk" was generic for "renegade" and, eventually, to be a Turk meant to be a "cruel, hard-hearted man."[202] Not surprisingly biblical prophecy began to be directed at real

Turks, whose impending doom was thought to be sealed by the second coming of Christ.[203] Fresh after the fall of the Ottoman Empire, the fundamentalist diatribe of Sale-Harrison equates the "despicable Turk" with "the worst of the nations." These "heathen" were said to be so dire a threat to Israel's prophesied revival that Turkish control of Palestine had to be foretold by the prophet Ezekiel. Ezekiel's prophetic wheels also spun out the building of the "Mosque of Omar" on the site of Israel's temple.[204] How else might a literalist Bible believer interpret the plain King James English: "Wherefore I will bring the worst of the heathen, and they shall possess their houses; I will also make the pomp of the strong to cease; and their holy places shall be defiled" (Ezekiel 7:24).

Most travelers to the Middle East differentiated Arab from Turk, often preferring one over the other. David Hogarth, the wandering scholar par excellence, preferred Turks to Arabs, especially those Anatolian peasants showing courage, simplicity, fidelity, and loyalty.[205] Even in the grip of stereotyping, politics could generate strange bedfellows. Thus William Eton, writing in 1799, admitted: "I would answer a Turk: I was your enemy as long as you were friends of the French: now you are their enemies I, as an Englishman, am your friend."[206] Whether or not Eton was aware of the oft-quoted Arabic proverb that harbors the same Machiavellian sentiment, it is clear that labels should be read in context rather than as isolated and unchanging entities unto themselves.[207]

From Saracen to Muslim

> *Quae quidem olim diaboli machinatione concepta, primo per Arrium seminata, deinde per istum Sathanan scilicet Mahumet, prouecta, per Antichristum uero, ex toto secundum diabolicam intentionem complebitur.* [Indeed, that which was once conceived by the device of the devil, first propagated through Arius, then advanced by that satan, namely Mohammed, will be fulfilled completely, according to the diabolical plan, through the Antichrist.]
>
> —Peter the Venerable

One of the early preferences of Christian writers in describing what would later be known generically as Near Eastern Orientals was a serendipitous neologism, Saracen. "Saracen" is the word used by the Venerable Bede in the early eighth century as he describes the Muslim military incursion into France as "a very sore plague."[208] The term is apparently derived from a

Greek pun in *Genesis*, where several words spoken by Hagar were transformed into an ethnic identity for the Arabs and other Muslim progeny descending from her and Abraham. At least this is the early view of John of Damascus, who remarks: "They also call them Saracenes, allegedly for having been sent away by Sarah empty; for Hagar said to the angel, 'Sarah has sent me away empty.'"[209] In the lexical flux of the time, Isidore of Seville suggested that some people thought wrongly that these people came from Sarah.[210] Isidore himself did not realize that Saracens were the same as Arabs. The author of *The Travels of Sir John Mandeville* traces Saracens to a city called Sarras, a splendid example of geographical imagination.[211] Saracens were also known as Agarines or Hagarines, after Mother Hagar.[212] The etymological musings extended the level of asinine debate, such as the query by Angelomus of Luxeuil in the mid-ninth century of whether or not Sarah has one "r" or two. Sometimes the lexical musings were ugly, such as when writers derived this "perverted name" from the Arabic verb *saraq* (to steal), as that was what they presumably did.[213] Such usage could be less figurative and more to the point, especially when practicing knights ran their lances into a "saracin of wood."[214] It would be rash to define with precision who exactly was to be covered by this name. The term was in fact invented at least two centuries before the start of Islam.[215] At times it had a liberal stretch beyond the obvious Arabs to Copts, Greeks, Indians, Nestorians, Persians, Zoroastrians, and Jews,[216] as well as the generic sense of non-Christian heathen.[217] Nary a sin has not been covered by Saracen.

The most important Saracen was Islam's prophet, Muhammad. For the first millennium of Christian–Muslim interaction there was little resemblance between Muhammad, the flesh-and-blood individual, and the "Mahomet" trumped up as imp, quite literally in this case, and impostor. The Crusades eventually made the prophet of the Saracens a household name of legendary significance. How significant it is that the literary creation of Mahomet took place during a swirling surge of "medieval" hero stories. Mahomet took his wrongful place in the European imagination at the creative dreamtime for other hero stories about Charlemagne, King Arthur, and Virgil as well as the rediscovery of the wonders of Rome and the miracles of the Virgin Mary.[218] Epic was in the air all over Europe, even if so loosely grounded in fact.

The widely disseminated *Chanson de Roland*, of about 1100 CE, portrays the Saracens as pagans worshipping Mahomet, Apollyno, and Tervagant— a mythic triumvirate that expands to include Jupiter, Diana, Plato, the antichrist, and Lucifer himself.[219] There were certainly voices that stressed the absurdity of such a claim, including William of Malmesbury's comment in 1127 that the Saracens did not worship their prophet "as some people think."[220] But many persisted in the medieval attitude of Guibert of Nogent that Islam's prophet was someone "whose malignity exceeds whatever ill can be spoken."[221] At one point or another in the ongoing polemic, Muhammad was called an adulterer, barbarian, false prophet, *homo ydiota*, liar, low-born, murderer, necromancer, pagan, robber, swinish, traitor, violent, and wicked; indeed there is hardly one of the Ten Commandments he was not said to have broken.[222] Consider the invective of Englishman John Cartwright, writing in 1611, the same year as the publication of the *King James Bible*: "Concerning Muhammad, the people of Mecca (where he lies intombed [*sic*]) do altogether condemn him, both for his robberies and murders. And himself, in his Qur'an, confesses himself to be a sinner, an idolater, an adulterer, and inclined to women, above measure and that, in such uncivil terms that I am ashamed to repeat."[223] Some even claimed that Muhammad's mother was Jewish. Because the Jews were held responsible for the early success of Islam, this alleged alliance proved disastrous to Jewish communities in the pogrom-prone path of less charitable crusading knights. In one account of unbridled calumny it was alleged that a cunning Jewess seduced Muhammad to come alone to her bed at night. When he arrived, the woman's relatives killed him, cut off his left foot, and threw the rest of his body to the pigs—*et hec est causa odii inter Saracenos et Iudeos.* The clandestine lover then anointed and scented the prophet's foot, saying that this was all that remained in a tug-of-war with the celestial powers.[224]

It should come as no surprise that Muhammad was a chief candidate during the Crusades for anti-christ-ening, and routinely marked as either the "Beast" or "False Prophet"—or both of the above—of the apocalypse. The term "antichrist" has been used rather loosely in the vagaries of Christian theology for anyone who "denieth the Father and the Son," although at times a particularly "wicked" man is singled out.[225] Less than a decade after the death of Muhammad, Maximus the Confessor described the new Muslim faith as "announcing the advent of the Antichrist."[226] For Peter the Venerable, Muhammad was the impious middleman between the heretic Arius—who was vilified for denying the divinity of Christ—and the future antichrist who would usher in Armageddon. William of Tyre tendered Muhammad as the "first-born of Satan," a kind of arch-heretic who did the Devil's bidding in leading more men to hell than anyone else. In 1191, Abbot Joachim of Fiore told the heartily lionized Richard I, who was on his way to liberate the Holy Land, that the Saracens were apocalyptic instruments of the antichrist. Perhaps this was to spur on Richard, with God's help, to defeat Saladin.[227] In his crusading appeal of 1213, Innocent III proclaimed Mahomet the "Beast of the Apocalypse" and the bearer of that most unlucky number, 666.[228] Apparently, the fact that more than 643 years had passed since Muhammad's birth was close enough as a numerically significant sign of the end time. Muhammad was a major antichrist target, but contemporary Muslim figures were also sometimes seen as what might be called the seal of the antichrists. The medieval monk Ademar of Chabannes called the caliph al-Hakim the antichrist (as well as Rex Babilonius and Nabuchodonosor Babiloniae) for his role in ordering the destruction of the Holy Sepulchre in 1010.[229] It was perhaps fortunate for this mad monk that al-Hakim, a political incarnation of Saddam Hussein's stature, did not read Latin.

Finding negative commentary on Muhammad in almost all genres of Western literature and scholarship requires little effort. Consider the widely circulated pop mega-narrative by H. G. Wells, *The Outline of History*, first published in 1920. Although he was full of praise for the early Islamic community, Wells made it clear that Muhammad was a prophet to be put aside, not to be put alongside Jesus or Buddha. Rather than "throw all of our history out of proportion," Wells portrays Muhammad as "vain, egotistical, tyrannous, and a self-deceiver."[230] Total disdain for Islam abounds in hack historical biographies, such as the dabbling in R. F. Dibble's Roaring-Twenties reduction of Muhammad's character to "the furthest limits of charlatanism, demagoguery, bombastic egotism, and general intellectual incompetency."[231] But one need not dip into the archives to find defamation of Islam's Prophet. Following the tragic events of the September 11, 2001, attack on the World Trade Center, several prominent medialogues of the Christian right disparaged Muhammad as a "terrorist," "absolute wild-eyed fanatic," and "demon-possessed pedophile."[232]

A decidedly denigrating ploy of Christian apologists is to make Muslims into "Mohammedans," and its several variants. A Muslim is literally "one who submits" to Islam, the best way of describing how Muslims see their own religious faith. "Mohammedan," by designation from a Christian context, implies that Muslims worship Muhammad in a similar way to how Christians view Christ as a part of the Godhead. Indeed, one of the fabulous and totally spurious claims fueled by the Crusades was the idea that Muhammad was worshipped as an idol.[233] In an early-twelfth-century account of the First Crusade, the knight Tancred encounters an idol cast of heavy silver in a Jerusalem mosque and comments:

> "Is it Christ? These are not the insignia of Christ.
> Not the cross, not the crown of thorns, not the nails, not
>   the water from his side,
> Therefore this is not Christ: rather it is ancient Antichrist,
> Mahummet the depraved, Mahummet the pernicious."[234]

Variations of the very name Muhammad, such as mahimet, maumet, and mahum, were used generically into and beyond the Renaissance for any kind of idol or false god.[235] "Mahometry" and "maumetry" eventually became synonymous with idolatry. In Elizabethan England, "Mahometan" could also refer to a Christian who did not believe in the Trinity and might thus be leaning towards Islam.[236] Even the fired-up Protestant John Wycliffe, who dared to translate the Latin Bible into the vernacular, was deemed a "Mahomet" by his enemies.[237]

By the middle of the nineteenth century, scholars tended to write about Mohammedanism rather than Islam. This was the result of some minor academic housecleaning in which "Mohammedan" seemed less "disconcertingly archaic" than the Elizabethan usage of Mahometan.[238] *Mohammedanism* was the title of Margoliouth's classic 1911 survey of Islam; it remained unchanged in Gibb's re-edition through reprints into the 1970s.[239] By the 1960s most sensitive students of Islam had dropped this outmoded term. As Robert Slater noted, "Nor would the Muslim speak of 'Mohammadanism' [*sic*]. His faith is Islam, the faith of utter surrender to the Divine Will, which is what Islam signifies, as the term Muslim signifies one who voluntarily submits to the Divine Will."[240] "Islam" is now the preferred modern usage, whether pronounced with a politically correct "s" or an outmoded "z." This direct borrowing from the Arabic has not been documented in English before 1613, with French adoption apparently lagging behind until 1687. "Muslim," the politically and linguistically correct term for someone who practices Islam, was preceded by "Moslem," which is now rare in print.[241] Before that "mussulman" and its variants had evolved from Latin *musulmanes*. The poet Dryden punned "musselwoman" for a female in 1668. The *OED* notes that "musulman" was applied during World War II in concentration camps for individuals who were totally exhausted and reduced to skin and bones, thus reduced almost to an animal state. With apologies to Roger Bacon, there was a mountain of names to which Western writers took Muhammad and his followers.

The medieval Christian backlash against Muhammad represents, for Edward Said, a "perfect case in point" of the Orientalist desire to control the "redoubtable Orient."[242] Central to his thesis is that although the sources may change over time, their character remains dismissive of Islam through contemporary academic writing. Certainly there was no dearth of malevolent diatribe against Muhammad in earlier Christian texts, but the examples explored here demonstrate that Muslims served Christians as specifically threatening others rather than generic Orientals. We should not reduce the terminological attacks on Islam to religious rhetoric, but neither is it useful to generalize away a conflict inflamed by faith-based debasement. Said's polemical need blinds him to the fact that the very stereotypes he criticizes had already been dismissed as misconceptions by many of those trained in Oriental studies. In a review written at the time that Said was researching *Orientalism*, Charles F. Beckingham recounts a number of the same overt errors of Christian polemicists that infuriated Said, including the insult of reducing Islam to a mixture of pagan Arab notions and Judeo-Christian folklore. But, as Orientalist Beckingham observes and critic Said ignores, such gross opinions are "explicitly held by hardly anyone to-day and certainly not by any reputable scholar."[243] Beckingham may have underestimated the gullibility of public opinion, but he was correct in observing that specialists who studied Islam were no longer following in the missionary-minded prejudice of early generations.

IV The Growth (Benign, Cancerous, or Otherwise) of Orientalism

The "ism" in Orientalism serves to insist on the distinction of this discipline.

—EDWARD SAID, *ORIENTALISM*

Having like Adam named the verbal beasts around us, we can now trace the notion of Orientalism as a fixed vernacular term in European languages. A word is necessary about the ism-mania that infiltrated the Romance languages at the end of the seventeenth century. This Greek suffix, suffice it to say, was to modern scholarly rhetoric what rationalism was to philosophy. Here was the mechanism to make things abstract at a time when European discovery of the previously poorly known world around them was ripe for abstraction of both goods and ideas.[244] Where would the study of comparative religion be without "animism," a term popularized by Edward Tylor in 1871, or "agnosticism," a Huxleyan secular gem from the same era? Going beyond Christianity was certainly aided by the addition of "Hindooism"[245] and "Buddhism."[246] Try to imagine modern science without "Darwinism," political science without "Marxism," art without "Impressionism." We could certainly do without "racism" and "sexism," but to focus only on the abstracted word at the expense of the awful truth being represented would be the moral equivalent of bowdlerizing. How powerful would Said's critique of Orientalism be if there were no despotism,[247] imperialism, and colonialism to play it against? Indeed, sarcasm and witticism aside, without this linguistic tidbit would there be any criticism at all in modernism, postmodernism, and all future isms?

The most common academic sense for "Orientalism" in pre-Saidian prose focused on scholarship that studied and used Oriental languages, primarily those other than biblical Hebrew and Aramaic. In French, where the usage first appears, there is reference to that "incunabulum" of "orientalisme" in Barthélemy d'Herbelot's *Bibliothèque orientale* (1697).[248] The *Dictionnaire de l'Académie Française* finally includes an entry for *orientalisme* in 1838. Actually, the field of discourse, if such be the meaning of Orientalism, was preceded discursively, in a non-Foucauldian sense, by the "Orientalist" per se. The English sense of someone "versed in Oriental languages and literature" has been traced back to a 1799 reference about Edward Pococke (1604–1691), the first Professor of Arabic at Oxford.[249] For those who prefer the prose of poets, Byron, in *Childe Harold's Pilgrimage* (1811), calls a certain Mr. Thornton a "profound Orientalist." Such was Mary Shelley's Clerval, an "Orientalist" who went to the university to become a "complete master" of Persian, Arabic, and Sanskrit.[250] All of this precedes a self-reference in 1816 by the German poet Goethe to his "Orientalismus," and another later by Humboldt, the latter apparently borrowing philosophically from the French sense of someone who knows Oriental languages.[251] Yet, certainly there were individuals known to specialize in "Oriental" languages long before they came to be labeled "Orientalists."[252] More than a century before, in 1691, Anthony Wood used the term "Orientalian" to describe Samuel Clark because of his knowledge of Oriental languages.[253] Thus Said's title missed being *The Orientalians* by the accident of recorded usage.

By the middle of the nineteenth century, the term "Orientalist" was routinely applied in scholarly contexts to someone who not only knew an Oriental language but who knew it well enough to go beyond mere translation and comment authoritatively on things Oriental.[254] In characterizing Guillaume Postel (Postell) as the first French Orientalist, Gustave Dugat's reasoning is typical: "Quand je dis le premier orientaliste français, j'ai en vue le premier savant qui étudia quelque groupe de langues orientales, avec une tendance à la comparaison, à la synthèse."[255] In some cases the sheer number of languages studied serves as a mark of distinction. Consider Dugat's praise for the scholar Bernhard Dorn, who in addition to German, Russian, English, and French, read Hebrew, Syriac, Arabic, Ethiopic, Sanskrit, Pahlavi, and several Persian, Afghani, and Turkish dialects.[256] In the twentieth century, however, "Orientalism" tended more and more to refer to the philological study of "nonextant civilizations."[257] As Orientalism took shape, a student of Egyptian hieroglyphics was as likely to call himself or herself an Orientalist as a student of Arabic or Sanskrit.

Historically, it is important to separate several usages of "Orientalism" that are far more specific than either the generic study of Oriental languages or Said's expansive sense of virtually everything the West says about the East. One of the earliest usages in English is in reference to any style, trait, or idiom that is in some sense Oriental.[258] This linguistic penchant is provided by Samuel Johnson, who rendered "Orientalism" in his 1773 dictionary as "An idiom of the eastern languages; an eastern mode of speech."[259] A more generic extension beyond linguistic idiom to cultural trait is evident in William Beckford's reference to "sparks of Orientalism" in the journal he kept during his 1787–88 trip to Spain and Portugal.[260] As early as 1683, "Orientalist" specifically referred to a member of the Eastern or Greek Orthodox Church. In art criticism there are also distinct usages, one for an "orientalizing" style in Greek art for the eighth century BCE, and the other for the genre of nineteenth-century Western painting characterized by exotic harem beauties and Bedouin sheikhs on horseback. Ironically, the latter application was coined by Jules-Antoine Castagnary, an artist who belonged to a group that opposed French exploitation in the colonies. He popularized the term "Orientalism" for this genre of art by heaping abuse on it; in 1876 he declared the movement dead, but the term has remained very much alive.[261] Moving across the channel, historians of British colonial history coined "Orientalism" to refer to a distinct phase of British involvement in India from 1784–1835, before the minute-minded Macaulay inaugurated the succeeding phase of "Anglicanism."[262]

The multiple meanings of "Orientalism," as well as its various nuances across languages, are obscured in Said's generalized model of Orientalist discourse. Critics have been especially harsh, as shall be seen, regarding Said's idiosyncratic rendering of the term "Orientalism." Fred Halliday, for example, labels Said's broad sense of the term a "promiscuous application.[263] Bayley Winder considers Said's equation of Orientalism with racism and imperialism to be a "perversion."[264] The imaginary geographical coordinates posed by default in *Orientalism* come unglued as "Orientalism" becomes synonymous for Western domination through imperialism and colonialism.[265] The catachrestic conveyance of Orientalism, or at least the Orientalist attitude, has resulted in a convenient catchall category for "making gross and vaguely deprecating generalizations about other (especially non-Western) cultures and peoples."[266] Or, as Graham Huggan suggests, such usage turns Orientalism into "a codeword for virtually any kind of Othering process."[267]

Even the spectres of "Black Orientalism" and "Khmer Rouge Orientalism" have been raised.[268] Anthropologist Peter Schneider coined the term "neo-Orientalism" to expand application of Said's meaning to the "Southern Question" in Italy,[269] although this neo-term had earlier been applied in French to the view that the Islamic world is incapable of modernizing.[270] Anthropologist James Carrier, in one of the more far-ranging misappropriations of Said's [con]notation, argues that "Said's work is so influential that 'orientalism' has become a generic term for a particular, suspect type of anthropological thought."[271] Down such a slippery neologistic slope, it is not long before the serious reader must hurdle explanada—expletive deleted—such as "Orientalisms of the Noble Savage," "ethno-Orientalism" as "a way that alien people produce an essentialism notion of themselves" and "ethno-Occidentalism" for "essentialist readings of the West by members of alien societies."[272] Another anthropologist, James Lindstrom, carries Carrier's careless usage to the New Guinea highlands, where even indigenous cargoism becomes a type of "orientalist discourse."[273] Even Tarzan of the Apes and the creation of the Boy Scouts become examples of Orientalism's discursive stretch.[274] Several historians have also expanded the nearsighted horizons of Said's narrative to what might be called a Europeanized pan-Orientalism. Medievalist Kathleen Biddick writes:

> For the purposes of discussion in this paper, I use orientalism to refer to the historically situated Euroamerican project of producing an experience of scholarship, order, truth and management based on the textualization of imagining others exterior to Europe who inhabit an imaginary space constructed by Europeans through their scholarship, cartography, surveys, photography, exhibitions, administration.[275]

Orientalism, post-Said, has no boundaries. As a heavily laden word, "Orientalism" through its frequent appropriation "often becomes a substitute for clear thought."[276]

Post-colonial writers have been among the most vigorous re-users of Said's [con]version of Orientalism. There are some rhetorical brushstrokes that leave a potentially sympathetic reader in a virtual state of suspended aporia. Even Homi Bhabha might be challenged to match the linguistic obfuscation of Aziz Al-Azmeh:

> That territory is Orientalism, which transforms the senseless abstraction of their thematic givenness into determinate thematic and semantic coherence by giving them this territory which constitutes the conditions of possi-

bility of the statements studied, it is the *sine qua non* for articulating propositions about things Oriental into the form of statements. Orientalism it is that designates empirical material, Oriental material, draws it out of the well of inert images and signs that float unstructured in the obscure regions of Western collective representation, and validates it as a distinct and functional topos, and then further allows this topos to be transformed into determinate conceptual content with a determinate reference to the empirical manifold, i.e. into a unit of discourse, a unit of meaning and logical function.[277]

As map most certainly is not territory, the strained coherence of this unparseable and impassable topos tops them all. Further alienation, at least for this writer, is provided by odd pairings such as "Maussian Orientalism" alongside "skewed postcolonial Orientalist discourse on Sinhalese Buddhists."[278] Orientalism is evoked in some post-colonial thinking the way ether was in nineteenth century cosmic alchemy.

ORIENTALISM IN WORLDLY TEXTS

To speak of Orientalism as an academic field necessitates looking at the introduction of systematic teaching of Oriental languages and knowledge in European universities. From a practical standpoint there are several terminus a quo candidates. One is the pragmatic decision of the Church Council of Vienna in 1312 CE to introduce the teaching of Arabic—in addition to the already-taught Hebrew, Greek, and Chaldean—at universities in Bologna, Oxford, Paris, and Salamanca, and in the Roman Curia.[279] This was actually the culmination of a series of papal bulls begun by Innocent IV in 1248.[280] The stated purpose for teaching Arabic in the curriculum was Christianization of Muslims, although it is important not to underestimate the impact of political and diplomatic concerns, as well as the ongoing trade and pilgrimage networks.[281] This does not mean that Christian scholars, especially those able to visit Muslim courts in Spain and Sicily, had not already begun the pertinent task of translating Arabic texts into Latin. Pedro de Alfonso, a Jewish convert to Christianity in 1106, is regarded as one of the first Western writers who knew Arabic and wrote on Islam.[282]

An equal first-stake claim could be made for the first "official" Latin translation of an Arabic text, thought to be Adelard of Bath's 1126 rendering of al-Khwarizmi's hoary and horary astronomical tables. This was soon revised by Robert of Ketton, just before Peter the Venerable induced him to translate the entire Quran. I emphasize "induce" here because it appears that Robert was not too pleased at having to postpone an intended translation of Ptolemy's *Planisphere*, as rescinded in Arabic by al-Majriti. It took Robert about a year to complete the task of Latinizing the Arabic scripture; he finished by July 1143.[283] Peter's ecclesiastically eclectic interest in the Quran was perhaps more venomous than venerable. As Robert the translator informs his patron, "I have uncovered Muhammed's smoke so that it may be extinguished by your bellows."[284] The un-saintly Peter was not reluctant to bellow out his objections to an anti-Christian heresy that he saw as "this greatest error of all errors."[285] The summation of his *Summa* says it all:

> For thus the very wretched and wicked Mohammed has taught them who, by denying all the mysteries of the Christian religion, whereby particularly men are saved, has condemned almost a third of the human race by some unknown judgement of God and by unheard-of, raving-mad tales, to the devil and eternal death.[286]

As far as Peter was concerned, Muhammad was inspired by the Devil to forge "a diabolical scripture, put together both from the Jewish fables and the trifling songs of heretics."[287] The representation of Muhammad, drawing on earlier misinformed stereotypes, is one of a ruthless and wicked individual intent on "killing whomever he could by stealth" to increase the terror of his name.[288]

Yet for all his apologetic invective against the religion of Muhammad, some comfort is to be taken from Peter's clear desire to convince Muslims of the error of their ways rather than just condemn them pro forma. The venerable abbot addressed his theoretical Muslim readers: "But I do not attack you, as some of us often do, by arms, but by words; not by force, but by reason; not in hatred, but in love."[289] Compare this sentiment with that of Bernard of Clairvaux, Peter's contemporary, orderly rival, and friend. For the saintly Bernard it was fine for good Christian knights to slay for God's love, for "a Christian glories in the death of a pagan (i.e., Muslim) because Christ is glorified."[290] Peter was so bold as to write to Bernard that the Church had no right to use the sword, because Christ had told the Apostle Peter, "Put back thy sword into the scabbard; for all those who take the sword will perish by the sword."[291] Bernard clearly found abandoning of the sword hard to swallow. He was at least consistent in his multiculturally militant hatred of unbelievers and apostates, as witnessed by his persecution of poor Peter Abelard, who ironically was granted sanctuary in the last years of his life at Peter the Venerable's abbey in Cluny. But Peter's pet project to translate the Quran and provide a rational evangelistic response to Islam ultimately had little impact apart from providing a range of literary metaphors by Islamic writers as fodder for apologetic misrepresentation. For the greater part of European history during and after the Crusades, the sword turned out to be mightier than an abbot's pen.

The fact that translation was occurring is not as useful for tracing the historical trajectory of Orientalism as the choice and impact of the specific translations becoming available to anyone wanting to represent Islam and peoples of the Orient. What were the seminal texts? For Arabic writings, surely the Quran itself must be the starting point. Robert's work was followed by another Latin translation by Mark of Toledo in 1210. An Italian translation of the Latin came out by the middle of the sixteenth century, but published translations from the Arabic only appeared haphazardly: a French one in 1647,[292] and one in English in 1734.[293] It seems that the first Arabic edition of the Quran was printed in Venice before 1518, although no known copy survives. No copy of the Quran in manuscript or print arrived at Cambridge University until 1631.[294]

In terms of Arabic literature, the *Arabian Nights* is generally held up as the quintessential Oriental tale to be translated from Arabic into the major European languages.[295] Speaking of Galland's French version, *Les mille et une nuits* (1704–17), Maxime Rodinson reminisces: "Thenceforward Islam was no longer seen as the land of Antichrist but essentially that of an exotic, picturesque civilization, existing in a fabulous atmosphere peopled by good and evil, wayward genies—all this for the delight of an audience that had already shown so much taste for European fairy tales."[296] Entertainment had at last eclipsed evangelism and borrowed science.

A bowdlerized English rendering of the Galland version was available by 1792, but a literary translation into English did not appear until 1811. The appearance of the *Arabian Nights* in European languages spawned a cottage industry of prose and poetry that lured Westerners to visit the fabled Orient and lulled generations of children to the dream world of Aladdin. It is arguable that there has been no greater influence on impressions of travelers to the Near East than this single set of tales and its spin-offs.[297] Even Cardinal Newman, in his widely read *Apologia Pro Vita Sua* (1865), noted:

> I used to wish the Arabian Tales were true: my imagination ran on unknown influences, on magical powers, and talismans.... I thought life might be a dream, or I an

> Angel, and all this world a deception, my fellow-angels by a playful device concealing themselves from me, and deceiving me with the semblance of a material world.[298]

The cardinal's religious education was lit by the *Arabian Nights* before it turned inward. The tales of Aladdin and Sinbad did not reveal a real Orient, but then neither did children's fare accurately reflect the West in the thoroughly Occidental *Grimm's Fairy Tales*.

Another way of evaluating the genealogy of an Arabic text is to work backwards from classic European works. Take for example Dante's *La Divina Commedia* (ca. 1317), the seemingly immortal trove of European literature surveys for generations. A reasonable argument has been made that this avowedly vernacular Italian journey through heaven and hell was influenced in significant part by the Muslim legend of the *miraj*, Muhammad's legendary night journey to paradise.[299] French and Latin translations of the Arabic legend were made around 1264 by Bonaventura de Siena of Seville, with an earlier Spanish version now lost. Although it would be overly de rigueur to slight Dante's literary genius as unduly inspired by an Oriental text, it is well worth noting the irony of a text that damns Muhammad to the lowest rungs of hell having some affinity with one that raises him to the highest level of paradise.

Or, for those who prefer English, Defoe's unsinkable 1719 *Robinson Crusoe*—the premise as opposed to the text—may owe part of its inspiration to an English translation of Ibn Tufayl's twelfth-century allegory, *Hayy ibn Yaqzan*.[300] This philosophical reflection of a man reasoning his way to God on a deserted island was first translated into Latin by Edward Pococke the Younger, soon followed by an English rendering in 1674 by the Quaker George Keith. The inner light had been lit, it seems, even for an earlier Muslim author, in this case one whom Keith compared to the biblical Job. Thus, reasoned the proud Friend, any man could reach God without need for the ecclesiastical authority of the church.[301] Defoe was concerned less with reaching a knowledge of God than with a sense of what it meant to survive as an individual apart from society, but a link between the two texts is plausible. For those critics concerned that Defoe's reputation is being maligned, consider that Ibn Tufayl appears to have lifted his plot from an earlier text by Ibn Sina. God only knows where Ibn Sina stole the story from.

It is commonly accepted that of Bath Adelard effectively introduced *Arabum studia* among English scholars during the mid-twelfth century.[302] Among the things he had learned from exposure to Arabic texts and Muslim scholars was the potentially useful idea that the earth was round. But to the extent that there was an English strain of Orientalism in advance of its colonial expansion, it was an idiosyncratic and far-from-systematic endeavor for several centuries.[303] The first formal British chair of Arabic, the Sir Thomas Adams Chair, was established at Cambridge in 1632. The charter for the chair was threefold: first was the academic aim of "advancement of good literature by bringing to light much knowledge which as yet is lockt upp in that learned tongue"; second, "to the good service of the King and State in our commerce with those Easterne nations"; and third, quite overtly, the "propagation of Christian religion to them who now sitt in darkness."[304] There is little evidence that the earliest Arabic classes were overcrowded. Oxford, as usual, was not far behind, with Edward Pococke, professor of Arabic, spending more than five years in Aleppo and another three in Istanbul before publishing his seminal *Specimen historiae Arabum* in 1650.[305] However, the English were once again trumped by the French, as Henry III had founded a chair for Arabic at the Collège de France in 1539. It was a later French initiative in 1795, quite revolutionary at the time, that led to one of the first schools devoted exclusively to contemporary Oriental languages.[306] For C. E. Bosworth, this last establishment is the beginning of "scientific orientalism."[307]

Like Said's *Orientalism*, this description of Orientalism's textual genealogy is far too skewed to the Near Orient. The first Sanskrit text translated into a European language was a 1651 paraphrase of Bhartrihari's *Maxims*.[308] In this respect the English were far more direct: Charles Wilkins is credited with producing in 1790 the first English translation from a Sanskrit text. The first German chair in Sanskrit was established at Bonn in 1818 for August Wilhelm von Schlegel; this was same year that Hegel began as Professor of Philosophy in Berlin. There was no chair for Sanskrit in England until the one established at Oxford in 1833, which was followed soon after by chairs in Copenhagen, Helsinki, Leiden, Zurich, Brussels, Geneva, and Turin. If a watershed moment is sought for the coming-of-imperial-age of Sanskrit studies, it is probably, as Schwab suggests, the publication in 1875 of Max Müller's *Sacred Books of the East* series, which brought the previously hidden wisdom of the East into the Victorian parlor and public library.[309] Farther afield, the field of Chinese studies was inaugurated in France in 1814 with a chair granted to Abel Rémusat at the Collège de France. Chinese had first been taught in France by E. Fourmont in 1732. The real history of Orientalism is full of these kinds of dates and founders— these are but the fragments of a rather uncoordinated and disparate trajectory towards established academic fields.

For there to be an active arm of imperialist policy, at least in the sense Said would have it, it was not enough for learned monks to sit in monastic libraries or exchange philosophical chatter while visiting tolerant courts. One of the perks of colonial control was the potential for collecting manuscripts. Thus, the building of Oriental collections in major university libraries is another useful indicator of an expanding academic enterprise oriented to Islam. Postel, the reputed founder of French Orientalism, brought back some 300 Arabic manuscripts after a visit to the region. A bequest of about a thousand manuscripts came to Leiden University in 1644. In 1718 Abbé Bignon, the royal librarian at the French court, invited missionaries to obtain and send back Oriental manuscripts.[310] Perhaps an even more relevant measure of Orientalism as a cohesive discipline would be the settling in the field—obviously because they could, in a colonial context—of trained linguists. Not as a missionary calling the Orientals to Christ, but as an Enlightenment scholar pursuing a quest for origins, William Jones arrived in India in 1783. Even this founding father had been preceded by the French linguist Anquetil-Duperron in 1754. Before that there were, of course, all those indomitable Jesuit missionaries.

Orientalism gained societal acceptance with the rise of professional societies devoted exclusively to Oriental Studies. In 1784 the Asiatic Society of Bengal was established by British scholars; this was the year that Herder published his seminal *Ideen zur Philosophie der Geschichte der Menschheit.* David Kopf cites this doubly significant date for the birth of modern Orientalism.[311] The first European organization was the Société Asiatique (1821) in Paris, whose *Journal Asiatique* appeared two years later. The British Royal Asiatic Society of Great Britain and Ireland, originally founded in London in 1823, inaugurated its journal in 1834. The Americans followed suit in 1842 with the American Oriental Society, which likewise issued a journal. The Deutsche Morgenländische Gesellschaft was formed in Leipzig in 1845, again with a prominent *Zeitschrift* to follow. The first journal devoted to Oriental Studies, Josef von Hammer-Purgstall's *Fundgruben des Orients* (1809–1818), originated in Austria. It was not until 1895 that a journal was exclusively devoted to Islam.[312] Similar societies sprang up not only in Europe, but in several prominent cities of the Orient. In 1873 the first International Congress of Orientalists was held in Paris.[313] The discourse was becoming guilded, as Said rightly notes, during the age of European expansion.

Great discourses need political backing to salvage intellectual invention from the fantasy that scholars often fancy themselves capable of transcending. For Said, Orientalism in the modern sense began with Napoleon's fleeting occupation of Egypt in 1798. "The entire modern experience of the Orient" is given a radical new start in the "universe of discourse" founded by Napoleon.[314] The discourse said to be founded textually by the Greek lines of Aeschylus is then jump-started by Bonaparte, with equally imperialistic British lords and travelers not far behind. The French invasion, capped by the completion of the Suez Canal, ushered in an era of active colonialism that fueled the ethnocentrism of most European travelers. Said, however, is so fixated on Napoleon as a textual agent of imperialism that he fails to see the impact of the Oriental man—Muhammad Ali Pasha, the Albanian cum Egyptian ruler—who set in motion the quest for Arab nationalism. Ironically, what Said sees from one side of the imperial divide as an invasive muting of real Orientals, other Arab scholars previously heralded as a "great awakening."[315]

ORIENTALISM BY NATION

> Therefore I study Orientalism as a dynamic exchange between individual authors and the large political concerns shaped by the three great empires—British, French, American—in whose intellectual and imaginative territory the writing was produced.
>
> —EDWARD SAID, ORIENTALISM

As a critical exercise in intellectual history, the preceding text-search for Orientalism's presumed birth has been purposely expanded—at times beyond sound reasons. The need to fix a starting point for this discourse easily succumbs to the sin of originism, in which quick-fixing a beginning becomes an end in itself rather than an appreciation of the problematic process of birthing. As Said eloquently argued before he wrote *Orientalism*, "Beginning is not only a kind of action; it is also a frame of mind, a kind of work, an attitude, a consciousness."[316] Thus, any scholar inevitably starts with an "attitude" when he or she retro-begins Orientalism through historical detection. But, and here is the haunting part, any beginning we could agree on for such a discourse of power will have its own murky prehistory. As archaeological critics, we may never know if our material grasp of Orientalism or the imagined Oriental fantasy is elusive and thus—in a pragmatic sense—imaginary, a product of textual relics for a process underlying all possible texts.

A glaring example of this problem is the virtual lack of concern in *Orientalism* with German Orientalist scholarship.[317] This omission strikes Robert Irwin as "something too bizarre and unbalancing to be accounted for" by Said's acknowledgment and apology.[318] The works of some German scholars, notably Goldziher and Brockelmann, were seminal in shaping the study of Islam and Arabic texts; their contributions have not entirely faded, nor are they likely to. The progress of German-speaking scholars in philology, philosophy, and history was so substantial that it might be said, albeit facetiously, that German is the first Semitic language.[319] Raymond Schwab notes that Victorian England looked to German universities for its chief Sanskrit Orientalists, Max Müller and Friedrich Rosen, much as Said describes modern American universities raiding the don dens of Oxford and Cambridge.[320] Even though German scholars were dismissive of Islam's ultimate authenticity, the Tunisian scholar Hichem Djait still calls much of their work "serious Orientalism," a discourse that was more appreciative of Islam because of Germany's national allegiance with the Ottoman empire.[321] Fuchs-Sumiyoshi notes that German usage of "Orient," unlike the British and French, did not focus just on the Near East.[322]

Said offers a superficial excuse for this neglect of German scholarship by saying that it had no "protracted, sustained national interest in the Orient." Along the Rhine, such scholars are assumed by Said to only have the crumbs, texts "almost literally gathered from the Orient by imperial Britain and France."[323] Ironically, the fact that German Orientalism flourished before Germany had imperial ambitions in the Orient suggests to Nadim al-Bitar that Said is wrong in assuming that Orientalism always served imperialism.[324] German imperial politics certainly had a sustained national interest in Britain and France, even if its formal intrusion into the Orient came later and at times with less resistance. Said, however, narrowly confines nationalism to overt colonization. The Germans may not have created their own Raj, but their intimate ties with Ottoman Turkey in World War I are perhaps worthy of comment.

Having been called on his omission of such a germane set of Orientalists, Said is content to summarily dismiss his critics: "Other observations— like my exclusion of German Orientalism, which no one has given any reason for me to have included—have frankly struck me as superficial, and there seems no point in responding to them."[325] I suggest that there is reason enough in excluding a country that had a different imperial relationship to the real Orient. It is true that early on some German scholars did go to France to learn Oriental languages. Wilhelm Schlegel, for one, was taught Sanskrit in Paris in 1803 by the Englishman Alexander Hamilton (not to be confused with the American patriot of the same name).[326] But to suggest that German Orientalism was, in effect, a byproduct of French scholarship is a careless error.[327] A frustrated critic might wonder if Said omitted German Orientalism precisely to highlight the complicity of the academic discourse with imperialism on the ground à la France and Britain.

What of the other continental European Orientalisms? The Dutch scholar Snouck Hurgronje is referred to in several passages of Said's text as the lone example of "a non-British and non-French instance where the scholar's sense of national identity is simple and clear."[328] Nowhere is the context of Dutch economic colonialism in the Orient spelled out by Said. Although the Netherlands was not a military power, Dutch trade with the Orient was of major importance. And what of the Spanish tradition closely associated with eight centuries of interaction with Muslims?[329] The Spanish *Reconquista*, culminating just as Columbus set out for the East, was an event of defining influence in the subsequent growth pangs of Oriental Studies. For Spanish Orientalism, comments Mahmoud Manzalaoui, "the study of the East is precisely not a study of the Other, but a recovery of part of the Self."[330] Julia Kushigian argues that Hispanic Orientalism is not an elaboration of the Anglo-French version but is notable for its spirit of veneration and absence of condescension.[331] Imagine how the field would have evolved if Muslim and Jewish scholars had carried on in Granada without an Inquisition. Also lacking in Said's selective sweep is any mention of Italian Orientalism, despite the Islamic influence in Sicily and the way in which modern Italy Mussolinied a colonial presence in North Africa.[332] The noted Italian historian Leone Caetani was abused in his native Italy for opposing Mussolini's conquest of Libya.[333] Other countries also produced prominent Orientalist scholars: Portugal, Russia,[334] Switzerland,[335] Scandinavia,[336] and several states in Eastern Europe. Orientalism was far more multicultural than Said supposes it to have been.

A key disconnect in the logic of Said's polemic is in how he fails to fit the abstract textual transgression of Orientalism as discourse with the concrete historical progression of politics, economics, and cultural exchange. The problem starts with the notion of nation. Nations, real and imagined, have all kinds of borders, but beyond the shifting fortunes of politics a key distinguishing boundary is language itself. In what Said suggests is only a "possibly misleading aspect" of his study, he chooses to almost exclusively examine Orientalist texts written in English or French, yielding the infertile mutant of an "Anglo-French" Orientalism superseded by an American offshoot in allegedly authoritative complicity with German Orientalism.[337] By presenting a solidified Orientalist discourse, Said ignores the rivalry and alternative cultural styles of European powers.[338] French and English Orientalists are closely linked not so much because they borrowed from each other's texts as because their respective nations clashed over "civilizing" the Orient.[339] Yet, if Said thinks that Renan resonated more in Oxford and Cambridge than did Wellhausen or Goldziher, he has read very few texts in either national tradition. To assume that national or cultural contexts were of no influence due to an alleged endemic and omnipresent anti-Orient mentality is to deny that texts have intentional authors, a Foucauldian *faux pas* that Said insists he is at pains not to commit.

What makes the English–French connection compelling, apart from geographical propinquity and historical engagement? Were French and British imperialism similar in the real Orient? Were both equally dogmatic in stressing their national superiority?[340] Was the mode of colonialism cloned in each? These are questions that a historian should ask, but that the textually laden Said steadfastly refuses to consider. As Basim Musallam observes, French colonial power in the Maghreb—which is virtually ignored by Said—yields a different sense than the French experience of loss in the Levant.[341] In a historically informed analysis, Madelaine Dobie argues that Said's focus on the Napoleonic expedition as the virtual start of French Orientalism overlooks a longer discursive tradition following French colonization of the New World.[342] Muhammad 'Abduh, a nineteenth-century Egyptian, considered French colonialism a greater enemy of Islam than the English variety because the French tried to destroy the Muslim personality, whereas the English were more flexible.[343] Furthermore, James Clifford criticizes *Orientalism*'s failure to consider modern French Orientalist currents, as these can not be castigated in the same way as the nineteenth-century scholarly run of Renan and Muir.[344]

This brief excursus into words and their all-too-poorly documented usages across languages is hardly definitive, but it does provide a context for considering how the idea of Orientalism might profitably be read back today. Setting aside its descriptive uses in art and colonial history, the issue is whether the history of Orientalism's basic vocabulary conveys a unified discourse of power à la Said, an unsalvageable academic label, or a slippery set of deeply embedded stereotypes that solid scholarship cannot whittle or wish away. There is no denying—and I am not sure who in the last several decades would foolishly try to do so—that one prominent connotation of historical Orientalism is the fantasy of mixed exotic and erotic projections summed up eloquently by Rodinson. Rummaging through dusty books and galleries of vividly colored imaginations in the skeleton-infested Orientalist closet rather quickly uncovers a specious typing of *Homo orientalisticus*, a fossil we cannot deny is a relative, however distant, of scholars who study both Islam and the real Orient today. Nor are negative images appreciably less present across the various modern media and Internet. But the question remains: is the entire frame of Western representations of Islam and points East only to be viewed as part of a unified discourse so powerful that otherwise rational and sincere individuals had not been able to transcend it until Edward Said came along?

2

The Said and the Unsaid in Said's *Magnum Opus Orientale*

Indeed, my real argument is that Orientalism is—and does not simply represent—a considerable dimension of modern political-intellectual culture, and as such has less to do with the Orient than it does with "our" world.

—Edward Said, *Orientalism*

The most astonishing thing in Said's *Orientalism* is that it is so much built on speculation.

—Douwe Fokkema, "Orientalism, Occidentalism and the Notion of Discourse"

I   Dissing *Orientalism*:
All That Said Has Done

> *Orientalism* is a *tour de force* of its kind: written from personal feeling so savage as to be virtually out of rational control; a vainglorious parade of learning, paradoxes, half-truths, evasions, fake relationships, and non-sequiturs; and a specious pleading to a readership, avid for intellectual scandal and cultural self-mortification, and incapable of scrutinising much of the evidence at firsthand, even if willing to do so.
>
> —G. M. WICKENS, "WESTERN SCHOLARSHIP ON THE MIDDLE EAST"

THE POLITICAL ART OF RHETORIC

> Thus it turns out that rhetoric is, as it were, a kind of offshoot of dialectic and the study of ethics and is quite properly categorized as political.
>
> —ARISTOTLE, *THE ART OF RHETORIC*

The debate over *Orientalism* has not been allowed to die.[1] The simple fact that the text now exists in some three dozen languages suggests that it needs to be continually reviewed as it is renewed. Its citational involution in post-colonial studies is second to none. Said's reconsidering and repositioning in lectures, articles, and interviews demonstrated that his own engagement with the text had not abated, even though he moved on to other issues. It is not surprising that, by targeting the establishment of scholars in Oriental studies and including in that a wide range of researchers who were unaware that they qualified as Orientalists, Said's polemic has engendered its own counter-polemic. Unfortunately, most of the substantive criticism is spread out in small doses. There are of course the reviews that are recycled in an almost canonical sense—those of Bernard Lewis, James Clifford, Aijaz Ahmad, Homi Bhabha, for example— but the time has come for a sustained look at how both the rhetoric and content of *Orientalism* are represented interdisciplinarily.

As befits the narrative of a literary critic, it is wisest to begin with attention to the text's rhetoric. I refer to the classical sense of rhetoric, as defined in Aristotle's canonical, mid-fourth-century BCE *Art of Rhetoric*, in which rhetoric is fundamentally the political art of persuasion. One pervasive quality of *Orientalism* in almost everyone's eyes is Said's ability to persuade so convincingly that even the most innocent-looking Orientalist texts can be reread as generated by a latent political bias of conspiratorial potential.[2] In assessing Said's rhetorical skills, the best that can be said is that he is an "erudite scholar of intellectual imagination,"[3] who wrote a "rhetorically brilliant book";[4] the middling that he exhibits "sometimes muddled eclecticism";[5] and the worst that he has a "tendency to be frightfully repetitive at times"[6] and exhibits an "epithet-laden, slightly stiff and formal voice."[7] Although some readers express frustration at the obscurity of his prose, at times a kind of over-articulation, it is obvious that he knows how to write.[8] Marrouchi goes a step further in insisting that Said's writing is "always full of insight."[9] For historian Willem Otterspeer, reading Said's *Beginnings* "has the same intoxicating effect as smoking a Havana cigar on an empty stomach."[10] Such glowing tribute to the author's style and effective use of language is due regardless of the merits or flaws of his arguments. In homage to Said's own neologistic contributions, I suggest that he be dubbed the literary knight-errant of "erudiction."

Most discussions of the rhetoric in *Orientalism* work backward into Said's style after they initially accept or reject what is being said. Thus, when a critic protests that "Said's rhetoric results in far more than distortion, exaggeration, and overgeneralization," the focus is clearly on Said as an author who distorts, exaggerates, and overgeneralizes.[11] One of the more sustained critiques of Said's rhetorical tropisms is by Victor Brombert, whose lengthy review in *The American Scholar* is almost never cited, certainly not in the general effluvium of post-colonial theorizing.[12] Brombert, a fellow specialist in comparative literature, does not speak from a base in Orientalist scholarship; there is no disciplinal axe to grind. Indeed, he agrees with Said that there is an "essentially hermeneutical relation between Orientalist and Orient," and finds *Orientalism* a provocative book inviting a "fresh approach." It is the method that attracts Brombert's critical eye, which sees through the rhetorical aim to a narrative that induces Said "to do what he objects to in the Orientalist discourse," a common complaint of the book's critics. Although several of Said's "stylistic observations about the inscrutable Orient" are praised as "to the point, even far-reaching," Brombert faults the text for providing detailed arguments on the flimsy basis of broad generalizations, questionable analogies, a tendency to caricature, and highly charged figures of speech. "But when polemical fervor so notably colors a discourse," concludes Brombert, "there is some cause for concern."[13]

Several of the specific examples noted by Brombert demonstrate the ways in which *Orientalism* transgresses the canons of established literary logic. For example, one of Said's "highly charged figures of speech" relates to his characterization of Silvestre de Sacy's approach to studying and publishing Oriental texts. "As a European he [de Sacy] ransacked the Oriental archives," asserts Said. "What texts he isolated, he then brought back; he doctored them; then he annotated, codified, arranged, and commented on them."[14] As Brombert asks, "Why use the verb 'ransack' instead of 'examine,' 'study,' 'scrutinize,' or a dozen other possibilities unless to connote a plundering and pillaging?" I might add that the notions of isolating and doctoring texts primes the reader to assume that Orientalists needed to quarantine their exotic subject first. Said continues to push the false consciousness of the Orientalist who "produced a whole field" by reducing philological production to a "pedagogical tableau," implying that the educational use of Orientalist texts is a frozen scene, picturesque rather than pragmatic. Furthermore, Brombert notes Said's sylleptic metaphorizing of Orientalism as both an abstract discourse and an institutionalized political system, as when he claims that Orientalism has a fatal tendency "towards the systematic accumulation of human beings and territories." As Brombert argues, "Not only is the metonymic shift a clever trope; the transcription is transmuted into an indictment. The gatherer of knowledge appears fated to become the aggressor." There is no way to be an Orientalist in anything but bad faith. This is an example of Said's "almost protean slipperiness," as David Gordon phrases it.[15]

The reader of *Orientalism* is led over rhetorical hill and dale in which a dogmatic assertion at one moment is softened in the next. Consider the following wrap-up passage near the end of *Orientalism*:

> Of itself, in itself, as a set of beliefs, as a method of analysis, Orientalism cannot develop. Indeed, it is the doctri-

nal antithesis of development. Its central argument is the myth of the arrested development of the Semites. From this matrix other myths pour forth, each of them showing the Semite to be the opposite of the Westerner and irremediably the victim of his own weaknesses. . . . For every Orientalist, quite literally, there is a support system of staggering power, considering the ephemerality of the myths that Orientalism propagates. This system now culminates in the very institutions of the state. To write about the Arab Oriental world, therefore is to write with the authority of a nation, and not with the affirmation of a strident ideology but with the unquestioning certainty of absolute truth backed by absolute force.[16]

This passage reduces "Orientalism" to the level of racist bias and ethnocentrism, but it goes beyond this to insist that Orientalists are bound by an "unquestioning certainty of absolute truth." If Orientalist discourse posits that all Orientals are inferior and incapable of civilizing themselves out of the "tent and tribe" hole dug for them by Western stereotypes, then such an ideological stand must by default be the "antithesis of development," as Said contends.[17] For Said the "matrix" of Orientalism only pours forth false and distorted myths. The matrix as a culminating "system" metamorphoses into "the very institutions of the state" to such an extent that Orientalist discourse becomes unquestioned as the authoritative voice of the state. Orientalists thus provide an "absolute truth" backed by the "absolute force" of the uncritical institutions that serve the state. This might be styled a rope-a-trope attack that pummels an entire field of academic discourse without leaving any breathing space for an opposing point of view.

Is it true that major scholars of Islam and the Arab World were not questioning the discourse against the Orient? Consider, for example, historian Marshall Hodgson, who is totally ignored in *Orientalism* and in the entire Saidian corpus. Edmund Burke III suggests that Hodgson anticipates both Foucault and Said in recognizing the "essentializing tendency in Western scholarly precommitments."[18] Hodgson's *The Venture of Islam*, published before Said started writing his book, represents the best contemporary historical assessment of Islam available in the 1970s. Over two previous decades Hodgson had criticized in print the ethnocentric assumption of lumping all of the civilizations of the Eastern Hemisphere together as "Orient" and making the West appear more important. The term "East," observes Hodgson, results from "profound ignorance of world history," and a historian should never use the concepts "Asia" or "Orient."[19] Hodgson, as a trained historian, has little sympathy for philologically-driven Orientalism. "It is absurd for scholars in Islamic studies to be sharing conferences with those in Chinese studies more readily than with those in Medieval European studies," he states.[20] How did an Orientalist historian like Marshall Hodgson escape from the matrix? How did such antithetical scholarship escape notice in *Orientalism*?

When confronted about his failure to acknowledge critical commentary from within the ranks of those he labels Orientalists, Said responds that his failure to include them does not conflict with his argument in *Orientalism*. Instead, he counters that "the guild of Orientalists has a specific history of complicity with imperial power, which it would be Panglossian to call irrelevant."[21] The relevant point, however, is that Marshall Hodgson does not fit Said's model of a guild member. Nor do many of the prominent scholars writing about the Arab World at the time Said wrote against Orientalism.[22] Given that Said insists the guild is incapable of development or of self-critique, I suggest that omitting scholars like Hodgson borders on the Pantagruelian. The impression that Orientalism cannot possibly change is Said's "grand problème," as French reviewer Jean-Pierre Thieck suggests.[23] It is this problem that perpetuates the very binary of East vs. West that Said so vigorously attacked.

If the methods of analysis employed by those who study the Orient are so totally antithetical to development of a fair or accurate representation, there would seem to be nothing of redeeming value in the long trajectory of Orientalist discourse. Yet Said strategically retreats from the dogmatic trajectory of this polemical excess, perhaps to convince his readers that he is not out to bash Western scholarship. "On the other hand, scholars and critics who are trained in the traditional Orientalist disciplines are perfectly capable of freeing themselves from the old ideological straightjacket."[24] This is a welcome and I think unassailable observation, but how is this possible if Said means to stand by his earlier assertion that Orientalism is incapable of developing from within? If a generic Orientalism is to be used in one passage as a discourse inherently incapable of transforming itself, how could any scholar rigorously trained as an Orientalist in Said's terms be able to successfully develop a "methodological consciousness"? And if, as Said emphatically claims earlier, Orientalism is not affirmed as a "strident ideology," what makes the manacle to be cast off into an "old ideological straitjacket"?[25] My argument is not that Said suffers from an occasional inconsistent slip of phrasing but that he quite systematically engages the reader through a rhetoric that asserts a claim as absolute and then qualifies it as not being meant to be dogmatic.

Saidian caveat-prone prose relies on a number of adverbial cushions.[26]

At times the reader is confronted directly with what would seem a commendable scholarly trope of caution. "Having said that," "that" being that "the Orient is an idea that has a history," Said immediately disarms the skeptical but sympathetic reader by writing, "one must go on to state a number of reasonable qualifications."[27] Not much later, Said's unidirectional disarmament resorts to "Nevertheless there is a possibly misleading aspect to my study."[28] What Said carefully labels as possibly misleading—the failure to include German Orientalism—is taken by many critics as outright misleading, whether by design or default.[29] Said proceeds to give a half-hearted mea culpa, reproaching himself for such an omission as if his awareness of the problem justifies ignoring it. Later he disguises the "embarrassingly incomplete" aspects of his own study by saying it is the first installment, and enjoining others to "undertake studies."[30] The operative trope here is one in which the author can admit a methodological problem without having to rectify it. Beyond this, Said suggests that the goal of his thesis about Orientalism is modest: "all I have done is to describe parts of that [Orientalist] fabric at certain moments, and merely to suggest the existence of a larger whole, detailed, interesting, dotted with fascinating figures, texts, and events."[31] I think that Said's readers invariably see far more than descriptions of parts and mere suggestion in *Orientalism*. That Said would be satisfied with such a pedantic aim, as though he were studying the history of Oriental carpets, is decidedly out of his published intellectual character. That Said is aware of the "perhaps self-flattering" nature of his methodological apologetic only compounds the rhetorically embedded inconsistency.[32]

The reader of *Orientalism* will find an almost constant framing with "almost." The classic example is in the oft-quoted line that "The Orient was almost a European invention."[33] Near the end of the book, Said observes that the Middle East experts advising policy-makers "are imbued with Orientalism almost to a person."[34] Other qualifying adverbial twists, from the book's introduction alone, include "all too frequently," "but this is not to say," "in a sense," "in part," "in some vague way," "mainly, although not exclusively," "more or less," "nearly every," "not for me an exclusively," "perhaps," "something more . . . than," "a sort of," and "virtually," as well as healthy doses of "however," "nevertheless," "whereas," and "yet."[35] There is enough rhetorical play here to replace the appropriate Latin dictum *caveat emptor* with *caveat auctor*.

These and more caveats applied throughout *Orientalism* serve in an ironic way as a form of involuted oppositional critique. Said has consistently opposed what he sees as a sea of dogmas in disciplinal methodologies, theories, and metatheories. There is no dogma that Said is philosophically willing to adopt, theoretically not even his own. Yet his narrative style is replete with dogmatic statements. "Everyone who writes about the Orient must locate himself vis-à-vis the Orient," asserts Said, with no exception in sight. "Every writer on the Orient (and this is true even of Homer) assumes some Oriental precedent."[36] When Said continues by saying that he does not think treating the "exteriority" of a text separate from what it describes "can be overemphasized," such rhetorical hubris denies wiggle room for caveat.

A survey of Said's rhetoric cannot avoid his careless, and at times mischievous, citations of contemporary scholars. As an example of "assertions of the most bizarre sort," sociologist Morroe Berger is accused of "presuming that since the Arabic language is much given to rhetoric Arabs are consequently incapable of true thought."[37] In the corresponding endnote, no direct quote is provided, perhaps because no smoking slogan could be found in the original text. Berger does say "An Arab political scientist, perhaps exaggerating out of dissatisfaction with Arab politics, has gone so far as to claim that esthetic appreciation of the language has hindered its use as a means of conveying ideas clearly."[38] I am not interested in defending Berger's biased and outmoded 1960s psychologistic portrait of Arabs and Muslims, but Said should fault the Arab scholar being quoted and not simply presume Berger is concocting the idea. How can it be assumed that Berger is agreeing wholeheartedly with a sentiment that says an author has "gone so far"? I do not find sufficiently disarming the half-hearted caveat in *Orientalism* that "Here one is speculating, of course"; the "one" speculating in this specific case is clearly Edward Said. As Charles Butterworth comments in a perceptive review, Said sometimes "tortures a passage until it yields a meaning quite distinct from that which it originally seemed to have."[39]

As a voracious reader across textual genres, Said is adept at eliciting damnable quotations. A particular penchant is the doubly damning quote, damningly out of context and dangling to convince the reader that no more need be said. Quotes drive the narrative in *Orientalism*, from the epigraphs at the opening of the book and at the start of each chapter to the steady narrative drizzle of excerpts, some up to half a page in length. Indeed, as van Nieuwenhuijze argues, the quotations are methodically meted out as in a trial, although "they do not really serve to nail one particular culprit *in flagranti delicti* so as to win a case against him."[40] The quotable include a veritable who's who of British imperialism. From the start of Said's book, British lords are virtually leaping off the page. Indeed, the first sentence of the first chapter begins with a quote from Lord Arthur James Balfour, an understandable target for an ardent critic of Israeli politics.[41] Balfour is succeeded in the opening rhetorical salvo by Lord Evelyn Baring Cromer, another late-Victorian curmudgeon ripe for quote shopping.[42] As a colonial administrator, Cromer was utterly unsympathetic to Muslims and Egyptians. But Cromer was not uniformly admired back home. In Sir Arthur Conan Doyle's *The Tragedy of the Korosko* (1898), a Frenchman about to be captured by Dervishes insists: "I repeat to you that there are no Dervishes, they were an invention of Lord Cromer in 1885."[43] And there are more lording-over-the-nativisms from the likes of Lord Salisbury (a.k.a. Robert Arthur Talbot Gascoyne Cecil),[44] Lord George Nathaniel Curzon[45] and Lord Horatio Herbert Kitchener.[46] Surely literary license admits Lord George Gordon Byron into the rank and file of Orientalists as well.[47] Nor does Said slight the Sir-prized initiants into British aristocracy.[48]

Here is the oppositional literary critic at his best, allowing the words of his victims to literally hang them.[49] Of course, at times it is Edward Said who supplies the rope. To hammer home his points, Said frequently turns to the blatantly racist and ethnocentric rhetoric of a few ideal [mis]fits. Thus the section on "Orientalism's Worldliness" begins with reference to a Kipling poem:

> Now, this is the road that the White Men tread
> When they go to clean a land—
> Iron underfoot and the vine overhead
> And the deep on either hand.
> We have trod that road—and a wet and windy road—
> Our chosen star for guide.
> Oh, well for the world when the White Man tread
> Their highway side by side![50]

Without doubt the zealous and print-happy Rudyard Kipling burdened popular imperialist rhetoric with the pretense that the British Raj was good for the natives. The academically uninclined Kipling, however, is an "Orientalist" only in the broad sweep that Said suggests. A "popular" writer of poetry and fiction gets pressed into service by Said, while the various poet-laureates of the British Empire are ignored. Lord Tennyson, for one. To add conjury to insult, Said later uses Kipling's Colonel Creighton as a paradigm for the anthropological ethnographer.[51] The fictional Creighton is simultaneously the "ethnographer in charge of the Survey of India" and "the head of British intelligence services in India." The overt operator of colonial policy is also colonial mapmaker of folklore. This fictional Victorian officer, an armchair collector of ethnographic facts at best, easily represents the worst in anthropology's pre-modern-fieldwork days. For Said, Colonel Creighton is as rank as swashbuckling Captain Richard Burton, both in the [dis]service of empire. However, by the late 1970s anthropology had evolved beyond the undisciplined ethnological muckraking of the late nineteenth century.

The irony for this exercise in "new criticism" is that Said appears to have no ear, and certainly no eye either, for irony. Quotes are taken at their limited face value, usually faceless after being lifted gingerly out of context. Thus, a quote by the French traveler Lamartine is introduced by Said as having "no trace of irony."[52] How an author who cavalierly remarks that Jesus is to Palestine as Rousseau is to Geneva could easily suspend a sense of the ironic—consciously or not—is not explained. If the notion of hyper-irony has any validity here, it is interesting how Said is at pains to portray Lamartine's literary concoction of an imaginary Orient as a prime example of Orientalist representation. This traveler gloried in not resorting to the skills of philologists and learned doctors—he was the quintessential amateur. Lamartine's willful avoidance of objectivity may make for an entertaining read, but how exactly did it inform the evolving scholarship about the Orient in the way that the work of an academically inclined scholar like Edward Lane did?

Being an amateur is the ultimate goal of Said's intellectualism. A common fault of the amateur is linguistic misuse or accidental catachresis. I am not referring to typographical errancy or naive word choice. In classical rhetorical usage, catachresis is generally reserved for the manifestly absurd howlers minds naturally generate, from humble pie to taking arms against a sea of troubles. American writers in particular are prone to bet their ass and not lose a donkey. The post-colonial catachrestic negligence on the part of Said refers to words and bundles of words that tend to be politically meaningful rather than consciously malapropistic. Thus, his expansion of Orientalism beyond an academic field to a "Western style for dominating, restructuring, and having authority over the Orient," strains the meaning of a generic literary term.[53] Textual rhetoric does not forge or maintain empires. "Catachresis" became somewhat of a catchphrase in and against post-colonial writing with its overwrought use by Gayatri Spivak *et alia subalternalia*.[54] Consider the comments of Gyan Prakash, who criticizes subaltern studies as "a catachrestic combination of Marxism, poststructuralism, Gramsci and Foucault, the modern West and India, archival research and textual criticism."[55] The Gramsci and Foucault combination alone suggest that in *Orientalism* the catachresis has been let out of the bag.

Much of the debate over Orientalism proceeds as a metaphorical strain of medical materialism. Anthropologist Mary Douglas uses "medical materialism" to label a tendency in comparative religion to reduce religious statements to a purported medical function, as in the case of the Mosaic dietary laws.[56] This trope effectively demythologizes religious belief, so that the biblical ban on pork can be rationalized in hindsight as a health intervention rather than a symbolic act of ambiguous origins. Said similarly reduces Orientalism to "a form of paranoia, knowledge of another kind, say, from historical knowledge."[57] In doing this, Said fits into an established critical trajectory of dis-ease with Western views of Oriental others. The Tunisian Albert Memmi refers to the "colonizer" as "a disease of the European."[58] Further east, the Iranian Jalal Al-i Ahmad dubs admiration of the West as a mutant "Occidentosis," a disease on the order of tuberculosis.[59] As for Orientalism as such, Ziauddin Sardar sees it as a "pathology,"[60] Aziz Al-Azmeh as "congenitally incapable,"[61] Nicholas Thomas as "the guild member's narcotic,"[62] and Brian Turner as a "syndrome."[63] Even Said himself gets caught up in the metaphor when Aijaz Ahmad suggests that Said dismisses entire civilizations as "diseased formations."[64] Said has even been uncritically diagnosed with paranoia, "an authentic madness in his method, and a psychosomatic tendency to the disease he describes."[65] Such polemical metaphors ill serve healthy understanding of a common rhetorical malady. The narrator, in each case, becomes the authority making the diagnosis.

The logic of rhetoric leads beyond style and disease to the soundness of Said's seminal text as a mode of argumentation. It is not simply that there are errors in the text, but Said consistently falls into certain kinds of errors. It is a pity that Said did not consult David Hackett Fischer's historiographic masterpiece on *Historians' Fallacies*.[66] While some fallacies may lie in the eye of the beholder, the criteria for properly making propositions are not dispensable for any author. Consider, for example, the fallacy of negative evidence as proof. In raw terms this is a shift from the position that there is no evidence against an idea to asserting that such an idea can, even should, be accepted as proven. Said claims that Orientalists were incapable of escaping the latent bias inherent in Orientalist discourse and then proceeds to prove this by citing only those who—apparently—did not. This fallacy was pointed out by Nadim al-Bitar, who chides Said for generalizing about Orientalism without having made a comprehensive survey of the texts.[67] Said himself estimates that some 60,000 Orientalist texts appeared between 1800 and 1950, but quite obviously only a tiny fraction of those could feasibly be examined. The point is not whether there is enough time to read everything—there never is—but that his argument is based on an assumption supported only by a limited set of texts rather than demonstrated through a comprehensive search of the literature. For al-Bitar, Said's approach is unscientific and relies on only carefully selected examples.[68]

Furthermore, Said's insistence that Orientalist discourse is a style for dominating primes it for Fischer's "furtive fallacy," in which history [read Orientalism] is "a story of causes mostly insidious and results most invidious."[69] Said's presumptions not only get in the way of his analysis, they drive it. The oppressive and hegemonic discourse of Orientalism is exemplified piecemeal, text by text, but the counter-argument that such a broad swathe of historical thought and political action might have been less than totalizingly instrumental is not allowed. In the process, the unfruitful but perennial apples-and-oranges fallacy surfaces. This is an academically sinful flavor of faulty reasoning so common that it almost seems in bad taste to mention it. Consider the critique by Fischer of a historical study by Daniel Boorstin, in which the latter historian lumped together a host of eighteenth-century intellectuals (including Kant, Hume, d'Alembert, Diderot, Voltaire, Condorcet, Holbach, and Ferguson) as part of a unique "contemplative tradition of European man" opposite the activism of American colonial experience at the time.[70] Excepting the fact that Boorstin in 1958 had not heard of Foucauldian discourse, such an indiscriminate bundling is mirrored by the even larger grouping from Aeschylus to Bernard Lewis in *Orientalism*. Fischer's dismissal of Boorstin's work as "simple-minded, uninformed, and seriously inaccurate" would apply equally to Said's text.

HATCHET JOBS AND STRAW TEXTS

> It is not, however, acceptable to extrapolate from the existence of these shortcomings a picture of entire careers and entire disciplines as obscene and shameful conspiracies.
>
> —WILLIAM E. NAFF, "REFLECTIONS ON THE QUESTION OF 'EAST' AND 'WEST' FROM THE POINT OF VIEW OF JAPAN"

As those who have felt the sting of his no-holds-barred, wit-held pen know only too well, Said's rhetoric frequently crosses the borderline of political correctness. Like a bull in Orientalism's china shop, Said forges ahead with Proustean abandon. For some critics this is actually an endearing quality of his work, leading to "delectable oases in a desert of pretentious prose."[71] But it is far more deleterious than delectable when Said broadly brands almost any anti-Arab, anti-Palestinian, or anti-Islam statement as Orientalist. For example, in *Orientalism*'s afterword, Said labels Golda Meir's polemical remark that there were no Palestinian people as "deeply Orientalist."[72] Deeply Zionist, yes; offensive to all but staunch partisans, indeed. However, this political comment was not arrived at after a thorough reading of primary texts, nor does it depend on academic authority for its power. Said's spectre of Orientalism becomes schizophrenic, harboring both the

Zionist ideology of an Israeli prime minister and the anti-Semitic sentiment of a nineteenth-century scholar such as Ernest Renan.

A notable feature of Said's prose is his tendency to deny, or at least trivialize, anything of value in the writing of those he opposes. The evidence for the prosecution is trotted out in rapid-fire detail, but without serious thought that it might effectively be cross-examined. One way he does this is by simply ignoring any statements or work contrary to his point. For example, in stressing his own dogmatic assertion that the prejudicial dogmas of Orientalists against Islam still exist "today"—"in their purest form" no less—he argues that there has been no significant challenge to these dogmas by academics, so that biased doctrines function unrevised.[73] Whether he simply did not know the full range of the literature being so dismissed or did not wish to know it, Said might have benefited from reading Jacques Waardenburg's earlier review of post–World War II "changing perspectives in Islamic studies."[74] Waardenberg shows how a more flexible image of Islam had developed to counter earlier dismissive acounts, with a hermeneutic shift from what Islam "is" to what Islam "means." This contemporary scholar proceeds to argue that scholars of Islam were now "painfully aware" of the political conflicts in places like Pakistan and Israel. Among contemporary scholars not in the dogmatic Orientalist mode but with best-selling books on Islam at the time were Wilfred Cantwell Smith and Fazlur Rahman; both fail to qualify as quintessentializing Orientalists and neither is mentioned in *Orientalism*.[75]

Another dimension of Said's dismissal of difference is guilt by association, a tendency to cite a litany of all-alike Orientalists. One of the longest such lists comes in a passage explaining how individuals such as Gertrude Bell and T. E. Lawrence were Orientalists even though they were not established academic scholars. They were, in Said's eyes, the beneficiaries of establishment Orientalism because their "scholarly frame of reference" included William Muir, Anthony Bevan, D. S. Margoliouth, Charles Lyall, E. G. Browne, R. A. Nicholson, Guy Le Strange, E. D. Ross, and Thomas Arnold.[76] Earlier he lists Muir as part of the "official intellectual genealogy of Orientalism," which is an even more cosmopolitan set comprising Gobineau, Renan, Humboldt, Steinthal, Burnouf, Rémusat, Palmer, Weil, and Dozy— "a few famous names almost at random from the nineteenth century."[77] Said simply names these earlier and increasingly obscure men as card-carrying members of the guild, as though that would be sufficient to define a scholarly frame of reference. The result is a scenario in which all listed Orientalists must be bad simply because they appear in the same random lineup.

The case of William Muir is illustrative of Said's tendency to conflate all varieties of bias as generically Orientalist. What we learn about Muir is that he wrote two major texts in English about Muhammad and the Caliphate, and that these texts are—by virtue of one damning quote—thoroughly biased against Islam. Indeed they are. "Swathed in the bands of the Coran, the Moslem faith, unlike the Christian, is powerless to adapt itself to varying time and place, keep pace with the march of humanity, direct and purify the social life, or elevate mankind," wrote Muir in what could easily serve as a sum of the kind of ethnocentric Orientalism Said's book rightly attacks.[78] Muir was an unabashed Christian apologist, whose prose is full of self-righteous invective against Islam and whose scholarship was to a large extent derivative. However, his biography of Muhammad can best be understood not as a latent Orientalist drive derived from overreading Homer and Dante, but as a text written to address the crisis of the Indian Mutiny of 1857, when negative stereotyping of Muslims became rampant.[79] Said is wrong to assert that this author's nineteenth-century accounts "are still considered reliable monuments of scholarship" by the 1970s. Serious historians had long since relegated Muir's work to the rarebooks sections of their libraries. For example, the major bibliographic survey of the Middle East and Islam edited by Derek Hopwood and Diana Grimwood-Jones in 1972 does not include Muir among the hundreds of texts cited.[80] Muhammad Haykel pinpointed the problem as early as 1935: "It should be remembered that our author, Muir, is a Christian, an *engagé* and proud Christian, as well as a missionary who never misses occasion to criticize the Prophet of Islam or its scripture."[81]

It appears that Said failed to read the major texts of the authors in his scholarly lineups, apart from a few pages in Muir, as none of the others are referenced in the text. Had he discovered what is perhaps the most famous text by Edward G. Browne, his canonical Orientalist survey of Persian poetry, Said might have paused to consider the following critical admission:

> For Islam and the Perso-Arabian civilization of Islam I have the deepest admiration; an admiration which it is especially incumbent on me to confess at a time when they are so much misunderstood and misrepresented by Europeans; who appear to imagine that they themselves have a monopoly of civilization, and a kind of divine mandate to impose on the whole world not only their own political institutions but their own modes of thought.[82]

As far as Said is concerned, Browne suffers from the same "imaginative perspectives" as Rudyard Kipling, who spoke of British dominion "over palm and pine." Again, had Said read all of the Orientalists he was dismissing, he might eventually have discovered that Browne defended Islam in a major review on Islam and its development during the early twentieth century in the French periodical *Questions diplomatiques et coloniales*. "To my mind," Browne warned, "Asia is right to be wary of Western civilization."[83] A century later, we need to be wary of Said's cavalier listing of individual scholars as pan-theoretically shackled by a latent discourse of domination.

As a critic, Said often pays less attention to what an author is saying than to what can be quoted to further his own agenda. A good example is his review of an essay on Arabic literature by French Arabist Charles Pellat. Said, whose career trajectory had been oriented away from Arabic literature, claims that Pellat "informs us that Arab poets couldn't be 'sincere,' that Arabs are 'reserved,' and that the popularity of certain literary forms indicates the Arabs' poor taste."[84] My reading of Pellat's essay finds no such extended bias, nor indeed would it be found in the substantial output of this respected scholar. Pellat does not dismiss Arab poets in general as insincere, as Said suggests, but specifically describes a genre of panegyrics composed to please powerful patrons; the imputed lack of sincerity refers to a defining hallmark of this one genre.[85] The poems themselves indicate why such a judgment would be made, and why it would be made by earlier Arab scholars before Western scholars. As to Arabs being "reserved," consider the actual phrase by Pellat: "While the Bedouin women celebrated at the beginning of the qasîdas had always enjoyed great freedom, the women of the cities had hitherto been more reserved."[86] My major reservation here is about Said's acontextual bait and switch that substitutes all Arabs for an urban elite of women at a particular point in time. Far from essentializing "Arabs" as having bad taste, as Said claims, Pellat was focusing in this passage on the "verbal acrobatics" of a particular genre that had devolved into an "artificial convention."[87] The only bad taste I find here comes from the oppositional critic who prefers to suit his own distaste.

In addition to Said's adept desquamation of damnable quotes, his critique of Orientalism, as Bernard Lewis observed early on, "has receted a row of straw men."[88] The straw man that most breaks the critic's back is Raphael Patai, a self-defined anthropologist whom Said—fortunately, from my position as an anthropologist—only labels an Orientalist. Patai is accompanied by a straw woman, Sania Hamady. Their respective straw texts—*The Arab Mind* (1973) and *Temperament and Character of the Arabs* (1960)—are rightly trashed by Said as "general nonsense." Two more damaging books would be hard to find, although the differences between them are worth noting. To my knowledge, this is Hamady's only book; Patai is described on the book jacket of *The Arab Mind* as an author of 600 articles and 20 books. Hamady, an Arab Druse, was born and raised in Lebanon but trained in the United States. Patai, a Hungarian Jew, specialized in Rabbinic studies and Semitic languages in Budapest and Breslau; he arrived in Palestine in 1933 and eventually emigrated to the United States. Like Said, both Hamady and Patai write in exile from their native culture, yet it is hard to imagine two writers more unlike him.

As a self-taught "anthropologist," Patai began his academic career as a folklorist collecting tales and documenting speech patterns. His limited fieldwork was among Persian and Kurdish Jews in Jerusalem (1948), as well as later work among "Indian Jews" in Mexico after he emigrated from Israel and taught anthropology and folklore at several major universities in the United States.[89] Said ignores the important role Patai played in Mandate Palestine in forming the Palestine Institute of Folklore and Ethnology (1944) and later writing the first modern anthropology textbook in Hebrew. Despite Patai's prolific corpus, his impact on the anthropology of the Middle East, especially regarding either Arab culture or Islam, has been negligible and is nonexistent today.[90] The reason for this is not hard to fathom, for Patai worked under the now-outmoded Kroeberian paradigm of distinct "culture areas," and retained the essentialist Fraserian zeitgeist that carelessly misread folk narrative as social science.[91]

In labeling Raphael Patai an Orientalist, Said fails to provide any other information on his personal or academic background that might explain his orientation. This is an odd oversight, given that Patai's personal note prefacing his first edition articulates the archetype of the Orientalist "scholar" Said sets out to epitomize. "When it comes to the Arabs," Patai begins, "I must admit to an incurable romanticism; nay, more than that: to having had a life-long attachment to Araby."[92] One of his first memories is shaking the hands of Ignaz Goldziher, whom his father called the greatest Orientalist alive. As a young boy, Patai read German adventure stories by Karl May about the Arabian Desert.[93] At age fourteen he drew a portrait of himself in Arab headdress. His Orientalist training with the distinguished Carl Brockelmann included Hebrew, Arabic, Aramaic, Syriac, Persian, and South Arabic. When he arrived in Palestine in 1933, he was the quintessential philological dabbler, his academic Arabic instruction not having prepared him to actually speak the language. There in the Old City he relished sitting in Arab cafes drinking Turkish coffee and listening to storytellers. His house was soon stuffed with Arab folk art, from hands of Fatima to inkwells. Patai does not hesitate to mention how many Arab friends and colleagues he had, including an al-Azhar graduate from a prominent Jerusalem family. On reuniting with this man after the 1967 war and a twenty-year absence from Israel, Patai reminisces that they "fell on each other's necks and wept" like Jacob and Esau.[94] Patai represents just about everything Said disdains in Orientalist discourse.

The Arab Mind is an apologist's dream, at least for those who either over-idealize or genuinely dislike Arabs. Patai's pathetic palaver was latched onto by eager racists, Zionist propagandists, and neocon artists.[95] Its over-all effect for understanding Arabs—at least from a perspective almost two decades after the last revision—is an academic, but no less virulent, variant of what the Protocols of the Elders of Zion informs about Jewish culture.[96] Patai's narrative, for all its enormous faults, is witty and eminently readable, a factor not unrelated to its publication by such a popular press as Scribner's.[97] It is also thick with descriptive detail that is presented with statistical panache. Patai draws on Arab texts as well as Orientalist and biblical scholarship interspersed with political commentary and dazzling anthropological argot such as the linguistic Sapir-Whorf hypothesis and Ralph Linton's idealized "basic personality types." Although he frequently refers to his own knowledge of Palestinian Arabs, this is almost entirely anecdotal. Admittedly, there was only a small corpus of ethnographic research available on the Arab world before 1973, but hardly any of this is to be found in the text or its subsequent revision.

Sania Hamady's text is also a convenient a target for Said, as it lends itself to the propaganda of anti-Arab apologists.[98] Said could have chosen an excerpt from almost any page to illustrate the kind of unoriginal and simplistic generalizations perpetuated by Hamady. Yet the two excerpts Said does provide show his lack of concern for textual nuance. In both cases he has chosen paragraphs that immediately follow extensive quotations, so that in fact he is quoting Hamady's summaries of what someone else said or implied.[99] Thus, the reader of Orientalism would be unaware that Hamady's quote beginning with "Thus" is not an original idea of her own but a paraphrase of a long quote by Patai. I am not defending what she or Patai is saying, which is indeed patent nonsense. The problem is that nowhere does Said contextualize Hamady qualitatively as a scholar. Is it enough simply to publish a book about Arabs to be considered an Orientalist authority? Here is an entirely derivative study of term-paper-level journalism, so poorly written that it is clear why it was not published by a reputable academic press. Hamady indiscriminately patches together the works of travelers, historians, folklorists, anthropologists, and a handful of Arab writers. On top of this she adds her own class prejudices as a Westernized Arab, and it is important to note that she did not undertake any original field research.[100]

A frequent criticism of Said's book is that it treats all texts as equal, not just comparing novels with academic treatises or political polemics, but also failing to assess the caliber and acceptance of a given work. To return to noted nineteenth-century scholars such as Muir or Renan is fair, if it is also recognized that they were long out of date by the time Said was writing, but to place this sad and faulty book by Hamady as a serious piece of scholarship in contemporary Oriental Studies is decidedly unfair. Certainly it had some influence on the general public, but this was not a book taken seriously by knowledgeable scholars or the students being trained in Oriental Studies or anthropology by the 1970s. Said also fails to indicate what Hamady, who dedicates her book to "the Arabs in this stage of transition," was trying to do in her book. Despite the flawed rhetoric, Hamady herself clearly thought she was contributing to a better understanding of Arabs by making their behavior "less mysterious, less unintelligible and less immoral."[101] Unfortunately, she was writing within an outgoing paradigm of national character studies, related to the personality and culture fad of Margaret Mead, Geoffrey Gorer, and Clyde Kluckhohn in midcentury American anthropology. Critiques of this approach were already well underway in anthropology and the approach had been thoroughly trashed by Said's Columbia colleague Marvin Harris.[102]

By sheer indexical bulk, the most significant Orientalist writers discussed in *Orientalism* are the Englishman Edward Lane and the French savant Ernest Renan.[103] For Said, Lane's scholarly rigor and Victorian manners make him a less blatant proponent of ethnocentric Orientalizing than the notoriously anti-Semitic Renan. Indeed, Said situates the intellectual writing of Renan in the 1840s as the tentative *terminus post quem* of Orientalism and defining a system of ideas "unchanged as teachable wisdom (in academics, books, congresses, universities, foreign-service institutes)" up through Said's literary present in the United States.[104] It is Renan, we are told, whose contributions were "to solidify the official discourse of Orientalism, to systematize its insights, and to establish its intellectual and worldly institutions." Renan, as described in *Orientalism*, becomes an embodiment of just about everything that is wrong with the field. Thus we learn that Renan is a racist who applauded British suppression in Egypt, wanted to reconstruct and even redeem the Orient, and provided much of the fodder for the "canonical pseudoscientific prejudices" of French, British, and Italian Orientalists.[105]

The focus on Renan as an archetypical Orientalist is telling in large part because it is very much Said's unique choice. In an endnote Said acknowledges that Renan is mentioned only in passing by Schwab, one of his most important sources on French Orientalism.[106] Renan is rarely cited by Orientalist scholars; when this happens the French author is usually disparaged. W. Montgomery Watt, for example, dismisses Renan's racist notion about the austere desert origins of Islam as having "little foundation in fact."[107] In the rather large literature on Renan's role in intellectual history, the focus is generally on his critical approach to Judaism and Christianity or the idea of the nation, all mitigated by his overtly prejudiced pronouncements on race. As Norman Daniel asks, "Wasn't the 'Semite' an incidental casualty in Renan's war on Christianity?"[108] Nikki Keddie is more to the point: "Professional Orientalists other than the unusually famous Renan did not play the main role in spreading these attitudes among the public; they were spread more by politicians, missionaries, journalists, and artists and writers."[109] Said uses a rhetorical smokescreen to burn Renan's textual attitude into the reader's mind.

Renan provides Said with a vehicle for Foucault's de-authorizing of the author. We learn little about what Renan actually said about the Orient, or how others responded to what he said, but rather encounter him as "a figure who must be grasped, in short, as a type of cultural and intellectual praxis, as a style for making Orientalist statements within what Michel Foucault would call the archive of his time."[110] The grasping here does not require extensive reading, for the gist is all we are given to digest. Said suggests we look at how Renan wrote, what he chose to include, and what he excluded because of his "background and training." In an extended passage following this suggestion, Said provides his idiosyncratic reading of Renan. It is worth rereading this critical passage in a similar critical spirit.[111]

The main point Said wishes to make manifest about Renan is that he merged the emerging scholarly discourse of Orientalism with the already highly regarded discourse of philology. Renan is first and foremost a philologist, not a specialist on the Orient. In order to explicate the role that philologizing played, Said reveals what he disdains most about the whole discourse he labels Orientalism. It is not Renan's overt racism, hardly a novel notion to deconstruct, but rather the assumed neutrality, the guildish and self-agrandizingly guiltless ivory-toweredness of establishment scholarship. I suggest that Said's argument is revealing because we are immediately teased with a paradox. Do not think, suggests Said, that philology connotes "dry-as-dust and inconsequential word-study," but listen rather to the dire warning of Nietzsche; the herd of philologists is damned to a Sisyphean word-hunt in which the essence is "setting oneself off, as great artists do, from one's time and an immediate past even as, paradoxically and antinomically, one actually characterizes one's modernity by so doing." We are, as Said seeks to demonstrate with a lengthy quote from Renan, not dealing with philology in the general sense but rather with a rationalistic philology-as-philosophy that Renan posits in grandiose terms as the key to understanding mental objects (*des choses de l'esprit*). Philology, as scientific praxis, becomes Renan's dogmatic replacement for religion.

Said elaborates Renan's stamp on philological Orientalism for about eighteen pages, one of the most sustained critical vignettes in *Orientalism*. What comes out of this is a portrait of Renan the rabid racist, who is responsible for creating the formal family of "Semitic" as a language group and at the same time denigrates everything Semitic as an inferior part of human nature. "Read almost any page by Renan on Arabic, Hebrew, Aramaic, or proto-Semitic and you read a fact of power," argues Said. This power refers to Renan as a library-bound dilettante who uses his philologist's authority to summon Semitic words and phrases in a rhetorical style that "points out defects, virtues, barbarisms, and shortcomings in the language, the people, and the civilization." Thus Renan constructs Semitic or Oriental culture out of his philological laboratory without ever actually going to the Orient, without ever needing to speak in an Oriental language to an Oriental. Said's selective application of Foucault's author function reduces Renan to an "act of construction," which is a "sign of imperial power." Furthermore, Renan's construction of the Orient denied any possibility that it could be generated or brought to life outside "the philological library."

Said tells us over and over again that Renan hates the "Semites" he has constructed. Yet nowhere do we find a measured investigation of why Renan was such a racist. Was it simply the tenor of his time? Is it a case of scholarly ethnocentrism in which his own Indo-European roots required downgrading Semitic languages?[112] Or did Renan so despise his own Judeo-Christian experience that its roots had to be demonized? Could this alleged French agent of imperial power have been afraid of Muslim military threats? All of these are theoretically possible, but how can we know which are probable if Renan as an author with a biography is, with Foucault's apparent authorization, simply ignored? Having fixed Renan as a "style" for construction and domination, Said is free to focus solely on carefully selected passages. Yet it is Said as a real author who constructs a "philological laboratory" from Renan's metaphorical French. This allows him to draw an analogy between Renan's linguistic analysis and that of an anatomist's laboratory.[113] The metaphor-driven implication, not stated directly, is that just as nineteenth-century scholars sorted human skeletons to construct races— an odious concept indeed—so Renan drew examples from his philological laboratory to create an equally artificial and power-laden category, the Semite, or Oriental. If you question the very idea of race, then you must also question any of the philologizing done by Renan, no matter his pretense of scientific objectivity. Yet this all-important "laboratory" never really existed except as a turn of phrase in Renan, and now as a clever rhetorical trope that defines Orientalist discourse. The bare bones of the metaphorical laboratory are spun by Said as the dry bones of an Ezekielian imagination.

The choice of Renan as an architect of Orientalism bares a fundamental flaw in Said's hindsight othering of the archetypical Orientalist. Renan, unlike his predecessor de Sacy, was not a renowned Arabist. His early philological expertise was oriented to ancient Near Eastern languages, predominantly Hebrew. The reason he merits so little mention in treatments of the history of Orientalism is that he is more properly seen as a contributor to biblical and religious criticism. In that tradition he made a mark, long faded, but Renan's biblical criticism was hardly the catalyst for modern Orientalist discourse. Renan did in fact come around to speaking about and against Islam. His 1883 article on "l'Islamisme et la science" took the avowedly racist tack that the Arabs must have borrowed all of their science and philosophy from the Greeks and Persians.[114] Oddly enough Said excludes this text from his analysis, yet it is certainly one of Renan's works most concerned with the Orientalism of de Sacy (with whom he is repeatedly paired in Said's text) and their British counterpart Edward Lane. Renan's "authority" did not prevent those far more knowledgeable about Islamic sources from registering disagreement. Ironically, the most immediate "refutation" was published in the same French journal by the Islamic scholar Jamal al-Din al-Afghani. Nikki Keddie, who translated and studied the exchange between Renan and al-Afghani, observes that the latter's ideas are "more in line" with twentieth-century Orientalist thinking than is Renan's original argument.[115] Ironically, Bandali Jawzi, a fellow Palestinian writing in Arabic half a century before Said, also saw through the racism of Renan, but noted that such an extreme view was at that time (1928) passé, there was no benefit in refuting it![116]

After arguing that Renan established the scholarly bias that "no Semite could ever shake loose the pastoral, desert environment of his tent and tribe," Said turns to the work of theologian William Robertson Smith as "a crucial link in the intellectual chain connecting the White-Man-as-expert to the modern Orient."[117] Smith is portrayed as an extension of Renan with the twist of actual travel out of the study to the Orient. "The crucial point is that everything one can know or learn about 'Semites' and 'Orientals,'" writes Said in reference to Smith's research, "receives immediate corroboration, not merely in the archives, but directly on the ground." Just as Renan is the prototype of philologists in the library, Smith serves as the forerunner of Western "anthropologists" who are said to essentialize from present, unpleasant cultural realities to primitive stocks.

In pairing these respective French and British—in fact, Scottish—scholars, Said acknowledges parenthetically that Smith issued a "savage attack" on Renan's *Histoire du peuple d'Israel*.[118] Apparently, the content of Smith's criticism is not relevant to the author of *Orientalism*. In his seminal text *Religion of the Semites*, Smith takes Renan to task for reducing the origins of Israelite religion to fear and superstition rather than communal bonding. "Religion is not an arbitrary relation of the individual man to a supernatural power," argues Smith, "it is a relation of all the members of a community to a power that has the good of the community at heart, and protects its laws and moral order."[119] This distinction, which Smith suggests had escaped contemporary theorists such as Renan, constituted a major step forward in the study of religion as such. Unlike Renan, Smith does not reduce religion to a racial ideology; he draws attention to its social function rather than unctuously dismissing the whole category of religion as irrational. It is not without reason that William Robertson Smith is regarded by many as a founder of the sociology of religion.[120]

Throughout his book Said continually elides the trajectory of biblical criticism with the philological study of "Oriental" languages. This is nowhere more evident than in his loose use of "Semitic" as virtually synonymous with "Oriental." Smith was primarily a biblical scholar, most noted for introducing critical German scholarship to the English-speaking world. Rather than standing in awe of Renan's philological authority—surely Smith would be astonished to hear Said's elevation of Renan to the quintessential instigator of modern Orientalism—Smith castigated him for bending facts "to suit his hypotheses." In particular, Smith judged Renan to be guilty of the very fault Said pins on Smith:

> A generation ago it was fashionable to call Abraham an Arab sheikh: M. Renan is content to say that he is the type of an Arab sheikh; but in point of fact it would be difficult to specify a single feature of resemblance between the patriarchal life, as described in Genesis, and the life of the modern Bedouin, which is not either superficial or part of the general difference between eastern and western society.[121]

Contrary to Said's claim, Smith does not look at the modern Bedouin and see the biblical patriarch, nor does he think that the Abraham-Isaac-Jacob lineup helps to understand the modern Bedouin or Turk.[122] Even though Smith operated within the general stereotypical frame of East and West, he was able to discredit the false analogy proposed by Renan.

The distinguishing feature of Smith's *Lectures on the Religion of the Semites*, as well as the more Orientalism-relevant *Kinship and Marriage in Early Arabia* (first published in 1885), is Smith's adoption of an evolutionary approach to the study of religion. Indeed, the aim of the latter text is to use pre-Islamic Arabian culture as an illustration of a relatively new theory of totemism and the origin of marriage.[123] As Emyrs Peters warns in his modern preface to Smith's study of Arabian kinship, "facts that were available then were of poor quality, and it is easy nowadays to show the unsoundness of the theories on which they were built."[124] Smith's evolutionary assumptions and naive views are indeed woefully out of date more than a century later, yet this does not invalidate the novelty of his meticulous methodology and linguistic insights any more than modern biology negates the originality of Darwin's *On the Origin of Species*. Said is wrong to assume that Smith wished to reduce the variety of Judaism, Christianity, and Islam to a generic and ahistorical "Semite." Smith's point was that none of these monotheisms could be understood apart from the older traditional religious institutions that preceded them. Surely this was a reasonable assumption in the 1880s for furthering academic study.

In critiquing Smith, Said draws his material primarily from a popular series of letters about a brief ten-day excursion Smith made to the Hejaz in 1880.[125] Said selects two damnable quotes from this chatty travel narrative written for a popular periodical as paradigmatic of the binary "us" vs. "them" that is said to be endemic to all Orientalist writing. In these quotes, Smith comes across as dogmatically opposed to Islam and biased to the Victorian limit about local Orientals. As Said interprets,

> Smith is able without the slightest trepidation to speak about "the jejune, practical and . . . constitutionally irreligious habit of the Arabic mind," Islam as a system of "organized hypocrisy," the impossibility of "feeling any respect for Moslem devotion, in which formalism and vain repetition are reduced to a system."[126]

Without question, Smith was no relativist when it came to Islam, about which he wrote very little and claimed minimal expertise. He was, after all, an ordained minister in the Free Church of Scotland, having followed the steps of his father. But Said's elliptical dismissal here pulls words and phrases out of context as though the mere use of certain terms now deemed pejorative is a sound guide to what a person thinks. How can Said judge Smith's intent as speaking "without the slightest trepidation" without probing Smith's rhetoric and thoughts beyond one incidental writing sample of this prolific scholar? Would it not be judicious to at least look at the available biographical literature on Smith? Ironically, this opinionated Scot wrote the remarks quoted by Said while he was under investigation for a heresy charge in his own denomination. My contrapuntal reading of Smith's 1880 letters suggests that Smith's own theological skirmish flows into his terse comments on Islam. Much of his commentary is on the hypocrisy of political and religious officials, such as the extent to which the Ottoman regime in Arabia did not represent "true Mohammedanism." Based on the situation he found during his brief visit to Arabia, Smith was in fact making a distinction among various forms of Islam. His own religious preference and ethnocentrism did not prevent him from recognizing the political and economic dimensions of Islam as praxis. Indeed, the quote Said provides to smoke out Smith's racism turns out to be a poor screen. Smith does not say that Muslims are incapable of "genuine religious feeling," but that much of what he was seeing in the Hejaz was in fact not based on the Quran and antedated Muhammad. In this regard the Wahhabis at the time would have concurred.

Smith's interest in going to the Orient is implied by Said to be no more than a ploy to achieve Orientalist expertise. The Hejaz is said to have been chosen because it is the *genius loci* for Islam, a place both historically and geographically "barren and retarded."[127] However, Smith spent most of his time in Cairo learning Arabic and talking with Muslim scholars; he only made a very short trip to the Hejaz. Beyond the stereotypic remarks about "Mohammedanism" and Arabs in the abstract, Smith is clearly able to recognize the humanity of Ismail, an Oriental he actually encountered. "He separates the essence of religion from the forms of Mohammedanism, and has no objections to worship with Christians," Smith comments on his guide. "He longs, like all thinking Moslems, for justice in the State, honesty between man and man, and an end to the ceaseless oppression of the poor by the rich."[128] This is hardly a dismissal of the real Oriental, nor is Smith imbued with a missionary zeal to convert and civilize the Muslim. His candid remarks suggest that the Orient was not that different from home. Said's insistence that Smith could serve as a precursor to T. E. Lawrence "preserving the Orient and Islam under the control of the White Man" is contrived.[129] Smith is under no illusion about the realities of imperialism: "It is the steamers, the telegraph, the diving-bell, and things like these that raise our name," observes the pragmatic Scot.[130]

Do Renan and Smith really fit as individuals who gave modern Orientalism its authority as a dogma that could not be challenged? If Renan's role was so seminal in Oriental studies, why is his contribution not recognized by anyone other than Edward Said? If his philologically authorized word was so powerful, how is it that there were refutations readily available, even in French? In addition to al-Afghani, a booming Oriental voice excluded by Said from the entire sweep of *Orientalism*, Renan had prominent Orientalist critics in the West. If, as Said suggests, power dripped from every page of his philological construction, how exactly did it serve the interests of a French government with limited imperial might at the time among contemporary Semites? Renan's racist rendering of the Semite, by no means shared by all those whom Said would call Orientalists, would seem to serve less as a signet for imperial power than a sign of wishful intellectual ambition. Renan's racism is not as Orient-oriented as Said assumes. In his Eurocentric racial profiling, Renan considered Semites "white" along with Aryans; civilization was in their blood even if an inferior form, unlike Negroes and Chinese.

Said's demonization of Renan can be constructively compared to Hichem Djait's treatment of Renan in his analysis of essentially the same subject at precisely the same time that *Orientalism* appeared.[131] Unlike Said, Djait does not elide Renan's focus on Semitic languages, especially Hebrew, with the Orient as a whole; nor does he fail to point out at the start that Renan was hardly an expert on Islam. Renan's ideas about Islam are described as unjust and sketchy, perhaps even incompetent, and certainly tainted by a static view of history. Djait provides a nuanced reading of Renan, who, Djait says, read Islam as antagonistic to science, and philosophy as a parallel to the Catholic church resisting Western science. For Renan, the enlightened views of the Muslim philosopher Averroes were akin to those of Galileo—both stood against religious dogmatism. Thus, it is not the Muslim as such that Renan vilifies, but rather what Renan deemed the barbaric handlers of a religion he had little express interest in studying. Unlike most Orientalists who were experts on Islam, Renan did not see the Orient as unchanging, but as necessarily bound up in an evolutionary progress in which rationalism would ultimately prevail, as it already had in Europe. Significantly, Renan even viewed al-Afghani's critique of his own work as that of an enlightened Asiatic who shared the same sense of reason.[132]

His Ahistorical Story

> His primary goal is not to understand the past but to understand the present; or, to put the point with more nuance, to use an understanding of the past to understand something that is intolerable in the present.
>
> —Gary Gutting, "Michel Foucault: A User's Manual"

Although these words were chosen by Gary Gutting to introduce the intellectual achievement of Michel Foucault, they apply equally to Edward Said. As an eclectic critic trained to read fiction, Said totally ignored historiographic logic in his literature-driven zest to historicize Orientalism as a discourse that fundamentally changed his own ethnic history. There is no evidence, either indexical or in the narrative, that in preparing *Orientalism* Said actually read a twentieth-century text of historiographic method. His approach appears to be that any scholar who can read can thus read a historical text as well as, or even better than, a trained historian; by this same token, Bernard Lewis could successfully navigate Conrad's *Heart of Darkness*. Indeed, it is this methodological antinomianism rather than the specific thesis that so frustrates many historians. As Donald Little explains, Said shows a basic lack of familiarity with the history, in contrast to other non-Western intellectual critics such as A. L. Tibawi and Anouar Abdel Malek, "so that it is unclear, when he accuses Orientalism of dogmatism, for example, whether he has merely failed to read as widely in orientalist scholarship as he should or whether he has simply chosen to ignore the vast body of literature which he cannot conveniently cut to his pattern."[133]

I can only wonder how different a text *Orientalism* might have been if Said had absorbed, for example, Herbert Butterfield's deservedly well-traveled *The Whig Interpretation of History*, which made studying the past for the present a present and future problem. A succinct, prescient, and ironic critique of both Said and Foucault can be found in Butterfield's early warning:

> The danger in any survey of the past is lest we argue in a circle and impute lessons to history which history has never taught and historical research has never discovered—lessons which are really inferences from the particular organisation that we have given to our knowledge.[134]

The whiggish historian reads the past through the present, and outside of any contextual details that might blur such a reading. For Dorothy Figueira, this is symptomatic of Said's contra-contextual reading of Orientalism: "By linking texts with certain cultural practices, Said imposes a systematized coherence on the historical past that presupposes experience of the twentieth century."[135] Thus the hegemony inherent in Orientalist discourse is read back through rather than read out of texts by the literary critic.

Along with the whiggish pseudo-historian at the short end of his own rhetorical stick, Butterfield's critique extends to any scholar who charts a shortcut through complexity and personifies ideas in themselves "as self-standing agencies in history."[136] "Behind all the fallacies of the whig historian," continues Butterfield, "there lies the passionate desire to come to a judgment of values, to make history answer questions and decide issues and to give the historian the last word in a controversy."[137] Yes, this does apply to a number of the Orientalists discussed by Said. Bad historiography crosses critical perspectives and crosses up all claims for total objectivity. In candid retrospection, Butterfield concludes that "the eliciting of general truths or of propositions claiming universal validity is the one kind of consummation which it is beyond the competency of history to achieve."[138] This could easily be the final sentence of either *Orientalism* or a review of it.

Said had much to gain from reading the ongoing critical assessment within the long history of Western historiography. Historians had already begun to recognize what David Hackett Fischer forcefully denigrates as the "extravagant holism of metahistory."[139] To the extent that Orientalists of any era follow Hegel, Spengler, or Toynbee in the quest for an essentialized whole or real truth, they are guilty of employing what has been recognized for some time now as a faulty methodology.[140] Said's insistence that Western scholars were not aware of their own faults speaks more of his ignorance of contemporary historiography than it does of the novelty of his pronouncement. There were indeed competent historians who did not attempt to "dig themselves into wholes."[141] I note with irony the similarity between Said's criticism of the *Cambridge History of Islam* as an enormous "intellectual failure"[142] and David Fischer's earlier critique of UNESCO's 1960s world history project as "a catastrophe on an appropriately monumental scale."[143] What gets published as authoritative history is immune to neither fine-tuning nor outright trashing by other trained historians.

Notably absent from *Orientalism* is discussion of contemporary historiographic texts about Islam and the Middle East. One of the most important of these was Jean Sauvaget's 1943 *Introduction à l'histoire de l'Orient musulman: Élements de bibliographie*, updated in 1961 by Claude Cahen and eventually translated into English.[144] Sauvaget recognizes the need for Orientalist scholars to collaborate with historians for a study of history as "a feeling for exactitude and accuracy and, above all, critical judgment."[145] Recognizing that the "Islamic world is by no means homogeneous," Sauvaget faults earlier Orientalists who produced uncritical and biased studies.[146] Unlike those Orientalists whom Said correctly characterizes as hating Islam, Sauvaget writes: "Needless to say, whether one subscribes to the Muslim faith or not, one should study the life of Muhammad with the sympathy due all great and sincere efforts on the part of man to attain a higher mode of life."[147] It is hard to imagine how any book could attempt a review of Orientalist discourse without examining two of the central resources of trained Oriental Studies scholars in the 1970s: the multilingual *Encyclopaedia of Islam* and the massive *Handbuch der Orientalistik*.[148] Said leaves both out of *Orientalism*. Nor does he show awareness of the major bibliographic reference, the *Index Islamicus*.[149] Similarly, Said's penchant for listing national Orientalist societies does not extend to analysis of the content of their major journals.

A number of fellow literary critics cite *Orientalism* as a text that prompted a shift from textuality to historicity.[150] Some go so far as to describe Said's achievement as "a vast, almost encyclopedic repertoire of evidentiary material."[151] Mustapha Marrouchi avows that Said is writing histories rather than accepting a grand notion of history, but I suggest that both should be judged by accuracy in details rather than truth-to-power claims. It may be a rule of thumb in literary studies, however in the field of history it is somewhat suspect to "improvise a convincing argument," as Marrouchi suggests about *Orientalism*.[152] For Moore-Gilbert et al., "It is Said's demonstration of the apparent consistency of Western regimes of knowledge and their associated will to power, across very diverse historical periods, cultures of origin and disciplinary and aesthetic domains which, more than anything else, gives *Orientalism* its extraordinary power."[153] Here is an extraordinary misunderstanding of how historians work. Crisscrossing of historical eras—already a problematic concept—and culture hopping all too readily lead to armchair analysis. Sir James Frazer's monumentally futile *The Golden Bough* exudes a similarly apparent consistency as long as no historian is around to dredge up the context that gets left behind in the flow of argument. The mere fact that Said finds grist for his polemical mill in historical personages—from Herodotus to Napoleon—hardly makes his understanding of history historical. What bedlam results when literary critics let loose their canons in an undisciplined raid on historical context.

"But history is not Said's forte," concludes historian Sir John Harold Plumb in his *New York Times Book Review* comments on *Orientalism*.[154] A common complaint of critics—not just professional historians—is how ahistorical this book is despite its expressed will to read literature in a historical mode.[155] In a lengthy review for the *Journal of Asian Studies*, David Kopf is blunt: "The reader should be warned that this is not a work of historical scholarship."[156] Some point out Said's "wilful misreading of the historical record,"[157] or his "vacillation between historical and ahistorical perspectives,"[158] while others speak more charitably of his "historical naiveté."[159] Medievalist Kathleen Biddick concludes that Said's confusion of representation and history suggests he "did not think through Orientalism with history."[160] The only scholars who seem oblivious to the innumerable historical gaffes in Said's corpus are those who similarly succumb to Said's rhetorical denial of the proverbial dictum that those who ignore history[ography] are destined to repeat it[s faults].

The historical woes of *Orientalism* revolve around a central thesis that defines a historically complicit discourse in Europe from the classics of Greece through the darkness of medieval unenlightenment to Napoleon and beyond, culminating in the Zionist leanings of contemporary American Middle East policy. As John MacKenzie argues, "The modern critique of Orientalism has generally committed that most fundamental of historical sins, the reading back of contemporary attitudes and prejudices into historical periods."[161] Medievalists in particular have not been enamored with Said's thesis. Kathleen Davis criticizes Said's insistence on an inherent West-vs.-East opposition, arguing that "it instates a core 'reality' that privileges the very discourse he critiques."[162] The simplistic notion that a homogeneous discourse of the Oriental other glided through medieval Europe on its own momentum is not convincing. Davis is particularly opposed to the assumption that the Middle Ages contributed textually to a latent discourse of Orientalism prior to its actual practice.[163] In the specific case of Chaucer's "Man of Law" tale, Davis shows that Chaucer was influenced by actual English experience with the East. To view Europe as "an absolutely self-constituting object," à la Said is to ignore the complexity of medieval representation of Oriental others.

Another medievalist, Gabrielle Spiegel, takes to task the kind of intellectual history in which the past is viewed merely in its discursive dimensions. "Literary critics," suggests Spiegel, "have been accustomed to get their history secondhand and prepackaged and have tended, in practice if not in theory, to treat it as unproblematic, something to be invoked rather than investigated."[164] Criticizing Foucault in particular, Spiegel notes that treating the imaginary as real—which Said does by ignoring the "real" Orient—and the real as imaginary leaves "no epistemological grounds for distinguishing between them" or "establishing a causal relationship between history and literature."[165] A specific example that refutes Said's contention of an omnipresent West-vs.-East dimension is mapped out by Suzanne Conklin Akbari.[166] Before the end of the Crusades, it was not the case that East was East and West was West. Not until the fourteenth century, Akbari argues, were maps routinely oriented with north at the top. Before then it was the East that was the focal point of a sacred geography in which Jerusalem and the eastern roots of the Christian faith took precedence. "For it is commonplace that Jerusalem is in the middle of the earth," writes the author of the mid-fourteenth-century *The Travels of Sir John Mandeville*.[167] Far from being the imagined locality of an inferior other, East pointed to the center of spiritual origin and the hallowed point of return. Such an East was a center rather than a location opposed to an emerging West.

Said fits comfortably among the literary analysts and historians that Nabil Matar accuses of a post-colonial reading back through the sixteenth and seventeenth centuries when the Ottoman Turks, not England and France, were the successful imperialists of the moment.[168] In positing a homogeneous discourse of latent Orientalism, Said sidesteps the unpleasant realpolitik of shifting alliances. From the fall of Byzantine Constantinople in 1453 until the lifting of the seige of Vienna in 1683, the Ottomans held any latent dreams of European imperialism at bay. Where is the endemic East–West binary drive behind King Francis I preferring the magnificent Ottoman "infidel" Sulayman over rival Charles V, the Spanish–Ottoman peace treaty of 1580, or Queen Elizabeth's request for help from the Ottoman Sultan Murad III against the Spanish Armada in 1588? A historian would be prone to argue that Elizabeth's stately confrontation with Catholic Europe drove the English Crown to seek trade and political alliances with the Ottomans, damned Turks though the clerics said they were.[169] Martin Luther thought the Catholic pope a greater nuisance for Germany than the Turks.[170] An Oriental or Islamic other was at times simply a good-to-hate surrogate for local passions; English Catholics and Protestants cursed one other for acting like Turks.[171] Provincial European Christians were too busy killing each other to unite in opposition to an Islamic Oriental other.[172]

The accusations that Said uniliterally butchers history relate to details as well as theory and method. If the devil is indeed in the details, then Said would have a devil of a time extricating himself from his loose canonical sins of historical commission as well as the wide off-the-mark range of outright omission. One of the more glaring examples of Said's ignorance of "Oriental" history is his casual note about the expansion of Islam to Turkey after Egypt and before North Africa.[173] Muslim armies did not wrest Asia Minor from the Byzantines until the Seljuk Turks in the late eleventh century, long after Arabs had crossed the Maghrib and settled in Spain. In the same passage, Said suggests that "Christian authors witnessing the Islamic conquests had scant interest in the learning, high culture, and frequent magnificence of the Muslims," apparently forgetting the extraordinary amount of medieval borrowing from Islamic scientific, philosophical, theological, and astrological texts. Said wrongly refers to Harun al-Rashid's inner thoughts about the capture of Baghdad by Ma'mun's army; rather than "sulking in Merv," as Said suggests, proper chronology would place Harun in his grave four years earlier.[174]

Said fares no better in recounting the Napoleonic invasion of Egypt, an event that he insists inaugurated the modern discourse of Orientalism. This is given more space in *Orientalism* than any other single historical event.[175] From the endnotes it is evident that Said derives most of his information about the imperial French savant-garde from Jean Thiry's *Bonaparte en Égypte décembre 1797–24 août 1799*, a relatively minor historical study.[176] This explains in part Said's uncritical assumption that Napoleon's "learned division of the army" was regimented in "teams of chemists, historians, biologists, archaeologists, surgeons, and antiquarians."[177] More than half of these "scholars" were in fact young civil engineers and technocrats who came to Egypt thinking they would be building roads and bridges.[178] Surgeons were there to put back together the broken bones of the troops. Had Napoleon been able to sustain his foothold, these practical concerns would have occupied much of their time. Only five of their number were "established" scientists, nor were there any archaeologists or antiquarians as such.[179] These were raw recruits rather than the established intellectual elite of Paris. These instant savants came, they saw, and they drew, but they did not conquer. Of the original hundred or so men (out of 38,000 troops), the toll was high: "five killed in battle, five assassinated, ten dead of the plague, five dead from dysentery, one drowned, and five dead in Europe from the lasting effects of the experience."[180]

On October 21, 1798, a jihad-fueled rebellion in the streets of Cairo took the French by surprise and prompted Bonaparte to bombard the mosque of al-Azhar. Less than a year later, Napoleon led his army north to thwart an alliance of Ottoman and British forces, his troops lingering on in w[e]ary isolation until October 1801. Was it that no eighteenth-century Egyptian dared raise a voice against the invincible Napoleon? The Egyptian scholar Mahmoud Shakir argued in 1936 that one of the aims of Napoleon's invasion had been to stop an age of enlightenment underway among scholars in the Islamic world.[181] It might be argued that the opposite occurred, with scholars like 'Abd al-Rahman al-Jabarti providing a spirited critique of the European interlopers. In a sarcastic and ironic chronicle of the French occupation, al-Jabarti not only described the French as "rabid hyenas," but laid out a detailed critique of the grammatical errors riddling the first French proclamation in Arabic.[182] In his afterword to *Orientalism*, Said argues that the Napoleonic *Déscription de l'Égypte* "dwarfs the individual testimony" of al-Jabarti.[183] If this were simply because of the fact that al-Jabarti's chronicle was not available to European Orientalists when the expedition's belated *Déscription* appeared, it obviously did get dwarfed. But it was the Egyptian Pasha Muhammad 'Ali, rather than Orientalists, who prevented al-Jabarti's major chronicle from being published until much later. When it was finally available in the 1870s, European Orientalists not only consulted it but praised it. Historian David Ayalon, in the guild-defining *Encyclopaedia of Islam*, calls al-Jabarti's text "one of the most important chronicles of the Arab countries during the Muslim period."[184] By ignoring how al-Jabarti has been cited in Orientalist historical texts, Said becomes the one who dwarfs the relevance of al-Jabarti's critical text.

Even with official patronage, it was still a decade after Napoleon's debacle in Egypt before the first of twenty-three volumes of the *Déscription de l'Égypte* appeared. It is relevant to point out that more than half of these volumes were devoted to illustrations. The editor Denon included some of the first Western drawings of ordinary Egyptians ahead of a major series on monuments, indicating that there was indeed life beyond the ruins.[185] From a "text" in which the illustrations outweigh the narrative, Said reads the *préface historique* by Fourier as a paean to ascendant Orientalism, conveniently leaving out the historical context in which the congratulatory words provide euphemistic cover for a humiliating military defeat. In historical hindsight, how is it possible to miss the irony in Fourier's concluding statement that "Égypte fut le théâtre de sa [Napoleon's] gloire, et préserve de l'oubli toutes les circonstances de cet évènement extraordinaire."[186] Mindful of his patron, the author snatches a rhetorical but Pyrrhic victory out of a failed mission; in this extraordinary reversal, the emperor's robe of glory has no closure. Even that goldmine of a linguistic fleece, the Rosetta Stone, was among the spoils of war that ended up in the British Museum rather than the Louvre.

"Quite literally," argues Said, "the occupation gave birth to the entire modern experience of the Orient as interpreted from within the universe of discourse founded by Napoleon in Egypt, whose agencies of domination and dissemination included the Institut and the monumental *Description* [*sic*]."[187] From Said's description, one would think that Napoleon was more interested in imagining the Orient than in conquering land and people for his omnidirectional political and economic aims. Just before his arrival in Alexandria, Napoleon issued a directive to his army that begins with the order, "You will strike the surest and most painful stroke possible against England until you can deal her final death-blow."[188] Apart from a glancing comment that France and Britain were fighting each other in the real Orient—and most certainly not just in an imagined space—there is little in *Orientalism* to explain why these two super-imperialist powers were constantly at war, or how both played with and against the powerful Ottoman presence. Instead, Said insists that Napoleon's project "acquired reality in his mind" from "ideas and myths culled from texts, not empirical reality."[189] Would the same rationale hold for his later eastward thrust into Russia? Was Waterloo but a figment of a fading emperor's pre-Tolstoy night reading?

Inattention to historical detail allows Said to romanticize Napoleon as making Egypt "totally accessible to European scrutiny."[190] Napoleon is portrayed not as a military general with territorial lust but as a museum director making sure that his intellectual army of savants held their meetings, conducted their experiments, and recorded "everything said, seen, and studied."[191] This just-so story for the discursive origin of modern Orientalism is accepted and at times embellished by admirers of Said's thesis. Mustapha Marrouchi, for example, births the French Oriental gaze as follows: "This close alliance and mutual interdependence between scholarly research on the one hand and military administration and State policy-making on the other was such that the scholars, in Said's words, became the 'learned division' of the army."[192] While Napoleon pushed propaganda to aid his military mission, the day-to-day realities of the short-lived French occupation hardly needed less than a hundred savants drawing the Sphinx. Had the French actually established a colony, as would later be the case in Algeria, then there would be a case for examining the role of scholarship in the service of imperial power. But the monumental *Déscription de l'Égypte* no more defines Egypt as a homogenized and inferior Oriental other than do the pyramids. The text, read contrapuntally, is pure paean to a failed empire-maker. Said and Marrouchi whiggishly aggrandize a post hoc narrative of political propaganda as though it were a colonial charter.

Said assumes that Napoleon's failure to conquer the real Orient proves that the only important result of the expedition was its "textual children,"[193] a rather wide-ranging family resemblance that Said applies equally to Gustave Flaubert and Richard Burton. Napoleon is forced to play the dramatic role—perhaps comic and tragic at the same time—of prototype to just about anyone who came after and wrote about the Orient. Binding these textual progeny of the Emperor-with-no-Oriental-Clothing "is not only their common background in Oriental legend and experience but also their learned reliance on the Orient as a kind of womb out of which they were brought forth."[194] A kind of womb? Said's fertile and fervid metaphor has poetic potential but fails to achieve historical fit. The valorization of a discrete historical event epitomized by a distinct text over subsequent literary productions that do not even discuss that event should be suspect from the start. To suggest that travelers as different as Flaubert and Burton, let alone Chateaubriand or Lane, were validated by Napoleon's unsuccessful expedition and tardy *Déscription de l'Égypte* requires more proof than Said's injudicious poetic assertion.[195] If Napoleon had not brought along any savants, would there have been no birth of Orientalism?

An even greater lack of familiarity with the genre he criticizes shows up in Said's assumptions about Orientalism in India during the British Raj. Said is aware via Raymond Schwab of several Sanskritists, most notably Abraham Hyacinthe Anquetil-Duperron and William Jones.[196] Several pages of his narrative discuss the British colonial rule of India, predicated upon the duplicity of Orientalists in justifying that rule. "The more Europe encroached upon the Orient during the nineteenth century, the more Orientalism gained in public confidence," concludes Said in lumping Jones into the same critical genealogy with de Sacy, Renan, and Lane.[197] This was certainly not the case for India. In his thorough review of *Orientalism*, David Kopf, whose earlier work on the British in India was apparently not known to Said, notes with irony that Said has the wrong target. Jones was indeed an "Orientalist," a term applied by British historians to the early scholars who went to India, but Said's objections are more properly suited to the anti-Orientalist "Anglicists" like Lord Macaulay, who consciously shunned the earlier Orientalists' desire to develop education in the vernacular.[198]

The colonialist debate over how to rule was far more complex than can be appreciated by an alleged uniform academic discourse justifying colonial presence. The earlier generation of British scholars and administrators came to India under a parliamentary mandate issued in 1772 to "Indianize" the East India Company. Although himself hardly a lover of Indian culture, Governor General Warren Hastings implemented a policy that advocated enlightened self-rule for the Indians and a form of diversity training for the visiting English civil servants.[199] Far from viewing the local elites merely as barbarians who must be civilized, a number of the so-called Orientalists—those who were studying the local Oriental languages— enraged the conservatives back home by defending Indian civilization. Certainly Friedrich Max Müller, the eminent academic authority on India, does not fit Said's mold. "The more I see of the so-called heathen religions," Müller wrote in a letter from 1878, "the more I feel convinced that they contain germs of the highest truth. There is no distinction in kind between them and our own religion."[200]

A prime response to this budding British Orientalism was James Mill's *History of British India* (1817), a political treatise highly critical of scholars like Jones for glorifying India—in effect, valuing India over Britain—as a site of mythical origin. Said correctly observes that the influence of Mill was "considerable" on British rule in India, but he is wrong to conclude that "the cornerstone of the whole system was a constantly refined knowledge of the Orient."[201] Mill wrote his history without actually visiting India. His armchair history was directed as "first and foremost an attack on the ruling British ideology of the time" rather than being an Orientalist text.[202] Mill was diametrically opposed to the emerging academic Orientalism, which he correctly viewed as not emphasizing the inherent inferiority of all things Indian. Although outmaneuvered politically, these academic Orientalists were among the staunchest defenders of the indigenous population and severest critics of the colonial mentality. For example, Horace Hayman Wilson, a prolific Indologist who eventually occupied the chair of Sanskrit at Oxford, later added a "corrective note" to Mill's *History of British India*, criticizing Mill for his ethnocentrism and shoddy scholarship. By ignoring the critical role of these Orientalists, Said ends up visiting the sins of avowedly anti-Oriental administrators on the very scholars who stood against them. This is a major methodological blunder—published sources on Jones and this period of colonial history were widely available. Said made no attempt to use archival sources, even published letters and memoirs, to determine if a single isolated quote reflected a pattern in the author's corpus. The one extensive quote he provides of Jones, for example, is taken from a secondary source rather than from the original essay.[203] My point is not that these early academics were free of ethnocentrism and racism, but that Said intuits his point rather than establishing it through historiographic research.

The minute examination of the rhetorical battle over British rule in India is often reduced to the most infamous quote of a British administrator in Raj rhetoric; this is Lord Macaulay's "Our native subjects" speech that could easily serve as the *Magna Carta* of colonial paternalism. Macaulay fits the archetype of the worst kind of "Orientalist" described by Said, although he was in no way an academic. Hear the noose tighten in the cadence of this self-in[dis]criminating statement:

> "I have no knowledge of either Sanscrit or Arabic. But I have done what I could to form a correct estimate of their value. I have read translations of the most celebrated Arabic and Sanscrit works. I have conversed, both here and at home, with men distinguished by their proficiency in the Eastern tongues. I am quite ready to take the oriental learning at the valuation of the orientalists themselves. I have never found one among them who could deny that a single shelf of a good European library was worth the whole native literature of India and Arabia. The intrinsic superiority of the Western literature is indeed fully admitted by those members of the committee who support the oriental plan of education. . . . It is, I believe, no exaggeration to say that all the historical information which has been collected from all the books written in

the Sanscrit language is less valuable than what may be found in the most paltry abridgments used at preparatory schools in England."[204]

Here is a poster child for Eurocentric dismissal of the Oriental other. Macaulay is not absent from the pages of *Orientalism*, although his glancing presence gives the reader no indication of his influence in shaping the debate over how to rule India. Surprisingly, Said does not provide more than the bland "Our native subjects" title of this self-inflected quote, although the reader of his endnotes learns where to find the whole cloth.[205] In *Culture and Imperialism* Said alludes to Macaulay's Minute as "a famous example, a haughty but still somehow personal obduracy," but again does not give the reader an actual taste.[206]

Avoiding Macaulay's damnable quote, although probably not out of a sense of overkill, parallels the absence of those Orientalist scholars at that time and since who have excoriated Macaulay's sentiments. The exception is a reference to Richard Burton, who Said suggests was against "Macaulay's simple-minded assertions."[207] Yet the reference cited has little to do with Macaulay, nor does Said examine Burton's numerous writings on India to see what he found objectionable. What exactly would make an Orientalist like Burton disagree with another Orientalist named Macaulay, if they were both part of the same Renan-induced guild? Indian intellectuals, who protested vigorously at the moment of the Minute, knew the difference between British Orientalism and British Imperialism, even if Said did not more than a century later.[208] So did the real Orientalists. Raymond Schwab, for example, defends the Orientalist Henry Thomas Colebrook as an outspoken critic of British colonial policy in India.[209] Colebrook, in a 1788 letter to his father, wrote: "Never mixing with the natives, an European is ignorant of their real character, which he, therefore, despises. When they meet, it is with fear on one side, and arrogance on the other."[210] In a slight that shows that Macaulay was not just an East–West ethnocentrist, Alfred Lyall complained that as a magistrate in Ireland, Macaulay had refused to procure Irish manuscripts for the British Museum: "If he [Macaulay] thought ancient Celtic literature mere rubbish, it was not likely that he should set much store by Sanskrit and Arabic treatises, which have not even an antiquarian value."[211] Said conveniently ignores Arthur J. Arberry's critique of Macaulay's Minute as a "partly malicious and, one fears, wholly ignorant misrepresentation of facts" although Said cites Arberry's text.[212] Similarly, in a work recommended by Said, Norman Daniel concludes unambiguously that "Macaulay's argument is indefensible."[213] Said's neglect of this consistent criticism by academic Orientalists is equally indefensible.

Said thus misreads William Jones, whose approach as a student of Oriental texts was more complex and ambivalent than the Anglicizing evangelism of Macaulay.[214] This philologist became the bête noire both for utilitarians like James Mill and for British missionaries.[215] Jones's ultimate role in legitimating the kind of chauvinism that contributed to the racist ideology of the Aryan myth is not to be denied, but there was no uniform "Oriental" to Oriental Jones; he at times denigrated Arabs, Tartars, and Chinese, but held Indians and Persians in great respect. Ironically, Jones once criticized Voltaire for saying that Arab poetry was in bad taste.[216] A poet himself, Jones argued that "the poet of Asia has as much genius as ourselves."[217] Jones rarely used the term "Oriental," calling it a Western term that "conveys no very distinct idea."[218] Said overstresses the extent to which Jones's argument was compromised because it was "philological." In accusing Jones of having the "principal goal" of grounding "the European languages in a distant and harmless Oriental source," Said misses the revolutionary implication of Jones's assertion: Sanskrit is not only a sibling of classical Greek and Latin, but a superior one![219] This in fact was a major breakthrough in the comparative study of language, rescuing philology from the banality of Babel. As Bruce Lincoln argues, Jones was a pioneering student of myth and religion, which led him to speculate about an Indo-European protolanguage.[220]

It is unfortunate that Said represents the British Raj through derivative texts such as the popular account by Victor G. Kiernan.[221] One result of this lack of critical judgment is Said's tendency to fix on any stray point that illustrates his position. As a case in point, it is taken without the grain of an old salt that the reason why Britain retired its administrators in India by age fifty-five was so that "no Oriental was ever allowed to see a Westerner as he aged and degenerated."[222] Granted that this was a ripe age which many Britons had trouble reaching in India, why did the Crown reappoint Lord Cornwallis as Governor-General in 1805 when he was sixty-seven?[223] Said does not probe the rationale for retirement age, match the assertion against the historical record of British administrators, or ask if such a policy could influence local opinion. Did real Orientals think that old diplomats went back to an enchanted island where they lived forever?

Crossing the Channel and the Rhine, Said provides multiple references to Johann Gottfried von Herder, the German romanticist who offered a coherent, if idyllic, representation of the Orient in his worldly philosophical history.[224] Along with Giovanni Battista Vico, the Italian savant idolized by Said in *Orientalism* and elsewhere, Herder did work that had a profound influence on historical studies outside his homeland. Said appears to have encountered Herder exclusively through Isaiah Berlin's treatment of both scholars, although Said is dismissive of Herder's views and Berlin definitely is not. Herder's rather extensive comments on the Near East and on the biblical world are ignored in *Orientalism*; it only matters for Said that Herder perhaps fostered an Orientalist interest in "artificial entities" rather than individuals,[225] and that he was a "populist."[226] Herder's classic *Ideen zur Philosophie der Geschichte der Menschheit* is mentioned briefly as "a panoramic display of various cultures, each permeated by an inimical creative spirit, each accessible only to an observer who sacrificed his prejudices to Einfühlung."[227] The relevance for Said is that such a view of culture allows Napoleon or Mozart "to breach the doctrinal walls erected between the West and Islam and see hidden elements of kinship between himself and the Orient." Herder's problem, it seems, is that he is too sympathetic.

What Said neglects to mention is that Herder was a relentless critic of the kind of imperialist propaganda that divided the world into "civilized" and "barbarian." As Berlin explains, "There is nothing against which he thunders more eloquently than imperialism—the crushing of one community by another, the elimination of local cultures trampled under the jackboot of some conqueror."[228] In a passage quoted by Berlin, Herder's sympathy is presciently post-colonial in tone:

> Can you name a land where Europeans have entered without defiling themselves forever before defenceless, trusting mankind, by the unjust word, greedy deceit, crushing oppression, diseases, fatal gifts they have brought? Our part of the earth should be called not the wisest, but the most arrogant, aggressive, money-minded: what it has given these peoples is not civilization but the destruction of the rudiments of their own cultures wherever they could achieve this.[229]

Said summarily dismisses Herder without digesting the German historian's *summa*. Ironically, one of the first examples cited in *Ideen* of a people adapted to its specific climate is the Bedouin, or Arab of the Desert. Here the Arab is not the usual victim of negative stereotyping, but rather is described as "indefatigable in supporting labour, bold and enterprising, faithful to his word, hospitable and magnanimous."[230] Similarly, Herder's discussion of Muhammad and the rise of Islam is remarkably free of apologetic prejudice and vilification.[231] Herder may not have been accurate in his depiction, which over two centuries suffers from the inevitable ebullience of a romantic working with limited data, but there is little evidence of his disparaging the Oriental for not being Western.

Said wrote *Orientalism* on the heels of the breakup of more than a century of active European policies of colonialism and imperial intrigue in the real Orient. Western influence continued unabated as a political and cultural counterpoint to the "Communist East," but by the end of the 1960s the formal presence of France in Algeria and Britain in Aden became *post forma* and the Israeli occupation of Palestine graduated to *pro forma*. The Age of Empire, the imperial stage on which Napoleon, Lord Cromer, and Lord Balfour played starring roles for Said, was dead; long live the age of analyzing imperialism.[232] Although the entry for "imperialism" in *Orientalism*'s index is almost as lengthy as the one for "Orientalism," the interested reader is not given Said's definition of imperialism. This is later laid out by Said in *Culture and Imperialism*:

> As I shall be using the term, "imperialism" means the practice, the theory, and the attitudes of a dominating metropolitan center ruling a distant territory; "colonialism," which is almost always a consequence of imperialism, is the implanting of settlements on distant territory.[233]

In *Orientalism*, Said uses the term "imperialism" interchangably for British, French, and American "involvement in the Orient," with little attention to actual practice, and no discussion at all of imperialism as a political theory.[234] Said's focus on the discursive justification of imperialism blurs the technological factors that directly aided the political and economic expansion of Europeans: strong and durable ships, powerful weapons (cannons), efficient forms of communication (telegraph), industrial machinery (printing press), and new scientific instruments (telescope). Consider, for example, that it was largely the superior galleon, a three-masted square-rigger that could stay at sea for months, that not only brought the Portuguese to the Indian Ocean but allowed them to destroy the Mamluk and Gujerati fleets at Dieu in 1509 CE. The later invention of the steamship coincided with the expansion of British colonial power in Asia. One does not need to be a Marxist to appreciate the economic stimulus surrounding European empire building. The only imperialism that seems to matter to Said is that which can be read in texts.[235]

In praxis, *Orientalism* assumes from the start that Orientalism is—and can only be—"an imperialist tradition" that provided a "broadly imperialist view of the world."[236] As Said reiterates in his afterword, the "interests of the Orientalist . . . can never be unilaterally detached from the general imperial context."[237] If this were simply a reference to the obvious interrelation of scholarship and politics, it would be hard to find any dis-

THE SAID AND THE UNSAID

agreement with such a truism. Charges against the hubris of self-serving "objectivity" had already been filed by several of the scholars Said pools together under his umbrage-laden umbrella of Orientalist discourse. But Said approaches Orientalist discourse as though it were totally un-nuanced, uncomplicated by internal and competing economic and political interests, unfazed by criticism from within or without. Even Basim Musallam, a favorable reviewer of *Orientalism*, views Said's assumed identification of Orientalism with imperialism as "a highly problematic conclusion."[238] As Peter van der Veer concludes: "The relationship between the production of Orientalist knowledge and the imperialist project is therefore much more twisted and complex than one would gather from Said's study."[239]

Said's one-way view of imperialism is exemplified in his brief discussion of Turkey, the land that has straddled East and West since the siege of Troy.

> But at no time did the convergence between latent Orientalist doctrine and manifest Orientalist experience occur more dramatically than when, as a result of World War I, Asiatic Turkey was being surveyed by Britain and France for its dismemberment. There, laid out on an operating table for surgery, was the Sick Man of Europe, revealed in all his weakness, characteristics, and topographical outline.[240]

Here, laid out on Said's Orientalist[ed] table of nations, is the last chronological glimpse the reader will have of this Western-doctored victim.[241] The only Turkey Said is comfortable with, for the sake of his argument, is the stereotypical Asiatic version, the one too sick to make the full transition to being European. Nowhere in *Orientalism* is there reference to the revolution initiated by Ataturk or to the secularization process in modern Turkey. An Oriental nation that engages or embraces the West, as problematic as that obviously must be, does not fit the mold. Meltem Ahiska suggests that Said was silent about the earlier Ottomans because this "disrupts the binary opposition of East and West, colonizer and colonized that inform his analysis."[242] Said prefers to remember the history of the real Orient only as the West dismembering it; the hacked body parts of an imperialized Osiris sinking to the bottom of an academic Nile. Had the walls of Vienna come tumbling down before the Ottoman janissaries in 1529, the young Amadeus Mozart born a little more than two centuries later might have played the *tanbur* rather than the violin; Beethoven might have composed "The Sultan's Concerto." The Sick Man of Europe was well enough to penetrate far into Europe in its glory days.

As numerous critics have noted, part of the problem with *Orientalism* is that Said makes a virtue out of not "advancing a completely worked out theory" of the connection between culture and literature or imperialism, as if one can construct a theory by simply opposing a part of what is already there.[243] Thus, "imperialism" as an ideology and "colonialism" as a historical reality are conflated.[244] For example, although North African lands were indeed colonized by nearby European powers, most parts of the region either were under indigenous political tutelage or maintained relative independence.[245] There is certainly a major contrast between America and Australia, where the colonizers carved out states by replacing the indigenous populations, and Egypt and India, where the colonized ultimately ejected the Europeans. And what should be done with Japan, where there was no imperial intrusion prior to World War II, and certainly no colonization by Europeans? The Meiji Restoration emulated the trappings of Western political and economic power so well that this "Oriental" state almost brought Western imperialism to its knees. By approaching imperialism and colonialism as epithets to which he is opposed, Said in effect denies the relevance of historical context.

The Race Against Eurocentrism

> Since the Oriental was a member of a subject race, he had to
> be subjected: it was that simple.
>
> —Edward Said, *Orientalism*

The default theory in *Orientalism*, as well as of *Culture and Imperialism*, is that somehow Europe is uniquely imperialist and colonialist; Said is willing to take the binary of West dominating East as a given, even if only to deconstruct it rhetorically. Treating the abstract Oriental as a subject race thus becomes a seemingly simple matter, especially when race takes on a scientific rather than a merely ethnic us-vs.-them character. But lost in the fire of writing back against empire is the problem faced by all colonizers, East or West, North or South. "Those who identify colonialism and empire only with the West either have no sense of history or have forgotten about the Egyptian empire, the Persian empire, the Macedonian empire, the Islamic empire, the Mongol empire, the Chinese empire, and the Aztec and Inca empires in the Americas," argues Dinesh D'Souza.[246] Empires have always subjected the people they conquer to discrimination, and racial identity was not exclusively a European invention.

As Aijaz Ahmad observes, Said misleadingly uses the term "Orientalism" for what could more accurately be called "modern, cultural Eurocentricity."[247] This umbrella is opened even wider by Said to include what might be called "Americentricity," at least in the sense of the United States of America. The more specific concept of "Eurocentrism" is the subject of a book by Samir Amin, who describes it as " a phenomenon that did not flourish until the nineteenth century" and as constituting "one dimension of the culture and ideology of the modern capitalist world."[248] As commonly marketed, this term elides the realpolitik in which the "West" since World War II has less of a geographical border than the ideological boundaries hardened in postwar Eastern Europe. Regardless of the manifold differences among human societies past and present, the prefix before "-centrism" is invariably determined by who holds the power. Europe and, now, the United States have dominated world power from the nineteenth century on; the problem in Said's usage is that whereas Orientalism has certainly suffered from Eurocentrism, Eurocentrism can only be imagined as Orientalist. Logically, this is less a chicken-and-egg argument than one about how you like your eggs.

Damning—and seemingly Said means to do so—virtually any Western writer who has ever written something intellectual on the Orient is in the end a clever trap set for the sympathetic reader. It is one thing to expose the rhetoric that encouraged and rationalized domination of real Orientals; it is quite another to assume that ethnocentrism and racism are unique to a given imaginary. It is arguable that elements of ethnocentrism and racism can be documented for any known human society. As Thomas Greene notes in an early review of *Orientalism*:

> It should not be an article of this indictment that the Westerner will see the Easterner in terms of "some aspect of the West." The Westerner has no other equipment. What one can ask of him is that his construct, his perspective, his myth, be flexible, open, respectful, and informed. But in the last analysis it must be ethnocentric, and to require that it be otherwise is to set him a trap.[249]

Orientalism shows how certain scholars and texts have been overtly ethnocentric and inevitably reflect cultural biases, but this does not logically prove that academic Orientalists must always have been or remain trapped as Eurocentric in a way that either misrepresents real Oriental others or prevents these others from representing themselves. When Irvin Cemil Schick comments that "the critique of orientalism must not be the domain of demonology but of history," the demonstrable demonizing in Said's text must be acknowledged.[250] In the abstract, ethnocentrism and racism are merely noxious notions; it is the impact of their concrete historical application on real people that causes so much suffering.

A key historical lapse in *Orientalism* is the starting assumption of a consensual union between Western writers and Western polity. The best that an Orientalist can be said to have is sympathy, which in the end is also subsumed and consumed by the dominant discourse. Is it not unconstructive to ignore shades and nuance, assuming a black-and-white ordering that must inevitably lead to a preordained civilizational clash? As it was perverse for Western scholars to do so to the Orient, it should be equally so for Said's representation of Orientalism as inherently imperialist, colonialist, and racist. If any given Orientalist, even an Oriental educated out of the East, operates within a colonial or neo-colonial state, then any dissent against colonial policy is doomed in this view as inauthentic, or at the very least ineffective. The discursive conditioning of the non-Western other is assumed to be absolute. This is perhaps why Said so consistently chooses to ignore counter-discourse. No Old World companion to the New World Bartolomé de Las Casas is uncovered, or even looked for, in the textual corpus of Orientalism.[251]

In addition to being impervious to what historians were already saying about the complexity of imperialism as a grab-bag concept, Said rails against racism as if it were the inevitable raison d'être for any statement by a Westerner about an Easterner. Indeed, one of the manifest qualities of Said's latent Orientalism, at least in its nineteenth-century irruption, was "the binary typology of advanced and backward (or subject) races, cultures, and societies."[252] David Cannadine includes Said among those literary scholars who assume that British imperialism was all about race, whereas it was also a reflection of class and status within Britain.[253] While Said talks at length about the racial theories of scholars such as Cuvier, Renan, and Gobineau, among many other names dropped in passing, his unfamiliarity with the evolution of both racial theory and racist practice results in a common, but misleading, summary execution that any Westerner who talked about race did so as a "racist," with all the emotional baggage that such a term carried by the 1970s in American culture. In the specific case of Gobineau, the German Orientalist Julius Wellhausen refuted his absurd racial depiction of Shi'a Islam as an Indo-European variant of Sunni Semite Arabs.[254] Consider Johann Friedrich Blumenbach, who is included by Said in an odd lineup of racial theorists from Linnaeus to Kant. Blumenbach specifically rejected the racist notion that one so-called race was superior to another. Blumenbach, whose eighteenth-century work was one of the first modern studies of "race," not only dismissed the idea that Negroes,

Indians, and Mongolians were hereditarily inferior, but satirized the racism of his day.[255] In Britain, the negative stereotyping of Indian Muslims took on a pseudoscientific racial dimension during the 1860s, thanks in part to the influence of Social Darwinism. But even there Humayun Ansari believes that, until the late nineteenth century, for Muslims in Britain class was a more significant issue than racialized skin color.[256]

At the time of Said's writing there was an extensive literature on the intellectual history of racial theory, especially among anthropologists Said places on the "wrong" side of the colonial divide.[257] Nowhere in *Orientalism* does Said compare the racial rationalization directed at specific varieties of Orientals with that directed at Africans or even fellow whites, such as the pre-Christian Slavs or the Irish. In a later essay, Said claims that among Western writers "there was virtual unanimity that subject races should be ruled, that they are subject races, that one race deserves and has consistently earned the right to be considered the race whose main mission is to expand beyond its own domain."[258] This was certainly behind the ideology of imperialist expansion, but it was by no means unopposed. Slavery was banned in the British empire before the golden age of British colonial growth in Asia. The success of the abolition movement suggests that "virtual unanimity" was more virtual than real. There is apparent unanimity among the writers that Said chooses to quote, but his claim goes far beyond the limited sampling of texts that have been selected precisely to prove his point.

Although Said carefully positions his target as the Orientalism that affected the nearby Orient, the absence of comparison to other forms of racism directed imperially beyond the Orient suggests to the reader that the history of racial theory was somehow especially virulent in reference to this small part of the world. It is disturbingly ahistorical to argue that Orientalism is one of the most profound examples of the machinery of cultural domination; it pales in actual historical impact next to the genocide of indigenous populations elsewhere. Can the imperialist carving up of parts of Asia be contextualized apart from the simultaneous dissection of the entire continent of Africa?[259] As Fred Halliday notes, Europeans did far worse things to the native peoples of America than to Muslims.[260] European exploitation of Native Americans proceeded without any need for an intellectual discourse of Indianism. Blaming the victimizers is easy to do, but little of the European presence in the real Orient can compare with the mass atrocities committed among the native populations of the Americas and in the slave trade from Africa.

A glaring omission in *Orientalism* is one that Said has discussed in other forums: anti-Semitism as a phenomenon targeting primarily and often exclusively Jews. How can a deconstruction of "Orientalism" as a racist rendering of an Oriental type not delve at the same time into the intimately related discourse of anti-Semitism against Jews, especially when Said announces that he is writing "the history of a strange, secret sharer of Western anti-Semitism"?[261] There are multiple references to "anti-Semitism" in Said's narrative, but virtually all of these reinforce the notion that "Semite" refers to both Jew and Arab in Orientalist discourse.[262] In a passage asserting that "the Arab is conceived of now as a shadow that dogs the Jew," Said suggests that out of the shadow of the Jew in pre-Nazi Europe there has evolved via Zionism "a Jewish hero, constructed out of a reconstructed cult of the adventurer-pioneer-Orientalist (Burton, Lane, Renan), and his creeping, mysteriously fearsome shadow, the Arab Oriental."[263] Not only is there no direct comparison here to the long and well-documented history of anti-Semitism against European, American, and Oriental Jews, but Said manages to blame Western Orientalists for the political domination of Israel over the Palestinians.[264] The political actions of Zionists in modern Israel hardly justify ignoring the centuries of overt prejudice directed periodically against Jews living through pogrom and holocaust inside Europe and the real Orient.

In giving carte blanche to Said's rhetorical intrusion into the history of racial theory, the reader may fail to see how the author puts the car[ro]t before the horse. In a taxonomical metaphor, Orientalism is presented as the genus and racism as the species, but it should be the other way around. Said writes as if racism needs an intellectual guild behind it in order to effectively influence political policy and cultural interaction. This is prefigured in his earlier critical review of several Orientalist volumes for the *New York Times*, in which he bluntly claims that "popular stereotypes about niggers, wogs, Semites, Ay-rabs, babus, gooks and the oriental mentality have derived not from uninformed lower middle-class Occidental red-necks but from the Orientalists' dogmas."[265] That an intellectual writing intellectual history should privilege the role that intellectuals play in making history—even as a result of their representing history unilaterally—is, I suppose, hardly surprising. But surely unenlightened plebeian greed can operate with or without canonical creed.

Some post-colonial writers read *Orientalism* with a combination of amnesia and dyslexia. Their admiration for Said's polemical stand against bias overcomes a critical engagement with the text as written and unrevised. It is easy to forget that Said is writing a history about a subject about which he has only a selective and superficial knowledge. To the extent that Said's Orientalism thesis becomes a paradigm for racism and ethnocentrism, it becomes possible for other non-Western scholars to do to virtually any other "ism" what Said tried to do to the specific discourse on the Orient. In the process, Said's rhetorical pairing of Orientalism and racism, regardless of the classificatory order, results in a widespread belief that Orientalism is in essence just another way of being racist. Even critics of Said's thesis fall into this trap. Thus Mani and Frankenberg comment: "One does not look to Orientalism to learn about the Orient any more than one looks to discourses of racism to learn about peoples of colour."[266] This implies that Orientalist texts are intrinsically racist, as were the nineteenth-century theories on race. However, if everything written about the Orient is Orientalism, where else could one look? Rhetorically, a kind of terminological miscegenation results here. The term "racism" has no pretence of scientific objectivity in academic circles, so of course it could not be resorted to for accurate information about the modern sense of "race," one that at the time had already been widely deconstructed as a social construct rather than a meaningful biological given. Orientalist discourse, however, was not automatically assumed to be prejudicial and racist before Said wrote *Orientalism*. There is still value in much of the descriptive detail, documentation, and critical insights of individuals Said calls Orientalists. Edward Lane, for example, may have shared the prejudices of many of his fellow Englishmen, but his description of contemporary Egyptian customs is nonetheless a valuable historical resource.

In a critical review of *Orientalism*, David Kopf mused that "If we can somehow overlook his unfortunate choice of the term 'Orientalism' to represent a sewer category for all the intellectual rubbish Westerners have exercised in the global marketplace of ideas, then surely the book has considerable merit."[267] But in hindsight, after a quarter of a century surely this is a big "if." Said travels into theoretical territory with a single-minded chart uninformed by the actual lay of the historiographic method. Should a historian who plies his craft to analyze the history of Western interaction with the rest of the world accept Said's caveated escape hatch in the following statement from *Culture and Imperialism*?

> To the best of my ability to have read and understood these "structures of attitude and reference," there was scarcely any dissent, any departure, any demurral from them: there was virtual unanimity that subject races should be ruled, that they are subject races, that one race deserves and has consistently earned the right to be considered the race whose main mission is to expand beyond its own domain.[268]

At issue here is Edward Said's attitude as a polemicist who does not read beyond the texts that prove his point. He refuses to apply methodological lessons from disciplines that study history and culture. Said introduces *Culture and Imperialism* by saying:

> Most professional humanists as a result are unable to make the connection between the prolonged and sordid cruelty of practices such as slavery, colonialist and racial oppression, and imperial subjugation on the one hand, and the poetry, fiction, philosophy of the society that engages in these practices on the other.[269]

This is certainly a useful point, but it is also important to know what is being connected. Formal slavery was almost out of the picture by the time Napoleon invaded Egypt. In the nineteenth century, European powers invaded the Orient not for slaves, but for economic advantage. Clearly there was more than a semantic difference between being a British subject and a British slave, but this is a nuance that Said's representation of imperialism fails to register.

How has Said managed to get away with writing intellectual history when it is the intellectualizing rather than the history that takes precedence? In part he has ridden a wave of scholastic relativism in which the act per se of criticizing an establishment truth puts the critic's truth-telling on equal footing. Said's point about the "interpenetration of truth and power" dismisses a priori any response by those he calls Orientalists.[270] In a critique of Said's secular criticism, William Hart applauds him for ignoring those who attack his qualifications to write about Orientalism. Falling back on the rhetorical posturing that "expertise is a presumption," Hart accuses critics such as Albert Hourani of "pulling scholarly rank," a ploy that has been "proven ineffective."[271] This guildy-until-proven-innocent trope is the real presumption here. When Bobby Sayyid argues that "Attempts to reduce the critique of Orientalism to the problems of scholarship and other textual problems is [*sic*] completely inadequate," both his point and his grammar are in error.[272] If there are no acceptable criteria for determining scholarly rank, why should any other scholar accept what apparently-unranked scholars Said or Hart think is less rank than those they criticize? Is a biologist who dismisses as unscientific a fundamentalist's belief in literal creationism pulling rank by pointing out that the latter is woefully ignorant of scientific theory and method? It is the lack of sound historiographic method, evident in the innumerable ahistorical statements, that marks *Orientalism* as a rank-and-file attempt that, for those with recognizable expertise, fails muster.

II   Drawing the Fault Lines

> From the beginning of Western speculation about the Orient,
> the one thing the Orient could not do was to represent itself.
>
> —EDWARD SAID, *ORIENTALISM*

> Sometimes, in his obdurate determination that Orientalism
> silenced opposition, Said, ironically, silences opposition.
>
> —LEELA GANDHI, *POSTCOLONIAL THEORY:*
> *A CRITICAL INTRODUCTION*

> Can the subaltern speak?
>
> —GAYATRI CHAKRAVORTY SPIVAK, *A CRITIQUE OF POSTCOLONIAL*
> *REASON: TOWARD A HISTORY OF THE VANISHING PRESENT*[273]

Can the subaltern speak? Said is so busy speaking for the Oriental in *Orientalism* that this question is essentially elided. Whether or not real Orientals can speak or even represent themselves, Said does not allow them permission to narrate. Subaltern voices are occasionally heard off in the wings, but never center-stage, in the production of *Orientalism*. The European almost-invention of the Orient, Said states emphatically, demands that a real Orient be absent.[274] "From the beginning of Western speculation about the Orient, the one thing the Orient could not do was to represent itself," he insists.[275] Not only does Said make the muted Oriental a pillar of his analytical framework; this is how others read him. "In fact," relates Arif Dirlik, "one of his basic goals is to demonstrate how such representations of the Orient have silenced the 'Orientals,' and undercut their ability to represent themselves."[276] Aslı Çirakman goes farther, suggesting that Said's notion of discourse "excludes a potential dialogue between the Orient and the Occident."[277] One question that Said fails to ask in his interrogation of colonial discourse is the one posed by anthropologist Mary Louise Pratt: "How have Europe's constructions of subordinated others been shaped by those others, by the constructions of themselves and their habitats that they presented to the Europeans?"[278] Apparently, given Said's more recent reflections, he decided not to look at such interaction in *Orientalism* because he "was talking of something quite different."[279]

If Said is only referring to the imagined "Orient" invented by Orientalism, then his representation becomes a tautology. If he is implying, as seems to be the case, that real Orientals were unable to represent their own identities, he is choosing to ignore a substantial published literature, as well as the active oral and behavioral resistance all along. If he assumes that none of this representation had an influence on specific scholars who studied the Orient, he needs more than negative evidence to make his case. It is bad enough that Oriental voices are absent in a work that purports to deconstruct the Western discourse primarily implicated in speaking for them. Why did Orientals need to be construed by Said as incapable of representing themselves? In *Orientalism*, Said was aware of some of the scathing critiques of Orientalism from earlier Arab intellectuals. Yet, whether consciously or not, he tries to convince the reader that there is virtually no textual voice before his own that can withstand the dominance of an Orientalist-induced imperialism. Even when he later acknowledges "active resistance" from the non-Western native, Said "stubbornly refuses to elevate anti-colonial resistance to the status of anti-colonial critique."[280] This is accomplished less by direct assertion than by ignoring available texts from within indigenous traditions. By default, the only voices encountered in *Orientalism* are the canonical Orientalist texts that are asserted to have muted the Oriental other. Paralipsis paralyzes analysis.

The most prominent complaints emanating from post-colonial scholars relate to Said's failure to recognize a "vast cacophony of multiple voices and interpretations."[281] As Nasrin Rahimieh argues, "the Orient has never been and is not now a silent addressee."[282] What is notably absent in almost all of Said's corpus, especially *Orientalism*, is the historical point–counterpoint of representing the other. Julie Codell and Dianne Sachko MacLeod counter that "colonized peoples engaged the Orientalizing discourse, resisting its stereotypes, subverting its epistemology, amending its practices and sometimes even re-applying its stereotypes to the British themselves."[283] In effect, Said's failure to consider indigenous resistance to imperialism and colonial policy forecloses the very agency of the people he assumes cannot represent themselves.[284] Xiaomei Chen believes that "Said's claims do not provide for even the possibility of an anti-official discourse within 'Oriental' societies."[285] The real Orientals implicated in *Orientalism*, primarily Arabs, are consumers of blue jeans and Coca-Cola and are victimized through "intellectual acquiescence in the images and doctrines of Orientalism."[286] It is unlikely that Said is naively ignorant of indigenous resisters out there; the question that lingers is why he did not attempt "to do more than mention them or allude to them quickly"?[287]

Although Said floats the idea that he represented "an Oriental writing back at the Orientalists,"[288] he was hardly alone. At the same time there appeared a number of similar critical studies by "Orientals" written in Arabic, Persian, and French.[289] Just before the Khomeini revolution, an acerbic assessment of "Occidentosis" (*gharbzadagi*) appeared in Iran. The author, Jalal Al-i Ahmad, explores the imaginative space between the poles of Orient and Occident. "The 'West' began calling us (the area from the eastern Mediterranean to India) the 'East' just when it rose from its medieval hibernation, when it came in search of sun, spices, silk, and other goods," muses Ahmad.[290] The West, continues Ahmad, awoke to an industrial resurrection just as the East "passed into the slumber of the Seven Sleepers."[291] Referring to the quintessential Orientalist rendering of Islam, the *Encyclopaedia of Islam*, Ahmad laments that the Easterner remains asleep while the Westerner "has carried us off to the laboratory in this encyclopedia."[292] Unlike Said, Ahmad is not interested in deconstructing Orientalism as a discourse but in assessing its impact on the vitality of his own culture:

> This is the ugliest symptom of occidentosis: to regard yourself as nothing, not to think at all, to give up all reliance on your own self, your own eyes and ears, to give over the authority of your own senses to any pen held by any wretch who has said or written a word as an orientalist. I haven't the foggiest notion when orientalism became a 'science.' If we say that some Westerner is a linguist, dialectologist, or musicologist specializing in Eastern questions, this is defensible. Or if we say he is an anthropologist or sociologist, this again is arguable to an extent. But what does it mean to be an orientalist without further definition? Does it mean to know all the secrets of the Eastern world?

Are we living in the age of Aristotle? This is why I speak of a parasite growing on the root of imperialism.[293]

Not surprisingly, Hamid Algar introduces *Occidentosis* by noting that Ahmad's comments anticipate "with remarkable precision" points made in Said's *Orientalism*.[294]

More than a half-dozen influential critiques in Arabic also appeared at the same time as *Orientalism*: the poet Adonis in *Al-Thabit wa-al-mutahawwil* (*The Permanent and the Changeable*, 1978), 'Abd al-Kabir al-Khatibi's *Al-Naqd al-muzdawij* (*Double Critique*, 1980),[295] Khalida Sa'id's *Harakiyat al-ibda'* (*The Dynamics of Creativity*, 1979), Tayyib Tizini's *Min al-turath ila al-thawra* (*From Heritage to Revolution*, 1978), and 'Ali Zayur's psychoanalytic *Al-Tahlil al-nafsi li-al-dhat al-'Arabiya* (*The Analysis of the Arab Self*, 1977). In French, Hichem Djait produced *L'Europe et l'Islam* (1978); in English Samir Amin contributed *Arab Nation* (1978). Although none of these books engaged as wide a Western audience or generated as much debate as *Orientalism*, the corpus suggests that the Oriental intellectual could speak, even if not in the Ivy League English that contributed to Said's success.[296] Also at this time, an anthology of contemporary Middle Eastern literature in translation appeared in popular paperback form, as did an academic volume in which Middle Eastern Muslim women speak.[297] The Orient that Said found it necessary to represent had already been represented when *Orientalism* appeared in the bookstores.

Edward Said later acknowledges that he was not the first scholar to see through *Orientalism*:

> At bottom, what I said in *Orientalism* had been said before me by A. L. Tibawi, by Abdullah Laroui, by Anwar Abdel Malek, by Talal Asad, by S. H. Alatas, by Frantz Fanon and Aimé Césaire, by Sardar K. M. Panikkar and Romila Thapar, all of whom had suffered the ravages of imperialism and colonialism, and who, in challenging that authority, provenance, and institutions of the science that represented them to Europe, were also understanding themselves as something more than what the science said they were.[298]

This was no doubt written in response to the wide range of criticism from all sides that Said had given short shrift to previous indigenous critiques of the stereotypes and entrenched intellectual hegemony of much scholarship on the colonized cultures of the Orient.[299] In citing this litany of counter-colonialist critics, Said satisfied many who were wondering how he could ignore such figures in the first place. In later writings, especially *Culture and Imperialism*, he draws on the work of several of these precursors. However, an enduring fault of *Orientalism*, stubbornly unrevised in its many translations and printings, is an absence of such acknowledgement.[300] Of the nine scholars mentioned above in Said's later quote, only Laroui and Abdel Malek rate attention in the narrative of *Orientalism*. Indeed the voices of Césaire and Fanon, so resonating for Said in other contexts, are nowhere to be heard.[301] In *Orientalism*, the bottom of Said's "at bottom" defense simply drops out.

Orientalism appeared only a few years after Abdallah Laroui's *La crise des intellectueles arabes* (1974), a critical study Said cites as the only "serious critique" of the Orientalist views of Gustave von Grunebaum.[302] It may be the only critique known to Said, but serious criticism of von Grunebaum's ideas appeared earlier in texts by the Algerian scholar Mohammed Arkoun and by "Orientalists" Elie Kedourie and Albert Hourani.[303] Said, following Laroui, points out a critical flaw in von Grunebaum's overtly Hegelian reading of history. In addition to what Said sees as an unflinching antagonism to Islam, von Grunebaum is criticized for adopting an outmoded "culturalist theory" that leads to a "political, not even euphemistically impartial" view.[304] Von Grunebaum, the transplanted German historian, is the primary example given of a specifically "American" brand of Orientalism. But in the process, Said contradicts his earlier view that "the new American social-science attention to the Orient" operated with a "singular avoidance of literature."[305] Von Grunebaum was not only recognized as a leading figure who sought to combine historical and sociological approaches, but he was an individual thoroughly grounded in the study of Arabic literature.[306]

Ironically, Said says nothing further about Laroui's basic thesis, even though it covers much of the same ground as *Orientalism*. Like Said, Laroui discusses the deleterious impact of European historicism in representing Islam and Arabs; questions the value of Orientalist texts as a starting point for Arabs to define their own sense of history; finds it fallacious that Islam must be reinterpreted from a Western perspective; borrows ideas from Gramsci on the relation of intellectuals to culture; finds much contemporary Marxist criticism problematic; and observes that Arab scholars all too effortlessly accept Western notions of modernity. Laroui is uncompromising in pointing out the ideological nature of most Orientalist works, thus judging them "for the most part" without value. He also attacks the "caste of Orientalists" as a bureaucracy—one might say guild—that cannot create new approaches or even apply valuable approaches that already exist.[307] Again, like Said, Laroui asserts that the Western historian is never objective, "for in speaking of others in the past it is always of himself and his own destiny that he really speaks."[308]

Perhaps Said neglects Laroui's argument because it follows a different rhetorical tangent than his own. "A serious critique must be founded upon a methodological choice; that much is relevant," declares Laroui. This much is certainly parallel to Said's own approach. "It should also remain within the framework of accepted epistemological rules," continues Laroui, the trained historian, who adds that "we must not forget to submit to the laws of modern historiography."[309] With Foucauldian [discon]intent, it may have been difficult for Said to borrow too much from a scholar who warns against self-indulgence in criticism that "can easily lead to the dismissal of every scientific undertaking."[310] In his 1996 lecture at the Middle East Studies Association (MESA) convention, Laroui cautioned that he had "no intention to open a new chapter in the old and often gratuitous campaign against Orientalism."[311] He then proceeds to define "Western Orientalism" without reference to Said. Laroui is an "Oriental" scholar who is quite capable of representing himself.

The earlier critic who receives most attention in Said's book is Anouar Abdel Malek, praised by Said for providing a new departure for "decolonizing" area studies.[312] Abdel Malek is so well regarded by Said for having "perfectly characterized" the Orientalized Orient that there is a full page quote of his writing in *Orientalism*.[313] Abdel Malek distinguishes two general groups of Orientalists. The first, exemplified by academic scholars such as William Jones, Michelangelo Guido, and A. J. Arberry provided a "fruitful and diverse" contribution imbued with methodological habits and philosophical concepts that often compromised the scientific value of their work. A second group includes colonial functionaries, missionaries, adventurers, businessmen, and even academics who were out to blatantly ensure the subjugation of the Oriental to European power.[314] However, Said misrepresents the nuance in what Abdel Malek says by inserting his own bracketed gloss in two parts of the quoted passage. In the passage quoted, Said leaves out Abdel Malek's original language about "both groups," and substitutes the generic "Orientalists" in its place; in addition, Said actually changes an active sentence to a passive. The result is that the quote does not show the qualification that makes Abdel Malek's approach more than a simple blanket othering of all who study the Orient.

Said neglects to mention that Abdel Malek is an unabashed Marxist who draws inspiration in part from Gramsci's notion of hegemony.[315] In two places in *Orientalism*, Said reproduces Abdel Malek's line about "the hegemonism of possessing minorities," which also appears in the long excerpt cited.[316] It is understandable why Said would focus on such a phrase, as it captures the thrust of his own thesis. But the dropping from the quote of its original emphasis on the fact that Marx and Engels exposed such hegemonism seems less than accidental for an author who proceeds to label Marx as a swept-along victim of hegemonic Orientalist discourse. Equally problematic is the failure to note that Abdel Malek was talking about a Eurocentric attitude directed against all non-Europeans, not the exclusive West-vs.-East binary to which Said reduces Orientalist bias. By not addressing the historian's explicit Marxist approach, Said is free to borrow phrasing suitable for his purpose without drawing attention to a major difference between his own use and that of his source.[317]

Coincident with Said's *Orientalism* is another critique of colonial representation by a member of the colonized group; this is Syed Hussein Alatas's well documented and well received *The Myth of the Lazy Native*.[318] The similarities between the two studies are striking, an indication that Said's general thrust was shared by significant "others" at the time of his writing. Alatas focuses on the farther East, specifically Malaysia, the Philippines, and Indonesia, in contributing a sociology of knowledge about the potent colonial trope of the lazy native. Like Said, Alatas locates the source of the "ideological denigration of the native" in "refined scholarship" as well as with colonial administrators.[319] In delineating this persistent myth over the course of two centuries, Alatas comments: "What we are concerned with here is the negative influence of ideology, the distorting, uncritical, inconsistent streak in a scholar's reasoning which arises from an unconscious attachment to his ideology."[320] Alatas recognizes that no scholar is free from the influence of ideology—a fair cousin of discourse in this context—but, quite unlike Said in his perpetually oppositional criticism, Alatas believes that an acceptably objective scholarship is possible if one is aware and counteracts prejudice. "Thus the statement that scholarship is conditioned by ideology should not be taken in the absolute sense that each and every scholar is necessarily and unconsciously influenced by his ideology," cautions Alatas.[321] Said argues the opposite in *Orientalism*. Alatas is critical of Marx and Engels, perhaps more so than Said. He recognizes, however, that one need not be a Marxist to understand the domination of a ruling elite and the fundamental significance of economic conditions.[322] What distinguishes the work of Alatas tarnishes the historical analysis of Said. The former applies a rigorous methodology based on a comprehensive examination of source material, and targets a specific stereotype rather than flailing away with a polemical hammer at the mythmaker writ large.

Who exactly was silenced by Orientalism? Said systematically ignores Marxist and Arab nationalist voices as though they cannot be effectively counter-hegemonic simply because he does not agree with them. There is not even a passing nod to Muslim intellectuals who learned from Western education yet saw through to the core of the prejudice and intolerance. Although Said does not explicitly state that Orientals were prevented from writing or unable to write their own histories, he suggests in the strongest terms "an intellectual acquiescence" in which "the modern Orient, in short, participates in its own Orientalizing."[323] This is asserted on the basis of Said's own presentational authority as an Arab intellectual, validated by his birth and early upbringing rather than by reading across the range of historical and critical texts written in the Orient at large. Said further contends that history journals in the Arab world are mere clones of Orientalist paradigms, although no specific examples are cited.[324] The assertion in *Orientalism* that there was not a "single decent library" in the Middle East is a clear indication of Said's ethnocentric taste in texts.[325] Garland Cannon observes that a similar claim cannot be made about India, in large part because of Orientalist scholars such as William Jones.[326] Must we assume that there was no indigenous critique of Western intrusion and Orientalism simply because Said fails to find the counterpart of an Ivy League library or antiestablishment academic journals?

Given his focus on a very selective part of the "Near Orient," Said ignores the large literature of resistance from India, Central Asia, China, and Japan. We are asked to assume that the unbounded discourse that supposedly muted Near Orientals functioned with equal effectiveness all the way to the farthest eastern shores of the imperial colonies. "Indeed," argues Sinologist Xiaomei Chen, "Said's Orient is a half-Western Orient, and it is inevitable that 'real' Orientals from China and Korea are likely to see how one-sided Said's arguments really are."[327] In reviewing the influence of Christian missions in India, Norman Daniel argues that by the end of the nineteenth century Muslim writers "were giving back as good as they got in the way of religious propaganda."[328] Japan's total rejection of Christian colonization was an effective challenge to the presumption that Western missionaries had a right to import their religion and cultural baggage.[329] The literary resistance was just as relevant. Consider the words of Muhammad Iqbal, arguably the most famous Urdu poet under the British Raj:

> This land of Syria gave the West a Prophet
> Of purity and pity and innocence;
> And Syria from the West as recompense
> Gets dice and drink and troops or prostitutes.[330]

The imagined Orient should not be reduced to the silent Orient.

Even for that part of the Orient actually covered by Said, his text shuts out the important role of Arab intellectuals in what Albert Hourani calls the "Liberal Age."[331] As analyzed with critical insight by historians such as Hourani, Nikki Keddie, Malcolm Kerr, and Hisham Sharabi, nineteenth-century Arab reformers did not systematically acquiesce to the West's presentation of superiority. Nowhere in *Orientalism* is there space for the Egyptians Jamal al-Din al-Afghani (1839–97),[332] Muhammad ʿAbduh (1849–1905),[333] ʿAli Mubarak (1823–92),[334] Mahmud Shakir (1909–97),[335] and Rifaʿa Rafiʿ al-Tahtawi (1801–73),[336] nor the Syrian Sheikh Tahir al-Jazaʾiri (1851–1920), nor the Palestinian Bandali Jawzi (1872–1942).[337] The impact of indigenous Arab, Persian, and Turkish newspapers and journals in writing back against cultural as well as political imperialism does not even warrant a sentence in Said's polemic.[338] The penetration of French and British imperialism neither converted the masses nor muted critical response. Nor did everything "Western" get rejected out of hand.[339] Indeed, it can be argued that the extreme anti-Western response in the Arab World developed near the end of direct colonial rule, in large part because of the formation of the state of Israel.[340]

It is one thing to wonder if the subaltern can speak, and quite another to question whether or not what is said is recognizable as the right kind of speech act. Some Saidians echo Said's own approach in treating the voices of dissent as ipso facto absent if they are not heard and utilized by the dominant colonial power. Ali Behdad, for example, considers earlier "counterdiscursive practices" as inauthentic because "they were working within the system as effects of its power relations."[341] In a book that travels along the same theoretical blind alleys as Said's *Orientalism*, Behdad engages in antonominous antinomialism: absense becomes presence. "As an 'amateur traveller' I began searching for something I unconsciously knew was absent: opposition and counterideologies in a hegemonic discourse. I discovered consciously the presence of their absence," says Behdad.[342] Relying on post-colonial intellectual-in-exile intuition, this scholar is relieved of the task of investigating whether or not counter-hegemonic trees were falling in the colonial forest. Resistance must be absent—all absence, as Said suggests—because the only thing presenting itself today is an absence. Is it that anti-colonial trees did not fall? Did they fall so deep in the forest primeval that no one heard? How exactly can we discover an absence that is assumed to be there—or not be there—from the start? Self-discovery here serves as self-delusion.

If Orientalist discourse was so emphatically hegemonic, how did nationalisms and revolutionary ideologies evolve in the Orient? Historian Edmund Burke describes the Algerian Revolution as a rejection of colonialism "from the native's point of view," in which a nationalistic movement cohered into a self-conscious "decolonization of history."[343] Said makes no pretense of defending the various Middle Eastern regimes near the time of his writing. Even Nasser of Egypt appears only once in *Orientalism*, where Said says that the revolutionary colonel needed to "activate Egypt's taking over of the canal by pronouncing the name of de Lesseps."[344] Arab political discourse, it would seem, was only a clone of Orientalist discourse, neither a serious counter nor a viable alternative to it. "In fact," notes Aijaz Ahmad, "it is one of the disagreeable surprises in *Orientalism* that it refuses to acknowledge the vast tradition, virtually as old as colonialism itself, which has existed in the colonized countries as well as among the metropolitan Left traditions, and has always been occupied, precisely, with drawing up an inventory of colonial traces in the minds of the people on both sides of the colonial divide."[345]

Nor does *Orientalism* engage the numerous Muslim intellectuals who have leveled broadsides in Arabic against earlier Western Orientalism (*istishraq*).[346] It is curious that Said avoids this extensive literature that reflects what many Muslims saw as Orientalist-influenced erosion of faith in the Quran as revelation. Many of the more popular Orientalist books on Islam were available in Arabic translation, so it was not difficult to find out how Islam was being imagined in the West.[347] Some indigenous scholars were fluent in English, French, or German. One of the more accessible counter-texts is Muhammad Haykel's *Hayat Muhammad* (*The Life of Muhammad*), first published in Arabic in 1935 and translated into English in 1976.[348] Reviewing European commentary on Muhammad, Haykel concluded: "What a nether world of degradation have the writers of the West sunk to!"[349] Haykel responds directly to the prejudice of William Muir's mid-nineteenth-century *Life of Mahomet*, a work that Said similarly cites for its overt anti-Islamic tone.[350] The influential Haykel, whose biographical text sold ten thousand copies in its first three months, was hardly a muted voice among Arab intellectuals just prior to World War II. Nor did he think that Orientalist discourse held hegemonic sway in his own intellectual milieu:

> However clever and adept such orientalists may be in formulating their slander, they will never be able to pass it as genuine scientific research; nor will they ever be able to fool any Muslims, except perhaps those young men deluded enough to think that free research demands of them the denial of their tradition and the naive acceptance of any nicely presented falsehood and attacks against their legacy, regardless of the validity or falsity of its premises and assumptions.[351]

Much of what Said says about Western bias against the Orient refers specifically to invective leveled against Islam. Earlier Muslim authors were not silent about this ideological affront. Haykel correctly labels Muir's nineteenth-century work an *argumentum ad hominem* fallacy.[352] In 1976, Mohamed Arkoun leveled a similar charge about the Western study of Islam: "L'islamologie classique est un discours occidental sur l'Islam; le mot et le concept d'islamologie—un discours que vise la rationalité sur l'Islam—sont, en effet, une création occidentale."[353] However, unlike Said, Arkoun proposes an agenda for an "islamologie appliqué." A similar and wide-ranging critique of Orientalist scholarship on Islam also appeared in 1976; this was 'Ali Husni al-Kharbutli's *al-Istishraq fi al-ta'rikh al-Islami* (*Orientalism on Islamic History*). Al-Kharbutli challenges the Western notion of the "Orient" (*sharq*) as one that is obscure (*ghamid*) and loose (*ghayr thabit*); he is particularly critical of those scholars who write about the Orient without actually having visited the region or knowing the relevant languages.[354] Al-Kharbutli defines three categories of Orientalists. Rather than rejecting all Western writing, he argues that some Orientalists provide Muslims with analysis of great scholarly value (*dhat qayma 'ilmiyya kubra*), other Orientalists should be consulted with caution because they offer honey sweetened with poison (literally, *al-samm fi al-'asal*), and yet others are simply without redeeming value of any kind (*bi-dun qasd wa-'amd*).[355] He praises Franz Rosenthal, Wilfred Cantwell Smith, and Edward Lane, whose *An Account of the Manners and Customs of the Modern Egyptians* he himself translated into Arabic. William Robertson Smith is cited as an example of the kind of scholar to be used with caution. The Belgian Jesuit priest Henri Lammens and the Irish scholar De Lacy O'Leary are both seen as utterly antagonistic to Islam.[356]

Said's erudition puts his polemic on a different level than a large portion of the vociferous anti-Orientalist rhetoric that has often flowed from angry Oriental voices. Although Said purposefully distances himself from "blanket condemnations of 'the West'" by many Muslim writers, he fails to explicate the legitimate grievances in the rhetoric of Muslim intellectuals and polemicists.[357] This becomes a condemnation in reverse. His dismissal of the desirability of an "Occidentalism" assumes that it could only be as pejoratively essentialist as the Orientalism it would oppose.[358] Not all Arab critics would agree that the Orientalist gaze sui generis prevents legitimate self-recognition by real Orientals. More than a century ago the Egyptian writer 'Ali Basha Mubarak wrote a novel, *'Alam al-din* (1882), in which the Orientalist is imagined as an advocate for the East in the West.[359] The contemporary Iraqi scholar Muhammad Al-Da'mi takes issue with Said's seeming desire to end Orientalism as a scholarly enterprise.

"Orientalists have offered us foreign perspectives and coercive challenges which have enriched our approaches to our culture and history," he argues.[360] Some of the "pioneering" Orientalists, as Mohamad Tavakoli-Targhi points out, commissioned works by Arab, Persian, and Indian scholars.[361] William Jones, for example, acknowledged the contributions of local pandits. More recently, the poet Adonis confides: "I find no paradox in declaring that it was recent Western modernity which led me to discover our own, older, modernity outside our 'modern' politico-cultural system established on a Western model."[362] Some Oriental scholars have found it useful to mine the silver lining in the clouded texts of Orientalism.

The manifest content of Orientalist discourse can be used for either oppression or liberation, more than simply as a style for domination of the other. As Xiaomei Chen suggests in her analysis of Chinese representation of the West, a nuanced discursive practice that constructs the Western other "has allowed the orient to participate actively and with indigenous creativity in the process of self-appropriation, even after being appropriated and constructed by Western Others."[363] Anthropologist Richard Fox makes a similar point in discussing the "affirmative Orientalism" in Mahatma Gandhi's resistance, which "depended on an Orientalist image of India as inherently spiritual, consensual, and corporate."[364] Fox also cites the example of Sikhs in northern India to show how the Western idea of Orientalism could be used against that very domination, and in fact enable resistance.[365] In a similar vein, David Kopf argues that "the Bengal Renaissance and Indian national awakening would have been inconceivable without the British colonial experience."[366]

"To speak of scholarly specialisation as a geographical 'field' is, in the case of Orientalism," writes Said casually, "fairly revealing since no one is likely to imagine a field symmetrical to it called Occidentalism."[367] Such a field has not only been imagined. Japan, for example, established an Institute for Western Learning in 1856, and the government sent a formal embassy to Washington in 1860.[368] Obviously Said had not yet met the Egyptian academic Hasan Hanafi, who at the time of *Orientalism*'s writing was creating just such a mirror-image academic field of "Occidentalism" (*istighrab*).[369] Hanafi, like Said, is an Arab educated in the West, having received a degree from the Sorbonne in 1966. Also like Said, he has been influenced by French philosophy, although Said's Foucault was Hanafi's Husserl. Unlike Said, the Egyptian Hanafi is a returned exile: after numerous years teaching around the globe in Philadelphia, Khartoum, Fez, Tokyo, and the United Arab Emirates, he went on to solidify his project of Heritage and Renewal (*al-turath wa al-tajdid*) at Cairo University. His aim has been to directly oppose and point out the weaknesses of Orientalism through a systematic and discursive othering of European intellectual history. Here is the direct writing back that Said found absent: a seemingly subaltern intellectual on the periphery looks back at the center that defined the need for peripheral vision. Hanafi mentions Said as one of the individuals who brought attention to Orientalism as an object of study. But he argues that because the Saidian reading of the "West" adopts Western secular humanism by default, it ultimately serves the same role in the modern Arab university as Said attributed to Orientalist texts in the Western academy.[370]

In later commentaries by Said, when he finally does recognize other anti-Orientalist writing, he fails to probe its rhetoric in the way he tried for Lane's descriptive study of Egypt or Austen's novel *Mansfield Park*. A case in point is the work of Abdul-Latif Tibawi, a fellow Palestinian to whom Said refers in *Orientalism* as a "distinguished Muslim scholar,"[371] and later includes in a list of like-minded "Oriental" critics who came before him. Ibrahim Abu-Lughod acclaims Tibawi's 1963 critique as the "first significant and major assault on Orientalist scholarship," one that paved the way for Said's *Orientalism*.[372] In 1963, Tibawi was a Harvard research fellow, cautiously chiding Western scholars in general as having "insufficient scientific detachment" in writing about Islam, although he cites Lane and Gibb as scholars who in his mind avoided meddling and patronizing.[373] The primary target of Tibawi's critique was the continuing prejudice of English-speaking Orientalists who maintained the momentum of earlier Christian hostility to Islam and were not impartial about Arab nationalism. In a later and blatantly apologetic piece written primarily for fellow Muslims, Tibawi exclaims his unwillingess to accept any scholarly claim that challenges his own devout view of the Quran as revelation.[374] Tibawi's indignation leads to the dangerous suggestion that only Muslims should be teaching about Islam, lest Muslim students have their faith challenged.

The widespread criticism that Said soft-pedals earlier challenges to what he calls the discourse of Orientalism elicited a fair amount of rhetorical backpedaling in Said's ongoing responses to his critics. "What I left out of *Orientalism*," admits Said somewhat belatedly, "was that response to Western dominance which culminated in the great movement of decolonization all across the Third World."[375] A litany of earlier Arab and Third World writers—whose voices are largely absent in *Orientalism*—is later offered as proof that others had been "challenging the authority, provenance, and institutions of the science that represented them to Europe."[376] Hegemony, says post-*Orientalism* Said, is never total, and "there are always resistances, however ineffective."[377] "My account here," he continues in *Culture and Imperialism*, "speaks of largely unopposed and undeterred will to overseas dominion, not of a completely unopposed one." In a chapter entitled "Resistance and Opposition," Said proceeds to do what was not done in *Orientalism*: he works both sides of the colonial divide. Novelists such as Austen, Kipling, Gide, Forster, and Conrad are played off against Ngugi and Tayeb Saleh, but Said labels the last two as "post-imperial writers of the Third World."[378] Said positions himself squarely on the "Western" edge of this divide as the secular humanist who has little use for nativistic resistance, and as the literary critic who cannot read a Third World text "except as embedded in its political circumstances" of imperialism and resistance to it.[379] Critics clearly on the other side of such a divide understandably wonder why the critique of Eurocentrism must itself be confined to the avowedly "Western" academic scene.

It is ironic that a literary scholar of Arabic heritage should essentially ignore the fiction genre in Arabic, especially given that there are well-known novels written back at the biases targeted in *Orientalism*. A notable example would be Tayeb Saleh's *Season of Migration to the North*, first published in 1969.[380] Saree Makdisi argues that this novel, far from being silenced by an overarching Orientalist discourse, actually rewrites imperialism—a "writing back" that is in itself a process of re-inventing through a heavy dose of sheer venting.[381] In this novel the Oriental, a Sudanese student named Mustafa Sa'eed, reverses the direction of domination and exemplifies the futility of trying to become a Westerner. The dirty secret about Mustafa is how he picks up the worst habits of the colonizer, playing the drunk and womanizer. The women in London are easy prey for the exotic student. "The women I enticed to my bed included girls from the Salvation Army, Quaker societies and Fabian gatherings. When the Liberals, the Conservatives, Labour, or the Communists, held a meeting, I would saddle my camel and go," reminisces Mustafa to the novel's Conradian narrator.[382] In reverse Orientalism, all Westerners looked alike and all their daughters were up for grabs, literally. The son of the imagined seraglio was returning the favor with interest.

In the novel, one girl at first rejects the young and impudent Sudanese sleaze. She recognizes his ugliness even though she is still tragically drawn to his bed. This is Ann Hammond, daughter of a military man and a moneyed mother; her aunt is married to a member of Parliament. Ann Hammond is also a young and impressionable girl studying Oriental languages at Oxford. "When she saw me, she saw a dark twilight like a false dawn," mused Mustafa. "In her eyes I was a symbol of all her hankerings." The Orient becomes the dream of an unfulfilled West. In his graveyard of a bedroom, where he sleeps with this budding Orientalist as if he "slept with a whole harem simultaneously," the Oriental man transforms the daughter of the Western Man into a harlot. "One day they found her dead," recounts Mustafa with a rare sobernesss. "She had gassed herself." And there is a suicide note, a crisp, ringing final rattle: "Mr Sa'eed, may God damn you." But which God? And was he not already damned?

The spectre that comes out of the Orientalist mirror is a cold-blooded seducer and accessory to murder. When discovered, he is advised by lawyers not to plead insanity but to hide his guilt behind nonexistence. "This Mustafa Sa'eed does not exist. He's an illusion, a lie. I ask of you to rule that the lie be killed." This is what the court should be told. He is, after all, an Oriental, an invention, a phantasm, a representation. Here is a ready-made defense: "Mustafa Sa'eed, gentlemen of the jury, is a noble person whose mind was able to absorb Western civilization but it broke his heart. These girls were not killed by Mustafa Sa'eed but by the germ of a deadly disease that assailed them a thousand years ago." That disease, reader and jury of *Orientalism*, is what Said calls Orientalism. But the trial Tayeb Saleh creates for Mustafa Sa'eed is not about truth, and ultimately is not concerned with justice. The trial, the novel's narrator informs us, is turned into a "conflict between two worlds."

THE BIND OF BEING GENDER-BLIND

> Why the Orient seems still to suggest not only fecundity but sexual promise (and threat), untiring sensuality, unlimited desire, deep generative energies, is something on which one could speculate: it is not the province of my analysis here.
>
> —EDWARD SAID, *ORIENTALISM*

> In short, by embracing the East, white women found new ways of being women. In this sense, Orientalism offered liberation and empowerment for white women.
>
> —MARI YOSHIHARA, *EMBRACING THE EAST.*
> *WHITE WOMEN AND AMERICAN ORIENTALISM*

Orientalism is a man's book. The author is a male; the vast number of writers and other individuals either analyzed in depth or mentioned in passing are men. A quick count of names in the index finds that some 440 men, mostly cited authors, are listed. Only 10 women are to be found.[383] For those who value statistics, a ratio of 44 to 1 would seem to lend credence to the complaint that Said does not penetrate the gender issue. Of these ten women, one is a sensational literary creation (Flaubert's Kuchuk Hanem), one a woman who is notable because she received a letter from Flaubert

(Louise Colet), one a very unladylike Queen (Victoria),[384] one a female who uses a male pseudonymn (George Eliot), and two are travelers/Orientalists (Gertrude Bell and Lady Hester Stanhope); the rest are modern authors (Hannah Arendt, Sania Hamady, Dorothee Metlitzki, and Barbara Tuchman). Of all these, only Bell gets more than a brief name-dropping in the narrative. Understandably, several critics have accused Said of being blind to gender issues.[385]

One of the specific feminist criticisms of *Orientalism* is that Said portrays an establishment in which there are virtually no women. Orientalism, writes Reina Lewis, is for Said "a homogeneous discourse enunciated by a colonial subject that is unified, intentional and irredeemably male."[386] Although it is true that women were almost exclusively excluded from what Said would call the guilds of Orientalist power, there were nevertheless women who wrote about their travels in the Orient, who imagined an Orient in their writing, and who painted this imagined Orient. Women were among the producers in this broad discourse of Orientalism just as they were surely among the consumers. One survey notes that some 187 women authors are known to have written travel books in English on the Middle East between 1821 and 1914;[387] also relevant is a study of accounts by some 200 European women.[388] Blindly following Said, Rana Kabbani offers the pessimistic claim that such women authors are merely "token travellers."[389] However, after examining nineteenth-century female travel and missionary narratives, Mari Yoshihara suggests that women revised as well as reinforced the dominant discourse of Orientalism at the time.[390]

My point is that in *Orientalism* almost all women authors are simply token for granted. The one apparent exception to this glaring omission in Said's analysis is the English traveler Gertrude Bell. Her name appears on ten different pages in Said's narrative, always in intimate association with T. E. Lawrence, and at times in the same literary bed as D. G. Hogarth.[391] Bell of Arabia, modeled after the iconic stereotype of Lawrence, is a rhetorical trope used by Said to illustrate that Orientalist writing blindly followed Kipling's "White Man" motif. After finding two damnable quotes in Bell's work, Said does not discuss what she is saying, but moves directly into his point that what appealed to Lawrence—and thus by implication Bell as well—was "the clarity of the Arab, both as an image and as a supposed philosophy (or attitude) towards life."[392] The irony is that while Said criticizes Lawrence and Bell for wiping out "any traces of individual Arabs with narratable life histories," he proceeds to do exactly that to Gertrude Bell, whose identity disappears as merely an alter-male-ego agent of empire.[393]

Were all the women who wrote about the Middle East tightly laced by a latent Orientalist discourse, which Said insists was a "peculiarly (not to say invidiously) male conception of the world"?[394] To be sure, most women had little expressed agency in the Victorian era, but does that mean women writers were as trapped by the sexualization of the Orient as the male voyagers and voyeurs? As Judith Mabro observes after reading numerous travelogues by women and men: "Only women travellers have been able to visit harems, and their reactions are complicated and often extremely critical."[395] For example, Lady Mary Wortley Montagu's *Turkish Embassy Letters*, published in 1763, challenged the Orientalist image of the veiled woman of the harem even as it was being elaborated.[396] "As to their morality or good conduct," Lady Mary wrote to her sister in 1717, "I can say like Harlequin, 'tis just as 'tis with you, and the Turkish ladies don't commit one sin the less for not being Christians."[397] The eighteenth-century feminist Susanna Rowson used Algeria as a setting for her novels that allowed her to break free of the conventions preventing her from writing about sexuality as a woman at home in the United States. In Rowson's 1794 *Slaves in Algiers*, the masculine construction of the harem-as-prison is turned inside out as "an enabling sexual space for women."[398] Instead of moralizing over the sad plight of the *femme odalisque*, Rowson reorients the image of the sensual freedom denied her to challenge the chauvinist discourse in her own society. The harem, much to male chagrin, was a unique social space where women could form strong bonds on their own and critique the manhandled world at the time.

Admittedly, access to writings by Oriental women writing either against the West or in critique of their own societies was limited at the time *Orientalism* appeared. More recent research provides evidence that some women were able to put themselves in a position to write back. An example is Fatma Aliye Hanim (1862–1936), who contributed three books to the 1893 Columbian Exposition. One of these works was an analysis of women in Islam written as a direct response to European distortions about the harem. Although the text was inaccessible to American fairgoers because it was written in Turkish, the mere fact that an educated Muslim woman's books were on display is worth noting.[399] Obviously her work would have been accessible to members of Ottoman society, however. Despite Said's consistent silence on critique from within the ranks of those represented, here is an example of an Oriental woman perfectly capable of representing herself. Several female authors in the Middle East used the West as a vehicle for self-definition in combatting the sexism embedded in their own societies.[400] Among indigenous feminist writings, the journals of the Egyptian Doria Shafik come to mind.[401] Ironically, Orientalist critique of Oriental male chauvinism, even if exaggerated, did inspire some Muslim women to seek reform of culturally embedded biases against women from within their own societies.

A second sin of gender omission by Said is the reduction of the fanta-
sized *femme orientale* to the preeminent symbol of oppression. A major
thrust of feminist criticism of *Orientalism* relates to Said's silence, what
he does not say about women beyond their sexploitation. If the Orient is
so intertwined in sexual fantasy with the feminine, why are real women
left out? Are we to assume that women were only capable of being silent,
mute victims of Orientalist discourse? Is it not problematic to situate
power with Western masculinity and assume only males capable of
agency? As Jane Miller remarks, women in Said's narrative are "apt to dis-
solve into metaphor."[402] An awareness of the penetrating gaze inherent
in sexist Orientalist stereotyping does not make Said into a closet feminist. As Sara Mills cautions, it is not enough to simply "add" gender into
Said's argument.[403]

The main female figure in *Orientalism* is an Egyptian dancer dallied with
by a French novelist who is presented as the paradigm of Orientalist domination of the Oriental other.[404] The passionate Flaubert slept with a real
Kuchuk Hanem, and other available Egyptian women, if his bravado is to
be believed.[405] I do not doubt Flaubert had sex with more than a figment
of his imagination, but the name he chose to record for his most-cited
exploit is in fact a Turkish honorific that means "little madam."[406] Said's
narrative frames Kuchuk Hanem as "a famous Egyptian dancer and cour-
tesan," euphemistically missing the point.[407] She was in fact a well-known
prostitute who had enticed several European travelers. Her real name
was Safiya. She had served as the mistress of the Pasha Muhammad Ali's
grandson before she danced for Flaubert. She reportedly had a verse from
the Quran tattooed in blue on her right arm. When Flaubert and his traveling companion, Maxime Du Camp, arrived by boat at Esna, a messenger
approached the foreigners and invited them to watch Kuchuk Hanem dance.
The invitation was not folkloric, but an offer of sex for money.

Under the cloak of literary criticism, Said focuses on Flaubert's fascination with "Oriental sex," which results in a twentieth-century man commenting in intellectually florid prose about a nineteenth-century man's privately
expressed wet dreams. Such dreams are not merely testosterone-driven,
but allegedly tainted by the Orientalist texts that first exposed the Oriental
woman to Flaubert's imagination.[408] Opposing a voyeur—red-letter-handed
in Flaubert's case—does not make Said a voyeur, but it does beg a question. How is Flaubert, the archetypically "Perverse Traveler," a poster-
enfant terrible for academic Orientalism when he does not even serve as
the norm for the genre in French Oriental travelogues?[409] I suggest that
this is a proposal most malapropos, given that Flaubert speaks directly of
Kuchuk Hanem in private letters that did not circulate in the Orientalist

repertoire and were not publicly available in the nineteenth century. The private musings of an exotic bohemian do not sum up an entire field of academic discourse except as a quite unworldly and private aide-mémoire. As Dennis Duncanson notes, "It is surely exaggerated for the literary critic to blame the scholars for these novelists' preoccupation with sex: it is their trade, and Chateaubriand and Flaubert wrote from experience not study."[410] Beyond the literary prototypes and apart from the colonially possible encounters with prostitutes (to which I seriously doubt trained Orientalists were for the most part inclined), how many Oriental women would be likely to retort "Je ne suis pas une femme, je suis un monde" when they were supposedly not allowed in the world?[411]

Imposing Flaubert as an Orientalist icon, Said misreads a passage that is offered as an example of the French voyeur of *bizarreries*. "In what he writes (or perhaps because he writes)," argues Said about Flaubert, "the premium is on the eye-catching, translated into self-consciously worked-out phrases: for example, 'Inscriptions and birddroppings are the only two things in Egypt that give any indication of life.'"[412] The implication here is that Flaubert saw nothing alive in Egypt apart from its glorious inscribed past and the fecal flutter of disrespectful fowl. Such a reading is aided by Said's careless omission of ellipses and avoidance of context. The passage in its original French actually reads:

> À Karnac nous avons eu l'impression d'une vie de géants.
> J'ai passé une nuit aux pieds du colosse de Memnon,
> dévoré de moustiques. Ce vieux gredin a une bonne balle,
> il est couvert d'inscriptions; les inscriptions et les merdes
> d'oiseaux, voilà les deux seules choses sur les ruines d'É-
> gypte qui indiquent la vie. La pierre la plus rongée n'a pas
> un brin d'herbe. Ça tombe en poudre comme une momie,
> voilà tout. Les inscriptions des voyageurs et les fientes
> des oiseaux de proie sont les deux seuls ornements de la
> ruine.[413]

Left out of Said's quote are the words "sur les ruines," even though they are present in the quoted English translation. Such an omission suggests that Said read Flaubert mainly for suitable quotes. Whatever Flaubert thought of contemporary Egyptians, and I certainly have no desire to defend Flaubert's self-absorbed prose, the sentiment in this passage is wrought with an irony that Said fails to appreciate. Here is the French voyager at the foot of the imposing Colossus of Memnon, a monument to a past not only forgotten but profaned by nature (indifferent birds and pesky mosquitoes) and by the graffiti of modern travelers.[414] The tragedy, for Flaubert, is that not only is this once-great civilization in ruins, but there is no current respect by anyone for its greatness. Echoing Shelley's "Ozymandias," a contrapuntal approach to this letter would capture Flaubert's reflections on "the decays of that colossal wreck," rather than turning a sense of loss into a desire on his part to deny that Oriental others still exist.[415] As Warren Rosenberg observes, "Said is taking Flaubert's view of a part for the whole, distorting the contextual meaning for the wider purposes of his argument."[416]

In *Orientalism*, we are only permitted to see how Orientalist men gazed at the imagined Oriental woman for sexual fantasy. Said's emphasis on the Western male's gaze at the woman of the harem takes part in what Ruth Yeazell criticizes as "the wishful ignorance of the commentators, with any representation of more than one woman in a vaguely Oriental setting constituting a harem for the purpose of some long-lived masculine fantasies in the West."[417] The exclusive focus on Flaubert's prototype for later fictional exotica implies that there was no other voice to be found. Even though Said wishes to expose the insidiousness of the harem sterotype, *Orientalism* offers no counter-image. Thus, to the extent that "Oriental woman is an occasion and an opportunity for Flaubert's musings," she ultimately serves the same purpose for Edward Said's thesis.[418] The harem fantasy, appealing as it could be to Western men, is presented in *Orientalism* only as a Western invention. Yet segregation and sexual exploitation of women had evolved in the real Orient prior to the intrusion of perverse travelers and Orientalist scholars. Western writers often embellished the harem for fantasy's sake, but they certainly did not invent it out of nothing.

Like Kuchuk Hanem, Flaubert serves Said primarily for his iconic stature as sexual exoticist. Said does not follow through on the extent to which Flaubert uses the Orient as a foil for speaking to the discontents of his own repressive bourgeois society. Ironically, one of Flaubert's targets is the French scholar Ernest Renan, bane of Said's discourse; in addition, Flaubert's inspiration stems from the work of honorary historian Vico, bard of Said's theoretical voice. As Dennis Porter argues, Flaubert not only poses the East–West dyad, but "more often than not reverses the traditional Eurocentric hierarchy in order to contrast Oriental wisdom with Western cultural smugness."[419] E. L. Constable expands on this point to argue that Flaubert's novel *Salammbô* persistently critiques the academic historical writing of his day even as it represents it.[420] The novel itself does not pose an East-vs.-West binary, nor does it glorify Europe at the expense of an Oriental other. Carthage represents the civilized order that Flaubert sets out to criticize, but the "others" in the novel are European and African.[421] *Salammbô* draws on classical sources via the work of historian Jules Michelet to portray civilized Carthage as excessively cruel. Countering Said's romanticizing of Flaubert, Ikdikó Lörinsky suggests that Flaubert's image of the Orient is posed as "vivent et réel" and not simply the mundane Oriental afterlife of distant Pharaonic glory.[422] Unlike the academic Orientalists critiqued by Said, Flaubert had no pretense of objectivity. How interesting that Flaubert muses about Kuchuk Hanem to his French lover Louise Colet: "We are weaving an aesthetic around her, whereas this particular very interesting tourist who was vouchsafed the honors of her couch has vanished from her memory completely, like many others. Ah! Traveling makes one modest—you see what a tiny place you occupy in the world."[423] Yet what a large place Flaubert's lustful tryst plays in *Orientalism*.

The "ready demand for coarsely piquant anecdotes of exotic sexual customs," as Samuel Chew puts it, was well supplied by Western representation of the Orient and Islam.[424] Said, however, ignores two pertinent points about this erotic imbroglio over the seraglio: male lust needed no East–West divide, and the prurient is almost always countered by the prudish. The pornographic trope held little regard for geography; imperialists in the field lusted after women wherever and whenever they crossed cultural boundaries in Africa, America, and the Pacific. "In myriad ways," writes Anne McClintock in her review of Western male imperialism worldwide, "women served as mediating and threshold figures by means of which men oriented themselves in space, as agents of power and agents of knowledge."[425] Indeed, lust on the home front in England and France was mitigated only by being a class act. Western governments frequently were involved in undoing the perceived excess of lurid literature at home. Isabel Burton, for example, feared that her husband's erotic flair would be a ticket to an English prison under the 1857 Obscene Publications Act, coincidentally the same year that Flaubert was charged with offending public decency with *Madame Bovary* and Baudelaire was convicted for the contretemps in *Les Fleurs du Mal*.[426] Earlier in 1851 a French art dealer in Paris named Malacrida had been sentenced to a year in prison and a fine of 500 francs for selling lewd photographs of nude French women; the photographer involved was also imprisoned.[427]

To insinuate that "'Oriental sex' was as standard a commodity as any other available in the mass culture" of nineteenth-century Britain and France is a malcontextual claim, unless the critic is prepared to probe plebeian prose and the impolitely oral vulgarities well outside the literary canon.[428] For whom was the Orient, as Said insists, "a place where one could look for sexual experience unobtainable in Europe"?[429] Real sex in the European male domain was as obtainable for the well-off as anything imagined in an Oriental mode. Speculating even further, Said claims that "Virtually no European writer who wrote on or traveled to the Orient in the period after 1800 exempted himself or herself from this quest."[430] How can Said justify "virtually" here, since he has sampled only a few travel writers and none of the far larger number of religiously motivated visitors? The examples he provides from Flaubert and Burton are poor witnesses, because these two also afforded themselves of sexual experience at home.[431] But were the numerous missionaries and pilgrims who flocked to the Holy Land also intent on knowing the locals in the biblical sense? Was Gertrude Bell a sex-crazed libertine?

If Flaubert is the Orient's premier Perverse Traveler, then Sir Richard Francis Burton should qualify as the second-to-none Perverse Translator. Burton engages Said's attention as the Orientalist who is a wild-mannered adventurer, would-be pilgrim, scholar, and sexual pervert all wrapped up in a Victorian jacket that is anything but straight.[432] I detect a note of grudging respect in Said's emphasis on Burton's combativeness. "He seems to have taken a special sort of infantile pleasure in demonstrating that he knew more than any professional scholar," writes Said, adding "that he had acquired many more details than they had, that he could handle the material with more wit and tact and freshness than they."[433] How, Said wonders, could such a rebel also be such a staunch imperialist at heart? The solution propounded and, I think, confounded by Said is that Burton was able to absorb the language and lifestyle of the real Orient so much that he himself became a living representation of it. He penetrated the forbidden mosque in Mecca; he mastered the figurative Arabic of the *Arabian Nights*. Indeed, Burton's texts, voluminous as they were, almost pale in significance next to his own persona. As the most successful Orientalist of all, Burton succeeded in translating himself into an Oriental, at least to his own satisfaction. Said appears to argue that in the end, Burton comes across as better than an Oriental precisely because he is really an Englishman.

The common thread between Flaubert and Burton is their seemingly excessive and therefore expressly unseemly pursuit of "Oriental Sex," which took the latter into the sexual manuals of Hinduism as well as the perfumed gardens of Arabic prose. Said mentions Burton's original and highly controversial "Terminal Essay" to his ten-volume *The Book of the Thousand Nights and a Night* (1885–86).[434] Burton's translation, especially the essay, details the kinky and unmentionable aspects of sexual performance and perversion that respectable publications dared not touch. Burton's was not the first major English translation of the epic tales—that privilege belongs to Edward Lane—but it was the first unexpurgated, not-for-the-ladies version to come along. At the time, the *Edinburgh Review* reflected the establishment view in recommending Lane for the library and Burton for the sewers.[435] Yet the story behind the translation and publication, as Dane Kennedy has perceptively documented, goes well beyond the voyeuristic drubbing Burton received from many critics.

Burton conceived his monumental translation while languishing for more than a dozen years in an administratively boring backwater Adriatic post in Trieste. Such an undertaking as the translation obviously consumed a great deal of time, and Burton was partly driven to it by frustration and anger at having effectively been shelved by mediocre administrators he much disliked. In a sense Burton was determined, as Kennedy suggests, "to tell truth to power." That "power" was the guilded establishment that kept the yet-to-be-knighted Burton outside the club. The open warfare between the translator of *The Arabian Nights* and the academic intelligentsia of the day spills over into the appendices of the edition. One particularly nasty battle was over Burton's request to borrow an Arabic manuscript from the Bodleian Library at Oxford. In laying out his side of what he called the *ineptiae bodleianae* Burton reproduces a series of formal letters, which he reads contrapuntally and attacks vehemently for everything from the head librarian's insistence on receiving a free copy of Burton's privately published edition to the sad state of the physical structure of the library.[436] He even drags out the all-great-men-come-from-Cambridge canard, charging that Oxford places "a dishonest obstacle to students learning anything which may be of use to them in after-life, such as modern and Oriental languages, chemistry, anthropology and the other -ologies."[437]

Faithful to the Foucauldian spin on discourse, Said views the combat between the individualistic Burton and the Orientalist establishment of his day as reducible to "the problem of knowledge of the Orient." The main and virtually the only problem is that Orientalist knowledge "becomes synonymous with European domination of the Orient, and this domination effectively overrules even the eccentricities of Burton's personal style."[438] A more judicious reader might raise an objection to such an overdetermined ruling, given the wider moral debate into which Burton's no-holds-barred translation of *The Arabian Nights* was introduced. This translation was consciously meant to be subversive. "His orientalism was intended above all to offer a mirror to his own society," argues Dane Kennedy, "exposing its various imperfections to itself."[439] The translation appeared the same year as a major attack on the laxity of British morals by William T. Stead, editor of the *Pall Mall Gazette*, an attack that led to the passage of the Criminal Amendment Act of 1885 and the creation of the National Vigilance Association.[440] Burton had more than a passing interest in the editorial views of the *Pall Mall Gazette*, which described his translation as a "muck heap." Comments appended to the *Supplemental Nights* reveal that he was concerned less about domination over the Oriental as other than about competition with rival Europeans as others:

> Mr. Stead's unworthy clap-trap representing London as the head-quarters of kidnapping, hocussing, and child-prosecution, the author invoking the while with true Pharisaic righteousness, unclean and blatant, pure intentions and holy zeal for good works, was welcomed with a shout of delight by our unfriends the French, who hold virtue in England to be mostly Tartuffery, and by our cousins-german and rivals the Germans, who dearly love to use us and roundly abuse us. In fact, the national name of England was wilfully and wrongfully defiled and bewrayed by a "moral and religious" Englishman throughout the length and breadth of Europe.[441]

Ironically, by reducing Burton's expressed concerns about his own society to the abstract notion of a will to dominate through knowledge, Said's own act of knowing Burton as author is in itself reduced to a polemical ploy. The text that Said chooses as the epitome of imperial-era British Orientalism has its own textual children, especially in the rise of the scientific study of sexuality by Havelock Ellis and Edward Carpenter. Dane Kennedy assesses Burton's critique of the prudish self-righteousness of Victorian society as "not all that different from the self-proclaimed project of post-colonial theorists" to do a critical ethnography of the West.[442]

In limiting himself to the Western gaze, Said implies that lust is endemic only to the Western traveler going East. In so doing he ignores a number of Oriental "voy[ag]eurs" who visited Europe in the eighteenth and nineteenth centuries.[443] After analyzing a number of Occidentalist Persian travelogues, Mohamad Tavakoli-Targhi concludes that European women were often represented in these texts as the houris of paradise here on earth. Some of these Muslim travelers described the beauty and mystery of European women with Sufi-like ecstasy. Mirza Abul Hassan Khan found his poetic muse when bedazzled by the beauties of London:

> Like a cypress you proudly stand, but when did a cypress walk?

Like a rosebud your ruby lips—but when did a rosebud
talk?
Like a hyacinth's blooms are the ringlets of your sweet
hair—
But when were men's hearts enslaved by a hyacinth's
stalk?[444]

Another reverse Oriental traveler, Mirza Fattah, alleged that not only were English women insatiable, but the men appeared to be sexually impotent and unable to satisfy them.[445] In his condemnation of the French, the Egyptian scholar 'Abd al-Rahman al-Jabarti claimed that French women were loose and without modesty to the point that some would enter a public barbershop to have their pubic hair shaved.[446] Titillation has been a male entitlement in which the gaze could veer as easily East to West as West over East.

The most visual focus for the lustful gaze is artfully ignored in Said's *Orientalism*.[447] A more fitting visual emblem of modern imperial lust for the Orient is harder to imagine than the sensual icon of the odalisque, often an Oriental beauty reclined for ravaging by the Western male gaze. *The Grand Odalisque*, painted in 1814 by Jean-Auguste-Dominique Ingres, launched the genre. This "cooly seductive" oil painting, viewed from many angles by art critics over several generations, shows a reclining naked girl who looks over her right shoulder at the viewer and grasps an exotic peacock-feather fan somewhat teasingly in her right hand.[448] There is little emotion in her face, barely a hint of what she feels. How convenient for Western domination of a feminized East. How odd that Said should ignore it. Such an image begs to be gendered. Ironically, there is little ethnographically "Oriental" about her boudoir; the royal blue curtains here will not be found in future harem scenes of the genre. The model, most definitely not a Semite, reproduces a young Italian girl. The penchant of Ingres for Oriental sexpots is an exercise *in volupté* in the tradition of Titian's paintings of Venus; the artist never visited a real boudoir in the Middle East.[449] His later canvases, especially the exotic harems and steamy bath scenes, are situated in a realistic Oriental context despite the fancied acts of painter and viewer. For example, Ingres's unisexually orgiastic *The Turkish Bath* (1862), even with the pale, blonde bodies, leaves little room for enlargement in the male imagination. This painting was considered so shocking by its commissioner, a relative of Napoleon, that it was returned to the artist, upon which it was almost immediately bought by the Turkish ambassador to Russia. It was not exhibited publicly until 1905.[450]

The apparent fit between Orientalist discourse and Orientalist art is at times a panoptic illusion. It was not so much the "Oriental" in the frame that excited as it was the naked female form. This is vividly illustrated in the famous pairing of Francisco de Goya's 1797–98 *Naked Maja* and *Clothed Maja*, both ironically depicting an arrogant beauty of Madrid, painted just as Napoleon was gathering his fleet. When a woman is fully clothed and surrounded by realism—as in the paintings of John Frederick Lewis—the impulse is not erotic but can tame the wildly exotic into the mildly mundane.[451] In another sense, depictions of the Oriental female form conflated a host of stereotypes that could effectively "steamroller differences" between Jewish, Turkish, Greek, and Spanish women.[452] Carol Ockman shows how representation of the "sensualized female Jew" became so widespread in 1840s French art and literature that the Jewish press responded with alarm. The naked female body, including its specific facial features, did indeed have far more to do with what was going on in France and Western society than any triggering events in the real Orient. The nineteenth-century emphasis on the female nude reflected, for Ockman, a "radical redefinition of the male body in the wake of the French revolution."[453] Napoleon may have failed to conquer Egypt militarily, but revolutionary change in France helped recontour the image of women in all sorts of drawing rooms.

The corpus of Orientalist painting should not be reduced to its most erotic examples.[454] There are numerous paintings of this style that do not coincide with the notion of a pervasive Orientalist gaze as penetratingly masculine. The nineteenth-century artist Henriette Browne portrayed the woman of the proverbially Orientalist harem as respectable, a domestic challenge from within to the male fantasies that dominated the genre.[455] Even male artists were capable of seeing beyond gender stereotypes. Eugène Delacroix, whose *The Death of Sardanapalus* (1827) is the archetypal linking of despot-erotica in Orientalist art, also drew the non-erotic *Chef arabe couché sur un tapis* (1832).[456] Ironically, the inaugurator of the art form could see his own society's faults in contrast to the real others he painted. Commenting on the differences in clothing between himself and the subjects of his art, Delacroix observed that men in Moroccan robes "are closer to nature in a thousand ways: their dress, the form of their shoes. . . . As for us, in . . . our ridiculous pinching clothes, we are pitiful."[457] Eugène Fromentin, who travelled widely in Algeria during the mid-nineteenth century, refused to enter a mosque just to paint it, even though he could: "To describe a woman's apartment or to paint the ceremonies of the Arabs' religion is in my opinion graver than fraud: it is to commit, in the matter of art, an error of point of view."[458] These subtle and gendered elements of self-critique are left out of Said's panopt-iconic rhetorical stance. Prominent nineteenth-century male artists did not necessarily take an unthinking siesta in the arms of odalisques.[459]

A major drawback to Said's homogenizing portrait of Orientalism is the assumption that Orientals could only be the subjects of artistic imperialism. A case in point is the Turkish painter Osman Hamdi Bey, who studied in France with the masters Gustave Boulanger and Gérôme. As part of the Ottoman contribution to the World's Columbian Exposition in Chicago in 1893, Hamdi's paintings in effect "painted back" against Orientalist bias. This real Oriental artist absorbed his mentors' technical advice but not their ethnocentric Orientalist mentality. Instead of a seductive odalisque, Hamdi Bey painted *Girl Reading*, in which a fully clothed young female is stretched out, absorbed in a book. This Turkish woman, as Zeynep Celik argues, "is thus given back her thinking mind and intellectual life, which had been erased by Orientalist painters."[460] Also included in the 1893 Ottoman exhibit were photographs that depicted the Orient from a positive, non-Orientalist perspective. One of these photographs shows a religious scholar reading in the modern Imperial Library in Istanbul. "Compared with Gérôme's paintings of Islamic worship or the innumerable nineteenth-century photographs of wandering dervishes, for example," observes Celik, "the theologist of the Abdul-Hamid albums brings forth the intellectual and scholarly aspects of the religion."[461] As the rightfully indignant voices of many Orientals were not hegemonically muted, neither was their ability mooted in reversing the biased image, answering the negative with a positive.

But why does Said stress the exoticizing of the Orient only as a focus on the female? For a book that is visually introduced by a quintessentially homoerotic portrait of a naked white boy holding up a snake, one would expect some coverage of the homosexual fantasies that can be found in Orientalist discourse. It is not just that the Orient is represented as an odalisque begging to be penetrated by the colonial gazer in pith helmet; the Orient could also be a place of unloosed sexual desires of all kinds. "For these European men," observes Alex Owen, "an apparent acceptance of *le vice contre nature* was part of the lure of the Arab world."[462] In addition to dallying with the prostitute Kuchuk Hanem, Flaubert was also florid in his description of Hasan al-Belbeissi, a homosexual male dancer. He even claims to have buggered a boy in a male brothel in Egypt.[463] The heterosexed Don Juan image was tolerated in both nineteenth-century France and Britain, but the image of two Oxford dons in bed was a rather different matter. Even Richard Burton, who was certainly no candidate for a who's who of Victorian prudes, refers to *le vice contre nature* as "one of absolute obscenity utterly repugnant to English readers, even the least prudish."[464] Given such surface resistance to the very idea of male homoeroticism, the Orientalist as voyeur should not be confined to the seraglio.[465] By averting the reader's gaze from sexual orientation, Said reinforces "a poetics and a politics of the closet."[466]

As Marjorie Garber argues in her analysis of the "chic of Araby," the otherness of the Orientalized object was not just men on top of women. On the level of image, the harm of male intrusion into the all-female harem needs to be balanced by the charm of male exclusion from a sensual haven where women could freely love other women. What Said sidesteps as "an almost uniform association between the Orient and sex" is uniform only from a unisexually male point of view.[467] He writes as though sexual fantasy were the exclusive domain of men and boys. Homoerotic impulses of women, especially through the filtering cultural subterfuge of transvestism, challenge the notion of a "feminized Orient subservient to the heterosexual masculinity of the Western observer."[468] Emily Apter argues that exotic Oriental stereotyping in French theatrical productions about powerful and erotic queens such as Cleopatra, Semiramis, and Thaïs may have served as a form of outing for feminist and lesbian reappropriation.[469]

Feminist critics have noted the unpleasant irony, not unique to Said by any means, of a deconstruction of Orientalism without targeting the broader and more invasive patriarchal denigration of women as indigenous others within the cultures producing Orientalists.[470] As Christine Holmlund observes, "Said on the whole ignores the female racial other in his analyses of Orientalism, and thus, despite his support for feminist projects elsewhere, perpetuates in *Orientalism* the patriarchal definitions of women as 'lamentably alien' which he seeks to critique."[471] By default, in his text (though not through any moral fault of his own) Edward Said contributes to the Western commodification of woman as object simply by not presenting—nor in any tangible way representing—her agency. "The narrative of the Muslim woman," writes Mohja Kahf in a critique of Said's proposed uniform Orientalist discourse, "had to be more than just a function of European relations with the Islamic world."[472] Ironically, medieval European representations of Oriental women often stress their agency rather than their assumed slavery. As a definitive termagant, the medieval Oriental queen is at times measured against Christian morals and found wanton precisely because of her active sexuality. Such queens openly display their sexual ornamentation rather than being forced to veil it; they rule the whole kingdom rather than being slaves in a secluded seraglio. Contra Said, Kahf proceeds to show that medieval "Saracen" women were not Orientalized but in fact made the same, a process of "same-ing" rather than othering.[473] However, after the Renaissance was underway, an imaginative seraglio entrapped the Oriental woman in much of European literature. It is under the gaze of the European Enlightenment, with its reasoned focus on human liberties, that the Oriental woman is laid out for the scopophiliac. By the time of Napoleon's penetration into Oriental regimes, the posterior charms of Oriental odalisques were ready to be painted by men for an admiring male posterity.

As feminists routinely and reluctantly note, Said "withholds his interest" from feminist works, especially in *Orientalism* and *Culture and Imperialism*.[474] Sara Mills faults both Said and Foucault for being theorists who are "inspiring yet disappointing for feminists."[475] On more than one occasion Said has admitted that he is uncomfortable with feminist scholarship, which he tends to essentialize away as a radical and exclusionary framework.[476] Said responded to a question from Jacqueline Rose about his lack of engagement with female intellectuals by saying that he resented having to give a list of "approved feminists."[477] In a self-serving defense of his own privileged exilic status, he cites Gramsci as an authority on it being "an inadmissible contradiction" that "only women can understand feminine experience."[478] Ironically, as Billie Melman points out, in Gramsci's sense of hegemony, "Women, associated with social rather than political history, are admitted to the experience of the empire only as spectators, or as victims."[479] The point Said misses is not that only women can understand, but that the unique way a woman understands within her sexist-cultured worldli-mess is worthwhile and unique when the issue is that very cultural sexism.

Reservations expressed by feminist scholars who by and large admire Said's general thesis are due less to what he says than to what he leaves out. I can think of no scholar sympathetic to gender equality who would find fault with the frank assessment that "Orientalism itself, furthermore, was an exclusively male province; like so many professional guilds during the modern period, it viewed itself and its subject matter with sexist blinders."[480] Because that is so true, it should have been worth exploring whether such blinders extend to all male scholars, including contemporary literary critics. In this respect, the nuance in Said's personal reflections "as a child growing up in two British colonies"[481] belies the relevant fact that he grew up not as just "a" child but as a male child. In *Orientalism* Said described himself as caught in a "web of racism, cultural stereotypes, political imperialism, dehumanizing ideology holding in the Arab or the Muslim." The fact that he was also a privileged male in a profoundly male-dominated world does not occur to Said as a relevant reflection to round out his personal dimensions.[482] I suggest that had Edward

Said been Edith Said, a female born at the same time and into the same cultural context, she would not have been in a position to gain an audience for her *Orientalism*.

READING THE CLASSICS WITHOUT CLASS

> Marx is no exception. The collective Orient was easier for him to use in illustration of a theory than existential human identities.
>
> —EDWARD SAID, *ORIENTALISM*

> I think that this account of Marx's views and analyses of highly complex historical processes and situations is a travesty.
>
> —SADIQ JALAL AL-ʿAZM, "ORIENTALISM
> AND ORIENTALISM IN REVERSE"

For many critics, Said reads the classics without any class. In textualizing Orientalist discourse, Said first turns to Flaubert's *Salammbô*—alongside H. A. R. Gibb's less titillating *Modern Trends in Islam*—to show that even the aesthetic was not immune from politics.[483] Flaubert, the libertine author, symbolizes the Orientalist who "must bring the Orient to life" and "must deliver it to himself and his readers."[484] What is especially appealing about Flaubert is that he actually went to the Orient. That this Frenchman could be in the Orient, live out his sexual fantasies, and report on them for his own amusement and economic betterment clearly grips Said's imagination. But Flaubert visited Egypt because he could afford to, *tout court*. It is ironic that Said is aware of Flaubert's unfinished satire *Bouvard et Pécuchet*, about two bourgeois clerks, yet does not follow up on the fact that Flaubert himself was a privileged man of means. To speak of Flaubert's writings and not to find class written between the lines is an egregiously unworldly example of critical negligence.

A first-class example of the role of social standing and privileged wealth is mentioned obliquely by Said and then ignored. This is William Beckford's *Vathek*, a widely read fantasy of "popular Orientalism" based in part on tales from the *Arabian Nights*.[485] Beckford's life is in itself a fantasy almost as exotic, in terms of its distance from reality, as the idiom in which he wrote. His father was twice Lord Mayor of London; his great-grandfather was Lieutenant Governor of Jamaica. On the maternal side, Beckford could claim descent from all of the barons—at least those who sired descendants—who signed the *Magna Carta*. At age eleven he became the wealthiest commoner in England through inheritance, but young William was hardly content to stay home alone. Touring Europe at age seventeen, Master Beckford received music lessons from Mozart and was patted on the head by Voltaire. When he finally settled down, William built a house, to the tune of 273,000 English pounds, that was fit for a sultan. Fonthill Abbey, as it was dubbed, was enclosed by a stone wall eight miles long and twelve feet high. The Long Gallery in the mansion was one-third the length of an American football field. A tower of similar proportions was erected. Beckford was a man of all means, picking up the entire library of Edward Gibbon to flesh out his own collection of volumes from monarchs and popes.

The wealthy Beckford was stricken with a passion for things Oriental. "Don't fancy, my Dear Sister, I am enraptured with the orientals themselves," he confided in 1788. "It is the country they inhabit which claims all the admiration I bestow on that quarter of the Globe."[486] Just after he turned twenty, Beckford hosted a Christmas party at Fonthill that featured an Egyptian hall and a Turkish room for a performance by Italian opera stars. The next year he wrote *Vathek*, according to legend, in the biblical measure of three days and two nights. Add to this that the Englishman wrote in French, the English translation was published without authorization under the translator's own name, and the author was also accused of being a homosexual, and you might see a literary—and otherwise—scandal in the making.[487] The novel itself is a mixture of Oriental lore—caliphs, dervishes, genies, and the like—and biting satire of opulence and political expediency.[488] The plot revolves around a caliph and his princess, who are tempted by the vanities of hell and succumb. The moral of the story is to not give in to the selfish drive for "empty pomp and forbidden power," because the punishment for "blind ambition" is "an eternity of unabating anguish."[489]

What sets Beckford's *Vathek*, like George Herbert's *Dune* series, apart from other fantasies based on Arabian themes is the extent to which Beckford textually bases his musings on "real" Orientalist knowledge. Much of this is derived from d'Herbelot's *Bibliothèque orientale*, almost a century old by the time of Beckford's writing. Yet it is not Beckford who studiously collected the footnotes. Rather the translator, Rev. Samuel Henley, plays the Orientalist detective, spinning out extensive footnotes on Arabic terms and customs. The noteworthy emphasis is on the exotic, bizarre, and sensual, which was true of much British writing of the day, including the mischievous midwife theory of Lord Kames. Beckford, who put off Henley from publishing the translation, was not particularly enamored of the meticulous detail outside the narrative, as he wrote to Henley in 1786:

> Upon my word, you pay Vathek much more attention than
> he deserves, and do you not think we shall usher him too

> pompously into the world with a dissection of his soul
> and machinery? Notes are certainly necessary, and the
> diss[ertation] I myself should very much approve but fear
> the world might imagine I fancied myself the Author, not
> of an Arabian Tale, but an Epic Poem.[490]

What makes William Beckford an Orientalist in Said's broad sense is the simple fact that he wrote about an Oriental subject and, through an odd publication sequence, included notable tidbits from canonized texts. The point that needs to be made is that Beckford's social position and wealth allowed him to both devour and create "Oriental" fantasy, but not in any sense as an academic Orientalist.

Class is no less a relevant issue in Orientalist art. Jean-Léon Gérôme, whose *Le charmeur des serpentes* graces the original paperback cover of *Orientalism*, was one of the most influential painters in the Orientalist genre. Gérôme's tenure as professor at the École des Beaux-Arts ensured his stamp on a generation of artists. But a major facet of Gérôme's success was his ability to travel extensively and collect art objects. With elite family connections, including an affine who ran an art dealership in New York, where his paintings and engravings sold well, he "represented the pinnacle of power in the art establishment."[491] Fame was also not unrelated to fortune in the case of the French artist Eugène Delacroix. After trekking across Morocco, Delacroix exclaimed to a friend: "The picturesque here is in abundance. At every step one sees ready-made pictures, which would bring fame and fortune to twenty generations of painters."[492] I assume that Said would subsume both these artists under the sway of a latent Orientalist will-to-dominate, but I see franc signs through the mirage. The Occamist option of simple greed is not within Said's field of explanatory vision.

Class position, elitism, and the bourgeoisie are elided in *Orientalism* into an establishment Orientalism.[493] The book's discussion of Sylvestre de Sacy is illustrative of Said's failure to analyze the privileged positions of the authors he cites.[494] We learn that de Sacy was the major teacher of most of the early French Orientalists, including many of Napoleon's expeditionary translators. In all, his positions came to include prominent professor at the Collège de France, resident Orientalist at the French Foreign Ministry, curator of Oriental manuscripts at the Bibliothéque Royale, first president of the Société Asiatique, and eventually formal peer of France. Here is the man whom Said associates with the beginning of modern Orientalism, the scholar who rigorously set the tone, the authoritative figure whose lasting achievement was "to have produced a whole field." As a discursive mover of awesome proportions, de Sacy figures as the sacrificial synechdoche for all that went wrong with academic Orientalism: "In time, the Orient as such became less important than what the Orientalist made of it; thus, drawn by de Sacy into the sealed discursive place of a pedagogical tableau, the Orientalist's Orient was thereafter reluctant to emerge into reality."[495] De Sacy's legacy is emphasized, his textual style dissected. But nowhere does Said consider the class dynamics of late-eighteenth-century France that promoted de Sacy and framed his worldview. Even Raymond Schwab, the source for most of Said's information on the early French Orientalists, discusses the class "psychology" involved in de Sacy's resignation from one appointment in order to avoid taking the republican oath.[496] Economic position and political affiliation are ignored by Said in favor of an ascribed, overarching latent prejudice.

This passion for the literary further privileges an elitist or intellectualist rendering of history. It is not hard to appreciate the lucrative potential for Flaubert, Gérôme, de Sacy, or Lord Curzon in othering the Orient. Said is right in saying that scholars, writers, and artists contributed to an imagined Orient—and politicians were pleased to promote such imagining—but what did the Orient mean to the poor sod on an English schooner heading east in the late seventeenth century? A brilliant analysis of Elizabethan English converts to Islam by Nabil Matar rescues the study of Orientalism from the great-books pedestal used by Said. Matar concludes that there was no cross-the-classes uniform view of Islam in premodern England, and certainly not throughout Europe as such. Probing beyond Rodinson's suggestion that Islam was a mystique, and past Bernard Lewis's contention that it served as an obsession, Matar looks at the rationality behind leaving Christianity for Islam, abandoning the West for the East. If Said's model of an inherent antipathy between West and East is wholly accurate, then such renegades would have to be lunatics. It turns out that there were many Englishmen, among others, who decided to switch civilizational allegiance. Why? Matar focuses on an allure of Islam and Oriental locales that some of the masses felt for very practical reasons.

> Rather, Islam projected an allure that promised a common
> Briton social and political power, and turned a poor European soldier into a well-paid rais (corsair captain: it was
> the allure of an empire that changed an Englishman's hat
> into a turban)—with all the symbolism of strength associated with the Islamic headdress—a Christian "John" into
> a Muslim "Ramadan," and allowed converts to Islam to
> fulfill themselves in worldly power and glory: ". . . in the
> great Turkes Soray," asked Francis Knight rhetorically,

"who are his Courtiers? who his Councellors? who his Vissiers? and his Bashawes? who his greatest Instruments, but these denyers, the sonnes of Christians."[497]

Matar makes the case that for Britain, France, and Italy in the sixteenth and seventeenth centuries, there were more Christians converting to Islam than vice versa.[498] This was recognized as a problem in the writings of major religious figures from Pope Pius II to Martin Luther, and authors from Cervantes to Dryden. Some no doubt converted out of convenience when their ships were captured. To a certain extent, Englishmen became Muslims because they could get away with it. The Ottoman Sultan Murad dictated to Queen Elizabeth that in any trade agreement, captured Englishmen who remained Christian would be returned to England, but those who converted to Islam were free to remain within the Ottoman Empire. The allure of Islam brought out a concerned response from some Christian apologists, such as John Cartwright, known as "The Preacher," who visited Aleppo in 1600 CE.[499] Kenneth Parker observes that the Turks were not necessarily the "embodiment of everything that is the antithesis to Christianity" in sixteenth- and seventeenth-century England.[500] The Englishman Robert Sherley served as a mercenary and later as an ambassador for Shah Abbas.[501] As European powers gained greater control in the Middle East, the incentive for escaping a less-desirable situation at home would have decreased. My argument is that Said's model trivializes the role of historical context by assuming that the discourse of Orientalism was unaffected by specific political sentiments and class conflict. Nor was the willingness to enter into the mirror of that surrogate other confined to the down and out. When it suited their Machiavellian purposes, even popes and European royalty dallied with sultans against local enemies.

Lost in the shuffle of a stifling Orientalist discourse is the role of economic self-interest crosscutting cultural ideologies. To say that Europe developed an unstoppable urge to dominate the Orient says little unless the material benefits of such domination are explored.[502] Had Napoleon never read an Orientalist or proto-Orientalist text, would he not have tried to establish imperial control of the Holy Land for the potential economic returns? "Presumably," retorts Sadiq Jalal al-'Azm somewhat facetiously, "had the long tradition of Cultural-Academic Orientalism fashioned a less peculiar, more sympathetic and truthful epistemological framework, then the powers would have acted more charitably and viewed the Orient in a more favourable light!"[503] Consider that by the 1830s, one of the biggest cash crops flowing from the Far East to European ports was opium; with apologies to Marx, opium became for a time the religion of American merchants, who were quite pleased to trade with the infidels.[504] The notion of an ideologically latent unity of discourse ignores the enduring and manifest lure of filthy lucre. Consider also that Christian or Jewish European merchants seldom let stereotypes of inferior Orientals or an avowedly ignominious Muslim prophet interfere with the profits of trade. Rather than following an interior binary split, all three peoples of the book—Muslims as well as Christians and Jews—adopted a co-conspiratorial policy of a pagan other eminently suited for the widespread medieval slave market.

Orientalism begins with Marx: "They cannot represent themselves; they must be represented," an apt adage for an author who proceeds to assume the first part and arrogate to himself the second.[505] Citing Marx before all else leads to an incongruity, when Said dismisses Marx's economic analyses as "perfectly fitted thus to a standard Orientalist undertaking"[506] and Marx himself as a well-meaning dupe unable to fully empathize with the suffering of the Asian masses because of "the lexicographical police action of Orientalist science and even Orientalist art."[507] Said's proposed mode for Marx's production stems from Goethe's lines on "the rule of Timur," but the well-known Marxist concept of an Asiatic mode of production is not even mentioned. Marxist critics have found little to praise in Said's use of Marx as a paradigmatic case of how a scholar's humanity can be "first dissolved, then usurped by Orientalist generalizations."[508] The Lebanese scholar Mahdi 'Amil, for example, provides a point-by-point rebuttal of Said's interpretation of Marx's views on the Orient.[509] 'Amil argues that Said conflates the beliefs that constitute a Marxist approach with a few select passages by Marx about the political context of the "Orient." It seems odd to this Marxist critic that Karl Marx would be implicated as defending rather than exposing British imperialist ambitions.

In *Culture and Imperialism*, Said continues his dismissal of "Western Marxism" as part of the "same invidious 'universalism' that connected culture with imperialism for centuries" and indeed remains "blinded to the matter of imperialism."[510] The irony is more than academic when Said stoops to conjure up Marxists of the American "Left" for having "surrendered their true radical prerogatives."[511] Such criticism was not unusual even within circles sympathetic to Marxism and socialism, but why throw out the class-conscious baby with the soiled Marxist bathwater? Not being an overt Marxist myself, I am not offended by Said's reluctance to engage in a classic Marxist interpretation of Orientalism as an ideological function of the global expansion of European capitalism. However, Said seldom expresses his reasons for disagreeing with such an approach except that it is used by avowed Marxists. It appears that the "ism" in Marxism is oxymoronic for the literary critic.[512] However, the genealogy of Marxists is quite varied.[513] In practice, Said overlooks the Marxist underpinnings of Gramsci and Raymond Williams, for example, but then misreads Adorno because of his allegiance to Marxism.[514]

But could Said be a southpaw Marxist and not know it? One of the more bizarre claims I have found in the ensuing debate about Said and Marx is that the former is really a Marxist.[515] William Hart's assessment goes even further: "Said is a Marxist-oriented thinker with Arnoldian sympathies."[516] I am not sure which of the two, Karl Marx or Matthew Arnold, would roll over the farthest in their graves if they were able to hear of such a posthumous pairing. An equally apoplectic critical illiteracy is evident in the evangelical Robert Frykenberg's remark that Said bashes the West with a "blending of Marxist and postmodernist language."[517] Ihab Hassan also seems to have his directions askew in describing Said as a "leftist critic."[518] Said himself was understandably bemused by those who have closeted him as "an undeclared Marxist."[519]

Of relevance here is Said's difficulty in reading beyond the neo-Marxism of Maxime Rodinson. Rodinson and Jacques Berque are singled out for rare praise in *Orientalism* as contemporary scholars who provide "instructive correctives" to "so-called Oriental problems."[520] Although Rodinson has a "vastly detailed knowledge of the Muslim World," his Marxist approach is said to be theoretically tainted. His descriptive analysis of Marxist movements is praised, but Said wonders why Rodinson is so unable to see the Orientalist side of Marx. "Is it entirely a coincidence," asks Said, "that Marx himself regarded the East with unfeigned dislike and was most unlikely to have viewed Islamic ferment with much interest?"[521] Like Orientalist father, like Orientalist son? Ironically, Said seems oblivious to the impact of anti-Marxist Cold War politics on Orientalist scholars. Some of the Western hubris in scholars like Bernard Lewis and Francesco Gabrieli can be explained by their strong feelings against Soviet and Chinese visions of the world order. Is there imaginary space for the realities of Soviet communism in Said's Orient?

The debate over Said's spin on Marx extends to fellow critics who have challenged his anti-Marxism. One of the most-read Marxist readers of *Orientalism* is Aijaz Ahmad, whose 1992 *In Theory* rebuts Said's views in strong terms, without being unduly inflammatory. Ahmad's main point of disagreement is with colonial capitalism taking less-explanatory precedence over "some transhistorical process of ontological obsession and falsity."[522] He accuses Said of fashioning a "rhetoric of dismissal" that fails to consider the complexities of Marx's thought.[523] Precisely because Ahmad spells out his objections in detailed refutations of Said's statements, these deserve better treatment than some critics fearful of Marxism have been willing to give. William Hart, in criticizing Said's secular rejection of religious rhetoric, preaches against Ahmad's critique as "Stalinist-inflected ranting against Said," adding the ad hominem insult that Ahmad "despises Marxist heretics more than capitalist infidels."[524] A 1993 special issue of *Public Culture* became a forum for a post-colonial dressing down of Ahmad for daring to criticize Said.[525] The most negative bluster in the issue comes from Marjorie Levinson, who derides Ahmad's "hostility that functions as the formal signature of the exercise, marking it as a harangue, jeremiad, flyting, ethnic cleansing: not to make a mystery of it, jihad."[526] In his response, Ahmad fires back: "Would the form of my rhetoric earn the term 'jihad' if my name were derived from Judeo-Christian traditions?"[527]

Said is sensitive to the hits he has taken critically from the Marxist left, but he simply dismisses anyone interested in Marx as part of an essentialized "orthodoxy."[528] "What I'm really trying to say," Said reflects in an interview, "is that the rhetorical and discursive accounts in Marxism, the accounts that are given by Marxists in this setting we are discussing, strike me often as less interesting than other theoretical and political possibilities that are not comprehended by those statements."[529] Said the critic is not interested in Marxism, but as di Leonardo comments, such "unthinking, reflexive anti-Marxism" results in a negation of the efforts of Marxist writers against imperialism and a generalized dismissal of the many variants of Marxism because of specific failings in the writings of Marx."[530] One need not find Marxist rhetoric interesting to acknowledge that it can be useful in combatting the kinds of prejudice Orientalism may encompass.

As Samir Amin, a critic who is otherwise favorably disposed to Said's work, laments: "Alas, those who proclaim the death of Marxism, far from surpassing its contributions to the understanding of the world, have simply shifted into reverse gear in order to return, without the slightest critical spirit, to the comfortable fold of the constructs that legitimate capitalism."[531] A related problem, as noted by Arif Dirlik, is that Said fails to separate Eurocentrism as an exploitative view of the other from capitalism as an exploitative economic system.[532] Anouar Majid suggests that the issue is not so much cultural difference, as Said assumes, but "the relentless penetration of capital into every sphere of human life."[533] The failure of Said's Orientalism thesis is that it prefers speculation about the intentions of Marx to the extraordinarily suggestive literature that Marx inspired on the fundamental economic disparity that fuels historical conflict.

III   Self-Critique More Than Mere Image

> Said does not seem to envisage the possibility that more
> directly counter-hegemonic writings or an alternative canon
> may exist within the Western tradition.
>
> —Dennis Porter, "Orientalism and Its Problems"

> I observe Europeans; I listen to them; I don't believe they
> understand what life is. Their imagination must be praised for
> having invented the devil. But since his death, they seem to
> be prey to a more chaotic divinity: the intellect.
>
> —Ling, in André Malroux's *The Temptation of the West*

"Indeed, my real argument," claims Said, "is that Orientalism . . . has less to do with the Orient than it does with 'our' world."[534] This intriguing suggestion, now so commonplace that it hardly requires comment, underlies Said's notion of Orientalism as a coercive will to power that refuses to define the Orient as it really is. A hegemonic manacle, Said's rhetoric infers, muted meaningful self-critique from within the ranks of trained Orientalists. But he fails to consider that a mirror image may be more than a distortion of the other; an image may also be consciously directed back as a critique of self. Throughout *Orientalism*, there is a failure to acknowledge Orientalist discourse as capable of self-criticism in order to protest an aspect of Western society or contest inaccurate understandings of the

Oriental other.[535] It is an odd, almost theological, position to assume that resistance to a distorted image of the Orient, or of imperialist goals as such, was structually impossible from within the European intellectual community. Arif Dirlik, in disagreement with Said's overall thesis, argues that self-critique was "almost a discourse within a discourse of Orientalists."[536]

Said would have us believe that Orientalists looked into the mirror of the Orient for a surrogate, but did so in vanity: "Mirror, mirror on the wall" becomes the mantra that any Westerner trying to look eastward is allegedly scripted to recite. Aijaz Ahmad counters that to the extent that the Orient becomes a kind of self-defining mirror for any given Westerner, the complexity of defining across time and space yields a virtual "wilderness of mirrors."[537] Why assume that every Orientalist only saw his own biased reflection? Why conflate the face-to-face encounter many Westerners experienced with the reflective mirroring of any text representing that encounter? It is one thing to critique the rhetoric of a travelogue, for example, but quite another to say that the individual writing it was utterly incapable of having an authentic understanding of any real Oriental other. There is a lived reality beyond representation.

Said's superficial familiarity with the history of Oriental studies explains in part why he fails to find scholarly Orientalist texts that critique flaws within the tradition. As his own endnotes indicate, Said's critical remarks about several nineteenth-century scholars were taken from a 1962 article by historian Johann Fück.[538] Said misrepresents several of the points made by Fück. For example, the reuse of Fück's wording is sloppy when Said writes that Burckhardt speaks of Islam as "wretched, bare, and trivial." Fück places both "wretched" and "bare" in quotes, as translations of Burckhardt's actual words, but there is no reference to "trivial" apart from a mention of triviality in a later sentence. A quote regarding the scholar Nöldeke's "low opinion" of Orientals refers to Fück's own characterization, but nowhere does Said indicate that the Orientalist Fück is the one drawing attention to the bias of an earlier scholar. Said might have looked at what would have been the most recent state-of-the-art survey of the field at the time he was starting to write *Orientalism*. This is Leonard Binder's 1976 edited volume *The Study of the Middle East: Research and Scholarship in the Humanities and Social Sciences*. "The fact is that Middle Eastern Studies are beset by subjective projections, displacement of affect, ideological distortion, romantic mystification and religious bias, as well as by a great deal of incompetent scholarship."[539] Such is Binder's critical read of an expanding and improving field of study that could no longer comfortably fit into the mold of a guild as baggage-laden as "Orientalism." Similar criticisms of faults in Western treatment of the East had been raised more than two decades earlier by Charles Malik in the journal *Foreign Affairs*.[540] Even earlier, in 1935, the famous historian Arnold Toynbee called the idea of an "Orient" an "egocentric illusion" and wondered "how this vulgar error can ever have obtained its hold."[541]

Although invidious apologetic against Islam and defamation of Muhammad were endemic to medieval European representation, it is possible to find texts that attempted to overcome the subjective bias in representation of the Orient.[542] Among well-known texts that are sympathetic in treatment of Islam and the Ottomans are Jean Bodin's 1576 *Les six livres de la république* and Adrian Reeland's 1705 *Of the Mahometan Religion*. One Italian historian, G. T. Minadoi, was so turned off by the distorted reports reaching him from the Levant around 1594 that he refused to write anything not from his own personal knowledge of events in the region.[543] Characterizing the 1636 travel account of Sir Henry Blount, Samuel Chew notes: "His unprejudiced outlook upon the world of Islam and his dispassionate desire to observe independently and report fairly upon the admirable features as well as upon the shortcomings of that alien civilization appear often in his narrative."[544] In his 1684 *Histoire critique des créances et des coutumes des nations du Levant*, the Catholic Richard Simon wrote on Islam "which he expounded clearly and soberly on the basis of a work by a Muslim theologian, without vituperation or disparagement and occasionally with real appreciation and even admiration."[545] Henri de Boulainvilliers' 1728 *La vie de Mahomed* presented the founder of Islam in a favorable light even though it was based on secondary sources. De Boulainvilliers lamented that so few "learned men" studied Arabic, given that Arabic texts were such an important source for understanding Muhammad.[546] Positive accounts were also given by some of the Jesuits describing Chinese philosophy in the eighteenth century.[547] Such assessments obviously failed to stamp out the negative stereotypes, so an explanation should be made based on the context of their reception rather than on a blanket condemnation of all Western writers as captive to a latent discourse.

In Said's thesis, Orientalism is assumed to be incapable of self-correction because it has no will not to dominate the other. A relevant and amusing historical anecdote can be cited to show how the seemingly obvious "truth" in such a polemical assertion amounts to a half-truth. Consider *Ezourvedam*, the Sanskritist scandal that could be called the Piltdown hoax of early Orientalist scholarship.[548] In 1760, the French savant Voltaire obtained a copy of what was assumed to be a French translation of a Vedic text written by an eminent Brahmin. So impressed was the normally skeptical Voltaire that he deposited the unique manuscript in the royal library, where Anquetil-Duperron eventually read it. The French text was finally published in 1778, followed by a German edition. With virtually little else available from the Hindu genre, a point that invites comparison with the initial scientific acceptance of Piltdown Man in England, this seemed a notable contribution to emerging Orientalist philology.

The true origin of the text went back more than a century before, but not to a Hindu theologian. The most likely culprit—if only one was involved— would be Robert de Nobilis, a Jesuit missionary who helped found the Catholic college at Pondicherry in India. The text was intentionally written, as Schlegel was later to label it, to be *ein frommer Betrug*, a biased account of Hindu beliefs to assist in converting them.[549] Among the first to expose the hoax was fellow priest Paulinus a Sancto Bartholomaeo, whose ridicule is worth quoting at length:

> And what do modern European scholars do with it? With singular zeal and effort they scrutinize the Brahmanic law, i.e. the Ezourvédam; they comment on it, interpret it, build philosophical structures on it, and like bags inflated and distended by the wind, with rattling cheeks, knitting their eye-brows, they educate the people and the king alike. But behold! one gust of wind, and the whole structure of the building lies in ruin![550]

Orientalist scholars could be accused of fraud, or at least naiveté, but not all scholars chose to cover up the falsehoods and inconsistencies generated in the emerging representations of the Orient.

A careful reading of *Orientalism* reveals several scholars who rise above meanness and deliberate distortion: Massignon, for instance. Yet Said insists that overriding the intentionality of even the most sympathetic voice is "a dogma that not only degrades its subject matter but also blinds its practitioners."[551] There are of course levels of degradation and stages of blindness in the real world. It would be absurd, as Said frequently reminds his critics, to assert flat out that all Orientalists were equally ethnocentric, prejudiced, or racist. The issue becomes whether or not individual scholars were capable of recognizing their own bias, correcting distortions enshrined as noble truths, and seeing through specious arguments and propaganda even if not with perfect 20/20th-century vision. Were at least some of the Western men and women who encountered real men and women in the Orient and read authentic Arabic, Persian, Sanskrit, or Chinese texts capable of revealing more than a self-serving surrogate in the mirror? Concluding *Orientalism*, Said notes that the "worldwide hegemony of Orientalism and all it stands for can now be challenged." Indeed, his book is proposed as a "modest contribution to that challenge."[552] Contra this contention, the challenge can be found from the very beginning of a field called Oriental studies.

One way to test Said's assertion is to examine specific individuals he identified as major contributors to Orientalist discourse. One of the earliest scholars receiving attention in *Orientalism* is Abraham-Hyacinthe Anquetil-Duperron, who translated the *Avesta* and the Upanishads into French. This philologist is presented by a lengthy half-page quote from the secondary text of Raymond Schwab.[553] For Said, Anquetil-Duperron and the English Indologist William Jones were "contributors to modern Orientalism," but came along before this was distinguishable as "a field, a group of ideas, a discourse."[554] Anquetil-Duperron is said to be an able philologist, "eccentric theoretician of egalitarianism," and biblical apologist who helped set in motion the higher criticism of the Bible. What, then, did the eccentric Anquetil-Duperron do wrong, apart from being an Orientalist and "all it stands for"? Said does not specify anything negative, unless "opening large vistas" by revealing the materiality of Oriental texts, languages and civilizations counts as a step back from medieval worldviews.[555] Schwab in fact is full of praise for the pioneering scientific expeditions of this philologist, through whom "the mysterious dimensions encompassed by the vagueness of the term 'Orient' were repatriated from the empire of hearsay and from the wings of court theater."[556] There are few better prescriptions for sound philological scholarship than that given by Anquetil-Duperron: "The only way to know the truth is to learn the languages well, to translate oneself the fundamental works, and to confer subsequently with the scholars of the country on the subject-matters treated therein, the books in hand."[557] Here was a man who "obstinately adhered to the best course of action, which is to treat all men as equals."[558] Schwab further notes that Anquetil-Duperron "was not sparing in his criticism of British imperialism."[559] Likewise, Thierry Hentsch praises this eighteenth-century savant for allowing the Orient to represent itself in his 1778 *Législation orientale*.[560] Anquetil-Duperron is clearly no Renan.

One of the few German Orientalists allowed into the narrative of *Orientalism* is Ignaz Goldziher, whose main failing appears to be that his "appreciation of Islam's tolerance towards other religions was undercut by his dislike of Mohammed's anthropomorphisms and Islam's too-exterior theology and jurisprudence."[561] Apart from the criticism that he did not like Islam enough that he would be willing to convert, it is not clear why Goldziher's quite substantial corpus of writing about Islam warrants being dismissed as "highly tendentious" and "hostile." Said apparently takes this characterization directly from Jacques Waardenburg without actually reading any texts by Goldziher.[562] Of all the Western books on Islam from the nineteenth century, Goldziher's *Muhammadischen Studien* has probably weathered the best. Said may be unaware that Goldziher criticized Renan's overt anti-Semitism.[563] Goldziher was also a critic of European intervention in Egypt, arguing that "the European in the Orient represents the class of the worst kinds of rascals who were spit out by European society."[564]

It is hard to insert some two centuries of scholars with different sets of prejudices and various intentions squarely into a whole and immutable discourse in which all commentators on the Orient are assumed to drown. Yet Said insists that Orientalism could remain "unchanged as teachable wisdom (in academics, books, congresses, universities, foreign-service institutes) from the period of Ernest Renan in the late 1840s until the present in the United States."[565] A cursory check of major texts and the innumerable book reviews and critical commentaries shows that so-called Orientalist scholars routinely argued against what they saw as distortions and errors by other scholars. Criticism of the work of Renan, Said's arch[etypal]-Orientalist, is a case in point. Even Ziauddin Sardar, who reiterates the Saidian mantra that there is "nothing about Orientalism that is neutral or objective," cites two books that he says were so objective that they had to be hushed up in European academic circles: Hans Prutz's 1883 argument that the Crusades gave the West access to rationalism, and Gustave Le Bon's 1884 thesis that Europe borrowed ideas of education from Islam.[566] Similarly, the Spanish Arabist Julián Ribera in 1928 challenged the notion among Romance specialists that Arabic influence had been minimal on Spanish literature.[567] Then there is George Wickens's blistering critique of prominent Arabists and Persianists who translate poetry as though they were trying to outdo Thomas Moore's romanticized *Lalla Rookh*.[568]

A PERSIAN MIRROR

> "Good Heavens!" I exclaimed to myself; "must we be forever blind to our own folly? Perhaps, after all," I argued, "it is a blessing that we should find consolation in the absurdities of others."
>
> —RICA, IN MONTESQUIEU'S *LETTRES PERSANES*

One of the most gaping holes in Said's Orientalism thesis is an almost total avoidance of the well-known literary mode of creating an Oriental metaphor to critique aspects of Western society.[569] Perhaps Said avoids this genre because he assumes that any Western representation of an Oriental is paradigmatically a statement of cultural domination and thus false by its very nature. But is it the case that such representation assumes that the real Orientals cannot speak for themselves, is it that anything they might say would be false, or is it that what they say would be difficult to translate? Said poses for a one-way mirror in which the West only stoops to conquer the image of the East, but that image can just as easily be refracted as purposeful self-critique. If indeed such representation says more about the one doing the representation, then it is important to know the intentions of the authors. Putting words in the mouths of exotic others can be a useful mode for criticizing certain shortcomings and flaws in one's own society. The result may be a kind of inverted ethnocentrism, a laundering process that makes foibles public even if the damned spots of prejudice are never fully cleansed. The satirical surrogate, as opposed to the false representation of an other's putative reality, is certainly no less relevant than the racist propaganda Said trumps as the essence of Orientalist discourse.

By far the most influential satire in which Orientals serve as Western mimesis is Montesquieu's 1721 *Lettres persanes*, a witty social self-critique that literarily defines the genre.[570] It is curious that Said would ignore a book that another literary critic, Dena Goodman, calls "the first attempt at political writing for the modern age."[571] Montesquieu is justly renowned as a defender of radical individualism and a "determined foe of imperialism."[572] Although *Lettres persanes* is a light work, Montesquieu proposes through the dilettante[alizing] dialogue of two Persian travelers many of the arguments that are later solidified in the political philosophy of his 1748 *Esprit des lois*. The plot revolves around Usbek, an older and presumably mature man who has to deal with his harem, which has been left in the hands of eunuchs, and Rica, a young man recently arrived in Paris who has yet to taste the delights of the Oriental harem but is confronted with the exotic civilization of eighteenth-century Parisian society. Montesquieu offers a disjointed series of some 161 letters exchanged by various combinations of the two main travelers, their friends at home, the eunuchs and women of Usbek's harem, Usbek's nephew, a mullah, and a Jew. Commentators generally view Usbek as a reflection of the more conservative, graver, and reflective side of Montesquieu, whereas Rica is sarcastic and delightfully harlequinesque. Ironically, as the letters coming from Persia describe the destruction of Usbek's harem in his absence, the Parisian letters playfully deconstruct French social mores, philosophical speculation, and politics.

Rica's first letter illustrates the newly arrived naif in a cosmopolitan world he can scarcely believe.[573] "Paris is quite as large as Ispahan," writes Rica in awe to his friend Ibben. "The houses are so high that you would swear they must be inhabited by astrologers." This is no simple monologue joke—astrology was for Montesquieu an irrational practice shared foolishly by Persians and French alike. Rica is first impressed by the technology: tall buildings and fast carriages. Because Rica's self-proclaimed nature is "not made for such hurry," he walks the streets, only to be jostled and splashed by the passing carriages. Thus he first discovers Paris not only as an outsider, but in the way a poor French peasant might. Rica quickly proceeds to the King of France—Montesquieu had Louis XIV in mind— who is said to be much wealthier than the King of Spain, as the former can draw "from a more inexhaustible source, the vanity of his subjects." The French king is compared to a great magician, for he can actually make his subjects think what he wishes, as by suggesting that a piece of paper he issues is as good as a gold or silver coin. But there is an even greater magician, the pope.

Relations between the French court and the papacy were seldom stable, but Montesquieu did not dare to openly satirize the pope, let alone the powerful Jesuits (called "dervishes") and Jansenists (called "invisible foes"). As it was, his Oriental tale was placed on the *Index Expurgatorius* in 1761. Montesquieu, like his sibling satirist Voltaire, did not idly choose to phrase rationalist critique through a foreign voice. It was precisely because a Muslim would be expected in vulgar stereotype to say outrageous things about the church that a cover could be provided for critique. It is not that Montesquieu feared burning at the stake, as he might have only a century before, but that the conservative establishment could make his career short and not so sweet. As Rebecca Joubin shows in a sensitive analysis of Diderot's 1751–72 *Encyclopédie*, "the philosophes used the topos of the Oriental as Other as a lens through which to engage in cultural self-criticism as a key method of subterfuge to shield themselves from the watchful eyes of the censors."[574] Joubin cites Said approvingly for drawing attention to the point that Orientalist works say more about the Orientalist's own culture than about the reality of an Orient. Yet her own research contrasts the negative portrayal of Islam with the recognition in the West of a positive role for Arab civilization in science and philosophy. This important finding contradicts Said's insistence that all "Orientals" were treated with the same disdain.

In *Lettres persanes*, Rica, the twinkle in Montesquieu's eye, goes to the core of the rationalist critique of Catholic Christianity by repeating the major objection Muslims had to this tolerable religion of the book. Concerning the pope, muses Rica, "Sometimes he makes the king believe that three are no more than one; that the bread which he eats is not bread; the wine which he drinks is not wine; and a thousand things of like nature."

Not only is this an accurate charge Muslims leveled against Christianity, but one shared by Enlightenment rationalists. Rica then brings up a contentious papal bull, the *Unigenitus* of 1713, which among other things forbade French women to read the Bible, which is "indeed, their Koran." The women of the French court openly rebelled against this stricture, but Rica thinks that the pope "does not reason amiss." Perhaps, Rica speculates, he was covertly instructed by Islamic teaching, in which "women are inferior creatures compared to us [men], and may not, according to our prophets, enter into Paradise." If Rica's tongue is not planted in his cheek, Montesquieu's is.

Like all effective satirists, Montesquieu counts on the reader to already share stereotypes—in this case, about Islam, Persians, and Turks. In one sense, Rica responds the way an average Frenchman would expect a Muslim infidel to sound. The Persian visitor believes that his own religion is superior and that the French other must be too uneducated or too obstinate to appreciate the difference between state policy and trickery, between theology and superstition. The parallels made in *Lettres persanes* between Islam and Christianity bring the shared anti-Islamic and ethnocentric prejudices of readers to the surface. The narrative dredges up statements and ideas that, if taken literally, would offend almost all Muslims and Persians. However, Montesquieu is not writing to tell off Orientals or add to the apologetic corpus of the church. The target is not the "other." In the outward ridicule riddling this text, the foibles and absurdities of Montesquieu's Paris are omnipresent. As Diana Schaub explains, Montesquieu uses the satire "to tame prejudice, temper fanaticism, and promote toleration."[575] Perhaps the man was not a social activist except in the salons to which this satire ensured an entry, but his embedded sentiments served subversive criticism of the status quo.

Exposing religious absurdity is not the only, and perhaps not the main, aim of these letters. Advancing through the seemingly mundane comments of Rica and Usbek, one finds Montesquieu's highly finessed spinosity on pop culture at the time: the lens of the supposedly inferior other de-focuses the ordinariness of the theater, opera, almshouses, coffeehouses, gambling, the Versailles palace, forms of government, social classes, fashion, marriage and divorce, academics, physicians, and even suicide. At one point Rica aphoristically defuses the gravity of the yet-future voyeuristic sins of odalisque-oglers: "The French seldom speak of their wives," he observes, "they are afraid to do so before people who may know them better than themselves."[576] Center-stage in the concern of Usbek and for the Western reader is the harem, the *roman du sérail* that serves as the domestic version of Oriental despotism writ small.[577] The correspondence between

Usbek and his wives, as well as their high-voiced overseers, reveals the intrigue and jealousy of an institution that Enlightenment men of Montesquieu's own world were at times as likely to encounter in their neighbor's boudoir as in a neighborhood bordello.[578] But even with the icon of slavery Montesquieu overwrites the triumph of liberty: Usbek's favorite wife, Roxana, has the last word, penned under the influence of the poison she—quite Socratically, in a way—takes to maintain her independence. Her death can be read as an act of agency, a defiance that forces the reader to question the institution and circumstances that create such tragedy.

How is a scholar today to read the impact of this satire, whatever the always debatable intentions of the author? In a recent mis-deconstruction à la Said, Mohja Kahf contends that Montesquieu's overt harem-slave image of the Muslim woman "partakes of the 'self-containing, self-reinforcing character of a closed system' that is Orientalism."[579] The point Kahf wishes to make is that whatever subversive intentions or latent liberationist sentiment the author entertained, his text has only been read as a reinforcement of the stereotype. Indeed, according to Kahf, *Lettres persanes* "was intended to be read, was read, and amazingly, is still read as straight ethnography as much as philosophy or anything else. The clincher is that even modern scholars will enter into the text's assumptions about the Muslim woman as if they were self-evident."[580] The charge that this clever satire could be mistaken for serious Orientalist scholarship, particularly an on-the-spot ethnographic account, would no doubt please Montesquieu. Perhaps by now some of the original Persian letters that Montesquieu never had a chance to translate have been found in a lost trunk in the Bibliothèque Nationale or a retired ayatollah's library in Isfahan. If *Lettres persanes* can pass as ethnography, I propose that equal validity be given to Rica's critique of the pompous Orientalists mentioned by Montesquieu. Rica once met a *decisionnaire*, "a man very well satisfied with himself," whose mind "was not once troubled with the least doubt."[581] As Rica describes the encounter, "I spoke to him of Persia; but hardly had I opened my mouth, when he contradicted me twice, basing his objections upon the authority of Taverner and Chardin. 'Ah! good heavens!' said I to myself, 'what kind of man is this? He will know next all the streets in Ispahan better than I do!'" Montesquieu via Rica appears to have trumped Said's critique of Orientalism more than two and a half centuries earlier.

The most memorable phrase in all these letters is the query of a puzzled Frenchman: "Comment peut-on être Persan?" Surely, if Montesquieu was seeking to persuade the reader of his ethnographic authority, this would be a strange question to pose. It must have been easy to "be a Persian" in the French mind—since all one had to do was assume that a Persian was the opposite of a civilized gentleman in a Parisian salon. The more difficult quandary, not explicit in Montesquieu's seemingly ethnographic comment, is how one could possibly be a Frenchman. Read literally, the Persians come off as naively perceptive, but certainly not evil or irrational. They share many of the passions of the French, even in bed, love to chatter about politics, and seem to appreciate life despite the seeming absurdity of everything going on around them. There is a positive self-critique stemming from the Persian letter-writers' awareness of the abuses associated with harem life. Usbek draws attention to the apparent contradiction between the Islamic allowance for up to four wives and Muhammad's call to satisfy all of them, "a precept which renders the life of a true Mussulman very laborious."[582] Dangling a concern about depopulation, Montesquieu allows Usbek to speak out against both the slavery of women and the castration of eunuchs: "You see how many persons of both sexes one man employs in his pleasures, causing them to die to the state, and making them useless for the propagation of the species." As a Persian seriously reacting to Western and Christian thinking, Usbek portrays the Oriental as a rational man; indeed, I suspect most readers would find Usbek rational enough to have been a creation of Montesquieu.

Kahf, like Said, takes the seeming fit with "reality" too literally, as though it could only have been meant to be taken seriously, or as though most readers would be unable to see fiction as fiction. Because the letters read as though they could have been written by a Frenchman, the reader's interest is not in learning about a "real" Usbek or Rica, or even about real ladies of the harem. Montesquieu is sharing a joke with his audience, which does not need to see the twinkle in his eye as he holds forth like a pundit. Thus when Usbek, the traveling philosopher, tells his nephew, "Men ought to stay where they are: the change from a good climate to a bad one produces diseases, and others spring from the mere change itself," the reader intuits that this will not stop people from travelling, even though the scientific rationale may have been somewhat sound at the time.[583] The successful satirist needs to stay close enough to probability that the text could at moments pass for reality, at least a reality imagined by the reader. Irony is served in these letters by a rhetoric of deadpan demeanor. But Montesquieu always turns the table on anyone who would take his brushes with reality too seriously. Just read the hilarious prescriptions of the country physician.[584]

It is curious that anyone should think these letters an ethnographic portraiture of Oriental lifestyle. In fact, there is in them a dearth of detail about Persia, especially the physical setting of the harem. Montesquieu backdrops the musings and emotional banter of his letter writers with a stage bare of almost all Orientalismic relish. Usbek, for example, is never home with his ladies. Usbek's wives and eunuchs complain about each other and gush over their fidelity and longing, but their letters could have been written anywhere. It is true that Montesquieu works in generic information about Islam, even quoting the Quran at times, but almost always this is as a contrast to what the Persian travelers encounter in Europe. Whether or not Montesquieu intended to fool the reader, the very order of the letters is not strictly chronological according to the Muslim calendar. There are also several references to Turks, usually contrasting the French king to the Ottoman sultan, but much of what the Persian Usbek says about the Turks borders on pure disdain.[585] It would be difficult to elicit a generic "Oriental" man or woman from these letters.

Montesquieu was not the first, and certainly not the last, to use the vehicle of an "Oriental" visitor to say something meaningful about Western society. The idea of using the voice of an other to point out shortcomings and blatant errors in one's own society is probably universal. The Greeks did it, as in Pseudo-Callisthene's dialogue between Alexander the Great and Indian wise men.[586] Medieval and Renaissance writers in Europe wrote poems and prose narratives that often included the voice of a foreign observer as an echo of the author. A number of admirers of Montesquieu's contribution shifted to other types of Oriental visitors. The most famous example is probably Oliver Goldsmith's 1760 *The Citizen of the World; or Letters from a Chinese Philosopher*, in which a traveler named Lien Chi Altangi writes back to China about the bizarre life he observes in England. At one point Goldsmith offers a scathing critique of English ethnocentrism in lumping Orientals together:

> Is it possible to bear the presumptions of these Islanders, when they pretend to instruct me in the ceremonies of China? They lay it down as a maxim, that every person who comes from thence must express himself in metaphor, swear by Alla, rail against wine, and behave, and talk, and write, like a Turk or Persian. They make no distinction between our elegant manners and the voluptuous barbarities of our Eastern neighbors.[587]

At the same time and place, and in the same spirit, Horace Walpole used his 1757 *A Letter from Xo Ho* to assail the political anarchy of England's Seven Years' War. On the other side of the Atlantic, Washington Irving's 1808 *Salmagundi* applied Oriental imagery, via Irving's experiential knowledge of Spain, to satirize American politicians.[588]

Orientals were frequently employed in the development of European drama. Thomas Kyd's 1588 *The Tragedye of Solyman and Perseda* may be the first English drama about a renegade Christian convert to Islam. The hero Basilisco "goes Turk" because the Ottomans better appreciate his skills as a soldier, a point that would hardly be lost on English infantry-men who at the time grumbled at their poor lot.[589] Christopher Marlowe's 1587–90 *Tamburlaine* stereotypes Islam as cover for the playwright's own antagonism to Christianity. In this adaptation of Machiavelli to the Elizabethan stage, the Oriental despot becomes "a superb means of masking the here with the there."[590] Yet, contra Said, Tamburlaine and the Muslim women in the play are represented in panhuman terms rather than as a Muslim/pagan other.[591] Pagan Tamburlaine, the saucy Tartar starring as the "Scourge of God," turns out to be a reformer at heart:

> Now, Casane, where's the Turkish Alcoran
> And all the heaps of superstitious books
> Found in the temples of that Mahomet,
> Whom I have thought a god? They shall be burnt.[592]

This is not a theological statement; Marlowe's target is hypocrisy, not heresy. The words were not bound to sit well with the local clerics, but they certainly made marks with like-minded social critics.

MANGLING AND DANGLING MUHAMMAD

> Mohammed no longer roams the Eastern world as a threat-ening, immoral debauchee; he sits quietly on his (admittedly prominent) portion of the Orientalist stage.
>
> —Edward Said, *Orientalism*

As a character of mythic proportions in the combustible mix of religion and politics, the Prophet Muhammad served well as a foil, a surrogate "fanatic" in criticism of both religious and political abuses in European society. Even while real Muslims were enemies or potential enemies to various European polities, the enemies nearer home, as Hourani puts it, included Protestants arguing against Catholics, freethinkers against dogmatic theologians, Anglicans against Deists, Quakers against Anglicans, and the like.[593] In the late-fourteenth-century allegory *Piers the Ploughman*, the English cleric William Langland dredges up the apologetic canard of Muhammad as a renegade Catholic priest, but it is clear that his real target is neither Muhammad nor the Saracens, who are praised for their monotheism, but the Catholic Church. The ultimate aim of Langland, suggests Dorothee Metlitzki, is to portray Muhammad as "a corrupted Christian abusing the power of the Holy Ghost."[594] Muhammad, we are told, after failing to become pope, went to Syria, where he fooled people into thinking that he was a messenger from God. This was accomplished with the ruse of a tame dove that was touted as a kind of avian Gabriel bringing the word of God, but in legendary fact was only a hungry bird snatching grain from his master's ear. "So," says Piers, "by means of a white dove and a little ingenuity, Mohammed led men and women into heresy, and in those countries learned and ignorant still follow his doctrines."[595] The Saracens who fall for this false Christian's message are dupes rather than savages. But Muslims are not Langland's audience. As his narrative unfolds, the equating of Muhammad with a reprobate Christian priest leads into a condemnation of the Catholic Church's failure to convert Saracens and Jews in a part of the world where the pope ordains hundreds of prelates. This account should not be read merely as a cleric's sounding off at a distant enemy, whether Saracen or papist. The Muhammad thus rendered is but a foil for "how English priests also feed a dove, whose name is Avarice, and behave so like Mohammed that no one knows what honesty means anymore."[596]

The most theatrical example of a text that uses Muhammad as foil is no doubt Voltaire's 1741 *Mahomet, ou le fanatisme*, a pre-Rushdie rendering of Islam's founder as the ultimate, fanatical tyrant.[597] Whether Muslims were to read this tragedy literally or take it at less than fa[r]ce value, this would seem yet another vitriolic attack from Christendom on their prophet. But Voltaire, needless to say, was no friend of the church, and not the kind of man who tolerated the widespread abuses only too visible in his own society. The entire satirical thrust of his interest in Islam is summed up well in a passage from the *prêtre* (priest) entry in his 1764 *Dictionnaire philosophique*:

> The Turks are wise in this respect. It is true that they journey to Mecca; but they do not allow the sherif of Mecca to buy permission not to observe ramadan, and to marry their cousins or their nieces. They are not judged by imans delegated by the sherif. They do not pay the last year of their revenues to the sherif. What things could be said about all this! Reader, it is for you to say them to yourself.[598]

The reader he addresses, of course, is any thinking reader, perhaps as rare a species in Voltaire's time as in the present.

As satire, *Mahomet* sets the story of Muhammad's conflict with Zopir, the ruler of Mecca, against the backdrop of Greek tragedy and Roman politics. Apart from names such as Omar and Seid, there is virtually nothing that creates an imagined Oriental landscape. The target of Voltaire's vicious wit here is hardly the real prophet of Islam; this was a tract intended neither to appease Jesuit missionaries to the Holy Land nor to convert Muslims through enlightened reason. Consider that Voltaire's own dearly held moral philosophy is expressed in the words of Omar, the duplicitous accomplice of Mahomet. "Mortal men are all equal," Omar chides the ruler of Mecca, "birth does not count—virtue alone determines the difference between them."[599] The ultimate evil, as stated unambiguously in the subtitle, is fanaticism. For this champion of reason, fanaticism is an almost incurable disease of epidemic proportions; the only remedy is "the spirit of free thought."[600] The only religion he exempts from serving as an inducement to fanaticism is the wisdom of another Oriental, Confucius. It is not the demons of the Orient that concern Voltaire, who finds the most detestable case of fanaticism to be the 1572 massacre of Saint Bartholomew, in which Parisians "cut in pieces their fellow citizens who did not go to mass."[601] The figure of Mahomet in this play has long been recognized as a foil for the abusers in his own time and place. Indeed, Mahomet is an only thinly disguised prototype of the Jesuit order's founder, St. Ignatius Loyola. That such an obvious trick could actually work is shown by the fact that Pope Benedict XIV, to whom the play is dedicated, naively accepted the honor of the play's dedication. Clerics closer to home, especially Parisian Jansenists, pressured the local authorities to force Voltaire into closing the play soon after its first staging in August 1742.[602]

Apart from the genre of Oriental tales, Western writers periodically valued the mores of various Oriental surrogates as moral lessons for the home front. Thus George of Hungary, a fifteenth-century Dominican imprisoned by the Ottomans for two decades, contrasted the modesty of Turkish women with the far less modest Christian women in his own society.[603] J. A. de Savigny, in the 1606 *Discours sur le choses turques*, contended that "those whom we call Turks are, for the most part, half-Christians and possibly closer to true Christianity than many among us."[604] Even the philosopher David Hume, certainly no lover of Islamic dogma, uses the example of a Muslim prisoner who says there is no God in Christianity—because he just ate Him in the Eucharist—as a "positive critique" of the absurdity of miracle-mongering Christian doctrine.[605] In his famous 1840 lecture *On Heroes, Hero-Worship, and the Heroic in History*, Thomas Carlyle contrasted the sincerity of Muslims with the laissez-faire faith of Victorian Christianity: "These Arabs believe their religion, and try to live by it," writes Carlyle. "No Christians, since the early ages, or only perhaps the English Puritans in modern times, have ever stood by their Faith as the Moslems do by theirs,—believing it wholly, fronting Time with it, and Eternity with it."[606] Carlyle adds, "Our current hypothesis about Mahomet, that he was a scheming Imposter, a Falsehood incarnate, that his religion is a mere mass of quackery and fatuity, begins really to be now untenable to any one."[607] In the realm of religious architecture, consider Owen Jones's 1835 lecture in which he praised the Muslim Alhambra palace as a site that reveled in the Creator more than the creature comforts in the churches of reformed Protestants.[608] Apologetic did at times give way to didactic.

SATIRE TO THE RESCUE

> Cynics like Mark Twain visited and wrote about it [the Orient].
>
> —EDWARD SAID, *ORIENTALISM*

> I bring you the stately nation named Christendom, returning, bedraggled, besmirched, and dishonored, from pirate raids in Kiao-Chou, Manchuria, South Africa, and the Philippines, with her soul full of meanness, her pocket full of boodle, and her mouth full of hypocrisies. Give her soap and towel, but hide the looking glass.
>
> —MARK TWAIN, "A GREETING FROM THE NINETEENTH TO THE TWENTIETH CENTURY," *NEW YORK HERALD*, DECEMBER 30, 1900

Renderings of the Oriental need not be sanctimonious or philosophical. One of the largely unplumbed resources of self-critique in the golden age of British imperialism was the pungitive caricaturing of officialdom in the pages of *Punch*. In 1845, the novelist William Thackeray contributed a parody of official British political correspondence to the Orient. A certain Viscount Pumicestone imperially instructs the English ambassador in Constantinople to inform the sultan that the British government requests that, in the spirit of civilized cooperation, he send back 499 of his 500 wives, convert to the Anglican faith, and add modern reforms such as the use of gaslights, trial by jury, weekly and Sunday newspapers, and Harvey sauce.[609] An official response is also recorded from the Sublime Porte's Grand Vizier Kabob Pasha. Some critics might dismiss the pages of a satirical rag as little more than humor for humor's sake, but it would be disingenuous to rule out the subversive effect of critique delivered within the colonial machine. In another example, an 1872 *Punch* political cartoon shows the Mikadoesque Japanese ambassador asking the archbishop of

Canterbury if religious rioters in the background are "heathen," to which the reverend archbishop replies that they are not heathen, but rather "our most Enthusiastic Religionists!"[610]

Having paid only limited attention to the American imagination of the Orient, Said thinks it safe in his analysis to ignore satirist Mark Twain, who is dismissed as a "cynic," a curious designation for the man who wrote one of the most widely read American travelogues of all time.[611] "Certainly, Mark Twain, like other nineteenth-century American travelers, never participated in the processes that rendered the East to the Western mind as re-presentation of the Orient in the same manner as the Holy Land travel narratives of Lamartine, Nerval, Thackeray, or the other French and English travelers Said describes," concludes Hilton Obenzinger after a romp through the raucous prose of the author guilty of punning *The Innocents Abroad*.[612] Twain shows little respect for the Orientalist travelers and biblical scholars who had prepared the Holy Land for the kind of beast he was paid to be, the modern tourist. His reader is invited on an excursion to the "real" Holy Land in expectation of the hallowed space where Jesus walked, but Twain chose to ride an ass. After detailing the squalor and misery in the real Palestine at the time, Twain remarks that Jesus might have come once, a long time ago when it looked like a Bible land, but would hardly want to come again and see the hypocrisy.[613]

There is little evidence of innocence in Twain's satirical rendering of stereotypes about non-Americans, whether Oriental or European. It is not hard to find quotes that perpetuate the worst kind of image of Arabs, Turks, and Muslims in Twain's no-holds-barred narrative. "The Damascenes are the ugliest, wickedest-looking villains we have seen," the humorist drawls as he enters Damascus.[614] Of course, he might have been describing Dodge City, which may very well be the model he had in mind. I am struck by the irony in Twain's discussion of riding tourist donkeys through the narrow streets of Damascus. Not only are the "men and women in strange Oriental costumes" knocked right and left and plowed through, but Twain and his party are so jostled and injured that Twain compares it to riding a Damascus "streetcar." Compare this to the imagined experience of Montesquieu's Rica, who is similarly pushed this way and that by carriages during his first days in Paris.[615]

It would be a mistake to simply laugh at Twain's iconoclastic humor and not recognize how his repetition of Oriental stereotypes serves more than one purpose, whether intentional or not. The Holy Land itinerary, as Obenzinger points out, is a backdrop for writing a narrative of mid-nineteenth-century post-bellum colonization of the American West. Bedouin Arabs become stand-ins for California's Digger Indians, and the Sea of Galilee drains straight into Lake Tahoe.[616] Yet, unlike most pilgrim narratives in search of a biblicized Orient, Twain's text reports current economic and political dilemmas among real Orientals. In doing so it spreads the blame for problems over the "damned human race" rather than pinning it on any singular racial or religious defect in Arabs, Turks, or any socially contrived group. The fanciful Arab on his desert steed is seen as a benighted tall tale; the Selim of romance turns out to be nothing but a pirate who never thinks of washing a horse's back.[617] Twain may start with the enmeshed East–West binary familiar to his readers, but the end result is a de-constricting of the stereotype in which it is not some mythologized Orient that is at fault but rather shared human nature.

"I claim the right to correct misstatements," says Twain as he gleefully takes to task earlier descriptions of the "beautiful" Sea of Galilee, a vista that has become in Twain's opinion "a scene of desolation and misery."[618] Far from recycling the textual wisdom of Orientalist discourse, Twain proceeds directly to the source of the problem in the Oriental travel genre:

> I am sure, from the tenor of books I have read, that many who have visited this land in years gone by were Presbyterians, and came seeking evidences in support of their particular creed; they found a Presbyterian Palestine, and they had already made up their minds to find no other, though possibly they did not know it, being blinded by their zeal. Others were Baptists, seeking Baptist evidences and a Baptist Palestine. Others were Catholics, Methodists, Episcopalians, seeking evidences endorsing their several creeds and a Catholic, a Methodist, an Episcopalian Palestine. Honest as these men's intentions may have been, they were full of partialities and prejudices, they entered the country with their verdicts already prepared, and they could no more write dispassionately and impartially about it than they could about their own wives and children. Our pilgrims have brought their verdicts with them.[619]

Although Twain does not set out to undermine the authority of an Orientalist establishment, nascent as it was, he consistently pans the penchant of writers, even sincere sinners like himself, to definitively render the other. For perspective, remember that Mark Twain wrote these words more than a decade before the deaths of Disraeli, Flaubert, Renan, and Burton, four authors Said discusses as paragons of the nineteenth-century Orientalist.

In *Tom Sawyer Abroad*, Twain offers a vivid critique of the kind of Orientalism that Said rightly views as a style for dominating the Orient. Ironically, this goes straight to the core of the contemporary political crisis over Palestine. The dialogue, as is often the case in Twain's homespun rendering, speaks for itself:

> "Huck Finn, do you mean to tell me you don't know what a crusade is?"
>
> "No," says I, "I don't. And I don't care to, nuther. I've lived till now and done without it, and had my health, too . . ."
>
> "A crusade is a war to recover the Holy Land from the paynim."
>
> "Which Holy Land?"
>
> "Why, *the* Holy Land—there ain't but one."
>
> "What do we want of it?"
>
> "Why, can't you understand? It's in the hands of the paynim, and it's our duty to take it away from them."
>
> "How did we come to let them git hold of it?"
>
> "We didn't come to let them git hold of it. They always had it."
>
> "Why Tom, then it must belong to them, don't it?"
>
> "Why, of course it does. Who said it didn't?"
>
> I studied over it, but couldn't seem to git at the right of it, no way. I says:
>
> "It's too many for me, Tom Sawyer. If I had a farm and it was mine, and another person wanted it, would it be right for him to—"
>
> "Oh shucks! you don't know enough to come in when it rains, Huck Finn. It ain't a farm, it's entirely different. You see, it's like this. They own the land, just the mere land, and that's all they do own; but it was our folks, our Jews and Christians, that made it holy, and so they haven't any business to be there defiling it. It's a shame. and we ought not to stand it a minute. We ought to march against them and take it away from them."
>
> "Why, it does seem to me it's the most mixed-up thing I ever see! Now, if I had a farm and another person—"
>
> "Don't I tell you it hasn't got anything to do with farm-

ing? Farming is business, just common low-down business; that's all it is, it's all you can say for it; but this is
higher, this is religious, and totally different."

"Religious to go and take the land away from people
that owns it?"

"Certainly; it's always been considered so."

Jim he shook his head, and says:

"Mars Tom, I reckon dey's a mistake about it somers—
dey mos' sholy is. I's religious myself, en I knows plenty
religious people, but I hain't run across none dat acts like
dat."[620]

Perhaps the most widely read twentieth-century version of the Oriental traveler as cultural critic is André Malroux's *La tentation de l'Occident*
(1926). In this updated correspondence, a fictitious Chinese visitor observes
that "at the core of European man, ruling the important movements of his
life, is a basic absurdity."[621] Malroux counterposes the letters from China
by a young Frenchman, given the timely name of A.D., and the Chinese Ling,
who is visiting the bookish culture of Europe. The French intellectual reflecting on the incessant materialism of his own society, speaks in despair of
Europe as a "great cemetery where only dead conquerors sleep. . . .Unsta-
ble image of myself," he confides, "I love you not at all."[622] "Go East, young
man" was the spirit he followed. The angst that A.D. cannot escape when
reflecting on what Western civilization has become is echoed—more Confucian than confused—in the willing-to-admire innocence of Ling:

> What then shall I say about these men of your race? I
> study them; I try hard to escape from books. I know that
> our translators, in their effort to make known to us the
> manners and morals of Europe as well as her literature,
> by selecting Balzac, Flaubert, the French naturalists, the
> early works of Goethe, the works of Tolstoy and Dos-
> toievski, by analyzing the genius of Baudelaire, have
> shown wisdom and great care. But aren't these excep-
> tional, even almost insane Christians, who scream and
> weep with anguish, from Emma Bovary to the Brothers
> Karamazof?[623]

For Malroux, both A.D. and Ling wrestle with the temptation of a Western
image that asserts itself as more advanced, yet is paradoxically lacking a
vitality that the "Orient" may be able to offer. But the notion of a unified

Orient is a chimera in this cross-cultural parable. "There is no China," confides Ling to his fellow seeker, "only a few élite Chinese."[624]

Malroux warrants only a one-sentence cameo appearance in *Orientalism*'s discussion of early-twentieth-century French concerns about "Oriental claims for political independence."[625] For Said these claims were only received as a civilizational challenge to "the West's spirit, knowledge, and imperium." A full-page quote from Sylvain Lévi, a French professor of Sanskrit and president of the Société Asiatique, is then produced to support the claim that the Orientalist "has no difficulty in connecting Orientalism with politics."[626] But what Said through one scholar's old-age reflections characterizes as the threat of Asian upheaval in a superior European civilization, Malroux presents as a fundamental problem in the soul of modern Western man. The conflicted sentiments of both Lévi and Malroux could better be understood by considering the impact of Pierre Loti's 1902 *Les derniers jours de Pekin*, a popular French text that had gone through fifty printings by 1914. Loti, who is cavalierly dismissed by Said as a minor writer of exotic fiction that furthered the racial division of East and West,[627] wrote from his own experience in China as it was forced to cope with the intrusion of Western civilization. Jonathan Spence argues that Loti speaks of the "sense of loss that came from knowing too much about China, from having penetrated too deeply into a hitherto forbidden terrain, now powerless to resist the assaults of a Western sensibility."[628] Given that all three authors operated in the existing context of French colonies in Asia, it is hard to imagine how they could write anything that was not in some sense about political realities. It is certainly unfair to assume that the "expressed humanism" of someone concerned about the deleterious effect of French colonization on real Orientals must be disingenous simply because that person wrote about the East from the West.[629]

The satirical splash of the Oriental as foreign observer need not be a mirror for foibles. One of its more calculated-to-be-ingenious applications in the twentieth century serves both to praise the contributions of Islamic mathematical science and inspire students in Western schoolrooms to appreciate the potential delight of mathematical reasoning. This is Júlio César de Mello e Souza's 1972 *Homem que calculava*, a eulo-algebraic tale about Beremiz Samir, the "Man Who Counted."[630] Rising from Persian shepherdhood to eventually match arithmetic wits with the pedantic savants of the caliph's court, Beremiz solves a number of conundrums not to keep his head but to turn heads, especially that of the caliph's daughter. In the process, Islam is portrayed as a rational and tolerant religion, and the scientific insights from the wider Orient are recognized as transcending all culturally imposed boundaries. Yet in Said's totalizing definition, even de Mello e Souza, a Brazilian mathematician clearly attracted by the allure of Oriental tales, must be numbered among the Orientalists.

Curiously, one well-paved road, that of the French literary critic Roland Barthes, is not taken by Said in *Orientalism*. Apart from a brief appearance as a bit player in which Said cites *Mythologies*, on the power of myth to ceaselessly invent itself,[631] Barthes is literally although not literarily absent in the text. There is no sign of *L'empire des signes*, a reflective Oriental tale from 1970 that imagines "Japan" quite consciously as a fictive entity. Rather than treating the real Japan as symbolic of something else, Barthes says he is seeking the "very fissure of the symbolic," exemplifed in the Zen concept of *mu* (emptiness) as that which is exempt from meaning yet creates all meaning.[632] Having made a brief visit to Japan, Barthes writes candidly as someone who does not understand the language and who is feeling his Occidentalness jarred. He tries to appreciate in print the mundane elements of being Japanese that he cannot seem to grasp: chopsticks, sukiyaki, pachinko slot machines, a city map, Sumo wrestlers, Bunraku dolls, a transvestite, calligraphy, bowing, haiku poetry, the eyelid, and *Zengakuren* riots. As Dennis Porter observes, this innovative text avoids "Orientalism" as Said would have it because Japan is not presented as an essence "but as a difference that merely serves to throw light on the peculiar ideology of the sign to which we cling in the West."[633]

As a scholar who lived in and wrote about Morocco as well as Japan, Roland Barthes should be included in a Saidian who's who of Orientalists. Diana Knight, reflecting on Barthes's homoerotic experiences in Morocco, asks, with more than a modicum of intrigue, "Does Barthes himself become an Orientalist exhibit for analysis?"[634] But it would be perverse to lump Barthes with Renan, Lewis, or even Flaubert as yet another bright mind warped by a latent discourse of domination. Barthes's own words challenge Orientalism-as-usual almost a decade before *Orientalism* appeared:

> Hence Orient and Occident cannot be taken here as "realities" to be compared and contrasted historically, philosophically, culturally, politically. I am not lovingly gazing toward an Oriental essence—to me the Orient is a matter of indifference, merely providing a reserve of features whose manipulations—whose invented interplay—allows me to "entertain" the idea of an unheard-of symbolic system, one altogether detached from our own. What can be

addressed, in the consideration of the Orient, are not other symbols, another metaphysics, another wisdom (though the latter might appear thoroughly desirable); it is the possibility of a difference, of a mutation, of a revolution in the propriety of symbolic systems.[635]

Barthes was not writing a book about Japan, and certainly not a travelogue in the accepted sense. It was not an Oriental other that mattered, but the very notion of what it means to be othered in words. Said as polemicist fails to grasp this point, perhaps because his passionately personal deconstruction of Orientalist discourse would not mesh with a fellow critic's book that concludes that "there is nothing to grasp."[636]

IV A Novel Argument out of Blurred Genres

> But, one might ask, why give so much emphasis to novels, and
> to England?
>
> —EDWARD SAID, *CULTURE AND IMPERIALISM*

> Said does not read literary texts—he reads into them; and his
> misinterpretation of works by Forster, Orwell, and T. E. Lawrence
> inspires a profound mistrust of his method.
>
> —JEFFREY MYERS, "UNDER WESTERN EYES"[637]

think that Said's question is important enough that it needs a response, as the caustic rejoinder of Jeffrey Myers indicates. The novel is clearly the literary form Said knows best and loves dearest. That reading novels, especially by canonical authors, could give rise to his textual attitude about history is thus no surprise; that it should pass for historical interpretation is by no means proven in *Orientalism* or later books. My point is not to disparage literary criticism, but to challenge Said's emphasis on fiction in trying to prove how academic Orientalists get their facts wrong.[638] Contemporary literary studies similar to the liberated analysis of religious myth have flourished because no single reading can be hegemonically established as definitive. Debating truth claims thus becomes a philosophical exercise of ways one might read a passage in order to probe possibilities. To the extent that history should be read through probabilities, backed by rigorous and systematic methods of sorting out the less probable, the novel would seem an unlikely place to establish what happened, especially—contrapuntally between the lines—in a given historical context.[639] Just as there really is an "Orient" independent of the imagined fantasies of Orientalists, so there must be a continual flow of historical events regardless of whether they are documented, merely re-membered, or even dis-membered through re-presentation of the past. To bring it down to earth, Said hardly needs to re-cite an exclusion in *Mansfield Park* to demonstrate the complicity inherent in imperialist exploitation of a sugar plantation.

A Novel Reading of Counterpoint

> The "departmental view" of the world that Said attributes to the novel aligns fiction too closely with the agendas of the state, as if fiction were a government department charged with the construction of tendentious geopolitical imaginings that exalt Britain and marginalize the rest.
>
> —James Buzard, *Disorienting Fiction: The Autoethnographic Work of Nineteenth-Century British Novels*

Said counterimposes upon the discourse he calls Orientalism the reading of the fiction genre as fueling imperialism. In *Culture and Imperialism*, the novel as the mega-text of imperialism replaces the more mundane historical sources of treaties, archives, and memoirs. "Without empire," claims the critic of novels, ". . . there is no European novel as we know it, and indeed, if we study the impulses giving rise to it, we shall see the far from accidental convergence between the patterns of narrative authority constitutive of the novel on the one hand, and, on the other, a complex ideological configuration underlying the tendency to imperialism."[640] This is, as John Sutherland points out, a "sweeping proposition."[641] Said positions the "novel" as both a product of empire and a productive shaping of imperialist ambitions. As a product, the novel understandably rises from a bourgeois public of authors who have the leisure to write and readers who have the education and time to read. For Said it is enough that the novel, "as a cultural artefact of bourgeois society, and imperialism are unthinkable without each other."[642] If this only means that the novel and imperialism "fortified each other" so much that it is impossible "to read one without in some way dealing with the other,"[643] then we are only being asked to admit that fiction is not divorced from social context and that the study of history can be informed by contemporary fictional narratives. Few historians would doubt this in the abstract. The problem is that Said goes well beyond the abstract without making an adequate concrete case for his chosen particulars.

Said appeals to establishment literary texts to explain the origin of the canon: "By the 1840s the English novel had achieved eminence as the aesthetic form and as a major intellectual voice, so to speak, in English society."[644] On closer inspection, this Defoe-defying claim follows from the fact that Jane Austen and George Eliot, among others, were then writing texts that later critics have relentlessly lauded as aesthetic genius. For the record, Said goes on in *Orientalism* to cite novels (*Adventures of Hajji-Baba of Ispahan, Bouvard et Pécuchet, Les Chimères, Daniel Deronda, Don Quixote, The Guermantes Way, Heart of Darkness, Louis Lambert, Middlemarch, Les Orientales, A Passage to India, La Peau de Chagrin, Salammbô, The Talisman, Tancred, Victory*), plays (*The Bacchae, The Persians, Mahomet, Othello*), epics (*The Arabian Nights, Chanson de Roland*), poetry (*The Divine Comedy, Don Juan, El Cantar del Mio Cid*, the *Rubaiyat of Omar Khayyam, Westöstlicher Diwan*), and operas (*The Abduction from the Seraglio*, the *Magic Flute*), among other imagined texts.

The issue is not, or certainly should not be, whether these authors were creating great literary works, but the extent to which such texts were actively shaping imperialism rather than reflecting personal spins on the obvious empireness the authors and their readers at the time experienced by default. Did the British admiralty—at least before Gilbert and Sullivan— need to be inspired by subliminal readings of *Mansfield Park* before setting sail? Does the mere fact that novels were being written and read prove that they were indispensible to the imperial ambitions of the British Crown abroad? If Said is right about the Anglo-French attitude to the Orient, how had England, Spain, Portugal, and France colonized the New World without requisite novels as an aid to conquest? Were all novels equally complicitous in abetting imperial ambition? A great deal of Western literature, even more so at the vulgar level of dime novels and tabloid prose ignored by Said, has been unflattering to Muslims, Arabs, and virtually all Orientals. But did every writer of fiction necessarily add to the friction between East and West?

. The point has come to provide counterpoint. In *Culture and Imperialism* Said points to contrapuntal reading as a critical lens for reading between the lines to note what is revealingly absent. There is a considerable discussion of this literary coinage with widely different views on what a contrapuntal criticism could mean.[645] The aim is to get underneath the skin of the text, to expose the conscious or unconscious choice of the author by searching for what is missing and at the same time overwhelmingly unrepresented by its absence. This is not simply another reading of the text, but another way of reading. "By looking at the different experiences contrapuntally, as making up a set of what I call intertwined and overlapping histories," states Said, "I shall try to formulate an alternative both to a politics of blame and to the even more destructive politics of confrontation and hostility."[646] Who could fault such a goal? Said wants the reader to join with him in reading with a purpose. That purpose, overtly stated, takes both imperialism and resistance into account "by extending our reading of the texts to include what was once forcibly excluded."[647] Nowhere does Said elaborate a concise methodology for such reading-into; he develops his reading by forcing an example, such as why "a colonial sugar plantation is seen as important to the process of maintaining a particular style of life in England."[648]

Even though Said continually cautions the critic to read completely through novels like *Mansfield Park* and not just select what one wants to see, he seems not to have done this alongside his contra-punting of Austen's text. Susan Fraiman argues that Said does not give a close reading of *Mansfield Park*, that he sacrifices the "complexity" of the text and thus misses Austen's use of irony.[649] The problem starts with Said's assumption that this particular novel must be a synecdoche of the author's imperial culture, and is compounded by the insinuation that British colonialist culture was, perhaps not in Arnoldian terms, far too sugar-coated. The most telling note in Said's contrapuntal reading is that Austen's imagined English estate must have been sustained by exploited slaves in England's colony. "Sir Thomas's property in the Caribbean would have to be a sugar plantation maintained by slave labor (not abolished until the 1830s)," claims Said, adding that "these are not dead historical facts but, as Austen certainly knew, evident historical realities."[650] The British sweet tooth that legitimized slave labor in Jamaica is indeed a reprehensible historical reality, one that Austen might have found as wrong as do her modern-day readers. But Said's reading simply fills in a lacuna he thinks significant with a possibility he finds relevant on Whiggishly modern moral grounds. To the previously unasked question—"Why does Austen neglect to mention what kind of plantation Thomas Bertram owned?"—Said draws on a shared sense of outrage at colonial-era slavery to imply that Austen was trying to hide an unpleasant element of her own society. Ironically, Said's Orientalist extraordinaire, Sir William Jones, need not be read contrapuntally, given that he stated in a 1780 speech that it would be better not to eat any sugar "than rob one human creature of those external rights, of which no law upon earth can justly deprive them."[651] Did the archetypical Orientalist have a keener moral sense than the canonized novelist?

Yet—and this is the fundamental flaw in Said's approach—any number of other readings can answer the same open-ended question. For one, Thomas Bertram might have been that rare gentleman who in fiction owned a different kind of plantation, at least in Austen's mind. He may have been a benevolent master who would eventually decide under moral conviction to free all his slaves and become an abolitionist. Or, even if he ran a sugar plantation with an iron fist and closely shackled slave labor, the actual operation of his English estate may not have required such input from abroad. In an archival study of estate records, Trevor Lloyd concludes that recorded practices at the time indicate that Said is wrong in assuming there must have been an input of plantation profits.[652] As George Wilson points out in critiquing the logic of contrapuntal reading, any particular reading of significance on the basis of what is not said "is less the result of sensitive but responsible attention to the text and more the product of an adamantly insisted upon outside agenda."[653] Said's agenda is to give voice to the resistance he insists needs to be represented.

As a paradigmatic case for contrapuntal reading, the *Mansfield Park* example turns negative evidence into circumstantial evidence. In the process, Austen as author is impugned for ignoring or, even worse, trying to cover up a facet of colonial policy she did not devise, could not change, and perhaps did not know very well. If Said is really concerned about the "truth" of this reading, would it not make sense to let Austen's corpus speak in its own defense? Does she make a habit of soft-pedalling the unpleasant aspects of her own society? What about characters in her novels who were abolitionists? Said makes no attempt to see if this is a pattern in her other, far more widely read novels. Nor does Said consider it relevant that Austen finds fault with Bertram for his harsh ways of dealing with his own family. George Wilson notes that such critique of this male character within the domestic sphere might in a contrapuntal sense extend to his undiscussed actions in Jamaica; thus *Mansfield Park* may be "a very early exemplar of an anticolonial novel."[654] A historian might have considered looking at the documentation about the author's views on abolition before assuming malicious or unconscious intent.[655] Is the English author's crime not being Harriet Beecher Stowe? As Susan Fraiman complains about Said, "His inattention to Austen's feminist critique of authority is both the logical result and an ideological cognate of his failing, similarly, to remark upon the last two decades of intensive feminist commentary on this writer."[656] Austen, the intentional female author, is essentially raked over the postcolonial coals by an indignant male critic.

The inspiration for reading against the grain comes from a major passion of Said's: the harmony that is music to his Western-tuned ears. This is Bach rather than Stravinsky, a fugue to be intellectually admired rather than a rite of spring to be obsessively danced:

> In the counterpoint of Western classical music, various themes play off one another, with only a provisional privilege being given to any particular one; yet in the resulting polyphony there is concert and order, an organized interplay that derives from the themes, not from a rigorous melodic or formal principle outside the work.[657]

This metaphor, for surely that is its aesthetic appeal to the reader, is revealing about Said's own ethnocentric intellectualism. Disparate parts of equal value, potentially clashing sounds brought under control: all of this results from simply allowing themes to play with and around each other rather than privileging a particular set of notes. The power here is that such music seems to be natural, as though the notes were meant to play off each other for a grand purpose. This is of course the genius of Bach, but it highlights a major flaw in the comparison. The notes are arranged according to a rigid pattern composed in an intentional act, but the polyphony results only because of the composer's acumen and the performer's skill. More significantly, and this is a point Said must ignore, the order is in the ear of the listener. Play Bach in an Amazon village, and the locals will scarcely be able to appreciate the cacophony over their alarm at such unfamiliar sounds.

There is, apart from the virtuosity of style, nothing to read between the lines of a fugue. Said notes that Glenn Gould has recorded markedly different performances of Bach's "Goldberg Variations." However, Gould succeeds by applying his style to the score, not by filling in musical notes that Bach for whatever reason failed to include.[658] Play it creatively and with feeling, but do not substitute notes and expect it to be recognized as the same piece. Imagining what notes Bach left out is not, I think, what Said is thinking about in a concert hall. But the inappropriate application of a musical metaphor to a literary text demands just such an imagining when Said adds notes of resistance that are not in the original score. I suggest that Said "Bachs" himself into a corner by attempting to read Austen for what she appears to choose not to write.

Shifting to a literary form, it is possible to approach a given novel or poem as equally polyphonous, a capable combination of themes and characters in a plot that can somehow merge contrasts into a sensed unity. This is for many literary critics the genius of Jane Austen or Joseph Conrad. It can also be said of a "great" work of art, such as da Vinci's *Mona*

Lisa, which captures a scene with more nuance than the reality it theoretically depicts. The ability to make the artificial, contrived arrangement seem natural is key to such aesthetic appreciation. In no sense is this natural or eternally fixed. An audience that enjoys the Brandenberg Concertos can move on to Philip Glass; the old guard does not rule out the avant-garde.

Said's fascination with certain forms of the Western musical canon could by his own terms be read back against him contrapuntally. Why does he not give equal weight to the musical forms of the real Orient? What does it mean that a book on *Culture and Imperialism* by a native Arab who once lived in Egypt privileges the Italian composer Giuseppe Verdi over the Egyptian singer Umm Kulthum? When Said, in "Homage to a Bellydancer," finally does turn to Umm Kulthum, this is only as a setup for the cinematic idol of his youth, Tahia Carioca. Said is indignant that Tahia, the "tawny seductress" of old Egyptian films, lowers herself from a *danse du ventre* diva to a political farce in becoming "a 220–pound swaggering bull."[659] When he finally has an opportunity to meet the film and stage star, his representation of the encounter revolves around his condescending query: "How many times have you been married, Tahia?" This seems a rather "Orientalist" form of homage.

If novel narratives are always encrypted with political nuance, so must be the metaphors and rhetorical tropes employed by those who critique novels. Rhetorically, Said's contrapuntal reading fades into an unfinished symphony when he moves from unwritten text to imperialist culture:

> In an important sense, we are dealing with the formation of cultural identities understood not as essentializations (although part of their enduring appeal is that they seem and are considered to be like essentializations) but as contrapuntal ensembles, for it is the case that no identity can ever exist by itself and without an array of opposites, negatives, oppositions: Greeks always require barbarians, and Europeans Africans, Orientals, etc.[660]

If the purpose of counterpoint is to play off specific notes to produce a pleasant harmony, then the notion of a "contrapuntal ensemble" would seem to mix metaphors, replacing the score or text with the ensemble of performers who would presumably only play the notes assigned them. But Said shifts here from music to language. The "identity" he refers to is semiotic rather than sonorous, a word to be defined rather than a note to be heard. Greeks "require" barbarians in the sense that Greeks distinguished those who spoke proper Greek from those who did not. Such barbarians may have come to function as generically inferior others, but there were other ways to invent such others. In the strict sense, Europeans did not require Africans, they acquired them just as they did American "Indians" and even other Europeans. So-called Europeans did not intrinsically need either Africans or Orientals, because until relatively recently there was no need for a specific European identity. Portuguese slavers took advantage of Africans because they had the opportunity and the means, not in order to create some essentialized and abstract identity.

If Said is only saying that any particular ethnic or language group's identity demands someone else to consider inferior or dominate, then this is hardly a novel reading, nor is there anything contrapuntal about the common dichotomization of self and other. Said's ultimate goal for contrapuntal criticism is not to harmonize the diversity inherent in human culture but to map the underlying "cultural topography" in formerly imperialist metropolitan cultures such as those of Britain, France, and the United States.[661] What starts out as an attempt to write in what the author of a text left out purposefully or not ends up as a project to highlight ambiguous "structures of attitude and reference." Rub hard enough on a novel written during the zenith of British colonization and that structure magically reappears as the attitudes and references that offend the contemporary critic. Whether or not the author herself was complicit in that offense does not really matter; it is only the text that survives and only the text that can be read for meaning.

Said fixates on texts that celebrate imperialism, such as Kipling's *Kim*, a white man's novel oozing with colonialist self-congratulation. In his own reading of *Kim*, Said in *Culture and Imperialism* refers more than once to the fact that this late-nineteenth-century novel was preceded by Sir Walter Scott and others.[662] In *Orientalism*, the novelist Scott is included in a number of Saidian lineups,[663] but appears as part of his overall argument only in a cameo role to show how a prominent author with no expertise on Islam writes about the Crusades with "the airy condescension of damning a whole people," i.e., the Saracens, while praising Saladin as the lone good Saracen.[664] From one brief measure of dialogue in one novel, Said attempts to establish how Scott succumbs to the latent Orientalist trope that an individual Oriental is "first an Oriental, second a human being, and last again an Oriental."[665] What if we apply this scenario to Scott's *Ivanhoe*, a work addressing English anti-Semitic sentiment against the generalized Oriental Jew? What is the political implication of Rebecca's refusal to convert to Christianity and take advantage, as Rowena naively suggests, of her nursing of Ivanhoe, for which "she can have nothing to fear in England, where Saxon and Norman will contend who shall do her honour"?[666] Is Rebecca, in the Scottish author's eyes, not here a human first and a Jewess second, and at last a fine specimen of humanity? I note Scott's closing irony that Rebecca as a Jewess chooses to be "secure of peace and protection" under the Muslim King of Granada. If not Scott, who then speaks through Rebecca in saying that "the people of England are a fierce race, quarreling ever with their neighbors or among themselves, and ready to plunge the sword into the bowels of each other"? Is this novel kin to *Kim*?

Authors do not only write novels, but also provide other avenues of fiction and personal memoirs. In *Ivanhoe*'s satirical dedicatory epistle to the Rev. Dr. Jonas Dryasdust, F.A.S., Scott gives his clan venue its due venting on the person of an English reader. Regarding the Englishman, Scott's alter-ego prologuist confides:

> If you describe to him a set of wild manners, and a state of primitive society existing in the Highlands of Scotland, he is much disposed to acquiesce in the truth of what is asserted. And reason good. If he be of the ordinary class of readers, he has either never seen those remote districts at all, or he has wandered through those desolate regions in the course of a summer tour, eating bad dinners, sleeping on truckle beds, stalking from desolation to desolation, and fully prepared to believe the strangest things that could be told him of a people, wild and extravagant enough to be attached to scenery so extraordinary. But the same worthy person, when placed in his own snug parlor, and surrounded by all the comforts of an Englishman's fireside, is not half so much disposed to believe that his own ancestors led a very different life from himself; that the shattered tower, which now forms a vista from his window, once held a baron who would have hung him up at his own door without any form of trial; that the hinds, by whom his little pet farm is managed, a few centuries ago would have been his slaves; and that the complete influence of feudal tyranny once extended over the neighboring village, where the attorney is now a man of more importance than the lord of the manor.[667]

As vintage Scott, certainly as good a cropping of his prose as that provided by Said, how exactly is imperialism abetted here?

A rather monstrous omission from Said's literary allusions is Mary Shelley's *Frankenstein* (1818), an epic novel created just as a more imperialist-minded Orientalism was getting underway. Joseph Lew argues that this book is "obsessed with the impact of Oriental texts upon western minds."[668] Victor Frankenstein reads the *Arabian Nights*, Clerval aspires to be an Orientalist, a Turkish merchant is unjustly imprisoned in Paris, and his daughter Safie dreams of marrying a Christian in Europe rather than returning to the walls of the harem. It would seem an ideal target for Said's agenda. But, argues Lew, *Frankenstein* should be read as an anti-imperialist text, a critique of the system that would later use Orientalist scholarship in the interest of empire. In an intriguing comparison of Said's depiction of Orientalism with Shelley's characterization of Frankenstein, Lew suggests that both have no "true" other.[669] Even the "mixed Oriental" marriage of Safie to a Frenchman is more a statement of the miscarriage of Western justice than of Turkish despotism. "Having peeled back layer after narrative layer," comments Lew, "we find only the bourgeois nuclear family in Oriental drag."[670]

DISRAELI: A MATTER OF DISTASTE

> The failure of Disraeli's *Tancred* can easily be ascribed to its author's perhaps over-developed knowledge of Oriental politics and the British establishment's network of interests.
>
> —EDWARD SAID, *ORIENTALISM*

> We think better of Europe than to suppose it rotten at the core and hastening to decay. We cannot think sufficiently well of the nations of the East to suppose them now the living fountains of all that is consolatory and good in life, the pure and immaculate possessors of celestial privileges and divine prerogatives.
>
> —REVIEW OF *TANCRED* IN *THE TIMES*, APRIL 2, 1847[671]

If epigraphs are meant to punctuate beginnings, then Said's choice of a quote from Benjamin Disraeli's *Tancred* (1847) is worth examining in detail. "When Disraeli said in his novel *Tancred* that the East was a career," explains Said, "he meant that to be interested in the East was something bright young Westerners would find to be an all-consuming passion; he should not be interpreted as saying that the East was only a career for Westerners."[672] Rhetorical license aside, this passage is not a direct quote from the lips of the future British Prime Minister Disraeli, but part of the dialogue that the author Disraeli creates for a certain Mr. Coningsby in casual dinner conversation about young Tancred, the future Lord Montacute. Tancred, the hero of the story, had decided to make a pilgrimage to the Holy Land as a spiritual quest, partly as a nostalgic following in the steps of his crusading ancestors, and partly because of his dissatisfaction with the way England was governed at the time. As Said spins it, Tancred went east with a "pilgrim's somewhat capricious impulses," characterized in *Orientalism* as an "ingenuous desire to go to Jerusalem."[673]

Poor Tancred, literary figure that he is, is allowed no voice in *Orientalism*. Resurrecting that voice in the best contrapuntal sense suggests that Said has not probed the author's intent as expressed in the words of his protagonist. In the novel we first learn of Tancred's desire to go east in a dialogue with his father. Tancred makes it clear to his surprised father that he does not wish to enter Parliament in large part because he is disillusioned by the "moral deterioration" of his age. Citing an impulse he believes came from above, Tancred tells his father he must travel:

> "I wish, indeed, to leave England; I wish to make an expedition; a progress to a particular point; without wandering, without any intervening residence. In a word, it is the Holy Land that occupies my thought, and I propose to make a pilgrimage to the sepulchre of my Saviour."[674]

Tancred's father reminds him that their estate had sent forth a crusader knight some six centuries earlier. The elder duke's response is stoic, but the impact on Tancred's mother is devastating:

> "And it ends in this!" exclaimed the duchess. "The Holy Land! Why, if he even reach it, the climate is certain death. The curse of the Almighty, for more than eighteen centuries, has been on that land. Every year it has become more sterile, more savage, more unwholesome, and more unearthly. It is the abomination of desolation. And now my son is to go there! Oh! he is lost to us for ever!"[675]

After this outburst the duke promises not to sanction such a trip and resolves to consult one of Tancred's tutors at Oxford, a certain Mr. Bernard. After praising his student as intelligent and morally immaculate, Bernard avers that Tancred's religious motives are "of no light and equivocal character."[676] A subsequent interview between Tancred and the local bishop results in the bishop declaring the young man a "visionary."[677] Then the matter is taken to a man of this world, Lord Eskdale, who suggests a practical way to seduce Tancred out of his folly. The plan is simple enough: demand that the trip be made in a private yacht that will take a year to build. In the meantime Tancred will have changed his mind and start to enjoy the benefits that his wealth and station provide him. To create that change of mind, Tancred is convinced to frequent the social circuit, in the hope that the young man will fall in love and have the matter end on a romantic note.

Romance follows soon after, with young Tancred much admiring the Lady Constance Rawleigh, who plots to capture his heart and thereby stop the rest of his body from making a foolhardy trip. Her plan is summed up by the narrator:

> "Why should Tancred go to Jerusalem? What does it signify to him whether there be religious truth or political justice? He has youth, beauty, rank, wealth, power, and all in excess. He has a mind that can comprehend their importance and appreciate their advantages. What more does he require? Unreasonable boy! And if he reach Jerusalem, why should he find religious truth and political justice there? He can read of it in the travelling books, written by young gentlemen, with the best letters of introduction to their consuls. They tell us what it is, a third-rate city in a stony wilderness. . . . A mother's tear may be disregarded, but the sigh of a mistress has changed the most obdurate."[678]

Yet in this case the sigh of the well-read but far too liberal Lady Constance does not have effect. Soon there are the tears of a second paramour, Lady Bertie, with whom Tancred falls madly but briefly in love. When he discovers that this second lady is "the most inveterate female gambler in Europe," he sails away; the remainder of *Tancred* takes place in Syria and Palestine.

Was this trip, as Said implies, a career move for young Tancred? Did Disraeli design an Orientalist, or is the accusation really that Disraeli himself must be an Orientalist? The quote worthy of *Orientalism*'s second epigraph appears in a casual conversation at a dinner party between Lord Henry and his brother-in-law, Mr. Coningsby. Lord Henry has just returned from an unsuccessful parliamentary vote. The conversation turns to Tancred:

> "I have been talking with Montacute," whispered Lord Henry to Coningsby, who was seated next to him. "Wonderful fellow! You can conceive nothing richer! Very wild,

but all the right ideas; exaggerated of course. You must get hold of him after dinner."

"But they say he is going to Jerusalem."

"But he will return."

"I do not know that; even Napoleon regretted that he had ever re-crossed the Mediterranean. The East is a career."[679]

From the perspective of Tancred's family and friends this was anything but a desirable career trajectory. Disraeli goes to great lengths to show how Tancred's pilgrimage for spiritual and political regeneration in the Holy Land was not approved by those around him. Multiple readings are possible, but Coningsby's remarks here warn that this trip could destroy Tancred. The link to Napoleon, which ironically Said does not mention, makes it clear Coningsby's concern was with the futility of surviving the real Orient, not the sensational dreams of multiple *Arabian Nights*.

Tancred's own words indicate that he takes his pilgrimage seriously, but they also express a major theme in Disraeli's criticism of English society at the time. "'Then,' says Tancred, with animation, 'seeing how things are, that I am born in an age and in a country divided between infidelity on one side and an anarchy of creeds on the other; with none competent to guide me, yet feeling that I must believe, for I hold that duty cannot exist without faith,'" the young lord resolves to visit the Holy Sepulcher.[680] Once in the Holy Land, Tancred ascends to the top of Mount Sinai, where he finds two ruins, a church and a mosque. Here the pilgrim prays, "O Lord God of Israel, Creator of the Universe, ineffable Jehovah! a child of Christendom, I come to thine ancient Arabian altars to pour forth the heart of tortured Europe. Why art thou silent?"[681] In the vision that follows, the Angel of Arabia warns Tancred that brooding Europe is "in the throes of a great birth" but is now miserable because it has turned its back on the sovereign God. The message from on high is that humans need to overcome their racism and follow a doctrine of "theocratic equality." In short, Jews and Christians should recognize what they have in common. To achieve the purity of mind necessary to pursue such doctrine, Tancred must return to the desert, the cradle of his own faith.

In Said's reading, Disraeli is of the same fabric as Renan. We are told that *Tancred* is a novel "steeped in racial and geographical platitudes" in which "everything is a matter of race."[682] The proof given for this is merely an allusion to sentiments expressed by certain characters in the novel. *Tancred* may not be an abolitionist tract, but it is a serious distortion to imply that it does not rise above the level of racist diatribe. In a 1997 interview Said accuses Disraeli of asking, "Arabs, what are they?" and then answering "They're just Jews on horseback."[683] This paraphrase of a line in *Tancred* is earlier cited in *Orientalism* without providing the context.[684] In the novel, these are the words of Baroni, an Italian attendant of Besso, a Jewish merchant to whom Tancred takes a letter of credit. Baroni makes this comment after Tancred expresses surprise that the tribesmen who kidnapped him followed the laws of Moses. Throughout the novel Disraeli is bitterly critical of the kind of anti-Semitic remarks he has Baroni utter here. The words are spoken by one character in the novel, not by Disraeli as narrator. There is bitter irony in Said's failure to mention either the lack of antagonism in Disraeli's writings about Islam or the biting critique given in *Tancred* of European anti-Semitism. Where is the Renanesque racism in the following?

> Conceive a being born and bred in the Judenstrasse of Hamburg or Frankfurt, or rather in the purlieus of Houndsditch or Minories, born to hereditary insult, without any education, apparently without a circumstance that can develop the slightest taste, or cherish the least sentiment for the beautiful, living amid fogs and filth, never treated with kindness, seldom with justice, occupied with the meanest, if not the vilest, toil, bargaining for frippery, speculating in usury, existing forever under the concurrent influence of degrading causes which would have worn out, long ago, any race that was not of the unmixed blood of Caucasus, and did not adhere to the laws of Moses; conceive such a being, an object to you of prejudice, dislike, disgust, perhaps hatred.[685]

The passage concludes with a vulgar dialogue between two "respectable" Anglo-Saxons passing by a Jewish household on the Feast of Tabernacles:

> "I say, Buggins, what's that row?" "Oh! it's those accursed Jews! we've a lot of 'em here. It is one of their horrible feasts. The Lord Mayor ought to interfere. However, things are not so bad as they used to be: they used to crucify little boys at these hullabaloos, but now they only eat sausages made of stinking pork." "To be sure," replies his companion, "we all make progress."

It is worth noting that Disraeli, a second-generation convert from Judaism, supported the idea of a Jewish homeland in Palestine. During his life he was a constant target of anti-Semitic attacks, especially in the pages of *Punch*, but also in respectable papers such as *The Times*.[686] A key twist in the plot of the novel has the hero Tancred fall in love with the Jewess Eva, whom he would not be allowed to carry home to England as a bride under English law.[687] Does Said think Disraeli would approve of such overt racist practices in his own country?

It is hard to read *Tancred* and not appreciate the wry commentary on the vanity of utilitarian social values and Whig politics in England at the time.[688] Not only was a yacht to be built for the would-be pilgrim, but it would be commanded by an officer of the royal navy and crewed by an expedition of three English gentleman, as well as servants directed by a "trusty foreigner accustomed to the East." The first part of *Tancred* glows with criticism of English society and politics. "England is the only country which enjoys the unspeakable advantage of being thus regularly, promptly, and accurately furnished with catalogues of those favoured beings who are deemed qualified to enter the houses of the great," Disraeli writes with none too subtle sarcasm of the high society pages in the English press.[689] Disraeli is at his best in lampooning the aristocrats who simply could not fathom Tancred's motives. A brilliant example of this is in the Mesdemoiselles de Laurella, fashionable young ladies who had spent a year in school at Marseilles. "This had quite turned their heads; they had come back with a contempt for Syria, the bitterness of which was only veiled by the high style of European nonchalance, of which they had a supreme command, and which is, perhaps our only match for Eastern repose."[690]

Disraeli continues his digs at the haughty demeaner of aristocracy in the description of those serving in the real Orient. At times the level of self-critique is acute. Consider the dialogue between two Englishmen settling down to dine on roast gazelle under a Syrian sky:

> "And the most curious thing," said Freeman to Trueman, as they established themselves under a pine tree, with an ample portion of roast meat and armed with their traveling knives and forks, "and the most curious thing is, that they say these people are Christians! Who ever heard of Christians wearing turbans?"
>
> "Or eating without knives and forks?" added Trueman.
>
> "It would admonish their weak minds in the steward's room at Bellamont, if they could see all this, John," said Mr. Freeman pensively. "A man who travels has very great advantages."

"And very great hardships too," said Trueman. "I don't care for work, but I do like to have my meals regular.". . .

"I should not like to turn Turk," said Trueman, very thoughtfully.

"I know what you are thinking of, John," said Mr. Freeman, in a serious tone. "You are thinking, if anything were to happen to either of us in this heathen land, where we should get Christian burial."

"Lord love you, Mr. Freeman, no I wasn't. I was thinking of a glass of ale."[691]

There is also Occidentalist polemic that Disraeli places in the mouth of Tancred's benefactor, the Emir Fakredeen:

"We ought never to be surprised at anything that is done by the English," observed Fakredeen; "who are, after all, in a certain sense, savages. Their country produces nothing; it is an island, a mere rock, larger than Malta, but not so well fortified. Everything they require is imported from other countries; they get their corn from Odessa, and their wine from the ports of Spain. I have been assured at Beiroot that they do not grow even their own cotton, but that I can hardly believe. Even their religion is exotic; and as they are indebted for that to Syria, it is not surprising that they should import their education from Greece."[692]

Clearly, Disraeli is not manacled by latent hatred of anything Oriental, nor does his novel glorify Europe at the expense of the Orient. Commenting on Downing Street's 1842 decision to force sectarian government in Lebanon, Disraeli as narrator shows how that action did indeed succeed in uniting the population of Lebanon, but "unfortunately against its own project."[693]

Said leads his reader to view *Tancred* as a failed novel in which the author is mired in "ludicrously complex descriptions" due to an "over-developed knowledge of Oriental politics and the British Establishment's network of interests."[694] Without providing a direct quote or considering that other characters may express opposite sentiments, Said sums up the contribution of Disraeli's novel as a paradigm of Oriental stereotyping: "An Oriental lives in the Orient, he lives a life of Oriental ease, in a state of Oriental despotism and sensuality, imbued with a feeling of Oriental fatalism."[695] But where in *Tancred* does Said find such an essentialized Oriental? Much of the novel is about Jews and Christians both east and west. In Disraeli's narrative we come across a Holy Land populated by Arabs, Bedoueen, Moslemin, Rechabites, Maronites, Armenians, Druze, Ottomans, Turkman, Kurds, and even a mountain retreat of Astarte-worshipping idolaters. Instead of depicting a homogenized life of ease under despotic rule, the novel shifts locales from desert to mountain forest, from tent to city. The few general references to Oriental manners are positive rather than negative. Patrick Brantlinger suggests that *Tancred* opposes racial stereotyping and ethnocentrism, despite being caught up in the racial categorizing of the time.[696] John Vincent calls Disraeli "a subversive enemy of received ideas," a phrase that might equally be used for Said.[697] Tancred, the hero, spends much of his time defending the Orient against Eurocentric stereotypes; he is unwilling to accept the archetypal Orientalist notion that "the East is used up."[698]

Giving precedence to the novel over other genres is in itself bourgeois. But to what extent did canonized novels reread more than a century later resonate across classes at the time? If the novel is "an incorporative, quasi-encyclopedic cultural form,"[699] were other popular formats—fairy tales, satires, allegories, memoirs, travel accounts, song lyrics—not equally cultural artifacts? Were they also unthinkable without imperialism? Were more Britons sitting at home reading long novels without the benefit of literary critics to explain how classic some of these novels would become, or standing in public houses listening to bawdy stories? And how does the limiting factor of distribution beyond the literate elites combine with the commercial interest of publishers in shaping the ideological success of any novel in any age? Texts may indeed serve the interests of empire, but in a pragmatic sense they also serve themselves.

The Absence of Poetic License

> These fools by dint of wisdom most crass,
> Think they in wisdom all mankind surpass;
> And glibly do they damn as infidel
> Each one who is not, like themselves, an ass.
>
> —Omar Khayyam, *The Rubaiyat of Omar Khayyam*

> Stocked with Pachas, Seraskiers,
> Slaves, and turbaned Buccaneers;
> Sensual Mussulmen atrocious,
> Renegados, more ferocious.
>
> —William Wordsworth, "Mary Barker's
> Lines Addressed to a Noble Lord"

It is odd to privilege the novel over poetry as an agent of imperial design. The political tenor of a poem can be as overt as metaphor is ambiguous. Surely there is an unmistakable patriotic beat to Thomas Campbell's "Ye Mariners of England":

> Britannia needs no bulwarks,
> No towers along the steep;
> Her march is o'er the mountain-waves,
> Her home is on the deep.[700]

If, as Said suggests, it is hard to imagine the novel apart from imperialism, what is to be done with such poetry? Britain expanded at first unaware of the complicity of its novel genre, but did recognize as poet-laureate Wordsworth in 1843 and Tennyson in 1850. Just as the drum and bugle corps led soldiers to battle, noted poets archived the fame and shame of building empires. Throughout history, tyrants were the fodder for poets before anyone imagined the expanded genres of modern Western prose. On the surface, would not Tennyson's "Charge of the Light Brigade" have served the cause of empire more than an ancient chivalric duel in *The Talisman*? In Shelley's "Ozymandias of Egypt," is the Oriental potentate on the pedestal now a "colossal wreck, boundless and bare" because of a unique Oriental despotism? Is this phrasing itself not a poetic monument to all mortal fools who dare to say, "Look on my works, ye Mighty, and despair!"?[701] But of course poetry was hardly a Western invention, nor was its employment as panegyric.[702]

Emily Haddad notes, in her survey of nineteenth-century poetry on Oriental themes, that British and French poets "made reputations and even a living from writing poems on oriental topics."[703] Oddly, the art form most advanced in the Near Orient of Said's interest is virtually ignored in *Orientalism*, where the dryest of academic scholars only briefly rub literary elbows with poets. Dante, Goethe, Hugo, and Byron are selected as the only well-versed examples of Orientalizing the Orient, which in a way is tantamount to criticizing them for writing poems rather than politically correct tracts. But it would be hard to find any major poet during the early nineteenth century who did not invest in Oriental themes. Wordsworth, Shelley, Coleridge, Keats, Southey, Tennyson, Moore, Gautier, and Matthew Arnold mined the fantasy of the Orient. Even Edward Lear, master of the limerick, visited and quite literally drew on Oriental scenes.

A major poet in Said's Orientalist conspiracy is Dante, the Italian humanist. There is probably no more hideous and biased representation of the prophet Muhammad in the Western canon than the *Inferno*'s eternal fating of Islam's prophet to be

split from his chin to the mouth with which man farts.
Between his legs all of his red guts hung
with the heart, the lungs, the liver, the gall bladder,
and the shriveled sac that passes shit to the bung.[704]

This insidious rendering symbolizes for Said the Orientalist vision that is "the common possession of all who have thought about the Orient in the West."[705] Dante is supposedly poeticizing what prosaic Orientalists intimate in less vulgar terms in their scholarly treatises. Although Said is aware that Dante places admired Muslim philosophers Ibn Sina and Ibn Rushd in more temperate zones of the allegorical netherworld, Aijaz Ahmad chastizes Said for not grasping the full force of this discrepancy.[706] Muhammad's sin, for Dante, was not just that he founded the heresy of Islam; he lacked the rationality of Averroes that budding humanists found to outweigh a latent East–West binary. To simply read *The Inferno* as a variation on the Islam-hating Orientalist theme ignores the complexities of a literary context in which Dante's topography of hell follows a rational axis that cleaves right through an imagined geography of Christian West vs. Islamic Orient.

Besides the bombast of Dante's infernal journey and the burden of Kipling's rhymes, the only other poetry Said quotes in *Orientalism* is Goethe's *Westöstlicher Diwan*. "In the Orient," argues Said in a swipe at the icon of German romanticism, "one suddenly confronted unimaginable antiquity, inhuman beauty, boundless distance."[707] Goethe appears as a poet who returns to the Orient, "seeing it as completion and confirmation of everything one had imagined." Said envisions Goethe as a worldly-minded artist restructuring the Orient, provoked but not guided by the "real" Orient.[708] Goethe is in effect dismissed as a co-conspirator of Orientalists for invoking "with veneration" the name of de Sacy and as a corrupter of Marx with "Romantic and even messianic" conceptions.[709] Said [en]lists Goethe throughout *Orientalism* as a meddling fabricator of Orientalist discourse, but nowhere gives evidence of having read the extensive commentary available on this well-studied German poet. Goethe is thoroughly divorced from his literary and historical contexts.

Through an egregious translation error, Said bolsters his argument of a Goethe-imagined Orient. In Said's own translation of several lines from Goethe, the phrase "Gottes ist der Orient!" is garbled as "God is the Orient." Said would have benefited from consulting the English translation by the poet Robert Browning: "God is of the east possess'd, / God is the ruler of the west;/ North and south alike, each land,/ Rests within his gentle hand." Far from expressing pantheistic tendencies in this passage, as Said implies, Goethe was simply stating that "To God belongs the Orient!"[710] The irony is heavily weighted here because Goethe was in fact citing a translated verse of the Quran, which reads "The East and the West are God's" (*li-Allah al-mashriq wa-al-maghrib*).[711] Goethe appears to have taken this directly from von Hammer-Purgstall's German translation published in *Fundgraben des Orients*.[712] As Wilhelm Halbfass remarks, "Certainly, the Koran itself can hardly be denounced as a 'contribution to Orientalist discourse;' but neither should Goethe's quote from that text."[713] In retrospect, Goethe might be expected to roll over in his *Grab* at the suggestion by Kathleen Biddick that Said could be celebrated as "the modern Goethe!"[714]

The subsequent genealogy of this poetic mistranslation is a poignant example of the uncritical acceptance of Said's critical evidence. The twenty-fifth anniversary edition of *Orientalism*, published in 2003, steadfastly maintains the error. An earlier (1980) British edition corrects the mistranslation without comment. The Hebrew, Norwegian, and Turkish versions transcribe Said's mistake literally. The 1981 Arabic translation corrects the error without comment; Goethe's original German is not included. In the Italian version (1991), Said's translation is left out of the narrative and an accurate Italian version of Goethe's lines is included by the translator in a footnote, but no indication is given of Said's error. Correction by emendation with established translations of Goethe is also made in the French (1980) and Polish (1991) versions. "Errors of this type," Fedwa Malti-Douglas notes, "are particularly damaging when one is attacking a discipline which made a fetish of textual accuracy."[715] As C. F. Beckingham retorts in responding to Said's linguistic and historiographic errors, "An attack on scholarship carries no weight if it is itself so unscholarly."[716] Unfortunately, Beckingham did not consider the dead weight that such a polemic might carry for decades.

The earlier Arab critic Abdullah Yusuf-Ali portrays Goethe's "Orientalism" as a subverter of the academic Orientalist essentialism of his day: "There is not one Eastern world, but many Eastern worlds, all living in watertight compartments, and here comes a man to open the flood-gates and confound the thoughts which had been carefully classified and ticketed!"[717] If Goethe's literal reading of an incontrovertible Islamic truth is only to be seen as an imaginative trope, Said is the one who refuses to recognize another's reality. Nor is Goethe a political polemicist in the service of any European imperial quest. As Sarah Roche-Mahdi retorts, "If Marx misuses the *Divan*, it is not Goethe's fault."[718] Consider the irony that former President Khatami of Iran recently read the same passage in Goethe and saw "no signs of colonialistic intentions and hegemonic interests."[719]

Said also reproaches the English romantic poet Lord Byron, but less for his origin-seeking than for having "a political vision of the Near Orient."[720]

Certainly Byron was not confined to a non-engaged armchair; his involvement in the Greek resistance put him more than poetically on the front lines. But many lines in Byron's corpus deal at length with the divide within the West. For example, the 1813 poem "The Giaour," mentioned only in passing by Said, probes the metaphorically sustained East–West divide through a monstrous battle between a European warrior and an Oriental harem master.[721] In one sense this can be read as a poetic re-enactment of Napoleon's penetration of Egypt, but Byron disrupts a single-minded reading by having the Western victor take on the evil traits of the vanquished villain.[722] Like Coleridge and Wordsworth, Byron at first admired the free spirit of Napoleon but later turned against the imperialist dictator.[723] Several specialists on Byron's work dispute Said's claim that the poet was an Orientalist faithfully producing a to-be-dominated Orient.[724] Speaking of the Ottomans, for example, Byron said: "they are not treacherous, they are not cowardly, they do not burn heretics, they are not assassins, nor has an enemy advanced to their capital. They are faithful to their sultan till he becomes unfit to govern, and devout to their God without an inquisition."[725] "Byron's Oriental space, in other words," argues Saree Makdisi, "offers liberatory possibilities for the critique of Western, European, English concepts, taboos, norms, and standards—political, social, sexual, poetical, economic, and cultural."[726] Is Byron's political vision, obsessively romantic and contradictory as it seems in hindsight, necessarily another Orientalist power play?

Romantic English poets, who would be surprised to be lumped into a discursive genre with pedantic Orientalists, oft wrestled with the biases of their day. Robert Southey's "Thalaba" (1801) "made an intelligent attempt to convey the spirit and principles of the Islamic faith as it really exists," argues Mohammed Sharafuddin, a Muslim literary scholar.[727] In "To the Nile" (1818), John Keats "sees the Nile neither as an underused arena for exploitation nor a purely imaginary realm in which an antecedent history is wiped out," contends Gregory Wassil.[728] There is also Coleridge's revolutionary 1816 "Kubla Khan," in which Xanadu becomes the paradise weeded out of a vivid romantic dream. Here the imaginary is liberated from a desire to distance the other. Contrary and prior to Said's model, as E. S. Shaffer cogently argues, the combination of a rationalist literary criticism of the Bible and a new non-theological approach to myth inaugurated by Orientalist scholars such as William Jones allowed the poet to probe primordial myth as a symbolic path to self-understanding.[729] Said refers to the "impressive" and "indispensable" study by Shaffer on the political implications of Coleridge's poem, but then dispenses with Shaffer's insights for his own study.[730] Shaffer does to a specific poem what Said fails to do— he examines in explicit detail the context in which it was actually written:

where Coleridge wrote the poem, what he was reading at the time, what other poems he was working on, etc. Given that Said insists authors do have a life, it is curious that the complexities of their lives fail to inform his analysis in *Orientalism*.

Some poets rode the stereotypes of *Arabian Nights* fantasy to exotic peaks unscaled by Said. How could a critique of nineteenth-century English-language depictions of the Orient not entertain Thomas Moore's 1817 epic romance *Lalla Rookh*?[731] In Britain at the time, this poem's romantic appeal was such that it saw seven illegitimate printings in its first year. Across the Atlantic in United States, it became an immediate bestseller, running through twenty editions by 1841.[732] Here is the ultimate Orientalist fantasy overlaying the expansion of British imperialism in the real Orient. An Oriental potentate named Abdalla, King of the lesser Bucharia, sets out from somewhere in Central Asia to make the pilgrimage to Mecca. Stopping to be entertained at Delhi, the pilgrim ruler finds a match for his son with the daughter of the Indian emperor. She is Lalla Rookh, "described by the poets of her time as more beautiful than Leila, Shirine, Dewilde, or any of those heroines whose names and loves embellish the songs of Persia and Hindostan."[733] The plot is an excuse for an extended epic poem that makes light verse of the storytelling artistry that saved Scheherezade from a despotically despoiled denouement. When the princess finds her journey away from the comforts of the palace a trifle boring, her guardian, "having refreshed his faculties with a dose of that delicious opium," unveils a young poet to recite "The Veiled Prophet of Khorassan." The poet, as graceful as Krishna, becomes the fated lover whom the princess is soon charmed into preferring over a promised royal bridegroom. For those who like happy endings, the young poet turns out to be the prince and bridegroom in disguise. In decidedly un-Oriental fashion the lovers' dreams are realized.

Moore more than most writers merges Muslims with Hindus, Near Easterners with Far Orientals, documentable legends with spontaneous fantasy. This is not a tale of East vs. West, but an [im]morality play pitting good against evil within a boundless East. Moore grounds his fancy with innumerable footnotes referring to Orientalist texts. The authorities cited include Anquetil-Duperron, William Jones, d'Herbelot, various travelers, and even the Quran. Here is a poem unthinkable in its textual form except as informed by academic Orientalism.[734] The homogenized Orient that emerges from Moore's belabored rhymes replaces hints of a real Muslim world with an ethereal menagerie:

> There to recline among Heav'n's native maids,
> And Crown the Elect with bliss that never fades—

Well hath the Prophet-Chief his bidding done;
And ev'ry beauteous race beneath the sun,
From those who kneel at BRAHMA'S burning founts,
To the fresh nymphs bounding o'er yemen's mounts;
From persia's eyes of full and fawn-like ray,
To the small, half-shut glances of kathay;
And georgia's bloom, and azab's darker smiles,
And the gold ringlets of the Western Isles;
All, all are there;—each Land its flower hath given,
To form that fair young Nursery for Heav'n!"[735]

This is the invented Orient Said so rightly disparages. And here is a text that was endlessly recycled in popular culture, not just among academics with access to esoteric libraries.

Moore's romance is enhanced in an 1861 edition with lithographic illustrations by John Tenniel.[736] The frontispiece encapsulates the studio overlay of a poetic text that bears little relation to reality. The scene is the interior of a luxurious tent with the canopy opening in the center. All the viewer is allowed to see outside are an elephant and a horse, both saddled and watched by several turbaned servants. Inside, a poet/prince standing to the left balances the cross-legged, wazir-like guardian lost in a poppy-eyed rapture on the right. Elevated behind the guardian sit two servant girls who almost serve as a cushion for the reclining Lalla Rookh. The "gaze" within the scene is as thinly disguised as the shapely curve of the princess's thighs and the subtle line of her nipple-less breasts that a flimsy veil fails to cover. The poet looks down demurely at his "kitar," his eyes seemingly closed in concentration. Lalla stares, her small mouth seductively open, at the poet's hands so skillfully in charge of his instrument. But beyond all this is a collection of perspectival orientations that could be read contrapuntally in a most vivid Freudian manner. The neck of the "kitar" is parallel to the vaginal canal of this quiescent odalisque. Her eyes are fixed not only on the poet's hands but also in direct line with his male organ, which is totally covered by his robe and further obscured in the shadow cast by the instrument. The music he plays cannot be heard by the viewer, but the sensual delight in her eyes hides little. The poet recites, he plays the melody on the strings; at some point all this poetry must lead to on-the-ground passion.

Lalla Rookh should be read as a striking confirmation of the complicity of popular entertainment framed with Orientalist credentials. This is not the real Orient, at least not for someone who had actually been there. Even Lord Curzon, vilified by Said as imperialist administrator, saw through the fanciful depiction and dismissed *Lalla Rookh* as totally inaccurate.[737] Yet the circle of imaginary diffusion was completed when part of the poem was eventually translated into Persian. This prompted one cynic to retort:

> I am told, dear Moore, your lays are sung,
> (Can it be, you lucky man?)
> By moonlight in the Persian tongue
> Along the streets of Isfahan.[738]

Moore's success owes more to the sensual tenor of his tale than to his uncanonized poetic genius. His book was attacked in conservative circles as pornography. Some critics suggested that he hid behind the Orientalist detail, so meticulously referenced to reputable sources, in order to escape the censors. Here then would seem to be the English poetic mirror of Flaubert, but with an important difference. Moore wrote not simply as a purported pervert—by the standards of the day—but as a fervent Irish patriot. Outside his poetry he stressed the real Oriental roots of Irish culture. In this politicized venue, Moore was hardly arguing for the colonial expansion of the Queen's navy; Islam becomes a surrogate for Protestantism, an alleged reform that slid into bigotry and imposture.[739] As G. M. Wickens notes, although Moore claimed to be adhering to Orientalism, "at the same time, character, posture, motivation and action are all grotesquely Romantic and European."[740] *Lalla Rookh* is certainly all about the West, but not in any tangible way for domination of a real East. The very success of *Lalla Rookh* may be viewed as a subversion of the British Orientalism that Moore as an Irish patriot despised.[741]

ACCOUNTING FOR TRAVEL THEORY

> For the rest the sun made me an Arab, but never warped me to Orientalism.
>
> —CHARLES DOUGHTY, *TRAVELS IN ARABIA DESERTA*[742]

> Wherefore I, desiring somewhat to inform myself of the Turkish nation, would not sit down with a book knowledge thereof, but rather (through all the hazard and endurance of travel), receive it from my own eye, not dazzled with any affection, prejudacy or mist of education, which preoccupate the mind, and delude it with partial ideas, as with a false glass, representing the object in colours, and proportions untrue.
>
> —SIR HENRY BLOUNT, *A VOYAGE IN THE LEVANT*

Privileging the novel in order to pillory Orientalism allows Said to blur differences with other forms of narrative entertainment that are critical in establishing Western views of the Orient. One nonacademic form of literature is the travel narrative that for Said is exemplified in the "obvious examples" of Gustave Flaubert, Mark Twain, Benjamin Disraeli, Alexander Kinglake, and Gérard de Nerval.[743] Yet these are anything but obvious, given the thousands of Oriental travel accounts published by Western authors. Flaubert never wrote a travel book for publication; his letters and notes were published posthumously, and not even in the nineteenth century.[744] Twain wrote a popular and overwhelmingly successful travel satire, but Said ignores it completely. Disraeli wrote novels, not diplomatic tourist books. Kinglake is a good Victorian example, just as Nerval is a classic from the French side.[745] Yet none of these works is representative of the pilgrim or the less-than-canon-material tourist. Said's choice is idiosyncratic, avoiding the widely read travel classics by Burckhardt and Doughty and the plethora of mundane "look what I saw" pedestrian pilgrim narratives.[746]

"To be a European in the Orient always involves being a consciousness set apart from, and unequal with, its surroundings," asserts Said.[747] As a statement of the inevitable displacement that any traveler represents, this is tautological. But there is a difference between being disoriented as a foreign traveler and automatically viewing the others visited as inferior and barbaric. Said seems to recognize this in positing three "intentional categories" of writing travelers. The first is the "professional" Orientalist, using residence as a form of "scientific observation." This describes Lane's *Account of the Manners and Customs of the Modern Egyptians*, which provides a level of detail not possible to absorb from a brief touristic visit. As the great popularity of Lane's work suggests, such texts were rather rare. The second category is arbitrarily defined as following the same purpose but characterized with "eccentricity," the paradigm being Burton's narrative of his surreptitious trip to Mecca in 1853. I find Said's classification here arbitrary because it is based on the difficulty the reader is supposed to have in disentangling description from "the personal vagaries of style." The final category is a traveler who follows a "personal aesthetic" rather than setting out to objectively describe; the French writer Nerval is said to fit this bill. Surely, the spiritual journey of Doughty would stem from an equally personal aesthetic. Said confuses intent with style, as though the latter can be said to inevitably override the former.

Having laid out these three categories, Said proceeds to argue that despite their differences they "are not so separate from each other as one would imagine," nor should they be seen as representing "pure" types. True enough, but the problem is that Said offers straw categories, the blurred boundaries of which do not represent the full range of travel narratives on the Orient. Why, for example, does Said make no attempt to peg his "obvious examples" into these quasi-categorical wholes? Would not the quite disparate writings of Flaubert, Twain, Disraeli, and Kinglake all fit a "personal aesthetic"? Said suggests that all three categories include recurring motifs of "pilgrimage" and a "vision of Orient as spectacle." Yet Flaubert, Twain, and Kinglake are hardly pilgrims, unless the meaning is stretched outside religious devotion to personal ambition. Said fails to explore the religious nature of most Oriental travel texts. The kind of bibliolatry that saw living Oriental people as a window into biblical characters would fit Said's Orientalism thesis. There is not one example in *Orientalism* of this genre, which is exemplified by the Protestant missionary William Thompson's 1859 *The Land and the Book*, a travel narrative based on years of residence as a missionary in the Levant. Thus the reader is not informed of the long-standing division between Christian apologists who functioned as Orientalists (e.g., Muir) and scholars who rejected the devotional nature or biased apologetics of much of the travel genre.[748] Nor is it clear how a travel narrative ever avoids treating its visited location as spectacle; is it not the goal of writing to make the *tableau vivant*? The problem is that Said narrows down a broad range of travel accounts to focus narrowly but intensively on texts that support his thesis.

I am concerned with the many kinds of travel texts Said passes over. For example, there is no discussion in *Orientalism* of *The Travels of Sir John Mandeville*, probably the most widely traveled of any text about the Orient after the mid-fourteenth century.[749] Whether an English knight by the name of Mandeville traveled to any part of a real Orient or a very clever author imagined such an exploit, this was arguably the seminal text that defined a penetrable Orient from Constantinople to Cathay. The words of the text do not dwell on a seamless Orient, but rather depict a plethora of "many kingdoms, lands, provinces and isles" specified, even if not accurately named, by the author.[750] There is no sense of Europe or the West except insofar as the various peoples and polities mentioned along the way partake in Christendom. Mandeville sets out to describe "the land beyond the sea, that is to say the Land of Promise which men call the Holy Land," with nary an "Orient" in sight.[751] Kenneth Parker argues that European travel accounts prior to the eighteenth century are ignored by Said and others "because such stories resist being fitted neatly into a model of cultural encounter that conforms to a colonizer/colonized model of the world, one in which Europeans can impose upon the peoples whom they encounter."[752]

The central focus of Mandeville's text is on those aspects of the "Land of Promise" that would be of interest to Christians. Would-be pilgrims are instructed on how to get to the Holy Land and about the biblical sites and holy relics to be found there. Having mentioned the Saracens who control the region, Mandeville then provides one of the most accurate and least judgmental views of Islam in all medieval Western accounts up to that time.[753] There is an elaborate passage on what the Quran says about Christian belief; the author suggests that Muslims "come so near to our faith" that they might easily be converted by preaching. In fact, the narrative includes a speech attributed to a sultan in which Christians are criticized for not following thé moral principles of their faith. This leads to a homily that is anything but a simplistic piece of Orientalist sentiment:

> It seemed to me then a cause for great shame that Saracens, who have neither a correct faith nor a perfect law, should in this way reprove us for our failings, keeping their false law better than we do that of Jesus Christ; and those who ought by our own good example to be turned to the faith and law of Jesus Christ are driven away by our wicked ways of living. And so is it no wonder that they call us sinful and wicked, for it is true. But they are very devout and honest in their law, keeping well the commandments of the Koran, which God sent them by His messenger Muhammad, to whom, so they say, the angel Gabriel spoke often, telling him the will of God.[754]

Here is an intentional pilgrimage even if largely framed in fable, but the author is no Orientalist.

By focusing mainly on nineteenth-century travel texts, Said relegates to literary prehistory the earlier travelers he mentions as the sources for later Orientalist writing. As a result, he is unable to chart the differing contexts of travel from West to East. The Orient beckoned long before imperial ambitions of a European label took shape. Consider the conditions of Elizabethan travel in the Levant. As Samuel Chew observes, before the era of British colonialism it was not more difficult or arduous to travel from England to Syria or Egypt than to travel just about anywhere. Thieves were as common at the time outside London as in Jerusalem, and there were few modern conveniences left behind. Many English travelers who made their way east were impressed that the Turks were cleaner and more civil than their own countrymen.[755] Examples abound of accounts in which Muslim manners are described in a far more positive light than those of certain fellow Europeans. Another critical point missing from Said's analysis is the endemic concern of many Western travelers with correcting previous travel accounts. Voyagers such as the Elizabethan Joseph Hall, for example, delighted in satirizing "sweet-sauc'd lies of some false traveller."[756]

Said's insistence on inherent Orientalist bias among all Western travelers blinds him to exceptions that weaken his overall argument. A case in point is that of Wilfrid Scawen Blunt and Lady Anne Blunt. Wilfrid Blunt makes a cameo appearance in *Orientalism*, but we learn nothing about him other than that he was an exception to those Orientalists who expressed hostility and fear of the Orient.[757] An exception indeed he was, although Said's subtle dismissal gives little indication of how un-colonialist both Blunts were. Said's total ignoring of Lady Blunt is yet another example of his failure to read female authors; in this case it is her *Bedouin Tribes of the Euphrates* (1871) and *A Pilgrimage to Nejd* (1881), which were more widely read and admired than Wilfrid's own writings.[758] One would have thought that simply being the granddaughter of Lord Byron might have secured her a berth, even if only on a list, in a literary critic's analysis of the imagined Orient.

Wealthy and well-connected Wilfrid retired from the foreign service in 1869, and soon the traveling Blunts went east. As Wilfrid noted about his first visit to Egypt in 1879, he was still "a believer in the common English creed that England had a providential mission in the East."[759] After learning about Bedouin customs firsthand in Syria, Lady Anne spoke for both travelers about their interest in no longer looking at the people "with the half contemptuous ignorance" of Europeans.[760] Not only were the Blunts aware of and appalled at Eurocentric attitudes, but Wilfrid wrote of Islam as a "true religion" that certainly had far more to offer African converts than Christianity.[761] In 1881 Blunt bought an estate in Cairo, where he and his wife became neighbors and friends of the Islamic reformer Muhammad 'Abduh. On a visit back to England, Blunt arranged a visit between 'Abduh and the reigning social philosopher, Herbert Spencer; the Egyptian reportedly told Spencer that the East was learning the evil rather than the good from the West, but the best of both was the same.[762]

Blunt was perhaps the most famous aristo-critic of British imperialism in Egypt. With the impunity his elite upbringing bequeathed at the time, he admonished Lord Cromer, whose "wrong-headed administration" only served to Anglicize Egypt.[763] He used his impeccable social connections to lobby British politicians, including Prime Minister Gladstone, whose "Oriental" policies he deplored.[764] Blunt's radical critique of the colonial transgressions committed by the burdensome white race is second to none, including Fanon and Césaire. Consider his prescient diary note at the close of the nineteenth century:

The old century is very nearly out, and leaves the world
in a pretty pass, and the British Empire is playing the devil
in it as never an empire before on so large a scale. We
may live to see its fall. All the nations of Europe are making the same hell upon earth in China, massacring and
pillaging and raping in the captured cities as outrageously
as in the Middle Ages. The Emperor of Germany gives the
word for slaughter and the Pope looks on and approves.
In South Africa our troops are burning farms under Kitchener's command, and the Queen and the two houses of
Parliament, and the bench of bishops thank God publicly
and vote money for the work. The Americans are spending fifty millions a year on slaughtering the Filipinos; the
King of the Belgians has invested his whole fortune on
the Congo, where he is brutalizing the negroes to fill his
pockets. The French and Italians for the moment are playing a less prominent part in the slaughter, but their inac-
tivity grieves them. The whole white race is reveling
openly in violence, as though it had never pretended to
be Christian. God's equal curse be on them all![765]

In addition to speaking out for Egyptian self-rule and against British stereotypes of Islam, Blunt had little patience for Orientalists such as Sir Henry
Rawlinson, whose views he found to be of "the strongest Anglo-Indian
official type."[766] He also distrusted Richard Burton, who "showed little true
sympathy with the Arabs."[767] How then did this prominent traveler escape
the manacles of a totally hegemonic Orientalism?

Wilfrid Blunt was not the only Westerner to disagree with colonial policy.[768] A similar story revolves around the Swiss agronomist John Ninet.
Originally charged by Muhammad Ali in 1839 with overseeing Egypt's cotton crop, Ninet fell in love with his adopted country and lived on a Nile
farm for the next half-century. In 1869 he drafted a manifesto protesting
British colonial rule, and by 1882 his activism was judged so dangerous
that he was expelled from Egypt. He thus became, as Thierry Hentsch
phrases it, "the ultimate personification of 'benevolent' colonialism."[769] Said
might also have considered the career of the Italian Orientalist Leone Caetani, especially in light of remarks by Johann Fück in an article Said cites:

His [Caetani's] deep insight into the interplay of relations
between Occident and Orient led him to condemn colonialism, and when Italy annexed Tripolitania and Cyre-

naica he issued a warning, in an essay, *La fonction de l'Islam dans l'évolution de la civilisation* (1912), against all attempts to Europeanize the eastern peoples; in a stimulating study of the century-old conflict between East and West he defended the right of the Muslims to lead an independent life in accordance with their own traditions.[770]

Said suggests that thinking of Orientalism "as a kind of Western projection onto and will to govern over the Orient" will result in "few surprises."[771] Here is a surprise. The Blunts, Ninet, and Caetani were among those courageous Europeans who wrote back against empire during its heyday.

In addition to those who admired the Orient but remained European, some Westerners converted to Islam as a lifetime commitment. A French convert to Islam, Jean d'Ivray, arrived with her Egyptian husband in Cairo in 1879. She later published a French text on Napoleon's invasion, citing Arabic sources and criticizing the atrocities against Egyptians.[772] Another important example is Mohammad Asad, born Leopold Weiss, who converted to Islam in 1926. "Islam appears to me like a perfect work of architecture. All its parts are harmoniously conceived to complement and support each other; nothing is superfluous and nothing lacking; and the result is a structure of absolute balance and solid composure," wrote Asad.[773] Befriended by Saudi King 'Abd al-'Aziz and Pakistani poet Muhammad Iqbal, Asad eventually served as the newly created Pakistan's minister to the United Nations. His *The Road to Mecca* (1954) provided a distinctively un-Orientalist view of Islam, and his English translation of the Quran was widely read in Europe and America. Here are two examples of individuals who not only adopted Islam as a personal faith but effectively wrote back against Western prejudice and imperialist politics.

TEXTS WITHOUT CONTEXT

> Said does not just juxtapose fiction with works of history, he equates the two; it's as if a quotation from Joseph Conrad has precisely the same historical validity as one from Lord Curzon— and a good deal more, it might be added, than one from Bernard Lewis.
>
> —ANDREW J. ROTTER, "SAIDISM WITHOUT SAID: *ORIENTALISM* AND U.S. DIPLOMATIC HISTORY"

A key criticism of *Orientalism* is that Said tears his texts out of their contexts, as he weaves a seamless discourse over time and place. As K. E. Fleming observes, "Indeed, the boundary-crossing, if not boundaryless, quality of Said's work has been identified as the ur-source of its power to move, annoy, influence, and enrage, as well as to elude concrete analysis."[774] In part this may be because of its stated yet incomplete reliance on Foucault's sense of discourse.[775] But I think a more likely explanation is that the blurring of textual genres opens up a wider range of texts from which to narrowly select self-serving quotes. By invoking Flaubert before analyzing Lane, Said teases the reader to associate travel to a real Orient with the seemingly straightforward matter of writing about it. Yet Flaubert was no Orientalist, even by the wildest stretch of the term, any more than thousands of other pilgrims and tourists who visited the Holy Land and lived to write or tell about it. Said is guilty of "injudicious elision," as Fred Halliday puts it, when he treats private journals, travel writing, fiction, and social science texts as equally applicable to his polemical aims.[776] As Bart Moore-Gilbert protests, it is "highly problematic" to collapse Kipling's *Kim*, written in 1901, with Thévenot's seventeenth-century travelogue, or with a legal edict on Hindu widows from the 1820s.[777]

The greatest limitation of Said's analysis may be the tunnel vision inherent in his "textual attitude." The polemical argument employed to establish a specific discourse of Orientalism privileges texts as such in order to avoid any demonstrable link to a reality outside the texts. This leads to the two prongs of his text-first argument that many of Said's critics turn upon as two essential wrongs. The first is that treating textuality as a closed unit of analysis results in a problematic blurring of genres.[778] Were Said arguing for a technological feature such as print culture, it would be viable to match text to world, the mode of representation to what is present. But Said proceeds as though any text, indeed any discursive act, can be linked to any other text without the need to contextualize intentionality, rhetorical style, or audience reception. Thus Flaubert's published novels and his private letters are discursively equal for the purpose of argument, even though the latter did not enter the accumulative public mainstream that Said insists Orientalists constantly drew from. Similarly, a shoddy and sloppy specimen of term-paper quality such as Hamady's *Temperament and Character of the Arabs* is treated as indicative of Orientalist scholarship, yet such a widely read and heralded study as Marshall Hodgson's *The Venture of Islam* does not even warrant an endnote. Any kind of text is fair game for Said's analysis, because discursive complicity in inventing a fictional Orient and dominating muted Orientals is assumed from the start. In a second analytical error, time becomes irrelevant, so that a long outdated text by Ernest Renan is presented alongside a contemporary conference paper by Bernard Lewis. If Orientalism marches discursively from Aeschylus to Henry Kissinger, contextualized time readily fades as a historical condition.

One of the more convenient charges of Said and other literary scholars who focus on the text in the contest of cultural "context" is what might best be labeled the use-is-abuse fallacy. Any Western writer who cites the imagery of a fanciful Orient thus becomes complicit *expressis verbis* in the verbal misrepresentation of real Orientals. "Orientalism overrode the Orient" is the overarching motto of *Orientalism*; "an observation about a tenth-century Arab poet multiplied itself into a policy towards (and about) the Oriental mentality in Egypt, Iraq, or Arabia."[779] Goethe's discursive crime is that he romanticizes an Oriental in poetry with the same words that prose writers might adopt for a politically sinister purpose. This careless attribution of motive according to a particular critic's own reading leads to the possibility of virtually any text being tainted as imperialist propaganda. Where is the logic in an exaggerated claim such as that of post-colonialist Hager Ben Driss: "Using, like representing, entails a coercive abusing and misrepresenting of the other."[780] Is all representation of an other necessarily misrepresentation? If so, then criticism itself devolves into nothing more than verbal solipsism. If citation of words or notions is by itself a criminal act, language offers little hope for resolving human problems. Semantically and ethically, use is not the same as abuse, but misuse is certainly sentence-able as a literary crime.

Western scholars of the Orient are damned by Said if they read Arabic texts too pedantically, and damned for not reading Arabic literature at all. "The other problem is that Orientalism for the most part has had very little to do with Arabic literature, or at least with literature as in some way an expression of Arab life," claims Said in a 1976 interview.[781] He adds: "Statistically, I am positive you will find literature to be the least represented of the Orientalist subspecialties, for obvious reasons, since literature muddles the tidy categories invented for Oriental life by Orientalists. The plain fact is that Orientalists do not know how to read, and therefore happily ignore literature."[782] Said is only right about the dearth of Orientalist scholars who had the fluency and competency to properly study literary texts if one accepts his generous promotion of anyone who taught about the Orient as an Orientalist. Certainly the cumulative contributions of literary experts outweigh the run-of-the-grist-mill narratives rehashing the history of the caliphate and Islam. In English alone there are Lyall's 1885 *Ancient Arabian Poetry*, Browne's 1902–06 *A Literary History of Persia*, Nicholson's 1907 *A Literary History of the Arabs*, and Arberry's *Aspects of Islamic Civilization as Depicted in the Original Texts* (1964). Does Said think that Arberry, whose lyrical translation of the Quran is still widely used, did not know how to read Arabic, let alone translate it? I find it ironic that Said ignores the valuable translation by Bayard Dodge of the tenth-century scholar al-Nadim's monumental compilation of Arabic texts, including poetry and prose literature.[783] Was Dodge unwittingly muddling the "tidy categories" by providing direct access to the names and works of major Arab literary figures before the tenth century CE?

In addition to the hole in Said's textual universe, there is in *Orientalism* the age-old methodological fallacy of building up a whole from a few carefully chosen parts. Said mines vulnerable texts for damnable quotes of glaring racism, glowering ethnocentism, and glib insensitivity.[784] Smoking excerpts and ellipsis-ed passages seduce the reader into agreement. The sheer crassness of what is being quoted can override a critical caution about what has been left out. Those critics who do know better, who know what Said so often leaves unsaid, get blamed for attacking the messenger because the vast majority of *Orientalism*'s readers have no independent knowledge of the message piecemealed in Said's carefully minced rhetoric. The material argument, for those of us who actively do the kind of research Said over-labels Orientalism, is literarily blind-sided.

3

The Seductive Charms
of and Against *Orientalism*

> Ontological Orientalism in Reverse is, in the end, no less reactionary, mystifying, ahistorical, and anti-human than Ontological Orientalism proper.
>
> —SADIQ JALAL AL-ʿAZM, "ORIENTALISM AND ORIENTALISM IN REVERSE"

> In retrospect, there were in fact many forms of orientalism and it was inadequate to lump so many diverse traditions into a single orientalist tradition.
>
> —BRYAN TURNER, *ORIENTALISM, POSTMODERNISM, AND GLOBALISM*

I Presenting and Representing Orientalism

They cannot represent themselves; they must be represented.
—KARL MARX, *THE EIGHTEENTH BRUMAIRE OF LOUIS BONAPARTE*[1]

How does one *represent* other cultures?
—EDWARD SAID, *ORIENTALISM*

The intellectual maelstrom that has kept the debate about *Orientalism* swirling across disciplines is a persistent metaproblem of much post-just-about-everything discourse: how can or should reality be represented? Look under any philosopher's stone from almost any era and you will find an opinion. Read canonical historiographic treatises and you will come across methodological insights and oversights. The various twentieth-century isms as structurally adjusted or existentially exhibited did not end on a positive[ist] note, although a pragmatic assessment would be that reality—whatever *it* really is—was little affected by what intellectuals in university chairs and students on bar stools thought it might be. Reality is not an academic issue for Said, whose worldli[fi]nessed watchword has been to speak truth to the rude reality that he steadfastly opposes. *Orientalism*, Said reflects, is a book that would not have been written had he not been "politically associated with a struggle."[2] He is after all a literary critic who proposes that texts are "in" the world, which is to say they are "enmeshed in circumstance, time, place, and society."[3] His polemic was not offered as the 1,002nd tale of an ongoing fantasy in which his world only *seems* to be suffering. His problem is with reality, not about it.

The main problem that permeates the superstructure of Said's prose and infiltrates the basal drive underlying his discourse is that the real Orient in which he has a stake has been represented in such a way that it is absented. Indeed, "Orientals themselves" are not only misrepresented, but said to be pervasively denied the possibility of making themselves present. Hence, as the lead epigraph from Karl Marx implies, "they must be represented." Is it the case that, at the time when Said wrote *Orientalism*, no existing presentations about the Orient properly or adequately represented the real Orient? Had no scholar yet succeeded in opposing the many misrepresentations? Does Edward Said have the authority—apart from being an author who was born an Oriental—to represent individuals imagined out of their reality? Are real Orientals unable to represent themselves, or is it that such self-representation is ignored or hard to find? These are the relevant questions that I address to a thesis based on a "set of historical generalizations" and a critical style that scoffs at any need to be "exhaustive."[4]

As Patrick Williams suggests, representation may be the most "abiding concern" of Said's work.[5] But Said is clearly not enamored with Marx's literal meaning, so what does he mean by "representing"? The main clue is provided in a passage from *Orientalism* that discusses the Marx epigraph:

> My analysis of the Orientalist text therefore places emphasis on the evidence, which is by no means invisible, for such representations *as representations*, not as "natural" depictions of the Orient. This evidence is found just as prominently in the so-called truthful text (histories, philological analyses, political treatises) as in the avowedly artistic (i.e., openly imaginative) text. The things to look at are style, figures of speech, setting, narrative devices, historical and social circumstances, not the correctness of the representation nor its fidelity to some great original. The exteriority of the representation is always governed by some version of the truism that if the Orient does represent itself, it would; since it cannot, the representation does the job, for the West, and *faute de mieux*, for the poor Orient. "Sie können sich nicht vertreten sie müssen vertreten werden," as Marx wrote in *The Eighteenth Brumaire of Louis Bonaparte*.[6]

A reader of *Orientalism* might assume that Said is representing the un̺
resented against the backdrop of real history. Modern Orientalism is ⸗
to begin with Napoleon's invasion of Egypt. Surely Napoleon really existed.[7]
However, the point of *Orientalism* is to read that history only through texts.
Said opens no unexplored mounds, measures no standing ruins, recon-
structs no jumbles of ancient shards. His discursive archaeology, attributed to historian Michel Foucault rather than Egyptologist Sir Flinders
Petrie, is one that allows him to proceed unsoiled by the disturbed fac-
ticity in artifacts of the past and unsullied by contradictory facts.

Despite serving as a validation for Said's representation of Orientalism,
Marx's epigram gets short shrift. My interest goes beyond the presence of
the quote to what Said meant by quoting it at all.[8] As an epigraph in English
it fits brilliantly: just as Orientalism must represent the Orient, so Said
intends to represent Orientalism. But what is the reader, especially the
English reader, to make of Marx's original intention? The full paragraph
from which Marx's quote is taken reads:

> In so far as there is merely a local interconnection among
> these small land-holding peasants, and the identity of
> their interests begets no community, no national bond
> and no political organization among them, they do not
> form a class. They are consequently incapable of enforc-
> ing their class interest in their own name, whether
> through a parliament or through a convention. They can-
> not represent themselves, they must be represented.
> Their representative must at the same time appear as
> their master, as an authority over them, as an unlimited
> governmental power that protects them against the other
> classes and sends them rain and sunshine from above.[9]

The "they" in the original quote refers to the class of petty landowners who
are "represented" in a political sense by a scoundrel who silences and
destroys them. In his English use of the Marx quote, Said conflates two
senses of "representation" in German; Marx refers to political representation, not the abstract philosophical sense used by Auerbach, for example. Such political representation, indicated by the German verb *vertreten*,
is fraudulent for Marx on almost every level. Said no doubt chose the quote
to accentuate the falseness of Orientalist discourse as symbolic representation, but unlike Marx he never defines who exactly is being represented.[10] Russell Jacoby finds Said's use of the quote inappropriate

because it implies that Orientals delivered themselves to adventurers representing them, as the French peasants did to the insincere politicians of their time.[11] Grewgious also criticizes Said for twisting the original meaning for his own rhetorical use, noting that "Marx is not making some essentialist judgment but offering an intricate analysis of social forces in their strengths, struggles, alliances, failures, at a particular historical moment."[12]

To make sense of representations *as representations* requires first knowing what the word "representation" represents both in an author's writing and within the reader's lexical grasp. The *Oxford English Dictionary* (*OED*) suggests the range of ambiguity that such a notion portends. The least figurative meaning given is to actually be or make present in the presence of someone or something else. Such is an image or a reproduction as presented in some material or tangible form. A political representative is chosen to go where the ones being represented cannot be, or do not really want to be. Less physically damaging is the connotation of bringing something clearly or distinctly to mind, a kind of reminding or remembering. This may be with the intention of persuading or as a kind of protest. Representations—visibly present or invisibly made to seem present—can come in the form of stand-ins, substitutes, performances, examples, specimens. To be pristine in a literary sense, the bottom line is that words bring both material and imaginary things to mind. The visible structure of any text is linguistic. The simple fact that literary critique involves using the medium to understand both the message and the medium it represents becomes, as no literate person of this century should need to be reminded, an ambiguous conflict of interests.

With flirtatious rather than reflective candor, Said admits his deep suspicion of the very idea of representation, citing the near-nihilistic mantra, "All representation is misrepresentation of one sort or another."[13] This suggests that representation is by nature artificial and invented, always a poor substitute, only a degree away from being a misrepresentation. The great sin of representation as such is that it "is *eo ipso* implicated, intertwined, embedded, interwoven with a great many other things beside the 'truth,' which is itself a representation."[14] Said is tempted by Nietzsche's quodlibetal comment that "truths are illusions about which one has forgotten that this is what they are."[15] This citation more than any other endears Said to some critics and thoroughly frustrates others. Said "seems to question the basic value of objective induction," complains Mahmoud Manzalaoui.[16] Not comfortable teetering on the brink of nihilism, Said draws back in humanist alarm and suggests that such an absurdly subjective view of language can at least "draw attention to the fact" (as though Nietzsche and fact can be casually balanced in the same phrase) that the word "Orient" is not necessarily the "real Orient." The immediate wall that Said's argument runs up against is, as Gyan Prakash asks, "How can Orientalism be just a representation that bears no relation to the Orient and yet shape and exercise power over it?"[17] As discourse, Orientalism must be more than discourse, more than the sum of its texts; the universal cultural determinants of economic, political, and psychological dimensions must at some point touch a real Orient.

Aijaz Ahmad is one of several critics who chide Said for being inconsistent on the difference between representation and misrepresentation because Said also insists that Orientalism is not a misrepresentation of some Oriental essence.[18] It is as though any truth that is not pure is sullied and of no redeeming epistemological value. In attempting to reform[ulate] Said's argument, Mahmut Mutman argues that "the actual Orient is not a natural guarantee of a non- or anti-Orientalist knowledge, for, as the site of a struggle, it is always already contaminated by representation."[19] Once again, unless it be assumed a priori that the only thing natural in representation is that it contaminates, attention is shifted from the degree of distortion to a winless whining that an absolute clone of reality is impossible. Although some of his followers find themselves or at least imagine themselves intellectually boxed into a relativist corner, Said holds out hope for getting at the truth being represented, at least the kind of truth that speaks back to the power said to be holding back an alternative truth.

Said's views on the moral implications of all representation need to be read against his statements on actual misrepresentation with what he sees as demonstrable inaccuracies. The pragmatic point, for those of us who are put off by endlessly splitting hairs, is the degree of fit between any representation and the assumed reality it attempts to represent. This is ultimately where Said ends up when he admits that *Orientalism* tries to demonstrate that "Islam *has* been fundamentally misrepresented in the West."[20] Said's methodological error is in shifting the issue to that of truthfulness for any representation rather than demonstrating the ways in which specific representations distort something knowable about reality. It is relevant to note that in *Covering Islam* Said proceeds as though the essential problem is that journalists are badly trained rather than that they are suffering from latent and terminal Orientalist discourse. "By using the skills of a good critical reader to disentangle sense from nonsense, by asking the right questions and expecting pertinent answers," argues Said, "anyone can learn about either 'Islam' or the world of Islam and about the men, women, and cultures that live within it, speak its languages, breathe its air, produce its histories and societies."[21] The same must then be true of something known as "the Orient." There is a world of meaningful difference between saying that something cannot be represented in its natural state and suggesting that it has been misrepresented and can be corrected. Only in the latter case is there hope for the cultural understanding Said so eloquently championed. As anthropologist Abdellah Hammoudi reminds us, "We cannot know what the object reality we are striving to discover is, but we can know which statements about it are more valid than others and those statements bring with them partial truths we did not know before, or partial truths which are more sustainable than others."[22]

Straddling the fence of representation presents real problems for readers of *Orientalism*. "In *Orientalism* his method is cumulative and repetitive, but it is difficult to contradict him since he does not allow for a concept of reality," argues Douwe Fokkema.[23] The real Orient must exist, for two significant reasons. First, Said cannot afford his own involvement in the contemporary world to be relativized to mere illusion. Because he toys with Nietzsche and Foucault, Said could be faulted for offering a truth claim that is no more objectively true than the representations he is so adamantly claiming to be false. Second, as Fokkema astutely observes, "in practice he cannot avoid referring to reality, if only to substantiate his claim that certain statements of Orientalism are false."[24] If the Orientalists have so consistently misrepresented Orientals, Said must have access to a truth the specialists do not have, or else demonstrate that his representation of Orientalism squares with the worldly consensus of the reality that he cares about.

Those who still doubt Said's belief in a real Orient, inconsistent rhetoric aside, should take seriously his introductory caveat that "it would be wrong to conclude that the Orient was essentially an idea, or a creation with no corresponding reality."[25] When Said states that it "is not the thesis of this book to suggest that there is such a thing as a real or true Orient," it should also be noted that neither it is his thesis to deny such a real Orient.[26] Indeed, Said immediately describes it as a "brute reality obviously greater than anything that could be said about them in the West." The issue for Said was never the reality of an Orient but rather how representation could reclaim that reality for him and his reader in a Western context. His purpose in *Orientalism* is not philosophical; this text in no way contributes to the ontological question of what it means to be real.[27] Nor does Said seriously propose to match existing Western representation to a real Orient, as a trained historian might. By limiting his focus to the contrived discourse of Orientalism, the textual locus that represents the Orient in the West, Said is content to simply assume the obviousness of a meaningful reality and move on exclusively to the realm of representation, the realm in which all texts participate by default. He cites real people and real historical events, but only to explicate textual understanding about an imaginary geography. A lot of misunderstanding about *Orientalism* would be cleared up if it were approached as an exegetical work, a textual commentary in which textuality, including its notional counterpart, discourse, is itself held sacred.

Because Said ultimately accepts the enlightened secular consensus of a reality, the philosophical angle becomes epistemological rather than ontological, hermeneutical rather than theological. The fact that there is something to be represented in texts makes them worth reading as long as there is something more to life than simply reading texts. So what, then, is visible through critical sleuthing about a representation as such? Said expresses interest in textual representations because they are not "'natural' depictions of the Orient."[28] The semantic nature of "natural," like the remonstration of "real," is quite naturally a real problem in *Orientalism*. Although Said equivocates on the tricky question of whether or not any representation can be "true," his train of thought is blandly Barthesian rather than radically Nietzschean. Language for both Roland Barthes and Edward Said deforms textual representation; this does not necessarily make representation false, but it does make the textual way of getting at truth—in a given context rather than in the abstract—distorted. In sum, the fact that Said does not believe in an "Oriental essence" does not mean that he fails to accept a real Orient that has been profoundly distorted in Orientalist discourse.

For Said there are texts, but there are only texts. Some are so-called truthful, and include histories, philological analysis, and political writing. Apparently, the common denominator of this bundling of genres is that they attempt to be accepted as truthful when they are in fact, or in principle, not so. Said leaves open the door to the possibility that such kinds of texts could be truthful under different circumstances. The criteria for what would make a text "truthful"—apart from opposing an untruthful text—are not spelled out in *Orientalism*. The reader is likely to have notions of several kinds of truth, from the idealized standard of "God's truth" to the more pragmatic rule of a reasonable fit with available evidence. At the time when *Orientalism* was published, historians who valued accuracy in writing history no longer succumbed *en masse* to the idea that a reconstruction of history is an exact match with the truth. The history of the discipline of history and its ongoing critique are replete with a concern to root out the long accretion of untruths recorded as what really must have happened. Herodotus may be revered in principle as the father of history, but he has also been [de]contextualized many times over as furthering many lies. What makes the modern study of history relevant and interesting is that examples of untruth, bias, and simple misunderstanding can be exposed in a credible way. The historical Jesus, for example, may never be known with anything approaching universal scholarly consensus, but the staggering deconstruction of the innumerable ahistorical representations of Jesus as prophet is a credit to the power of criticism to erode dogmatically based discourse.

A Tongue Lashing for Philology

> Indeed, it is not too much to say that Renan's philological laboratory is the actual locale of his European ethnocentrism; but what needs emphasis here is that the philological laboratory has no existence outside the discourse, the writing by which it is constantly produced and experienced.
>
> —Edward Said, *Orientalism*

Representation is a product of language, but philology as the methodological handmaiden for the discourse of Orientalism is singled out by Said for much abuse. In a negative way, this precursor of modern linguistic study is represented solely as a pedantic pastime of dilettantes out of touch with the reality outside texts. Said's sophomoric dismissal of the crucial impact of philological breakthroughs and methods in shaping the modern intellectual world is breathtaking and at times sudorific. The study of Oriental languages as something other than the profusion of tongues initiated in a fit of Jehovian jealousy at Babel unloosed the grip of a bibliocentric Christian theology over Western thought. Yet Said finds this shift from a dogmatized divine-origin model of language to early exploratory steps in a scientific approach problematic rather than a positive leap forward.

Said's spin on the origins of philology is a rhetorical slashing that well illustrates his skill in persuading the reader that evil intent lurks even in the dry-as-dust tomes of philology's modern founders:

> What is the category, Nietzsche will ask later, that includes himself, Wagner, Schopenhauer, Leopardi, all as philologists? The term seems to include both a gift for exceptional spiritual insight into language and the ability to produce work whose articulation is of aesthetic and historical power. Although the profession of philology was born the day in 1777 "when F. A. Wolf invented

for himself the name of *stud. philol.*," Nietzsche is nevertheless at pains to show that professional students of the Greek and Roman classics are commonly incapable of understanding their discipline: "they never reach the roots of the matter: they never adduce philology as a problem." For simply "as knowledge of the ancient world philology cannot, of course, last forever; its material is exhaustible." It is this that the herd of philologists cannot understand. But what distinguishes the few exceptional spirits whom Nietzsche deems worthy of praise—not unambiguously, and not in the cursory way that I am now describing—is their profound relation to modernity, a relation that is given them by their practice of philology.[29]

This lengthy excerpt from *Orientalism* follows a quote from Balzac's *Louis Lambert*, which sets up the three quoted excerpts taken by Said from Nietzsche's "Wir Philologen."[30] The thrust of the paragraph is to explain why philology, the discipline of guild-maker Renan, was anything but "inconsequential word-study." It leads to a pronouncement that philology, analogous to his view of Orientalism, is "a way of historically setting oneself off, as great artists do, from one's time and an immediate past even as, paradoxically and antinomically, one actually characterizes one's modernity by so doing."[31] In this scenario the early Enlightenment philologists might as well have been medieval, denying the imperially designed motives surrounding their own emerging modernity.

Because the average reader of *Orientalism* is not likely to know much about the early history of philology, Said is able to persuade with an idiosyncratic view of this field. Here the "profession of philology" begins with a single obscure individual who "invented for himself" a label. But that label stands for a significant departure from an intellectual straitjacket in which debate had stagnated over what now seem the most frivolous of issues. Which son of Noah bequeathed which new tongues in the biblical Table of Nations? How fluent was Adam's Hebrew? What language did the uneducated wild man of the forest speak naturally? The profession of philology became a discipline in the modern sense as techniques were developed to study language beyond such scripturally involuted questions. Glossing over the liberating effect that such a shift had in biblical scholarship, philosophy, and the developing sciences, Said reduces the "new philology" to the nascent and clearly racist speculation of Renan on the development of Semitic languages.[32] The racist linking of language and culture, as in the Aryan myth and in anti-Semitism, has a long and sordid history, but it was hardly the creation of modern philology. Said is apparently unaware that the linkage between language and race in Renan's work was rejected by major comparative philologists such as Max Müller.[33] There is little room in Said's fictive "philological laboratory" for the breakthroughs in translation of ancient Oriental written languages such as Egyptian hieroglyphs and Assyrian cuneiform; these efforts represent a continuing contribution of philology.

For Said, the sole interpreter of philology as a modern science is Friedrich Nietzsche, one of the masters of aphoristic writing, rather than the founding philological fathers themselves. Yet Nietzsche for all his brilliance was a philologist by default; he was trained in classical languages but can hardly be held representative of those individuals such as Jones, de Sacy, and Renan, who actively analyzed Oriental languages.[34] Nietzsche's highly polemical dismissal of philologists as a "herd" delegitimized the philology of his day, just as he defamed much intellectual endeavor. Throwing in the immodest caveat that his description has been given in a "cursory way," Said still implicates philology, as practiced by Orientalists, as a racist Eurocentric field. Having downplayed the scientific and comparative aspects of philology, Said proceeds to ridicule Renan's claim that philology is a method that could liberate the human mind. I suggest as counterpoint that this liberation through reason has been essential for the evolution of the humanities in the modern academy in which Said made his home.

In the history of intellectual exchange between Europe and the Orient, the first and foremost goal of philological study was to provide a textualized way of understanding the various languages used in the Orient, from the dead and liturgically life-supported languages of the West's religious texts to the diplomatic correspondence of contemporary sultans. The quintessential philological texts in Orientalist scholarship were not racist tomes or racy travelogues but grammars and linguistic commentaries. Yet *Orientalism* is less concerned with Edward Lane's *Arabic-English Lexicon*, which has informed almost all Arabic-language learning in the United States and England during the past century, than with Lane's dated description of an Egypt no longer modern in the way it seemed when Lane visited it so long ago. "Does this mean that products of philologists in general, including dictionaries, etc., are inherently and inevitably prejudicial and pernicious and an expression of the latent imperialism of scholars?" asks Wilhelm Halbfass.[35] As a nonspecialist in the subject, Said was seemingly unaware that the sine qua non of a well traveled text in the nearer variety of Orientalist philology is Wright's *Grammar*, rather than Renan's *Histoire générale et système comparé des langues sémitiques*. There is a reason why some texts stay in use and others drop out.

REPRESENTING THE TEXTS THAT FIT

> *This* Orientalism can accommodate Aeschylus, say, and Victor Hugo, Dante and Karl Marx.
>
> —EDWARD SAID, *ORIENTALISM*

Some texts are overtly political. A political treatise by its very nature is a truth to be believed with passion or under coercion rather than naively accepted without fault. Certainly there is a world of difference between Plato's *Republic* and Hitler's *Mein Kampf*, as there is bound to be between any narrative explaining politics and the range of documents produced in the political process. The *Magna Carta* and the U.S. *Declaration of Independence* are less relevant for representing historical truth than as pragmatic catalysts of the political process. *Orientalism*, however, is written as a text about the political reading of any imaginable kind of text, including novels and poems. The problem is not that virtually any kind of text can be read politically, as the culturally studious suggest, but that Said fails to read specifically political texts and historical documents generated in the exchange between European polities and actual Orientals. Thus Napoleon's invasion of Egypt is read through the introductory afterthoughts of *Déscription de l'Égypte* rather than through the available and relevant archives about the invasion and its reception.

Orientalism explains Orientalism as a literary critic reviews a novel; style and rhetoric are paramount, but historical accuracy and a credible fit with the real world being imagined upon are lacking in Said's narrative. Texts are approached first and foremost as texts, because any attempt to go beyond this is said to lead to a governed "exteriority," governed it seems by the claim that the Orient cannot represent itself. Said problematizes his representation of Orientalism from the start with his self-serving dismissal of the need to undertake a systematic and thorough investigation of the field. Consider the paragraph concluding the first section of the introduction:

> It should be said at once that even with the generous number of books and authors that I examine, there is a much larger number that I simply have had to leave out. My

argument, however, depends neither upon an exhaustive catalogue of texts dealing with the Orient nor upon a clearly defined set of texts, authors, and ideas that together make up the Orientalist canon. I have depended instead upon a different methodological alternative— whose backbone in a sense is the set of historical generalizations I have so far been making in this Introduction— and it is these I want now to discuss in more analytical detail.[36]

This critical passage indicates just how uncritically Said's thesis is going to be framed. Here is the author chatting up-front with the reader, dropping caveats and glossing assumptions in order to eventually move on to the discussion "in more analytical detail." The ever-present "I" of the author is introduced here in the passive sense. "It should be said at once," begins Said. But why? Why do we not have the active voice of an author stating "I need to state" or "I want to state"? What exactly is the "it" referring to? Could "it" be a fear that the three interdependent meanings proposed for Orientalism will need a certain degree of coaxing in order to become clear to the reader? And why the urgency? Should "it" be said "at once" because "it" is something so important that it cannot wait until after the analysis is under way? Is it the author's intention to get "it" over with once and for all?

The assumptions come at once. Said informs the reader that the number of books and authors will be "generous." A casual glance through the 403 notes over 22 pages indicates that this is indeed a generous amount. This is particularly ironic for an author who critiques Orientalists for their anal-retentive citational involution. What exactly is the cutoff point for having a generous helping of references in a scholarly text?[37] If there had been half the number of sources cited, would the effort still be generous? Should any academic study by someone reading texts that range well beyond his own field of expertise be judged on how many references are cited throughout the text? Would it be less generous to offer the reader a range of relevant, appropriate, or even representative texts? The phrasing here sets up the admission that "a much larger number," as Said generously puts it, "I simply have had to leave out." Why? Was it the author's seeming lack of knowledge of references not in English or French? Were the university libraries he frequented inadequate? Did a publisher's deadline compromise the scholarly goal of being comprehensive? Said immediately suggests that it does not matter anyway because his argument is not going to depend on "an exhaustive catalogue of texts." It is not surprising that, for a literary critic used to probing the meaning in a single text or the works of a single author, the need for being exhaustive is of little import. However, Said has just described a project to analyze a discourse replete with innumerable texts stretching back to Aeschylus and including such major intellectual icons as Karl Marx and Goethe. Surely the criteria for the sources chosen deserve more attention than simply being somewhere between the gratuitous minimum of generous and the absurd maximum of exhaustive. When all is said and done, what Said says undoes what has been done by leaving much of the discourse of Orientalism unsaid. The issue for an intellectual historian would be to work with a comprehensive range of relevant texts rather than the illusory goal of an exhaustive catalogue.

The dismissal of the need for a catalogue is accompanied by an equal disdain for staying within the "clearly delimited set" that makes up the Orientalist canon. Said proposes from the start not to limit himself to a select cadre of Orientalists, yet nowhere does he indicate where such a set is to be found except in the circular sense that Orientalists quote each other.[38] The implication of a "clearly delimited" canon is that it has fixed boundaries, the image of a guild with registered members. This sets up the reader by redefining any text treating the Orient as Orientalist by default. At the time when he was writing, who could argue with a literary scholar attempting to open up a delimited canon to fresh analysis?[39] The problem in probing the intellectual history of Oriental studies is that this history extended over many disciplines and fields before they became officially disciplined. The examples used in *Orientalism* include philologists, biblical scholars, religious scholars and theologians, social philosophers, historians, and social scientists even before Said mixes in travelers, novelists, poets, and colonial administrators. A vaguely delimited canon is replaced with a virtually unlimited *corpus vile*.

In all of this the basic criticisms that can be leveled at the methodology of *Orientalism* are deftly deflated from the start. Said does not need to base his analysis on a comprehensive and representative number of texts, nor does he have to define the precise boundaries of the canon he wants to cross out. Instead, a "different methodological alternative" is mentioned. This turns out to be little more than the "set of historical generalizations" already made in Said's threefold definition of Orientalism. This is circular [un]reasoning. The generalizations are the very assumptions Said intends to prove in his analysis. But who says that the "most readily accepted designation" of Orientalism can be reduced to anyone teaching, writing or researching the Orient? This implies a consciously undelimited and theoretical pool of Orientalists without differentiating the criteria for what is considered acceptable or authoritative. Is anyone who writes about health a physician? The ground is just as quicksanded in the further claim that anyone who has ever written in the West about the East necessarily filters everything through the binary lens of an ontological distinction between two imagined and opposed pseudo-geographical poles. Finally, Said offers the vague condemnation of Orientalism as a style fueled by a latent and potent will to dominate. All three of these generalizations are contestable and certainly not constitutive of a methodological breakthrough. Said's alternative is polemical smoke that repeats what was assumed in the first place. Hidden in the rhetorical shuffle is the proffering of an inconsistent method which substitutes select textual analysis for the rigorous and critical methods available at the time in history and the social sciences.

.II   The Essential[ism] Problem

Isn't there an obvious danger of distortion (of precisely the kind that academic Orientalism has always been prone to) if either too general or too specific a level of description is maintained systematically?

—EDWARD SAID, *ORIENTALISM*

In charging the entire tradition of European and American Oriental studies with the sins of reductionism, he commits precisely the same error.

—MALCOLM H. KERR, REVIEW OF *ORIENTALISM* IN THE *INTERNATIONAL JOURNAL OF MIDDLE EAST STUDIES*

The essentialist's significant facts are not windows through which an observer may peek at the inner reality of things but mirrors in which he sees his own *a priori* assumptions reflected.

—DAVID HACKETT FISCHER, *HISTORIANS' FALLACIES: TOWARD A LOGIC OF HISTORICAL THOUGHT*

In the ever more postmodern intellectual milieu, the essential unpardonable sin—what Bedouin sheikhs would brand an unredeemable *'ayb aswad* (black sin)—has been essentialism. The *OED* defines "essentialism" as a "belief that things have a set of characteristics which make them what they are, and that the task of science and philosophy is their discovery and expression." As a useful alternative to assuming that the world about us has no order at all or is totally beyond our material grasp, this concept is bland enough to evade serious criticism if the right caveats are applied. But taken to extremes, such characterizing can rapidly decline into an abysmal, chicken-egged-on debate in which ontology decapitates philosophy. If we are to escape such an apodictic free fall, the bottoming-out line should be how we use and abuse meaning rather than clinging to the rhetorical alibi of what the meaning of "is" is. Whether or not things really have essences, it is sufficient to start from the premise that many scholars assume other scholars have essentially wrong or distorted views about those essences that most concern them.

The quintessential criticism of *Orientalism* is a claim that Said most forcefully, and at times ruthlessly, resents: that Said represents Orientalism in the way he claims that Orientalists misrepresented the real Orient. As Arab scholar Nadim al-Bitar observes, Said brings through the back door the very myth about the essentialist, innate properties of the imagined "Orient" that he wants to demolish.[40] "In other words," argues Aijaz Ahmad, Said "duplicates all those procedures even as he debunks the very tradition from which he has borrowed them."[41] Ahmad adds: "Said quite justifiably accuses the 'Orientalist' of essentializing the Orient, but his own essentializing of 'the West' is equally remarkable."[42] Or, as Robert Irwin phrases it, "Said's vision of the Orient is in fact as monolithic and ethnocentric as that of any of the orientalists he denounces."[43] According to the most extreme critical view, Said constructs a misrepresentative conceptualization of Orientalism, "as pure an example of 'Orientalism' as one could wish for!"[44] The problem is that Said's specious *Homo orientalisticus* is for many critics a revolutionary dead end.[45] Such criticism extends both to the assumptions attending a conscious borrowing of Foucault's term "discourse" and to Said's insistent reduction of virtually all "Western" attempts at representing the Orient to a set of all-pervasive and all-powerful latent principles. To amplify, by only treating the imagined Orient and overtly refusing to situate the myriad Oriental images in the historical context of real people and real cultures, *Orientalism* reifies by default—by not in fact representing a real other—the powerful discourse Said is so much against.

The words of multiple critics from varied backgrounds speak to the fallout emanating from this articulation of Orientalism as a Western-styled discourse. A pervasive assumption underlying Said's depiction of Orientalism-as-discourse is an unchanging, unifyingly hegemonic and pervasive influence that individual agency and self-critique by individual Orientalists were powerless to stop. It is wrong, many critics say, to assume that such a proposed discourse could be "all-powerful,"[46] "structurally coherent,"[47] congruous,"[48] "homogeneous,"[49] "coherent imposition,"[50] "monolithic,"[51] "monologic,"[52] "all-consuming,"[53] "self-constituting,"[54] "static,"[55] "uncontested inscriptions of the hegemonic,"[56] "unvarying,"[57] "enduring, transhistorical hostility,"[58] "unidirectional,"[59] or of "unilinear conception."[60] In short, Said's characterization of a discourse he calls Orientalism is critiqued as either theoretically naive, flawed, or plain wrong. "Despite its importance and élan, however," remarks Fred Dallmayr kindly, "*Orientalism* was not free of quandaries or theoretical dilemmas."[61] As Valerie Kennedy phrases it, "Said's failure to acknowledge the heterogeneity of Orientalism may be one reason why his analysis of it becomes embroiled in contradictory definitions and redefinitions."[62]

Most critics contend that what Said molds together into Orientalism, and by extension into the political discourse of Western culture itself, was not or could not have been that singular and that discursively omnipotent. "There does not exist an Orientalist 'science' whose limits have been defined by God or by the nature of things," argues Maxime Rodinson. "What does exist is a multiplicity of issues coming under the jurisdiction of many general disciplines."[63] Another respected historian, Muhsin Mahdi, argues that Orientalism was a byproduct of general currents in Western thought, so that the politicization of knowledge rightly criticized by Said was "not created but merely confirmed by Orientalism."[64] Anthropologist Ernest Gellner simply dismisses Said's "Orientalism" as a "bogey."[65] David Kopf drags out another mythic analogy by saying that Said "transformed Orientalism into a dragon that might be destroyed with his book."[66] The whole complex of studying and representing something called an Orient should not be reduced to the discursive essence that Said suggests.

FOUCAULT'S DISCOURSE AND THE CRITICS

> We should not consider these concepts molds cast in iron, but tools to be used in each instance in the most productive way, otherwise I would discard them, for what is the value of any concept if it is used only as an ornament?
> —MUHAMMAD ABID AL-JABIRI, ON FOUCAULT'S DISCOURSE[67]

The essential site for probing Said's trenchant rhetorical exploration is Michel Foucault's antimetaphysical literary archaeology. For the record, Said informs the reader of *Orientalism* that he finds it useful to employ Foucault's "notion of discourse" to examine Orientalism.[68] Discourse is said to have a "material presence or weight" that is "really responsible for the texts produced out of it," thus superseding the originality of a given author.[69] "Most important," Said continues in Foucauldian spirit, "such texts can *create* not only knowledge but also the very reality they appear to describe." In *The World, the Text, and the Critic* Said reiterates his attraction to Foucault's notion: "The power of discourse is that it is at once the object of struggle and the tool by which the struggle is conducted."[70] Discourse is said to operate from the level of base rather than superstructure, giving it an uncanny ability to appear as truth. Thus Said lends an evaluative but nevertheless invisible hand to his analysis of specific texts. One implication is that discourse can be traced by linking its manifest effects to a set of necessary but latent defects. Foucault provides a missing link "by making the text assume its affiliations with institutions, offices, agencies, classes, academies, corporations, groups, guilds, ideologically defined parties and professions."[71] A text becomes meaningful not because of its demonstrable fit with a reality called historical truth, but simply because it can be shown to create a subtle but false appearance of truth in the service of some obvious power ploy.

From the beginning, Said was quite explicit about what he saw as shortcomings and even inconsistencies in Foucault's work. "Yet unlike Michel Foucault," writes Said the literary scholar, ". . . I do believe in the determining imprint of individual writers upon the otherwise anonymous collective body of texts constituting a discursive formation like Orientalism."[72] As a result, Said pledges to "reveal the dialectic between individual text or writer and the complex collective formation to which his work is a contribution."[73] Such is Said's stated goal, but throughout *Orientalism* there is a decidedly one-armed dialectical shakedown in which an author's intentions are either thoroughly suspect or incapable of making any sustainable imprint. As Sara Mills observes, Said retains some notion of the author's intentions "if only to be able to castigate someone for the racism of their texts."[74] Said believes that Foucault was aware of the overall "problem of the relationship between individual subject and collective force" but unable to resolve it.[75] I believe that Said was also aware of the same problem but is equally unable, perhaps unwilling, to resolve it. If Said in fact demonstrates no practical possibility that an individual Orientalist textually challenged the dominant discourse of Orientalism, then what is gained by his analysis of specific texts except as pieces of a whole that is defined from the start?

Apart from the meta-problem of intentionality, Said faults Foucault for a number of sins that critics in turn find present in *Orientalism*. There is more than a little irony in Said's accusation that Foucault ignores the roles of class, economics, and state power because of his "eagerness not to fall into Marxist economism."[76] Said's own eagerness to distance himself from Marxism, especially academically American Marxists, is evident from his dainty inferno-ization of Marx, along with Aeschylus, Victor Hugo, and Dante, as an accommodating Orientalist.[77] That complex interaction is missing in his Orientalism thesis; commentators on *Orientalism* find a lack in Said's own work, in that "in referring to the power of Orientalists, he does not in any simple and limited way refer to the economic, political, and administrative institutions of colonial domination."[78] Adding additional insult to his own injury, Said later finds that Foucault "does not seem interested in the fact that history is not a homogeneous French-speaking territory but a complex interaction between uneven economies, societies, and ideologies."[79]

By the time *Culture and Imperialism* appears, Said seems to have abandoned a totalizing and deterministic concept of power.[80] I suspect that what always disturbed him about Foucault—more than any theoretical fault—was the latter's public refusal to be a political activist, the ultimate sign for Said of an incomplete intellectual. In *The World, the Text, and the Critic* Said expresses concern about "Foucault's unwillingness to take seriously his own ideas about resistance to power."[81] As John Meeks phrases it, Said came to view Foucault as being "theoretically predisposed to submission."[82] This may explain the relevance of pairing the avowed Marxist Gramsci with the a-meta-theoretical Foucault. Said admits, "What one misses in Foucault is something resembling Gramsci's analyses of hegemony, historical blocks, ensembles of relationships done from the perspective of an engaged political worker for whom the fascinated description of exercised power is never a substitute for trying to change power relationships within society."[83] Perhaps he sensed what others have more recently charged, that Foucault's work appears at times to be "scrupulously eurocentric."[84]

The theoretical success of *Orientalism* is due in theory to the claim that Said melded Foucauldian "discourse" with Gramscian "hegemony." Ironically, the very citation of these two prominent critics of the establishment is analogous to the citational involution Said identifies as a major constitutive factor of Orientalist authority. Certainly his "explicit invocation of Foucault" enhanced *Orientalism*'s "essential prestige in avant-gardist cultural theory," as Aijaz Ahmad observes.[85] By introducing Foucault, Said runs afoul both of those who think he is not Foucaldian enough and of those who think he is too much so. A key genealogical twist, for Timothy Brennan, is that Said's text became a major source for the influence of Foucault in post-colonial studies even though this was "an *Orientalism* that Said did not write."[86] Regardless of how major a role Foucault actually plays in Said's argument, virtually everyone, including Said, agrees that a pure sense of Foucault's discourse is not in evidence.[87] Lisa Lowe maintains that *Orientalism*'s monolithic polemic "falsely isolates the notion of discourse."[88] Uta Schaub states that Foucault allows for counterdiscourses in the West whereas Said does not.[89] William Cain goes so far as to argue that Said must disagree with Foucault in order to be able to represent Orientalism.[90] The criticism on this fulcrum is both widespread and recycled, so I will concentrate here on three of the more prominent critics: James Clifford, Aijaz Ahmad, and Homi Bhabha.[91]

Clifford chides Said the humanist for borrowing methods from Foucault, the radical critic of humanism, and thus failing to be a full-fledged Foucauldian.[92] Or, as Cain comments, "Said depends on influential theorists and yet commits himself to values that these theorists expressly disallow."[93] Said's pick-what-you-like approach to Foucault is peculiarly American, a liberal blend in which Nietzschean ersatz is effectively drained away.[94] Aijaz Ahmad likewise avers that in *Orientalism* Said borrows the apparatus of Foucault's discourse but refuses to use it the way Foucault does. As a fellow literary critic, but one who has neither chosen nor needed to live in American intellectual exile, Ahmad offers what is perhaps the most systematic and sustained critique of *Orientalism*, in an entire chapter of his *In Theory*.[95] Because Ahmad's Marxist critique is so unabashedly oppositional to Said's use of theory and history, it has sometimes been dismissed as "shrill" and "a savage attack."[96] Ahmad understandably disagrees with Said's cavalier rejection of Marxism, as well as his practical indifference to the nature of bourgeois economic and ideological underpinnings with which Marxists are fundamentally concerned. Beyond this theoretical conflict, Ahmad reads Said's reading of Foucault as a misreading:

> And at that point Foucault never spoke of a full-fledged
> discourse before the sixteenth century because what he
> then called "discourse" presumes, as coextensive corol-
> lary, a rationalism of the post-medieval kind, alongside
> the increasing elaborations of modern state forms, mod-
> ern institutional grids, objectified economic productions,
> modern forms of rationalized planning. Said's idea that
> the ideology of modern imperialist Eurocentrism is
> already inscribed in the ritual theatre of Greek tragedy—
> or that Marx's passage on the role of British colonialism
> in India can be lifted out of the presuppositions of polit-
> ical economy and seamlessly integrated into a transhis-

torical Orientalist Discourse—is not only ahistorical in
the ordinary sense but also specifically anti-Foucauldian
in a methodological sense.[97]

Foucault, unlike Said, did not try to derive discourse from master texts,
nor was he preoccupied by canonical authors.[98]

The most psychoanalytic, indeed Lacanian, critique of Said's (mis)cours-
ing of Foucault's discourse is by literary critic Homi Bhabha, who finds the
argument in *Orientalism* revealing and relevant, but in need of a rereading.
Bhabha argues that Said is guilty of "psychologistic reduction" in reducing the content of Orientalism to a latent or unconscious repository of fantasy and the form of Orientalism to a historically based, manifest aspect.[99]
By opposing content over against form and confusing essence with appearance, Said subverts the power of Foucault's approach by returning to an
instrumentalist notion of power. "The productivity of Foucault's concepts
of power/knowledge lies in its refusal of an epistemology which opposes
essence/appearance, ideology/science," argues Bhabha. "'*Pouvoir/Savoir*'
places subjects in a relation of power and recognition that is not part of a
symmetrical or dialectical relation—self/other, master/slave—which can
then be subverted by being inverted."[100] Said's East/West binary is thus
challenged as a misapplication of the Foucauldian approach to power. Further, for Bhabha there are contradictions and conflicts in colonial discourse
that Said does not appreciate in his insistence on Orientalist discourse as
homogenized and unidirectional.

Bhabha proposes a solution by drawing on the ideas of two other household F-names in post-colonial studies, Freud and Fanon.[101] Freud provides
the fable of fetishism as "the disavowal of difference" in a titillating, even
towering, sweep of Bhabha-speak:

> For fetishism is always a "play" or vacillation between the
> archaic affirmation of wholeness/similarity—in Freud's
> terms: "All men have penises"; in ours: "All men have the
> same skin/race/culture"—and the anxiety associated with
> lack and difference—again, for Freud "Some do not have
> penises"; for us, "Some do not have the same skin/race/
> culture." Within discourse, the fetish represents the simul-
> taneous play between metaphor as a substitution (masking
> absence and difference) and metonymy (which contigu-
> ously registers the perceived lack). The fetish or stereo-
> type gives access to an "identity" which is predicated as
> much on mastery and pleasure as it is on anxiety and

defence, for it is a form of multiple and contradictory belief in its recognition of difference and disavowal of it. This conflict of pleasure/unpleasure, mastery/defence, knowledge/disavowal, absence/presence, has a fundamental significance for colonial discourse.[102]

Readers of Bhabha's quasi-pornographic panopti-concept render his main point as ambiguity or ambivalence.[103] In a sense, Bhabha and others who derive theoretical insight from psychoanalytic theory are forcing Said's use of terms such as "latent" and "manifest" back into the channels created for them. The colonizing imperialists not only can then be seen with their pants down, but the very source of their power is deactivated. If Flaubert's mal[e]odorous prose speaks of penetrating a feeble and feminized Orient, Bhabha's recasting of Freud's castration complex conjures up anxiety in the very act. Such depoliticizing has brought down more than a fair share of counter-critique that Bhabha is essentially reconstructing collaboration with power. As Youssef Yacoubi laments, "Bhabha's reading can only throw us back on the imperial soap box shouting and forcing rational infiltrations, evidentiary demurrals, detours of splits, *corpus delecti*, and stoppages."[104]

Fellow Freudian Frantz Fanon enters the post-colonial canon by the powerful rhetorical teeth of his skin. "My contention," writes Bhabha, "is splendidly caught in Fanon's title *Black Skin, White Masks* where the disavowal of difference turns the colonial subject into a misfit—a grotesque mimicry or 'doubling' that threatens to split the soul and whole, undifferentiated skin of the ego."[105] Such stereotyping becomes an arrested or fixated representation that denies the possibility of difference. But, argues Bhabha, this presents a problem for the colonizer as well as the colonized. Bhabhan Orientalism, unlike the Saidian homogenized and hegemonic variety, has within it internal contradictions and generates the seeds of its own subversion. For all the merits of Bhabha's redirecting of Said's argument, his use of Fanon raises the eyebrows of more than a few critics. Bhabha's rendition turns Fanon into "le Lacan noir," complains Henry Louis Gates Jr., who accuses both Bhabha and Said of treating the pre-post-colonial icon as "a Rorschach blot with legs."[106] In revising Said's binaries, Bhabha adds untested, occasionally contested, pairings of his own.

From the other side, Said's thesis is said to be spoiled by his reliance on Foucault, whose discursive "archaeology" was not universally admired in the humanities and social sciences.[107] As Michael Dalby observes, by choosing Foucault's discourse Said is "freed from the burdens of conventional historical explanation" that focuses on change over time: Foucault will only get Said to the "how" rather than the "why."[108] Anthropologist Christa Salamandra notes that "Said's excursion into Foucauldian questions of knowledge and power" has resulted in a "political correctness" that makes it almost impossible to portray Arabs and Muslims in anything but a positive light.[109] The most virulent critical visitation in this regard is Bryan Turner's bizarre genealogical link backward from Said through Foucault to Martin Heidegger, the German philosopher who is damned as inaugurating deconstruction within the legacy of fascism.[110] For sociologist Turner, *Orientalism* is another example of socially deviant deconstruction and solipsistic textualism, both borne on an anti-modernist fascist error that would appear to contaminate anyone who uses such methods; in essence "guilt by association."[111] Historian Sir John Plumb, less controversially, urges Said to read more Karl Marx and less Claude Lévi-Strauss or Foucault, as the "thesis" about Orientalism "bred its own antithesis."[112]

From both sides there is a somewhat pedantic concern for how Said scores on some pristine Foucauldian scale. This line of disagreement all too easily becomes a put-up-with-Foucault's-deconstruction-of-humanism-as-usual-or-shut-up condemnation. Perhaps now that the uncritical faddishness of Foucault has subsided it is possible to ask if it is not worth an attempt to salvage important elements of humanism from its poststructural iconoclastic savaging. My own reading of the extensive reviews and critiques of *Orientalism* suggests that more energy has been spent on discussing whether Said properly understands Foucault than on whether or not his argument is sound on its own terms. After all, Said does not claim to adopt Foucault's archaeological methodology in situ; at bottom, why must Said or anyone copy Foucault lock, stock, and over a philosophical barrel? William Hart, for example, notes that such criticism of Said is limited, because it begs the question of subjecting "Foucauldian 'scripture' to 'high criticism.'"[113] It makes little sense to fault Said's thesis just because it "falls short of Foucauldian orthodoxy," as Neil Lazarus observes.[114]

Discourse is not the same as ideology, a term Said repeatedly rejects in his writings. In explaining Foucault's views on the "struggle for domination," Said finds "ideology" to be "too constraining a term" for "systems of belief and universes of effective performance and discourse."[115] Yet throughout Said's corpus an adjectival form of "ideology" continually emerges, as in the "system of ideological fictions I have been calling Orientalism."[116] Said's inconsistent return to ideology is well illustrated in a passage at the end of *Orientalism*: "But there is no avoiding the fact that even if we disregard the Orientalist distinctions between 'them' and 'us,' a powerful series of political and ultimately ideological realities inform scholarship today."[117] If other politically informed biases are ultimately ideological, how can Orientalism not also be an ideology? No matter what the author's semantic preference, readers often read *Orientalism* as a thesis about an ideology.[118] The submergence of ideology in Said's rhetoric no doubt relates to his disdain for much of Marxist literary theory. This in turn alarms many of his critics. "Why is it that in a world racked by ideological conflict," contends Terry Eagleton, "the very notion of ideology has evaporated without trace from the writings of postmodernism and post-structuralism?"[119]

GRAPPLING WITHOUT GRAMSCI'S CONSENT

> In any society not totalitarian, then, certain cultural forms predominate over others, just as certain ideas are more influential than others; the form of this cultural leadership is what Gramsci has identified as hegemony, an indispensable concept for any understanding of cultural life in the industrial West. It is hegemony, or rather the result of cultural hegemony at work, that gives Orientalism the durability and the strength I have been speaking about so far.
>
> —EDWARD SAID, *ORIENTALISM*[120]

Orientalism consciously incorporates Gramsci's concept of cultural hegemony alongside Foucauldian discourse. Where some see a postmodern marriage of convenience, others condemn a theoretical "yoking together by violence."[121] Said was certainly not the first Arab scholar to find Gramsci's ideas useful for studying how intellectuals serve to legitimize political ideology. Gramsci's *The Modern Prince* had been translated into Arabic in 1969. As Abdallah Laroui observes: "The Arab revolutionary intelligentsia can profit greatly from Gramsci's remarks, provided that it takes care to reinterpret them in the context of the Arab political tradition."[122] Writing about the ideological role of European intellectuals without reference to Gramsci is almost like discussing Orientalism and not mentioning Said. Beyond the disorienting affront of seeing a non-leftist humanist shacked up with a radical icon of the left, there is the legitimate question of how the revolutionary content of Gramsci's theory can be domesticated without acknowledging the relevant fact that Gramsci was, after all, manifestly a communist.[123]

The key concept—indeed, the only item borrowed for *Orientalism* from the Gramscian corpus by Said—is hegemony. Said finds Gramsci's view of civil society a "useful analytic distinction," but there is no indication in his text of the controversial interpretive history of *egemonia*.[124] There is general agreement that Gramsci proposed the concept to explain the proletariat's ability to rule as a class with the seeming approval of subaltern groups in the same society; manipulating consent became an alternative to overt coercion. However, Said adopts the term without Gramsci's philosophical consent and leaves out its contextual meaning. Seldom in *Orientalism* is there an explication of how Orientalist discourse manipulates the consent of real Orientals. The closest Said comes to this is his blank-listing dismissal of unnamed "Oriental students" who want to sit at the feet of American Orientalists and repeat the dogmatic clichés.[125] There is no discussion of the ways in which real Orientals consent to Orientalist dogma from within their own worldly contexts.

To speak of the "hegemony of European ideas about the Orient" and the "umbrella of Western hegemony over the Orient," and "saturating hegemonic systems like culture" harks back to the generic and wide use of the term as a mere synonym for political domination.[126] As Dennis Porter notes, what is absent from *Orientalism* is "a sense of hegemony as process in concrete historical conjunctures, as an evolving sphere of superstructural conflict in which power relations are continually reasserted, challenged, modified."[127] Similarly, Nicholas Dirks finds a problem with Said's direct application of Gramsci's hegemony in the colonial process, because this would imply both the possibility of assent and a political capacity to generate that assent through the institutional structure of a civil society that is absent, not allowed, in a colonial context.[128] The ability to dominate, a privilege of imperialism and colonialism, does not define hegemony, because the whole point is that there be a form of consent from those most affected.[129] The irony is that Said would have to modify his position that a totalizing Orientalism mutes the other in order to explore how consent is in fact created synergistically among the colonized.

THE KNOWLEDGE-VS.-POWER STRUGGLE

> Ceci dit, Said n'a pas à mon avis analysé méthodiquement les divers savoirs et formations de pouvoir que comprend l'orientalisme. Leurs différences qualitatives et fonctionnelles, leurs hétérogénéités et leurs conflits restent obscurcis.
>
> —PERCY KEMP, "ORIENTALISTES ECONDUITS, ORIENTALISME RECONDUIT"

What Said attempts to do in *Orientalism* is wed two seemingly symbiotic, but clearly not identical, views about the relation of power to knowledge.

Setting aside exegesis of Foucault and Gramsci, how does Edward Said inscribe the contested power-knowledge continuum in *Orientalism*? His closing warning about "the seductive degradation" of "any knowledge, anywhere, at any time" is certainly a bitter admission for a humanist.[130] Power corrupts, and absolute power corrupts absolutely—so goes the old saw. So is all intellectual knowledge corrupting? Is any claim for objective scholarship just a de facto justification of oppression? It was certainly no novelty at the time to point out the power inherent in discourses of knowledge, but Said is not simply recycling Nietzsche in the abstract. The polemical anger girding Said's rhetoric suggests at times that Orientalism is akin to smallpox, a fire that needs to be put out, a fallen Edenic apple rotten to the core. At least this is how many of his critics read *Orientalism*.[131] Lines such as "To have such knowledge of such a thing is to dominate it, to have authority over it" encourage such a reading.[132] Or, "He [the Orientalist] is never concerned with the Orient except as the first cause of what he says."[133] "Never?" asks John Whalen-Bridge.[134]

Rashmi Bhatnagar tries to rescue Said's power failure by suggesting that Said "only meant to suggest the suspicion of a relationship" rather than asserting that all Orientalist texts have a will to power.[135] But, as Abdirahman Hussein argues, "in Said's writing, the will to truth and the will to power are almost always directly implicated in each other."[136] How else is a reader to understand Said's insistence that an "unbroken arc of knowledge and power connects the European or Western statesman and the Western Orientalists," or that the "scope of Orientalism exactly matched the scope of empire"?[137] Paul Armstrong reads Said as denying validity to knowledge "because of the very will to power which motivates it."[138] Said's hermeneutic self-enclosure rules out any potential for self-disclosure. This suggests that the self can be independent from an other, thus reinforcing the kind of binary reasoning Said and so many others deplore. Said's polemic would hardly have bite if it were only about raising intellectual suspicions. Such a suspicion, already flagged within the circles Said labels Orientalist, would hardly be novel. Such would not be a fair reading of what Said actually says over and over again. The texts narrated in *Orientalism* are judged guilty even when the author appears to be sympathetic. Even if Said was simply raising suspicion, his admirers brought out the rope and quickly strung up the perceived culprits.

But surely, most readers wonder, there is a more subtle message beneath the anger. Victor Brombert asks the question that Said chooses to duck: "Granted that a relationship between knowledge and power exists, does it follow that the will to knowledge is synonymous with the will to power?"[139] A pragmatic response, one of many, is offered by Terry

Eagleton: "It is perfectly possible to agree with Nietzsche and Foucault that power is everywhere, while wanting for certain practical purposes to distinguish more and less central instances of it."[140] This nuance is precisely what Said fails to provide in his polemic. The power inherent in Orientalist discourse is bad by default: the West always dominates the East, whether from a position of strength or weakness. Even Roger Owen, an admirer of *Orientalism*, observes that there is more to the problem than seeing Orientalist studies through their "association with power."[141]

A recent attempt to rescue Said's Orientalism thesis from his critics has been made by anthropologist Nadia Abu El-Haj, who argues that Orientalism should not be viewed as an essentialism, because Said grounded it in the actual history of empire. She criticizes those who would reduce his thesis to "a discursive practice stripped of its entanglement with specific forms and institutions of power in which Orientalist discourse was and remains embedded."[142] Yet it is precisely the sympathetic fellow literary critics and post-colonial scholars who are the most guilty of ignoring the history cited by Said. An essentialism is not simply the result of "dehistoricizing cultural forms," as Abu El-Haj suggests, but also the result of faulty historicizing, and it is the latter that compromises *Orientalism* as intellectual history.[143] As I noted in chapter 2, Said's history of empire is selective and seriously flawed because he did not approach that history with critical historiographic insight. When a discourse asks one to imagine an Orientalist discourse from Aeschylus to Kissinger, it is not hard to see why so many readers view that discourse as a textualized essentialism distorted out of historical context.

THE OCCIDENTAL CRITIC

> Above all, I hope to have shown my reader that the answer to Orientalism is not Occidentalism.
>
> —EDWARD SAID, *ORIENTALISM*

Said insists that he is not out to combat one essentialism with another. Certainly almost all of Said's readers, apart from those who advocate an ethnocentric anti-Westernism, agree that the story needs to be more than "dueling essentialisms."[144] Heartfelt as it clearly was, this plea did not stop many Arab and Muslim readers from assuming that any critique of Orientalist bias against Islam was in effect a defense of Islam and by default a blanket condemnation on the West.[145] As Stein Tønnesson observes, "Assuming there really is something we may call a Western cultural hegemony or cultural imperialism, then 'orientalism' is its literary and social scientific form, and 'occidentalism' is a programme for revenge."[146] As a consequence of failing to designate what Islam "really" is outside its Orientalist vilification, *Orientalism* seduces some sympathizers into responding with an equally polemical "anti-orientalism."[147] Said, by the default[y] incompleteness of his deconstruction-minus-reconstruction, thus becomes "an apologist of sorts."[148] One of the unfortunate and unforeseen results of Said's Orientalism thesis is that a variety of visceral forms of anti-Western rhetoric can claim equal rhetorical space for resistance.

Said, like a number of binary-blinded writers, errs in assuming that the opposite of the Orientalism he is describing would be an Occidentalism, a kind of linguistic tit for tat à la Orient vs. Occident. This is the implication in Ziauddin Sardar's charge that "Said's reduction of this diversity and heterogeneity actually amounts to Occidentalism—a stereotyping in reverse," a parodic paraphrase of Sadiq Jalal al-ʿAzm's "Orientalism in reverse."[149] As Orientalism is reduced to what Westerners hate or reject about the Eastern other, so an equally complicit Occidentalism can be seen merely as what Orientals hate about the West. Consider the popular media usage following the 2001 bombing of the World Trade Center. Such an Occidentalism, exemplified in a *New York Review of Books* article by Ian Buruma and Avishai Margalit, becomes the "creed of Islamic revolutionaries" as well as the propaganda of imperial Japan on the way to a ballooned—in my view baloneyed—conceptual amalgam of anti-urbanism, anti-bourgeois, anti-reason, and anti-feminism.[150] This quadrivial trivialization of what is cross-geographically a reaction to certain fundamental aspects of modernity is ill-served under the banner of Occidentalism. The absurdity in this privileging of a variety of concerns as inherently anti-Western is belied, as the authors themselves observe, when a Christian fundamentalist such as Jerry Falwell becomes "not so far removed " from the radical Islamists.[151] A spade is a spade, but what is passed off here as Occidentalism is a specific kind of anti-modernism; a temporal rather than a spatial metaphor is needed.

Even in defining "Occidentalism" it is hard to escape the epistemo-illogical Westocentrism Said sees underlying the discourse of Orientalism.[152] Couze Venn, for example, redefines Occidentalism as "the conceptual and historical space in which a particular narrative of the subject and a particular narrative of history have been constituted; these have become hegemonic with modernization having effects throughout the world because of the universal scope of the project of modernity and the global reach of European colonization."[153] Venn's Occidentalism is for all authorial intents and rhetorical purposes Said's Orientalism. If the West's East is really more about the West than the East, then Venn is quite right to redirect Orientalism to the Occidentalism it cannot escape being. Both Said and Venn see a thick post-colonial discourse embedded in the West, but this terminological anarchy is compounded even further—in what might be called an occi-moronic mode—by Venn's insistence that there is already a "post-occidentalism" in place.[154] Anthropologist James Carrier follows the Venn diagram, spinning theoretical wheels over a claim that *Orientalism* "encouraged an easy inversion, to occidentalism," although this inverse is seen as thoroughly perverse.[155] For anthropologist Fernando Coronil, Orientalists should be called Occidentalists to emphasize that they bear "the conceptions of the West animating these representations."[156] In the scholarly debate over the terms, it appears that not only can East meet West, but they also end up rhetorically being one and not the same.

The standard pre-post-colonial definitions of "Occidentalism" in English all refer to the process of making something Western, just as the earlier meaning for "Orientalism" originally connoted an Oriental custom. The dominant lexical usage, at least before *Orientalism*, is for someone who emulates or at least adopts Western custom or speech. Thus a writer/traveler/editor such as the nineteenth-century Ahmed Midhat is styled an "Ottoman Occidentalist" not because he rejected what Europe offered but because he eagerly accepted technological and educational advantages.[157] To clarify the confusion, Samir Amin coins "Occidentalocentrism" for those Arabs who basically turn Western.[158] In establishing respectability for a formal field of studying the West from the East, Hasan Hanafi proposes a distinction between Occidentalism (*istighrab*) as the academic study of the West and "occidentalisation" (*taghrib*) as the process of emulating or becoming like a Westerner.[159] Lost in this translation is a poignant linguistic irony, for the Arabic term *istighrab* also means "wonder" or "astonishment." For generations of Arabic speakers, becoming a Westerner has figuratively been something odd, strange, or absurd.

Opposition to the kind of Orientalism alleged by Said as a Western style for domination wavers between Occidentalism, anti-Westernism, and anti-modernism. Dueling ethnocentrisms between East and West have been in place from the start, no matter when that start is imagined. For example, medieval Christian diatribe against Islam was matched in equal force by Muslim invective against the Franks.[160] Writers on both sides have long treated each other as proverbial scapegoats. There were always authoritative reasons for mutual violence, just as there were brave individuals who saw through the malice and advocated tolerance and mutual understanding. When Ayatollah Khomeini called America "the Great Satan," he was not creating an Eastern style for domination or a counter- "Occidentalist" discourse, but was flatly rejecting what he saw as immoral aspects of Western influence on his own society. When so-called Islamists condemn sexual license in Europe and America as eroding religious values, they are hardly differing in principle from conservative Catholics, fundamentalist Protestants, or Orthodox Jews. The claim that contemporary Western civilization is evil in theory and practice is not intrinsically an Oriental idea. But the tendency to bundle together essentialized enemies goes on. In a particularly egregious cataloguing of the forms of anti-religious Western modernism, Muslim convert Maryam Jameelah includes "Communism, Socialism, Capitalism, Pragmatism, Positivism, Fascism, Nazism, Zionism, Kemalism and Arab nationalism."[161] She misses being a Christian fundamentalist only by negating two members of the trinity.

So after all this criticism in the literature, how does Said deny aiding and abetting militant anti-Western sentiment through his Orientalism thesis? Unfortunately, he blames the readers:

> One scarcely knows what to make of these caricatured permutations of a book that to its author and in its arguments is explicitly anti-essentialist, radically skeptical about all categorical designations such as Orient and Occident, and painstakingly careful *not* 'defending' or even discussing the Orient and Islam.[162]

In this deflective reflection, Said maintains that his critics are incapable of getting his point and must resort to caricature and distortion. At the same time, he shifts the focus from what critics have identified as a methodological problem to a matter of intent. As a proud humanist speaking from one of the academic bastions of Western intellectualism, Said has indeed been careful not to condemn the "West" that nurtures heroes such as Vico, Foucault, and Gramsci, not to mention Said himself. If he did believe that the West is evil, then his role as an American intellectual would be a glaring inconsistency. If some read Said's rhetoric as suggesting that Orientalism serves as a synecdoche of the West, this is due in large part to his polemical excess. American and European critics do not think Said is trying to "defend" Islam at all; his secular criticism is evident throughout his entire corpus. If even the most sympathetic scholars must be branded as victims of this hegemonic discourse, then it is clearly Orientalism rather than Western culture as such that Said ipso facto views as an essentialism.

III   What Is Said (but True?) About Said

> He [Said] is one of those figures who, if he did not already exist,
> the philistines would need to invent.
>
> —MUSTAPHA MARROUCHI, "ROOTPRINTS"

> "What do you think of Edward Said?" Like anyone writing on
> the Middle East—or other subjects—I have learnt that this is
> never an innocent question, but is always taken as a litmus test
> for a whole range of political and intellectual issues.
>
> —MICHAEL GILSENAN, "THE EDUCATION OF EDWARD SAID"

> So intent has Lewis become upon his project to debunk, to whit-
> tle down, and to discredit the Arabs and Islam that even his
> energies as a scholar and historian seem to have failed him.
>
> —EDWARD SAID, ORIENTALISM

*O*rientalism, the text, reminds me of a staged boxing match, with some undeniably clean points, but with a foul share of low blows.[163] Said's fresh rhetoric, designed from the start to bloody the nose of old-school academic experts, climaxes with a perfunctory mid-ring clinch, as though it is up to the ringside audience to determine who has won the match. After all, Said insists that he was not writing for—as he certainly was against—the Orientalists he was pummeling.[164] Even his fiercest critics would have to admit that the literary pugilist was still standing, eruditely, while certain Orientalist scholars could be imagined as grabbing for the ropes. In round one, Said shares his fears as an author not wishing to succumb to distortion and inaccuracy, not wanting to generalize his way through "a coarse polemic."[165] His confessional, by way of introduction, ends with the hope that his work will contribute to "a better understanding of the way cultural domination has operated" and stimulate "a new kind of dealing with the Orient."[166] In both respects this hope has been fulfilled in the extraordinary, though hardly exemplary, debate that has followed. Whatever else one can say about this single text, it has not been ignored.

After some three hundred pages of dazzlingly dense literary criticism, Said reiterates his fundamental aim of challenging the "worldwide hegemony of Orientalism and all it stands for."[167] Whatever Orientalists claim to stand for, Orientalism stands in the way of Said's own aspirations as a Palestinian, a flesh-and-blood Oriental. There is little evidence of defeatist cynicism or paralyzing pessimism in this stance. Said provides an urgently needed warning "that systems of thought like Orientalism, discourses of power, ideological fictions—mind-forg'd manacles—are all too easily made, applied, and guarded."[168] And then, on an ultimately ironic note for an individual whose career revolves around words and ideas, Said warns us about the "seductive degradation of knowledge, of any knowledge, anywhere, at any time."[169] For those who hear the bellwether echo of Foucault in this parting shot, Said's own seductive rhetoric is equally at work. It is as though the boxer wins the purse and then admits that the whole sport is, or at least probably is, rigged. But Said, as his later writings and lectures demonstrate, had no interest in putting down his gloves.

Critical commentators on *Orientalism* come in all shapes and sizes, from left and right, liberal and conservative, secular and religious, Muslim and non-Muslim. Despite the initial surprise of established historians and Arabists at the time, the ongoing debate has been most pronounced, by sheer volume, in literary studies and its poststructuralist offshoots of cultural and post-colonial studies. It is hardly the case that "Orientalist" scholars had no defense or that the establishment would rise or fall with the debating skills of any particular individual. Many scholars shook their heads at Said's brash naiveté and assumed that *Orientalism* would soon be forgotten. For younger initiates at the time, including myself, the revolution Said was calling for was already underway. Those who wanted the heads of old-guard stalwarts epitomized by Bernard Lewis found in *Orientalism* a manifesto. Rallying around Said, some Arab and Persian graduate students no doubt felt they could now storm the Bastille that had dis-oriented them so authoritatively. Anyone who knocked Said too harshly was simply a caught-in-the-discursive-act Orientalist or, worse, a closeted Zionist. More than two and a half decades later, his more adamant defenders still argue that Said's opponents "have corrupted his positions with predictable histrionic misrepresentations."[170] The polemic drags on with no end in sight.

Looking back on the overall landscape in the wake of *Orientalism*, it is possible to distinguish several general ways in which Said's critique has itself been critiqued. The first relates to Edward Said himself, an author whose driven agency does not easily allow separation of the man from his arguments and rhetorical style. His self-acknowledged "personal involvement in having been constituted as 'an Oriental'" underlies his passion from the outset, although it is clear that it is more precisely his life as an Arab Palestinian in largely pro-Israel United States that is the most "disheartening."[171] Said did not just bash an established Orientalism; he did so unabashedly as a Palestinian in exile. For many of his detractors and defenders, this fact prevents an objective reading of any argument he might make.[172] From an extremely nasty Zionist angle, Said is demonized as the "Professor of Terror," Arafat's Man Goebbels in New York.[173] Liberal Jewish writers such as Leon Wieseltier try to navigate between the extremes by not collapsing Said into an Abu Nidal so as not to end up themselves in bed with a Meir Kahane.[174] Ironically, as Ella Shohat observes, it is Said-as-Palestinian's public appropriation of the "cultural signifiers of Jewishness— exile, diaspora, wandering, homelessness" that makes him more dangerous in the long run to some Israelis than a suicidal Hamas terrorist.[175] It was his overt political visibility on the Palestine vs. Israel issue, rather than anything negative he said about dead Orientalists and their dust-covered tomes, that occasioned the most vitriolic verbal attacks and threats of violence against him.[176]

The ad hominemization of Said followed his own attack-dogmatic tactics, which at times reached the fever of a "summary exercise in character assassination."[177] The bad-guy Orientalist singled out the most has been historian Bernard Lewis, a doyen of the old-style academic establishment at an Ivy League haven. This began, at least in accessible print, in Said's spirited 1976 *New York Times* review of ten books about Islam and the Middle East, including three edited by Lewis. Said's unmitigated disgust for the work of Lewis is evident throughout this review; Lewis's ideas about Islam are not just called wrong, they are said to amount to "utter and categorical nonsense."[178] Lewis as the archetypical living Orientalist is singled out in *Orientalism* for half a dozen pages of invasive invective, in which he is said to have a "project to debunk, to whittle down, and to discredit the Arabs and Islam."[179] It is Said the intentional Palestinian critic who speaks of Lewis's ulterior polemical mission to brand Islam as an "anti-Semitic ideology" rather than merely a religion. Based on carefully selected passages, including those from conservative opinion forums such as *Commentary*, the sum total of academic production by Lewis is summed up as a dogma that "Islam does not develop, and neither do Muslims; they merely are, and they are to be watched, on account of that pure essence of theirs (according to Lewis), which happens to include a long-standing hatred of Christians and Jews."[180] That Lewis does not state this flat out, Said insists, is due to a cleverness that serves as a cloaking device of academic objectivity over what Said sees as partisan political propaganda.

As a major proof provided for this rather serious charge of academic distortion, Said turns to Lewis's etymological excursus on *thawra*, a contemporary Arabic term for "revolution," in a minor conference-proceedings paper. *Orientalism* reproduces an entire paragraph in which Lewis notes that the root meaning in classical Arabic of the form *thawra* referred to rising up or being excited.[181] In Lewis's text, the example of a camel is provided parenthetically. Said calls this typical Orientalist bias. Yet, as Arab author Hazim Saghiyya rightly observes, Lewis is simply repeating what the major Arabic lexicons say.[182] With regard to the "bad faith" of Lewis in pointing out what medieval Arab lexicographers wrote, Dennis Duncanson suggests facetiously that this is "not a bad image, if you know the habits of those irascible beasts."[183] The quoted paragraph does not dwell on the camel but shows how *thawra* was used historically in Arabic texts to refer to political excitement and sedition. Lewis actually begins his study with the Arabic term *dawla* because that was used to describe the early Abbasid overthrowing of the Umayyad caliphate. He proceeds to show how this term was used in the Quran and a number of early historical and lexical texts. Yet another term, *fitna*, was used prior to *thawra*, the latter term more recently applied to the French revolution. "At no point in the essay is one sure where all these terms are supposed to be taking place except somewhere in the history of words," complains Said.[184] Yet this is no haphazard menagerie of quaint Orientalist musing on words. Why excoriate Lewis in a most unappealing way for not mentioning the modern term until near the end of his short article, when Lewis's stated point is to discuss the various Arabic terms in chronological sequence? Said's categorical rejection of Lewis also ignores the fact that the overall goal of the conference at which the paper was presented was to avoid looking at "revolution" in Arab or Ottoman contexts as a clone of the European sense.[185]

But this sleeping camel is not left to lie. "Why introduce the idea of a camel rising as an etymological root for modern Arab revolution except as a clever way of discrediting the modern?" queries Said rhetorically in branding the entire passage as "full of condescension and bad faith." Quoting camels, according to Said, is a sadistic way of dismissing Arabs as incapable of serious political action. We are enticed to read [into] along with Said that Bernard Lewis has a pornographically political motive in reducing the Arab to "scarcely more than a neurotic sexual being." "Instead of revolution there is sedition," writes Said famously, "setting up a petty sovereignty, and more excitement, which is as much as saying that instead of copulation the Arab can only achieve foreplay, masturbation, coitus interruptus."[186] "These, I think," muses Said, "are Lewis's implications, no matter how innocent his air of learning, or parlorlike his language. For since he is so sensitive to the nuances of words, he must be aware that *his* words have nuances as well."[187] It is enough, Said assures us, that he as critic can elicit such a "nuance" contrapuntally. My unexpurgated reading of the same passage fails to discover the blatant sexual innuendo that Said supplies between the lines.[188] Bearing in mind Said's closing reminder of the "seductive degradation of knowledge," it is hard to imagine how Lewis, or any other academic author, has a chance to respond rationally to such simultaneously titillating and titivating rhetorical flair. With this insertion of latent phallocentric intent into prosaic philology, Lewis is given—so to speak—the shaft. There is not even the redemptive coda of a "Go, and sin no more!" in sight. I blush to think what Said would make of a more recent attempt by Lewis to classify Middle Eastern alimentary practice as "the finger zone."[189]

Said's lust-laden camel trope is worth examining for the finessed stroke of odalisque phrasing that makes it so delectable to dis-like-minded voyeuristic critics. An established scholar is portrayed in principle, yet without principle, as a kind of ideological peeking don. As a result of overwrought polemic, both the literal pen and the metaphorical penis appear to be mightier than the sword for rendering the body politic in Orientalist narrative. For rhetorical bait Said sets up Lewis by characterizing the introductory remarks of the proceedings editor, P. J. Vatikiotis, as "purple writing" that links revolution with "a bad kind of sexuality." We are led, line by line, to think that Vatikiotis, like Lewis, is ultimately referencing Arab sexual ability, or lack thereof: an exercise in Lacan-like pseudo-political castration. I suggest that Vatikiotis is more Platonic than Sadist in his prose. Nor is there any specific reason to assume, as Said insists, that Vatikiotis is presenting a "quasi-medical definition of revolution" as a "cancerous disease."[190] It is Said who reads a sexual slant into the editor's prose, which is stilted and forgettable to be sure.[191] Vatikiotis's own spin on the ideology of revolution in European usage is that "it attempts to create substitutes for reality: to control the known world by bringing it under its history-moulding will."[192] The irony is how closely this resonates with Said's view of Orientalism as discourse. The "bad kind of sexuality" that Said teases out of the passage would, if an accurate claim in the first place, tarnish the revolutions in Europe rather than the Middle East.

Throughout his analysis of the Vatikiotis introduction, Said recreates the dichotomy of a superior West versus an inferior "Arab" stand-in for the East. Vatikiotis, clearly drawing on the papers he is introducing, talks about "revolution" as applied to Turkey and Iran as well. It is Said who shows bad faith by insisting that the authors are denigrating Arab politics as inferior, when it is the applicability of the Western concept of "revolution" that is being challenged in the volume. The main point of Vatikiotis's introduction is that the kind of revolution that transfers power from one social class to another had not yet occurred in the Middle East; the various coups d'état, insurrections, and rebellions had for the most part just changed the actors without revising the structure. Vatikiotis points out that revolutionary uprisings in the Middle East have not happened because of change in the economic basis of society, but primarily as a result of military coups.[193] Several of the papers in the book, most explicitly the one by Roger Owen, focus on Marxist theory of revolutionary change and class structure. The question for these authors is what the term "revolution" should mean, which is why the conference was held in the first place. The first article in the volume, by A. T. Hatto, argues that the term "revolution" has been so loosely applied that its usefulness is still an open question. In the last article, John Gardner, a specialist on Communist China, calls revolution "one of the vaguest words in the political scientist's vocabulary." Albert Hourani, in a historical overview of political movements in the Middle East from 1798 to 1962, questions whether these were "true revolutions" at all.[194] The point of all these papers is not to dismiss Middle Eastern politics as inferior, but to examine whether a vague Western term like "revolution" really serves cross-culturally. The volume in which the offending article by Lewis appears is poor evidence for Said's dis[cuss]ing of Orientalism-as-usual. Said confounds the discussion of how politics and economics integrate in producing and sustaining revolutionary change by arbitrarily teasing out a story about Western superiority.

One of Said's rhetorical means for a polemical end is to partially— certainly not impartially—quote a phrase while judiciously neglecting words that would qualify and at times refute what the phrase alone might imply. After criticizing Lewis for not starting his historical etymology with one of the most recent terms, Said insists: "The point there is mainly that 'the Western doctrine of the right to resist bad government is alien to Islamic thought,' which leads to 'defeatism' and 'quietism' as political attitudes."[195] Were this really what Lewis was saying, he would fit the bill of the bad Orientalist like a trial lawyer's glove. But consider what Lewis actually wrote: "The Western doctrine of the right to resist bad government is alien to Islamic thought. Instead, there is an Islamic doctrine of the duty to resist impious government, which in early times was of crucial historical significance."[196] Lewis's qualification, omitted by Said in his selective quoting, is turned into a simplistic denial by its deletion in the quote. It is not Lewis who suggests that a lack of resistance to bad government leads to a "defeatism" and "quietism"—these two terms appear three paragraphs later in his article, in a summary of a long quote by the famous ninth-century writer al-Jahiz and in an elaboration of a point made by the fourteenth-century scholar al-Iji, respectively. Said's cut-and-paste job makes Lewis seem to say something utterly outrageous, when in fact Lewis in this passage is discussing documented nuances in Islamic discussions on the duty of civil disobedience in the face of tyranny.

Said vs. Lewis became a comic and at times tragic sideshow to the issues underlying the polemic. Indeed, as Michael Gilsenan post-prophetically observes, the combative tone of Lewis's responses no doubt contributed substantially to the making of *Orientalism* as a phenomenon.[197] I would go so far as to venture that without Lewis as a convenient target, the polemical force of *Orientalism* would have been far less. Before the publication of *Orientalism* Lewis responded to Said's blistering attack on his work by looking beyond the "personal abuse" and expressing his alarm at Said's desire to scrap the entire sweep of Orientalist—a term Lewis considered somewhat archaic at the time—scholarship.[198] Said contends that Lewis is the scholar of animosity who is "there to oblige" when someone needs a "knowledgeable attack on the Arabs and Islam."[199] In Said's relentless bashing, few literary punches are pulled. Even in *Orientalism*'s later afterword we read:

> Lewis's verbosity scarcely conceals both the ideological underpinning of his position and his extraordinary capacity for getting nearly everything wrong. . . . He proceeds by distorting the truth, by making false analogies, and by innuendo, methods to which he adds that veneer of omniscient tranquil authority which he supposes is the way scholars talk.[200]

Lewis is the poster child not so much for "obfuscation" as for "active insinuation" by his learned presence in partisan political forums.[201] The Princeton historian is maligned as a secular Great Satan.

Said is certainly not alone in targeting Lewis as an Orientalist hired gun for Israel. Mustapha Marrouchi, for example, ranks him with Daniel Pipes as one of those who "blather on in places of weak scholarship."[202] Historian Rashid Khalidi more diplomatically suggests that Lewis holds high the "torch of urbane, condescending contempt for Arabs, Muslims, and Middle Easterners."[203] Given his discernable support of Israel, there have been many Muslim intellectuals who could not see past Lewis as a "Jewish writer" and "Zionist," especially for his early mass-marketed paperback *The Arabs in History* (1966).[204] We are even informed that Lewis "operated as an intellectual agent of the British Foreign Office" with a "cavalier James Bond instinct for scholarly manipulation" while at London University.[205] Admittedly, apologists against Islam frequently use careless comments in the Lewis corpus to buttress their polemic. Ibn Warraq, for example, repeatedly cites Lewis, along with the more blatantly biased Renan and Muir, to explain why he is not—or at least no longer—a Muslim.[206] For an academic such as Lewis with inevitable personal opinions and a career extending back into the World War II and Cold War academic milieux, there are many points that scholars today can criticize and should correct in the rather large corpus of this over-stretched historian.[207] But it is one thing to disagree with what a scholar says in particular passages and another to accuse him of a lifelong conspiratorial plot of pornographic scope.

It is not hard to find statements by Lewis that without being twisted out of context would justify Said's indignation. What can one say about a scholar who, as late as 1998, writes that "the first, primal and indelible mark of identity is race"[208] or, in analyzing the rhetoric directed by Muslims at Salman Rushdie, adds that he is not quite sure what the phrase "insulting to Muslims" means?[209] Lewis writes and rewrites and yet again rewrites the history of the Arabs and Muslims—more often the Turks—as a once-upon-a-time great civilization that simply failed to keep up with the enlightened West, even despite Ottoman overtures to European modernity. An extinct Islamic civilization that for centuries was "in the forefront of human civilization and achievement" is sharply distinguished from the one that produces Osama Bin Laden and suicide bombers.[210] Indeed one of the things that goes very wrong with the post–September 11 rambling of Lewis in *What Went Wrong?* is his penchant, page after page, to imagine Orientals calling Europeans and Christians "infidels."[211] How great they were, how close-minded they became, how irrational they are now: this is the Oriental history that media-made Bernard Lewis tends to provide the general reader.

Such political bias should be exposed and corrected without silly Freudian asides.

A critical blind spot in much of Lewis's indignant rhetorical response to Said is an unending insistence on his own objectivity when writing about Islam and Middle Eastern culture. In part this stems from Said's total dismissal of Lewis's previous writing against a number of blatant stereotypes about Islam and the Middle East. For example, in an essay titled "The Study of Islam" that serves as introduction to his book *Islam in History*, Lewis derides the Western tendency to view the Islamic world through "a distorting glass of European and, later, North American, categories and terminologies."[212] The literature of anti-Islamic Christian polemic, Lewis continues, "shows little sign of intellectual curiosity or detachment." Noting that Oriental studies has largely been the domain of missionaries and theologians, Lewis is rhetorically quite Saidian in noting that "The prejudices of the medieval schoolmen may still at times be detected lurking behind the serrated footnotes of the academic apparatus." Ironically, Lewis is largely critical of what he calls "the odd term, 'orientalist,' significantly with a small 'o.'" For Lewis, Orientalism "designates, with extreme vagueness, the object of the scholar's studies, but gives no indication of his method or purpose." Lewis, of course, sees himself as the ideal combination of a trained historian who also knows the languages, not just a philologist lost in his study. His point is that Orientalists need to become better historians rather than undergo a discomforting public psychoanalysis. Credible scholars should stay above the fray. Indeed, Lewis takes this methodological principle so much to heart that he almost entirely ignores the merits in Said's thesis.[213]

Bernard Lewis took almost three years before responding in print to Said's sustained attacks, in a belated review of *Orientalism* in the *New York Review of Books*.[214] Attempting to match the rhetorical shrills of Said, low blow by low blow, Lewis drowns his valid points in a vat of sour grapes. The sarcastic tone of the opening Hellas-bent metaphor actually serves to highlight Said's charge that Lewis is an out-of-touch academic snob:

> Imagine a situation in which a group of patriots and radicals from Greece decides that the profession of classical studies is insulting to the great heritage of Hellas and that those engaged in these studies, known as classicists, are the latest manifestation of a deep and evil conspiracy, incubated for centuries, hatched in Western Europe, fledged in America, the purpose of which is to denigrate the Greek achievement and subjugate the Greek lands and people.[215]

The point missed entirely in this scenario is that no one has to imagine the racism of Renan or the political opportunism of Lord Curzon. There was a side to "Orientalism" that Said's charge fits well. Lewis fails to make a persuasive argument here, not because his specific points are always wrong, but because of his lecturing and snobbish tone.[216] The effect is that of a learned master peering down his nose at a brash young student. Such a patronizing tone is tonic only to those who do not like Said to begin with. As Juan Cole concludes: "Lewis can never admit that *Orientalism* is, for all its faults, a powerful and theoretically sophisticated piece of writing that has had a profound and in many ways salutary impact in cultural studies and anthropology and on the study of the Middle East itself."[217] Lewis simply does to Said what Said does to Lewis, and both end up the lesser for it.

The Said vs. Lewis face-off was followed by a thriller redux in the mid-1980s between Said as Palestinian-American and Michael Walzer as Jewish-American. The exchange between these two scholars started with Said's caustic review of Walzer's *Exodus and Revolution*, in which yet another pro-Zionist scholar was depicted by Said as wearing the mantle of academic objectivity only to disguise a justification for the continued exploitation of Palestinians. Their vitriolic point and counterpoint became the pretext for an entire book on Said's view of religion by William Hart. In his own exegesis of the verbal jousting, Hart notes: "One gets the sense that Said is circling his prey, reconnoitering and reconnoitering again before going in for the kill."[218] This image of Said as a mercenary critic with venomous ink dripping from his canine-ish, if not Canaanite-ish, pen is a disturbing reminder that because of his intent as an intellectual activist the messenger overrides the message. As Charles Butterworth remarks about Said's polemical excess in *Orientalism*, "Where a deft slash with a razor would effectively dismantle an argument, Said wades in with a pick ax."[219] Enough blood has been spilled in print.

THE INTELLECTUAL AS AMATEUR

> Hence my characterization of the intellectual as exile and marginal, as amateur, and as the author of a language that tries to speak the truth to power.
>
> —EDWARD SAID, *REPRESENTATIONS OF THE INTELLECTUAL*

> The narrowness of the Saidian exploration, on the other hand, arises from its inclination towards reductionism, and its tendency to ignore much of the richness and complexity of ori-

> entalism and of its accompanying motivations and impulsions, or else to constrain these to fit into an overtly simple mould.
>
> —J. J. CLARKE, *ORIENTAL ENLIGHTENMENT: THE ENCOUNTER BETWEEN ASIAN AND WESTERN THOUGHT*

Said is reverently lauded by admirers as the "consummate intellectual" with a "theoretically eclectic practice."[220] Representative of such acclaim is Paul Bové's opening remark in *Edward Said and the Work of the Critic: Speaking Truth to Power.* "Said's work embodies three values essential to intellectual responsibility: breadth and depth of knowledge, historical and scholarly rigor, and a profound basis in political morality of a kind that alone makes civilization possible."[221] Breadth is a judicious measure, rhetorically. In terms of scholarship, this implies intellectual work of broad scope, ranging beyond the normal boundaries of a discipline or theoretical paradigm. This is why breadth needs to be paired with depth, representing a field of vision that has full 3–D play. When Said's corpus ranges outside his original training, its breadth easily becomes a cavorting with anything concerning the Orient; the depth, which is not to be denied, is only of textual dimensions. "Rigor" is an odd category for summing up Said's historical and scholarly achievements. If the meaning here is the rigor of being rigidly and scrupulously accurate, this is a characteristic that Said faults Orientalists for privileging above concerned activism. Few, if any, historians who have reviewed Said's reading of history find it rigorous; even Said's sympathetic admirers find a lack of scholarly attention to accurate detail in much of his work. In terms of intellectual history, his interdisciplinary rigor borders on the mortis.

One word that haunts the phenomenon of Edward Said the critic is "animosity." Early on, this Anglicized appropriation from Latin via French dealt with the *anima*; animosity meant that someone was spirited and courageous. The more modern sense is that of enmity and hostility, the Said who is animated against the world against him. One man's animosity, of course, is another man's poison. This is the legacy to which Said's spirited rhetoric has come. He does not just see himself as an Oriental writing back against Orientalism, but as a man whose anger could be excused by righteous indignation.[222] Unkind critics say he bites the hand that feeds him by flailing away at an established form of humanities from within the academic halls that shelter him. Said's lashing of those who do not move with him, or simply move too slowly, made this a lonelier battle. Lewis and Waltzer make perfect foils for Said as the heroic defender of the downtrodden, but Said loses potential allies when he trashes Arab students as stooges of Western Orientalists.[223] In later contexts it is Fouad Ajami, a fellow Middle East media expert, who is said to not "know anything about the Arab world. He doesn't care about it. What he writes is simply used by the Zionist lobby and the establishment in this country against the Arabs."[224] Said often speaks as though he were personally under siege every time someone has a different view.[225] In the end, this willingness to turn on those with whom he disagrees devolves into a form of rhetorical Saido-masochism.

Said loves to see himself as an amateur; so do his critics. The problem is that Said thinks of amateurism in light of the positive Latin origin of an *amator*, or lover, whereas many of his readers find sufficient cause to label him depreciatingly as amateurishly unprofessional. Both meanings are usable in English, although the academic establishment and the commercial-sportification of professionalism have cast a long shadow over the sense Said prefers. Few of even his fiercest critics would quibble with Said's sentiment that a responsible intellectual should exhibit "care and affection" in his work and by his demeanour.[226] Nor is there cause for objection to a scholar having a "committed engagement with ideas and values in the public sphere."[227] Who can argue with the abstract aim of opposing "every form of tyranny, domination, and abuse"?[228] Indeed, taking a moral stand in a decidedly unequal world is one of the most commendable aspects of Said's intellectual legacy. But Said at times goes a step further in assuming that fellow professionals do not share such a goal simply because they belong to a corrupt guilded establishment.

The most objectionable aspect of the intellectuals Said criticizes is the narrow focus of academic training and practice. The amateur can only care if he or she is vigorously opposed to specialization, which Said thinks "kills your sense of excitement and discovery" by routinizing intellectual query in an "inevitable drift towards power and authority."[229] The opposite of amateurism thus becomes professionalism in the pejorative sense of a "cult of the certified expert."[230] In his constant characterization of the academic establishment as a guild, Said reinforces the notion that most other scholars belong to a closed club and are resistant to change from the outside. Yet it is Said's own membership in the guild, as a tenured professor at Columbia University, that allowed him a voice not crying in the wilderness of oblivion.[231] In this sense the intellectual life membership validated through his own tenure was not a barrier to being a caring amateur; why must it be for those with whom he disagrees?

There are indeed those scholars who hole up in the unworldliness of a tenured ivory tower, and others who readily sell their "professional" souls for Mammon, or foster politically expedient patriotism. What must be resisted, however, is the assumption that training or professional expertise is inevitably bad or corrupt. Said suggests that an amateur status "releases critics from the barriers imposed formalistically on them by departments, disciplines, moribund traditions of scholarship, and opens up the possibility of an aggressive study of the realities of discourse."[232] But how exactly are these barriers imposed on individuals? Does being accepted to a graduate program in itself squelch curiosity? Is entering a university faculty always the kiss of moral death? Is testifying before Congress evil in itself?[233] Are all scholarly ideas moribund just because they appear in peer-reviewed journals? The academic world is far from a trouble-free paradise, and certainly not devoid of small-minded politics and uncollegial behavior. Said compounds his a priori conspiratorial view of the "establishment" by focusing on an essentially political litmus test rather than the criteria for professional standards. I suggest that it is a rank amateur gambit to assert that professionals and specialists of any kind are incapable of being caring intellectuals or legitimately disagreeing over specific political or social issues. Suggestive metaphors aside, the academic community should not be rhetorically reduced to a closed guild of doddering dons lacking intellectual integrity.

Justifying the need for an amateur's insights, Said positions himself between the powerful hegemonic sway of the dogmas he disagrees with and the failure of earlier critique of that domination. In *Orientalism* he writes as though he were both the first "Oriental" and the first Western intellectual to speak truth to the power of Orientalism. Indeed, this is the force of his rhetorical power. There may have been a few John the Baptists— Abdallah Laroui, Hamid Algar, and Talal Asad—but Said promotes himself as exposing "what Vico called the conceit of nations and of scholars."[234] The early-eighteenth-century historian Vico, Said's tutelary historical consciousness, is especially important to Said. "We must take seriously Vico's great observation that men make their own history," Said reminds the reader, and "that human history is made by human beings."[235] Yet the central argument of his Orientalism thesis is that individuals are driven by a latent discourse. Neither Louis Massignon nor Bernard Lewis is allowed to make his own history as Vico saw it.

In insisting on the ambiguous term "amateur," Said seems oblivious to the obvious irony this carries for the role of the amateur both in his chosen field of literary studies and in the aesthetics of performance, where his wider interests lie. A student in a literature class may be motivated by a particular author yet lack critical tools to evaluate a literary work. Understandably, a literary journal would be more apt to publish an essay by Edward Said than a term paper by one of his freshman students. The point is not that a beginning student is incapable of providing useful insights but that critical skills can be profitably honed to the point of greater competence. Similarly, one can look at the example of the virtuoso pianist Glenn Gould, a most unworldly icon for Said's elaboration of musical genius. When Gould stepped onstage with a major orchestra, he did so after years of training that combined with a peculiar artistic genius that cannot be taught. At the start of *The World, the Text, and the Critic*, Said marvels at Gould's uncanny ability to play such diverse composers as Bach and Liszt in their own distinct idioms. "If one thinks about Gould and his record," argues Said, "parallels will emerge with the circumstances of written performance."[236] I suggest that a compelling contrast also emerges. Gould's recordings are valued because he is a competent professional and not a mere amateur; it takes more than love and that feeling that one is right to play well. The point of these examples is that competence does not grow on trees; specialization and professionalism based on the proper training and the right personal motivation should be valued rather than contemptuously dismissed.

Despite his emphasis on being an unspecialized amateur, Said insists that he is not against competence.[237] "I would not have undertaken a book of this sort," he remarks at the very end of *Orientalism*, "if I did not also believe that there is scholarship that is not corrupt, or at least as blind to human reality, as the kind I have been depicting."[238] Individual scholars, including the anthropologist Clifford Geertz and the Orientalists Jacques Berque and Maxime Rodinson, "are perfectly capable of freeing themselves from the old ideological straitjacket."[239] Said's rhetorical emphasis here, apart from serving as a cautious caveat to a long and pounding polemic, is that there is an overpowering establishment guild that must be critically put in its place. Unfortunately, Said provides little detail of what these approved scholars were doing differently except drawing from "the contemporary human sciences."[240]

It is not clear how carefully Said read Geertz's influential *Islam Observed*. Geertz may not be a trained Orientalist, but his approach to Islam echoes the essentialized ideal types of Weberian sociology rather than presenting Muslims on their own terms.[241] Geertz, the only anthropologist singled out for praise in *Orientalism*'s narrative, dissed Said soon after by genre blurring him to an undisclosed level of epistemological hell reserved for "ideological arguments cast as historiographic inquiries."[242] Said, not surprisingly, returned fire with fire by attacking the criticism from Geertz as "rather trivial" and implying that he had been treated by Geertz as a "wog."[243] The renowned French scholar Maxime Rodinson describes *Orientalism*'s "great merit" as shaking the "self-satisfaction of many Orientalists," a welcome appeal to stop seeing their ideas as "a natural, unprejudiced conclusion of the facts, studied without any presupposition."[244] Yet Rodinson continues to point out the methodological problems with Said's "militant stand," including Said's unyielding rejection of Marxist criticism. Another scholar favorably mentioned, Jacques Berque, is an established scholar with rigorous training in the guilded halls of professional Orientalism. Ironically, all three examples mentioned by Said are assumed to be competent to address, rightly or wrongly, the faults of prejudicial views of the real Orient because of their specialized expertise.

But what if Rodinson stepped outside his field of expertise and wrote a polemical critique of the entire American field of literary studies in which Said was trained? Suppose he defined "Lit-Criticism" as a dominant discourse of elitist intellectuals perpetuating a closed canon of Western texts? Add to this the theoretical premise, borrowed from Marx, that class warfare has been the latent legitimizing force behind all the manifest differences between practitioners in the Western humanities. Perhaps the "Renan" trope in this thesis would be that since the pioneering work of Victorian Matthew Arnold, European literary critics have fostered the suppression of "low" literary forms in order to justify a state-engineered and tiered educational system of privileged elites served by the tax dollars of unintellectual working-class laborers. It could then be argued that the genealogical trajectory of Ivy League candidates gave tenurial precedence to men who read texts that they were taught but that the common populace deemed highbrow. Of course, now and then an individual scholar would come along who could resist the guild's straitjacket, but only after having achieved tenure at one of the top universities in the world. Follow along with the scenario that a major publisher would publish and promote a sensational accusatory text without having it vetted by critical scholars with expertise on the subject. This, I suggest, is *Orientalism* in perverse.

The example just given is an exaggeration, a gross parody and a cavalier dismissal of a seminal text by a scholar who has reached far beyond one single, controversial narrative. As a satirical retort it is at the same time the act of an amateur in both Said's sense of concerned engagement with an issue and the more common sense of a trivial pursuit. I care that Said reduces an imagined discourse he idiosyncratically mislabels "Orientalism" without elaborating a critique informed by competent and open-ended analysis of sources. I am disturbed when Said subsumes biased and shoddy scholarship under the umbrage-laden umbrella of disciplines in which he has no credible experience. I certainly do not share the essentialist notion that centuries of political and representational exploitation in European and American policies can best be explained as driven by a nebulous will to dominate a surrogate "other." My flippant writing back at *Orientalism* has a purpose. My immodest proposal illustrates the danger of ignoring the central issues of competence and the capability of scholars to learn from past mistakes. Just as Rodinson, Berque, or Geertz would not have the methodological tools and experiential background to competently survey the entire imagined field of Literary Criticism, so Said does not demonstrate in his text a recognizably adequate understanding of many of the texts, individuals, and historical events he alludes to and analyzes. There are innumerable specific flaws in *Orientalism*, but above all the essential problem is the overt polemical thrust of an intelligent and inspiring writer onto a range of ideas and historical contexts he enters into undaunted as a polemicized and thus insufficient lover.[245]

Even critics who acknowledge methodological flaws and historical inaccuracies in *Orientalism* often buy into Said's argument that his freshness as a non-Orientalist allows him a critical outside perspective lost to most on the inside. Surely it is amateurish to claim, as do Ashcroft and Ahluwalia, that Said "has displayed an extraordinary command" of disciplines such as "History" and "Geography," and that Said's province includes "Sociology" and "Anthropology."[246] Said cites historical information, often errantly, but nowhere does he apply the wide range of methodologies available within Western historiography or the social sciences. Said's geographical expertise is Near-East-sited; he shows a distinct lack of understanding of other parts of the Orient. Said's use of sociological and anthropological concepts has never developed beyond that of an undergraduate student; nor does he care to engage with the swirling theoretical and reflexivist debates in these formal disciplines. Said may be widely read and a superb writer, but his forays into other disciplines are always met with resistance and at times with outright rejection. Roger Owen cautiously suggests that Said's lack of training in the field "gives him all the advantages of an outsider who can go straight to the matter and say at once what is wrong."[247] In itself, this would be the same logic followed by earlier Orientalists who assumed that only their outside secular perspective could explain Islam. The point is not the ability to look in from the outside, which even the most bigoted and biased scholars can do, but an approach to controversial issues with an open mind and no overt political agenda. Edward Said, by his own admission, is not a disinterested outsider, nor does he express any sustained interest in how to resolve the problem he identifies. Indeed, it is evident from the first page of *Orientalism* that Said is offering polemical persuasion and is anything but conflicted about the moral correctness of his own position. I suggest that Said's outsider amateur credentials ill prepare him for a surgical critique of those who wrote about the Orient. The patient under such a well sharpened knife is also under the gun; intellectual malpractice is the inevitable result.

> Yet when I say "exile" I do not mean something sad or deprived.
> On the contrary belonging, as it were, to both sides of the impe-
> rial divide enables you to understand them more easily.
>
> —EDWARD SAID, *CULTURE AND IMPERIALISM*[248]

Said's intellectual perch is "a double perspective that never sees things in isolation," the privileged perspective of voluntary exile.[249] He foregrounds *Orientalism* as "an attempt to inventory the traces upon me, the Oriental subject, of the culture whose domination has been so powerful a factor in the life of all Orientals."[250] The same exilic trope introduces *Culture and Imperialism*, which Said labels "an exile's book."[251] This autobiographical emphasis is politically charged. By entering an Ivy League university Said followed quite a few intellectuals who had come earlier as adults fleeing the repressive acts of World War II Nazism and Fascism. The main differ-ence is that whereas several noted scholars, including Orientalists criti-cized in his book, had to flee Germany to save their lives, Edward Said was not forced by persecution to migrate from Egypt to an elite American finish-ing school, nor did he choose to permanently return, though eventually able, to the Arab world or Palestine.[252] Many Palestinian Arab immigrants, Said's father included, came to the United States seeking a better life regard-less of the political and economic conditions at home. Some have been wealthy or lucky enough to cross borders; others were literally forced out of their homes with guns at their backs. There is no reason why Edward Said should not have freely preferred to live in America, but his freedom to choose resulted primarily from class advantage and career commitment.

Exile for Edward Said is less a position than a positioning. As the linch-pin of Said's secular criticism, exile becomes for him a "permanent state" leading to a "transcendental homelessness."[253] Said defines this stance as the distance enabled through crossing borders and allowing him to escape the seduction and dogmatics of any single perspective; "belonging, as it were, to both sides of the imperial divide enables you to understand them more easily."[254] The logic here is the premise underlying the modern ethno-graphic method of "participant observation" in a foreign culture. Knowing the lay of the land across borders certainly provides the opportunity to understand each other better, especially if border crossing becomes a life-long passion. But if simply being in two "theres" is the critical point, then those Orientalist scholars such as Robertson Smith and Richard Burton who actually went to the region, and anthropologists who make an academic career out of doing so, must be allowed the same border-passing savvy as other intellectuals. If, as Said argues at length, neither Orientalist scholars nor anthropologists have been able to escape the strictures of a hegemonic discourse, it would seem that only those exiled from the colonized to the imperial culture are privileged to see it both ways. The imperial divide posited by Said, the secular and "specular" border intellectual, thus becomes a one-way mirror in which only those crossing against the grain can see truth; the others just see themselves in a self-reflective mirror, darkly.[255]

The border-crossing metaphor provides an imaginative geography in which Said is able to isolate himself as an intellectual who can theoretically free himself from the shackles of establishment discourse. The exemplar of this role is a twelfth-century Saxon monk, Hugo of St. Victor. Hugo was induced by family circumstances to leave a difficult situation at home and study abroad. Not only did Hugo join an established order, he eventually became its head. His intellectual achievements, synthesizing medieval theology and science, assured him a founding role in the development of Christian scholasticism. Said is fond of the abbot's sentiments: "From boyhood I have dwelt on foreign soil, and I know with what grief sometimes the mind takes leave of the narrow hearth of a peasant's hut, and I know, too, how frankly it afterwards disdains marble firesides and panelled halls."[256] Hugo was hardly the only man or woman of his generation to dwell on foreign soil, but it is less the fact of exile than the insight of having a humble origin that informs his recollection here. He had risen from peasant to prelate, but still appreciated the simplicity of rustic life. There is certainly exilic parity between Hugo's twelfth-century Paris, even a monastery, and Said's late-twentieth-century New York, especially a major university. But there is little else in common between a monk who seeks escape from the world and the critic who values worldliness as the greatest good.

Hugo comes to Said via Erich Auerbach, the mimetic archetype for his secular criticism.[257] Setting his own life against that of a Jewish refugee sheltered in Istanbul from the Nazis, Said reverses the process: a Palestinian denied a homeland by Zionist fascism makes himself a home in a Western mega-library of great books. But the contrasts are relevant. In Istanbul, Auerbach was "out of place, exiled, alienated" from the West, whereas Said's separation from his native "Orient" leads him to prefer New York to anywhere else. Crossing borders in exile allowed Auerbach to transcend the narrowness of being at home and at the same time to appreciate all the more his own roots. Yet those very roots—being Jewish in early-twentieth-century Europe—made Auerbach an outcast in the anti-

Semitic European home where he was born. The difference is that Auerbach knew he would return, whereas Said chose the role of representing from abroad those he assumes could not effectively represent themselves. Auerbach learned little of the non-West in exile; Said brings little about the non-West into his critical opposition to Western discourse. Auerbach had been separated temporarily from the only land he wanted to recognize as home. He returned to make his home, prejudiced as it was, a better place.

The "executive value of exile," Said's ringing phrase in his essay on "Secular Criticism," avoids an uncomfortable reality faced by Arabs trained or teaching in the West.[258] Consider the following scholarly assessment from 1962:

> Even now there is no denying the fact that the Arab intellectual understands himself and his situation best, not in Cairo, Damascus or Beirut, writing or speaking in Arabic, but rather in Paris or London or New York, writing or speaking in French or English.[259]

This was the view of Gustave von Grunebaum, a German historian of Islam and target of Said, in American exile from Nazi Germany. Said rightly criticizes the essentialist categorization endemic in the scholarly work of this "Orientalist," but he himself exemplifies this stark assessment. Underlying the words of Auerbach, von Grunebaum, and Said is a privileging of the Western intellectual tradition as the only ground from which to assess and critique a specifically Western discourse. The possibility of an indigenous knowledge not informed by Western reason and science is not broached. Said's "executive" privilege becomes a mantle of authority for speaking out, despite his acknowledged distance from those he would speak for. He claims to speak as an "Oriental," but in fact he is able to speak mainly because he is a Western-educated Oriental. Not surprisingly, this leads to a view of exile that has a "slightly peculiar angle."[260] He brandishes Arab identity when it can be used to explain the passion in his conviction, but he does not situate himself with those Arab intellectuals who have not chosen exile in the West. In *Orientalism* he is at best an "amateur" Oriental.

OPPOSING SAID'S CRITICISM

> If criticism is reducible neither to a doctrine nor to a political position on a particular question, and if it is to be in the world and self-aware simultaneously, then its identity is its difference from other cultural activities and from systems of thought and

> method. In its suspicion of totalizing concepts, in its discon-
> tent with reified objects, in its impatience with guilds, special
> interests, imperialized fiefdoms, and orthodox habits of mind,
> criticism is most useful and, if the paradox can be tolerated,
> most unlike itself at the moment it starts turning into organ-
> ized dogma.
>
> —EDWARD SAID, *THE WORLD, THE TEXT, AND THE CRITIC*

In his BBC Reith Lectures, Edward Said represents himself as an amateur, exiled ideal for intellectual criticism. When Said is criticized for being inconsistent, he insists with Zarathustrian zest that this is the essence of his critical stance. Standing in one theoretical place, whatever the strength offered by that theoretical ground, is assumed to lead down the path of organized dogma unless the critic relentlessly refuses to be pinned down. Said thus privileges his own oppositional criticism against all comers and goers. Earlier critics are either so far removed from present realities that they serve merely as forebearing icons (Vico or Nietzsche), are flawed in a worldly sense (Foucault), or are useful mainly for citing in lists and endnotes (Talal Asad). Said continually writes as though he were the lone cultural critic. "Yet most cultural historians, and certainly all literary scholars, have failed to remark the geographical notation, the theoretical mapping and charting of territory that underlies Western fiction, historical writing, and philosophical discourse at the time," he asserts.[261] To argue this in the early 1990s, especially given the impact Said's *Orientalism* had already had on many literary scholars, is a self-serving stretch of rhetoric. Said provides a minor caveat for cultural historians, but certainly not for fellow literary scholars. So either Said's effort to that date had fallen on completely deaf ears—certainly news to his many critics—or other literary scholars were not being critical according to Said's standards.

Even when Said grudgingly admits that some scholars are doing what he says they mostly do not do, their efforts are characterized as "only slightly more than rudimentary."[262] For example, Said confesses that postcolonial critic Homi Bhabha's elaborations "just don't speak to me."[263] "And Baudrillard! It's just nauseating. It's just gobbledegook," exclaims Said. "No, Lacan is a serious man, I don't mean that. Both Baudrillard, and what's the name of that other guy—Lyotard, it's a kind of provincial atavism of a very very unappealing sort, and I feel the same way about postmodernism. I think it's the bane of Third World intellectuals, if you pardon the expression."[264] But should we pardon such self-served expression? Must the oppositional critic be opposed even to those who admire the critical insights of his own work? Why does Said have so little patience with the "Third World intellectuals" who draw inspiration from the rhetorical power of *Orientalism*?

By his own admission, Edward Said as oppositional critic does not take oppositional criticism of himself very well. Patrick Williams introduces a range of critical assessments of the Saidian corpus by saying that "in general Said has not been well served by his critics."[265] The reverse, I think, is also the case. Said regards "a fair amount" of *Orientalism*'s critical wake as "hostile," and some of it as "abusive."[266] In the afterword to the 1994 edition of *Orientalism*, Said dismisses a considerable amount of criticism by scholars in Oriental studies as "no more than banal description of a barony violated by a crude trespasser."[267] In his preface to the twenty-fifth anniversary edition of *Orientalism*, Said's last word on the subject, there is no reference to any of the substantive criticism of his original text. Said writes as though the only relevant explicators of Islam are Bernard Lewis and Fouad Ajami, his perennial straw Orientalists.[268] As Graham Huggan observes, Said all too often "lets his impatience get the better of him, launching into an all-out attack on the 'programmatic ignorance' of his readers."[269] It is as though no one who disagrees with him could possibly have critical self-awareness.

While Said has few qualms in asserting that some of his critics get "nearly everything wrong" or "literally everything wrong,"[270] he appears perplexed but not surprised that there is even a fair amount of criticism of his work. When Said states in his afterword that he "shall try to correct misreadings and, in a few instances, willful misinterpretations," he has in mind only the comments of his critics, not the content of his own text.[271] When asked if *Culture and Imperialism* was written to redress conceptual problems in *Orientalism*, Said responds, "Well I don't know about conceptual problems, but I expand the notion." Although intellectually assenting to the admirable principle that criticism be "reflectively open to its own failings," Said effectively closes the door to self-critique by systematically ignoring specific criticisms and wishfully proclaiming that most of the attention to his book has been "positive and enthusiastic."[272] The problem is that in claiming to have progressed beyond all "isms" Said fails to examine the "ism" inherent in his own criticism. Mustapha Marrouchi, despite his admiration for Said's work, complains that "Said negatively defines his rivals as partial, even stunted intellectuals."[273] As a "doctrinaire oppositionalist," cautions Judith Shulevitz, Said "never has to rethink his position or perform a fresh moral calculation."[274] His will to be against power is apparently enough to establish the truth of his truth.

The problem is that Said's oppositional approach prevents the consensual achievement of synthesis in academic thought. As Leela Gandhi observes, Said is "disablingly impervious to the accomplishment and value of the theories and knowledge he chooses to critique."[275] Orientalism as Said defines it cannot be reformed because it is so discursively deformed. This leads to a brand of intellectual fatalism that defies finding common ground. In an interview about his political opposition to the Oslo Accords, Said reflects: "I got the most hostile mail I've ever gotten," all from Arabs. "That's impossible for people to understand—that there are irreconcilables and that it's the job of the intellectual to show that they can be irreconcilable, but they exist, unreconciled, next to each other."[276] But certainly if an issue is irreconcilable there is no need for intellectual critique at all; a priest issuing last rites would seem sufficient. If the discourse of Orientalism is irredeemably irreconcilable with truth, then it is always going to be power rather than truth that wins out. Unfortunately, despite Said's humanist training, this is more like Machiavelli than Vico.

If criticism is always oppositional, then it must at some point even oppose itself, a philosophical corner no intellectual can comfortably dwell on or in. Said thinks he avoids such a reductio ab absurdum by assuming that an opposition to all forms of dogma is not capable of being a dogma as well. In a laudatory essay, Andrew Rubin argues that Said's lack of a defined methodology "avoids hardening into the lapidary forms of static orthodoxies, theoretical dogmas, and provincial forms of professionalism."[277] But surely no one can oppugn continually with impunity. It is absurd to be constantly oppositional rather than, as George Woodcock nicely phrases it, "merely oppositional when necessary."[278] Anti-dogma can easily become dogma, a rigid refusal to move toward reconciliation of opposing views. "To express one's solidarity with Said's position leads one to the logical necessity of somehow disagreeing with it, or modifying it in the interests of the production of criticism, and in the interests of escaping its 'domination' of one's critical practices," cautions Thomas Docherty.[279] Should academics and pundits be forever disagreeing among themselves as the real world turns and churns on?

An Occamist would look at the inconsistencies and contradictions in Said's writing as evidence of a problem, the lack of a clear and replicable methodology. Yet some of Said's defenders valorize his idiosyncratic approach to criticism. Most notable in this regard is Abdirahman Hussein, whose exegesis of Saidian prose is denser than the original. In making the case that Said's intellectual contributions have been misrecognized by critics both sympathetic and hostile, Hussein spins the following explication of Said's notion of criticism:

> Rather it involves a multiplicity of disjunctions which
> inscribe themselves as irreducible paradoxes: it is intended

to act as an insurrectionary form of energy—an index of congenital crisis that at once unmasks and dissolves dogmatic ossification; yet at times it acquires the properties of a measuring rod, a positive criterion. It partakes of methodology, often very eclectically; yet it is meant to negate—or at least problematize—method as such: perhaps it would be more precise to say that method is turned inside out, upside down, or against itself.[280]

If criticism is condemned to irreducible paradoxes and a congenital crisis, would it not be useful to seek better methods rather than hypocritically assuming that an anti-methodical antidote is free of the limitations of all other methods? Hussein immediately asks "Is such a slippery, nomadic concept useful at all?" The apparent answer is that Said's criticism cannot be reduced to a doctrine or political position, as though doctrines and politics can be avoided by will. I suggest that Hussein's admiration here dulls Occam's razor, blunting the cutting edge of critical theory as a never-ending process.

By choosing to be a public intellectual, an untiring polemicist, and a critic who opposes tropistically, it is his own perceivable persona in all its potential variance that Edward Said does not allow the reader to forget. That Said could be generous, courageous, open, charming, and admirable in countless ways no one should dispute.[281] Nor do I think it productive to dismiss Said because of his strongly held political stance regarding Palestine. My argument is that the incessant blending of Said's corpus with Said himself does little to serve the interest of constructive scholarship. Defending or attacking Said himself can all too easily take precedence over the merits and demerits of his arguments. The print trail of the debate over *Orientalism* is an unfortunate case in point. The sight of learned dons slinging erudite mud pies across guilded conference halls, no less than the more consciously made-up media journalists on cable news, yields little travelworthy intellectual insight. It is time, I suggest, to move on.

IV   Beyond the Binary

> It is time to move beyond the ideological framework in which
> even Marx found it possible to say: They cannot represent
> themselves; they must be represented.
>
> —CHANDRA MOHANTY, "UNDER WESTERN EYES:
> FEMINIST SCHOLARSHIP AND COLONIAL DISCOURSE"[282]

n sum, the essential argument of *Orientalism* is that a pervasive and
endemic Western discourse of Orientalism has constructed "the Orient,"
a representation that Said insists not only is perversely false but prevents the authentic rendering of a real Orient, even by Orientals themselves. Academicized Orientalism is thus dismissed, in the words of one critic, as "the magic wand of Western domination of the Orient."[283] The notion of a single conceptual essence of Orient is the linchpin in Said's polemical reduction of all Western interpretation of the real or imagined geographical space to a single and latently homogeneous discourse. Read through *Orientalism* and only the Orient of Western Orientalism is to be encountered; authentic Orients are not imaginable in the text. The Orient is rhetorically available for Said simply by virtue of not really being anywhere. Opposed to this Orient is the colonialist West, exemplified by France, Britain, and the United States. East versus West, Occident over Orient: this is the debilitating binary that has framed the unending debate over Orientalism.

A generation of students across disciplines has grown up with limited challenges to the polemical charge by Said that scholars who study the Middle East and Islam still do so institutionally through an interpretive sieve that divides a superior West from an inferior East. Dominating the debate has been a tiresome point/counterpoint on whether literary critic Edward Said or historian Bernard Lewis knows best. Here is where the dismissal of academic Orientalism has gone wrong. Over and over again the same problem is raised. Does the Orient as several generations of Western travelers, novelists, theologians, politicians, and scholars discoursed it really exist? To not recognize this as a fundamentally rhetorical question because of Edward Said is, nolo contendere, nonsense. No serious scholar can assume a meaningful cultural entity called "Orient" after reading Said's *Orientalism*; some had said so before Said wrote his polemic. Most of his readers agreed with the thrust of the Orientalism thesis because they shared the same frustration with misrepresentation. There is no rational retrofit between the imagined Orient, resplendent in epic tales and art, and the space it consciously or unwittingly misrepresented. However, there was and is a real Orient, flesh-and-blood people, viable cultural traditions, aesthetic domains, documented history, and an ongoing intellectual engagement with the past, present, and future. What is missing from *Orientalism* is any systematic sense of what that real Orient was and how individuals reacted to the imposing forces that sought to label it and theoretically control it.

ASLEEP IN ORIENTALISM'S WAKE

> I have avoided taking stands on such matters as the real, true or authentic Islamic or Arab world.
>
> —EDWARD SAID, "ORIENTALISM RECONSIDERED"

Orientalism is frequently praised for exposing skeletons in the scholarly closet, but the book itself provides no blueprint for how to proceed.[284] Said's approach is of the cut-and-paste variety—a dash of Foucauldian discourse here and a dram of Gramscian hegemony there—rather than a how-to model. In his review of *Orientalism*, anthropologist Roger Joseph concludes:

> Said has presented a thesis that on a number of counts is quite compelling. He seems to me, however, to have begged one major question. If discourse, by its very metanature, is destined to misrepresent and to be mediated by all sorts of private agendas, how can we represent cultural systems in ways that will allow us to escape

the very dock in which Said has placed the Orientalists? The aim of the book was not to answer that question, but surely the book itself compels us to ask the question of its author.[285]

Another cultural anthropologist, Charles Lindholm, criticizes Said's thesis for its "rejection of the possibility of constructing general comparative arguments about Middle Eastern cultures."[286] Akbar Ahmed, a native Pakistani trained in British anthropology, goes so far as to chide Said for leading scholars into "an intellectual *cul-de-sac*."[287] For a historian's spin, Peter Gran remarks in a favorable review that Said "does not fully work out the post-colonial metamorphosis."[288] As critic Rey Chow observes, "Said's work begs the question as to how otherness—the voices, languages, and cultures of those who have been and continue to be marginalized and silenced—could become a genuine oppositional force and a usable value."[289] Said's revisiting and reconsidering of Orientalism, as well as his literary expansion into a de-geographicalized *Culture and Imperialism*, never resolved the suspicion that the question still goes begging.

There remains an essential problem. Said's periodic vacillation in *Orientalism* on whether or not the Orient could have a true essence leads him to an infinity of mere representations, presenting a default persuasive act by not representing that reality for himself and the reader. If Said claims that Orientalism created the false essence of an Orient, and critics counterclaim that Said himself proposes a false essence of Orientalism, how do we end the cycle of guilt by essentialization? Is there a way out of this epistemological morass? If not a broad way to truth, at least a narrow path toward a clearing? With most of the old intellectual sureties now crumbling, the prospect of ever finding a consensus is numbing, in part because the formidably linguistic roadblocks are—or at least should be—humbling. The history of philosophy, aided by Orientalist and ethnographic renderings of the panhumanities writ and unwrit large, is littered with searches for meaning. Yet, mystical ontologies aside, the barrier that has thus far proved unbreachable is the very necessity of using language, reducing material reality and imaginary potentiality to mere words. As long as concepts are essential for understanding and communication, reality—conterminous concept that it must be—will be embraced through worded essences. Reality must be represented, like it or not, so how is it to be done better?

Neither categorical nor canonical "Truth" need be of the essence. One of the pragmatic results of much postmodern criticism is the conscious subversion of belief in a singular "Truth" in which any given pronouncement could be ascribed the eternal verity once reserved for holy writ. In rational inquiry, all truths are limited by the inescapable force of pragmatic change. Ideas with "whole truth" in them can only be patched together for so long. Intellectual activity proceeds by characterizing verbally what is encountered and by reducing the complex to simpler and more graspable elements. A world without proposed and debated essences would be an unimaginable realm with no imagination, annotation without nuance, activity without art. I suggest that when *cogito ergo sum* is melded with "to err is human," essentialization of human realities becomes less an unresolvable problem and more a profound challenge. Contra Said's polemical contentions, not all that has been created discursively about an Orient is essentially wrong or without redeeming intellectual value. Edward Lane and Sir Richard Burton can be read for valuable firsthand observations despite their ethnocentric baggage. Wilfrid and Anne Blunt can be appreciated for their moral suasion.

The *j'accuse* of criticism must be tempered constructively with the *touché* of everyday human give-and-take. In planed biblical English, it is helpful to see that the beam in one's own rhetorical eye usually blocks appreciation of the mote in the other's eye. Speaking truth to power à la Said's oppositional criticism is appealing at first glance, but speaking truths to varieties of ever-shifting powers is surely a more productive process for a pluralistic society. As Richard King has eloquently put it, "Emphasis upon the diversity, fluidity and complexity within as well as between cultures precludes a reification of their differences and allows one to avoid the kind of monadic essentialism that renders cross-cultural engagement an a priori impossibility from the outset."[290] Contrasted essentialisms, as the debate over Orientalism bears out, do not rule each other out. Claiming that an argument is essentialist does not disprove it; such a ploy serves mainly to taint the ideas opposed and thus tends to rhetorically mitigate opposing views. Thesis countered by antithesis becomes sickeningly cyclical without a willingness to negotiate synthesis.

The critical irony is that Said, the author as advocate who at times denies agency to authors as individuals, uniquely writes and frames the entire script of his own text. Texts, in the loose sense of anything conveniently fashioned with words, become the meter for Said's poetic performance. The historical backdrop is hastily arranged, not systematically researched, to authorize the staging of his argument. The past becomes the whiggishly drawn rationale for pursuing a present grievance. As the historian Robert Berkhofer suggests, Said "uses many voices to exemplify the stereotyped view, but he makes no attempt to show how the new self/other relationship ought to be represented. Said's book does not practice what it preaches multiculturally."[291] Said's method, Berkhofer continues, is to "quote past persons and paraphrase them to reveal their viewpoints as stereotyped and hegemonic." Napoleon's savants, Renan's racism, and Flaubert's flirtations serve to accentuate the complicity of modern-day social scientists who support Israel. *Orientalism* is a prime example of a historical study with one voice and one viewpoint.

Some critics have argued in rhetorical defense of Said that he should not be held accountable for providing an alternative. "The voice of dissent, the critique (of Orientalism or any other hegemonic discourse) does not need to propose an alternative for the critique to be effective and valid," claim Ashcroft and Ahluwalia.[292] Saree Makdisi suggests that Said's goal in *Orientalism* is "to specify the constructedness of reality" rather than to "unmask and dispel" the illusion of Orientalist discourse.[293] Timothy Brennan argues that Said's aim is not to describe the "brute reality" of a real Orient but rather to point out the "relative indifference" of Western intellectuals to that reality.[294] Certainly no author is under an invisible hand of presumption to solve a problem he or she wishes to expose. Yet, it is curious that Said would not want to suggest an alternative, to directly engage the issue of how the "real" Orient could be represented. He reacts forcefully to American literary critics of the "left" who fail to specify the ideas, values, and engagement being urged.[295] If, as Said, insists "politics is something more than liking or disliking some intellectual orthodoxy now holding sway over a department of literature,"[296] then why would he not follow through with what this "something more" might be for the discourse he calls Orientalism? As Abdallah Laroui eloquently asks, "Having become concerned with an essentially political problem, the Arab intelligentsia must inevitably reach the stage where it passes from diagnosis of the situation to prescription of remedial action. Why should I escape this rule?"[297] This is a question that escapes Edward Said in *Orientalism*, although it imbues his life work as an advocate against ethnocentric bias.

Clash Talking Ad Nauseam

The questioning of whether or not there really is an Orient, a West, or a unified discourse called Orientalism might be relatively harmless philosophical musing, were it not for the contemporary, confrontational political involvement of the United States and major European nations with buyable governments and bombable people in the Middle East. One of the reasons Said's book has been so influential, especially among scholars in the emerging field of post-colonial studies, is that it appeared at the very moment in which the Cold War divide reached a zenith in Middle East politics. In 1979, the fall of the United States–backed and anti-communist Shah allowed for the creation of the first modern Islamic republic in Iran, even as the Soviet Union invaded Afghanistan to try to prevent the same thing happening there. Almost three decades later, the escalation of tension and violence sometimes described as "Islamic terrorism" has become a pressing global concern. In the climate of renewed American and British political engagement in Afghanistan and Iraq after September 11, 2001, the essential categories of East and West continue to dominate public debate through the widely touted mantra of a "clash of civilizations."

The idea of civilizations at war with each other is probably as old as the very idea of civilization. The modern turn of phrase owes its current popularity to the title of a 1993 *Foreign Affairs* article by political historian Samuel Huntington, although this is quite clearly a conscious borrowing from a 1990 *Atlantic Monthly* article by Said's nemesis, Bernard Lewis. Huntington, speculating in an influential policy forum, suggests that Arnold Toynbee's outdated list of twenty-one major civilizations had been reduced after the Cold War to six, to which he adds two more. With the exception of his own additions of Latin America and Africa, the primary rivals of the West, according to his list, are currently Confucian, Japanese, Islamic, Hindu, and Slavic-Orthodox. To say, as Huntington insists, that the main criterion separating these civilizations is religion, given the labels chosen, borders on the tautological.[298] But logical order here would suggest that the West be seen as Christian, given its dominant religion. In a sense, Huntington echoes the simplistic separation of the West from the Rest, for secular Western civilization is clearly the dominant and superior system in his mind. The rejection of the religious label for his own civilization, secular as it might appear to him, seriously imbalances Huntington's civilizational breakdown. It strains credulity to imagine that religion in itself is an independent variable in the contemporary world of nation-states that make up the transnationalized mix of cultural identities outside the United Sates and Europe.

Following earlier commentary of Bernard Lewis, Huntington posits a "fault line" between the West and Islamic civilization ever since the Arabs were turned back in 732 CE at the Battle of Tours.[299] The fault of Islam, however, appears to be less religious than political and ideological. The fundamental clash Huntington describes revolves around the seeming rejection by Islam (and indeed all the rest) of "Western ideas of individualism, liberalism, constitutionalism, human rights, equality, liberty, the rule of law, democracy, free markets, the separation of church and state."[300] In citing this neoconservative laundry list, Huntington is blind to the modern history of Western nations. He assumes that these idealized values have in fact governed policy in Europe and America, as though divine kingship, tyranny, and fascism have not plagued European history. Nor is it credible to claim that such values have all been rejected by non-Western nations. To assert, for example, that the rule of law is not consonant with Islam, or that Islamic teaching is somehow less concerned with human rights than Western governments, implies that the real clash is between Huntington's highly subjective reading of a history he does not know very well and a current reality he does not like.

Huntington's thesis was challenged from the start in the very next issue of *Foreign Affairs*. "But Huntington is wrong," asserts Fouad Ajami.[301] Even former U. N. Ambassador Jeane Kirkpatrick, hardly a proponent of post-colonial criticism, called Huntington's list of civilizations "strange."[302] Iron-ically, both Ajami and Kirkpatrick fit Said's vision of bad-faith Orientalism. Being wrong in the eyes of many of his peers did not prevent Huntington from expanding the tentative proposals of a controversial essay into a book, nor from going well outside his field of expertise to write specifically on the resurgence of Islam. Soon after the September 11, 2001, tragedy, Edward Said weighed in with a biting exposé on Huntington's "clash of ignorance." Said rightly crushes the blatant political message inherent in the clash thesis, explaining why labels such as "Islam" and "the West" are unedifying: "They mislead and confuse the mind, which is trying to make sense of a disorderly reality that won't be pigeonholed or strapped down as easily as all that."[303] Exactly, but the same must therefore be true about Said's imagined discourse of Orientalism. Pigeonholing all previous scholars who wrote about Islam or Arabs into one negative category is discursively akin to Huntington's pit-ting of Westerners against Muslims. Said is right to attack this pernicious binary, but again he leaves it intact by not posing a viable alternative.

Both Edward Said and Fouad Ajami, who rarely seem to agree on any-thing, rightly question the terms of Huntington's clash thesis. To relabel the Orient of myth as a Confucian-Islamic military complex is not only eth-nocentric but resoundingly ahistorical. No competent historian of either Islam or Confucianism recognizes such a misleading civilizational half-breed. Saddam Hussein's Iraq and Kim Jong Il's Korea could be equated as totalitarian states assumed to have weapons of mass destruction, but not for any religious collusion. This is the domain of competing political ideologies, not the result of religious affiliation. And, as Richard Bulliet warns, the phrase "clash of civilizations" so readily stirs up Islamophobia in the United States that it "must be retired from public discourse before the people who like to use it actually begin to believe it."[304] Unfortunately, many policy-makers and media experts talk and act as if they do believe it. The best way to defeat such simplistic ideology, I suggest, is not to lapse into blame-casting polemics but to encourage sound scholarship of the real Orient that Said so passionately tried to defend.

The Orient and Its Nodalities

> Thus there was (and is) a linguistic Orient, a Freudian Orient,
> a Spenglerian Orient, a Darwinian Orient, a racist Orient—and
> so on.
>
> —Edward Said, *Orientalism*[305]

In *Orientalism* the nuanced meanings of "Orient" are adjectival, most literally in a bizarre set of idiosyncratic concoctions that bear little relation to the real world. Given that Oriental studies evolved primarily as a philological field, it is almost redundant to speak of a linguistic Orient; even in King James biblical English the Tower of Babel remains an Oriental trope. Said ignores the fact that Western philologists recognized a variety of Oriental languages as well as coming to terms with the discovery that their own Western languages owed much to Oriental linguistic roots. The proper study of language, post-Nimrud, has been keeping up with the William Joneses ever since. A Spenglerian Orient can be theorized, given that Oswald Spengler theorized about the role of the Orient in world history, but consider how far the force of his 1918 *The Decline of the West* had declined by the time *Orientalism* was published.[306] If there could be a Spenglerian Orient, then there could be an equally long line of individually surnamed variants: Herderian, Schlegelian, Hegelian, Toynbeean, Vicoan, and so on *ad historiam*. Freud had little to say about the Orient, unless his musings on *Moses and Monotheism* are taken outside their biblical context. Had Freud probed Hindu myth for an Oedipal clone, perhaps psychoanalysis would have been tilted into the Orientalist camp. Darwin's *H.M.S. Beagle* coursed through the Orient on its admiralty mission to chart the waters for imperialist expansion, but Tierra del Fuego is a long way from Terra Sancta. Or is Darwin's name sullied here as a surrogate for the scientific racism unjustly laid at the feet of this Victorian author of natural selection?[307]

Said's rhetoric posits and positions the genus *Orient*, lumping together its varying species as essentially the same for argument's sake. Only by peeling off layers of nuance can Said's notion of Orientalism as a unified and holistic discourse be superseded. Perhaps a more fruitful approach than collapsing diversity into the unity of a single discourse is to follow up on Said's suggestion that Orientalism is a "style," and admit that styles, like fashions, are modal, definable by form rather than content, by means rather than ends. Representation of the Orient thus becomes a matter of fashion, in which any particular mode is meaningful only in comparison to others. The potential styles for saying something about an Orient are legion, as even Said is forced on occasion to admit. In the narrow guild sense there are nuance-able differences by nationality, which often follow linguistic lines—British or German for example—as well as the specific intellectual trajectories of disciplines. In the broader sense conceived by Said, the number of approaches is as wide as the range of individuals placed under Orientalism by default. Consider the various ways any given individual could appropriate the Orient as pilgrim, crusader, hardened mercenary, merchant, missionary, colonial administrator, poet, novelist, satirist, artist, mystic, tourist. It is precisely this tinker-tailor-candlestick-maker hetero-genus-ness in discourse that is obscured in the argument of *Orientalism*.

The danger in isolating particular styles surfaces when an overriding commonality is allowed to mitigate the relevance of differences. This is convenient for polemical works, where categories can be chosen to persuasively frame the outcome of an argument. Said's *Orientalism* is built quite consciously on the seemingly narrow "Anglo-French-American experience of the Arabs and Islam," but when this is taken as a unit, the broad range of possible orientations is reduced to a simplistic quasi-national base.[308] The narrowness results from leaving out the dominance of German philological scholarship; the over-breadth by assuming that a bohemian such as Gustave Flaubert can be pictured in the same bed with a conservative academic such as Sir Hamilton Gibb. The unity for Said's unbounded unit consists of "what made that experience possible by way of historical and intellectual background, what the quality and character of the experience has been."[309] The historical and intellectual background is, unfortunately, only sampled in order to avoid the archival virus of knowing too much. Because Said makes no pretense of systematically examining the exhaustive corpus of texts or looking at other types of historical evidence, he ends up being the one who inscribes, as he ascribes, the quality and character of the experience.

Without providing an engineer's flow chart, Said presents a number of differing styles by which he thinks the Orient has been represented. Within the vested Anglo-French-American unit, the tribe of Orientalism is nested in a segmentary system similar to that used by anthropologists to analyze Arab tribal kinship. Of primal importance for Said are the primary lineages of Britain, with Gibb as principal icon, and France, figured with Louis Massignon. "Yet even after making all the proper qualifications about the difference between an individual and a type (or between an individual and a tradition)," argues Said, "it is nevertheless striking to note the extent to which Gibb and Massignon were representative types."[310] It is very useful for his Orientalism thesis that such carefully selected individuals "were" ideal types, but they only "are" at Said's forced suggestion. Said's discussion of Gibb and Massignon avoids qualifications and portrays each scholar according to an assumption of differing political agendas by England and France. The stated purpose of counterposing the two scholars is to characterize "interwar Islamic Orientalism," but nowhere does he discuss the political agenda of each country between World Wars I and II. Such idealized typecasting is far from ideal for an attempt to explain intellectual history. It is little more than a dumping-on ground for polemical criticism, as necessary as such critique might be.

I am not suggesting that Said's classification of specific styles for representing the Orient be revised or replaced by an equally subjective set. Teasing out an unending progression of modal approaches to theoretically Oriental others would only lead to subjectively deadened ends. Rather than squeezing nuance out of every conceivable narrative genre to fit select statements into a manifestly artificial discourse broad enough to be labeled "Orientalism," is it not more instructive to look at points of convergence or divergence, where the fiction of willing the other into a fashionable form meets the friction of actual human contact, where ideas can be analyzed as more than proctored ideals by individual authors? Said molds Orientalism as a mode of domination. I suggest a switch in emphasis to nodality, the point at which various lines meet, less a characterizable style or fashion than an intersection through which ideas flow. The language of a text, for example, is one such nodality. No matter what their individual training or motives, all authors who write in English share what English as a language has to offer. Thus, Gibb can not be read the same as Massignon any more than Flaubert's *Salammbô* over against Disraeli's *Tancred*. There is a reason why translation is necessary and why few translated texts are ever thought to convey the same meaning as the original.

Nodes of contact cross literary genres because they necessarily cross in and out of written texts as such. Academic training, contra Said, is not simply the precursive positioning for writing about an other. For example, all modern linguists share certain commonalities of training, but none absorbs that training like a mechanical robot. The institutional context and basic textual tools in the programming of a linguist may seem similar in many respects—especially to an amateur looking in from the outside—but in a worldly sense there are bad scholars, adequate scholars, and good scholars. Experience inevitably challenges seemingly entrenched dogmas and overrides the rote dictation of book learning. Much of what Said criticizes in the history of Oriental studies is the bad and the ugly, positions that may have informed intellectual currents but which have in the inevitable course of reform been superseded. Because of what Said chooses to highlight in texts, the ability of individual scholars to think, reflect, and reform is negated.

It is possible to elicit numerous nodalities for tracing the multiple ways in which the notion of Orient has meant something. Yet such an effort, which would be a monumental undertaking that might make even the Pharaoh Khufu blush, is more likely to be entertaining than conclusive. I have no wish to counter *Orientalism* with a mere literary counter-punch, especially not a deconstructive scorched-earth rhetorical backlash. The literary tidbits presented by Said as stereotypical hors-d'oeuvres are, on the whole, just that: time-bound hoary diversions that detract from the progress made. Flaubert's pubescent Orient, [res]erected by a literary critic after more than a century, fascinates because of its stereotypic half-life, but does not resonate with the best scholarship available on a real Orient. The fact that other imperialist-era authors were horrified by the literary licentiousness of certain novelists and poets of their day, or that there were Europeans so sympathetic that they quite consciously became "Oriental" balances the picture that Said slanted for his own purpose. This is the kind of balance needed to redress the faults of *Orientalism* as an unrevised text.

Moving Beyond the Polemic

> On the other hand, scholars and critics who are trained in the traditional Orientalist disciplines are perfectly capable of freeing themselves from the old ideological straitjacket.
>
> —Edward Said, *Orientalism*

The haunting paradox that remains is how to negotiate the age-old conundrum of unity in diversity. How can there be a united discourse of imagination, perhaps even a conspiratorial plot, oriented eastward from Europe, and yet there be so many different ways in which the real Orient has been experienced in both directions? Orientalism as figured by Said ends up as an abstract fit of and for a polemic; Orientalism is judged to be proven guilty by type and literary testimony despite presentable protestations of innocence. In exposing the negatives in written Western depiction of an Oriental other, Said ends up making his case study more than the case calls for. Few scholars would disagree with the majority of examples he provides as proof of bad, even evil, representation. But it is a stretch to move from showing fault in selected examples to implying that there is something inherently rotten in academic discourse per se. Said virtually invents a horrid Orientalist whoredom of callous colonialists, a most discourteous discourse. However, processes of xenophobia, racism, political ploys, economic rationale, religious intolerance, and just plain bigotry have always crosscut regional, national, and ethnic boundaries and continue to do so.

My interest is not in defending the laurels of noted authorities and past-their-prime paradigms, nor in covering up the many ways in which Islam and the Middle East have been blatantly demonized and denigrated, let alone obscured, in academic narrative. Judging by the literature and venue of most professional monographs and conferences today—more than a silver jubilee after *Orientalism*—there is little evidence for a dominating intellectual hegemony of a hierarchically enclosed structure dictating what Islam and politically significant "others" oriented to our collective must dogmatically be. Nor is the voice of the subaltern, historically misrepresented and periodically muted, silenced in contemporary post-colonial scholarship; indeed it may be suffering coming-out pains from overexposure in the academy.[311] Blatant bias has by no means disappeared, whether among highly opinionated scholars or in the popular media, but bias bashing is a politically expedient part of the ongoing critical canon. Sound scholarship is moving on, as I have demonstrated through copious examples in this book.

I have no desire to repeat Said's uncritical mistake and stop short of suggesting an alternative to the polemical path of *Orientalism*. We need to escape the faults of bias and distortion in representation of real people and their real history as well as the imaginative discourses that invade all historical understanding. This can best be accomplished by adapting rather than rejecting the available tools developed within the very guilds Said relegates to the latrines. Much of the available criticism documented here offers ways in which the target of Said's rhetoric can be more credibly analyzed. Linguists are far more capable today of analyzing Oriental languages in a comparative sense because of the insights of earlier philologists and the sheer force of experience in diverse contexts. Historians, like archaeologists, have improved methods for looking at the material remains of daily life, including scraps of ordinary writing, to create a better understanding than canonized texts afford on their own. It is still necessary to read Herodotus, for example, but what a more enlightening reading is possible given the fragments still visible of the real world that writers like Herodotus recorded. Anthropologists, never comfortable sitting above it all in academic armchairs, both learn and unlearn through the dialectic of living with real Orientals and speaking in their native languages. Increasingly, ethnographers work with native intellectuals rather than simply parroting an outsider's perspective. Contemporary historians of Islam, no longer motivated by a desire to defend a beleaguered Christian view, study the diversity of Muslims as well as the trajectory of their complex textual tradition. Political scientists and economists debate views from the far right to the far left. Contrary to what a reading of *Orientalism* today might suggest, the right kind of scholarly work is there; some of it has been there all along.

In reading *Orientalism*, I have not only shown the many rhetorical excesses and historical flaws in Said's thesis but have also suggested ways in which scholars have contributed to a less biased and more nuanced understanding of the real Orient. Moving beyond the East–West binary requires an academic approach that emphasizes the continued improvement of methods to reach a less biased representation of the other while recognizing the inevitable ethnocentricity in us all. Moving beyond the politics of blame requires a switch from the rhetoric of polemic to civil academic debate with a measure of intellectual tolerance for opposing viewpoints. It would certainly help to shift the focus away from demagogic cultural criticism to informed analysis of cultures through refined methodologies. No single specialization has the answers. But this should be a call to cooperate in a joint concern for ferreting out discernable truths rather than disparaging individuals and academic disciplines. Rather than the lone oppositional critic lashing out at an untidy world, I propose the model advocated by my colleague Jacques Berlinerblau, that "a public intellectual/scholar establishes the trust of an audience, treats adversaries with consideration, writes in lucid prose, clarifies complex issues, apprises readers of 'inconvenient facts,' advocates unpopular opinions, questions and reveals his or her own motivations in doing so, and yes, ultimately, if possible, comes to a decision about the issue at hand."[312] The challenge at hand is to contribute to a better, not eternally fixed, understanding of the other.

If the idealized notion of Orient is an invention through discourse, it should also be capable of being reinvented through sound scholarship. Serious academic study of Middle Eastern cultures and Islam, despite the limitations and prejudices of individual scholars, is not hostage to a latent hegemonic discourse in which representation of an imagined Orient or East is condemned to be inherently racist, sexist, and ideologically driven. Rather than succumb to the hubris of polemicists who make dogmatic assertions or manipulate history with Whiggish intent, the contemporary student of Middle Eastern cultures, or of any cultural setting, should focus on the question of fit with an assumed and irreducible reality worth studying. The dreaded fork in the road to recovery need not be reduced to a choice between orthodoxic *nihil obstat* and Nietzschean ortho-toxy. There is something real that is worth being conceptualized by and beyond the term "Orient." Orientalism can be conjured, constricted, constructed, and deconstructed ad nauseam, tasks quite Herculean if done right but absurdly Sisyphean if carried on in the same old spirit of competitive intellectualizing. What was once a broad field of geographical and cultural specialization will not go away, Said's book notwithstanding, because the real Orient is not about to fade from view.

Let us agree, at least in principle, on the following truisms at the start of the third millennium. All scholars, no matter how careful and sincere, carry with them assumptions and expectations from their own cultures and individual socialization. All generalizations about people's ideas, beliefs, and behavior essentialize to some extent, invariably along an ethnocentric fault line. Representation, especially by someone writing in another language or from an outsider's perspective, is never going to be an exact duplication, nor one that can effectively distill manifest difference into a whole meaningful to all. I am not so naive as to assume that the damage of an opportunistic East-vs.-West clash can simply be wished away, but neither do I doubt our ability to whittle away at bias and misinformation by using the methodologies of critical scholarship from established but evolving disciplines. If we cannot lay to rest the ghosts of Orientalism past, at least we can stop being frightened out of our critical scholarship by such a troublesome spectre.

I conclude by suggesting that the best way to battle misleading binary thinking is to get on with sound academic scholarship and spend less time rhetorically damning the binary itself or reconstructing incomplete genealogies of intellectual history. This was the lesson learned in the twentieth century by biologists and anthropologists who researched human evolutionary development without constantly stopping to attack the biblical notion of creation. Scientific progress has not been retarded by the pulp[it]-fiction whims of religious dogmatists and demagogues. Even though American public opinion clings to belief that God created the universe in seven days, a vast majority of people accept the results of modern medicine rather than only opting for God to work a miracle. Certainly the scientific literacy of the American public has been undermined by efforts to substitute religious doctrine about creation, however intelligently designed by the current packagers, for scientific reasoning. But we must not let the public face reflected in the mirror of media mediocrity detract from an appreciation of advances in the sciences. There is a need to improve the teaching of science, just as there is to improve teaching about Islam and cultures and politics of the Middle East, but this is hardly the fault of those who conduct rigorous, peer-reviewed research. If we cannot blame Francis Crick for the appalling fact that half of Americans say they still believe in a literal Adam and Eve, how we can fault all Orientalist scholars by discourse default for the ongoing gross stereotypes perpetuated in the media and preached by pandering politicians?

Neither the social sciences nor the humanities will ever match the predictability of chemistry or astronomy, but a pragmatic scholar must admire how modern methods in all fields yield more consistently validated results than alchemical wizardry, astrological charts, and arsenic-based cures. Yes, "the Orient" was invented, but it continues in the process of analysis to be reinvented; real people in a real geographic space are being represented in responsible ways. The goal of serious scholarship should be to improve understanding of self and other, not to whine endlessly or wallow self-righteously in continual opposition. There is no need to posit a new direction for studying the Orient, for the "Orient" rightly critiqued by Said has long since ceased to exist academically as a meaningful object of study. The notion of Oriental homogeneity will exist as long as prejudice serves political ends, but to blame the sins of its current use on hegemonic intellectualism mires ongoing mitigation of bad and biased scholarship in an unresolvable polemic of blame. It is time to read beyond *Orientalism*.

Coda

Representing the East may have been Said's career, but why must it continue to occupy the careers of so many others, including, mea culpa, a brief swathe of my own? The publishing and conferencing world continues to generate discussion on this prominent intellectual, even after his passing. *Orientalism* is still to be found in most bookstores, and prospects of a long global shelf life are extended all the more by the sheer number of translations. Whether Edward Said is viewed as a quintessential cultural critic or as a professorial anti-don putting on airs, the author's presence will prevent his most traveled book from disappearing any time soon. To the practitioners of post-colonialism, Robert Young pleads, "Instead of objecting to Said and qualifying him by modifying his ideas in certain ways, what needs to be done is to re-theorize colonial discourse as such."[313] I offer this book as a prolegomenon to that weighty effort. For myself, an Orientalist by Said's fault-finding and an apparently wrong-side-of-the-divide anthropologist through the chosen fault of disciplinal training, I plan to revert to my continued study of Muslim and Arab cultures and my idiosyncratic historical passion for thirteenth-century Yemeni agricultural texts.

This has been, for me, a book that had to be written—although it may take a future literary thesis or two to suggest why—but it most certainly is not one that had to be read. So I end by begging your indulgence, *lecteur amical*, and return *ad finem* to a beginning. If *amantes sunt amentes*, so are all critics.

Notes

Acknowledgments

1   Berlinerblau (1999:xii).

To the Reader

2   Menocal is referring to Dante, but I think her comment applies equally to Said's *Orientalism*.

3   O'Hanlon and Washbrook (1992:163) refer to postmodern writers' penchant to question the power in all knowledge systems except their own.

4   W. J. T. Mitchell (2005a:366).

5   A. Ahmad (1992:160). John Mackenzie (1995b:91) is compelled to remind critics that "most of his contemporary political positions are also mine. But I do not see that such sympathies should neuter my critical faculties." B. D. H. Miller (1982:284) finds it difficult and embarrassing to criticize Said because of who he is: a Palestinian intellectual. Julia Kushigian (1991:111n2) confides that Said both inspires and encourages her in another direction.

6   Halliday (1999:200–201). A similar sentiment is expressed by Mackenzie (1995b:92).

7   Behdad (1994a:11). Madeleine Dobie (2001:16) travels with Behdad's course correction, but only to a point.

8   Majeed (1992:4).

9   Sayyid (1997:49n1): "I am very aware of my intellectual debt to Edward Said and his work, and any disagreements that I express in the following pages should be seen in the light of my acknowledgement of Said's influence in opening up these horizons for me."

10   Holmlund (1993:2).

11   Kramer (2001:22). Apart from repeating criticism already well known, Kramer offers no original insights on *Orientalism*. Although there is much to criticize in the large corpus of Said's work, simply dismissing it as ideological garbage renders Kramer's work virtually unusable. I devote space here to his political polemic in order to distance it from my own critique of Said's rhetoric, methodology, and thesis. As Richard Bulliet (2004:99) observes, Kramer writes "a bitter book devoted to disparaging the entire Middle East Studies enterprise."

12   Kramer (2001:32), who proceeds to argue that *Orientalism* gave a "step up" to Arab and Muslim scholars who thought they were "unspoiled" and "entitled" to university positions. Who hired them, if not members of the establishment?

13   Ibid., 39. It appears that in Kramer's view a scholar cannot be Arab and American at the same time. Does this mean it is not possible to be Israeli and American at the same time?

14 Ibid., 84.

15 Ibid., 46.

16 Ibid. Kramer finds "irony in the fact that the Beirut hostage-holders of Islamic Jihad should have offered Said's *Covering Islam* as reading to their captive audience of hostages." I see little irony in this irascible *ipse dixit* that would blame an author who without hesitation condemns terrorism in the very book mentioned.

17 Ibid., 47. "Just as ironic was the fact that Said—who had stoked the fires of suspicion in the Muslim world—had read Rushdie's book in manuscript and failed to see the risks in publishing it." It is not ironic but pathetic that a political scientist specializing in the Middle East could claim that these fires needed stoking by a book from an American secular scholar. I leave out of this list the sub[tle]plot that conjures Said's supposed sway over Middle East studies as complicit in not targeting Osama bin Laden from the start as a major threat and for the malicious claim that Said deserves part of the blame for the tragedy of September 11, 2001.

18 Ibid., 45.

19 Ibid., 44. At times Kramer views the few and largely marginalized pro-Palestinian voices, so clearly ineffectual in shifting American foreign policy, as spouting an anti-Semitic demagoguery that might be called *Protocols of the Dispossessed Against Zionism*.

20 Ibid., 32. As Ella Shohat (2004:56) notes, Kramer and a few other vociferous critics had for the first time scanned post-colonial theory on the "neocon radar."

21 Kramer (2001:36–37). Rather than questioning the ability of experts as such to "predict" politics or economics, Kramer uses the same rationale to describe quite different paradigms. One of the more bizarre claims in Kramer's grab-baggage is that "the Middle Eastern studies 'establishment'" had already been abandoned by right wingers in American foreign policy at the same time that it "came under assault from the left" (2001:87). It is not clear who was minding the store. Nor is it clear whom Kramer was reading. In almost any political science text of the late 1960s or early 1970s the handwriting was on the wall that "The Middle East is in a state of ferment," observed James Bill and Carl Leiden (1974:220). Ironically, post-colonial critics have applied a similar un-Nostradamus litmus test to earlier Western Orientalists (Horsley 2003:22).

22 Makiya (1993:317–318). He is seconded in a rambling and derivative personal attack on Said by Ibn Warraq (2002). Gordon (1989:95) makes a similar point that Said and other anti-Orientalists "encourage a sort of self-justifying apologia that has been detrimental to self-criticism."

23 Makiya (1993:324). Said (1994a:345) dismisses Makiya as one of Bernard Lewis's "epigones," yet fails to respond to the specifics of Makiya's critique. Ahmad Dallal (1994:89) echoes Said in describing Makiya's critique as a "quite irrational, attention-seeking desire to malign Arab and Islamic culture." Thus, in a most un-Foucauldian manner, an author's ascribed intention negates the need to discuss what is being said.

24 Sardar (1999:76).

25 Ibid., 74.

26 Ibid., 67.

27 Ben Jelloun (2002:item #28). Similarly, as reported in a *Seattle Times* interview (quoted in Amireh 2002:292), the Egyptian feminist Nawal El Saadawi calls Said "an arrogant intellectual who has a westernized interpretation of the Middle East."

28 Majid (2000:26). In an earlier piece, Majid (1998:341) states: "Few Western(ized) scholars have questioned the validity of secularism as a global project, although it is well
known that the concept is the intellectual product of a specific moment in European
history."

29 My position here is similar to that of fellow anthropologist Michael Gilsenan (2000:158),
who admires Said's courage as an advocate for Palestinian rights without feeling a need
to defend Said's arguments about Oriental studies or anthropology. Similarly, J. J. Clarke
(1997:8) is critical of Said's narrowness, but makes it clear that this "does not by any
means imply a total rejection of Said's attitude of suspicion towards orientalism or his
attempts to politicize it."

30 The phrase is from Dallmayr (1996:134).

31 Marrouchi (1997:72). Patrick Williams (2001:xxvii) faced a similar problem in deciding
what to include in his massive compilation of critical excerpts on Said, because many
of the critiques exemplify a "Said-as-straw-man syndrome."

32 Turner (1981:110).

INTRODUCTION

1 Said said this to describe structuralist *découpage* or *couper épistémologique*.

2 Prakash (1995:206).

3 Doniger (1999:943).

4 James Rice (2002:223) comments: "This is a time when seemingly every academic volume, paper, and conference panel uses Said's critical framework as the *de rigeur* point
of departure, a trope—positive or negative—for any critical exercise embracing Asia,
at least through the lens of culture or any of its manifestations." As Stuart Burrows
(1999:50) observes, "It is almost inconceivable to imagine someone receiving a humanities PhD today without having come to terms with Said's legacy."

5 The prepared remarks of Lewis, Said, Leon Wieseltier, and Christopher Hitchens were
published in Viswanathan (2001:291–312).

6 Although anthropologists appear first in Said's (1979:2) lineup of generic Orientalists,
the virtual absence of anthropology from *Orientalism* is an indexical fact. If anthropology is to be [em]bedded with Orientalism, I ask that the bedsheets covering all suspect Orientalists receive a fair airing.

7 A minimal list, extending into the 2000s, would include: Ansell-Pearson et al. (1997),
Aruri and Shuraydi (2001), Ashcroft and Ahluwalia (1999), Bové (2000), Hart (2000),
Sprinker (1993), and Williams and Chrisman (1994), not to mention Valerie Kennedy's
(2000) biographical account. More than two dozen interviews with Said have been published by Viswanathan (2001); see also Bayoumi and Rubin (2000:419–444), Jarah (1999),
Levine (1999), Rose (2000), Rushdie (1991), and Williams (2001). The interview with
David Barsamian (Said and Barsamian 1994) is partly available in Arabic translation in
al-Bahrayn al-Thaqafiyya (Kazim 2001:89–103). A major bibliography of Said's works is
available online (Yeghiayan 2001), but Marrouchi (2004:245–297) has surpassed all with
his database of books, articles, and reviews by Edward Said from 1966 to 2002. Much
relevant commentary is posted at the website called "The Edward Said Archive"
(www.edwardsaid.org). The extensive literature by Said and about Said—it is often a

challenge to find a post-colonial study that does not mention Said at some point—can also be entered through the excellent bibliographies compiled by Valerie Kennedy (2000:162–173) and Yasmine Ramadan (2005). There is a forty-minute video interview from 1998 called "Edward Said on Orientalism" (Northhampton, MA: Media Education Foundation). Among published forums devoted to *Orientalism* are a 1992 conference in Leiden reflecting on fifteen years of the book's critical life (Barfoot and D'haen 1998) and a 1994 international conference at Warwick University (Ansell-Pearson et al. 1997). The ultimate tribute is a multivolume compilation edited by Patrick Williams (2001); with "ultimate" I allude to the spread of more than 1,600 pages. This collection contains excerpts from eighty different texts, many of which are obscure and hard to find.

8   Milner and Gerstle (1994:3). Fred Dallmayr (1996:xi) writes that *Orientalism* "opened the eyes of readers to the complicity of much traditional scholarship with European colonial expansion." Said provided "a rather unflattering X-ray view of our intellectual selves," notes Warren Rosenberg (1979:109), who adds that, like an X-ray, *Orientalism* does not reveal the whole picture. Gordon (1989:xvii) suggests that writers "have often felt obliged to show their freedom from this sin," i.e., Eurocentrism, since *Orientalism*. Williams (2001:xx) thinks that Said's thesis created a self-awareness especially in academic departments of the humanities. More bluntly, Said rubbed culture's nose in the mud of politics (Gregory 1997:270). Aijaz Ahmad (1992:177) remarks that *Orientalism*, despite its blunders, opened up a space for oppositional work in Middle East studies. The mixed praise in even the more critical reviews belies Said's (1994a:332) claim that the motivation of critics has been one of "resistance and hostility."

9   Greene (1979:578).

10   Wahba (1989:187). Consider the similar sentiment of Prakash (1995:201): "Tossed into this maelstrom of indeterminacy and dubiety, the established authority of Orientalist scholars and their lines of inquiry have come undone." Of course, this is said by someone who does not wish to be known as an Orientalist scholar. A specialist in literary criticism, Steven Mailloux (1985:68), cites Said's *Orientalism* as an example of how literary theory can have "disruptive consequences."

11   Rodinson (1991:130). He continues to point out the methodological problems with Said's "militant stand." A similar point is made by Steenstrup (1985–86:237), who notes that the Saidian controversy "created the opportunity to haul onto the surface submerged prejudices." John Esposito (1990:4) notes that Said's critique, "though at times excessive, was insightful in identifying deficiencies and bias in scholarship of the past." Wilhelm Halbfass (1997:12), despite finding the book's argument exasperating, is still grateful for the debate it inspired. Historian D. K. Fieldhouse (1980:86) views *Orientalism* as a "valuable reminder that all historical writing is subjective." Or, as Muhsin Mahdi (1997:173) concludes, *Orientalism* "is the kind of book that Orientalists or Islamists or Arabists can ignore at their own peril."

12   Marrouchi (2003:55). Given criticism of Said for once having thrown stones toward Israel from inside southern Lebanon, this is a somewhat left-handed compliment from an admirer.

13   Young (2001:383, original emphasis). A similar point is made by Dirks (2004:39).

14   For discussion of literature, see Gordon (1989); for negative stereotyping in film, see Bernstein and Studlar (1997), McAlister (2001), and Shaheen (2001); for recent anti-Islamic representation on the internet, see Varisco (2001).

15 Rodinson's (1991:91–92) nuance is useful to stress: "While it may be pointless today to denounce this phenomenon and express righteous indignation at its legacy, it is still necessary to acknowledge it and to recognize its insidious influence." As Madeleine Dobie (2001:31) noted more recently, there is a need for "continuing critical reflection" because of the "abiding force of representations rooted in the Orientalist tradition."

16 Winder (1981:618). Among the numerous critics who describe *Orientalism* as an overdone polemic are Blank (2001:263), Butterworth (1980:175), Duncanson (1980:200), Gordon (1982:109), Kerr (1980:545), Schimmel (1980:149), and Van Keuren (1980:502). Marrouchi (2004:34) observes that Said has a "famous gift for polemicism." Even those who find Said's argument convincing often note its polemics (e.g., Tolan 2002:xviii). Brennan (2001:96, 98) believes that "the overall impression" of *Orientalism* is not polemical because Said provides so many palpable details and is not "offensively crude." Yet, to suggest that Said's purpose is not to aggressively challenge Orientalism in a controversial manner is unfair to Said's own oppositional stance.

17 Van Nieuwenhuijze (1979:10).

18 Schwartz (1980:21).

19 Waardenburg (1992:747). This does not stop other critics from viewing the anger as yielding a "principled piece of writing" (Malak 2005:5).

20 Said (1979:27).

21 Ahmed (1992:180).

22 Gordon (1982:112) labels Said "a brave and valuable, even if problematic, maverick." Yet Gilsenan (2000:152), reflecting a view more prevalent across the Atlantic, sees Said's implied bête noire status as a more recent phenomenon. Certainly James Brown (1999:550) sums up the reaction well: "*Orientalism* divides."

23 Said (1979:5). For a discussion of Said's treatment of Disraeli's novel, see chapter 2 of this book, pp. 210–217.

24 For example, in *The World, the Text, and the Critic*, Said foregrounds "the impressive constitutive authority in textuality" (1983:224) that can create a field of discourse with powerful worldly force.

25 Turner (1994:7). Ironically, fellow literary scholars sometimes regard Said as speaking against "the complacency of the textualist bed of literary theory" (Palmer 1990:42).

26 Said (1994a:330). Using a more mechanical metaphor, Said (1988b:33) reminisces: "What I was doing—this is something that I learned from Foucault—was producing things that become a box of utensils for other people to use."

27 Thomas (1991:4). Thomas thinks that Said is more cautious than his critics assert, yet he illustrates this by attacking the overwrought rhetoric of a negative critic rather than by parsing Said's own phrasing and choice of words.

28 Meyer (1991:663). Meyer accepts Said's premise of a dominant Orientalist discourse in his analysis of Byron and other romantic poets.

29 Said (in a 1976 interview for *Diacritics*, quoted in Viswanathan 2001:39). Another example of an Oriental writing back at Orientalism is Bassam Tibi (2001:21), who does so in part as a reaction to "suffering in German academia from the racism of German Orientalism."

30 Said (1979:27). Said (1994a:339) later admits he is "pleased and flattered that *Orientalism* often made a difference" in literary criticism, among other fields and disciplines.

Harootunian (2002:168), in a pragmatic assessment, suggests that "English departments everywhere should raise monuments and statues to Said for having saved English studies by giving it a new [imperial] lease on life."

31 Said (1994a:329), describing how he came to write the book, suggests that the topic "*might* interest a general audience." Duncanson (1980:201) predicted quite accurately that *Orientalism* would "have a vogue in non-specialist academic studies, where it will be taken for a comprehensive history of Oriental studies."

32 Said (1994a:340). Said (1988b:32) remarks that he also wrote *Orientalism* because of the poor quality of writing about the Middle East.

33 Said (1979:28). Oliver Leaman (1996:1144) suggests that many practitioners used Said's criticism as an opportunity to reappraise their approach to scholarship. As Norman Daniel (1990:189) observes, "Why has the attack on orientalism caused some heart-searching? It was not on the whole shrugged off." Despite the importance of examining claims of objectivity, Daniel warns that it should not encourage "the wildest fancies and speculations."

34 Said (1979:320); Said places this phrase in parentheses.

35 Said (1994a) makes this more explicit in his later afterword to *Orientalism*, in which new targets include Golda Meir, "Israeli Arabists and Orientalists," Samuel "clash of civilization" Huntington, Francis Fukuyama, and "retrograde social and political polemicist" Paul Johnson.

36 For a blistering critique of the penchant for "the writing of reviews upon reviews," see Frykenberg (1996:290). Young (2001:384), who calls this a "*mise-en-abyme* repetition effect," confides that he and other early post-colonial critics began "their postcolonial new life with a critique of Said."

37 The linking of Said with Bhabha and Spivak as the influential founders of post-colonial studies is both explicit and implicit in many surveys. Young (1990) perhaps fixed the pantheon of what he calls a "Holy Trinity" by devoting his last three chapters to these three critics; see also Young (1995:163). Moore-Gilbert et al. (1997) reproduce selections from Said, Spivak, and Bhabha back to back. See also Ashcroft et al. (1989:31), Baldick (1996:186), Bhatnagar (1986:3), Boyne and Rattansi (1990:35), Connor (1989:231), Crush (1994:334), Marrouchi (2004:73), Ning (1997:57), Quayson (2000:3), Roy (1995:102), Spencer (1997:14), Steele (1997:97), van der Veer (2003), Vasunia (2003:88), and Whalen-Bridge (2001:193). It would be politically—and more than politically—incorrect to over-psychoanalyze the sexual potential in Valerie Kennedy's (2000:117) observation that "Spivak takes a position on theory that locates her in between Said and Bhabha." Thus, it seems obvious that the road traveled by Homi Bhabha and Gayatri Spivak was imaginatively blazed by Said.

38 Excerpts from *Orientalism* are frequently provided in published readers of literary and cultural studies, such as Easthope and McGowan (1992:59–65). Said's works are so eminently reprintable that many of his original journal essays can be found in either a later text of his own or a laudatory collection.

39 On the back cover of Bhabha's *The Location of Culture*, Said provides the kind of praise Hollywood producers salivate over: "Homi Bhabha is that rare thing, a reader of enormous subtlety and wit, a theorist of uncommon power. His work is a landmark in the

exchange between ages, genres, and cultures; the colonial, post-colonial, modernist and postmodern." With such gracious hyperbole, Bhabha may not mind being called a "thing."

40 Gates (1991:465). Or, as Amin Malak (2005:15) more poetically suggests, "never-ending arcane discourses, to be followed by a set of arcane counterdiscourses, to be followed, yet again, by another set of equally futile discourses couched in recondite idioms."

41 In addition to those quoted in this paragraph, the "ayes" include Bawer (2002:620), Bayat (2001:151), Biddick (2000b:1234n1), Boehmer (1995:6), Crush (1994:336), Harootunian (2002:151), Kandiyoti (2002:281), Kazim (2001:110), Marrouchi (2004:xiii), Massad (2004:10), Parry (2002:67), Robbins (1992b:209), Sarkar (1994:205), Schick (1999:3), Sim (2002:336), Singh and Schmidt (2000:16), Smith and Godlewska (1994:6), and Young (2001:382). Said (1994a:348) is not shy about citing his *Orientalism* as an antecedent of both "post-colonialism and post-modernism"; the latter claim would probably come as a surprise to writers such as Derrida and Lyotard. Quayson (2000:4) refines Said's contribution to helping establish "colonial discourse analysis." Alam (2000:16) lauds Said as "the major post-colonial theorist of the colonial encounter." Ironically, as Calder (2000:13) observes, post-colonial theory—which primarily is written in English— derives its philosophical basis "from European 'post'-Romanticism—precisely the same source, that is, as the Orientalism denounced by Said." Definitions of post-colonialism are a rupee a dozen. I find the most useful that of Appiah (1991:348): "Postcoloniality is the condition of what we might ungenerously call a *comprador* intelligentsia, a relatively small, Western-style, Western-trained group of writers and thinkers, who mediate the trade in cultural commodities of world capitalism at the periphery." For recent surveys of post-colonialism's post-Said history thus far, see Gandhi (1998), Quayson (2000), and Young (2001). Moore-Gilbert et al. (1997) assemble selections from ten of the foundational post-colonial critics.

42 V. Kennedy (2000:2). Harootunian (2002:151) calls it "postcolonial discourse's canonical text."

43 Gandhi (1998:64).

44 Jacoby (1995:31).

45 Behdad (2005:10).

46 Ahmad (1992:14).

47 Schueller (1998:5). Any book written about for so long by so many people can easily be exaggerated. Robert Young, who has written three books with substantial commentary on Said, not surprisingly observes that "its influence can hardly be overestimated" (2001:384).

48 Thomas (1994:8).

49 This point is made by Ashcroft and Ahluwalia (1999:30).

50 Said (2002:2). However, Said's critical stance would fit well within Marrouchi's (2003: 37) noting of post-colonialism that "the mark of the movement is the disavowel of movements."

51 Prakash (1995:199).

52 Crinson (1996:6).

53 Plumb (1979:3).

54   This point is made by Aijaz Ahmad (1992:177). "Erudite" is a common denominator for those who review Said's writings. There are, however, some who find Said's petulant pedantry so pervasive that it seems perverse.

55   As of 1994, Thomas (1994:21–22) claimed that reviews had been either uncritical or hypercritical, with no balanced assessment; he ignores the useful "review of reviews" provided by Mani and Frankenberg (1985). As Kathleen Biddick (2000b:1234n1) rightly suggests, "A critical review of these retrospectives would be a study in itself." I heed the advice of Malti-Douglas (1985–86:52n40): "The best way to arrive at an accurate assessment of Said's *Orientalism* is to read all of the major reviews." I also take up the challenge implicit in Abaza and Stauth's (1988:343) comment that "the extensive reception of this book deserves a study of its own right." As my book was going to press, Robert Irwin (2006) published a blistering attack on Said in which a "lust for knowing" is liberated from any political baggage. Irwin rejects Said's effort without engaging with the theoretical issues that drive the critical value of *Orientalism*.

56   For a general overview of the main critics, see Valerie Kennedy's (2000:14–48) survey of Said's intellectual contributions, and also Gandhi (1998:64–80).

57   Clarke (1997:23).

58   Marrouchi (2004:4). Ironically, Marrouchi notes that Said saw his *Culture and Imperialism* as a more important book, indeed "his book" (12).

59   Ashcroft et al. (1998:167–169). In describing Henry Louis Gates's criticism of Said for creating a "Critical Fanonism," the editors add a sentence defending Said. Similarly, Said's analysis of Austen's *Mansfield Park* is presented as an established fact of "contrapuntal reading," with no indication that many Austen scholars have contested Said's representation (see Ashcroft et al. 1998:56). Venn (2000:53) assumes that Said's reading of Austen's *Mansfield Park* is now gospel, as does Boehmer (1995:25). A similar disengenuflection can be found in Bracken's (1998:505) reading of post-colonialism as a virtual invention of Said; even Bracken's section on Bhabha fails to note Bhabha's criticism of Said's *Orientalism*.

60   See, e.g., Venn (2000:3), whose sentence is worth quoting in full: "Edward Said established some time ago that colonial discourse was not just about the discursive construction of the colonized 'other' but that it was intrinsic to European self-understanding, determining how Europe and Europeans could locate themselves—as modern, as civilized, as superior, as developed and progressive—only by reference to an other that was represented as the negation of everything that Europe imagined or desired itself to be."

61   S. Makdisi (1998:226n6).

62   Said (2003:xv) and Bayoumi and Rubin (2000:64). Although a Dutch publisher bought the translation rights to *Orientalism*, the book has not yet been translated into Dutch (van der Veer 2003:33). Translators interested in contributing to worldwide expansion of my critique are encouraged by the author to contact my publisher. For my part, I would be willing to write a targeted foreword to be included with the translated original until such time as publishers would prefer a mature afterword. I solemnly pledge never to revise my original text; less than definitive translations can theoretically occur well into the future.

63   I am aware that many of these rubrics overlap, nor can this be an exhaustive listing.

Not all disciplines have reacted to Said's *Orientalism*; Rotter (2000:1205) suggests that American diplomatic historians have not been interested in Said's spin on post-1945 foreign policy.

64   When Akbari (2000:19) writes that *Orientalism* "has been the foundation of virtually every effort to characterize literary descriptions of the Near and Middle East," the fact that this statement is made in English is significant. There are analyses of Arab cultural criticism with no mention at all of Said (e.g., Sharabi 1990). The lack of reference to *Orientalism* in Obeidat's almost entirely atheoretical 1998 study of Orientalism in American Literature I attribute to a failure to read almost anything published after 1976, rather than to a radical disagreement with Said.

65   Bassin (1991:764), Brombert (1979:532–533), Delaney (1994:165), Dirlik (1997:105), Freitag (1997:620), Kopf (1980:498), Kushigian (1991:2), Mani and Frankenberg (1985:174), Minear (1980:507), Myers (1980:xlv), and Ning (1997:59). V. Kennedy (2000:147) concludes that *Orientalism* "continues to provoke debate," and Macfie (2000:ix) that it "continues to provoke great interest." Kopf (1980:498) speculates that perhaps a provocative style was needed to combat the endemic racial and cultural distortion of Asia in the West. Beyond all this, I note with irony the pregnant sexual nuance of "provocative," since Said is quick to contrapuntally thrust menacing genderisms into the grammatical construction of those he opposes (see chapter 3 of this volume, pp. 271–272.

66   These are the words highlighted in bold in the three review excerpts posted on the back cover of my 1979 Vintage edition. These particular quotes are by Albert Hourani (*The New York Review of Books*), Patrick Seale (*The Observer*), and Nissim Rejwans (*Jerusalem Post*).

67   Arac (1980:465).

68   Daniel (1982:221), who calls it "an angry book, stimulating, interesting, constantly vulnerable and I think often wrong." Brennan (2001:94) also notes that many passages are written with "a palpable anger."

69   Prakash (1995:199).

70   Inden (1986:410, 1990:38).

71   Owen (1979:59).

72   Bulliet (1994:95), Prakash (1992a:179).

73   Gare (1995:309), who claims that *Orientalism* "has been almost universally acclaimed by Western intellectuals as a brilliant critique of discourse on the 'Orient.'" Schaar (1979:67) labels the book "brilliant and bold;" Makari (1985:60) is content with "brilliant." Combs-Schilling (1989:13) praises it as a "brilliant exposé." More cautiously, James Brown (1999:551) observes: "*Orientalism* is in many ways a brilliant work; or, rather, it includes brilliant passages, which inevitably tend to be the ones that one remembers, burnt into one's memory by their coruscating passion."

74   Wahba (1989:189).

75   Bulliet (2004:96).

76   Baderoon (2002:367), Holmlund (1993:3).

77   Brombert (1979:536).

78   Quandt (1997:232).

79   Breisach (2003:138).

80   Steenstrup (1985–86:233).

81   Kemp (1980:162).
82   Whalen-Bridge (2001:193).
83   Hussein (2002:13).
84   Young (2001:383).
85   Turner (1984:24, 1994:4).
86   This was my earliest assessment (Varisco 1982b:8).
87   Hussein (2002:229).
88   Roussillon (1990:7).
89   Marrouchi (2004:75).
90   Brown and Theodossopolous (2004:3), Celik (2002:21), Chow (2002:104), Davis (2000:106), Easthope (1998:341), Hoogvelt (2001:206), Kahf (1999:15), V. Kennedy (2000:11), King (1999:82), Schneider (1998:5), Singh and Amritjit (2004:xviii).
91   Freund (2001).
92   Fieldhouse (1980:86).
93   Flanagan (1986:382).
94   Çirakman (2002:8), Crush (1994:335), Koptiuch (1999:124), Mills (1991:48). Lockman (2004:3) says "very influential," and Yeazell (2000:8) raises the stakes to "immensely influential."
95   Sweetman (1988:8), who suggests it is worth pondering for the visual arts.
96   Blythe (1993:221).
97   Dallmayr (1996:xv).
98   Rice (2002:223). Gilbert and Tompkins (1996:258) call it a "landmark analysis."
99   Abu-Laban (2001:76).
100   AbuKhalil (2001:100), Boyne and Rattansi (1990:35), Chow (2005:21), Marrouchi (2004:27), Turner (1981:107).
101   Akbari (2000:19). Bullock (2002:xviii) says that Orientalism is "masterfully analyzed" by Said.
102   Musallam (1979:19); specifically, "a meditation on the relations between societies in an age of unequal power."
103   A. Owen (1997:112). Schick (1999:3) calls the book a "milestone in the deconstruction of European perspectives on 'other.'"
104   Dirks (2004:50), Gandhi (1998:142), and Joubert (2000:199).
105   Abu El-Haj (2001:278), Ahiksa (2003:373n33), Confino (2000:182), Coronil (1996:54), Davis (2002:342), Dirks (2004:39), Katrak (2005:34), Sim (2002:329), Walia (2001:6). Starn (1992:157) refers to the "pathbreaking yet overly tidy polemics" of Orientalism.
106   Al-Azmeh (1984:95).
107   Mutman (1993:166).
108   Van Nieuwenhuijze (1979:10).
109   Clarke (1997:8). William Watson (2003:42) calls it a "powerful attack."
110   Abu El-Haj (2005:538).
111   Otterspeer (1998:194).
112   Mackenzie (1995:93).
113   Hess (2000:92), Parker (1980:5).
114   Behdad (1994b:4); see also Dobie (2001:xi), Keddie (2002:554), and Malak (2005:1).

Wahba (1989:187), on the other hand, characterizes *Orientalism* as having eloquent passion "with a minimum of *apparatus criticus*."

115 Bhabha (1994:71).

116 Rafael (1999:1210n1). Rotter (2000:1207) calls it "a sprawling book."

117 Breckenridge and van der Veer (1993:3).

118 Gaeffke (1990:72).

119 Rocher (1993:215).

120 Huggan (2005:125).

121 Butterworth (1980:176), Wickens (1985–86:62).

122 Dobie (2001:12).

123 Myers (1980:xlv). For a less balanced German variant—in which Said's book is reduced to Hobbesian dementions—see Hartmut Fähndrich's (1988:179) summing-up of the German translation: "die zum Teil unschön, zum Teil hässlich, zum Teil ignorant, zum Teil dümmlich und zum Teil schlicht und einfach falsch ist."

124 I Corinthians 10:33. I do not include women here because neither did the apostle.

125 Martin et al. (1997:3).

126 Moore-Gilbert et al. (1997:22).

127 Ghazoul (1992:158). Daniel (1982:211) asks, "Should this *succès de scandale* be also a *succès d'estime*?" Brennan (2001:95) is surprised that *Orientalism* "received the welcome it did in the academy" because it violated "collegiality." But is that not the perennial attraction of a scandal pulled off with aplomb?

128 Marrouchi (1997:74–75, 2004:38). I note this as someone with Sicilian heritage.

129 Gordon (1989:93).

130 Said (1994a:330).

131 Manzalaoui (1980:837).

132 Young (1990:126). Brennan (2001:94) makes a similar point: "*Orientalism* mattered because it allowed people spurred on by an uncomfortable awareness of contemporary empire to talk about such things in an acceptably humanist language."

133 Bhabha (1994:ix). Bhabha (1986:149) earlier remarked, "For me, Said's work focused the need to quicken the half-light of western history with the disturbing memory of its colonial texts that bear witness to the trauma that accompanies the triumphal art of Empire." Similarly, Mutman (1993:167) argues that his own critique of certain aspects of *Orientalism* "is possible only in the horizon" opened by Said.

134 Spivak (1993:56). Yegenoglu (1998:14) comments that *Orientalism* has served as a "fruitful arena" for raising questions about "the discursive constitution of otherness."

135 Sim (2002:330). Emphasis in original.

136 Chatterjee (1992:194). Her tribute is also quoted by Mackenzie (1995:93) and Alam (2000:16). For a critical view of Chatterjee's use of Said, see Sarkar (1994:210–214).

137 Alam (2000:34).

138 Biddick (2000a:35). Ananya Jahanara Kabir (2005:20) notes, "If I am a postcolonialist today rather than a medievalist, I am so because of Edward Said."

139 Prakash (1995:205). In an earlier critique of Prakash's use of Said, O'Hanlon and Washbrook (1992:142) argue that it is a "mistaken assumption that Edward Said's work provides a clear paradigm for a history that transcends older problems of representation."

They go on to suggest that both Said and Prakash are trying to ride two horses at once, to which Prakash (1992a) provides a spirited rebuttal; unfortunately, their mutual polemic is saddled with mutual misunderstanding.

140 "By depicting the glittering tradition of kingly orientalists as a procession of malevolent nudists, Said legitimized criticism of all sort," comments Bulliet (1994:100).

141 Prakash (1995:209). Sympathetic readers usually note faults as well: "All this is not to say that there are not problems with the book. There are. And they are substantial but not totally destructive by any means" (O'Hara 1980:277–278).

142 Huggan (2005:126).

143 Irwin (1981–82:106–107). Critics have also noted this for Said's other works, e.g., Gallagher (1985) on Said's inconsistent attitude about the political role of the intellectual in *The World, the Text, and the Critic*.

144 Freitag (1997:629–630).

145 Said (1994a:339).

146 Brown (1999:551).

147 Whalen-Bridge (2001:202n2).

148 Grewgious (1994:88, 96). Azmeh (1984:117) finds the "positive impulse" of Said's work the "advocacy of a deabstractionist humanism." A reluctant admirer, diplomatic historian Andrew Rotter (2000:1215), comments: "Yet the churlishness of Said's response to the earnest student who wished to understand the 'Orient' cannot overwhelm the more forceful vector of Said's work, which is both optimistic and humane." In other words, Said's human faults do not invalidate his humanist voice.

149 Prakash (1995:208).

150 Ashcroft and Ahluwalia (1999:25).

151 Said, in a 1993 interview quoted in Viswanathan (2001:174). For an author who finds theoretical sustenance in the metaphysical killing fields of Foucault and Gramsci, such a provocative admission might best be taken with a grain or two of salt.

152 Mitchell (2005b:471).

153 Said (1979:59).

154 Said (1993b:64).

155 See Said (1997), first published in 1981. In a critical review, Tehranian (1982:262) faults Said for failing to critique Muslim revolutionary rhetoric in the same way he does Western bias.

156 Said (1993a:228).

157 "Yet *Orientalism* has in fact been read and written about in the Arab world as a systematic defense of Islam and the Arabs, even though I say explicitly in the book that I have no interest in, much less capacity for, showing what the true Orient and Islam really are" (Said 1994a:331).

158 This label was coined by JanMohamed (1992:97).

159 O'Hara (1980: 274).

160 Kopf (1980:495).

161 E. Wilson (1981); it is notable that this was published in the *Journal of Palestine Studies*. By 1978, deconstruction of American racism had proceeded quite rapidly without needing insights from *Orientalism*, especially given that Said draws no significant comparison between colonial policy on slavery and Western racism directed at African-

Americans. Mudimbe (1988) draws on Foucauldian theory to examine "Africanism," but without explicit reference to Said. Unlike Said, Mudimbe probes Foucault's methodology rather than simply borrowing terms. Christopher Miller (1985:23) distinguishes Africanist discourse as not reducible to the binary of "ours" and "theirs" that Said assumes for Orientalism. Deutsch (2001:198) thinks that Said's concept can accommodate Elijah Muhammad and Muhammad Ali; thus it seems that any imagined Orient can be part of the same piece. More recently, Bill Mullen (2004) has coined the cross-continental hydrid term "Afro-Orientalism."

162   Arac (1980:468).

163   Starn (1992:176n3).

164   Minear (1980:515) observed that the field of Japanese studies needed a similar shaking up, as some of the seminal texts on Japan by Westerners "seem to resemble closely" Said's depiction of Orientalism. But Minear was troubled by the fact that there was no imperial interest or presence in Japan, thus calling into question a crucial argument by Said that Orientalism serves imperialism. Other scholars critical of Said's thesis for Japan include Naff (1985–86) and Steenstrup (1985–86). Citing Said sympathetically, Russell (1992) analyzes Japanese racial stereotyping of blacks.

165   See Rosengarten (1998:118) for an application to Italy's "meridionalismo."

166   Vasunia (2001). Vasunia (2003:96) argues that "the lesson we take from *Orientalism* is that how, what, and even why any one today thinks about ancient Greece is inseparable from two hundred years of European civilization."

167   Rubenstein (1998).

168   Herzfeld (1987:64).

169   Frantzen (1990).

170   McCormack (1985:219–238). Leerssen (1998) discusses the influence of *Orientalism* in Irish studies.

171   Wahba (1989:187). AbuKhalil (2001:106) suggests that Said is better known in the Arab world as a media personality than for his book on *Orientalism*. I am not convinced by the argument of Sabry Hafez (2004:82), who blames the negative reaction to a bad translation by Kamal Abu-Deeb. Hafez criticizes the "thick verbosity, pretentious terminology, and confused vocabulary" in the Arabic translation, but in fact the same criticism can be made of the English original.

172   The main studies of early responses in Arabic to *Orientalism* are Sivan (1985)—an analysis that AbuKhalil (2001:105) finds biased—and Roussillon (1990). Rudolph (1991:60–66) provides a brief review of the major Arab critiques. The Egyptian anthropologist el Sayed el Aswad sums up the response among Arab scholars: "Said has been criticized for putting together various and conflicting Orientalists' approaches into one category of knowledge overlooking their epistemological and historical conditions" (personal communication, January 15, 2002). As Radwan al-Sayyid (2001:6) argues, the decline in prejudicial Orientalism was due less to Edward Said than to the postmodern revolution in the social sciences and humanities. A critical study of the reaction to *Orientalism* in Arabic, Persian, Urdu, Chinese, and Japanese sources would be an important contribution.

173   Said (1994a:339). Said does not mention any of his major Arab critics by name, e.g., 'Amil (1985), al-'Azm (1984), and al-Bitar (1982). For an optimistic view of Said's critical influence in the Arab World, see Hafez (2004).

174   Said (1979:129). As Patai (1979:63) comments, Said's translation mistakes the noun
        jam' for a verb.

175   It is ironic that Said only uses translations of Arabic sources, when he is "disappointed
        to discover that Schwab [a major source for his text] knows oriental literature mainly
        through translation" (Said 1984:xv). Oriental studies scholars are routinely criticized
        by native speakers for not really knowing the language.

176   As White (1987:185) explains, older authorities such as Freud, Hegel, Marx, and Nietz-
        sche were still part of the intellectual's Mount Olympus, but "more as ancestral shades
        or sanctioning grandfathers than as models and guides to specific research tasks."
        Aijaz Ahmad (1992:194) places *Orientalism* as part of a trend in American scholarship
        within the Nietzschean world of questioning the very idea of facts.

177   See White (1978) and Hudson (1977).

178   For a sense of who was "in" in cultural studies, consider the authors excerpted in the
        reader by Ferguson et al. (1990). Aijaz Ahmad, JanMohamed, and Said also make the
        post-colonial sub-canon (e.g., in Moore-Gilbert 1997).

179   Y. Haddad (1991:1). She also includes a colleague's remark that the Iranian crisis cre-
        ated so many career opportunities for scholars of Islam that each should have a mes-
        sage imprinted on the forehead saying "Made by Khomeini." It is significant, no doubt,
        that she did not say "Made by Said." Said (1994a:334) suggests that the Islamic revo-
        lution was one of the reasons for the assumption by some Muslims that his book was
        essentially anti-Western. Ironically, as Christopher Hitchens (2003:153) observes, the
        revolution in Iran and the closely-following assassination of Sadat gave a "tremendous
        charge" to *Orientalism*. For a detailed assessment of the "watershed" events in the Mid-
        dle East during 1979, see Lesch (2001).

180   Ahmed (1992:35).

181   To this it is possible to add the observation by Gaeffke (1990:70) that the failure of
        social science models to predict the Iranian revolution gave credence to Said's cri-
        tique of the bad faith of American social scientists.

182   Consider Brennan's (2001:90) observation: "It was, after all, following the book's appear-
        ance in 1978, that a great outpouring of first-rate studies on imperialism and culture,
        race and representation began to emerge out of disciplinary settings as varied as anthro-
        pology, art history, film theory, sociology, and history." The belief in the "novelty" of
        Said's project often results in an acceptance of the manifest faults in *Orientalism* (see
        Thomas 1991:6).

183   White (1978). Most of the essays in that volume had been published in the decade before,
        but Said does not cite them in *Orientalism*. A glancing comment in *The World, the Text,
        and the Critic*, that for White "there is no way to get past texts in order to apprehend
        'real' history directly" (Said 1983:4), suggests to me that Said does not understand
        White's own appreciation of the importance of studying history beyond texts as well.

184   Stone (1981:74–96); the original article appeared in the journal *Past and Present* in 1979.
        Stone concludes: "If I am right in my diagnosis, the movement to narrative by the 'new
        historians' marks the end of an era: the end of the attempt to produce a coherent and
        scientific explanation of change in the past" (91). Iggers (1997:97–100) analyzes the
        impact of this article within the discipline of history.

185   Handlin (1979:18).

186   Lewis (1979:373).

187   Turner (1978:1). "Edward Said's book has deservedly become famous while my study remains marginal," reminisces Turner almost fifteen years later (1994:1). He goes on to observe that Said's book is "now obviously outdated." Turner's article was translated into Arabic by Abu Bakr Baqadir and published in the journal *al-Ijtihad* (no. 47–48, 2000, pp. 55–77).

188   Turner (1978:81).

189   Turner (1978:9).

190   Turner (1978:85); he specifically targets Talal Asad in his comment.

191   Prakash (1992b) has announced the onset of a "post-Orientalist" phase. I acknowledge, for the purist, that posted puns about recent discursive "posts" are endemic to the post-colonial and postmodern genres. I fear that the end of post-colonial discourse must await the exhaustion of all possible othering-back punditry. Given that most relevant book and journal titles in recent years begin with two words, followed by a colon—a form of redirected colon-ization, perhaps—mathematical logic alone would suggest that there is an upper limit, even with the lower standards employed. I have yet to see rhetorical coherence in the majority of post-colonial texts, so I prefer to maintain the hyphen in "post-colonial," as well as the hope that we can get back to work on making the "modern" meaningful rather than dismissing it with a prefix.

192   Mani and Frankenberg (1985:178) estimate that at least sixty reviews were published in Britain and America. For a critical reaction to their review of reviews, see Mutman (1993:193n19). The substantive reviews of the first edition include Arac (1980), Asad (1980), Beard (1979, 1980), Beckingham (1979), Beit-Hallahmi (1980), Biddis (1981), Brombert (1979), Chambers (1980), Daniel (1982), Dawn (1979), Duncanson (1980), Fieldhouse (1980), Flanagan (1986), Gordon (1982), Gran (1980), Greene (1979), Irwin (1981–82), Joseph (1980), Kemp (1980), Kerr (1980), Kiernan (1979), Kopf (1980), Lewis (1982a), Luckett (1982), Malti-Douglas (1979), Manzalaoui (1980), Miller (1982), Minear (1982), Musallam (1980), Myers (1980), Owen (1979), Padoux (1979), Parker (1980), Patai (1979), Plumb (1979), Rassam (1980), Rosenberg (1979), Ryckmans (1980), Schaar (1979), Schimmel (1980), Thieck (1980), Turner (1981), Van Keuren (1980), van Nieuwenhuije (1979), Wilson (1981), Winder (1981), and Woodcock (1980). Hitchens (2003) reviews Said's preface to the twenty-fifth anniversary edition; for his candid disagreement with Said, Hitchens has been accused by some of delivering the proverbial "kiss of Judas" (Brandabur 2003).

193   Bhabha (1994:73–74); see also Inden (1986:421).

194   Sayyid (1997:33). In an uncritical introduction to an otherwise useful anthology, Macfie (2000:3) makes the bizarre claim that Said's approach to Orientalism is based on Derrida's deconstruction. In fact, as Spivak (2005:520) comments, Said was turned off by Derrida. Said noted that Derrida's school seemed "to be somehow imprisoning, and finally uninteresting" (quoted in Viswanathan 2001:167).

195   Figueira (1994:3). Clarke (1997:12) finds Gadamer's sense of text as dialogue useful for recovering "a richer and often more affirmative orientalism."

196   Tanaka (1993). *Orientalism*, suggests Richard van Leewen (2001:198), would have been improved if attention had been paid to Bakhtin's idea of how dialogic systems can be constructed through a synthesis of opposing interpretations.

197   Krupat (1992:26).

198   Makdisi (1998:115–116). He adds that there are moments in *Orientalism* when Said "undermines" what Makdisi sees as his most important points, but concludes that Said's "central claims withstand the text's shortcomings."

199   Lele (1993:45).

200   Sinha (1995:13).

201   Thomas (1994:105); see also Thomas (1991:7).

202   McGowan (1991:170).

203   The phrase is from Rotter (2000:1213), who still thinks diplomatic historians can find insights in a work that is otherwise historically flawed.

204   Owen (1979); he also wishes Said had provided suggestions on how study of the real Orient "could be made better." In a later retrospective, Owen (2005:491) notes that he better appreciated the force of Said's work because Owen had taught in a Middle East center where he was engulfed with "misrepresentations, distortions, and belittlements" of the region.

205   Ahmad (1992:161). Van Nieuwenhuijze (1979:13) maintains that the picture Said develops of Orientalism "is marred by certain flaws." Beard (1980:177) calls it a "flawed and necessary book." For Fleming (1999:180) Said's theory "is not without its significant flaws and oversimplifications." Windschuttle (1999) considers *Orientalism* "seriously flawed."

206   Leys (1985:99); this author is also known as Pierre Ryckmans (1980:20), as quoted in Thomas (1994:22) and Chun (1995:49n2).

207   I will leave it to others to unveil the "real" Said; his elevation to intellectual notability guarantees a stream of such analyses for some time to come. Nor do I have an interest in treating Said's intellectual corpus as he indirectly does with Foucault, i.e., to "indulge ourselves in the practice of saving Foucault from himself in order to make self-interested use of him" (Said 1986:151).

208   Adams (1971:212).

209   Halliday (1999:200). This is certainly true when authors continue to write as follows: "Almost 25 years after it was published, Said's book remains a bracing and invigorating critique of the politics of knowledge" (Hansen 2002:3).

210   From 1978 to 1979 I carried out ethnographic research in a rural highland village of Yemen. My first engagement with Said's text was a commentary written soon after my return from the field (Varisco 1982b). As Lila Abu-Lughod (1990:119n1) observes, anthropologists with field experience in the Middle East or among Muslims tend to be the most suspicious of Said's text; she is one of the few exceptions (see Varisco 2004:107–110).

211   I had taken a graduate course on Arabic historiography at the University of Pennsylvania with the late George Makdisi, one of the preeminent "Orientalist" historians of the time, and my own experience in the class as an interlocutor from anthropology did not confirm the kind of establishment for domination that Said posed abstractly for institutional Orientalism as discourse. Makdisi, like several other good historians at the time, always encouraged critical engagement with earlier scholarship. Like a number of other competent specialists in the study of Arabic history, he did not enter the public debate over Said.

212 Hentsch (1992:xiii); he goes on to say that Orientalism "cannot be reduced to a preda-
tory extinct [*sic*] in academic clothing." James Brown (1999:550) notes that *Orientalism* "figures widely on undergraduate reading lists in cultural studies and social
theory."

213 Roussillon (1990:11).

214 Thomas (1991:4); he was responding to an overtly negative review by Richardson (1990).

215 Marrouchi (2004:xv).

216 For those who can stomach post-colonial double-speak, I offer the following summation: Thus, Humpty Dumpty [latent Orientalism] sat [with a will to dominate] on a wall
[of privilege over the colonial divide], Humpty Dumpty [manifest Orientalism] had a
great fall [thanks to *Orientalism*'s nudging], all the king's [Bernard Lewis, for exam-
ple] horses [meaning asses] and all the king's men [women are invariably absent] could
not put Humpty Dumpty [the guild that came unglued] together again. Or, in other
pedantic words, a de-construction that does not begin to attempt a re-construction
must ultimately be an ob-struction. Mea culpa for the logopandocie above. I proceed
with the caution of Friedrich Nietzsche (1974:54–55):

> In jener Gegend reist man jetzt nicht gut;
> Und hast du Geist, sei doppelt auf der Hut!
>
> (That region is not safe for strangers,
> And having wit doubles the dangers.)

217 The term "satire" is derived from the Latin *satura* in the sense of "a mixture full of
different things," commonly used in referring to food (Highet 1962:231); it is well to
remember that it has nothing to do with the rude, bestial, and hungry satyrs of Greek
myth.

218 Quoted in Highet (1962:234).

219 I do not wish to repeat the harmful hubris of Simon Leys (1985:97): "Some readers
may rightly feel that my approach to this serious topic is selective, arbitrary, incoherent, and flippant. I could not agree more with such criticism—I merely try to imitate Said's method." I intend to imitate Said's rhetorical style to a fault, but only to
point out the flaws in Said's methods.

220 Posner (2001:254). As a private—and thus marginal—intellectual myself, I am pleased
that the book offered here will have a ready niche in public-intellectual space.

221 Ockman (1995:127–28). Parody is more than a literary genre; it is also an art. This applies
even to parodies of postmodern criticism, including the anti–*Social Text* "experiment"
of physicist Alan Sokal (1996, 1998).

222 Said (1979:92). The same Voltaire whose *Candide* Said finds so essential to appreci-
ating the textual attitude underlying Orientalism is also the author of the politically
charged drama *Mahomet*, in which a blend of Oriental and classical characters serve
as a foil for eighteenth-century French society.

223 The fact that I am writing this book should be taken as evidence that I view this as a
rhetorical question. I do not agree with O'Hara, who irons the impact out of satire by
saying that Said in *Orientalism* is "writing a savagely ironic critical *satire* on the discourse of the Orientalist" (1980:277, original emphasis) The role of satire in an Oriental mode as self-critique is discussed in chapter 2 of this book, pp. 183–190.

224   Voltaire (1991:86). Note how in this passage the mentioned items originally came to Europe from the Orient. Voltaire is certainly not endorsing Islam, about which, as Daniel (1966:25) suggests, he is ambivalent.

225   Edwards (2000:12) notes that the boy's naked body was so seductive that the museum had to put it under a protective layer of glass to keep visitors from touching it. There is no substantive discussion in the book about the ways in which Western art contributed to Orientalist discourse; the index contains no entries for "art" or "odalisque." For a critique of Said based on the history of "Orientalist" art, see Mackenzie (1995a); see also Benjamin (2003).

226   Plumb (1979) describes the scene as paradigmatic of what Said wishes to say about Orientalism: "Here is the West's crude vision of the Orient—a mixture of barbarity and luxury, of military ferocity and unspeakable depravity, all bathed in a twilight glow of exoticism." Turner (1994:98) likewise labels this painting "a perfect illustration of this theme of sensuality in the traditional vision of oriental society." Kerr (1980:544) concurs that the purpose is to highlight the "luridness" of Orientalist stereotypes. More recent British readers may be a bit confused, as the 1995 Penguin edition substitutes a demure painting by Ludwig Deutsch, *A Guard with a Zither Player in an Interior*.

227   This phrase is used by Nochlin (1989:35), who enthusiastically endorses Said's Orientalism thesis.

228   Fraiman (1995:821) comments: "The effect of the cover, therefore, like the argument inside, is to leave out actual women while feminizing the wiles of imperialist culture, scorning them in a language indebted to sexist gender terms."

229   Benjamin et al. (1997:131). Following Roger Benjamin (2003:4), "To reconsider Orientalist art in the hands of 'oriental' subjects is to break free of the interpretative vise applied to painting by admirers of Edward Said's great study of European literary Orientalism." For the influence of Dinet on Muslim artists in Algeria, see Pouillon (1990).

230   The painting is titled *Judah and Tamar*, and currently resides in the Wallace Collection in London. The story is recounted in Genesis 38.

CHAPTER 1

1   Said (1979:1). The word "almost" is significant as a starting point for this critical study of *Orientalism*, because that part of the Orient that must then be "not quite" an invention of discourse needs to be represented.

2   Recently, one admirer of Said's work felt it necessary to remind his colleagues, "Just to be clear, Said didn't invent the term 'Orientalism'; it was a term used especially by middle east specialists, Arabists, as well as many who studied both East Asia and the Indian subcontinent" (Amardeep 2005).

3   For example, the Department of Oriental Studies at Princeton, home base of Said's nemesis Bernard Lewis, was divided in 1969 into Far Eastern Studies and Near Eastern Studies. However, the Department of Oriental Studies at the University of Pennsylvania was not changed to the Department of Asian and Middle Eastern Studies until 1992. Currently there are separate departments: East Asian Languages and Civilizations, and Near Eastern Languages and Civilizations. Europeans have not entirely abandoned Oriental studies: for example, the Berlin Center for Modern Oriental Studies was created in 1996.

4   Raymond (1994:6). The main thesis of this book was immediately criticized by Norman Itzkowitz (1958) in *Studia Islamica*. For an extensive critique of this last hurrah of old-style Orientalism as mainstream Orientalism, see Lockman (2004:104–108).

5   One example was the Colloque sur la Sociologie Musulmane, held in Brussels in 1961. Said is among numerous scholars who acknowledge the call for change by Anouar Abdel Malek (1963) in the journal *Diogenes*.

6   The new title chosen at the time for the organization was the International Congress of Human Sciences in Asia and North Africa. Bernard Lewis (1993a:103–104) complains that Said made the term "Orientalism" "polluted beyond salvation" after accredited Orientalists had already thrown it "on the garbage heap of history." Fleming (1999:181) notes that Said introduced the "connotations of naïveté, colonialist superiority, and cultural absolutism." As Richard Bayly Winder (1981:615) muses, Said "has probably destroyed a once respectable if rather fusty academic word, *Orientalism*." Said (1994a:340), however, takes great pride in quoting the remark by the historian Albert Hourani that *Orientalism* "had the unfortunate effect of making it almost impossible to use the term 'Orientalism' in a neutral sense, so much had it become a term of abuse."

7   Cahen and Pellat (1973:89): "Comme, à des degrés divers, en certains autres pays, les études islamologiques en France ont été handicapées par la coupure trop profonde qui sépare les études dites d'orientalisme, relevant essentiellement de l'apprentissage des langues, et les études historiques, sociales, etc."

8   Berger (1964:xv). The British Orientalist Gibb (quoted in Polk 1975:138) once wondered in print if Orientalism could ever produce a real historian.

9   Like Said, Lewis seems to endlessly and seamlessly recycle his words. Although this comment appears in Lewis (1973:22), he had used it in a 1954 conference publication (republished in 1970). Albert Hourani (1976:123–124) notes that historians were not comfortable in most Oriental studies departments because specialists in language and literature usually lacked the methods and vocabulary of historiography. Ironically, the same lament over deteriorating language study can be made by those who agree with the thesis of *Orientalism* (e.g., AbuKhalil 2001:103).

10   Breasted (1919:169).

11   White (1973:v).

12   Lane (1973:184).

13   From the "Editor's Preface" in Lane (1973:xxi–xxii).

14   Tibawi (1963:188). Arberry (1960:87–121) presents a colorful, but short, biography of Lane. For a contextualization of Lane's work in the historiography of folklore, see Schacker-Mill (2000), who describes the critical tradition that influenced Lane's translation of the *Arabian Nights*.

15   Said (1979:164). A number of Said's admirers have followed suit. Teltscher (1995:132), a specialist on India rather than Egypt, believes that Lane "was skilfully analyzed by Said."

16   Said (1979:8).

17   For example, Lane (1973:xxivn2) points out that the French study resulting from Napoleon's expedition had mistakenly described the Egyptian people by what their foreign Mamluk rulers did. Said (1979:159–160) dismisses this as little more than English conceit, although Said similarly rejects that French epitome of Orientalism as an agency

of domination (87). Said's condemnation of Lane is countered by Brown (1999:560–562), Daniel (1982:216–220, 1990:176), Rodenbeck (1998), and Watt (1991:108–110). Kiernan (1979:347) recommends that readers ignore Said's dismissal of Lane and read the biography of Lane published by Leila Ahmed (1978). Manzalaoui (1980:839) finds it ironic that Said writes Lane off as "sexless" when he in fact married a slave girl in Egypt. Crinson (1996:28) argues that Lane's depiction of the typical Egyptian as docile served as an antithesis of the local drive to promote the work ethic among the British working class.

18   Rodenbeck (1998:237). For example, despite Said's (1979:160) attribution, Edward Lane obviously did not comment on a proverb collection by Jacob Burckhardt, as the appropriate author was in fact the traveler John Lewis Burckhardt. For criticism of Said's attack on the wrong Burckhardt, see Rodenbeck (1998:235–237).

19   Said (1979:160).

20   Lane (1973:xxx) writes in his preface that he was often assumed to be Muslim, but that he avowed himself of belief in the Messiah in accordance with the words of the Quran. This was regarded, according to one of his companions, as a tacit profession of faith (Lane 1973:xxix). As related by Jason Thompson (2000:xxv), in 1835 a sheikh who was tutoring Lane in Arabic wrote out a *shahada* (statement of faith), giving half to Lane and placing the other half in a crack in Lane's Cairo house. The idea was that Lane must return to Egypt, because God would not allow the two parts of the statement of faith to remain divided for long. Lane did indeed return.

21   "Unless one concludes that when Said wrote his attack on Lane he had not read *Manners*, such incompatibilities are inexplicable" (Rodenbeck 1998:238).

22   Vague as the term "postmodern" can be, I would not use it to label Said's approach. Said warrants an entry in *The Routledge Companion to Postmodernism* (Sim 2002:354–355), but mainly as a poststructuralist. As Marrouchi (1997:70) suggests, "His *oppositional* criticism—eventually his anti-criticism—has sought in all seriousness to engage the chaos and pathos of the present without a single concession to the knowing smile of the postmodern drawing-room, the disaffected twitch of a Lyotardian eyebrow." Charles Freund (2002) observes: "While Said and many of his early followers approached their subject as public intellectuals seeking to persuade a general audience, later practitioners have pursued the matter as academics, writing in thick postmodern jargon and producing works that sit unread on research library shelves."

23   As Said (1975a:380) began to say a long time ago, "beginnings for the critic restructure and animate knowledge."

24   Said (1999:4). Said notes that the primary reason for his birth in Palestine was the family's desire for better health care than they thought they could get in Egypt. As Marrouchi (1997:67) observes, Said is a "scion of the Arab *haute bourgeoisie*."

25   Said (1999:111). The Howard Johnson is gone; Said's work remains.

26   Quoted in Wicke and Sprinker (1992:227).

27   Wicke and Sprinker (1992:229).

28   Said has addressed this turning point on numerous occasions, e.g., Said (2000:560). Lennard Davis (2001:2) remembers that, as late as fall 1968, Said's "Modern British Literature" course at Columbia did not deal with anything overtly political; even T. E. Lawrence's *Seven Pillars of Wisdom* was approached only as an example of egoism.

29   Said (2000:560) reminisces that his first essay on the politics of the region, "The Arab

Portrayed," was written in 1968. The germ of Said's critique of Orientalism was laid out in a 1975 article occasioned by the myths surrounding the October War. Rejecting physical violence, Said (1975b:112) called for "the intellectual equivalent of the war, which is sustained, antimythological, self-conscious thought." In this sense, *Orientalism* becomes Said's academic spin on critical *ijtihad*.

30   Said (1993a:64).

31   Marrouchi (1997:74). Or, as Ashcroft and Ahluwalia (1999:6) suggest, "The paradox of Edward Said's work, far from being disabling, is a considerable measure of its power, because such paradox locates his work firmly in a world in which ideology has material consequences and in which human life does not conform neatly to abstract theory."

32   Quoted in Williams (2001:ix). I think it safe to assume that such praise holds over into the current century as well.

33   Sprinker (1992:1). Sprinker proceeds to link Said to a litany of critical scholars including Auerbach, Curtius, and Spitzer. Bayoumi and Rubin (2000:xii) include Said among "the long tradition of engaged intellectuals," including Jean-Paul Sartre, Simone de Beauvoir, Angela Davis, Frantz Fanon, Noam Chomsky, C. L. R. James, James Baldwin, Malcolm X, and Huda Shaarawi. For Bové (2000:5), Said is in the line of "historical thinkers from Vico to Benjamin and beyond."

34   Many of the tributes can be found at The Edward Said Archive (http://www.edwardsaid.org). The Winter 2005 issue of *Critical Inquiry* was devoted to reflections on the legacy of Edward Said, as were special issues of *Mizna* (2004) and *Amerasia Journal* (2005); see Abu-Lughod (2005). Yet, as Vinay Lal (2005:39) suggests, "the near reverence with which he [Said] has been viewed, as the numerous obituaries and testimonies subsequent to his death so amply demonstrate, has precluded an engaged reading of Said's own intellectual legacy."

35   Cockburn (2003).

36   Barenboim (2003). A year before Said's death, he and Barenboim were awarded the distinguished Prince of Asturias Concord Prize in Spain. Among the previous recipients was King Hussein of Jordan in 1995.

37   Rubin (2003:861).

38   In a 1999 interview, Said (quoted in Viswanathan (2001:439) observes that his major interest is in writing new things rather than revising what he has already written.

39   The words of van Nieuwenhuijze (1979:12) are worth keeping in mind: "A much repeated and much amended definition is yet no theory."

40   Said (1979:1).

41   Hart (2000:x–xi).

42   Hourani (1991:1). Prior to writing *Orientalism*, Said (1975b:84) defined the discourse of Orientalism as "that school of thought and discipline of study whose focus includes 'the Arabs,' Arabism, Islam, the Semites, and the 'Arab Mind.'"

43   Adnan-Adivar (1953:276); this is an English translation of the 1939 original.

44   Lassner (2000:vii). Lassner is a rare scholar who has successfully combined a career in both Judaic and Islamic studies.

45   For a critical assessment of Said's modelling of culture after Arnold, see Varisco (2004:101–104).

46   In a major survey of what Said would call Orientalist scholarship, Binder (1976:4) drew

attention to this problem and cited statistics from an earlier report that most Middle East specialists lacked either the ideal of multiple language skills or extended experience in the modern countries of the region. Bernard Lewis (1979), a major target for Said's condemnation of Orientalism, lamented the lack of rigor in training students in Oriental languages.

47 Said (1979:2–3). Quotations not otherwise attributed in this section are taken from the introduction in the first edition. I shall use this section as an opportunity to introduce a number of specific criticisms elaborated in other parts of my book. For brief synopses of the thesis of *Orientalism*, see Cain (1984:209–215), Hussein (2002:236–241), and V. Kennedy (2000:16–17).

48 Compare Said's broad use of the term with Abdallah Laroui's (1976:44) straightforward designation of an Orientalist as a Western researcher "who takes Islam as the subject of his research."

49 There is an extensive literature on the "area studies syndrome" in the modern university. See, for example, Tessler et al. (1999) for a social science view. Asef Bayat (2001) offers an argument for the comparative advantages within areas studies.

50 Simon Leys (1985:97) takes umbrage at Said's assumption that Sinologists are Orientalists, as Western scholars did not routinely conflate China with other parts of the so-called Orient.

51 Bulliet (1996:809).

52 Some of Said's uncritical admirers follow suit in this pandoric opening of such a definitional black box; consider AbuKhalil's (2001:102–103) bizarre list of "theologo-centric" Orientalists that includes Bernard Lewis, Judith Miller, and Khalid Duran. Fedwa Malti-Douglas (1985–86:37), among others, notes the problem with this general reduction of Orientalism to any kind of study of the Orient.

53 This point is made by Morroe Berger (1976:36) in a commentary to which Said (1976b) responded. Said's (1979:18) dismissive note that he reproaches himself for not considering German Orientalists is unsatisfying in a work that implicates Goldziher, a native Hungarian who wrote in German, for the very fact that he was an "Orientalist."

54 Donald Little (1979:124) made this point based on a response to Said (1976a), before *Orientalism* was available. In a 1999 address at the American University of Cairo, Said (2005:27) acknowledged Makdisi's *The Rise of Humanism in Classical Islam and the Christian West* as a "remarkable book."

55 Said (1979:322–324) insists there is "some reason for alarm" at what he sees as the wholesale intellectual capitulation of Middle Eastern scholars who "still want to come and sit at the feet of American Orientalists, and later to repeat to their local audiences the clichés I have been characterizing as Orientalist dogmas." This patronizing attitude, like much of Said's rhetoric, is not documented with even a modicum of examples. Fred Donner (1996:49) describes the historian Philip Hitti, for example, as "among the first writers in the West to present a comprehensive overview of the Arabs and of Arab and Islamic culture as subjects deserving attention in their own right." Winder (1981:617) also notes that Hitti does not fit Said's charges. Said seems unaware that Hitti spoke before Congress about the Palestinian issue. For a critical reaction to Said's charge by an Arab scholar, see al-Bitar (1982:174–175).

56 At the time of Said's writing, anthropologists who clearly did not fit the description of

being text-loving Orientalists included Richard Antoun, Bernard Cohn, Donald Cole, Walter Dostal, Dale Eickelman, Robert Fernea, Clifford Geertz, and Michael Gilsenan, to name but a few. Bryan Turner (1981:110) adds E. E. Evans-Pritchard, Ernest Gellner, and Vanessa Maher to the list of exceptions. It is a pity that Said had not come across the constructively critical review of anthropological approaches to Islam by El Zein (1977); see Varisco (2005:146–150).

57   Said (1976a:4). Most scholars not trained in "Oriental studies," as it used to be called, find their own field offering a better approach; for example, Timothy Insoll (1999:7) points to his training in general archaeology rather than Orientalism.

58   Kerr (1980:545).

59   Kerr (1980:546). Winder (1981:617) thinks it inexcusable to ignore scholars like Nabia Abbott, Carl Brockelmann, Anne Lambton, R. A. Nicholson, and I. Y. Kratchkowski. Turner (1981:110) suggests that Marshall Hodgson and W. Montgomery Watt "cannot be regarded as Orientalist *manqués*." Said ignores Watt's *The Influence of Islam on Medieval Europe*, which closes with the following call: "Because Europe was reacting against Islam it belittled the influence of the Saracens and exaggerated its dependence on its Greek and Roman heritage. So today an important task for us western Europeans, as we move into the era of one world, is to correct this false emphasis and to acknowledge fully our debt to the Arab and Islamic world" (Watt 1972:84). Annemarie Schimmel (1980:149) mentions the German translator Friedrich Rückert as an Orientalist who does not fit Said's description. Henry Corbin, observes Hermann Landolt (1999), is a scholar of Islamic mysticism who anticipates some of the critical stance of Said. Woodcock (1980:301) would absolve British archaeologists on the Indian subcontinent, who accomplished "extraordinary feats of disinterested research." Bernard Lewis (1993a:111–112) also provides a list of those who should have been discussed.

60   Ahmed (1992:184).

61   Said (1994a:345).

62   Said (1979:19). It is enough for Said that political scientists "draw on the vestiges of Orientalism's intellectual position in nineteenth-century Europe." I suppose this would make them vestigial Orientalists.

63   Von Däniken (1971:27) claims that these were on display in the Baghdad museum. Perhaps the recent search for weapons of mass destruction in Iraq should have been extended to this pillaged museum.

64   Fischer (1970:49–51) provides a useful discussion of this fallacy in historical writing.

65   Said (1984:ix). Rhetorically, this is a grudging admission: Said attributes the distinction to a 1956 memorial tribute by André Rousseaux, and leaves the term in French with a significantly small "o." Ironically, Schwab was an amateur—like Said—rather than a specialist in Oriental studies (Halbfass 1985:800).

66   Said (1984:xi). Indeed, the ultimate compliment paid by Said (xvi) is that Schwab prefigures some of the ideas of Foucault: "Still more Schwab demonstrates with inexhaustible patience what it means in Foucault's sense (formulated nineteen years after *La Renaisssance orientale* in *The Archaeology of Knowledge*) literally for an archive to be formed."

67   Rahimieh (1990:9). She suggests that Said does not probe this point with any consistency because it would disprove his overall thesis of a totally dominant discourse.

68   Said (1979:264).

69   Said (1979:267).

70   Said (1979:271). As Sadiq al-'Azm (1984:359) suggests, Said assumes that Massignon's "original sin" was not abandoning the "essentialist separation of the world into two halves." Although enthusiastic about Said's overall project, Fakrul Alam (2000:18) writes that the specific example of Massignon "suggests that there can be an alternative to scholarship which blindly or blithely carries on as if it could not be bothered about human impulses and had no concerns except to serve power." James Brown (1999:564–566) notes a stark difference between the treatment of Massignon in *Orientalism* and in *The World, the Text, and the Critic*.

71   Said (1983:288). For a critical view of Said's treatment of Massignon, see 'Amil (1985:27).

72   Said (1979:273). In a later work, Said (1983:282) argues that "this great scholar defies routine analysis, but can still be apprehended as part of Orientalism." I find it difficult to accept Basim Musallam's (1979:24) overly generous assumption that Massignon "attracted Said's utmost generosity." Stuart Schaar (1979:71), a committed admirer of *Orientalism*, argues that Said fails to recognize the significance of Massignon's public criticism of French colonialism in North Africa. Francesco Gabrieli (1965:131–132) points out that Massignon was beaten by fascists and French police for his open support of Muslims.

73   Said (1979:23). In a 1976 interview (quoted in Viswanathan 2001:24), Said praises "Foucault's great discovery": "If we disabuse ourselves of the idea that 'writing' is something that can be reduced unilaterally, terminally, and univocally to an 'author' we open a new avenue of approach to the world." Certainly there is room for negotiation between Foucauldian discourse and the absurdly reductionist notion that authors write in a vacuum.

74   Said (1979:23–24).

75   Clifford (1988:270).

76   Sharafuddin (1996:ix).

77   Said (1979:61, 55, and 1976 [quoted in Viswanathan 2001:25]). Said thinks highly enough of Southern to include a quote amounting to a third of a page. Southern characterizes the earliest Christian imagination of Islam as an "age of ignorance," an intentional pun on the Islamic dismissal of pagan Arabia as *Jahiliyya*.

78   Southern (1962:1).

79   Said (1979:60). On the same page Said quotes from a historical study by Samuel Chew, apparently with approval.

80   Said (1979:65).

81   Said (1979:307).

82   Amin (1989:100–101).

83   Hamilton (1942:19, 28).

84   Fabian (1999:38). Said's cavalier usage of "ontological" ignores a wide range of debate on what this concept means, not only in Western philosophy. If he thinks he is on to a logical argument, I believe he is mistaken.

85   See Varisco (2004) for a critique of Said's updating of the culture concept from Matthew Arnold.

86   Ellingson (2001:129).

87   Grabar (2000:3).

88   Said (1988b:35).

89   Martin (1990:517).

90   Said (1979:3). The following discussion relates to the introduction of his text.

91   Said (1979:6).

92   Foucault (1984:112).

93   Mani and Frankenberg (1985:189) argue that Said shifts to "one" in order to slip from historically specific statements to a generalized level. In a related sense, Aijaz Ahmad (1992:171) and Valerie Kennedy (2000:43) discuss the rhetorical device of Said's we-ness.

94   Nygren (1993:178). See also Malti-Douglas (1979:729–730), who discusses Said's dependence on mental binary oppositions, and Crinson (1996:6), who observes that Said's general thesis depends on "a Manichean structure of opposition."

95   Durkheim (1965:53). It is interesting to note Durkheim's mix of awe and disdain for what he labels the "sacred," which is associated with terms like "irrational" and "mysterious" (Durkheim 1965:54, note 45). Bryan Turner (1978:83) also sees a connection between this East–West dyad and Durkheim, but notes that the "inadequacy of ideal type polarities" was already recognized in sociology.

96   Said (1976a:4); parts of this review are incorporated into chapter 3 in Orientalism (Said 1979:300–305). The assertion that the West categorically regards the East as inferior is assumed rather than probed.

97   Appiah (1991:354). There is widespread agreement on this point. Moore-Gilbert et al. (1997:5) note that the binarism of Europe or West vs. East or Third World is "no longer tenable or easily accepted." Chen (1995:12) insists that "neither East nor West is an essential and empirical category." Kushigian (1991:3) suggests that Said's fixation on binary opposition entraps the discourse. Rice (2002:237) calls for an Althusserian "epistemological break" from the "monolithic, mysterious, and ultimately inexplicable Other, which has become so familiar a fixture in contemporary discourse." For a nuanced examination of the "West" as myth, see Shohat and Stamm (1994:13–15).

98   Kandiyoti (1996:16).

99   Senghor (1994:30); originally published in 1970.

100   Said (1993:214).

101   Said (1993:228).

102   The original German reads: "Das ganze Phänomen gehört zu der Unzahl von vorgefassten schematischen Meinungen und Begriffsfixierungen, mit denen wir leben, unter denen wir leiden, die unseren Alltag und unsere Bildung erfüllen, und deren wir selbst nach generationslanger Abnutzung nicht überdrüssig werden" (Goldammer 1962:xx).

103   Steadman (1969:14). Dawson (1967:90–105) argues against the binary of East vs. West in the study of China. Similar pronouncements are not hard to find for scholars fluent in the literature.

104   Steadman (1969:30, 18).

105   Hay (1970:330).

106   Nanji (1997:xi).

107   Ironically, as Judith Tucker (1990:211) comments, the actual East–West encounter is "one of the most impoverished research areas" in the social history of the Middle East.

108	See Biddick (2000b:1238). The obsessive opposition between East and West comes long after the conflict between Christianity and Islam, as noted by Hart (2000:85).
109	Ohlmeyer (1998:131). For a flavor of Moryson's travel prose, see the excerpt published in Parker (1999:128–148).
110	Fleming (1999:149). Joseph Lenning (2004:264) notes that Said fails to recognize the anti-colonialist Orientalist writers in Ireland who were quite critical of British imperial Orientalism.
111	As James Buzard (1993:134) comments on nineteenth century European tourist books, northern writers often gendered the southern parts of the continent, especially Italy, as feminine.
112	For the former, see Said (1979:3–4, 18, 53, 290); for the latter, Said (1979:284, 294).
113	This point was originally made in 1946 by F. S. C. Northrop (1966:4).
114	This is by no means unique to Said. Even Goethe was prone to offset *Europäer* with *Orientaler* (Grimm and Grimm 1889:XIII:1346).
115	Said's insistence on using the broad term "Orient" while mainly focusing on the Near or Middle East is an inconsistency that has been frequently noted by critics, e.g., Halbfass (1991:10), Luckett (1982:274), and Sardar (1999:70). George Woodcock (1980:299) comments that Said focuses on "a very small slice" of the Orient. Consider the irony that Said's usage here follows the trajectory of Ary Renan, son of the historian he deems the major intellectual founder of Orientalist discourse; for Ary Renan the Orient was "a vague word defined quite clearly by the frontiers of the ancient Muslim conquests" (quoted and translated by Benjamin 2003:8).
116	Fieldhouse (1980:85).
117	Harootunian (2002:152).
118	Said (1979:3).
119	Ahmad (1992:185).
120	Said (1979:3). Said asserts it as a fact; I rephrase it as a question.
121	In his posthumous *Humanism and Democratic Criticism*, Said (2004:5) notes that he never taught anything but Western humanism and had no intention of teaching anything else.
122	Binder (1988:92).
123	These voices are surveyed in chapter 2, pp. 143–151.
124	Said (1979:82). Said quotes from a secondary source rather than reading the original text of al-Jabarti.
125	The phrase is from Said (1979:208), although I read its relevance back at the author. By failing to use local responses to European imperial and colonial power, Said effectively becomes as much a handler of the Orient as the Orientalists he critiques. The same can be said of Said's failure to recognize the possibility of an "allure" of Islam that enabled certain commoner English seamen in the Renaissance to escape their class victimization (see Matar 1998).
126	As Richard Bulliet (2005:41) argues, "If today one were to measure the long-term success of competing socioreligious systems, therefore, according to their demonstrative appeal over recent centuries, one would be forced to conclude that Islam pushed decisively ahead between 1500 and 1900 while, after an initial surge, European Christianity eventually declined, stagnated, and fell backward."

127   Said (1979:206). My analysis here is derived primarily from Said's discussion on pp. 206–225.

128   A. Ahmad (1992:179). Ziauddin Sardar (1999:68) finds seven different and "contradictory" meanings that Said uses for defining Orientalism. "As we shall see," argues Aslı Çirakman (2002:10), "it is hard to separate these three definitions or these three domains of Orientalist practice since they are articulated in such a manner that they all refer to an imagined, or orientalized Orient."

129   Said (1975, 1983) is familiar with the work of Lacan, but nowhere to my knowledge acknowledges or explains borrowing this distinction from psychoanalytic theory. I attribute rhetorical tidbits like "Psychologically, Orientalism is a form of paranoia" (Said 1979:72) to pop psychology. Elsewhere Said, in a 1993 interview cited in Viswanathan (2001:167), criticizes Lacan—alongside Althusser, Derrida, and Foucault—as being "prisoners of their own language." He is, of course, free to say that. See Yegenoglu (1998:23) for a discussion of Said's failure to explore the psychoanalytic usage of these terms.

130   Flaubert (1972:220); this is quoted in Said (1979:187). Flaubert made the comment about Kuchuk Hanem, an Egyptian prostitute with whom he had a tryst, in a private letter to his French lover. It is odd that Said is content to cite an existing English translation, given that he also consulted the original French texts (Said 1979:342n102). Said chooses a private letter as though this were a published text cited throughout the manifest Orientalist corpus. For the context of the letter, see Orr (1998:194–197).

131   Said (1979:6).

132   Having earlier broached the Western fetish of sexualizing the Orient as a constitutive element of latent Orientalism, Said (1979:188) decides that it is "not the province" of his analysis. Meyda Yegenoglu (1998:24–26) questions how such a significant part of his analysis could simply be dismissed. For further discussion of Said's gender blindness, see chapter 2, pp. 155–170.

133   These phrases are taken from chapter 3, part I, of *Orientalism*. In a later text, Said (1983:222) refers to Orientalism's "latent vocabulary" as "a set of enunciative possibilities." The "enunciatory act" attributed to colonial discourse is a major theme for Homi Bhabha (1994:128).

134   Said (1979:221).

135   Michael Beard (1979:4) notes that the extent to which the link between the discipline and discourse of Orientalism "is a willed, conscious and homogenous connection" remains "the central unanswered question" in the book.

136   As Asli Çirakman (2002:17) observes, "Thus Said's argument on Orientalism as absolutely anatomical and enumerative, engaging in particularizing and dividing things Oriental into manageable parts [Said 1979:72] was in fact the basic tendency of Renaissance imagination and style, not only for the Orient but also towards the Occident!"

137   Al-Sayyid (2001:6).

138   Said (1979:1).

139   Said (1979:203).

140   Said (1979:1–2).

141   In the index one is directed to Europe and the United States under "West."

142   Al-ʿAzm (1984:349). For the record, al-ʿAzm finds "a strong and unwarranted general anti-scientific bias" (345) in *Orientalism*.

143   Al-ʿAzm (1984:367).

144   This comes from the title of al-ʿAzm's 1984 article. Manzalaoui (1980:838) calls this tendency a "meta-orientalism" which repeats some of the same faults castigated in Orientalism.

145   Van Nieuwenhuijze (1979:14).

146   Halbfass (1991:12).

147   The phrase is from Rudyard Kipling, who is generally regarded by post-colonial writers as the populist Darth Vader of British imperialist writing.

148   Said (1979:57). Said follows Schwab (1984:1) in assuming that the idea of a meaningful area called "East" emerged in classical Rome because it appears in works of Virgil and Tacitus, among others.

149   See Drews (1973:32–33).

150   Al-ʿAzm (1984:351).

151   In a 1976 interview Said (quoted in Viswanathan 2001:37) traces the "family of ideas" characterizing Orientalism back to Herodotus. Beard (1979:8) and Parker (1980:9) find this claim dubious. For a thorough review of the ways in which Herodotus viewed the other, see Hartog (2001).

152   See Goldammer (1962:10–19) for a useful discussion of the Greek and Latin usage.

153   Dobie (2001:14).

154   Burkert (1992:153n2). Manzalaoui (1980:838) wonders why it never occurred to Said to call the imagined Orient a "pseudo-Orient."

155   The Greek word for Persia is derived from the Persian, unlike the broader term for Asia. It is important to remember that relations between Greece and Persia were not based only on hostility and confrontation. For example, Themistocles, the victor at Salamis in 480 BCE, later joined the Persians as a vassal (Halbfass 1988:11).

156   Such repetition of nonsense syllables is used in a number of languages to indicate people who cannot be understood. In the highland valley of al-Ahjur in Yemen, villagers would refer to those who spoke another language by saying *laghallaghallaghal*.

157   Romm (1998:95–96). This did not prevent Greeks from treating some barbarians with respect. In his *Anabasis*, Xenophon refers to a range of groups encountered in the famed march of the Ten Thousand, rather than to a generic oriental other. When the Macronians sold them needed supplies, Xenophon (1998:423) remarked that "we therefore regarded them as friends, barbarians though they were, and took by force not a thing that belonged to them."

158   Rosellini and Said (1978) argue that humans were seen as more bestial the farther away they were from Greece. As Denys Hay (1957:4) had noted long before, barbarians were "particularly troublesome in Europe itself."

159   Said (1979:56).

160   Aristotle (1971:396) from *Politics*, book VII, chapter 7. Compare the argument of Walter Burkert (1992:129) that, archaeologically speaking, "Hellas is not Hesperia."

161   Cardini (2001:3); he is drawing on Henri Pirenne's 1935 *Mahomet et Charlemagne*.

162   This assumption still finds its way into uncritical texts with undue regularity, *e.g.* Susantha Goonatilake's (2001:6) bland assertion that the Greeks invented both the Orient-

Occident dyad and the concept of Europe at the same time. In pragmatic terms, the term "West" generally refers to what David Gordon (1989:xiv) calls "the modern complex of states and peoples who, however diverse and however often they may have fought against one another, are conscious that they belong to a common civilization, rooted in the classical and Judeo-Christian eras, integrated in the High Middle Ages, and transformed after the Renaissance and Reformation into mainly secular cultures during and after the eighteenth century." Marshall Hodgson (1974:53–54) discusses several ways in which historians have used the term "West."

163   Among the numerous critics who have pointed out the inappropriateness of tracing an East–West divide to ancient Greece are al-'Azm (1981:10–11, [quoted in Sivan 1985:135]), Figueria (1994:3), Goldammer (1962:57), Hentsch (1992:20), Mani and Frankenberg (1985:178), Prakash (1995:206), and Sinha (1995:13). Drawing on the work of al-'Azm, Kaiwar and Mazumdar (2003:274) note that Orientalism is "entirely an artifact of modernity," fueled by capitalism more than by French savants. Dennis Porter (1994:152) is right to point out the absurdity of assuming a "continuity of representation" empowering Orientalism from Alexander the Great to Jimmy Carter. Said is hardly alone in this conceit; see Burkert (1992:1) on classicists. Phiroze Vasunia (2003:89) attempts to rescue Said by claiming that "the authoritative nature of the unbroken European cultural tradition was founded on massive denial and violence." But he misses the essential point that discourse as a "self-validating European construct" must at some point intersect a real history, or all we do is trade one fictionalization for another.

164   Goldammer (1962:37). Goldammer adds, "Der Osten ist das Land der Kindheit, Heiligkeit des Lebens, Gerechtigkeit, die Region, aus der Christus kommt. Der Westen dagegen gilt als 'Unglaube,' als 'defectus virtutis,' als Mangel eines höheren Lebens, ja sogar als Sünde" (43).

165   See Cardini (2001:59).

166   Higgins (1997:1).

167   For discussion of German romanticist views of the Orient, especially India, see Gerard (1963), Halbfass (1988:69–120), and Wilson (1964).

168   Halbfass (1988:83).

169   An 1803 letter quoted in Gerard (1963:92).

170   Schwab (1984:4).

171   Dobie (2001:21–22).

172   Sauvaget (1965: 216).

173   Hall (1929:341); he drones on poetically about Stalin: "His Tartar ears, head, eyes, and cheekbones, his poetic, Gallic mouth and his nose 'half of each' represent the amalgamation between East and West which, in soul and mind as well as in blood, is the vast merging-land of the world's two great civilizations." Kemal, or Ataturk, was the founder of modern Turkey.

174   Fleming (2000:1224). He adds (1232–1233) that Said made it possible to consider a discourse like Balkanism, but Orientalism as a model cannot show what that should be. Susan Layton (1997:82) suggests that Said's East–West division is similarly "ill suited" for looking at Russian Orientalism.

175   Lewis and Holt (1962:1). Mahan's suggestion appeared in the *National Review* for Sep-

tember 1902. Koppes (1976:95), however, records a usage from 1900 and suspects it could be even earlier.

176 Abdel Malek (1981:50; see also 130–138). Note that Abdel Malek is talking in broad terms about comparison between overlapping concepts of civilizations, cultural areas, and nations. He sees each cultural area as sharing a common *Weltanschauung*. Halbfass (1997:7) characterizes Abdel Malek's critique as "less sweeping and rhetorical" than that of Said.

177 Hegel (1953:43). This is from his 1837 *Geschichte der Philosophie*.

178 Halbfass (1988:84–99).

179 Gaeffke (1990:68).

180 Hegel (1975:162–163). See Todorov (1984) for a discussion of Hegel's views on America.

181 Kontje (2004:6).

182 See especially Hourani (1972a) and Owen (1973).

183 Djait (1985:80). Hentsch (1992:144) comments on Djait's praise by noting that Hegel did not practice anti-Muslim obscurantism or minimize Arab contributions, as Renan did.

184 Lyrics to a Top 40 hit in 1962. A similar sentiment can be found in Elvis Presley's song "Harem Scarum" (1965), in which he drawls "To say the least, go East, young men, You'll feel like the Sheik, so rich and grand, with dancing girls at your command" (quoted in Mernissi 2001:17).

185 Benjamin Braude (1997:111) argues that the later Christian tabling of nations from Noah's sons stems mainly from Josephus, although quite different origins are noted in Jewish Midrash texts, as well as in the widely circulated *Travels of Sir John Mandeville*.

186 The modern usage of "anti-Semitism" began in 1870s Germany in reference to the distinguishing of Jews on an assumed biological basis rather than by religion (Hess 2000:56).

187 Schwab (1984:22).

188 In a recent twist providing a gloss on the label of "Oriental Jew," "Oriental" is also the translation of Hebrew *Mizrakhim*, the term of self-identification used by Israeli intellectuals resisting the "Eurocentric" focus of Israel's recent history (Shohat 1992:141n4).

189 See Varisco (1995) for a discussion of the Arab genealogical links of the Prophet Muhammad.

190 The biblical basis for linking Arabs and Ishmael appears to stem from Josephus; Arabs are not mentioned as an ethnic group in the Old Testament (Ephal 1976:232).

191 The *OED* traces the earliest use of "Arabdom" to a 1949 article in *International Affairs*. I am not aware of any scholarly work that followed up on this coinage, apart from Marshall Hodgson's (1974:57) unrelated and ill-fated suggestion of an "Islamdom."

192 Hodgson (1993:174, original 1960).

193 Donner (2001:22).

194 See Edwards (2000:22) for an 1898 photograph by Jacob Riis with this title. Thomas Edison released a silent film in 1898 called "A Street Arab."

195 Western denigration of the term "Arab" follows a much older indigenous usage in which Arabs were sometimes seen by elites and urban dwellers as little more than savages, even if noble at times. For a discussion of how the term was domesticated for mod-

ern nationalist usage, see Haim (1964:52) and the various writings she edited on Arab nationalism.

196   This is the speculation in the *OED*, which also notes that it may be a derivative of "golliwog," a kind of black-faced doll with fuzzy hair.

197   Milligan (1976:125–126). Said (1982:45) sarcastically refers to his dismissal by critics like Lewis and Geertz (1982) as basically treating him as a wog. Fedwa Malti-Douglas (1985–86) counters that this is tantamount to blaming Orientalism for Western racism. Bayly Winder (1981:617) sympathizes with Said's victimization by "woggery" on every side.

198   See Matar (1998:21n2) and Parry (1962:280). Rodinson (1991:36) further notes that "Turk" effectively replaced "Saracen."

199   Matar (2003:9).

200   The verbal form of Arabized *f-r-n-j* literally means to become Europeanized; see Watson (2003:4) for a discussion of this.

201   Setton (1992:43).

202   Grose (1811). This early English slang dictionary equates "Turkish treatment" with "barbarous usage," perhaps in reference to application of the bastinado. For examples of the "Terrible Turk" in seventeenth-century English literature, see Parker (1999:17–20).

203   It is conceivable that some of the anti-Turk doomsaying was of Ottoman origin, to lure gullible Christians into confrontation (Deny 1936). Setton (1992:29–46) discusses an early-sixteenth-century Ottoman prophecy of end-time destruction; this was apparently read as widely by Christians at the time as the works of Martin Luther, whose *Vom Kriege Widder die Turcken* (1529) was prompted by the Ottoman siege of Vienna in the same year. For taking a soft stand on the Turks, Luther was himself linked with the antichrist by the English cleric Thomas More; see Dimmock (2005:26–28).

204   Sale-Harrison (1934:34).

205   Hogarth (1925:46). Beckingham (1985–86) discusses English texts that show admiration for Turks.

206   Quoted in Nasir (1976:50).

207   The Arabic proverb says, "Me and my brother against my cousin; me and my cousin against a stranger" (see Landberg 1883:63–64).

208   Quoted in Metlitzki (1977:14). As negative as the Saracens were usually depicted, Greek Orthodox Christians were at times treated more severely in the Crusades (Hentsch 1992:33).

209   Sahas (1972:133).

210   Quoted in Southern (1962:17–18n11). Cardini (2001:5–6) suggests: "The derivation of the word Saracens from Sarah is probably a piece of *a posteriori* pseudo-etymology, based on the first half of the word and the misinterpretation of a form from Arabic or Syriac." For extended discussion on the etymological history of the term, see Guérin Dalle Mese (1991:134–141), Shahid (1984:123–141), and Tolan (2002:126–134).

211   In his translation, Moseley (1983:109) suggests that this might have been in reference to Shiraz. Mandeville (1983:115) represents the Saracen as a proto-Christian sharing with Christendom the Jew as common enemy.

212   An apparent cognate also exists in Syriac as *Mhaggraye*, although perhaps this stems from the Arabic *muhajjirun* (Donner 2001:22). As the traveler Felix Fabri commented ca. 1500 CE, the descendants of Ishmael were *Sarraceni praesumti* and illegitimate (quoted in Guérin dalle Mese 1991:135).

213   Reported in Matar (1998:155). An attempt to identify the Arabic term as *sharqi* (easterly) seems far-fetched; see Cardini (2001:6) and the *OED* (14:479).

214   This usage is recorded by the Earl of Monmouth in 1637 CE (*OED* 14:479).

215   Rodinson (1991:5) notes that a fourth-century Christian text mentions Saracens as getting "by bow and plunder all they required to live."

216   Metlitzki (1977:3). In the late seventeenth century, newly introduced maize was called "Sarazin corn," an odd linguistic turn-about for a New World crop transplanted to the Old World.

217   *OED* 14:479. This was a thirteenth-century usage. In the *Chanson de Roland*, the term "Sarrazin" even applied to Ethiopians, "a cursed people, blacker than ink; their only whiteness is their teeth" (quoted in Friedman 1981:64). As Braude (1997:138–140) demonstrates, in some medieval sources Saracens and Jews were associated with the curse of Ham.

218   This important point is made by Southern (1962:29).

219   Jo Ann Cruz (1999:57) argues that this may not be as far-fetched as it seems on the surface. The Muslim commander at the Battle of Alhandega in 938–939 CE was evidently a Slav; but it seems a bit presumptuous to assume, as Cruz does, that Slavs "must have retained some of their pagan ways." Yet, it would not be surprising that elements of this epic predated the need to disparage Muslims and built on previous pagans wreaking havoc on Christian lands. Alauddin Samarrai (1999:144) notes that "Apollyon" may be a corruption of "Allah," and "Tervagant" of "Tariq," the Muslim leader who conquered Spain in 711. The claim that the Saracens worshipped Venus has been linked with the fact that the Muslim holy day is Friday, the day of Venus (Metlitzki 1977:206). Metlitzki (1977:209) and Tolan (1999) argue that identifying Islam with paganism helped justify the First Crusade.

220   Cruz (1999:65).

221   Quoted in Southern (1962:31) and Bosworth (1977:149). Muslims respected both Moses and Jesus as legitimate prophets mentioned in the Quran, but it was a commonly held belief among them that only Muslims were destined for Paradise (see, e.g., Ahmad ibn Qasim in Matar 2003:24).

222   I have taken these allegations from Daniel's (1960) discussion of Christian polemical texts.

223   Quoted in Parker (1999:124).

224   This thirteenth-century account by Pascual San Pedro is related by Daniel (1960:105); see also Setton (1992:1–3) and Tolan (2002:142–143). In some versions, the body of Muhammad is consumed by dogs, resulting in a link between Muslims and *Cynocephali* in medieval Christian iconography (Friedman (1981:67–69).

225   1 John 2:22. There are numerous books detailing the reputed antichrists in Christian apologetics; see especially Jenks (1991). Recent Muslim candidates from fundamentalist prophecy-watchers for the mother of all antichrists include Anwar Sadat, Yasir Arafat, Mu'ammar Gadhafi, Ayatollah Khomeini, and Saddam Hussein. Of course it

is hard to find a world leader or pope who has not been trussed up for this starring role.

226   Quoted in Lamoreaux (1996:14). Kenneth Setton (1992:11) believes that most medieval Christian prophecy did not claim Muhammad as the actual antichrist, but rather in the Dantean sense of a *seminator di scandalo e de scisma*. The exegetical damnation of Muhammad as antichrist is discussed by Tolan (2002:90–94).

227   Southern (1962:42n10). Saladin was generally viewed in a favorable light because of his renowned mercy on the battlefield, so he was not designated an "antichrist" candidate.

228   Southern (1962:42n10). The number 666 has figured in many configurations of the apocalypse. The original biblical reference is usually taken to be a word pun for the numerical value of the Hebrew variant of "Nero Caesar." Wild sightings of this number are common. My personal favorite is an early-twentieth-century anti-Semitic interpretation of the blue eagle emblem for Roosevelt's National Recovery Administration (NRA): "Now look at the N.R.A. emblem. Count the teeth in the cogwheel. It's fifteen. Five and one. Get it? Five and one is six. Count the tail feathers on the bird. Six. That's six and six. Now how many bolts of lightning are there (on the Eagle's claw)? Six! And that makes 666—the mark of the beast" (anonymous writer quoted in Fuller 1995:153).

229   Frassetto (1999:84–85).

230   Wells (1930:578).

231   Dibble (1926:44).

232   These statements were made in 2002 by, respectively, the reverends Jerry Falwell, Pat Robertson, and Jerry Vines. They were widely reported in the media and are archived at [http://www.beliefnet.com/story/116/story_11688_1.html], accessed April 2004.

233   For information on medieval and later Christian views of Muhammad, see Daniel (1960). Samuel Chew (1937:387–451) surveys sentiments in literary and travel sources from Elizabethan England.

234   Tolan (1999 :108).

235   Metlitzki (1977:208). She quotes a Middle English commentary on Isaiah in which Baal is referred to as the "principal maumet" of the Babylonians. Shakespeare cites the variant "mammet" in a line for Hotspur (quoted in B. Smith 1977:3).

236   Matar (1998:48).

237   Chew (1937:101). An additional example is the anti-Protestant tome of more than 1,000 pages, *Calvino-Turcismus, id est, Calvinisticae perfidiae cum Mahumetana Collatio*, published in Antwerp in 1597.

238   Chew (1937:viii).

239   Although he comments that no well-informed person still thought Muslims worshipped Muhammad, Gibb (1953:2) justifies continued use of this misleading term as a translation of *al-umma al-Muhammadiyya*, a far-fetched alibi echoed by Patai (1979:62). This is clearly an imposed category, although it would have relevance for more specific theological reference, such as the Sufi path called the Muhammadiyya (Schimmel 1985:24).

240   Slater (1963:123). Wilfred Cantwell Smith (1957) uses the modern term "Muslim" in his well-known study of contemporary Islam.

241   The term "Muslim" is hard to document before the twentieth century. A dictionary by Worcester (1874:295) records only Moslem, Mussulman, and Mahometan.

242   Said (1979:60).

243   Beckingham (1976:611). See, for example, the discussion by W. Montgomery Watt (1972:72–77) on the "distorted image of Islam."

244   I am tempted to say, with apologies to Frederic Jameson, that this single suffix, more than any other, has led to the modern pr*ism*-house of language. The *OED* provides an interesting history of the infiltration of Latin *ismus* through French *isme* to English *ism*, the last proliferating by the sixteenth century. Except in church matters, medieval and Renaissance scholars studiously avoided Latinizing the Greek ending, and the first usages often took on a pejorative aspect; one's enemy became an *ist* (see Koebner 1951:300–301).

245   The earliest recorded use in English is by Rammohun Roy in 1816 (Killingley 1993:60).

246   According to Almond (1988:14), this was first used in an English book title, soon after its first recorded usage, in Edward Upham's *The History and Doctrine of Budhism* (1829).

247   D. Schaub (1995:22) points out that *despotisme* as popularized by Montesquieu was the first ism designating a form of government, although the first use of the term is attributed to Pierre Bayle in 1704. This usage appears to have been developed with the Turkish sultan serving as a foil for Louis XIV (Koebner 1951:301–302). Montesquieu has been credited with placing the modern sense of "despotism" in the intellectual trajectory that led to the French revolution. For a survey of the concept of "Oriental despotism" in Montesquieu and others, see Grosrichard (1998). Oddly, Said ignores the influential *Oriental Despotism* of Karl Wittfogel (1957), which re-orients the earlier concept in a political attack on Stalinism (see Harris 1968:671–674).

248   Said is highly critical of this text as alphabetizing an invented Orient, but Wilhelm Halb-fass (1997:9–10) notes that the inspiration for this work was the encyclopedia of the Turkish scholar Hajji Khalifa. The *Bibliothèque orientale* does not treat all Orientals as equal—e.g., the Persians exhibit *politesse* in contrast to the *nation barbare* of the Ottoman Turks (see Longino 2002:44).

249   Rodinson (1991:57) pushes the English term back to 1779 and debuts the French usage in 1799, but apparently the editors of the *OED* have not read Rodinson or do not wish to revise an English etymology on the authority of a French author. Perhaps, of course, Rodinson errs in thinking that English Orientalists formally preceded French ones. The *Dictionnaire historique de la langue français* (Rey 1992:II:1383) premieres "Orientaliste" as a noun in 1799 and in adjectival form in 1803. The French *oriental* had been estab-lished in French from Latin as early as 1160. For more information on early French usage, see Reig (1988:9–22).

250   Shelley (1981:53); she adds: "Resolved to pursue no inglorious career, he turned his eyes towards the East as affording scope for his spirit of enterprise." This was origi-nally written in 1816.

251   According to the brothers Grimm (1889:XIII:1346). This seminal lexicon does not record "Orientalistik," the contemporary usage.

252   Given Said's impact on perception of the term "Orientalist," Kenneth Parker (1999:3–4) prefers to call early scholars such as Edward Pococke "Arabists," because their moti-vation was a new spirit of humanism rather than part of a Western "style" to domi-nate the Oriental other.

253   See Fuchs-Sumiyoshi (1984:3) and Arberry (1943:8). German scholarship also uses *Mor-genland*, a less literal rendering of "orient."

254   It appears that the Arabic neologism *mustashraq* (Orientalist) was coined at about the same time and for the same purpose.

255   Dugat (1868–70:I:xviin1). This sentiment is also held by Adnan-Adivar (1953:266) and Bosworth (1977:149). Postel lived from 1510–1581, and apparently was the first Orientalist to use an Arabic geographical text (Tolmacheva 1995:143). In addition to being a "thoroughly committed scholar," Postel was in Rodinson's (1997:40) estimation a mystic, a zealous French patriot, and insane. Dugat believes that the first known French translator of Arabic was Armengaud of Montpelier in the late thirteenth century.

256   Dugat (1868–70:I:99).

257   Binder (1976:9).

258   Ironically, the *OED* records the first instance as Holdsworth's *On Virgil* (1769) in reference to the literary style of the Greek author Homer. Greece was, and still is, east of Italy, so Greek could conceivably be an Oriental language for a native Latin speaker. This sense of adopting an Oriental manner or style parallels usage of the modern Arabic term for Orientalism (*istishraq*).

259   Webster's 1828 American dictionary paraphrases Johnson by inverting the earlier definition to an "eastern mode of speech; an idiom of the eastern languages." For Webster, copying continental reasoning as he obviously did, "orientalist" was both "an inhabitant of the eastern parts of the world" and someone "versed in the eastern languages and literature." The 1843 constitution of the newly formed American Oriental Society described the organization's principal aim as "cultivation of learning in the Asiatic, African, and Polynesian Languages" (American Oriental Society 1843:vi). This emphasis on language is evident in the society's inaugural address, delivered by John Pickering (1843:48), who referred to Oriental languages as "the key to all knowledge of the East."

260   This journal was not published until 1954; see Alexander (1954).

261   Benjamin (1997:17).

262   See chapter 2, pp. 128–129.

263   Halliday (1999:210).

264   Winder (1981:617)

265   This point has been made by Young (1995:166). The uncritical acceptance of Said's Orientalism as only a "discourse of false identity" continues in much post-colonial literature (e.g., Michael 2003:702).

266   This criticism is made by Fleming (2000:1231). Diana Schaub (1995:6) criticizes Said's misconceived use of the term "for an ethnocentric appropriation of the other." Jalal Ahmad (1984:28) expresses the expanded usage in noting, quite logically, that in an economic sense, much of Latin America should be considered part of the East.

267   Huggan (2005:125–126). The full quote reads: "Studies such as these, which Said welcomed ["Orientalism Reconsidered" 140; see also Viswanathan 220], risk emptying out the already mythologized category of the Orient, turning Orientalism into a codeword for virtually any kind of Othering process that involves the mapping of dominating practices of knowledge/power onto peoples seen, however temporarily or strategically, as culturally 'marginal,' economically 'undeveloped,' or psychologically 'weak.'"

268   Ali Mazrui (1999) uses the first term in a film review: "The question which has been raised by Skip Gates' television series is whether it signifies the birth of Black Ori-

entalism. Are we witnessing the birth of a new Black paradigm which combines cultural condescension with paternalistic possessiveness and ulterior selectivity?" This term is expanded upon by Trafton (2004:20–27) in analyzing the Egyptomania of African-American travelers such as Frederick Douglass. Kevin McIntyre (1996:758) suggests that Khieu Samphan, architect of the Khmer Rouge in Cambodia, was influenced by Orientalist assumptions while writing his doctoral dissertation in Paris. Thus, a perverse Orientalism in reverse is held to be partially responsible for the atrocities of this regime.

269 Schneider (1998:21). Nelson Moe, quoted in Rosengarten (1998:118), offers the more politically correct "meridionalismo."

270 Khosrokhavar (1990:123).

271 Carrier (1995:1).

272 Carrier (1992:10, 198).

273 Lindstrom (1995:35).

274 Walia (2001:43), quoting Rana Kabbani.

275 Biddick (1994:24).

276 Keddie (2002:555).

277 Al-Azmeh (1984:93). Al-Azmeh's (1984:110–111) hieroglyphic style of writing is at times cryptically formulaic. I await a future Champollion to decipher the following: "If we therefore represent the East by E and its specific thematic classes/categories by E1, E2, etc., and the West and its thematic classes/categories by W, W1, W2, etc., we can arrive at the following generative paradigm:

$$W\text{-}\text{-}\text{-}W1\text{-}W2\ldots\ldots$$
$$E\text{-}\text{-}\text{-}E1\text{-}E2\ldots\ldots\text{"}$$

As historian John Mackenzie (1995:95) observes, many who have followed in the rhetorical wake of *Orientalism* "write in an esoteric language designed only for a tiny coterie." This includes members of my own discipline, such as Kristin Koptiuch (1999:135), whose Said-inspired "Inconclusion" to a poetic ethnography of Egyptian potters reads as follows: "The nostalgia with which the simulacral informal sector must be invested to deflect attention from its new function in staging the reterritorialization of the class structure could best be validated by an imaginary historical authenticity supplied by the authoritative gaze of the (preferably Western) social scientist, now documentary witness to hyperreality." Selah.

278 Goonatilake (2001:200, 272). I suspect that any postmodern Orientalist representation must be skewed.

279 This event, mentioned by Southern (1962:72), is taken by Said (1979:49–50) to be the "formal" establishment of Orientalism as a "field of learned study." Turner (1994:37) follows suit. Adnan-Adivar (1953:262) refers to the early monkish Arabists as ancient Orientalists, citing Gerard of Cremona (died 1187) as one of the most important translators. Interestingly, Adnan-Adivar, a Turkish scholar, goes on to compare the Western interest in Arab science to contemporary work among Turkish scholars to translate and adapt ideas from the West.

280 See Dugat (1868–70:I:vii).

281 This important point has been made by Turner (1994:37), among others.

282 Waardenburg (1992:737). Pedro later went to England and became the king's personal physician.

283 Unfortunately for poor Robert's royalties, his translation was not available in print form until four centuries later, as *Machumetis Saracenorum principis eiusque succes-sorum vitae ac doctrina, ipseque Alcoran . . .* , published in Basel in 1542. The publisher, Johann Herbst, was promptly jailed for spreading blasphemy, but Martin Luther came to his rescue by arguing that it was best that Christians saw the "lies" of the Quran for themselves (Tolan 2002:275). The Latin version was full of errors and inconsis-tencies, far more so than Robert's later and less-at-stake translation of Al-Khwarizmi's algebra—an effort that brought mathematics to the Latin curriculum. An Italian ver-sion was published four years later in Venice.

284 Kritzeck (1964:65).

285 Kritzeck (1964:143).

286 Kritzeck (1964:123). Norman Daniel (1997:131) thinks that the translation work spon-sored by Peter the Venerable represents the beginning of "true Orientalism." But he immediately clarifies this by noting that they were only Orientalists as translators, with no interest in the language itself or the range of Islamic doctrine.

287 Kritzeck (1964:132). Peter goes on to say: "For in no way could anyone of the human race, unless the devil were there helping, devise such fables" (Kritzeck 1964:148).

288 Kritzeck (1964:126).

289 Kritzeck (1964:161).

290 Daniel (1960:113).

291 Matthew 26:52. Peter's letter is described by Kritzeck (1964:22). A similar sentiment is expressed a century later by Roger Bacon, who argued that "faith did not enter this world by arms but through the simplicity of preaching, as is evident" (quoted in Cruz 1999:69).

292 This was *L'Alcoran de Mahomet* by André du Ryer, Sieur de Malezair. As Kenneth Set-ton (1992:53) notes, this was the first translation in a vernacular language that most educated Europeans could read.

293 This was by George Sale. An earlier 1649 English edition attributed to Alexander Ross came directly from the French and was almost banned before it appeared (see Matar 1998:76–77). Ross's text is criticized by Arberry (1960:15) for being "as hostile and bigoted in intention as it was incompetent in execution."

294 The first, in fact, was a manuscript donated by William Bedwell, who in 1615 published the first list in English of chapters in the Quran (Matar 1998:74). Reading the Quran at this time would have been quite difficult for students, since the monumentally impor-tant *Lexicon Arabico-Latinum* of Jacob Golius did not appear until 1653.

295 See Robert Irwin's (2004) informative and entertaining companion guide to the *Arabian Nights* for details on this text's editing and reception in the West.

296 Rodinson (1974:36). A similar point had been made by Daniel (1966:20). Ironically, a major target of Galland was the audience of French duchesses and marquises (Mernissi 2001:63) rather than lusting males. It is interesting to note that the French translation was printed before the first Arabic publication, which was in 1814–18.

297 See Mabro (1991:28–39) for examples in English travel literature.

298 Newman (1908:1); the quote here is from a reprint of the 1865 edition.

299 Asín Palacios (1919, 1926). For the influence of this translated Muslim work in English literature, see Manzalaoui (1965) and Menocal (1987:115–135).

300 Defoe most probably knew of Ockley's 1708 translation. Riad Kocache provides a modern translation of the Arabic text (ïbn Tufayl 1982).

301 Even John Wesley admired this text. See Arberry (1960:21–28) and Matar (1998:99).

302 See Metlitzki (1977:26–55) for an extended discussion of the role of Adelard in promoting studies of Arab and Islamic knowledge.

303 Kenneth Setton (1992:13) notes that the study of Arabic "declined markedly" in Europe from about 1330 until the seventeenth century.

304 The quotes are from a letter written to Sir Thomas Adams by the vice-chancellor of Cambridge in 1636 (Arberry 1960:12). Adams was a businessman; the 1636 benefactor of the chair in Arabic at Oxford was an archbishop.

305 Pococke, who clearly admired Arabic literature, wrote a poem in Arabic to mark the restoration of Charles II in 1660 (Matar 1998:85). The English public had earlier been introduced to "Arab" culture. For example, one of the first printed books in England was William Caxton's *The Dicts and Sayings of the Philosophers* (1477), which included Arab authors (Parker 1999:4).

306 Dugat (1868–70:I:xxxi). The first article of the governmental decree establishing the school reads: "Il sera établi dans l'en ceinte de la Bibliothèque nationale une école publique destinée à l'enseignement des langues orientales vivantes d'une utilité reconnue pour la politique et le commerce."

307 Bosworth (1977:150). Adnan-Adivar (1953:269) also considers this the start of modern Orientalism. In terms of priority, it should be noted that schools for the study of modern Arabic had previously been established in Naples (1727) and Vienna (1754), according to Worrell (1919:191).

308 Wilson (1964:37). Schwab (1984) discusses the history of Indology, as do a number of more recent texts.

309 Schwab (1984:8). Carl Steenstrup (1985–86:233) cites Müller's series as an Orientalist exercise that "reduced rather than abetted prejudice."

310 Schwab (1984:29); he notes that it was not until 1731 that a complete text of the *Rig Veda* arrived in Paris.

311 Kopf (1980:499).

312 This was the *Revue de l'Islam*, first published in Paris. The German *Der Islam* was established in 1910, and the American *The Moslem World* a year later.

313 Fedwa Malti-Douglas (1985–86:38) suggests that one way of looking for the start of "Orientalism" is to see when it became the common term for self-determination, but she thinks it would be misleading to start with the international congresses.

314 Said (1979:87). In a 1976 interview Said (quoted in Viswanathan 2001:32) casually observes that "after 1798 the Orient was militarily an occupied territory." For the record, virtually every part of the Orient has been a militarily occupied territory since the pharaohs. The Ottomans remained very much the dominant military occupiers of the Middle East in the first half of the nineteenth century. Some parts were never occupied by a Western power, and much of the region only came under direct European political suzerainty after World War I. Lebanese cultural critic Charbel Dagher

disagrees with Said's valorization of Napoleon's entry as the start of Orientalism, and suggests that it really started with the beginning of Portuguese, Spanish, French, Dutch, and British empire building at the end of the fifteenth century (quoted in Chalala 2004:2).

315   Atiyah (1955:73) notes: "If any one date is to be chosen as marking the end of this long Arab sleep, it will be the day on which Napoleon set foot on Egyptian soil in 1798." Hourani's seminal study, *Arabic Thought in the Liberal Age, 1798–1939*, also begins with Napoleon's invasion. As Rashid Khalidi (2004:10–11) observes, this date is "both too early and too late" to define the modern history of Western intervention in the Middle East.

316   Said (1975:xi).

317   This failure is noted by Beard (1979:10), Beckingham (1979:562), Biddiss (1981:373), al-Bitar (1982:172–173), Conrad (1999:139), Figueira (1994:56), Joseph (1980:948), Kemp (1980:157), Kerr (1980:545), Leask (1992:104), Lewis (1993a:108), Manzalaoui (1980:838), Odell (1999:328), Owen (1979:61), Rocher (1993:215), Schimmel (1980:149), Thieck (1980:516), and Wahba (1989:188). Peter van der Veer (2001:107) refers to Said's ignoring of German Orientalism as an irony. Fuchs-Sumiyoshi (1984:156) and Johansen (1990:116) argue that Said's thesis about British and French Orientalism does not apply in the same way to German sources, whereas Nina Berman (1997:32) suggests that a fourth phase of German Orientalism, ending with the racism of Nazi ideology, fits Said's thesis. Phiroze Vasunia (2003:92) suggests that Said's failure to address German scholarship may explain why his Orientalism thesis has had such little impact in critical analysis of scholarship on classical Greece and Rome. For information on German and Austrian scholars, see Fück (1955:239–245, 254–260, 322–325); Said cites this historical study but does not draw much from it. Sheldon Pollock (1993) provides a reflective prolegomenon to the history of German Indology. For the impact of Orientalism in German literature, see Fuchs-Sumiyoshi (1984). See Waardenburg (1997b) for a study of German scholarship on Oriental studies.

318   Irwin (1981–82:108). Attempts to defend Said's conscious avoidance of the German tradition can be equally bizarre. Nadia Abu El-Haj (2005:545) dismisses Said's critics with the lame excuse that "the question or problem of where to begin haunts all writing." Indeed, this is the case, but Said's beginning and ending points are the same in that they only consider examples that support his broad notion of a hegemonic Western view of the Oriental other. Said was attempting to write history, not a novel.

319   This point is made by Malti-Douglas (1979:725).

320   Schwab (1984:43). "Ultimately," adds Schwab, "England was to welcome many more orientalists than she gave birth to."

321   Djait (1985:54, 74–96). However, Tibi (2001:33) goes so far as to label German Orientalism the "most arduous" variety in essentializing Islam as inferior.

322   Fuchs-Sumiyoshi (1984:4).

323   Said (1979:19). This is qualified for the first two-thirds of the nineteenth century. Such sentiment would have infuriated the German scholar Wilhelm Schlegel, who was critical of English Orientalists. Said appears to be reflecting some of the ethnocentric bias occasionally shown against German scholars by Raymond Schwab (1984:256), e.g., in comparing French and German romanticism by noting that "in France the fools and

sages were not the same person." Wilhelm Halbfass (1985:799) discusses the flawed treatment of Schlegel in Schwab's text.

324   Al-Bitar (1982:173). In fact, during the latter part of the nineteenth century, Germany had African colonies with sizeable Muslim populations.

325   Said (1985:1).

326   Schwab (1984:73) notes that Franz Bopp and Othmar Frank, who dedicated his 1808 *Das Licht vom Orient* to Napoleon, also studied in Paris.

327   "It is one of the greatest accidents of cultural history that the British 'discovery' of India coincided with the German search for a way to free themselves from the French," argues Sarah Roche-Mahdi (1997:108). Far from what Said assumed, German Orientalist scholarship was anything but an emulation of the French.

328   Said (1979:263). Said does not specify what this simple and clear identity is. Frederick de Jong (1986) and Johann Fück (1955:325–328) discuss the role of major Dutch scholars in Oriental studies. Manzalaoui (1980:838) regards many of the earlier Dutch Orientalists as "politically innocent." See Waardenburg (1997a) for a review of Dutch scholarship on Islam.

329   See Fück (1955:265–269). Spanish scholars have made notable and lasting contributions, such as Miguel Asín Palacios's *La Escatología Musulmana en la Divina Comedia* (1919), which argues that Dante borrowed from the legend of the night journey of Muhammad to paradise. Contrary to Said's dismissal, E. C. Graf (1999:72) argues that Cervantes's *Don Quixote* is "an important precursor in the task of diplomatically interpellating European orientalism."

330   Manzalaoui (1980:838). See Lezcano (1988) for a discussion of nineteenth-century Orientalism in Spain, and Menocal (1987) for a study of Romance rejection of the Arabic roots of Spanish literature.

331   Kushigian (1991:2–3).

332   Giorgio Vercellin (1991:100) criticizes Said for ignoring the Italian tradition of Michele Amari, Leone Caetani, Giorgio Levi della Vida, and others. Vercellin provides an interesting perspective on what he sees as the *hortus clausus* of Italian Orientalism in his time. For early Italian Orientalists, see Fück (1955:185–187, 220–222, 297–301). Amari is a particularly interesting example, because much of his research was on the Arab influence on his native Sicily (see Dugat 1868–70:I:12–24).

333   Gabrieli (1965:131) and Turner (1981:112).

334   Said's omission of Russian scholars is of concern to Manzalaoui (1980:838). Bernard Lewis (1993a:113) chides Said for not commenting on the abusive statements of Russian Orientalists against Islam, as though Said would be supportive of Marxist and Communist politics in the Middle East. Several chapters on Russian concepts of the Orient are included in Brower and Lazzerini (1997). Dimitri Mikoulski (1997) provides a brief overview of the Russian study of Islam. For an older and sympathetic survey of Soviet Orientalism, see Gafurov and Gankovsky (1967). Yet, as Shay and Sellers-Young (2003:20) comment, the artistic influence of Russian ballets with Oriental themes has not been acknowledged.

335   See Fück (1955:287–289).

336   See Fück (1955:305–309). In a commentary on the research of Finland's Edward Westermarck and Hilma Granqvist, Riina Isotalo (1995) concludes that "Westermarckian

sociology thus falls outside the Saidian definition of Orientalism, because its principles do not contain an ontological and epistemological difference between the Orient and the Occident."

337   Said (1979:18–19). British Orientalism, by no means a uniform field in its development, is discussed by Arberry (1943) and Fück (1955:278–286). The very idea of an "American" brand of Orientalism is, as Adrienne McLean (1997:133) notes, "as overarching and imprecise as *oriental* itself."

338   See Leask (1992:103–104).

339   A more cynical critic might wonder if such a limitation has more to do with Said's fluency in both languages and seeming lack of proficiency in German, Dutch, Italian, Russian, etc. Maxime Rodinson (1987:131), a less cynical critic, implies that Said focuses on English and French Orientalists because they make an easy target.

340   German authors such as Wilhelm Schlegel criticized the English for being too biased in trying to convert subjects in India rather than understand Hinduism in its own right; see Schwab (1984:44).

341   Musallam (1979:19).

342   Dobie (2001:17–18).

343   Djait (1985:76). Yes, this is a generalization—the opposite might also be argued—but it is not the truth of what is being said that is important as much as the feeling conveyed about what colonialism meant to the victims. 'Abduh's truth was also spoken to power, and still needs to be.

344   Clifford (1988:267); a similar point is raised by Boon (1982:280n10). Claude Cahen and Charles Pellat (1973) provide a concise review of French contributions to "Orientalism" in the first half of the twentieth century. Neither of these contemporary scholars, two of the most prominent in France at the time, is mentioned in *Orientalism*. There were numerous French scholars who did not carry on the racist agenda of Gobineau and Renan. French responses to Said's thesis are discussed by Roussillon (1990).

CHAPTER 2

1   I think the obituary by Brennan (2000:558), that the "history of *Orientalism* is already slipping away," is premature, but I agree with him that "some basic questions lingering about it have not yet been posed."

2   Young (1995:166) finds Said's argument so persuasive that it rules out alternatives. Norman Daniel (1982:212), on the other hand, thinks *Orientalism* would be more persuasive "if it were written with the light wit, irony, and I suppose gentle malice that occasionally break through," but adds that the purpose was more to shock than to persuade. Wickens (1985–86:63), who sarcastically rejects *Orientalism*, sees it as "an all-purpose pass key to diverse and complex structures of events and attitudes, and reducing them all to something near a conspiracy—witting or otherwise, it makes no difference."

3   Bové (2000:2). Van Nieuwenhuijze (1979:10) contends that "the considerable erudition it displays is mainly a matter of collecting ammunition."

4   Dalby (1980:491). Gregory (1997:270) speaks of the "uncommon eloquence of its prose."

5   Hart (2000:75). Said's eclecticism is discussed at length by Aijaz Ahmad (1992).

6   Aijaz Ahmad (1992:177). Michael Biddis (1981:373) also refers to Said's "tendency towards repetition and exaggeration."

7   Beard (1979:6). For Beckingham (1979:563), Said's prose contains "many phrases and sentences which are unintelligible or absurd."

8   As Ernest Gellner (1994:167) notes appreciatively, "Said writes well, though not always lucidly." B. D. H. Miller (1982:284) thinks that *Orientalism* "is sometimes evocative, but more often cumbrous, elusive, and opaque." Bryan Turner (1981:110) finds "bristling acumen" in the narrative. D. K. Fieldhouse (1980:86) captures a sentiment of most readers by noting that *Orientalism* is "not easy to read or to understand." Said's prose may often be dense, but it is certainly not anarchic. For the record, *Orientalism*'s afterword (Said 1994a:341, 351) has two Freudian slips of Voltaire-ic voltage, glossing the French scholar Claude Cahen as Claude Cohen and knocking the "h" out of Salman Rushdie.

9   Marrouchi (2003:39). In addition, Marrouchi (2003:44) praises *Orientalism* as a magnificent work of "polyphonic ingenuity."

10   Otterspeer (1998:189).

11   Frykenberg (1996:288); he fails to discuss how Said constructs rhetorical tropes or specific fallacies. Rhetorically speaking, how far out can Said be stretched to result in something "far more than" distortion, exaggeration, and overgeneralization?

12   The succeeding quotations of Brombert are all from his 1979 review. Maria Menocal (1987:16n1) comments on the value of Brombert's review. For a similar close reading of Said's tendency to misquote, see Brown's (1999) discussion of the treatment of Gibb, Lane, and Massignon in *Orientalism*.

13   In another review, Warren Rosenberg (1979:111) comments: "At times the reader feels manipulated." In subsequent exchanges Said can even be "vituperative," as noted by William Phillips (1989:344), who proceeds to ask "Could it be that his anger breaks into his prose?" Thomas Lippmann's (1981:647) succinct sum of Said's *Covering Islam* could as easily apply to *Orientalism*: "The cogency of Said's argument, however, is undermined by the narrowness of his focus, his arrogant and hectoring tone, unsubstantiated assertions and numerous inaccuracies."

14   Said (1979:127). Raymond Schwab (1984:32) notes that a number of Sanskrit texts sent to French institutions were simply forgotten about, literally buried in archives. Ironically, de Sacy's private library of more than 6,000 books and 364 manuscripts was auctioned off rather than preserved in a library (Foster 2002:19).

15   Gordon (1982:109). Van Keuren (1980:502) sums up the view of many critics in saying that Said "makes weighty judgments on the basis of often shaky textual analyses."

16   Said (1979:307). The missing sentences indicated by my ellipsis reiterate Said's identification of the "Semitic myth" with the image of "tent and tribe," which are cited as "instruments" that have a hold on the mind of the Orientalist.

17   In contrast to Said, J. J. Clarke (1997:211) argues that in the further reaches of the Orient, Orientalism "has been busily engaged in deconstructing the fabric of its own discourse by calling into question the essentialist East-West polarity on which it has often seemed to rest, and by investigating the social and political conditions of its own production." David Cannadine (2001:xix) rejects Said's claim that Orientalist discourse always saw those on the imperial periphery as inferior. As Susan Layton (1997:82) notes

for the case of Russian Orientalism, "We should thus be wary of Said's tendency to construe 'otherness' as something inevitably inferior and alien in the eyes of the perceiver."

18   Burke (1993:xv). David Gordon (1982:110) criticizes Said for ignoring scholars like Marshall Hodgson, who are clearly not trying to denigrate Islam. Zachary Lockman (2004:133) refers to Hodgson's rejection of Eurocentric views of Islam. Nicholas Dirks (2004:44) suggests that anthropologist Bernard Cohn, who worked in India, anticipated Said's argument about colonial knowledge.

19   Hodgson (1974:49, 38); he adds: "Whether it is the 'East' or the 'pre-Modern' that is being misperceived, the postulate of essential changelessness obscures the important question of how the particular posture in which various peoples happened to be at the moment of the Transmutation affected their destiny under its impact."

20   Hodgson (1974:I:31).

21   Said (1994a:341).

22   Compare the call by Arthur John Arberry (1960:255): "Before the truth about the East and its people can be established in the common consciousness of the West, a vast accumulation of nonsense and misapprehension and deliberate lies will need to be cleared away. It is part of the task of the conscientious orientalist to effect that clearance." In addition to the example given here, an analysis of self-critique by "Orientalist" scholars is provided on pp. 181–183.

23   Thieck (1980:515).

24   Said (1979:326).

25   Said's use and non-use of "ideology" are discussed in chapter 3, pp. 259–260.

26   Said's tendency to retreat from his caveats is noted by J. S. F. Parker (1980:6–7).

27   Said (1979:5). Said's use of "one" immediately follows his narrator presence as an "I" and part of a "we." Why is it that "one" must go on, rather than Said in a more rhetorically literal sense?

28   Said (1979:18).

29   Critical response to Said's exclusion of German Orientalists was discussed in chapter 1, pp. 89–90.

30   Said (1979:24). In a letter written to Roger Owen (2005:491), Said notes that he was in a hurry to finish his third chapter and "anxious to finish the manuscript as quickly as possible."

31   Said (1979:24).

32   Michael Beard (1979:6) describes Said's "theatrical honesty" as "a rhetorical device to disarm critics in a project to which he knows there will be hostile reaction."

33   Said (1979:1).

34   Said (1979:321).

35   I draw all of these examples from the introduction, although they can also be found throughout the whole of the narrative.

36   Said (1979:20). To cite Homer, whose Oriental others seem Greek to the core rather than Asiatically Persian, is to pull a Trojan horse here. My point is not about the accuracy of the proposition, but the way in which it is stated. However, Homer is in Foucauldian terms a "transdiscursive author," whether or not the real Greek ever existed (Foucault 1984:113).

37   Said (1979:310).

38 Berger (1964:140), quoting Elie Salem (1958). Berger's passage uses this quote to show the importance of oral testimony in Islamic law.

39 Butterworth (1980:176).

40 Van Nieuwenhuijze (1979:11).

41 Said (1979:31). Said's initial interest in Balfour is in reference to Egypt. The 1917 Balfour Declaration, which called for a Jewish state in Palestine, is not mentioned until the last section of the last chapter (Said 1979:294).

42 Direct quotes from Lord Cromer can be found on pages 37–39, 44–45, and 211–213 of *Orientalism*. Norman Daniel (1982:212) calls into question Said's (1979:211) "comic quotation" from Cromer about the "shy Englishman" and "semi-educated Oriental."

43 Quoted in Daniel (1966:416).

44 A direct quote from Salisbury can be found on page 41 of *Orientalism*. Lord Salisbury is indexed under his less ethereal family name of Cecil.

45 Direct quotes from Curzon can be found on pages 213–216 of *Orientalism*; Said mined these from Curzon's *Subjects of the Day: Being a Selection of Speeches and Writings* (1915), whose precious title is probably an unintended pun. For a sympathetic assessment of Curzon, who Said does not appear to know was critical of early Zionism, see Gilmour (1995).

46 Kitchener makes it into *Orientalism* (on p. 238) only as part of a quote from T. E. Lawrence.

47 Said pays list-service to Byron on several pages of *Orientalism*, but does not quote from him directly. For the Orientalism of Byron, see pp. 220–221.

48 The index records Sir Isaiah Berlin, Sir Richard Burton, Sir James George Frazer, Sir Hamilton Gibb, Sir William Jones, Sir Alfred Comyn Lyall, Sir Charles James Lyall, Sir John Mandeville, Sir Gaston Maspero, Sir William Muir, Sir Walter Scott, Sir Alexander Swettenham, and Sir Mark Sykes. It would be unfashionable if I neglected to mark the Marquis de Vogüe, duck the Duc de Broglie, embrace the Baron Georges-Léopold-Chrétien-Frédéric-Dagobert Cuvier, count the several cited Comtes, count in Cardinal John Henry Newman, prescind Prince Clemens Lothar Wenzel Metternich, or, earmark the first Earl of Beaconsfield, or cite the first Viscount Milner.

49 As Morroe Berger (1976:36) observes in comments on an earlier book review that eventually made its way into the narrative of *Orientalism*, "To sustain his critique, Professor Said has to select and exaggerate, thus misleading the non-specialist reader of a general review of books." It is difficult for the nonspecialist to see what is happening, because the accumulated evidence is meant to appear overwhelming.

50 Quoted in Said (1979:226). Kipling's prose is also quoted, e.g., on a mock chain of command for the Raj (Said 1979:45). As Lenning (2004:265) observes, Kipling's Orientalism is far different from that of the Irish writer Yeats (1956:304), whose burden is John Bull:

> John Bull is gone to India
> And all must pay him heed,
> For histories are there to prove
> That none of another breed
> Has had a like inheritance.
> Or sucked such milk as he,

And there's no luck about a house
If it lacks honesty.

51   Said (1989:217, 1993a:56). For a critique of this trope, see Varisco (2004). Other literary critics have begun to critique the designation of anthropology as a handmaiden of colonialism. For example, James Buzard (2005:14) writes: "I do not believe that twentieth-century anthropology's widely held and vehemently professed relativism, even if it represents a utopian, ultimately unsustainable position, deserves to be wholly dismissed as the false consciousness of imperial dupes and stooges, however much the projects of anthropological fieldwork were constructed within and constrained by imperial power structures."

52   Said (1979:178). For a perceptive treatment of Lamartine as a romantic Oriental traveler, see Brahimi (1982).

53   The phrase is from Said (1979:3). I analyze this part of Said's definition of Orientalism on pp. 53–56.

54   In the index of the curiously titled *A Critique of Postcolonial Reason*—curious because it is not primarily self-critique and Spivak has been post-colonially colonized whether she considers it reasonable or not—"catachresis" receives half as many entries as "colonialism." "The dictionary defines a 'catachresis' as, among other things, 'abuse or perversion of a trope or metaphor,'" comments Spivak (1999:14) parenthetically, suggesting that her literary acumen has degenerated to the point where critical terms are left to anonymous dictionary renderings. I interject Spivakian spin here because other commentary refers to catachresis "in Spivak's sense," e.g., Prakash (1994:1490). "Spivak, like most post-colonial theorists, cannot write a sentence," complains Jacoby (1995:36). It is argued by Hayden White (1987:106) that Foucault's style "privileges the trope of catachresis in its own elaboration."

55   Prakash (1994:1490).

56   Douglas (1966:29).

57   Said (1979:73).

58   Memmi (1991:147).

59   J. Ahmad (1984:27).

60   Sardar (1999:2). In a bizarre analogy that takes the disease image a step further, Sardar (71) tries to explain the sympathy and antipathy of Orientalists in the following terms: "A paedophile admires and reveres a child before he denigrates and depreciates it!"

61   Al-Azmeh (1984:116).

62   Thomas (1991:7).

63   Turner (1978:81): "By 'Orientalism', I mean a syndrome of beliefs, attitudes and theories which infects, not only the classical works of Islamic studies, but also extensive areas of geography, economics and sociology." Elsewhere, Turner (1981:110) also labels Orientalism a "disease."

64   Aijaz Ahmad (1992:182). In a mocking tone, Wilhelm Halbfass (1997:6) sums up Said's thesis in a medical minute: "Unfortunately, however, Orientalism is a contagious disease; it has infected the Orientals themselves." Patrick Wolfe (1997:408n77) calls for an "epidemiology" of Orientalism.

65   Luckett (1982:276); he is responding to Said's claim that Orientalism was a "form of paranoia."

66   Fischer (1970) divides his study into fallacies of inquiry (question-framing, factual verification, factual significance), explanation (generalization, narration, causation, motivation, composition, false analogy), and argument (semantic distortion, substantive distraction). An Arab scholar who has read Fischer is al-Bitar (1982:24).

67   Al-Bitar (1982:156–157); translated in Sivan (1985:134).

68   Al-Bitar (1982:160,170).

69   Fischer (1970:74). As Fischer observes, this harks back to the Christian notion of original sin. Fred Halliday (1999:210) complains that Said brands Orientalism "the root of all evil."

70   Fischer (1970:57).

71   Plumb (1979:28).

72   Said (1994a:337). Earlier, Said (1985:4) engages in rhetoric that suggests that "Arabs or Islam" as the objects of labels may not exist either.

73   Said (1979:300–301).

74   Waardenburg (1973). Said cites an earlier work in which Waardenberg examines five interpreters of Islam prior to World War II. The earlier examples, apart from Massignon, give ready support to Said's desire to find hostility in academic circles. W. Montgomery Watt (1972:1) similarly notes that a more objective picture of Islam was taking shape among European scholars. As Maria Menocal (1987:22n13) observes, some of Watt's statements about Eurocentric assumptions made in the past about Islam "might have been made by Said himself."

75   Smith's (1957) *Islam in Modern History* and Rahman's (1968) *Islam* are specifically identified by Pruett (1980:304) as anti-Orientalist texts rebelling against the excesses of earlier prejudices. Fred Dallmayr (1996:63) concurs that Smith is not an Orientalist in Said's mode; he also considers J. L. Mehta, R. Pannikkar, and Wilhelm Halbfass as positive examples of post-Orientalists. It is worth noting that Seyyed Hossein Nasr chose philosopher of religion Huston Smith to write the preface to his *Ideas and Realities of Islam* (1972). Seyyed Hossein Nasr (1972:10), as long ago as 1965, regarded the European Frithjof Schuon's *Understanding Islam* (1961) as "the most outstanding ever written in a European language on why Muslims believe in Islam."

76   Said (1979:224). V. G. Kiernan (1979:347) disparages Said for producing a "summary list of academic black sheep," noting that Browne championed Persian independence. C. F. Beckingham (1979:562) points out that Thomas Arnold wrote against prevalent misconceptions of Islam in his *The Preaching of Islam* (1896); Katherine Watt (2002) provides a detailed study of Arnold's style of Orientalism.

77   Said (1979:99).

78   Muir (1898:606). Yet writing about the same time as the first edition of Muir, the American Edward Salisbury (1860–63) contributed to a better understanding of the Muslim science of tradition without attacking Islam.

79   Ansari (2004:61, 74).

80   Hopwood and Grimwood-Jones (1972). Nor does this source mention any work by Renan.

81   Haykel (1976:lxiii). Because of this antagonism towards anything Islamic, Muir's text has continued to be a goldmine for outright anti-Islamic apologists, e.g., Ibn Warraq (2003).

82   Browne (1956:II:x); the original was written in 1906. This is quoted by Nasrin Rahimieh
      (1990:117), who admonished Said for failing to read Orientalist texts carefully. A brief
      biography of Browne is provided by Arberry (1960:160–196).
83   Quoted in Buheiry (1982:15). This was originally published in 1901.
84   Said (1976a:5). Said apparently saw no need to actually read any of Pellat's rather large
      corpus on Arabic literature in the author's native French.
85   Pellat (1976:145).
86   Pellat (1976:144).
87   Pellat (1976:150). Consider how Pellat (1976:143) praises the *Mu'allaqat* odes as "elo-
      quent relics of a consummate art," hardly a swipe at any ethnic lack of literary taste.
88   Lewis (1976:36).
89   These included visiting appointments at Columbia University, Ohio State University,
      the New School for Social Research, the University of Pennsylvania, and Princeton Uni-
      versity. Patai's main teaching position was at Dropsie College in Philadelphia, from 1948
      to 1957. For a short summary of Patai's academic career, see Winters (1991: 529–530).
      Patai provides a brief autobiographical statement in the preface to *The Arab Mind* (Patai
      1983:1–7), and a much fuller one of his early years in *Apprentice in Budapest* (Patai 1988).
90   In their respective surveys of the field, neither Dale Eickelman (2002) nor Daniel Bates
      and Amal Rassam (2001) refers to his work. Richard Antoun (1976:188) not only ignored
      Patai's *The Arab Mind* in his mid-70s survey of the field, but denigrated "pernicious"
      images, especially those given credence by social scientists, which fueled "neocolonial
      Propagandists."
91   A major critique of Kroeber's approach was provided by Marvin Harris (1968:319–342).
92   Patai (1983:1).
93   Nina Berman (1997) provides an overview of May's Oriental writings.
94   Patai (1983:5).
95   For critiques of *The Arab Mind* and similar studies of Arab modal personality, see
      Moughrabi (1978) and Barakat (1990). Malcom Kerr (1980:546) accuses Said of intro-
      ducing Patai to "establish the presence of an anti-Muslim or anti-Arab animus." Richard
      Bayly Winder (1981:617) agrees with Said's critique of Patai. In *Culture and Imperialism*,
      Said (1993a:260) returns to Patai as a writer who shows an implacable hatred of Arabs,
      without noting that the uncritical ideas promoted in *The Arab Mind* did not resonate
      at the time in critical historical or anthropological scholarship. Because Said neglects
      to mention the criticism of Patai's work by fellow scholars Said labels Orientalists, some
      scholars (e.g., Abu El-Haj 2005:539) are misled into thinking that Said was unique in
      blowing the whistle on the culturalist views of Patai. Though Patai's *The Arab Mind* may
      have served as the "bible of the neocons on Arab behavior" (Hersh 2004:42), it did not
      represent the best scholarship of anthropologists and historians.
96   Adding to the absurdity, Patai's mindless rendering of the "Arab" was followed in 1977
      by an equally egregious palindrome on *The Jewish Mind*, published as Said was writing
      Orientalism. In polite Latin, *hoc est ridiculum, hoc est absurdum*.
97   It is relevant that Patai claims friendship with Charles Scribner III, who was the book's
      editor.
98   Said (1979:349n145); Hamady's text is discussed on pp. 309–312.
99   The first excerpt from Hamady (1960:100) is text that follows a quarter-page quote from

physical anthropologist Carlton Coon (1951:153); Said (1975b:88) had quoted this previously. The second excerpt (Hamady 1960:197) follows a half-page quote from a 1955 *Middle East Journal* article by Patai; Said (1975b:89) had also used this quote previously. In the first excerpt Said omits Hamady's footnote on Sayegh's *Understanding the Arab Mind* (1953), a book published by the Organization of Arab Students in the United States.

100   The naiveté of the author is sadly displayed in her introduction: "My remembered knowledge of Arab characteristics had been communicated through relatively unbiased perception. My past observation had not been directed by any frame of reference; it had been spontaneous. Consequently it had raised no problem of confusion between facts and interpretation" (Hamady 1960:25).

101   Hamady (1960:235).

102   Harris (1968:393–421); he observes that "the main thrust of the methodological critique to which Mead, Benedict, and the other pioneers of the field have been subjected comes from within the field itself" (p. 415). Although singled out by Said as a discipline on the wrong side of the continental divide, anthropology does not succumb to the guild mentality posited for Orientalism.

103   I deduce this not from the author's own words, but from the length of lines assigned to each writer in the book's index: Lane has 28 lines and Renan 27 lines. The next authors in descending citational order are Flaubert (24 lines), Nerval and de Sacy (17 lines each), Massignon (15 lines), Burton (14 lines), and Gibb and Lawrence (13 lines each). Bernard Lewis, although oft cited by page, only receives 2 lines, with no sub-referencing by topic.

104   Said (1979:6). Renan appears, often in a cameo role alongside de Sacy, throughout *Orientalism*. Rather than note each page from which my following discussion cites, I direct the reader to follow the citations provided in the index of *Orientalism*.

105   Who these Italian Orientalists are is not clear from Said's text or endnotes.

106   Said (1979:338–39n44). In a later work, Said (1980b:66) also uses Renan to explain the "nature of modern Orientalism." This ignores the fact that Schwab does not think Renan played that singular a role in establishing Orientalist philology. Schwab (1984:26) emphasizes the role of Anquetil-Duperron as "establishing oriental studies in the full sense of the word." Perhaps Said assumes that Renan was important because of an isolated quote, quite idiosyncratic, in Lewis's (1966:36) *The Arabs in History*. Said's mis-valorization here is at times accepted uncritically by readers of *Orientalism* (e.g., Schaar 1979:68). For nuanced study of Renan's intellectual influence, see Conrad (1999) and Todorov (1993).

107   Watt (1972:15). Maxime Rodinson (1991:55) considers Renan only in passing as a successor for de Sacy, who he calls "the real innovator." Jacques Waardenburg (1992) sums up the canonical history of Orientalism without even a mention of Renan. As Zachary Lockman (2004:78–79) observes, Renan "was not trained or regarded as an Orientalist."

108   Daniel (1982:215). Compare the earlier remark of Oscar Wilde (1907:215): "The nineteenth century is a turning point in history simply on account of the work of two men, Darwin and Renan, the one the critic of the Book of Nature, the other the critic of the books of God."

109   Keddie (2002:554–555).

110   Said (1979:130).

111   The references in the next few paragraphs relate to Said's discussion of Renan on pages 130–148 of *Orientalism*.

112   Maurice Olender (1987:334) notes that Renan viewed Hebrew as plainly inferior to Indo-European or Aryan languages. Renan's view that Semitic languages were incapable of progress centered on his rejection of Hebrew; Arabic was simply a sibling of the older tongue.

113   Schwab (1984:300–306) writes of the link between biology and linguistics, especially in the works of Cuvier and Balzac, prior to Renan.

114   Rodinson (1991:142n123) comments that this lecture immediately inspired two racist works, against both Muslims and Jews, by a Greek anti-Semite.

115   Keddie (1968:86). She notes that al-Afghani's response was written in Arabic first and then translated into French. Goldziher and Jomier (1965:419) mention a German translation of al-Afghani's article that was published together with the German version of Renan's lecture. Fück (1962:308) draws attention to al-Afghani's critique of Renan in an article Said cites. Soon after the publication of *Orientalism*, Said (1980b:64n21) discovers Keddie's discussion of al-Afghani, whom he calls a "distinguished Muslim," although only in a footnote. Later, Said (1993a:263) suggests that al-Afghani was little more than a hand-picked elitist benefiting from the British colonial presence in Egypt. The German August Müller (1885:I:512) was also critical of Renan's assumption that the Arabs contributed nothing original to science.

116   Quoted in Sonn (1996:73).

117   The passage analyzed here is in Said (1979:234–239). Said (1979:277) reiterates his point that the same ideas get "repeated and re-repeated" from Schlegel to Renan and from Robertson Smith to Lawrence.

118   Said (1979:235). Said does not mention the specific source of this attack, which is a review published in the *English Historical Review* in 1888; this was republished in Smith (1912:608–622), the work that Said cites in his endnote.

119   Smith (1894:54–55).

120   Beidelman (1974:68); he provides a useful overview of the contributions of Smith to various fields. Mary Douglas (1966:14) goes a step further in citing Smith as the founder of social anthropology, despite the fact that his evolutionary assumptions have long been superseded. Said implies that a comparative approach on the basis of field observation—a key ingredient in Smith's contribution to a woefully biased field—is suspect in and of itself.

121   Smith (1912:613). Compare Said's (1979:237) misdirected claim about Smith that "a modern 'colored' man is chained irrevocably to the general truths formulated about his prototypical linguistic, anthropological, and doctrinal forebears by a white European scholar."

122   Said's reading of a false intention into Smith's work is parroted uncritically by pop historian Karen Armstrong (1992:511), who repeats the absurd claim that Smith assumed that "nothing had changed since the time of Mohammed and that it was, therefore, perfectly possible to see what the first umma was like by looking at modern Arabs."

123   Smith built on fellow Scot J. F. McLennan's 1865 *Primitive Marriage*. Interest in

totemism as a possible key for understanding the evolution of the earliest religion was later shared by Durkheim and Freud.

124 Peters (1967:xiii). Instead of explaining what was wrong with Smith's evolutionary perspective, Said (1979:235) pulls a partial quote out of context to imply that Smith's aim is to disparage Islamic sources. In fact, in that passage Smith is noting that it was difficult to prove his hypothesis about the origin of animal names for tribes as totemic, because the available Islamic sources routinely criticize earlier pagan rites without going into details.

125 Smith's (1912:484–597) letters were originally published in the *Scotsman* in 1880, at the time of the journey. Between 1878 and 1890, Smith spent about a year and a half visiting Egypt, Palestine, Syria, and North Africa. A primary reason for going to Egypt was to improve his Arabic—he was primarily trained in Hebrew. His visit to Taif in Arabia was one of his shortest excursions.

126 Said (1979:236–237).

127 Said (1979:235).

128 Smith (1912:500).

129 Said (1979:238). Nor is Lawrence as decidedly lost in a romantic haze as Said implies. The same Lawrence who could speak of "Semites" as "limited, narrow-minded people, whose inert intellects lay fallow in incurious resignation," could admit as well that living as an Arab "let me look at the West and its conventions with new eyes: they destroyed it all for me" (quoted in Porter 1994:155, 161n8; the quotes are taken from Lawrence 1962:36, 30).

130 Smith (1912:493).

131 I quote from the English translation (1985), in which Renan is discussed primarily on pp. 42–50. Djait's original text, *L'Europe et L'Islam*, was published in 1978.

132 See Renan's comments in Keddie (1968:92). Ironically, an Arab writer, ʿAbd al-Halim Mahmud, cited Renan's authority in refuting Orientalist bias against Muhammad (Malti-Douglas 1985–86:52n33).

133 Little (1979:121).

134 Butterfield (1931:22). Numerous critical historians were aware of the dangers of prejudice in historical writing. Bloch (1953:140), for example, draws from Montaigne in his own summation that "When the passions of the past blend with the prejudices of the present, human reality is reduced to a picture in black and white."

135 Figueira (1994:56).

136 Butterfield (1931:43). A latent Orientalist discourse that overwrites manifest differences and sympathies is, if not self-standing, at least self-generating, in Said's usage.

137 Butterfield (1931:64). As Fischer (1970:139) rightly observes, the same fallacy can as easily be committed by an anti-whig: presentism "appears in works by scholars of all political persuasions."

138 Butterfield (1931:65). MacKenzie (1995a:98) identifies Said's approach to history as "essentially Whiggish." As Franklin (1998:64) suggests, "It is dangerous to impose a twentieth century post-colonial sensitivity upon an earlier age; a species of historicism and relativism had and has to operate."

139 Fischer (1970:66). Or, as Jacques Berlinerblau (1999:23) classifies the polemical work of Martin Bernal, this kind of writing becomes "slap-dash big-picturism."

140 Arnold Toynbee (1961) provides a reflective reconsideration of his own reading of history in the light of his critics. Ironically, Toynbee (1961:473) defends the civilization
of Islam from its denigration, certainly not in a religiously apologetic sense, by the
anthropologist A. L. Kroeber. For a critical assessment of Toynbee, see Fück
(1962:312–314).

141 Fischer (1970:66–67). Good historians are also capable of making good puns.

142 Said (1976a:4). As Said (1979:348n124, 350n137) acknowledges in *Orientalism*, the critique of the *Cambridge History of Islam* had earlier been made by "Orientalist" historians Albert Hourani (1972a) and Roger Owen (1973). "'Event history' is not particularly
a Western conspiracy foisted on the Orient," comments Irwin (1981–82:110), who adds
that Said shows a critical tunnel vision here, as similar methodological problems have
been cited for Cambridge and Oxford histories of other areas.

143 Fischer (1970:67).

144 In an endnote, Said (1979:347n89) refers to the 1961 French version as "a very detailed
survey of the Islamic-Orientalist field" but does not examine its pivotal role in the field
of Oriental studies. For a more recent survey of the field in relation to "Orientalist"
study of Islam, see Humphries (1991).

145 Sauvaget (1965:5).

146 Sauvaget (1965:3). For example, Sauvaget (65) critiques Huart's *Histoire des Arabes*
1912–13 as "a hodgepodge of names whose success in its time is now difficult to understand and which should be avoided."

147 Sauvaget (1965:115). In Sauvaget's seminal text, Renan, Said's paradigm for modern Orientalism, appears only once, for his 1852 study of the Islamic philosopher Averroes.

148 *The Encyclopaedia of Islam* in English first appeared 1913–38. A new edition was begun
in 1960 and finally reached twelve volumes. Hodgson (1974:40–48) discusses the "philological bias" in this source. Early Muslim response to the first edition was largely
negative—e.g., Husayn al-Harawi (quoted in Saghiyya 1995:57), who in 1932 labeled it
painful slander (*al-ta'n al-jarih*). The *Handbuch der Orientalistik* series, also published
by Brill in Leiden, was begun in the mid-twentieth century and now has more than 150
volumes in several languages.

149 The *Index Islamicus* was first published in 1958, and included some 26,000 references
in Western languages from 1906 to 1955. It proceeded with a volume every five years
until 1977, when it became quarterly. By 2004, this resource was surveying articles on
Islam and related topics in about 2,500 periodicals.

150 See, e.g., Behdad (1994a:10; 1994b:3).

151 Hussein (2002:228). In a simlar manner, Nadia Abu El-Haj (2005:545) refers to Said's
notion of Orientalist discourse as an "archive of systematic statements and bodies of
knowledge," without acknowledging the extensive criticism by trained historians
regarding what Said left out or misread. To aggrandize Said's "marshalling of facts" as
proof for his empirical methodology, as asserted by Shelley Walia (2001:19), is apt only
in a histrionic—not historigraphical—sense.

152 Marrouchi (2003:54, 56). It is useful to keep in mind Russell Jacoby's (1995:32) query
about non-historians who rewrite history: "Are they serious students of colonial history and culture or do they just pepper their writings with references to Gramsci
and hegemony?" Consider the reflection of historian Jacob Lassner (2000:34): "Wax-

ing philosophical, many scholars talk endlessly of historical processes and/or the limits of interpretation, without demanding a detailed and informed picture of the past."

153   Moore-Gilbert et al. (1997:23). On the subsequent pages, the same authors aver (24–25): "Consequently, Said prevaricates damagingly over the degrees to which Orientalism varies over historial periods, between national cultures (for instance, France and the United States), across disciplines and between individual writers and scholars."

154   Plumb (1979:23). Victor Brombert (1979:536) adds that reverence is not Said's forte either. A more religious spin is provided by David Gordon (1982:112): "But gospel, as some would have it, Said is not."

155   This criticism is shared by many Western and Arab scholars, e.g., Burke (1998a), Dawn (1979:1334), Eickelman (2002:27), Fähndrich (1988:181), Halbfass (1991:10), Kiernan (1979:346), Kopf (1980:496), Sarkar (1994:220), and Wahba (1989:188). In a perceptive insight, D. K. Van Keuren (1980:502) predicts that Said's book will be of "lessened interest to historians" because it only expresses a "secondary concern with history." Julia Kushigian (1991:2) writes that Said has "rewritten" history. Madeleine Dobie (2001:15) refers to Said's "erasure of historical distinctions between different discourses and counterdiscourses." Saree Makdisi (1998:216n64), who is sympathetic to Said's central argument, notes *Orientalism*'s "occasional slippage into ahistorical and essentialist claims." E. San Juan (2005:63) refers to Said's "deliberate refusal to historicize power relations in concrete material conditions" as limiting his reading of literary texts. In response to critical historians, Said (1985:2) retorts, "as for my ahistoricity, that too is a charge weightier in assertion than in proof." I could not agree more with Said, which is why I have included this rather long section of proofs.

156   Kopf (1980:499); he explains that "Said's procedure of dropping names, dates and anecdotes to support a method which is profoundly structural and synchronic is diametrically opposed to history." For a discussion of Kopf's critique of Said, see King (1999:86–90).

157   MacKenzie (1995a:xix). For critical responses to an earlier critique by Mackenzie (1994) of Said, see Hildreth (1995), Robbins (1995), Young (1995), Castronovo (1995), and Simmons (1995), as well as MacKenzie's (1995b) reply.

158   Kennedy (2000:24).

159   Plumb (1979:28).

160   Biddick (2000b:1235). William Hart (2000:83) notes, for example: "Much of what Said attributes to Orientalism, especially during the Middle Ages, is better understood as religious discourse." Lucy Pick (1999:267) adds, "Said's understanding of the worldview of the medieval Christian is, in the end, as much or more the product of a stereotype as medieval Christian knowledge of Islam itself was."

161   MacKenzie (1995a:214); see also Matar (1998:13). Mohja Kahf (1999:6, 177) offers a similar criticism of historians who read back views of the veiled harem into medieval European literature.

162   Davis (2000:113). Similar points are made by Akbari (2000:19) and Biddick (2000b:1236).

163   Davis (2000:111). She writes: "Said's insistence upon a purely textual medieval Orientalism untainted by any experiential intercourse with the East safeguards one of the major arguments of his book: that European Orientalist representations had no

basis in a 'real' Orient." Mohja Kahf (1999:15) observes: "Nothing could be more misleading, however, than to subsume under the term 'Orientalism' the production of texts about the Islamic world that began to thrive in the High Middle Ages."

164   Spiegel (1997:20). As Douwe Fokkema (1996:238) notes, "Said does not refer to research that confirms his position."

165   Spiegel (1997:14).

166   Akbari (2000:20) is critical of Said's assumption of an East-vs.-West opposition: "It would be a mistake, however, to conflate a binary overtly based on religious difference with the binary of Orient and Occident." She also criticizes Said's reading back of a modern notion of Europe into the medieval period. A similar point is made by Samir Amin (1989:102). Paula Sanders (2003) argues that the category of "medieval" is more important than "Orient" in creating the Victorian image of Cairo.

167   Moseley (1983:129).

168   Matar (1998:12); see also Berman (2005:227, 242), Çirakman (2002:21), and Dimmock (2005:9).

169   The expediency of seeking political and trade agreeements between Elizabethan England and the Ottomans was recognized by an earlier English literature scholar, Samuel Chew (1937:104). Chew points out that rivalry with other European powers mitigated the idea of a specific Islamic enemy. As Jonathan Burton (2000:130) notes: "Elizabethan England never enjoyed the upper hand in its dealings with the East." See also Daniel (1966:12–13), Vaughan (1954), and Watson (2003:10–12).

170   Berman 2005:230). This was in 1518, before the Ottomans laid siege to Vienna, after which Luther became even more convinced that God had allowed the Turks to come that far as an apocalyptic warning to the church. A similar view was given by Luther's reform-minded compatriot Desiderius Erasmus in his De bello turcico (1530); see Dimmock (2005:20–21).

171   Cardini (2001:171). A case in point is Englishman William Lithgow's 1614 travel account, in which he is more hostile to Catholics than to Muslims (see Chew 1937:40).

172   DeVries (1999:546).

173   Said (1979:59).

174   Said (1979:303). The error is pointed out by Beckingham (1979:563).

175   A major excerpt from Said's text (1979:81–88) is reprinted as an addition to the English translation of al-Jabarti (1993).

176   Thiry (1973). Said appears to be unaware of the classic studies of Napoleon's expedition by de la Jonquière (1899–1907) and Charles-Roux (1925). For a recent survey of the expedition, see Laurens (1997).

177   Said (1979:84).

178   Prochaska (1994:73). For a thorough analysis of the savants, see Laissus (1998), who portrays them as generally sympathetic to Egyptians.

179   In the process of preparing the Déscription, some of the major scientists of the day were involved in analysis of the specimens brought back. However, contrary to Said's implication, Napoleon did not think of his conquest as a scientific venture from the start.

180   Wilson (1964:15).

181   This is discussed by Wahba (1989:195–196), with a focus on al-Jabarti. In addition to

al-Jabarti, Shakir cites al-Shawkani (died 1834) and al-Zabidi (died 1790) as relevant scholars in Yemen. Shakir's critique of Western Orientalism is discussed by Daniel (1990:177–182).

182 Al-Jabarti (1993:93, 29–33). For a discussion of al-Jabarti's view of the French, see Wielandt (1980:17–33). Said (1979:82) refers to al-Jabarti in *Orientalism*, but in reference to a secondary source. In *Culture and Imperialism*, Said (1993a:33–34) mentions al-Jabarti's *'Aja'ib al-athar*, although the author is effectively mooted into an uncompromising anti-Westernism.

183 Said (1994a:333). Ironically, French officer Jacques Menou, who took charge of French forces in Egypt in 1800, established that country's first Arabic-language newspaper, a vehicle that eventually became a primary source of intellectual resistance to Orientalist assumptions.

184 Ayalon (1965:355).

185 See Sweetman (1988:115), who notes that in 1817 Muhammad 'Ali invited Pascal-Xavier Coste, a French architect, to measure and draw all the main buildings of Islamic Cairo. These were later incorporated in his 1837–39 *Architecture Arabe ou monuments du Kaire*. Such valuable documentation is surely as relevant a contribution to Western representation of the Orient as the ethnocentric renderings focused on by Said.

186 Quoted in Said (1979:86), who provides only the French, although earlier quotes from the same source are translated into English for the reader. A free rendering of the French would be: "Egypt was the stage of his fame and [to this day] saves from oblivion all the circumstances of that extraordinary event." Even Said's carefully chosen quotes, when read contrapuntally as statements couched to salvage glory from a humiliating reversal of fortune, suggest that the *coup de théâtre* here is more Beckett than Bedwell or Burton. We would do well to remember that Napoleon started out with 400 ships and 38,000 men; virtually all the men were lost in this Waterloo warm-up.

187 Said (1979:87). On a note of irony, considering Said's insistence that real Orientals were mute, the samurai Omura Masujiro, the so-called "Father of the Japanese Army," in the mid-nineteenth century translated accounts of Napoleon's military strategy (B. Anderson 1991:94n25). Daisuke Nishihara (2005:242) suggests that Said's *Orientalism* was well-received in Japan precisely because there was a long history of academic resistance to Western misrepresentation. For further irony Nishihara also suggests that Said's work prompted a desire in the Japanese academy to read criticism in English.

188 Quoted in Lloyd (1973:58). British fear of Napoleonic influence in the Middle East and India is discussed by Daniel (1966:175–205).

189 Said (1979:80). Among the texts that Napoleon took with him to Egypt were Homer's *Iliad*, Xenophon's *Anabasis*, and Plutarch's *Lives* (Bernal 1987:185). Said's assumption that Napoleon viewed these texts as a "useful substitute for any actual encounter with the real Orient" is questionable; Napoleon certainly regarded the Greek texts as reflecting an actual history he hoped to replicate, if not supersede.

190 Said (1979:83).

191 Said (1979:84).

192 Marrouchi (2003:54).

193 Said (1979:87–88). Said does not consider the expedition's artistic children. The British

painter David Roberts, famed for his detailed illustrations of architecture, thought the plates in the French *Déscription* "quite inaccurate," and set out to correct them (Peltre 1998:102). Similarly, Emily Weeks (1998) shows how the English painter Sir David Wilkie does not fit Said's thesis of domination.

194 Said (1979:88).

195 I note with irony that Chateaubriand was no lover of Napoleon, and once paid for a royalist pamphlet against the dictator. Said does not actually provide examples from the *Déscription de l'Égypte*; Prochaska (1994:86) indicates that in this text Egypt is "often treated more individually and sympathetically than in later, more stereotypically Orientalist works." Philip Kohl (1995:241), a loose reader of Said's text, extends the Napoleonic moment of Orientalist hegemonizing to explain the Near Eastern archaeological interest in prehistoric sites, as if looking for the evolutionary origins of the cultures in the region validates the textual attitude of the Orientalists critiqued by Said.

196 Said (1979:22, 76–79, 122, 252).

197 Said (1979:122).

198 Kopf (1980:503); also in Kopf (1995:155). The same point is made by Saree Makdisi (1998:117), who adds that Edmund Burke does not fit Said's understanding of "modern" Orientalism. David Ludden (1993:251) points out Said's misunderstanding of the differing roles of Orientalists in British colonial policy before and after 1830. Tripta Wahi (1996) argues that Said fails to understand that British historians have treated medieval India the way they treated other "medieval" cultures. Richard Eaton (2000) suggests that Said and the post-colonial writers who follow him seriously misrepresent politics in India before the British arrrived. Peter Heehs (2003) outlines six different styles of Orientalism in India, while noting that Said vastly oversimplified his account. Wendy Doniger (1999:944) laments the anti-Orientalism "disregard" of the philological and textual analysis in early scholarship about India.

199 Schwab (1984:34) paints a far more nuanced portrait of Hastings than the stereotype of the colonial administrator assumed by Said.

200 Quoted in Chaudhuri (1974:358). Max Müller only appears in *Orientalism*'s lists (Said 1979:18, 246, 252).

201 Said (1979:215).

202 This analysis is from Majeed (1992:195), who examines the impact of Mill's book in detail. Kopf (1995:157) is critical of Majeed for defending Mill, a conservative who wrote his book without actually visiting India. Inden (1990:46) follows Said in labeling Mill an Orientalist or Indologist simply because he wrote a derivative book about India. If, as Inden suggests, Mill's book is "the hegemonic text on India," it does not achieve this status as a result of scholarly study of Indian language à la Jones and the Orientalists. Peter Heehs (2003:175) complains that Inden's work gives a "new lease on life to Eurocentrism." For a critique of Inden's appropriation of Said, see Halbfass (1997:18–21). For Scottish Orientalist critics of Mill, see Rendall (1982:67–69).

203 Said (1979:79). Neither of the two major biographies on Jones in English (Cannon 1964, Mukherjee 1968) were consulted.

204 This famous "Minute" is archived in a number of texts and internet sites. Macaulay positioned himself within a stauch classicist framework, as evidenced by his follow-

ing remarks: "The first instance to which I refer is the great revival of letters among the Western nations at the close of the fifteenth and the beginning of the sixteenth century. At that time almost everything that was worth reading was contained in the writings of the ancient Greeks and Romans. Had our ancestors acted as the Committee of Public Instruction has hitherto noted, had they neglected the language of Thucydides and Plato, and the language of Cicero and Tacitus, had they confined their attention to the old dialects of our own island, had they printed nothing and taught nothing at the universities but chronicles in Anglo-Saxon and romances in Norman French, would England ever have been what she now is? What the Greek and Latin were to the contemporaries of More and Ascham, our tongue is to the people of India. The literature of England is now more valuable than that of classical antiquity. I doubt whether the Sanscrit literature be as valuable as that of our Saxon and Norman progenitors. In some departments—in history for example—I am certain that it is much less so." A bold claim, considering that Macaulay could not read a word of Sanskrit. Kopf (1995:148–149) discusses Macaulay's views in light of his bitter disappointment at having to serve in India. Macaulay's viewpoint was hardly universal; Sir John Robert Seeley, author of an 1880s popular history of British colonial history, wrote about the Hindu: "He can match from his poetry our sublimest thoughts, even our science perhaps has few conceptions that are altogether novel to him" (quoted in Wahi 1996).

205   Macaulay is mentioned in Said (1979:14, 152, 196, 340). The first reference to the "Minute" is part of an aside in a discussion about Carlyle's apparently "salutary" construction of Muhammad as a hero. Said provides the actual quote in his famous essay on secular criticism (1983:12). In his critique of *Orientalism*, Sarkar (1994:208) observes: "Colonial domination gets robbed of all complexities and variations, and so Macaulay's notorious Minute is thought to be a sufficient description of more than a century of British cultural policy in India."

206   Said (1993a:99). The other references to Macaulay (Said 1993a:78, 102, 109, 133) are list-serving. In a curious indexical catachresis, if I may use the term not in the Spivakian sense, *Culture and Imperialism* elides the African anti-colonialist Herbert Macaulay with Lord Thomas Babington Macaulay.

207   Said (1979:196).

208   Kopf (1980:505). See Kopf (1969) and Rao (1939:143–147) for information on the Indian response.

209   Schwab (1984:37).

210   Quoted in Lanman (1920:234).

211   Lyall (1882:249). As Allen Frantzen (1990:28) points out, Macaulay's view was thoroughly Anglocentric, not broadly Eurocentric.

212   Arberry (1943:8).

213   Daniel (1966:273), cited in Said (1979:335–336n4).

214   This issue is discussed by Freeman (1998:144) and Teltscher (1995:194). There is a misquotation in a passage about the intentions of William Jones. "The use of quotation marks and lack of ellipsis make it look as if Said (1979:77–78) cites a continuous passage," observes Bruce Lincoln (1999:84). The passage is from Said (1979:77–78). In fact Jones jotted down these notes on the way to India, not after his arrival as Said says; nor is the list provided by Said complete. For a discussion of the context of Jones's

plans for his arrival, see Cannon (1990:195–221). Said's ahistorical misreading of the link between Jones and imperialist policies in India is further compounded by those who read Said; thus Stuart Schaar (1979:68) blindly repeats the absurd value judgment that Jones "felt absolutely no conflict of interest in serving imperialism and set the pattern which later Orientalists and area studies experts emulated." For information on the influence of Jones, see Arberry (1960:48–86), now somewhat out of date, Cannon (1990, 1998), and the articles in Cannon and Brine (1995). After a thorough study of the archives of the Asiatic Society of Bengal, O. P. Kejariwal (1988:28) calls Jones the "first scholar to have looked at the east without a western bias." Kaiwar and Mazumdar (2003:270) also note that Jones does not fit Said's model of Orientalism. Michael Franklin (1998:65) suggests that Jones's work on India was "earnestly combating provincialism, prejudice and complacency." Leela Gandhi (1998:79–80) cites a statement by Jones on behalf on the value of non-Western knowledge as an appeal that "begs to be accommodated in a less formulaic rereading of Orientalism." It is worth noting that Jones, the arch philologist, learned his Arabic and Persian from a Syrian in London rather than from his Oxford dons.

215   Van der Veer (2001:114). In addition, staunch advocates of evangelization in India vilified the French philosophers Montesquieu and Voltaire because they valorized Oriental wisdom to discredit Christianity; see the 1813 speech by William Wilberforce (Marshall 1968:187–188).

216   Cited in Franklin (1995:329).

217   Cited in Franklin (1995:320).

218   Quoted in Shaffer (1975:117).

219   Said (1979:78). Said reproduces a quote from a 1786 address by Jones, taken from Arberry (1960:65); the same quote can be found in Schwab (1984:41). How exactly is Jones waxing Orientalist in saying that Sanskrit was "more perfect than Greek, more copious than Latin, and more exquisitely refined than either" (cited in Franklin 1995:361)? Garland Cannon (1990:xv) notes that Said pays little attention to the impact of the Jones lecture on the development of European philology.

220   Lincoln (1999:95).

221   Said might have noted that Kiernan (1969:133–138) was quite iconoclastic in pointing out the flaws in Western representations of the Orient. As Bryan Turner (1994:5) observes, much of Said's criticism of Orientalism "had already been done in a more mundane way by writers like V. G. Kiernan."

222   Said (1979:42), who cites Kiernan (1969:55) for this point. Perhaps Said thinks all the English in India were appointed administrators. Many British scholars and administrators had difficulty reaching such an age; philologist William Jones died at the young age of 48. Myers (1980:xlvi) refers to Said's point here as one made in "a moment of blindness." Woodcock's (1980:299) caution is worth repeating: "Like many of Said's statements, this has to be taken with a little salt."

223   Cornwallis, in fact, died shortly after his second posting as Governor-General of India, so perhaps there was a practical rather than ideological reason for the age limit.

224   Said cites Herder on ten different pages, mostly as part of various lists. Herder's concept of the Orient is surveyed in depth by Gérard (1963:3–67); for Herder's views on India, see Wilson (1964:49–71).

225 Said (1979:154–155). Marshall Sahlins (2000:553), on the other hand, argues that Herder's culture concept was "empowering," unlike the domination inherent in the existing sense of "civilization." As Bruce Lincoln (1999:52) observes, Herder was one of the first scholars to develop the idea of cultural relativism. For an informative study of Herder as an "anthropologist," see Zammito (2002).

226 Said (1979:98, 118, 155, 336).

227 Said (1979:118).

228 Berlin (1976:158).

229 Berlin (1976:160). The excerpt is from *Briefe zu Beförderung der Humanität* (1793–97). Compare the remarkable self-critique from Herder's periodical *Adrastea* in 1802: "'Tell me, have you still not lost the habit of trying to convert to your faith peoples whose property you steal, whom you rob, enslave, murder, deprive of their land and their state, to whom your customs seem revolting? Supposing that one of them came to your country, and with an insolent air pronounced absurd all that is most sacred to you—your laws, your religion, your wisdom, your institutions, and so on, what would you do to such a man?' 'Oh, but that is quite a different matter,' replied the European, 'we have power, ships, money, cannon, culture'" (quoted in Berlin 1976:161). Herder was also a critic of the racial polemics against Jews (Hess 2000:61).

230 Herder (1968:8). This is from book VII, chapter 2. In a 1976 interview given while he was writing *Orientalism*, Said (quoted in Viswanathan 2001:27) remarks: "What I think we must note in Herder is the tendency always to compare the Oriental unfavorably with the Occidental," adding that both Schlegels, von Humboldt, Renan, and Bopp did the same thing. This is certainly not the view of Berlin, whom Said had just read, nor an accurate appraisal of Herder's work. To further claim that all these writers did the same binary essentializing because this is "almost always the practice of universalizing sciences like philology and comparative grammar in the early nineteenth century," shows that Said has no eye for nuance.

231 Herder (1969:337–339). In fact, the Eastern Christians of the time are singled out by Herder in very negative terms. I find Young (1995:36–43) unfair in criticizing Herder for not totally transcending the ethnocentrism of his time. Herder's flirtation with a naturalistic interpretation of historical differences was limited by his knowledge but not corrupted by overt racism; see Harris (1968:89).

232 As Said (1979:14) acknowledges, the relation of imperialism to nineteenth-century literary figures was at the time "a subject not very well studied."

233 Said (1993a:9). The word "distant" is ambiguous here; I assume that Ireland is, for the sake of the myth of imperialism, as distant as India or South Africa. James Boon (1982:280n10) suggests that Said "overgeneralizes" the role of imperialism in creating stereotypes of Orientals.

234 Said (1979:3). For example, Said fails to explore the shifting rationales for European imperialism as an ideology with economic as well as political ends; see Young (2001:15–43) for a discussion of this issue.

235 One of the few "technological" interventions mentioned by Said in *Orientalism* is the Suez Canal. Without this canal it is hard to imagine Britain's strategic interest in occupying Egypt.

236   Said (1979:15). My interest is in how Said continually links Orientalism and imperialism through his rhetoric. As Wendy Buonaventura (1998:55) argues about Said's thesis, "An obsession with European colonialism has unfortunately blinded many critics to the complex interrelationship which has existed between Europe and the Arab-Islamic world for hundreds of years."

237   Said (1994a:332).

238   Musallam (1979:24).

239   Van der Veer (2001:107). Maxime Rodinson (1991:131) expressed much the same sentiment soon after Said's book was published: "The growth of Orientalism was linked to the colonial expansion of Europe in a much more subtle and intricate way than he imagines." Albert Hourani (1991:63) similarly finds the unbreakable chain of links between Orientalist discourse and Western imperial policy "too simple."

240   Said (1979:222). In a thorough analysis of European views of the Ottomans, Aslı Çirakman (2002:2–3) disputes Said's portrait of a continuous Orientalist discourse: "Rather than perceiving a consistent and constant body of European thought and experience, I have found that there is variety and a mix of negative and positive ideas about the Turks." This echoes the earlier work of Schwoebel (1967) on Renaissance European images of the "Turk."

241   Strictly speaking Turkey does reappear, but only as the place of exile for Erich Auerbach (Said 1979:258). Robert Irwin (1981–82:108) chides Said for ignoring the role of Ottoman Turkey, especially its alliance with Germany in World War I.

242   Ahiska (2003:369–370). As Gerald Maclean (2001:87) writes in critique of Said, "Unlike 'the Orient,' the Ottoman Empire really existed." Albert Hourani (1972b:66), in a volume that also includes an article of Bernard Lewis attacked by Said, noted that the contemporary revolutions in the Middle East had all occurred in areas formerly under Ottoman control. For a concise historical survey of Ottomanism just before and during World War I, see Kayali (1997).

243   Said (1993a:14).

244   Parry (1992:24); see also Young (2001:18). Keith Windschuttle (1999) does not mince words: "Even Lenin has a more convincing explanation of imperialism than Said."

245   This point is discussed by Arkoun (1994:27).

246   D'Souza (2002:B8).

247   A. Ahmad (2000:47). In later years, Said (2000:xv) indirectly acknowledges this by reminiscing that his work has contributed to "the critique of Eurocentrism," a point also noted by admiring critics (e.g., Lindenberger 1996:207).

248   Amin (1989:vii). This sense is elaborated by Coronil (1996:57). In his study of European attitudes toward the Ottomans, Aslı Çirakman (2002:4) suggests that modern Eurocentrism evolved in the eighteenth century. However, Kamps and Singh (2001:4) warn against assuming a unified Eurocentrism in the early modern period. Stam and Shohat (1994:1) extend the concept to the "neo-Europes" of America and Australia. Wilhelm Halbfass (1997:13) argues that the idea of a specific European view of "others" is the real concern for Said.

249   Greene (1979:581). As James Brown (1999:552) asks, "What other terms were they to use? One necessarily starts from one's own particular cultural and historical location

in seeking to understand other people and other cultures." As Charles F. Beckingham (1979:562) adds, in *Orientalism* Said "does not seem aware that such absurd statements are often made about people other than orientals."

250 Schick (1990:367). In discussing Said's handling of Edward Lane, James Brown (1999:561) warns that Said "comes perilously close to demonizing Lane." For a balanced sense of the reception of Lane, see Roper (1998).

251 Bartolomé de Las Casas, a Spanish priest who closely followed Columbus—and his deeds—to the New World wrote one of the first and most devastating critiques of the Spanish conquest only a half century after the Americas were "discovered."

252 Said (1979:206).

253 Cannadine (2001:126).

254 Fück (1962:307); see Harris (1968:103–104) for a discussion of Gobineau's racism.

255 Gossett (1965:39).

256 Ansari (2004:65).

257 A notable example is the seminal study by anthropologist Ashley Montagu (1942), which was reprinted as late as 1998.

258 Said (1994c:30).

259 Using the index as a guide, I find in *Orientalism* twenty-four pages on which the term "Africa" or a variant occurs. A third of these are references to Africa in quotations, several of the references are specifically to North Africa—which has a separate entry in the index—and the rest are little more than casual comments. I find no specific comparison to British and French colonialism south of North Africa, the latter of which is, in a loose sense, a part of the imagined Orient. Recent studies have shown that cultural representations in the U.S. media and literature often use "Arabs" as foils for racist stereotyping of African Americans (McAlister 2001:84–124; Salem 2001:224–227).

260 Halliday (1999:211). Benedict Anderson (1991:93) acknowledges: "No one in their right mind would deny the profoundly racist character of nineteenth-century English imperialism." But he adds that the same kind of ethnocentric "Anglicization" promoted by Lord Macaulay in India was the policy in white colonies as well.

261 Said (1979:27). As Bryan Turner (2000:13) rightly suggests, "The study of Orientalism must also include an analysis of anti-Semitism." Said avoids the critique of anti-Semitism provided in Disraeli's *Tancred*, discussed below on pp. 213–215.

262 According to the index, "anti-Semitism" and its variants appear on twenty-four pages of *Orientalism*, ironically the same number on which "imperialism" is said to be mentioned. Most of these rhetorically link Jew and Arab or other "'low' Orientals" (Said 1979:99, 262, 286, 337). Said discusses at length the essentialized use of "Semite" as an essence in the work of Schlegel and Renan.

263 Said (1979:286).

264 Said does not develop his linking of Orientalism and Zionism by citing specific Israeli scholars, but Basim Musallam (1979:24–25) does.

265 Said (1976a:4).

266 Mani and Frankenberg (1985:186).

267 Kopf (1980:498). I suggest that Said's polemical dismissal of Orientalism as a sewer category is not flush with historical reality.

268 Said (1993a:53). Halliday (1999:210–213) accuses Said of the genetic fallacy: assuming

that an idea (Orientalism) is invalid because of the context (imperialism) in which it was elaborated.

269   Said (1993a:xiii).

270   Ashcroft and Ahluwalia (1999:74); their claim is quite inaccurate, as readers of my end-notes can see for themselves.

271   Hart (2000:xi). Hart fails to mention which historians actually validate the details of Said's thesis about Orientalism as a discourse. Hart should also include the French historian Maxime Rodinson (1987:131), who observes that because Said is "a specialist of English and comparative literature, he is inadequately versed in the practical work of the Orientalists."

272   Sayyid (1997:34).

273   This question first appeared in a 1985 article. A number of commentators who have read her subsequent writing are now asking, at least for her case: can the subaltern write and make sense? It would appear that all subalterns are not created unequal.

274   Said (1979:208) writes: "I mean to say that in discussions of the Orient, the Orient is all absence," and that "the Orientalist's presence is enabled by the Orient's effective absence." Yet, as Andrew Rotter (2000:1210) retorts, in *Orientalism* "There is no who there." Said (1994a:335) acknowledges in his afterword that "indeed, the subaltern can speak, as the history of liberation movements in the twentieth century eloquently attests." This after-the-fact defense does not disguise the fact that subalterns are not given voice in *Orientalism*; see Paul Armstrong (2003:111). Having finally made this admission, Said still does not consider the earlier anti-Orientalist critiques of subal-tern Arabs and Muslims.

275   Said (1979:283).

276   Dirlik (1997:107). "Most tellingly," conclude Marcus and Fischer (1986:2), "he acknowl-edges no political or cultural divisions among the subject peoples he is allegedly defend-ing. These last have no more independent voice in his text than in that of any other Western writer." Dorothy Figueira (1994:3) complains: "In Said's analysis, Western tex-tualities about the non-West are viewed in isolation from how these textualities have been received, accepted, modified, challenged, overthrown or reproduced by intelli-gentsias of colonial countries." See also P. Armstrong (1991:159) and Porter (1991:3–4). William Sax (1998:293) notes that this claim of no-agency "flies in the face of histori-cal fact."

277   Çirakman (2002:13).

278   Pratt (1992:6). Her concept of "contact zone" re-presents the subject as an active part of an interaction that Said insists is discursively one-sided. Arif Dirlik (1996) borrows Pratt's concept for "recasting" Said's analysis in relation to Chinese history.

279   Said (2002:5); he also falls back on the trite gripe that he wrote the book a long time ago, "attempting something for the first time, on a relatively open field as it were."

280   Gandhi (1998:81); she is responding to Said (1993a:xii). A similar point is made by Ajit Chaudhury (1994:46): "Collaboration by the colonized people is viewed either as an aberration—betrayal by the lackeys of colonial power—or as a myth produced by the colonizers."

281   Codell and MacLeod (1998:2). Julie Codell (1998) provides an example of local resist-ance in the life of Maharaja Sayaji Rao III (1863–1939).

282   Rahimieh (1990:2).

283   Codell and MacLeod (1998:3). David Ludden (1993:271) makes the same point. Confino (2000:185) shows how Said's own experience in an Anglophile Cairo school fostered a form of resistance.

284   Yegenoglu (1998:22). Similar criticism is leveled against *Orientalism* by Abaza and Stauth (1988:344), Dirks (1993:280), Fokkema (1996:232), King (1999:86), Mani and Frankenberg (1985), Parry (1992:34), van der Veer (1993:23), and Wilson (1981:64).

285   Chen (1995:9).

286   Said (1979:325). This assumption is shared by AbuKhalil (2001:108): "The authority of Orientalists had not been seriously questioned before Said's book, and many Arabs considered the assertions of Western experts on Islam and the Arabs to be definitive and true." Perhaps some did, but certainly many did not. This is analogous to saying that American slaves always took the masters' view as definitive and true.

287   Said (1979:325).

288   In a 1976 interview recorded in Viswanathan (2001:38); see also Said (1979:25). James Clifford (1988:256) places Said in a tradition of "writing back" that extends back to the critical work of Michel Leiris published in 1950 in the journal *Les temps modernes*.

289   For a brief introduction to Arab cultural criticism since the 1970s, see Sharabi (1990:22–44). The journal *Khamsin* was started in 1975 by Arab leftists in Paris, yet there is no mention in Said's text of its critical attacks on Orientalism.

290   J. Ahmad (1984:32). The English translation by Campbell is based on the 1978 Persian text, but the original was published privately in 1962. Two previous English translations had already appeared. Ahmad died in 1969. His name is rendered as All-Ahmad by Ali Behdad (1994a:ix).

291   J. Ahmad (1984:55). The reference is to a Christian legend mentioned in the Quran; for details, see Paret (1960).

292   J. Ahmad (1984:33). Compare Said's (1979:146) metaphor of Renan's philological laboratory.

293   J. Ahmad (1984:98–99).

294   Algar (1984:16); his earlier (1971) critique of the problems of Orientalism is ignored by Said in *Orientalism*. Said was apparently unaware of Ahmad's Persian text, although in *Culture and Imperialism* (Said 1993a:228) it is dismissed parenthetically as an "Iranian tract" that "blames the West for most evils of the world." However, most of Ahmad's critique is directed at Iranians for not shaping their own destiny. "So long as we remain consumers, so long as we have not built the machine, we remain occidentotic," states Ahmad (1984:31).

295   For a discussion of al-Khatibi's "double criticism," see Wolf (1994:62), who notes that both he and Said were "working out of comparable cultural archives at approximately the same time."

296   Wielandt (1980), writing at the same time as Said, provides a detailed history of Arab views of Europe in the nineteenth and twentieth centuries. For Occidentalist Arabic travel writing in the seventeenth century, see Matar (2003).

297   The anthology in translation is Hamalian and Yohannan (1978); it includes excerpts from Arabic, Armenian, Hebrew, Persian, and Turkish literature. The volume of women's writings was edited by Fernea and Bezirgan (1977).

298   Said (1985:4). The otherwise thorough *Orientalism* index does not include Asad, Alatas,
       Fanon, Césaire, Tibawi, or Thapar. Mentions of some of these are relegated to the end-
       notes—e.g., A. L. Tibawi is obliquely indicated in the narrative as a "distinguished Mus-
       lim scholar," but only identified by name in the endnote (Said 1979:272, 347n88). Aijaz
       Ahmad (1992:176) finds it "somewhat breathtaking" that Tharpar's seminal study on
       the history of India only appears to be known to Said via two textbooks written for
       middle-school students. Sardar (1999:65) complains that Said does not acknowledge
       Tharpar and these other scholars in *Orientalism*. Said (1979:350n137) praises "several
       more thoughtful scholars" for critiquing *The Cambridge History of Islam*, but they—
       Albert Hourani and Roger Owen—are again only named in the endnote. Nor does Said
       mention the work of Michael Suleiman and Ayad al-Qazzaz on stereotypes about Arabs,
       even though their papers were published in the same volume as an earlier treatment
       of Orientalism by Said (1975b). Roger Owen (1979:61), whose work is favorably men-
       tioned in *Orientalism*, thinks the listing of modern critics like himself "seems much
       too short." Said praises Talal Asad's pioneering work on colonialism in anthropology.
       Praising Said's *Orientalism* in return as more subtle and interesting than most schol-
       ars realized, Asad (1980) still wished Said had developed the argument to include other
       groups affected by European colonialism.

299   Aijaz Ahmad (1992:176) suggests that Said probably mentioned Tibawi, Laroui, and
       Abdel Malek in direct response to a criticism raised in a review by Robert Irwin. Tim-
       othy Brennan (2004:35n11) observes that Said "quite inaccurately" claims that he was
       the first to examine the relationship of culture and imperialism. David Gordon
       (1982:104) is correct to observe that although Abdel Malek and Laroui wrote earlier,
       "no one has produced so total and relentless a repost." Ziauddin Sardar (1999:66) reit-
       erates the charge that Said ignores earlier critiques and then provides a flawed one.
       David Kopf (1980:497) chides Said for not recognizing earlier Indian critics of British
       imperialism, such as Keshub Chandra Sen and Rabindranath Tagore; to these Peter
       Heehs (2003) adds Sri Aurobindo. S. N. Mukherjee (1996:69), in a paper presented at the
       1967 American Anthropological Association convention, suggested that the nineteenth-
       century British idea of the Indian village community was "more an idea than a fact." I
       would also add the critical attack on ethnocentric views of Western civilization by
       P. Konanda Rao (1939).

300   Moore-Gilbert et al. (1997:22) state that it is important not to devalue or marginalize
       earlier critiques of Orientalism as Said does in *Orientalism*.

301   In his later *Culture and Imperialism*, the watchword might as well be "Hail Césaire, full
       of quotes!" as Said hypercritically fans the flames of anti-imperialistic rhetorical
       crossfire.

302   Said (1979:297); he mentions both the original French edition and the English trans-
       lation of Laroui's book. Binder (1988:317–338) discusses Laroui's contributions. It is
       worth noting that Said misreads in the published instances the first name of Abdal-
       lah Laroui as "Abdullah." Although Said—or should I say "Sayyid"—is not the only
       scholar to make Abdallah into Abdullah, it indicates a carelessness in praising an
       admired fellow critic.

303   Kedourie (1956) questions both von Grunebaum's analysis and the "consensus among
       modern Orientalists" (1980:37), as do Hourani (1962:451–456), Arkoun (1964), and

Anawati (1970). For more recent assessment of von Grunebaum's influence, see Turner (1994:67–73) and Riedel (1999).

304 Said (1979:299).

305 Said (1979:291). By concentrating on American political scientists, Said ignores Arabists who taught Arabic literature in American universities.

306 This point was made by Gordon (1982:110). Richard Bayly Winder (1981:618) cites Pierre Cachia (misprinted as Caccia in his review) and Mouna Khouri as specific examples of scholars who promoted the study of Arabic literature. J. Derek Latham (1972) provides a survey of the major Western texts on Arabic literature available before the time *Orientalism* was written.

307 Laroui (1976:44); he suggests that Orientalism should be examined in the way C. Wright Mills critiqued the sociology of his time.

308 Laroui (1976:27); he returns to the same theme in Laroui (1997). Said ignores Laroui's (1976:32) relevant self-reference, first printed in 1968, that the problem of Palestinian resistance "is allowing the Arabs, while demanding much of them, to become truly conscious of history."

309 Laroui (1976:63).

310 Laroui (1976:62).

311 Laroui (1997:3). Perhaps this is why Laroui tends to ignore the work of Said in later writings.

312 Said (1979:325). A couple of pages later (327), Said includes Abdel Malek with Maxime Rodinson, Jacques Berque, and Roger Owen in a list of "critical readers, and students of what goes on in other fields." Yet it appears that Said finds Abdel Malek easier to quote than learn from. Apart from one 1963 article, none of the latter's corpus is utilized, even in *Culture and Imperialism*, which was published twelve years after an English anthology of Abdel Malek's work. For some reason—apparently not out of philological prudery—Said (1979:351, etc.) consistently alters the first name "Anouar," the chosen rendering in all of the Egyptian Abdel Malek's French and English articles, to "Anwar."

313 Said (1979:96–97), based on Abdel Malek (1963); the latter is reprinted in Macfie (2000:47–56). The English translation published in Abdel Malek (1981:73–96) differs from the original article. A formal response to Abdel Malek is given by the Italian historian Francesco Gabrieli (1965:134), who acknowledges the past colonial sins of some Orientalists but insists that it would be foolhardy to abandon the approaches of Western secular humanism and the scientific method. Ironically, Bernard Lewis (1993a:106) offers guarded praise for Abdel Malek's "careful, even if not sympathetic, study of Orientalist writings."

314 Abdel Malek (1981:74–76). This distinction between polemical Christian Orientalists and those interested in Islam and the Arab world in a more scientific sense is commonly employed by those writing the history of Orientalism, e.g., Bosworth (1977:148).

315 This was laid out in a 1972 article in which Abdel Malek (1981:21) stated his theory of "social dialectics" as a Marxist "vision of the world and as a method of analysing the dialectics of the real world." See also Abdel Malek (1981:97–117).

316 Said (1979:98, 108). In the first case, Said paraphrases Abdel Malek and then proceeds

to develop an account of the origins of Orientalist philology that is not part of Abdel Malek's analysis.

317   Abdel Malek begins his 1963 article by referring to a "crisis of conscience" within Orientalism due to the recent national liberation movements in Asia. Said's views on Marx are discussed on pp. 175–177.

318   Alatas (1977). In *Culture and Imperialism* Said (1993a:245) refers positively to the "assiduous archival research and scrupulously up-to-date documentation, argument, and generalization" in the work of Alatas. Whalen-Bridge (2001:200) suggests that Alatas is both "authorized and advertised" by Said's overtly polemic theorization, as though the world only knows the work of Alatas through a brief note in Said.

319   Alatas (1977:8).

320   Alatas (1977:16).

321   Alatas (1977:9).

322   Regarding Marx and Engels, Alatas (1977:232) is excoriating: "Their condescending attitude, their carelessness about facts, their misrepresentation of Asian institutions, and their ethnic pride were clearly revealed in their writings." He is particularly upset that both Marx and Engels view their own society in terms of class, but arrogate others to ethnicity and race.

323   Said (1979:325).

324   Said (1988b:34).

325   Said (1979:323). Such sentiment serves as an indictment of Said's disdain for the kinds of historical texts, especially archival and manuscript, in valuable libraries throughout the region. Victor Brombert (1979:538) chides Said for making this kind of subjective statement and at the same time censuring von Grunebaum for saying that Muslims were not vitally interested in the study of other cultures.

326   Cannon (1990:xvi).

327   Chen (1995:11). Similar criticisms are made by Ning (1997) and Spence (1992a:90). Donald Lopez (1995:11–12) points out that Said's thesis does not work for Buddhism, because there is no direct link to colonialism. J. J. Clarke (1997:26) finds Said's thesis too narrow to fit Japan and much of Southeast Asia. For rejection by a Japanese writer of the notion of a single Oriental culture, see Sokichi Tsuda (1955:96). See Nishihara (2005) for an overview of the book's reception in Japan.

328   Daniel (1966:281). Sara Suleri (1992:18) notes that the Oriental response was not invisible in colonial India. Antoinette Burton (1998) analyzes the contestation of British imperialism by Indians living in England.

329   Steenstrup (1985–86:241). Said's (1979:73) ignorance of Asian history surfaces in his remark that there was no challenge to Western dominance except by the Arab and Islamic Orient.

330   Iqbal's (1955:75) "Europe and Syria," translated by V. G. Kiernan. Akbar Ahmed (1992:30) mentions Muslim modernists such as Sir Sayyed Ahmed Khan and Muhammad Iqbal who used their understanding of British culture to "engage successfully with the colonial power." David Kopf (1980:497) cites Rabindranath Tagore (1915) as writing "one of the most devastating attacks in the English language on the sources of Western nationalism." See also Hay (1970) on Tagore. Richard King (1999:93) mentions

Vivekananda, founder of the Ramakrishna Mission, as an example of a Hindu reformer who transformed the colonial discourse against Western imperialism.

331   Hourani (1970). There were also Ottoman intellectuals, such as Ahmed Midhat (Findlay 1998), who resisted the cultural hegemony of the West.

332   See Keddie (1968).

333   See Kerr (1966).

334   For further discussion of this important book, see Alleaume (1982) and Wielandt (1980:41–72).

335   Magdi Wahba (1989) discusses the significance of Shakir's critique of Orientalists in his 1936 study of the Arab poet al-Mutanabbi. Orientalists were described as part of a conspiracy alongside Christian missionaries to further colonial interest; they had no scientific objectivity because they were not born into the language and cultural context of Islam. Shakir wrote: "These men visited the Middle East with their airs of innocence and wheedled and cajoled their Muslim hosts into yielding the secrets of their knowledge and many of their priceless manuscripts and books" (quoted in Wahba 1989:194).

336   For a translated extract from his travel account of Paris, see al-Tahtawi (2002).

337   Tamara Sonn (1996:11) argues that Jawzi's 1928 *Ta'rikh al-harakat al-fikriyya fi al-Islam* (History of Intellectual Movements in Islam) anticipates Said's argument in *Orientalism*. Sonn (viii) also suggests that the earlier Palestinian's critical Marxist perspective on reform movements in Islamic history prefigures the "neohistoricism" of Foucault and Derrida.

338   As Magdi Wahba (1989:191) rightly notes, "most of the lively controversies and polemics" of the twentieth century were carried out in Arab periodicals. None are cited in *Orientalism*. The Egyptian scholar al-Tahtawi (2002:33) recognized in 1834 the "great merits" of the newspaper in encouraging those who do good deeds and in restraining those who do evil. English-language periodicals in early-twentieth-century Britain gave a voice to Muslims living there (Ansari 2004:90).

339   According to Hisham Sharabi (1970:44), al-Afghani believed that all the East needed in order to resist and crush the West was its scientific knowledge. Consider the pragmatism in the verse of a nineteenth-century Moroccan traveler to Paris (al-Saffar 1991:152):

> Don't reject an idea if it is suitable,
> Or Truth even if it comes from error.
> Pearls are precious to acquire,
> But it is not the diver who decides their worth.

340   Rotraud Wielandt (1980:251–410) argues that blanket rejection of the West by Arabs largely developed between the two world wars.

341   Behdad (1994a:1). Similar emphasis on Said's point that all knowledge of the "Orient" is mediated by "the Orientalist canon" is made by Aamir Mufti (2005:479). Compare the comment by Said (1979:208) that the indigenous reaction to Orientalism was "all absence."

342   Behdad (1994a:1). The reader should be suspicious of any writer who is not quite sure

whether he is a tourist or not. Present in Behdad's narrative (17) are two writers who he admits did oppose the colonialist policies of France and Britain: Isabelle Eberhardt and Anne Blunt. Their writings, however, do not counter the bias because they "were appropriated by the colonial system as valuable information" that could effectively be used to "subvert" the insurgency of Bedouin tribes. Without citing any archival references and without demonstrating the strategic value of these romanticized travel accounts, Behdad assumes that the colonial administrator or military commander needed such "valuable" details for exercising political control. If in fact such texts were used to form colonial policy, this may explain why that policy was often ineffective at subverting opposition.

343   Burke (1998b:10). Ernest Gellner (1994:164–168) criticizes Said's understanding of French colonialism in Algeria, as presented in *Culture and Imperialism*, for "how much is left out, how much is misleading and how much is mistaken."

344   Said (1979:91). The quote comes from a parenthetical remark. The designing of the Suez Canal is described three pages earlier as a scientific project of a piece with Renan's philological work. So is Nasser really a closet Orientalist?

345   A. Ahmad (1992:174).

346   The most thorough analysis of the *istishraq* genre is provided by Rudolph (1991). Fedwa Malti-Douglas (1985–86) presents a survey of this genre, whereas the discussion by Nathan Sivan (1985) is highly selective. One of the best Arabic discussions of anti-Orientalist writing is by Hazim Saghiyya (1995), who bases his analysis on an astute and critical reading of Orientalism. Examples of this important indigenous genre have long been present in major American university libraries. In 2002, the Princeton University library contained some fifteen Arabic texts published on "Orientalism" before 1978, and more than twenty-five published after Said's text. There are also anti-Orientalist writings in Persian (J. Ahmad 1984) and Turkish (Dogan 1975).

347   These books include translations of Lane's work on Egypt, Gustave Le Bon's *La civilisation des Arabes* (1884), Adam Metz's 1935 *The Renaissance of Islam*, and the 1887 *Reste arabischen Heidentums* of Julius Wellhausen. In the late 1960s, Hamid Algar (1971:96) complained that a Persian translation of von Grunebaum's *Medieval Islam* was being used as a textbook at Tehran University.

348   Haykel (1976). The translation was made by Prof. Isma'il al-Faruqi, who notes that plans for such a translation had begun in the 1940s. Al-Faruqi's translation was approved by the Supreme Council of Islamic Affairs in Cairo. The original Arabic edition was introduced by Muhammad Mustafa al-Maraghi, the grand sheikh of al-Azhar.

349   Haykel (1976:xliv).

350   Haykel (1976:lxiii). For a more recent Muslim critique of Muir, see Buaben (1996:21–47). Said (1979:151) is wrong to assert that Muir's works were "still considered reliable monuments of scholarship" by Orientalists in the 1970s; this point has been made by Wickens (1985–86:69) and Winder (1981:617).

351   Haykel (1976:lxx).

352   Haykel (1976:lxxv).

353   Arkoun (1984:43).

354   Al-Kharbutli (1976:8, 16, 17).

355   Al-Kharbutli (1976:5). This argument is similar to that made by Abdel Malek

(1981:74–76). The noted Egyptian writer Taha Husayn found value in the works of several Orientalists (see Malti-Douglas 1985–86:51n22).

356   Similarly, in a 1963 article Maxime Rodinson (1981:26) severely criticizes Lammens, a scholar Said passes over in *Orientalism*, as "filled with holy contempt for Islam" and having "excessive prejudice." "The only accounts acceptable to him," claims Rodinson, "were those that reflected unfavorably on Muhammad and his family." Lewis and Holt (1962:5) also offer criticism of the extremism in Lammens's arguments.

357   See, for example, Said (1993a:275).

358   The issue of Occidentalism is discussed in chapter 3, pp. 263–266.

359   Basim Musallam (1979:25) mentions *'Alam al-din* as "the first full-scale treatment in Arabic of Orientalism and Orientalists."

360   Al-Da'mi (1998:3). A similar point is made by Radwan al-Sayyid (2001:8).

361   Tavakoli-Targhi (2001:23); he argues that both Edward Said and Raymond Schwab "fail to take into account the intellectual contribution of native scholars to the formation of Oriental studies."

362   Adonis (1990:81). Adonis suggests that it is only necessary to reject the ideological part of the West, not the West as a whole: "We can learn from the creative energy of the West and its intellectual inventions and construct a dialogue with them, as the West itself did in the past with the products of our civilization" (91). A similar validation of Western methods of research has recently been made by the Lebanese scholar Charbel Dagher, who concludes that "These methods are useful and effective analytical tools, and the fact that Said himself employed them to criticize the Western discourse illustrates my point" (quoted in Chalala 2004:2).

363   Chen (1995:4–5). She calls this counter discourse "Occidentalism." Compare Allen Chun (1995:28), who argues that "an Oriental Orientalism is not conceivable partly because it is not predicated upon an Other, which is the epistemological point of departure for its imagination, hence exoticism."

364   Fox (1992:151).

365   Fox (1992:146).

366   Kopf (1980:500)

367   Said (1979:50).

368   Miyoshi (1994:1).

369   For a French version of Hanafi's thesis, see Hanafi (1990). Boullata (1990:40–45), Esposito and Voll (2001:68–90), and Hildebrandt (1998) review the development and impact of Hanafi's work in the Arab world. For an Arab critique of Hanafi's project, see Saghiyya (1995:156–162). More than one real Oriental has imagined such a field: "Curiosity, that Faustian daemon of the mind, is bound to overcome anger in time, and we may perhaps look forward to the day when there will be an *Encyclopaedia of Christianity* written by Muslim 'occidentalists'!" (Wahba 1989:199).

370   Hanafi (1991:54).

371   Said (1979:272). Said does not mention Tibawi by name in the narrative, but does cite his 1964 critique published in *Islamic Quarterly*. Earlier in *Orientalism* (100), Said quotes from Tibawi (1961), but again without mentioning the author's name in the text.

372   I. Abu-Lughod (1982:vii). This piece was written in memory of Tibawi, who died in Octo-

ber 1981 at the age of seventy-one, when he was hit by a London truck as he was mailing a letter. Unless Abu-Lughod means only those critiques available in English, his comment ignores the role of earlier critics such as Haykel.

373 Tibawi (1963:189, 202). Both Edward Lane and Hamilton A. R. Gibb come under major criticism from Said, and Laroui (1997:7) singles out Gibb for his negative assessment of "liberal Islam." For discussions of Gibb's contributions, see Hourani (1991:61–73), Lapidus (1995), and Mahdi (1997). James Brown (1999:554–560) also critiques Said's reading of Gibb.

374 Tibawi (1979:11). Gordon Pruett (1984:82), in a pro[con]foundly superficial analysis of Orientalism as anti-Islamic, agrees with Tibawi. Speaking primarily in his role as an instructor in Arabic at Cambridge, Tibawi levels a scathing denunciation of Western "pseudo-orientalists" who are illiterate in Arabic. A similar complaint is voiced by Algar (1971:98) about Western experts who do not know Arabic well and yet pose as experts on Islam.

375 Said (1993a:xii). In his later afterword to *Orientalism*, Said (1994a:348) implies that resistance is at that point now quite striking, but that he only "had some sense of it" in the 1970s. The point remains that Said failed to discover and incorporate a sense of the level of resistance that had always been present against Western colonial interference.

376 Said (1985:4). In Said (1989) and in the afterword to *Orientalism* (Said 1994a), this direct claim is not made, although Said mentions the work of Abdel Malek and Fanon.

377 Said (1995:186). Earlier, in *Culture and Imperialism*, Said (1993a:xii) says that "in the overwhelming majority of cases, the resistance finally won out."

378 Said (1993a:212). When asked later why he did not devote as much attention to Ngugi and Achebe as he did to Kipling and Austen, Said (2002:8) responded that his book "was already far too long," as though his default valorization of the Western canonical authors were simply a matter of insufficient space.

379 Said (1993a:239).

380 It is ironic that Said should have ignored a novel that, as he later admits (Said 2000:381), is so like Conrad's *Heart of Darkness*.

381 Makdisi (1992).

382 Saleh (1989:30); the quotes in the two succeeding paragraphs are from pp. 30–33.

383 I am referring only to the quite comprehensive index. I note that Salomé and the Queen of Sheba make the text but not the index, but then the same fate befalls St. Anthony.

384 In the text (Said 1979:31), Victoria is not referred to by name but only as "a monarch" served by Lord Balfour.

385 Dane Kennedy (2000:37–46) devotes an entire section of his article to feminist critique of *Orientalism*. Graham Huggan (2005:132) laments that some feminists have "falsely assumed the gender-blindness of Said's methods."

386 R. Lewis (1996:17).

387 Reported by Billie Melman (1992:7), based on the *Bibliotheca Cisorientalia* of Richard Bevis. Melman provides a detailed analysis of female English travel writers on the Middle East.

388 Ueckmann (2001). For sources on female French travelers to the Middle East, see Ragan (1998).

389   Kabbani (1986:140n21).

390   Yoshihara (2003:11).

391   Said (1979:197, 224, 225, 229–231, 235, 237, 238, 246).

392   Said (1979:229).

393   Gertrude Bell is an easy target for Said, because she was instrumental in bringing Prince Feisal to Iraq after World War I. Said ignores her earlier work on Persia, including a well-regarded translation of the poems of Hafez. Said (1979:246) suggests that Bell's "expert-adventurer-eccentric" role was "created" in the nineteenth century by Lady Hester Stanhope. The only other reference in Orientalism to Lady Stanhope is that she served as the "Circe of the desert" to Lamartine (177). Again, the woman is only relevant because of her value to an Orientalist male.

394   Said (1979:207).

395   Mabro (1991:7).

396   See Heffernan (2000), Kahf (1999:118–125), Kietzman (1998:538), Lew (1991b:435), Lockman (2004:64–65), and Yeazell (2000). Donna Landry (2001:478) finds Lady Montagu "both Orientalist and mildly subversive of Orientalist conventions." Ella Shohat (1993:73) notes that Lady Mary Wortley Montagu records an awareness among Turkish women about the oppression of their European counterparts.

397   Lady Mary Wortley Montagu (2001:102). Compare the 1843 remark of Sophia Poole (2003:137), sister of Edward Lane and a fervantly Christian Englishwoman: "The ideas entertained by many in Europe of the immorality of the hareem are, I believe, erroneous." Similarly, Mary Eliza Rogers (1862:369), who lived in Palestine during the 1850s, spoke of the "matter-of-fact" Muslim women she met in harems.

398   Schueller (1998:65).

399   Celik (2000:92–96). Compare the writings of Halide Edib Adivar (1882–1964), who in 1930 advocated a separation of church and state for Turkey and elsewhere in the Islamic world (see Kurzman 2002:215–219).

400   Rahimieh (1990:54)

401   Shafik wrote La femme nouvelle and Bint al-Nil just after World War II. Her view that Islam was not opposed to modernity was harshly criticized by conservatives at the time; see Nelson (1998) and also the earlier writings of Bahithat al-Badiya in Kurzman (2002:70–76).

402   J. Miller (1990:164). In a related argument, Mari Yoshihara (2003:6) challenges the blanket notion that the West was figured as male and the East as female.

403   Mills (1991:57).

404   Said (1979:6).

405   Flaubert's Egyptian letters, especially those to his friend Louis Bouilhet, are replete with tales of conquest, usually with prostitutes with whom he is at times unable to communicate verbally. Flaubert had to cut short his trip to the Orient because of complications of venereal disease. For an alternative reading of Flaubert's eroticism, see Lörinsky (2002), Lowe (1995), and Orr (1998).

406   Valerie Kennedy (2000:38) notes the irony of Flaubert, Said, and herself in reproducing this term as though it were a standard name, when it signifies the inequality of the relationship. See Buonaventura (1998:71–77) and Wall (2002:173–174) for more information on this dancer.

407   Said (1979:186).

408   In his letters, Flaubert frequently refers to the texts he read about the Orient, especially about ancient Egypt. However, Myers (1980:xlvii) is not convinced that Flaubert's reading of Orientalist texts had greater effect on his work than his direct experience. Lörisnky (2002) demonstrates that Flaubert was greatly influenced by comparative mythology, especially about ancient Carthage.

409   "The Perverse Traveler" is a term used by Dennis Porter (1991:165, 180–181) to describe the unique kind of sensual travel accounts exemplified by Flaubert. In assessing travel accounts of Greece and Turkey, K. E. Fleming (1999:14) objects to Said's assumption that this literature was "voyeuristic, manipulative, distorted, and thoroughly bankrupt." Said's assertion of sexual penetration as an endemic trope of Orientalism is read back even further by Phiroze Vasunia (2001:39), in his analysis of pre-Alexandrian Greek texts, so that "the psychosexual demands of the Egyptian can be read as a projection of the Greek male's fantasies or as a mirror in which he can see the other and recognize the self." It would be perverse, I think, to suggest that such a projection only extends in what later generations would imaginatively call an Oriental direction. I note with irony an apparent self-reading of Flaubert quoted by Ali Behdad (1994a:55): "Don't comment on me, but write with me in my perverse fashion."

410   Duncanson (1980:201).

411   This line from Flaubert figures in Said's (1979:187) analysis of the French author's musings on the Oriental woman as "an occasion and an opportunity." For Flaubert, virtually any attractive woman, especially a prostitute, was both an occasion and an opportunity.

412   Said (1979:185). In copying the passage from Steegmuller (1972:200), Said drops the hyphen in "bird-droppings."

413   Flaubert (1926:204). In the translation quoted by Said, the full passage reads: "Karnak gave us the impression of a life of giants. I spent a night at the feet of the colossus of Memnon, devoured by mosquitos. The old scoundrel has a good face and is covered with inscriptions. Inscriptions and bird-droppings are the only two things in the ruins of Egypt that give any indication of life. The most worn stone doesn't grow a blade of grass; it falls into powder, like a mummy, and that is all." (Steegmuller 1972:200). The final sentence from the passage (not translated by Steegmuller) would be: "The inscriptions of travellers and the droppings of birds of prey are the only two ornaments of the ruin."

414   The ironic use of "inscription" here is in reference to the graffiti of modern travelers, as indicated in the last sentence of the passage quoted here. This combination of script and bird shit is encountered in several of Flaubert's unpublished notes (see Behdad 1994a:65–66).

415   Shelley wrote "Ozymandias" in 1817, based on a reference by Diodorus Siculus to the Pharaoh Ramses II. It is not clear if Flaubert was familiar with the poem. Elsewhere in his letters, Flaubert (1926:162) notes that the sight of the ancient ruins reminds him of his own insignificance: "toute cette vielle poussière vous rend indifferent de renommée" (all this ancient dust renders one indifferent to being renowned).

416   Rosenberg (1979:111). Said (1979:186) multiplies his careless errors by stating that Kuchuk Hanem was encountered in Wadi Halfa, when she lived in Esna (Rodenbeck 1998:243n26).

417   Yeazell (2000:41). See also Buonaventura (1998:82).

418   This point has recently been made by Stavros Karayanni (2005:123), who suggests that because Said reduces the dancer to "a monolithic representation of the available woman of the East," she is treated not as an individual but "a figure as vague and far-reaching geographically and temporally as the Orient in Said's work."

419   Porter (1991:169).

420   Constable (1996:625). This is reflected in a statement made by Flaubert in 1864: "L'histoire n'est que la réflexion du présent sur le passé, et voilà pourquoi elle est toujours à refaire," (quoted in Green 1982:117).

421   The novel is racist, but this is directed primarily at black Africans rather than at an imagined Oriental other. Martin Bernal (1987:358), loosely following Said, collapses the racism in the novel into the "Orient." In a response to his critics, Bernal (2001:33) notes that he differs from Said: "In the first place, his work is literary and allusive, whereas mine is historical and pedestrian. More important, I do not accept his view that Orientalism, or, for that matter, ancient history, is almost entirely self-referential."

422   Lörinsky (2002:40).

423   Translated by Steegmuller (1972:220).

424   Chew (1937:548). Irvin Schick (1999:91) argues that some of the classic erotic novels of eighteenth-century England were penned by men who had traveled abroad, such as John Cleland, who wrote *Fanny Hill* (1749) after having lived in Smyrna and India. Eroticism was not confined to Oriental harems.

425   McClintock (1995:24). Ella Shohat (1993:48) also discusses the tendency of nineteenth-century Romantics to figure the non-West as feminine. As Norman Daniel (1982:214) suggests, the Orient "was not essential to arouse literary sexuality" in nineteenth-century French literature. James Millward (1994:450–452), farther afield, shows how the Chinese sexualized their "Oriental" others through the Xiang Fei myth.

426   To avoid litigation, Richard Burton published his translation by private subscription and created a fictitious publishing house, the Kama Shastra Society, although the text was printed in Stoke Newington by Waterlow and Sons (D. Kennedy 2000:324); see also Brodie (1967:367–379) and Casari (1997). Lady Burton burned her husband's private notes, including extensive erotica, after his death.

427   Koetzle (2005:11); he adds that between 1840 and 1860, about 5,000 erotic daguerreotypes were produced, primarily in France (48).

428   The quote is from Said (1979:190). In a study of crime fiction with Middle Eastern themes, Reeva Simon (1989:92–93) found that Western stereotypes were not prominent in this literature before 1967, noting that the "truly outrageous villain of disgusting caricature" for Muslims and Arabs appeared only recently.

429   Said (1979:190).

430   Said (1979:190). As Madeleine Dobie (2001:124) notes, French travel writers before Nerval disclosed "only peripheral interest in exotic sexual practices and mysterious Oriental women."

431   Writing of Burton's sexual exploits, Fawn Brodie (1971:423) concludes "So we find in his life an Indian mistress, a passionate love affair with a Persian woman, an attempted seduction of a nun, and experimentation with native women in Africa and the Near East, as well as Fred Hankey's special variety of Paris prostitutes."

432 Burton is mentioned on twenty-four pages of *Orientalism*, often in a list mode, according to the book's index. There is extensive literature on Burton, as annotated by Casada (1990). Richard Luckett (1982:279) takes Said to task for dismissing Burton because of his firsthand knowledge and at the same time arguing that lack of such experience fueled the imaginative geography in Orientalism. Patrick Brantlinger's (1990:159, 165) misinformed call for Burton to be canonized as a founding father of anthropology "because of his thoroughness and seeming objectivity (or scientific ruthlessness)" notwithstanding, Burton had no impact on the evolution of the discipline, nor have his bizarre cultural theories stood up to critical scrutiny.

433 Said (1979:194).

434 Sexual matters occupy only about one-fifth of Burton's "Terminal Essay," which is primarily devoted to placing the translated text into context, but inculpatory non-readers of Burton only have eyes for the sex. Burton was well aware of how controversial his raw treatment of "turpiloquium" would be. It is fitting to reiterate his own retort, borrowed from Dr. Johnson's response to a lady complaining about naughty words in his dictionary: "You must have been looking for them, Madam!" (Burton 1885:X:204). For a nuanced and up-to-date consideration of Euro[ec]centric erotica on the Orient, see Schick (1999).

435 D. Kennedy (2000:339). As Robert Irwin (2004:24) observes, "True, Lane's translation is easier to read than Burton's, but that, as we shall see, is not saying much."

436 R. Burton (1888:IV:281–289). For an entertaining and enlightening review of Burton on his reviewers, see R. Burton (1888:VI:311–366). It is fair to say that in its day, Burton's translation occasioned as great a disturbance in the press and the academy as has Said's *Orientalism*.

437 R. Burton (1885:X:289).

438 Said (1979:195, 197).

439 D. Kennedy (2000:319).

440 Stead's article was published in the *Pall Mall Gazette* issues for July 6–8 and 10, 1885, and subsequently released as a widely distributed tract.

441 R. Burton (1888:VI:320).

442 D. Kennedy (2000:321); he refers specifically to Homi Bhabha. I suggest that this places Bhabhan fetishism in a whole new dark light.

443 The term "voy[ag]eurs" appears to have been coined by Tavakoli-Targhi (2001:54). Some of these travelers of the Oriental elite were apparently treated well by and gained respect as fellow elites among their British hosts (Ansari 2004:55–57).

444 Khan (1998:99); he then notes: "There were many lovely ladies and beautiful girls at the party, but I fancied none of them save this girl of noble birth whose beauty inflamed my heart with passion." Khan visited the court of King George III in 1809–10.

445 Tavakoli-Targhi (2001:67).

446 Al-Jabarti (1993:28).

447 Laurence Michalak (1985:52–53) finds it odd that Said did not include French Orientalist painting in his text, suggesting that Said's broad concept of representation may be useful for contextualizing this art genre. If W. J. T. Mitchell (2005b:467) is correct, this may be because the visual left Said "frequently baffled or panicky." Such an analysis of Orientalist art was begun in a limited way by Linda Nochlin (1983), whose work

has been critiqued by Christine Peltre (1998:158). For a thorough review of Orientalist art of North Africa, see Roger Benjamin (2003). Frederick Bohrer (1988:50–51) admits that Said's text is one that students of Orientalist art "must come to terms" with, but questions Said's "near-solipsistic view of orientalism." John Sweetman's (1988:249) major survey of British and American Orientalist art includes a call for "a careful narrowing down" of Said's strictures. More recent surveys (Beaulieu and Roberts 2002; Edwards 2000) find Saidian discourse difficult to apply to artistic production.

448 The characterization of "coolly seductive" is by Benjamin (1997:9). A detailed analysis of Ingres's style is provided by Ockman (1995). Unlike some painters in the genre, Ingres never visited the Orient. The painting was commissioned by the Queen of Naples, Caroline Bonaparte Murat, the younger sister of the emperor who painted quite a different picture in his unsuccessful invasion of Egypt.

449 See Sweetman (1988:2) for an elaboration of this point. This painting currently resides in the Louvre, where it has been one of the defining moments for garçon visitors (see Mernissi 2001:104).

450 Benjamin et al. (1997:70). Some artists of the time were critical of naked harem voyeurism, as in the comments of Antoine Castagnary on Gérôme's *Almeh*: "It is of a coldly calculating indecency, and I recoil from describing it" (quoted and translated by Benjamin 2003:25). Lynne Thornton (1985:3) notes that sexually excited women are quite rare in the harem scenes of Orientalist art.

451 This is especially the case for *Life in the Harem* (1858), where the agency of the Oriental woman is not denied. Even in Lewis's classic *The Hhareem* (ca. 1850) the wives and concubines participate in the scene, relaxed but not inviting the viewer into bed with them. Both illustrations can be seen in Benjamin et al. (1997:81–84). Unlike some Orientalist painters, Lewis had lived in Egypt for ten years.

452 Ockman (1995:73).

453 Ockman (1995:4).

454 Yeazell (2000:249–254) contrasts the Orientalist art of Gérôme and Ingres, arguing that the latter signals its status as fantasy.

455 R. Lewis (1996:126–190). See, for example, Browne's 1861 *Une joueuse de flûte* (R. Lewis 1996, plate 12). Other female artists who painted Oriental scenes are discussed in Benjamin et al. (1997).

456 Both paintings are reproduced in Peltre (1998:86–88, 112). Even an iconic representation of Orientalist mastery, such as Delacroix's *Les femmes d'Alger dans leur appartement* (1835) can be deployed to critique Orientalism (Celik 2002:38).

457 Quoted by Benjamin et al. (1997:56), who also provide a reproduction of the watercolor.

458 Quoted and translated by Roger Benjamin (2003:19), who argues that Fromentin was a major theorist in the ensuing debate over Orientalist art.

459 Matisse, for example, pursued cultural expression of the other that opened up a different cultural space rather than portraying the Oriental as inferior (Benjamin 1997:27–28). Hollis Clayson (2002:131) argues that later works in the Orientalist art of Henri Regnault (1843–71) "shatter the Saidean orthodoxy which holds that the nineteenth-century European artist routinely imposed a univocal and supremely self-confident Occidental colonial perspective on the Orient."

460 Celik (2000:83); see also Celik (2002).

461   Celik (2000:89).

462   A. Owen (1997:115). Although this remark was made for Aleister Crowley and T. E. Lawrence, I think it applies to a wider range of male travelers to the Orient.

463   Flaubert (1972:204–205). Jean-Paul Sartre (1981–94), on the other hand, suggests that Flaubert's homosexual banter was more a matter of joking to impress his friends at home.

464   R. Burton (1886:X:204). Although he does not shy away from discussing homosexuality, primarily pederasty, Burton introduces his topic with phrases in Latin from an English bishop, French from a book translated from Italian, and Greek. "I proceed," continues Burton (1886:X:205), "to discuss the matter *sérieusement, honnêtement, historiquement*; to show it in decent nudity not in suggestive fig-leaf or *feuille de vigne*." It appears that Isabel was more pragmatically disposed to abrogating references to homosexuality in her husband's edition of the *Arabian Nights* (Brodie 1971:393–394).

465   Joseph Boone (1995) criticizes Said for privileging heterosexual encounters and fantasies and ignoring homoerotic elements. Parminder Bakshi (1990) examines the role of homosexuality for the traveler Edward Carpenter. For similar points about colonial India, see Suleri (1992:16) and Colwell (1996:219–220).

466   Clark (1999:337).

467   The quoted phrase is from Said (1979:188) in reference to Flaubert.

468   Garber (1992:342).

469   Apter (1994:105). Apter's point is that agency can be provided by being an avatar on and off the stage, exemplified in such actresses as Sarah Bernhardt. A similar argument about the role of fan-magazine Orientalism for American women has been made by Gaylyn Studlar (1997:125).

470   There is further irony in the fact that Said's idealization of Orientalism parallels the work of some Western feminists who construct a hegemonic "Patriarchy" that ensures male domination and female exploitation across time and cultures; see Mohanty (1994). Rashmi Bhatnagar (1986:20), on the other hand, finds that Said's use of Foucauldian discourse helps her to resist being made into "a site for theory" as a Third World female scholar.

471   Holmlund (1993:1). Danny Colwell (1996:215) cautions that Said's trope of the West's male dominance over the feminine East "inadvertently replicates the colonial structures it seeks to criticize."

472   Kahf (1999:116). Kahf (1999:177) argues that "the Orientalism critique is not an adequate methodology for studying the representation of Muslim woman in Western texts" before the eighteenth century.

473   Kahf (1999:53).

474   Spivak (2000:64), although in a slightly later reflective piece on Said, Spivak (2005:522) claims that she did not remember taking Said to task "for not having sufficient sympathy for feminism," although she did encourage him to be "nice to women." Nancy Armstrong (1990:4), Anne McClintock (1995:14, 397n4), and Malika Mehdid (1993:19) include Said with other male post-colonial theorists who do not explore the gender dynamics of their subject. Thomas Prasch (1995:176) cites Said's failure to posit a non-sexist position on the role of women. The kindest remarks come from Lila Abu-Lughod (2001:101), who praises Said for opening up the way for others to go further in explor-

ing gender and sexuality in Orientalist discourse. It borders on the ludicrous to suggest, as does Sondra Hale (2005:5), that Said is an "accidental feminist."

475 Mills (1991:13).

476 In praising three works on the Middle East by female scholars, Said (1993a:xxiv) finds it necessary to qualify these as "feminist, but not exclusive."

477 Rose (2000:24). In responding to feminist critics, Said (1985:3,12) is willing to [en]list feminism as another example of an "un- or mis-represented" human group. Merely citing a feminist does not resolve his own gender blindness. Said's impatience with feminist critiques of his work shows in his condescending response to "a black woman of some eminence" who asked why Said focuses almost exclusively on white male authors. "I was guilty," writes Said (2000:374) in a published essay, "of not mentioning living non-European nonmales..." Compounding this slight, Said then proceeds to inform a black woman that as an Arab he himself is "nonwhite."

478 Said (1993a:31). Yet, Said has no qualms claiming that his Palestinian birth does indeed give him a special place (even though he admits to being out of place) for explaining Arab and Muslim grievances.

479 Melman (1992:6).

480 Said (1979:207).

481 Said (1979:25). My comments in this paragraph refer to pages 25–28 of *Orientalism*'s introduction.

482 It is not my intention to place Said on the psychoanalyist's couch. This has recently been done by Valerie Kennedy (2000:7): "Said's neglect of gender may be at least partially explained by certain features of his context and upbringing. Neither the Palestinian society nor the class into which he was born, nor the elite British and American educational institutions which he attended as a student and at which he later taught, encouraged any awareness of gender as an important theoretical factor or fact of real life. Indeed, Said has spent most of his life as a student and teacher in typical patriarchal institutions, all-male worlds where women's role and presence were negligible, at least until the recent past."

483 Said (1979:11). Said assumes that Flaubert's novel about ancient Carthage is Orientalist because it takes place in North Africa.

484 Said (1979:185). Timothy Mitchell (1991:21) also finds Flaubert the perfect foil for the bedazzled European visitor. Neither Said nor Mitchell compares what Flaubert says about the "Orient" with his accounts of travel elsewhere.

485 Said (1979:22, 101, 118) mentions Beckford three times, always in tandem with Byron, but does not discuss Beckford's fantasy. This is unfortunate, because *Vathek* is certainly more than a rich boy's literary idyll of *Arabian Nights* pretension. E. S. Shaffer (1975:116), in a work favorably cited by Said, argues that Beckford's gloss of Islam as a Christian heresy subverts "Christian civilization" itself as a heresy; El Habib Benrahhal Serghini (1998:57) reads *Vathek* as a critique of "Europe's mode of intervention and domination." Diego Saglia (2002:84), examining Beckford's journal from a trip to Spain and Portugal, argues that the English visitor viewed the Orient as "a material and discursive zone of overlapping of East and West." These comments would not appear to be Saidian Orientalism as usual.

486 Quoted in Gemmett (1975:xii).

487 The translator, Rev. Samuel Henley, claimed that the English version was a translation of the Arabic; he did not mention Beckford, probably to hide the latter's role
because he was told by Beckford not to publish it at the time (Melville 1910:139–140).
488 Beckford (1971:40) delights in ridiculing the spoiledness of the affluent. When the litters carrying the royal harem caught fire, the ladies were forced to jump out: "Full of
mortification, shame, and despondence, and not knowing how to walk, the ladies fell
into the dirt. 'Must I go on foot!' said one; 'Must I wet my feet!' cried another; 'Must I
soil my dress!' asked a third; 'Execrable Bababalouk!' exclaimed all; 'Outcast of hell!
what hadst thou to do with torches? Better were it to be eaten by tigers than to fall
into our present condition! We are forever undone! Not a porter is there in the army,
nor a currier of camels, but hath not seen some part of our bodies, and what is worse,
our very faces!'"
489 Beckford (1971:280). In the novel itself there are good and bad Orientals. Muhammad
is presented in a favorable light as a moral prophet whose warning is not heeded by
the vain Vathek.
490 Quoted in Melville (1910:135).
491 Benjamin (1997:17).
492 Quoted in Benjamin (1997:8).
493 As Tripta Wahi (1996) argues, "The notion of social formation is alien to Saidean orientalism which replaces class by the absolutized concept of nationality." I find it ironic
that Wahi refers to Said as "a brave warrior of the bourgeoisie." James Buzard
(2005:42) criticizes Said's approach, in *Culture and Imperialism*, to the British novel as
"blotting out so completely all those fine differentiations (of class, of region, of religion, and so forth) observable *within* the imperial nation."
494 This is primarily in Said (1979:123–130), but there are other scattered references in
the text.
495 Said (1979:127–128).
496 Schwab (1984:87). De Sacy was well connected at the French court.
497 Matar (1998:15). I note for purists that in this passage the closing parenthesis is lacking in Matar's prose, but I do not wish to interject yet another grammatical novelty
into an already beleaguered sentence.
498 Matar (1998:19). One could make the argument following María Rosa Menocal
(1987:46–47) that many of the earlier crusaders were "culturally converted" even if
not becoming Muslims themselves.
499 K. Parker (1999:106).
500 K. Parker (1999:3). Discussing early English travel narratives, Kamps and Singh
(2001:3) argue that these "do not produce Said's Orientalism, but instead recount cultural encounters in which self and other are not fixed in opposing positions but are
rewritten through discursive and social interventions." Shalev Zur (2002) thinks
Said's thesis not useful for understanding the seventeenth-century Oxford scholar John
Greaves, who wrote *Pyramidographia* in 1646.
501 Chew (1937:298–339).
502 Bryan Turner (1994:18) criticizes Said for privileging texts "rather than focusing on
the everyday nature of imperial penetration of cultures via the materiality of commodity
exchanges." For Percy Kemp (1980:172), Said avoids "toute réflexion sur les rapports

entre l'orientalisme et l'économie politique." Ernest Gellner (1994:165) likewise complains that Said is "more concerned with his general thesis—literature at the service of colonialism, or of resistance to it—than with the concrete society with which he is dealing." John MacKenzie (1995:93) is disturbed by Said's failure to consider economic contexts and class. A similar criticism is leveled by Arif Dirlik (1996:118): "A thoroughgoing historicism subjects cultures to the structures of everyday life, rather than erasing those structures by resource to a homogenizing culturalism." This point works equally well for Orientalist essentializations of Orientals and for Said's homogenizing of all Western writing on the Orient into one "discourse."

503   Al-ʿAzm (1984:354).

504   See Schueller (1998:28).

505   For a discussion of Said's rhetorical use of this quote, see chapter 3, pp. 237–240.

506   Said (1979:154). A similar knee-jerk rejection of Marx as anti-Orient is given by Sardar (1999:51).

507   Said (1979:154). Said implies that Karl Marx welcomed British imperialism in India. No attempt is made by Said to reconcile a seemingly out-of-character remark from a peripheral publication with the massive corpus and abundant exposition of Marx's views, evolving as they were, about the expansion of industrial capitalism in all directions. "Marx was certainly not driven by racist feelings or antihuman impulses," argues Anouar Majid (2004:7). "He clearly saw colonization as a necessary prelude to a better life for all humans."

508   Said (1979:156). For example, see the critiques by Aijaz Ahmad (1992:159–219) and Sadiq Jalal al-ʿAzm (1984:360–363). Michael Sprinker (1993:13) also criticizes Said for "slighting" Marx. James Brown (1999:563) finds Said's discussion of Marx "very strained," and wonders why a generalization such as the "Asiatic Mode of Production" is not even addressed. For a defense of Said's treatment of Marx, see Brennan (1992:94n20). Ernest Gellner (1994:163) somewhat facetiously says that Said lets the founders of Marxism off the hook "far too easily."

509   ʿAmil (1985); he is criticized by AbuKhalil (2001:108–109) for using the Arabic edition. AbuKhalil (2001:109) engages in a classic case of solipsistic ad hominem Marximus dismissal by asserting that ʿAmil's arguments are "simple and unsophisticated because they are." Nadim Al-Bitar (1982:183–185) is another early Arab critic of Said's spin on Marx. Hazim Saghiyya (1995:71–72) and Anwar Moghith (2005) also discuss the Marxist debate among Arab intellectuals over Orientalism. As Michael Gilsenan (2000:152) notes, Said's book was not widely read or taken seriously by the Left in the West; indeed it was rarely reviewed in left-leaning journals.

510   Said (1993a:278). Elsewhere, Said (1994a:338–339) admits that he was "upbraided" by critics for his comments on Marx, but his only response is that Marxism as "a coherent total system seems to me to have been a case of using one orthodoxy to shoot another." Yet he does not respond to the specific criticism that he only uses selected passages to represent Marx's position on British imperialism. For a discussion of this post-colonial confounding of Marxism by Said and others as adverse to social change, see Gandhi (1998:24–26, 70–74). Bryan Turner (1978) discusses Marx's attitudes toward British imperialism at length; Turner (1981:111) does not agree with Said's

Orientalizing of Marx. Abdallah Laroui (1976) and Sharabi (1990:29–31) offer a wide-ranging analysis of Marxism among Arab intellectuals.

511 Said (1983:160). In reference to Said, O'Hanlon and Washbrook (1992:166) note hostility in American political culture to any kind of materialist or class analysis. But as Ernest Gellner (1994:6) bluntly states, "History is the history of class struggle."

512 Said (1983:28).

513 I am not accusing Said of Marxist-baiting, which is common enough among more conservative writers. Such ideological diatribe can reach rather silly levels, as in the case of the French Arabist Bousquet accusing the Protestant clergyman W. Montgomery Watt of Marxism for considering the socioeconomic context in which Muhammad preached (see Rodinson 1981:47).

514 Varadharajan (1995:130). For a similar reading of Said's intellectual relationship to Adorno, see P. Williams (2001:I:xii–xix). Fred Dallmayr (1997) finds Said's exilic stance to be close to Adorno's negative dialectics, albeit with reservations. Moustafa Bayoumi (2005:51) thinks that Said came to identify with Adorno in large part because of their shared approach to criticism as reflexivist *Ansatzpunkt*.

515 Gaeffke (1990:71). Shelley Walia (2001:6) likewise uncritically lumps Said with "other Western Marxists" simply because he borrows from Gramsci and Foucault. Mustapha Marrouchi (2004:45) thinks that Said developed an "articulatory version" of Marxism.

516 Hart (2000:97).

517 Frykenberg (1996:288). Alas, on the same page Frykenberg's aim is notably off-target when he misreads the name of Said's early critic al-ʿAzm as al-ʿAim!

518 Hassan (1986:511). Giorgio Baratta's (1999) genealogical trajectory from Marx to Gramsci to Said is a further example of this imaginative geography.

519 Said (1983:28).

520 Said (1979:327); see also Said (1979:265–266). Said (1979:336n4) refers to Rodinson (1974), which is a major critique of old-style Orientalism, but does not draw from it or even highlight its significance in his narrative. Although Said has only positive things to say about Jacques Berque in *Orientalism*, Mustapha Marrouchi (2003:55) steamrolls Said's thesis over this French historian by describing him discursively as an Algerian variant of Napoleon's eighteenth-century army of savants.

521 Said (1980:389–390).

522 A. Ahmad (1992:184). It is useful to compare Said's uneconomic explanation with Benedict Anderson's (1991:190) thesis that "the world never saw the rise of New Basras" because Arab colonizers in the eighteenth and nineteenth centuries did not "successfully establish coherent, wealthy, selfconsciously creole communities subordinated to a great metropolitan core." Said focused solely on the imagined Orient rather than attempting to understand the historical development of modern nation-states in the region.

523 A. Ahmad (1992:224). For example, Said is said to rely primarily on brief journalistic accounts rather than sifting through the considerable corpus Marx left regarding colonialism. Related points are made by ʿAmil (1985:59) and Young (1990:138).

524 Hart (2000:xi). Hart admits that Said is not at his best in grafting Marx into Oriental-

ist discourse, but then accuses him of applying a "Marxist" interpretation to religion (76). Hart implies that any intellectual rejection of religion, especially the very specific religion Marx had in mind, must somehow be a form of Marxism; nowhere in my reading does Said reduce religion to the ideological role of justifying the elites or opiating the masses.

525 The set of response essays was introduced by Michael Sprinker (1993). See also Varadharajan (1995:135).

526 Levinson (1993:101).

527 Ahmad (1993:153).

528 Said (1993a:338–339).

529 Said, in a 1992 interview recorded in Viswanathan (2001:160).

530 Di Leonardo (1998:49). Wilhelm Halbfass (1997:5) notes with irony: "In a sense, the results which Said expects from the abolition of Orientalism are reminiscent of those which Karl Marx expected from the abolition of class and private property: a utopian state in which humans can exist without being confined to roles and identities imposed by others."

531 Amin (1989:118). In a reflection admiring the critical work of Said, Timothy Brennan (2005:415) wishes that Said had probed the critiques of capitalism.

532 Dirlik (1996:117).

533 Majid (2000:139).

534 Said (1979:12).

535 Among those who make this point, see Çirakman (2002:13), Clarke (1997:9), King (1999:97), Malti-Douglas (1979:732), Moore-Gilbert (1996b:18), Parry (1992:26), Rahimieh (1990:38), Schaub (1989:308), and Schueller (1998:x). Joseph Lenning (2004:xxviii) argues that Said's latent and manifest forms of Orientalism "do not allow for a rhetorical manipulation of established Orientalism to create an ironic critique of imperialism."

536 Dirlik (1997:110). K. E. Fleming (1999) provides a contextualized analysis of self-critique in Western travel accounts about Ali Pasha's Greece.

537 Ahmad (1992:184).

538 Said (1979:208–209), from Fück (1962:306, 308, 309, 311). Fück's (1962:306) designation of Ranke, Burckhardt, and Spengler as "non-Orientalist historians" is elided by Said as "General cultural historians" typifying a "static male Orientalism."

539 Binder (1976:16). The aim of this survey by experts from different disciplines was to look beyond Orientalism.

540 Reprinted in Malik (1964:221–223).

541 Toynbee (1935:164.

542 Daniel (1966:47). Daniel discusses numerous narratives on the Orient, and argues that "the Muslim world had its defenders and its opponents at all times."

543 V. G. Parry (1962:288).

544 Chew (1937:43). When queried by an Ottoman officer, Henry Blount (quoted in Vitkus 2001:40) admitted that an English Protestant in 1634 could lawfully serve the Ottoman sultan rather than the Catholic pope. For further details on Blount's travel narrative, see Maclean (2001).

545 This is the assessment of Rodinson (1974:37).

546   De Boulainvilliers (1731:6). Henri de Boulainvilliers is often singled out by Muslims as a Westerner who did not dismiss Muhammad as an imposter; see Amir (1998:4). A more historical and critical successor to Boulainvilliers's work was published by J. Gagnier in 1732 (see Holt 1962:300).

547   Clarke (1997:42).

548   The following information is derived from Rocher (1984).

549   The German phrase can be translated as "a pious fraud."

550   Quoted in Rocher (1984). The original source is Bartholomaeo's 1791 *Systema Brahmanicum*. Rocher notes that the hoax was suspected as early as 1778, although it was not until well into the nineteenth century that this was fully known.

551   Said (1979:319). This dismissal of Massignon as "blinded" is repeated in Said (1980b:60). In defending Said's differential respect for Massignon, Nadia Abu El-Haj (2005:543) notes that Massignon "represented a real attempt to understand the Muslim world," but adds "albeit always Eurocentric." It is obvious that as a European Christian Massignon is not, as he never claimed to be, totally objective, but should not the value of his representation be based on what he says rather than on the simple fact that he was European?

552   Said (1979:328).

553   Said (1979:77). Said's endnote suggests that this part has been translated from several passages in Schwab (1934:10, 96, 4, 6), but no ellipses are provided in the quote. Said (1984:xiii) repeats the same quote in his foreword to the English edition of Schwab's survey, but adds a clause at the end of the last sentence. This time the entire passage is taken from Schwab (1934:6). A paraphrase of this passage is included in Schwab's (1984:18) translation.

554   Said (1979:122).

555   Said (1979:77).

556   Schwab (1984:19). Schwab is quoting here from his earlier biography of Anquetil-Duperron. Raymond Schwab's enthusiasm was shared much earlier by Gustave Dugat (1868–70:I:xxix), who eulogizes Anquetil-Duperron as "la figure la plus remarquable de cette galerie d'orientalistes célèbres produits par le XVIIIe siècle."

557   Quoted by Halbfass (1988:66), who notes that the English translation (Schwab 1984:160) mistranslates this passage; see also Halbfass (1985:800). As physicians have their Hippocratic Oath, this quote might serve a similar function for philologists and historians.

558   Schwab (1984:26).

559   Schwab (1984:35).

560   Hentsch (1992:110–111).

561   Said (1979:209). Writing in Damascus in 1890, Goldziher saw Islam as superior to both Christianity and Judaism in that it "was the only religion in which superstition and pagan elements were proscribed not by rationalism but by the orthodox doctrine" (quoted in Patai 1987:20).

562   See Waardenburg (1963).

563   See Conrad (1999:144–145) and Hourani (1991:30).

564   Quoted in Patai (1987:141). This was written in Ismailia, Egypt, in 1873. It might be said that all that litters Orientalism with prejudice is not Goldziher.

565   Said (1979:6).

566   Sardar (1999:vii, 51). Said (1979:207) mentions Le Bon once in *Orientalism*, but only as someone who defined the Oriental as a subject race. Fück (1962:308–309) notes that Le Bon was not a racist in the mold of Gobineau and Renan, but viewed Arab Islamic history as tolerant: "Not surprisingly his work found widespread approval in the Islamic world and was frequently quoted by Muslim modernists." Timothy Mitchell (1991:122–125, 169–171), however, thinks that Le Bon's psychological theory was attractive mainly to Arab elites.

567   This is discussed by María Menocal (1987:xi) in a brilliant historical analysis of the Arabic etymological origins of the term "troubadour." Here it was the Orientalists who recognized the important influence, and the Romance scholars who systematically refused to accept such an origin.

568   Specifically, Wickens (1971:63) attacks Arberry, Browne, and Nicholson.

569   Said (1979:12). Victor Brombert (1979:538) is one of the critics who asks why Said does not explore the eighteenth-century use of the Orient as a mode for criticizing Europe. As early as the fourteenth century, Honoré Bonet wrote a satirical poem, "Apparicion Maistre Jehan de Meun," about a Saracen spy in France and Spain. Texts written before Montesquieu's *Lettres persanes* include Giovanni Paolo Marana's 1684 *L'esploratore turco e le di lui relazioni segrete alla Porta ottomana scoperte in Parigi nel regno di Luiggi il Grande . . .* , Jean Frédéric Bernard's 1711 *Réflexions morales, satiriques et comiques sur les moeurs de notre siècle*, François Augustin-Paradis de Moncrif's 1715 *Les avantures de Zéloïde et d'Amanzarifdine, contes indiens*, and Joseph Bonnet's 1716 *Lettre écrite à Musala, homme de loy à Hispahan*. Lord Lyttleton wrote *Letters from a Persian in England to his Friend at Ispahan* in 1735. For more information on this genre, see Barfoot (1998), Conant (1908), Dobie (2001:83–120), Roosbroeck (1972), and Yeazell (2000).

570   There were ten editions in the text's first year, plus eighteen more by 1784 (D. Schaub 1995:4).

571   Goodman (1989:2).

572   D. Schaub (1995:7). Montesquieu's depiction of Oriental despotism has been widely studied; see especially Çirakman (2002:116–132), Dobie (2001:35–60), Grosrichard (1979,1998), and Valensi (1993). It is clear that there was not a uniform attitude of various European polities to the Turks as despots. Lucette Valensi (1993:57–60) notes that Machiavelli offers a critique of tyranny, but exemplifies the Ottomans as reclaiming the virtue of the Roman Empire.

573   Montesquieu (1901:65–68); this is in letter 24.

574   Joubin (2000:210).

575   D. Schaub (1995:17). On the preceding page, Schaub describes Montesquieu's text as a "thoroughgoing analysis and critique of despotism in all its forms" (16).

576   Montesquieu (1901:115); this is in letter 55.

577   For a survey of discussions of the harem in *Lettres persanes*, see Dobie (2001:44–45, 61–82), Trumpener (1987), and D. Schaub (1995). It is interesting to compare this text with Horace Walpole's (1785:1–9) satirical reversal of the *Arabian Nights* plot, in which a new princess gets the better of the sultan by suffocating him in his sleep and then following suit with a new husband each night—only pardoning her husbands if they behaved.

578   Joubin (2000:198) suggests that the same vocabulary used in Diderot's *Encyclopédie*

to describe the Oriental woman was employed against the presence in public of women in France.

579 Kahf (1999:133), quoting Said (1979:70). I pass here on Kahf's odd lumping together of all depictions of "Oriental" women, especially women of the harem, as essentially being depictions of Muslim women. For an alternative view, see Trumpener (1987) and Yeazell (2000:66–73), who discuss the literary trajectory of Roxana as a symbol of female rebellion. Madeleine Dobie (2001:77–79) reads Roxana's final letter as unmasking the male authority that judges her. These views follow on Joyce Zonana's (1993:599) suggestion that Montesquieu's self-critique in the harem trope "inaugurates feminist orientalist discourse."

580 Kahf (1999:133). Kahf ignores the vast literature about Montesquieu's text, including earlier feminist analysis (D. Schaub 1995). In lefthanded sarcasm aimed at Katherine Rogers (1986), one of the many scholars who finds the satire to be subversive, Kahf asks: "How does she know this? If she is dealing with any work besides *Lettres Persanes*, she does not feel it necessary to cite it as evidence." Nor does Mohja Kahf.

581 Montesquieu (1901:147); this is in letter 72. The term *decisionnaire* was coined by Montesquieu to describe what in English slang might be termed a "know-it-all."

582 Montesquieu (1901:210); this is in letter 115.

583 Montesquieu (1901:220); this is in letter 122.

584 These prescriptions appear in letter 143. For example, for an emetic: "Take six harangues; any dozen funeral orations, carefully excepting those of M. of N.; a collection of new operas; fifty novels; thirty new memoirs. Put the whole in a large flask; leave it to settle for two days; then distil it on a sand-bath" (Montesquieu 1901:269). M. of N. refers to the Bishop of Nimes.

585 Throughout the text, Montesquieu (1901:83) heaps abuse on the Turks "who are to serve the Jews for asses." Thus there is not a unified view of an Oriental other presented in the letters.

586 See Roman (1992:47).

587 Goldsmith (1901:318).

588 Muhammad Al-Da'mi (1998:5), an Iraqi scholar of English literature, sees a "self image" in Washington Irving's writings on Islamic Spain.

589 Matar (1998:52).

590 Kirschbaum (1962:30). For analysis of the political motivations behind Marlowe's play, see Dimmock (2005:135–161).

591 This point is developed by Jonathan Burton (2000) and Mohja Kahf (1999:67–71).

592 *Tamburlaine*, Act 5, scene 1 (quoted in Kirschbaum 1962:262–263).

593 Hourani (1991:136); see also Hourani (1980a).

594 Metlitzki (1977:207). The legend of Muhammad as an apostate Catholic extends back to eleventh-century France (Metlitzki 1977:204).

595 Langland (1966:191).

596 Langland (1966:191). For a later English text that uses an attack on Islam as a foil for responding to deism, see Humphrey Prideaux's 1697 *The True Nature of Imposture*, the polemics of which are described by Holt (1962:290–294).

597 Voltaire (1964). The first English translation was made in 1763 by Rev. Franklin. The plot is an old one. Zopir, the ruler of Mecca, is losing his power to an upstart, Mahomet,

who has already been responsible for the destruction of Zopir's family. In one battle, Zopir captures a slave-girl, Palmira, with whom Mahomet is deeply in love. As Zopir is talking to his loyal senator, Phanor, the traitor Omar arrives to offer a peace agreement from Mahomet. As the dialogue unfolds, we see that both Zopir and Mahomet plan to use this truce as a ruse to kill the other and seize power. Meanwhile, in the amorous subplot, Omar leaves a slave named Seid as a pledge. Seid and Palmira are revealed to us as star-crossed lovers as Voltaire draws on his Oedipal instinct so the full extent of the tragedy can take its course. Palmira and Seid are really Zopir's children, abducted and raised as slaves by Mahomet so that their love can never be fulfilled. In her blind and fanatical devotion to Mahomet, Palmira convinces the uncertain Seid to go against his conscience and slay the idolator, Zopir. Before Zopir dies, both Seid and Palmira find out the truth, but Seid has been poisoned by Mahomet's henchman and thus meets the same fate as his father. Palmira, like Shakespeare's Juliet, then plunges into her own breast the same dagger that Seid used to kill their father.

598   Voltaire (1971:347). Voltaire's criticism does not depend on an accurate depiction of the Turk here, given that, as he was probably aware, Muslims did in fact marry their cousins.

599   Voltaire (1964:10).

600   Voltaire (1971:203).

601   Voltaire (1971:202). Voltaire was apparently so repulsed by this incident that he would get sick on its anniversary date, August 24.

602   An attempt to stage the play in Geneva, Switzerland, in the early 1990s brought a stinging protest from local Muslim groups and as a result it was not performed. The irony of a play about intolerance being shut down more than two centuries after its initial hostile reaction by the church did not escape European commentators at the time.

603   Daniel (1966:11).

604   Quoted in Setton (1992:51). Other examples of positive views on the Ottomans are provided by Çirakman (2002).

605   This point is made by Bryan Turner (1994:49).

606   Carlyle (1993:66). This piece was translated into Arabic in 1911.

607   Carlyle (1993:38).

608   Quoted in Crinson (1996:34).

609   Quoted in Daniel (1966:360–361). Said (1980b:55–56) fails to note the satire inherent in a passage quoted from Thackeray's *Vanity Fair*.

610   This September 28, 1872, cartoon is reproduced in Tanaka (1993:2).

611   Twain's best-selling *The Innocents Abroad* reached the same audience as those buying Bibles, as both books were originally peddled door-to-door. Twain once remarked to his friend William Dean Howells that his travel book "sells right along just like the Bible" (Obenzinger 1999:212). It could be argued that Twain reflects a broader American reading of the Holy Land part of the Orient than Flaubert's idiosyncratic letters speak for a French perspective or Richard Burton defines a publicly shared British view.

612   Obenzinger (1999:193). The literature on Twain is extensive, as it should be.

613   While at the Dead Sea, Twain recorded in his notebook: "No Second Advent—Christ been here once, never will come again" (quoted in Obenzinger 1999:178).

614   Twain (1966:340).

615   Montesquieu (1901:65).

616   This point is made by Obenzinger (1999:193). Consider Twain's (1966:382–383) description of a Bedouin Arab "as swarthy as an Indian" in a passage that seems to be modeled on a Sioux warrior.

617   Twain (1966:353). In this passage Twain recollects his boyhood dreams about the noble Arab and his horse, a hardy individualism that fits well with America's own mythic ethos of the cowboy.

618   My comments here relate to Twain (1966:378–380).

619   Twain (1966:379–80).

620   Twain (1894:18–22). Rana Kabbani (1986:139), in her uncritical post-Said trashing of Western travelers, speaks of Twain's "inhuman humour." Apparently she missed this passage.

621   Malroux (1992:40).

622   Malroux (1992:121).

623   Malroux (1992:13).

624   Malroux (1992:110).

625   Said (1979:248).

626   Said (1979:249). Said takes this from an interview in a memorial volume rather than from a professional article or text. Lévi, a specialist in Buddhism, is an odd choice for a villain, as he was involved in numerous collaborative projects with real "Oriental" scholars. He provided, for example, support for the first Hindu Nobel laureate, Rabindranath Tagore, to found the Institute for Asian Culture in Santinketan in 1921. Said neglects to mention that Lévi was a prominent French Zionist; he was also a friend of Raymond Schwab, who quotes him in the second sentence of *La Renaissance orientale*.

627   Said (1979:99, 252). Said does not quote Loti, but includes him in two lists of Orientalist writers.

628   Spence (1992b:viii).

629   Thomas Greene (1979:580) criticizes Said for ignoring "unprejudiced Westerners" such as Malroux.

630   The book was published under the pen name of Malba Tahan (the author's real name is Mello e Souza); for an English translation see Tahan (1993). The dedication of this book reads: "To the memory of seven great geometrists, Christian or agnostic: Descartes, Pascal, Newton, Leibniz, Euler, Legrange, Comte—Allah take pity on these infidels!—and to the memory of the unforgettable mathematician, astronomer, and Muslim philosopher Abu Jafar Muhammad ibn-Musa al-Khwarizmi—Allah preserve him in his glory!—and also to all who study, teach, or admire the prodigious science of scale, form, numbers, functions, movement, and the laws of nature."

631   Said (1979:308). The reference is to Barthes (1972:109–159). In other works Said only rarely refers to Barthes.

632   Barthes (1982:4).

633   Porter (1991:293).

634   Knight (1993:619). Ross Chambers (1994:26) thinks that Barthes's outing in his short essay "Incidents" reveals "a less self-conscious, more banal, touristic and colonialist

R. B." These homoerotic reflections are styled by Chambers as a reproduction of Orientalist repression rather than simply as a gay male sexual tourist admiring a young Moroccan man. Behind Barthes's lust, we are told, stand "Orientalist predecessors" such as Chateaubriand, Nerval, Gautier, and Flaubert. Is it possible, I wonder, for any European, even a critical specialist, to sleep with a gay Moroccan without being subsumed under a hegemonic discourse?

635   Barthes (1982:3). Compare the remark made by Oscar Wilde (1907:76) at the turn of the twentieth century: "Now do you really imagine that the Japanese people, as they are presented to us in art, have any existence? If you do, you have never understood Japanese art at all. The Japanese people are the deliberate self-conscious creation of certain individual artists....The actual people who live in Japan are not unlike the general run of the English people; that is to say, they are extremely commonplace, and have nothing curious or extraordinary about them. In fact the whole of Japan is a pure invention. There is no such country, there are no such people." Part of this is quoted—actually misquoted in part—by Kwame Anthony Appiah (1991:347). A similar sentiment, apparently not known to Said, was expressed by Foucault as early as 1960: "In the universality of Western reason, there is a partition, which is the Orient: the Orient, thought of as origin, dreamt of as the vertiginous point from which are born nostalgias and promises of a return, the Orient, offered to the West's colonizing reason yet indefinitely inaccessible, because it remains forever the limit: night of the beginning in which the West formed itself but in which it drew a dividing line, the Orient is everything for it that it is not, even though it still must try to find its own primitive truth in it" (quoted and translated by Racevskis 2005:94).

636   Barthes (1982:110).

637   Myers (1980:xlvii) adds: "The weakest part of Said's argument is the interpretation of literary texts. He is naively surprised to discover the obvious fact that writers have greater interest in themselves than in their subjects, that they are influenced by private myths and obsessions, that they prefer imagination to reality." Ironically, as Herbert Lindenberger (1996:208) notes, Said fails to mimic the "detailed analysis of brief passages" as Auerbach does in *Mimesis*.

638   I do not subscribe to the blanket dismissal of "lit-crit" by Ernest Gellner, who engaged in a venomous exchange with Said in the pages of the *Times Literary Supplement*, but Gellner (1994:162) is correct in noting that Said offers "no general discussion of cultural transformation" in his attempt to read novels contrapuntally.

639   As David Armitage (1998:102) suggests, "However, to apply modern models of the relationship between Culture and Imperialism to early-modern literature and Empire demands indifference to context and inevitably courts anachronism."

640   Said (1993a:70). This claim has been frequently criticized; see, e.g., V. Kennedy (2000:84).

641   Sutherland (2005). Some of Said's amateurish admirers go so far as to insist that Said is saying that the novel and the empire "were born at a stroke" (Walia 2001:9).

642   Said (1993a:70–71). A more nuanced view of the rise of the imperial-era novel is provided by Robert Young (1995:2), who argues that the English novel portrays English experience as "a sense of fluidity and a painful sense of, or need for, otherness"; see also the excellent critical history by James Buzard (2005).

643   Said (1993a:71).

644   Said (1993a:71–72). Norman Daniel (1966:61) suggests that many of the young men who served in colonial posts "formed their first ideas of the Muslim world" from translations, poetry, and travel accounts, as well as novels.

645   No matter how one reads Said's reading, Patrick Williams (2001:l:xvii) pegs it well: "The injunction 'to read what is there or not there' enjoins a particularly difficult intellectual labor." Paul Armstrong (2003:116) believes that this type of reading "assumes what needs to be established." Mustapha Marrouchi (2004:58), however, thinks it will be a "lasting contribution to the study of literature." Singh and Greenlaw (1998) draw inspiration for a "contrapuntal pedagogy" approach to literature. Said (2000:186) plays the term to the limit, even describing the condition of exile as contrapuntal. At this stage, I think the musical metaphor is baroque and quite counterproductive.

646   Said (1993a:18). Jonathan Arac (2000:67) views contrapuntal criticism as a form of loving or joining in opposition to aggressive polarization. As such it appears to be more a generalized inspiration for the critic than a specific method for reading.

647   Said (1993a:66–67).

648   Said (1993a:66).

649   Fraiman (1995:808–809). Fraiman provides a list of negative reviews of Said's interpretation of Austen; see also Dunn (1995) and Mee (2000). Critics such as Meili Steele (1997:101) think that "Said's contrapuntalism has no recuperative dimension." In a similar vein, Sutherland (2005) refers to Said's "error-ridden" treatment of Thackery's *Vanity Fair*; although Said's view of the novel has not had much influence among fellow literary critics, it has informed Hollywood film adapatations.

650   Said (1993a:89).

651   Cited in Franklin (1995:375). This was eleven years before the Quaker William Fox's famous speech calling on his fellow men to abstain from West Indian sugar and rum. A similar abolitionist attack on sugar consumption was delivered by the poet Samuel Coleridge in 1795 (Morton 1998:90).

652   T. Lloyd (1999:75). Ironically, the author William Beckford was forced to give up his stately Fonthill mansion in 1822, less than a decade after the publication of *Mansfield Park*, because of the depreciation of his West Indian properties after the abolition of the slave trade (Brockman 1956:170–171).

653   G. Wilson (1994:272).

654   G. Wilson (1994:272); he is consciously facetious in order to illustrate how unconvinced he is by Said's forced reading. Consider the irony at the start of the last chapter in *Mansfield Park*: "Let other pens dwell on guilt and misery. I quit such odious subjects as soon as I can, impatient to restore everybody, not greatly in fault themselves, to tolerable comfort, and to have done with all the rest" (Austen 1933:751).

655   Rajeswari Sunder Rajan (2000:8) thinks that Said misstates Austen's views on abolition.

656   Fraiman (1995:815). Fraiman concludes that "Said's typing of Austen is, I will finally suggest, symptomatic of a more general gender politics underlying his postcolonial project" (807). A similar point is made by Jon Mee (2000:85–86). It is hardly encouraging when Said (2000:381) complains that Austen has been added to the canon just to include a female author's name, objecting that such an inclusion "does not provide for intellectual process."

657   Said (1993a:51; 1994c:29).

658 Said (2000:219).

659 Said (2000:352). In an interview on Dutch television in 2000, Said reminisced about his first experience at an Umm Kulthum concert in Egypt, complaining that it lacked counterpoint and that he found it "very disturbing" (quoted in De Groot 2005:219).

660 Said (1993a:52).

661 Said (1993a:52). This broader goal is echoed in a tribute by Said's student Aamir Mufti (2005:482), who describes Said's contrapuntality as "the very nature and identity of human collectivities and the places they inhabit in the world." How does abstracting the already essentialized notion of cultures to collectivities ring in a new approach to go beyond textual analysis?

662 Said (1993a:75,78,135).

663 Sir Walter Scott is lumped together with less distinguished novelists (Disraeli), poets (Byron), and travelers (Burton, Lane), as well as established luminaries such as Goethe, Hugo, Flaubert, and Eliot (Said 1979: 99, 157, 169, 192).

664 Said (1979:101). Said assumes that the character of Sir Kenneth in *The Talisman* can unproblematically represent the author's own projected prejudices. Sari Nasir (1976:107), on the other hand, states that Scott depicts Arabs favorably in *The Talisman*. Norman Daniel (1966:60) also sees a certain fair-handedness in comparing Franks and Saracens in this novel. Paul Pelckmans (1998) argues that Said misreads Scott's stance in *The Talisman*. The German author Gotthold Ephraim Lessing also presents Saladin in a favorable light (see Fuchs-Sumiyoshi 1984:38).

665 Said (1979:102). Rather than demonstrate this as a pattern in Scott's novels, Said conveniently jumps to Disraeli's *Tancred*.

666 Scott (1997:518). The quotes here and following appear in the last few pages of *Ivanhoe*.

667 Scott (1997:xxviii–xxix). This epistle was first written in 1817. As argued by James Buzard (2005:44), a number of British novels present "skeptical questioning and testing" of Britain's "nation-making and culture-making procedures." Buzard examines Scott's *Waverly* as paradigmatic of this autoethnographic genre.

668 Lew (1991a:256). Unlike Said, who seldom probes the historial context of authors, Joseph Lew shows how texts, family history, and contemporary contacts influenced Shelley.

669 Lew (1991a:277–278).

670 Lew (1991a:283).

671 Quoted in Stewart (1975:233).

672 Said (1979:4). There is a further reference to this quote later in *Orientalism* (Said 1979:166).

673 Said (1979:192). The characterization of Disraeli's intent suggests that Said found such a plot "ingenuous" in a political sense as well as naive in an artistic sense.

674 Disraeli (1877:54).

675 Disraeli (1877:63).

676 Disraeli (1877:66).

677 Disraeli (1877:74). Tancred's mother blames the bishop for not talking her son out of his quest.

678 Disraeli (1877:105). Note the satire in Disraeli's dismissal of Orientalist travel accounts.

679 Disraeli (1877:141). Lady Isabel Burton (1897:2:360) also chose Disraeli's quote "The East is a career" as an epigraph for the last chapter in her autobiography.

680   Disraeli (1877:123).

681   Disraeli (1877:289).

682   Said (1979:102). The latter excerpt is quoted by Said from Monsieur de Sidonia, who goes on to suggest an Ibn Khaldunian view of race decay as inevitable unless one lives in the desert and has pure blood (see Disraeli 1877:149–150). Disraeli ranked both Jews and Arabs as Caucasians, along with Saxons and Greeks; he held the notion of a superior Aryan race to be absurd (Vincent 1990:28,34).

683   Said, quoted in Viswanathan (2001:424). Sari Nasir (1976:106) correctly notes that Arabs were a backdrop to Disraeli's plot but "nevertheless were pictured both colourfully and romantically with appreciation."

684   Said (1979:102)

685   Disraeli (1877:389).

686   See Stewart (1975:231–235). The anti-Semitism directed against Disraeli is discussed by Bernard Lewis (1995:32).

687   Disraeli (1877:439).

688   In a diary entry for 1903, Wilfrid Scawen Blunt (1923:II:72) admires Disraeli for "his smashing of those solemn rogues the Whigs, and his bamboozling of the Tories," but also insists that he is not a "Dizzy-worshipper."

689   Disraeli (1877:82–83). Unlike the quotes and sentiments provided by Said, these words are those of the narrative author himself speaking.

690   Disraeli (1877:381–382).

691   Disraeli (1877:364–365).

692   Disraeli (1877:436–437). The use of dialogue to critique the alleged superiority of the West was not uncommon in nineteenth-century writings. In the early nineteenth century, James Morier's 1824 *The Adventures of Hajji Baba* provided the following description of Europeans in the words of the character Mirza Ahmak: "In short, there is no end to what might be related of them; but most certain it is, that they are the most filthy people on the earth, for they hold nothing to be unclean; they eat all sorts of animals, from a pig to a tortoise, without the least scruple, and that without first cutting their throats; they will dissect a dead body, without requiring any purification after it, and perform all the brute functions of their nature, without ever thinking it necessary to go to the hot bath, or even rubbing themselves with sand after them" (Morier 1976:93).

693   Disraeli (1877:348). There are several passages in *Tancred* that come across as anti-colonial; see pp. 175–177, 226–227, 242, 259, 266, 302–303, 309–310, 378–379, 393.

694   Said (1979:192). Said (1979:169) also calls Disraeli an "unrestrained" writer and his novel "an exercise in the astute political management of actual forces on actual territories."

695   Said (1979:102). This characterization would better fit Disraeli's arch-rival, W. E. Gladstone, who was virulent in denigrating "Orientals" and "Mahomedans" (Ansari 2004:80).

696   Brantlinger (1992:256).

697   Vincent (1990:xi).

698   Disraeli (1877:302).

699   Said (1993a:71).

700   Excerpted in Palgrave (1994:205).

701   Excerpted in Palgrave (1994:251).

702   For a relatively recent survey of the multicultural dimensions of poetry as a genre contained by no national or political borders, see Brogan (1996), in which 106 "cultures" are represented.

703   Haddad (2002:1).

704   Dante Alighieri (1954:236).

705   Said (1979:69). But consider the retort in 1777 of William Beckford, author of *Vathek*, to Dante's allegory: "He must have been an uncomfortable wretch to have placed some of the best people that ever existed in this horrid Gulph" (quoted in Melville 1910:44).

706   A. Ahmad (1992:187–190). See also Biddick (2000b:1236), Cantor (1996:140), Greene (1979:580), Parker (1980:9–10), and Pick (1999:268). W. Montgomery Watt (1972:79) remarks that there is actually very little about Islam in Dante's work—Ulysses rates more attention than Muhammad.

707   Said (1979:167). Rhetorical license aside, the problem surely is that the antiquity of the East could be imagined and that the beauty there was worth imagining. James Boon (1982:280n10) argues that Said's "views of power as the determinant of discourse cannot explain the attraction of German early romantics to India." Consider the argument by Muhsin Mahdi (1997:151): "If there ever was an idea that was not intentionally political, or at least whose intention was neither massively nor directly political, and was self-centered rather than directed to the domination of others, that was the image of the East in early German Romanticism."

708   Said (1979:22). Several examples rescue the poet from textual limbo. The recently available poetry from the then-modern Orient was, for Goethe, an extension of the Hebrew Bible (see Shaffer 1975:106); Goethe encountered von Hammer-Purgstall's translation of the Persian poet Hafez on the day of Napoleon's defeat at Waterloo; the *Westöstlicher Diwan* was written as Goethe approached the age of seventy (Yusuf-Ali 1912:30–31). Andrea Fuchs-Sumiyoshi (1984:156) and Wilhelm Halbfass (1997:11–12) strongly disagree with Said's characterization of Goethe as aiding and abetting an abusive Orientalism. Todd Kontje (2004:123) suggests that Goethe's Oriental style flows from a "willingness to combine the incompatible." Walter Veit (2002:166) argues that Goethe's Orientalism was actually a critique of "the superficiality and hypocritical foundations of European culture." J. J. Clarke (1997:3) begins his study by contrasting Goethe's sentiment that "East and West cannot be separated" with Kipling's "never the twain" remark.

709   Said (1979:341n76, 154). The latter is a passage from Marx in which he quotes Goethe. However, Wilhelm Halbfass (1997:12) disputes Said's comment that Goethe was influenced by de Sacy; the German scholar von Hammer-Purgstall was clearly more important. Goethe was also influenced by Herder's views of the Orient (van Ess 1980:38–39).

710   Said's translation is in Said (1979:167). The discrepancy is pointed out by Charles F. Beckingham (1979:563) and Raphael Patai (1979:63). Readers of German will also wince at dropped umlauts in the passage. For a more recent translation, see Veit (2002:176).

711   *Surat al-Baqara* (The Cow), 2:142. The English translation here is from Dawood (1990:21). It is interesting to compare Said's misstep with a comment by classical scholar Walter Burkert (1992:1), originally made in 1984: "'God's is the Orient, God's is the Occident' says the Koran. Classical scholars have found it difficult to maintain such a balanced perspective and have tended instead to transform 'oriental' and 'occi-

dental' into a polarity, implying antithesis and conflict." The classicist did not make the same translation error as the self-appointed representative of Orientals.

712   This is according to Katharina Mommsen (1988:269–270). Mommsen published extensively in the 1950s and 1960s on Goethe's use of the Quran and other Arabic sources.

713   Halbfass (1997:12).

714   Biddick (2000b:1234n1).

715   Malti-Douglas (1979:725). In reading through *Orientalism*'s endnotes, I can find only two direct links that suggest that Said read in their original language any of the German texts cited. References to Nietzsche and Herder are all from translations. Dorothy Figueira (1994:57) suggests that Said is not fluent enough in Schlegel's texts to substantiate his claims, which dampens Kiernan's (1979:346) uncritical praise for Said's analysis of Schlegel. Regarding the Saidian upside-down translation of Nerval's "la mer d'Ionie" as "the Ionian sky" (Said 1979:182), the reader should be grateful that the transcription was not "la merde d'Ionie" and that the sky was not falling. Said's spell is such that admirer Gayatri Spivak (2005:520) accepts his earlier "impatient mistranslations" of French post-structuralist texts by noting that "this charming impatience was part of his signature."

716   Beckingham (1979:563).

717   Yusuf-Ali (1912:38). Karl Fink (1982:315) develops this point to argue that Goethe "anticipates Said's view that 'Above all, authority can, indeed must, be analyzed.'" For example, Goethe was dismissive of earlier scholars, such as Johann Reiske and Johann Michaelis, who thought the Orient inferior to the West.

718   Roche-Mahdi (1997:117). She explains: "For although Goethe was an early discipline [*sic*] of Herder and was introduced to Arabic, Persian, and Sanskrit poetry by Orientalist scholars, his profoundly creative encounter with another culture, with another poet whom he recognizes as mentor and brother, is far too subtle, at once far too personal and too universal to lend itself willingly to the nationalistic polemics which prevailed by the time it was published (1819)." The response is to Said (1979:154). Said seems to think that a Marxist mode of production must come from an ode of false reproduction.

719   From a speech given in Weimar in 2000 (Veit 2002:174–175).

720   Said (1979:192). Byron appears on seven different pages in *Orientalism*, but mostly in lists of writers. It is interesting that Samuel Chew began his study of Elizabethan views of Islam after an initial interest in Byron's Oriental imagery. Daniel Watkins (1987:146n1) speaks favorably of Said's general thesis on Orientalism, but uses Byron's "Eastern Tales" to argue that the poet's praxis was "doggedly committed to exposing social contradiction and injustices," hardly the hallmarks of an Orientalist inferiorizing the real Orient. I note with irony that Gayatri Spivak (2005:521) recalls her first sight of Said as of a "Byronic figure sitting alone all the way down on a narrow bit of vista that the old Naples Pizza in New Haven allowed."

721   Bernard Beatty (1999:77) notes: "But the 'them' and 'us' attitude with which Said accuses 'Orientalism' of inculcating itself is itself object of attention and source of narrative energy in The Giaour."

722   Meyer (1991:664). Meyer (1991:673, 676) recognizes the "self-undermining" of the poet and the "deconstructive propensities" in the poem, but still feels that the alleged hegemonic context in which Byron participated mitigates a "real overturning of the structure of dominance."

723 Watkins (1987:20–21).

724 Makdisi (1998:124). See also Kelsall (1998:245), Sharafuddin (1996:ix), and Triveldi (1995:96–97, 192). Norman Daniel (1966:57) observes that although Byron's poetry may exploit exotic knowledge, he saw little difference in the real world between East and West. Mohja Kahf (1999:160), on the other hand, views Byron's depiction of the Oriental harem beauty as paradigmatic even though the poet satirizes the whole seraglio scene in "Don Juan." It is interesting to note that in "Don Juan" Byron questions the nature of reality and how it can be represented (Haddad 2002:74).

725 Quoted in Daniel (1966:218).

726 Makdisi (1998:137); he adds: "The concept of imperialism underlying Byron's early Orientalism is hence torn with anxiety." For a discussion of Byron's depiction of the unnaturalness of the Orient, see Haddad (2002:141n88).

727 Sharafuddin (1996:131). Southey's Oriental poems are discussed by Majeed (1992:47–86). Ruth Yeazell (2000:34) notes that Southey's major poems do not exploit the infamous harem scene. For a less nuanced view of Southey's work, see Obeidat (1998:19–20).

728 Wassil (2000:433).

729 Shaffer (1975).

730 Said (1979:18). For a discussion of Said's reading of Shaffer, see Barfoot (1998).

731 Said's (1979:118) sole reference to Moore is in a list of writers in Gothic-tale-wagging "Popular Orientalism," alongside Beckford, Byron, and Goethe.

732 For those who think that American fashion runs behind Europe, it is worth noting that G. M. Wickens (1971:62) suggests that the lustre of *Lalla Rookh* had faded in England by 1840.

733 Moore (1915:340), from the prose introduction. The impact of Moore's epic is described by Wickens (1971). Moore's *The Loves of Angels* was given an Islamic coating in its fifth edition (1823) to escape attacks of indecency. As Wickens (1971:61) sees it, "making it possible for angels to be lecherous as Muslims rather than as Christians hardly constitutes a venture into poetic Orientalism."

734 There are some 387 notes citing more than 100 sources, though they are often irrelevant (Wickens 1971:65).

735 Moore (1915:345), from the first part of the poem.

736 Tenniel's illustrations were originally published in the 1861 Longman edition, and frequently reprinted in other editions in the latter half of the nineteenth century.

737 Searight (1970:179).

738 Quoted in Searight (1970:179).

739 This issue is discussed by Majeed (1992:96). Wickens (1971:63) notes that the Veiled Prophet represents Irish demagogue Daniel O'Connell. Joep Leerssen (1998:171) argues that Said fails to understand "Irish" Orientalism.

740 Wickens (1971:63).

741 Lenning (2004:157).

742 This passage is quoted in Said (1979:237). Doughty appears in *Orientalism* mainly in laundry lists of Orientalists. Yet this important author distinguishes "tales rather of an European Orientalism" from those "with much resemblance to the common experience" (Doughty 1936:I:96). Richard Luckett (1982:278) discusses Said's failure to appreciate Doughty's idiosyncrasies.

743   Said (1979:157).

744   The first edition of Flaubert's notes on his travels appeared in 1910, but this was expurgated; see Flaubert (1991) for a recent edition of the original letters. Zachary Lockman (2004:69) wrongly assumes that Flaubert wrote one of the "influential accounts of travel in the Levant."

745   After quoting a passage in which Said dismisses Kinglake as only a nationalistic ego, John Sweetman (1988:117) notes: "Such a comment seems to undervalue the book's charm and take a somewhat severe view of its prevailing tone, which is insouciant rather than openly aggressive." Madeleine Dobie (2001:129–130) states that Said fails to appreciate the "political engagement" of Nerval. Nabil Matar (2003:xxxii) argues that Said's theoretical approach to European travelers does not work for Arab travelers.

746   As Çirakman (2002:15) points out, "In travel literature and in many other writings of historians, political thinkers, astrologists and diplomats one can find images, details and vocabularies which can only reveal disparate, many-sided and even contradictory visions and these cannot be conceived as a unified western discourse about the East." Izabela Kalinowski (2004:10) argues that Polish and Russian travel writers did not necessarily reproduce a structure of "Western" dominance.

747   Said (1979:157).

748   This failure is echoed by Basim Musallam (1979:20–23), who discusses a late-nineteenth-century American book by a Syrian immigrant responding to the bias and stereotypes in the work of Henry Jessup. As a Protestant missionary writing in an apologetic vein, Jessup must be read not simply as a Western scholar but more specifically as having a religious axe to grind. It is not, as Musallam suggests, "literature that hides the truth," but writers who disguise one kind of truth through literature to promote another kind of truth.

749   Said (1979:58) simply refers to Mandeville as a "fabulist." For information on the distribution of this text, see the introduction by C. W. R. D. Moseley (1983:9–11). Columbus is said to have looked at this text before his first voyage. In like manner, Said mentions but does not explore the major texts of Marco Polo (ca. 1298) and di Varthema (1510) as ur-texts from which a set pattern of tropes and stereotypes emanates.

750   Mandeville, in Moseley (1983:44). The specific places cited by Mandeville include: Turkye, Lesser and Greater Ermony, Tartary, Perse, Sirie, Araby, Upper and Lower Egipte, Liby, Caldee, Ethiope, Amazon, and Lesser and Greater Inde. Disputing Said, Kenneth Parker (1999:13) notes that the idea of several Orients is common in seventeenth-century English travel texts.

751   Mandeville, in Moseley (1983:43). The focus is clearly on Palestine and Syria, or from the deserts of Arabia to Cilicia (Mandeville, in Moseley 1983:97). Said (1979:31) errs in stating that Mandeville used the term "Oriental" in a canonical sense.

752   Parker (1999:9).

753   This description is given in chapter 15 (Moseley 1983:104–110). Although much of the book is given over to fabulous stories, including one in which Hormuz is so hot that the testicles of the men there hang down to their thighs, the discussion of Saracens has few such legendary tropes.

754   Mandeville, in Moseley (1983:108).

755   Chew (1937:53).

756 Chew (1937:3–4).

757 Said (1979:237). Sari Nasir (1976:82–83), a fellow Palestinian scholar, views Blunt positively. Jeffrey Myers (1980:xlvii) criticizes Said for ignoring Blunt's opposition. Rana Kabbani (1986:10, 95–101) recognizes Blunt's challenge to British imperialism, but is content to note that it "did not capture the public imagination of the West." Thomas Assad (1964:53–94), a source mentioned by Said, devotes an entire chapter to Blunt. Oddly, Blunt is totally absent from Timothy Mitchell's (1991) spin on Britain's "power to colonize" Egypt. This allows Mitchell to follow Said in ignoring those who rejected the imperial ambitions of Britain.

758 The Blunts worked together as a literary team. Not only did Wilfrid help edit Anne's two travelogues, but they shared in a translation of the famous *Mu'allaqat* odes in 1903. Billie Melman (1992:283) and Ali Behdad (1994a:95) argue that this was an unequal team, in which Wilfrid's male authority validates Anne's female voice. Behdad then goes on to ignore Wilfrid's political activism against British imperialism and assumes that Lady Anne's travel narratives were ineffective because they could be appropriated and defused within the Orientalist establishment. But the readable accounts of Lady Anne were widely consumed.

759 Blunt (1922:7).

760 Blunt and Blunt (1879:I:28). If anything, Lady Anne (Blunt and Blunt 1879:II:225) is too idealistic about the Bedouin: "I do not think, incredible as it may sound to English ears, that the Bedouin exists who, if trusted with money by a friend, would misemploy it."

761 Blunt (1882:142, 26). In brilliant satire of the common stereotype, Blunt (1882:135) wrote: "I know, according to all rule written and spoken by the orthodox, that Islam cannot move, and yet in spite of it I answer with some confidence in the fashion of Galileo, 'E pur si muove.'" Richard Luckett (1982:278) argues that Blunt's pro-Muslim writing is [im]balanced by an anti-Semitic streak.

762 Blunt (1923:II:67).

763 Blunt (1923:I:213).

764 Blunt (1922:x).

765 Blunt (1923:I:375–376). In her preface to Blunt's diaries, Lady Gregory (Blunt 1923:I:xiii) confided: "An 'enfant terrible' of politics, indeed, he has kept to the resolve recorded in the first page of these Diaries of 'pleading the cause of the backward nations of the world' in and out of season." His grandson, Noel Lytton (1961:338), later wrote: "The 'false Darwinism' invoked by Englishmen as a title to their superiority over all other races (with an implied right to subjugate Orientals) was to him the most obnoxious doctrine of his time." In "The Wind and the Whirlwind," a poem written in 1883, Blunt (1922:409) condemned all imperialism in the Near East:

> The Turk that plunders and the Frank that panders.
> These are our lords who ply with lust and fraud.
> The brothel and the winepress and the dancers
> Are gifts unneeded in the lands of God.

766 Blunt (1922:172).

767 Blunt (1923:II:132). Norman Daniel (1966:55) argues that Burton's "unhappily, delib-

erately and ludicrously archaic" translation of the *Arabian Nights* "strengthened the image of Islamic quaintness."

768   Another British example is Major Arthur Glyn Leonard (1909:140), who in writing against the notion of a "Moslem Menace" noted, "For like the unfortunate victim in a Spanish bull-fight, tormented to its death by matadors, picadors, torreadors, and a host of other 'dors,' Islam is beset and heckled by the frothy vapourings of theocratic firebrands, and the unbridled licence of Europe's gutter press."

769   Hentsch (1992:137).

770   Fück (1962:311); see also Hourani (1980b:6). As Akbar Ahmed (1992:180) observes, "to condemn all orientalists as driven by a pathological hatred of Islam is incorrect."

771   Said (1979:95).

772   Ragan (1998:225).

773   Quoted in Nawwab (2002:11). Ironically, Muhammad Asad is the father of anthropologist Talal Asad, who wrote one of the more favorable reviews of *Orientalism*.

774   Fleming (2000:1231). The itinerant literatus trope of Said's traveling theory has traveled far within his own field. Ali Behdad (1994a:1), for example, rides this discursive omnibus "through literary texts, theoretical domains, images, photographs, signs, letters, and traces" with no caution signs or roadblocks in sight.

775   Porter (1994:153). For Said's use of Foucault, see chapter 3, section I, pp. 253–259.

776   Halliday (1999:213).

777   Moore-Gilbert (1996b:11). Jean de Thévenot, who visited the real Orient in the mid-seventeenth century, cautioned against thinking the Turks barbaric (Longino 2002:39–40).

778   Robert Young (2001:390) labels this a problem of historicity in which Orientalism "dehistoricizes, and treats all texts as synchronic, as if they existed in an ahistorical unchanging spatialized textual continuum." Young's omission of commas may be excused here as an ironic illustration of such a continuum.

779   Said (1979:96).

780   Driss (2001:163). In her examples of two early novels, Driss (2001:162–163) complains that although one female author "deliberately stifles" the native voice and the other "strategically undermines" it, both still "share the same colonial strategy of freezing the native female in her exterior appearance." The problem is that she reads real history only through a comparison of specific fictional texts. The circular reasoning here is dizzying. Enunciating a "colonial strategy" depends on reading the particular voices of authors and their fictional characters, so how can any given author's intentions be disallowed simply because a strategy has been presumed from the writings of other writers? By this reasoning, satire could not exist as a literary genre. *Damnant quod non intelligunt.*

781   Said (1976, quoted in Viswanathan 2001:33).

782   J. Derek Latham (1972) provides a survey of the major Western texts on Arabic literature available by the time *Orientalism* was written.

783   Dodge (1970).

784   As Basim Musallam (1979:20) notes in a favorable review, Said has an easy job in finding "self-condemning statements of Orientalists" because of the general agreement that much "scientific" writing of the time had been racist and ethnocentric.

CHAPTER 3

1   This is used as the book epigraph in *Orientalism*. Said repeats it on pp. 21 and 293 of that book, as well as in Said (1983:123).

2   Said, in a 1992 interview cited in Viswanathan (2001:374).

3   Said (1983:35).

4   Said (1979:4).

5   Williams (2001:xx). Robert Young (1995:161), after noting the major criticism of Said's views on representation, suggests that "the most productive revisions of Said's work" focus on this issue. Nadia Abu El-Haj (2005:540) views representation as "one of the widest influences of *Orientalism*."

6   Said (1979:21). Said's analysis of Marx's passage is critiqued by Aijaz Ahmad (1992:185–186). This is a very popular aphorism; e.g., Margery Wolf (1992:13) quotes Mohanty quoting Marx. In *Tristes Tropiques*, Claude Lévi-Strauss (1967:61) reflects that "rarely do I tackle a problem in sociology or ethnology without having first set my mind in motion by re-perusal of a page or two from the *18 Brumaire of Louis Bonaparte* or the *Critique of Political Economy*."

7   Said's Orientalism thesis does not question the real impact of Western imperialism, nor does it echo the philosophical doubt of Bishop Richard Whately, who presented his "Historic Doubts Relative to Napoleon Buonaparte" in 1819: "If we are disposed to credit all that is told us, we must believe in the existence not only of one, but of two or three Buonapartes; if we admit nothing but what is well authenticated, we shall be compelled to doubt the existence of any" (Whately 1958:154).

8   Said is otherwise very precise about footnoting the sources of quotes, but the edition and reference for this quote are not provided. I suspect that this quote was encountered first in English, a point Said intimates in *The World, the Text, and the Critic* (1983:300n12); here Said mentions that he is using the Fowkes translation in which the German quote also appears.

9   Marx (1963:124), translated by Daniel De Leon.

10 Aijaz Ahmad (1992:208) goes a step further, implying that "Said seems not to know the immigrant communities on whose behalf he speaks."

11 Jacoby (1995:33).

12 Grewgious (1994:91). See also Spencer (1997:11). Said is not alone in this appropriation of a political metaphor for discursive intent; see, e.g., Sim (2002:329).

13 Said, in a 1996 interview cited in Viswanathan (2001:236). Those who insist that Said is not out to show that Orientalism is false but rather to establish "how it creates truth" (Thomas 1991:5) fall prey to a semantic either/or.

14 Said (1979:272). Said toys with the epistemological problem here, but apart from his brief references to Foucault, the extensive debate over this very issue is totally ignored. Said is hardly the first writer to wonder what truth is. Richard Evans (2001:287) provides a pragmatic and razor-sharp solution to all this onto-illogic: "In the end, perhaps, no one has proved conclusively and logically that we do exist; but no one has proved that we don't either." As Stephan Fuchs (2001:72) comments, "About truth there seems to be no truth."

15 Said (1979:203).

16   Manzalaoui (1980:839).

17   Prakash (1995:207). This problem has been raised by several commentators, e.g., Owen (1979:62), Sardar (1999:72), and Young (1990:129).

18   Aijaz Ahmad (1992:193). William Cain (1984:213) notes Said's inconsistency in implying at times that everything is representation and no real reality can be viewed through any representation, while he still speaks of "human realities" and "direct encounters."

19   Mutman (1993:192n9).

20   Said (1979:272). Aijaz Ahmad (1992:195) overreacts in claiming that Said in any sense is denouncing "the whole of Western civilization." Boyne and Rattansi (1990:36, 37) agree with Ahmad and find Said's "epistemological ambivalence" over representation vs. misrepresentation to be "politically disabling." Consider also the kind of question raised by Rashmi Bhatnagar (1986:7): "Furthermore, if all roads lead to false origins, where does inquiry begin without being implicated in false origins?" Among those who take this rhetorical trope seriously is A. L. Macfie (2000:8). As Timothy Mitchell (1991:32) suggests, the question is a "bad one."

21   Said (1997:lix).

22   Hammoudi (1997:xvii).

23   Fokkema (1996:239–240). The same argument has been made by David Gordon (1982:111).

24   Fokkema (1996:233).

25   Said (1979:5). Later, Said (1985:2) reiterates his acceptance of a real Orient, saying that "there could be no Orientalism without, on the one hand, the Orientalists, and on the other, the Orientals."

26   Said (1979:322).

27   As Mark Bauerlein (1997:58) explains, literary critics borrow philosophically ontological concepts all the time without dealing with the textual genealogy of such concepts in philosophy. Whether or not this is due to an assumption that the philosophical issue has been settled or simply to ignorance of the philosophical debate, he cannot decide.

28   Said (1979:21).

29   Said (1979:131). As Peter Gaeffke (1990:69) observes, Nietzsche's own knowledge of the Orient owed much to the "painstakingly prepared" Orientalist texts he criticized.

30   Said (1979:337) cites a page number for Balzac's quote, but fails to identify the precise location of the excerpts from Nietzsche. It is apparently sufficient that "Nietzsche's remarks on philology are everywhere throughout his works."

31   Said (1979:132).

32   Said (1979:140–148). Compare the judgment of Albert Hourani (1980b:7): "We are conscious now of the dangers in this way of thinking, the ideas of superiority and inferiority to which it may give rise, but at the time it was a liberating force: religious systems were seen as human products, or as human efforts to express some experience of the divine, and they could be examined and judged with the same freedom as other expressions of the human spirit."

33   See van der Veer (2001:135).

34   Nietzsche's spin on philology has a decidedly religious flavor, as in his dismissal of Luther's German translation of the Bible for putting the text in the hands of "philologists, who are

the destroyers of every faith that rests on books" (Nietzsche 1974:311). It would seem that Nietzsche, like Goethe, must also be branded an Orientalist by Said's reasoning, for such sentiments as: "The European south has inherited this suspicion from the depths of the Orient, from primeval and mysterious Asia and its contemplation" (Nietzsche 1974:293). Nietzsche's own racism, not to mention his sexism, is apparently not relevant for Said; for an analysis of the former, see Bruce Lincoln (1999:64–66, 101–120).

35   Halbfass (1997:5); he notes that Said "does not give us a clear answer."

36   Said (1979:4).

37   Said borrows much of his information on the history of Orientalism from Johann Fück, whose 1955 index, for example, contains about 500 names of Orientalists, yet Said refers to only a select handful of these.

38   In restricting himself to readily accessible Orientalist texts, Said forgets that these have been canonized by a peer-review process that tends to weed out critical assessments, which are to be found through more probing scholarship; see Ragan (1998:227).

39   Some literary critics praise *Orientalism* for its "enormously broadened scope" of texts as valuable in itself without focusing on the methodological problems inherent in such genre blurring (e.g., P. Williams 2001:xii). Even negative reviews are prone to exaggerating Said's scholarly range: "Every page yields scholarship remarkable for its scope and, in general, for its accuracy," writes Richard Luckett (1982:272). This comes from a non-Arabist who proceeds to correct Bernard Lewis's philological observation about the Arabic term *thawra*; despite Luckett's objection, the root sense of "to rise up" was indeed applied to camels by Arabic lexicographers, and only recently borrowed for the sense of "revolution." Where some see signs of scholarly rigor, others cite "Said's procedure of dropping names, dates, and anecdotes" (Kopf 1980:499).

40   Al-Bitar (1982:8–9), quoted in Sivan (1985:136). I do not think that Said (1994c:29) avoids the critique by later restyling essentialisms as "contrapuntal ensembles." To say "Greeks always require barbarians, and Europeans Africans, Orientals, etc." may sound like an ensemble, but it is still a dangerous oppositional essentialism.

41   A. Ahmad (1992:167). Concurring on this point are numerous critics, e.g., Crinson (1996:5), Dimmock (2005:6), Eaton (2000:67), Figueira (1994:3), Franklin (1998:48), Hoenselaars (1998:9–10), Johansen (1990:73), Kalinowski (2004:184), O'Hara (1980:279), Simmons (1995:90), and Woodcock (1980:303). Robert Young (1990:127) accuses Said of "repeating the very structures that he censures." Rosane Rocher (1993:215) states that Said "does to orientalist scholarship what it accuses orientalist scholarship of having done to the countries east of Europe." Richard Martin (1985:15) comments that "Said offers an interpretation that is more blatantly ethnocentric and politicized than most of the targets of his own criticism." Ali Behdad (1994a:11) notes that Said "repeats" the very faults of essentialism and generalizing tendencies he denounces. Kathleen Davis (2000:113) says that Said "instates a core 'reality' that privileges and solidifies the very discourse he critiques." In James Brown's (1999:566) words, "To return to *Orientalism* is to find Said locked in combat with himself, furiously condemning in others the very ploys he uses himself." The Marxist scholar Mahdi 'Amil (1985:11) argues that by privileging Orientalism as a bourgeois creation, Said creates the same thing. Wilhelm Halbfass (1997:11) comments that *Orientalism* is "no less a construct and projection than the so-called Orient itself."

42   A. Ahmad (1992:183).

43   Irwin (1981–82:108). Çirakman (2002:30–31) and Gordon (1982:110) express similar
     criticism.

44   Richardson (1990:17).

45   For example, Fedwa Malti-Douglas (1985–86:43) suggests that Said reduces *Homo ori-*
     entalisticus to "an essence of nature" rather than a scholar. As Hichem Djait (1985:56)
     suggests, "So present-day Orientalism covers a gamut of positions, and the one most
     hostile to Islam is only a single minority view."

46   Mills (1997:119).

47   Van Leeuwen (2000:207).

48   Freitag (1997:622).

49   Dawn (1979:1334), Mills (1997:119), Schick (1999:96), Teltscher (1995:6), Woodcock
     (1980:301), and Young (2001:391). Sarkar (1994:206) characterizes the Saidian frame-
     work in *Orientalism* as a critique carried out "in the grossest of homogenizing ways."
     Sumit Sarkar (1997:17) further notes: "If histories written within the Saidian mould
     homogenize, they also often tend to impose closures by suggesting ready answers to
     issues that could have developed into interesting inquiries."

50   Thomas (1994:3).

51   Behdad (1994a:11), Edwards (2000:16), Kopf (1980:499), Lowe (1991:4; 1995:219), Majeed
     (1992:4–5), Mani and Frankenberg (1985:177), Nanji (1997:xv), Sardar (1999:70), Teltscher
     (1995:6), Ueckmann (2001:73), and Wassil (2000:447). As E. L. Constable (1996:628) notes,
     "Post-Saidian critiques have themselves moved away from his description of Oriental-
     ism as a monolithic series of representations." Not all have, unfortunately, as is evi-
     dent in Shelley Walia's (2001:38) claim that "Orientalism was never a disinterested
     science, but operated on the premise of unequal relations with the motive of deter-
     mining how lands could be occupied and managed."

52   Pathak et al. (1991:215), Young (1990:135).

53   Crinson (1996:228).

54   Davis (2000:113). For a critique of Said's insistence on the unilinear development of
     Orientalism, see Çirakman (2002:27–32).

55   Edwards (2000:16), R. Lewis (1996:237), Moore-Gilbert (1996b:23).

56   Parry (1992:27).

57   Moore-Gilbert (1986:2).

58   Halliday (1999:211).

59   Sinha (1995:19).

60   Al-'Azm (1984:352).

61   Dallmayr (1996:xvi).

62   V. Kennedy (2000:29).

63   Rodinson (1991:81). Madeleine Dobie (2001:15) finds "problematic" Said's claim that "the
     whole political apparatus and emergent bourgeois culture of the mid-nineteenth century
     constituted a single dominant discourse of which Orientalism was a constituent part."

64   Mahdi (1997:174).

65   Gellner (1994:159). For an analysis of Gellner's reaction to Said, see Varisco (2004).

66   Kopf (1995:156).

67   Quoted in Sharabi (1990:27).

68   Said (1979:3). The index shows how usable the term was: there are twenty-seven lines in the "discourse" entry. See Said (1975:279–343) for an earlier assessment of his views on Foucault, and Said (1986a) for a later view; the latter was translated into Arabic by 'Ala' al-Din Husayn (Said 2001b). I note with more than a modicum of multi-layered irony that Foucault's 1972 *The Archaeology of Knowledge*—which Said (1979:3) cites as the primary source for his understanding of "discourse"—was written while Foucault lived in Sidi-Bou-Saïd in Tunisia. To add to the Oriental flavor of the primordial theoretical soup out of which post-colonialism has risen, consider that Sartre, Althusser, Derrida, and Lyotard all, as Robert Young (1990:1) points out, either were born in Algeria or participated in the Algerian War of Independence. Even Frantz Fanon and Albert Memmi passed through Algeria. Other subalterns, especially those not privileged by ties to European academic institutions, may understandably feel as though the burdensome white-manned theory used to represent them post-colonially is too closely Oriental for indigenous comfort. Said is not the only "Oriental" commentator on Orientalism to find methodological value in Foucault's work. North African critics 'Abd al-Kabir al-Khatibi and Muhammad 'Abid al-Jabiri also borrow from the French anti-*philosophe*.

69   Said (1979:94). It appears as though Said viewed his analysis as part of the same project.

70   Said (1983:216).

71   Said (1983:212). It is useful to note that Said says this after he criticizes Jacques Derrida's deconstructionism as unable to move a text out of its intertextuality. Said dismisses Derrida's position as "an extremely pronounced self-limitation, an ascesis of a very inhibiting and crippling sort" (214). Robert Young (1990:137) comments that "only by rejecting Derrida *tout court* can Said continue to entertain the very possibility of a closed structure, system or method."

72   Said (1979:23).

73   Said (1979:24–25). Douwe Fokkema (1996:230) characterizes Said's rhetoric here as "a feeble attempt to rescue the notion of individual actor or agent from the swamp of determinism"—feeble because it only goes halfway.

74   Mills (1991:38). But, as Daniel O'Hara (1980:278) argues, Said leaves no room for authorial freedom despite his disclaimer.

75   Said (1983:187).

76   Said (1983:244). Said's failure to consider class issues is discussed in chapter 2, pp. 170–177.

77   Said (1979:3).

78   Yegenoglu (1998:15). Similar points were made earlier by Aijaz Ahmad (1992:199) and Sumit Sarkar (1994:207–209).

79   Said (1983:222). This criticism is reiterated in *Culture and Imperialism* (Said 1993a:41).

80   This point is made by several authors, including Alam (2000:23), Brennan (2001:91), V. Kennedy (2000:26), Marrouchi (2204:91), and Moore-Gilbert et al. (1997:25). It is not clear which imagined version of *Orientalism* Shelley Walia (2001:29) is reading when she argues that "Said pays full attention to Foucault's notion of discourse." The term "discourse" is in fact banished from *Culture and Imperialism* in favor of an Arnoldian definition of culture—a retro-discourse of high-cultural hypallage. Madeleine Dobie (2001:12) suggests that Said did not properly understand what Foucault meant by discourse, because "Said approaches Orientalism as a pure expression of the power exercised by one group over another." A similar point is made by Karlis Racevskis (2005:92), who notes that

Said misconstrues Foucault's view of power as a "thing" rather than a relation to control. Perhaps, as Moustafa Bayoumi (2005:47) suggests, this is because Said had "largely finished with Foucault" by the time he wrote *Orientalism*.

81   Said (1983:246). In *Culture and Imperialism*, Said (1993a:278) writes: "Foucault, perhaps because of his disenchantment with both the insurrections of the 1960s and the Iranian Revolution, swerves away from politics entirely." He makes the same point in a 1987 interview cited in Viswanathan (2001:77). Valerie Kennedy (2000:26) also sees Foucault's apolitical stance as something that irked Said. As noted by Karlis Racevskis (2005:83), Said's frustration with Foucault's personal politics was evident during a visit to Paris when Said met with Jean-Paul Sartre and Simone de Beauvoir in Foucault's apartment; Foucault apparently did not criticize Israel for its treatment of the Palestinians. Harold Weiss (1989), on the other hand, thinks that Foucault's work is more politically active than Said assumes.

82   Meeks (2003:131).

83   Said (1983:221–222).

84   Young (2001:395).

85   A. Ahmad (1992:177).

86   Brennan (2000:567). It has become axiomatic to assume that Foucault was "mediated" to post-colonial writers by Said, without consideration of how Said actually uses Foucault's notion of discourse (see Kandiyoti 2002:281).

87   Aijaz Ahmad (1992:165) acknowledges the affiliation between Foucault and Said but still wonders what the relationship between the two really is. Michael Beard (1979:4) characterizes it as slight. Timothy Brennan (1992:77) relegates Foucault to a relatively minor role in *Orientalism*. Grewgious (1994:88) finds Said's use of Foucault's discourse little more than a gesture. Vincent Leitch (1992:132) cites specific examples of how Said "backtracks" from a Foucauldian position. David Ludden (1993:252) discusses Said's views of Foucault's refusal to separate knowledge and power. Arran Gare (1995:316) sees Said as simply absorbing Foucault's anti-hermeneutic stance. On the other hand, Valerie Kennedy (2000:25) naively reiterates the uncritical assumption that "Foucault is perhaps the most important single theoretical source for Said."

88   Lowe (1991:8). Mahmut Mutman (1993:170) faults Said for not getting to the "constitutive aspect of discourse." John David Ragan (1998:227) argues that Said's Orientalism is not Foucauldian discourse, as it was not "an internalized language or system of thought which prevented people from thinking otherwise." Robert Young (2001:385) laments that despite the plethora of arguments about Foucault's sense of discourse, there is still no full theorization of the concept in post-colonial studies.

89   U. Schaub (1989:308).

90   Cain (1984:214). A similar point is made by Fokkema (1996:234).

91   Bové (1986:212–237), Dutton and Williams (1993), Chuaqui (2005), Hussein (2002:193–210), V. Kennedy (2000:27–31), Otterspeer (1998), and Young (2001:385–389) provide concise surveys of the critique of Said's use of Foucault. Basim Musallam (1979:25) argues that Foucault's "discourse" is "much weaker" when applied to relations among different societies rather than within a continuous cultural tradition. Anthropologist Marshall Sahlins (2002:2) is so little enamored with the value of Foucault's work that he labels the latter's modeling of power as "poly-amorphous perverse."

92   Clifford (1992:264). James Brown (1999:551) concurs that this is "an unresolved tension."

William Hart (2000:74) dismisses this critique by arguing that "every would-be antihumanism (which purports to be something other than fascist) is a form of humanism." Cain (1984:210). A similar point is made by Binder (1988:115).

93

94 Rorty (1991:193), referring to a critique by Vincent Descombes. See Brennan (2000; 2001) for further discussion of the "American" nature of *Orientalism*, and Marrouchi (2004:75–83) for a critique of Brennan.

95 A. Ahmad (1992:159–219). Earlier versions of this chapter were presented at seminars in both India, where Ahmad teaches, and the United States.

96 Prakash (1995:200n3). This is repeated, without direct attribution, by Mustapha Marrouchi (2000:20). Robert Young (2001:413) lashes out at Ahmad's tongue lashing of *Orientalism*. Timothy Brennan (2005:412) adds to the post-colonial avoidance of Ahmad's critical points by suggesting a psychologistical explanation that Ahmad "could not fathom how someone could be feted and flattered and, at the same time, a problem to power." Dismissal of Ahmad is resurrected by Neil Lazarus (2005:124), who asserts that Ahmad poisoned the debate over *Orientalism* within post-colonialism. Graham Huggan (2005:131) provides a nuanced view of Ahmad, who he admits "scores a number of palpable hits here," but then adds that "much like Said, he has a tendency to let his eloquence get the better of him." These critics of the critic ignore that Ahmad's (1992:159) expressed admiration of Said's courageous stand for Palestinian rights makes it difficult to voice such criticism.

97 A. Ahmad (1992:166). Bart Moore-Gilbert (1996b:17) finds "a certain degree of justice" in Ahmad's accusation, as does Aslı Çirakman (2002:14).

98 In Aijaz Ahmad's (1992:163) words: "The particular texture of *Orientalism*, its emphasis on the canonical text, its privileging of literature and philology in the constitution of 'Orientalist' knowledge and indeed the human sciences generally, its will to portray a 'West' which has been the same from the dawn of history up to the present, and its will to traverse all the main languages of Europe—all this, and more, in *Orientalism* derives from the ambition to write a counter-history that could be posed against *Mimesis*, Auerbach's magisterial account of the seamless genesis of European realism and rationalism from Greek Antiquity to the modernist moment." To put it bluntly, you can't bake a cake out of the high humanism Said admires in Erich Auerbach by using the vitriolic anti-humanist rhetoric of Foucault and expect not to be told to eat it. Rather than engaging Ahmad's critique, Said allegedly suggested that all copies of his book be thrown into an incinerator (see Brennan 2005:411).

99 Bhabha (1986:157–158; 1994:72–73). For an explicit view of "Oriental despotism" as fantasy in Lacan's sense, see Grosrichard (1998).

100 Bhabha (1994:72). As Paula Sanders (2003:179) suggests, the dynamics of power do not necessarily account for all meanings of "Orient."

101 Neither Freud nor Fanon is accorded intellectual space in *Orientalism*, although the latter plays a minor role as a global theorist in *Culture and Imperialism*.

102 Bhabha (1994:74–75). Antony Easthope (1998:341) regards Bhabha's critique of Said a "crucial and necessary intervention." Prior to Bhabha's enunciation, Said's failure to see stereotyping as a two-way process disturbed anthropologist James Boon (1982:280n10). For a series of anthropological studies on the ambivalent role of stereotypes in southeastern Europe, see Brown and Theodossopolous (2004).

103   Quayson (2000:63): "For Bhabha then, the colonial encounter is read as a series of tropes of ambiguity." Young (1990:141) entitles a chapter "The Ambivalence of Bhabha." See also Gandhi (1998:77–78), V. Kennedy (2000:119), and Moore-Gilbert (1996:5). Patrick Taylor (1995) prefers Said to Bhabha because the former avoids "the schizoid language of ambivalence in which the postmodernists indulge." Following Bhabha, Ali Behdad (1994a:135) focuses on the "ambivalence" of Orientalism as maintaining the "discourse of domination."

104   Yacoubi (2005:215); he adds: "Empire is irreducible to the excess of jargon and academic professionalism."

105   Bhabha (1994:75).

106   Gates (1991:462, 458). See also Young (1990:141–156).

107   I have no interest here in debating the overall relevance of Foucault, about which there is an extensive literature. P. Steven Sangren (1995) offers an anthropological rebuttal to Foucault's conception of power. Abdellah Hammoudi (1997:ix) faults Foucault for privileging "pure concepts and conceptual architectonics in the advent of discursive formations." Also among Foucault's critics is historian Hayden White (1987:104) who writes: "But the thorniness of Foucault's style is also ideologically motivated. His interminable sentences, parentheses, repetitions, neologisms, paradoxes, oxymorons, alternation of analytical with lyrical passages, and combination of scientistic with mythic terminology—all appear to be consciously designed to render his discourse impenetrable to any critical technique based on ideological principles different from his own." Historians would basically be out of business if Foucault's blurring of cause-and-effect explanation is taken to the extreme (see Rotter 2000:1211–1212).

108   Dalby (1980:488). Said thus ends up viewing Orientalism as an "explicandum in its own right" (Dalby 1980:489).

109   Salamandra (2004:63).

110   Turner (1994:7).

111   Turner (1994:7). Turner also argues that Foucault's sense of "no discourse-free alternative" (31) makes its difficult for Said to go beyond a vague hope for reform.

112   Plumb (1979). Jayant Lele (1993:70) likewise proposes moving with Marx and Gramsci rather than Nietzsche and Foucault.

113   Hart (2000:209n18).

114   Lazarus (2005;115).

115   Said (1976, quoted in Viswanathan 2001:15).

116   Said (1979:321). Of course, Said is rejecting a specific Marxist use of "ideology," but if he finds the noun unsuitable, why not the adjective as well? He is less reluctant to use a variant of "ideology" in interviews, e.g., Orientalism as a "disciplined ideological presence" (Said 1976, quoted in Viswanathan 2001:38).

117   Said (1979:327).

118   In his preface to the French translation of Said's *Orientalism*, Tzvetan Todorov (1980:8) comments: "L'idéologie est le tourniquet qui permet aux discours et aux actes de se prêter mai-forte, et *l'Orientalisme* raconte un chapitre des destins croisés du Pouvoir et du Savoir." Roger Owen (1979:58) describes the target of Said's thesis as "an ideology supported and seemingly legitimized by the facts of power." Benjamin Beit-Hallahmi (1980:69) describes Said's argument as an "ideology of imperialism." David

Gordon (1982:110) accuses Said of reducing literature to ideology. Writers who draw inspiration from Said often refer to what he calls discourse as "cultural ideology," e.g., Menocal (1987:6).

119   Eagleton (1991:xi). There are myriad explanations of what "ideology" might mean, but my favorite is Eagleton's (1991:xiii): "What persuades men and women to mistake each other from time to time for gods or vermin is ideology." Even non-Marxists rely on a generic sense of ideology; e.g., Schick (1990:349): "As an ideology of colonization old and new, orientalism makes use of male-dominant discourse."

120   Said does not indicate here the passage from which he obtains his information on Gramsci's hegemony. After hegemony is introduced as an important concept, it is basically dropped and never explicated in the rest of Said's narrative. The only direct quote of Gramsci (Said 1979:25) is from *The Prison Notebooks*, but this is in reference to justifying his discussion of a personal dimension. I also note a tendency to assume that other scholars are not reading the same seminal texts. Thus, in a later article, Said (1994c:26) complains that Gramsci's *Some Aspects of the Southern Question* has been "under-read and under-analyzed." If you will pardon the grammatical incongruity, under-read and under-analyzed by whom? By the non-Marxist commentators Said chooses to read? The first two volumes of the *Bibliografia Gramsciana* record 11,430 entries on Gramsci between 1922 and 1993. To add to Said's ignoring of the importance of Gramsci in Marxist and sociological theory, he compounds his unfamiliarity with the corpus of Gramsciana by claiming that *The Prison Notebooks* is the only sustained piece of political and cultural analysis Gramsci wrote.

121   V. Kennedy (2000:20). Kennedy's point is that Said tries to remain a humanist in the tradition that both Foucault and Gramsci attack. This, in itself, would be less of a problem if Said probed his own humanist orientation more reflexively. Patrick Wolfe (1997:408–409) notes that the yoking of Foucault and Gramsci leads Said to develop a unidirectional discourse. James Brown (1999:564) also faults Said's conjoining of Foucault and Gramsci. Dorothy Figueira (1994:56) criticizes Said's borrowing of Gramsci's "inventory of traces" concept because this is separated in *Orientalism* from other sorts of inventions and traces. On the other hand, Abdirahman Hussein (2002:14) finds Said's use of Gramsci more insightful than his use of Foucault.

122   Laroui (1976:105). See also Sharabi (1970). Ignoring the discussion of Gramsci in both Sharabi and Laroui, Said (2002:9) recalls that "he was the first to lecture on Gramsci at Columbia" some twenty years ago. Whether this is true or not—and I somehow doubt that students had to take an English literature class at Columbia to learn about Gramsci—Said avoids those who criticize his use of Gramsci by asserting what a "very, very assiduous student of Gramsci" he has been.

123   This point has been elaborated by Aijaz Ahmad (1992:169). Stuart Schaar (1979:79) chides Said for not recognizing the potential constructive function in Gramsci's concept. Meili Steele (1997:103) contrasts Said's interpretation of Gramsci with that of Cornel West, finding the latter more conducive to understanding cultural differences. The literature on the work of Gramsci is vast. For a feminist perspective on Gramsci, see Renate Holub (1992:191–203).

124   See Salamini (1981:126–153) for a survey of this history. Nadia Urbinati (1998) pro-

vides an overview of Gramsci's "hegemonic project" as not simply a description of power but also a possible means for social change.

125   Said (1979:322).

126   Said (1979:7,14). For example Mohja Kahf (1999:177) states that Europe did not have hegemony in the Middle East before the eighteenth century. A more nuanced use of hegemony as practiced by the West in colonialism is provided by Abdallah Laroui (1976:113–114, 117–118). Ajit Chaudhury (1994:44) targets Said, among others, in discussing "a particular (mis)reading of Gramsci in the colonial context." Gramsci, we do well to remember, carefully distinguished *egemonia* from *dominazione*.

127   Porter (1994:152). A similar point is made by Comaroff and Comaroff (1992:29).

128   Dirks (1992b:7). Arif Dirlik (1997:109) argues that although "Orientalism was an integral part (at once as constituent and product) of a Eurocentric conceptualization of the world," it is less clear if it had the complicity of Orientals. Said (1993a:51) mentions Gramsci's hegemony in *Culture and Imperialism*, but views consent only as something within the colonizing culture to aid its rule of others.

129   R. Williams (1976:118).

130   Said (1979:328). Benjamin Schwartz (1980) comments that Said's fear of knowledge as endemically corrupt rules out a Weberian sense of *Verstehung*.

131   For example, Bryan Turner (1994:21) complains that Said follows the discourse of "To know is to subordinate."

132   Said (1979:32).

133   Said (1979:21).

134   Whalen-Bridge (2001:197).

135   Bhatnagar (1986:14). Mustapha Marrouchi (2003:57; 2004:97) borrows the phrase and agrees with Bhatnagar.

136   Hussein (2002:11).

137   Said (1979:104).

138   P. Armstrong (1991:159).

139   Brombert (1979:538).

140   Eagleton (1991:8).

141   R. Owen (1979:62).

142   Abu El-Haj (2005:541).

143   Abu El-Haj (2005:542).

144   The phrase is from Lindstrom (1995:35).

145   In his later afterword to *Orientalism*, Said (1994a:331) laments that this is how his book has "in fact been read and written about in the Arab world"; see also Said (1985:4). It is interesting to note that Maxime Rodinson (1991:127) makes the same observation at the end of his personal reflections on the history of Orientalism.

146   Tønnesson (1994).

147   Sayyid (1997:35) .

148   The phrase is from Gordon (1982:110).

149   Sardar (1999:71); see al-ʿAzm (1984).

150   Buruma and Margalit (2002:7, 4). This is repeated in the book-length expansion of their argument (Buruma and Margalit 2004). In what I assume is a conscious restatement

of Said's earlier plea, these authors end their original article with the ironic note that "we should not counter Occidentalism with a nasty form of Orientalism." Their own retort is nasty, whether it qualifies as Orientalist or not. Nadia Abu El-Haj (2005:541–542) dismisses their work as ahistorical.

151 Buruma and Margalit (2002:6).

152 Clifford (1988:271) argues that "Said's discourse analysis does not itself escape the all-inclusive 'Occidentalism' he specifically rejects as an alternative to Orientalism." Andrew Rotter (2000:1207) notes that Said commits Occidentalism by assuming that "the American empire is little more than an inheritance from Europeans."

153 Venn (2000:2). Venn positions his book to break with this conceptual space. In the sense that a space can also be a void, this conceptual breach might best be a-voided.

154 Venn (2000:196). It is not always clear what this is in the place of, apart from the conceptual space that the writer does not wish to occupy.

155 Quoted by Lamont Lindstrom (1995:49), who also speaks of a "pseudo-occidentalism" in which Occidentals "tell stories about themselves using an oriental's voice."

156 Coronil (1996:56); he adds: "Occidentalism, as I define it here, is thus not the reverse of Orientalism but its condition of possibility, its dark side (as in a mirror)." This dark side is lit with global capitalism. Nancy Armstrong (1990:4) uses "Occidentalism" to refer to the effects of the practices of Orientalism on Orientals.

157 This is the phrasing used by Carter Findlay (1998). Meltem Ahiska (2003:368) proposes "Occidentalism" as an Ottoman elitist "answering practice to the construction of the West."

158 Amin (1989:xiii).

159 Hanafi (1990:117). In general Arabic usage, the translation for Occidentalism is *tagharrub* or *ghuruba*; in colloquial Egyptian this can also be expressed as *faranja*, which is derived from the ethnic term for the crusading Franks. Hanafi, like Said, is trying to reorient—or perhaps more accurately re-occident—the standard meaning. Bernard Lewis might be prodded to add that the cognate *gharib* refers to the withers of a camel.

160 For example, in 1845, the Moroccan Muhammad al-Saffar (1991:108), on seeing a large wooden crucifix in Aix, was appalled by the French Christian claim that Jesus was divine. "My God how they lie!" he exclaimed. "This is the cross set up in their churches to worship and glorify, and which Jesus, may peace be upon him, will break upon his return, refuting the falsehood of their belief and the wrongheadedness of the Christian religion." Identical sentiments about the fate of Muslims and unconverted Jews can be found in almost any Christian fundamentalist writing on the apocalypse; e.g., Hal Lindsay's mass-market paperback *The Late Great Planet Earth* (1973).

161 Jameelah (1966:14). Jameelah is an American who converted to Islam in 1961 and married a Pakistani publisher. For biographical information on her, see Esposito and Voll (2001:54–67).

162 Said (1994a:331). Abdirahman Hussein (2002:200) accepts Said's argument that his critics do not appreciate the complexity of Said's "idiosyncratic methodology." In an interview in 1995, however, Said (quoted in Singh and Johnson 2004:86), candidly admits: "Where I felt there was a lot more justification (although I don't think it's real justification but somehow it's a more salient criticism) is the notion that I was suggesting that the West was a kind of monolithic presence with a consistency to it. I talk

about that in the 'Afterword.' I don't think I even actually say that in the book but you could deduce that from what I am saying."

163   In debating Said at the 1986 MESA meeting, Bernard Lewis noted the event had been billed as an "American boxing ring," among other things (quoted in Viswanathan 2001:291). W. J. T. Mitchell (2005a:367) speaks glowingly about the intellectual ability of Said, "like a boxer carrying his opponent for an extra mile or two." William Phillips (1989:343) characterizes Said's writing as "more like the work of a street fighter than a scholar." David Gordon (1982:109) describes Said's tactics as those of an *engagé*.

164   Said (1993a:340). Ali Behdad (1994a:5), on the other hand, thinks that Said did choose Orientalists as one of these audiences "to present them with their 'intellectual genealogy' and question their false assumptions about the Middle East."

165   Said (1979:8). By my estimation, Said's polemic in *Orientalism* is not coarse, but he does generalize his way through it.

166   Said (1979:28).

167   Said (1979:328).

168   Said (1979:328).

169   Said (1979:328).

170   Merod (2000:115). As'ad AbuKhalil (2001:100–101) contends that Said's ideas are "deliberately distorted" and "frequently misquoted."

171   Said (1979:26–27).

172   In a review of *Orientalism*, Thomas Greene (1979:578–579) writes: "Its author is a Palestinian Arab who has personally suffered from Western prejudice and whose anger inflames, sometimes blurs, his analysis."

173   E. Alexander (1989). Other commentary in *Commentary* has been anything but complimentary to Said (e.g., Weiner 1999). Such inflammatory rhetoric explains why government officials took seriously threats on Said's life.

174   Wieseltier, quoted in Viswanathan (2001:309).

175   Shohat (1992:135); see Shohat (2004) for a recent assessment of Said's critical work in Israel.

176   Richard Posner (2001:57–58) scores rhetorical points by ridiculing the unphotogenic incident of Said's stone-throwing at the Lebanese border, but ignores the danger in which Said placed himself over the years by defending such a strong pro-Palestinian stance against hostile media.

177   Malcolm Kerr (1980:547) thus characterized Said's depiction of Gustave von Grunebaum.

178   Said (1976a:4).

179   Said (1979:316). In his subsequent afterword to the book, Said (1994a:341) makes it seem as though it were Lewis who is attacking him. It is somewhat disingenuous to claim that "Lewis has in a sense appointed himself a spokesman for the guild of Orientalists" when his character and scholarship have been totally maligned by Said on numerous occasions in print.

180   Said (1979:317).

181   Said (1979:315); the passage cited is from Lewis (1972:33). It is not clear why Said regards this short paper by Lewis as "the scholarly centerpiece" of the volume, except for his undisguised anatagonism for this historian. Said's critical comments here were given

in two versions of an earlier article (Said 1975b:92–94). Similarly, the 1972 paper by Lewis was republished in later books (1973, 1993b). For a different critique of Lewis's approach to the etymology of Middle Eastern terms for "revolution," see Halliday (1999:204–207).

182   Saghiyya (1995:123n10).

183   Duncanson (1980:201).

184   Said (1979:314). The "one" must be in reference to Said's own reading; the discussion by Lewis carefully provides his historical sources.

185   I do not wish to defend Lewis's specific argument on the evolution of political consciousness in Arab sources, but it is worth noting that at the time he was on record as strongly condemning the prejudicial claim that Arabs and Muslims were incapable of democratic government (Lewis 1964:57), as was Elie Kedourie (1980:37; original, 1956). If short phrases are so prone to condemnation, imagine what Said might have done with Abdallah Laroui's (1976:174) statement that "The Arab world has known but one revolution—the national revolution . . ."

186   Said (1979:315–316).

187   Said (1979:316); he had introduced this example earlier (1975b:91–94).

188   Lewis (1993a:192–193n7) responds by quoting the Duke of Wellington: "If you can believe that, you can believe anything." Victor Brombert (1979:540) brands Said's "irate contention" about Lewis questioning Arab sexual ability as "a travesty of textual explication." "And it is after this performance," states Brombert, "that Said speaks of the 'scandals of 'scholarship'!" As Brombert (1979:538) further suggests, the erotic symbolism of words such as "penetrate" "and embrace," along with the French *fouiller* and *étreindre*, is common practice and not simply related to an imagined Orient. Fedwa Malti-Douglas (1985–86:54) and J. S. F. Parker (1980:10–11) also chide Said for sexualizing the passage by Lewis. Daniel O'Hara (1980:279) notes Said's tendency in the book to see sexual metaphors everywhere. Norman Daniel (1982:214) thinks that the literary passages quoted in *Orientalism* do not illustrate Said's point of a "pervasive motif" of Oriental sexuality. Said ignores the fact that Oriental Jews, as well as Arabs, have been hypersexualized; see Loshitzky (2000:53). For a related, although not sexually explicit, critique of the untranslatability of key Western terms, see Larsen's (1995:234) comments on a contention by M. Finley that the Greek *eleutheria* and Latin *libertas* cannot be freely expressed in Oriental languages, ancient and modern.

189   Lewis (2002a:63). Presumably, in this case the right hand would not know what the left hand had been doing. C. F. Beckingham (1979:564) wonders how Said missed the sensuous implications of Muir's famous *The Caliphate, Its Rise, Decline, and Fall* (originally published in 1883).

190   Said (1979:312) claims that the title of the volume, *Revolution in the Middle East, and Other Case Studies*, is "overtly medical." This is apparently because of the subtitle's mention of "other case studies" as though case studies are exclusive to the medical establishment. The subtitle was in fact added to cover case studies from Eastern Europe, Latin America, and China that are included in a book that is otherwise about the Middle East and North Africa. The one medical allusion I do note in the introduction by Vatikiotis (1972:9) is in reference to the failings of political ideologues of the left and the right: "The activity of politics and its prescriptive variant is not therapeutic

but cathartic. It cannot leave untreated the uncertainties which derive from man's and society's stumbling continuity. Instead it seeks to treat the whole by demanding certainty. This is perhaps the essence of totalitarianism." Surely this is Said's point in condemning the excesses of Orientalism. It is curious that Said does not refer to any of the other articles in the volume apart from the brief introduction by Vatikiotis and the philological piece by Lewis. The other ten articles certainly do not view "revolution" as a disease, but focus on specific historical cases in Algeria, Morocco, Egypt, and Iran, as well as outside the Middle East.

191   Furthermore, Said (1979:313) distorts a straightforward statement by Vatikiotis at the start of a long quote. By subtracting the phrase "In this fundamental sense," which refers to a preceding quote from Camus's *The Rebel*, Said implies that Vatikiotis (1972:11) is accepting the quote as "having 'fundamental sense'" when he is in fact summarizing it. A page later, Said again quotes Vatikiotis misleadingly. He drops the first word ("Rather") in the start of the excerpt. Then he omits about three paragraphs in shoddy aposiopesis to imply that Vatikiotis thinks "revolution" cannot be attained in the Middle East.

192   Vatikiotis (1972:8).

193   Vatikiotis (1972:11). Bryan Turner (1978:67–80) is critical of much of the arguments of both Vatikiotis and Lewis, although his disagreement hinges on how the term "revolution" is defined rather than on sexual hang-ups.

194   Hourani (1972b:67).

195   Said (1979:314).

196   Lewis (1972:33). This important point is elaborated brilliantly by Richard Bulliet (2004:61–73).

197   Gilsenan (2000:152).

198   Lewis (1976b:37). The term "Orientalist" had fallen into disuse among many historians; Franceso Gabrieli (1965:130) earlier predicted that the "old generic term of orientalism was destined to disappear."

199   Said (1976b:38).

200   Said (1994a:342). Similar invective is delivered in Said (1985:6). Said (1994a:336) blames his critics for reducing his thesis to "an attack on Western civilization," but then proceeds to say that it is "entirely correct to read recent Orientalist authorities, such as the almost comically persistent Bernard Lewis" only as "politically motivated and hostile witnesses." Said, states Manzalaoui (1980:838), "too over-polarizes; he omits much and over-emphasizes much, so giving a distorted picture." When Mustapha Marrouchi (2003:41, 2004:77) insists two decades later that Said examines the scholarship of Lewis with a "fine-tooth comb," I think a rake is a more fitting metaphor.

201   Said's commentary at the 1986 MESA meeting, recorded in Viswanathan (2001:298).

202   Marrouchi (1991:66n1). See also A. Ahmad (1992:173), Fathy (2005:158–159), Lockman (2004:130–132, 173–177), Sharabi (1990:12–15), and Tucker (1990:209).

203   Khalidi (2004:209n20).

204   For example, see Sardar (1999:69) and Tibawi (1979:11, 28). See Motabbagani (1994) and Saghiyya (1995:161–162) for discussions of Arab attitudes toward the work of Lewis. Even Arab hip-hop artists have attacked Lewis, as in the Iron Sheik's (2004:49) song "Orientalism," which includes the lines

Empires employ academics
to tell leaders other cultures are nonsense
like Bernard Lewis . . .

205   Nyang and Abed-Rabbo (1984:279). The pairing of academic Bernard Lewis and spy icon James Bond is an odd combination, although they do both speak with British accents.

206   Ibn Warraq (2003:186). He asserts that Lewis has "clearly shown that Islam is incompatible with liberal democracy," but adds that Lewis is basically contradicting himself by allowing for "pluralism and tolerance" in Islam.

207   Mohammed Arkoun (1985–86:96–99) offers a wide-ranging critique of Lewis's views on Islam. Yvonne Haddad (1991:5–6) takes issue in the strongest terms with Lewis's "disingenuous" dismissal of American foreign policy as a cause of Muslim rage. Nasrin Rahimieh (1990:13) and Nabil Matar (2003:xiv) contradict Lewis's claim that Muslims once displayed an "extraordinary reluctance" to travel to Christian Europe. Matar (1998:16) also takes Lewis to task for assuming that only a few European adventurers converted to Islam. Albert Hourani (1991:139–140) points out a strong desire on the part of the Ottomans to know about the West. For example, the famous 1513 map by Piri Reis shows a newly discovered America. Fred Halliday (1999:201) contends that Lewis last wrote about the Middle East substantively in his 1961 *The Emergence of Modern Turkey*, and even that was flawed. For other critical commentaries on the work of Lewis, see Bulliet (2004), Hefner (2001:12), Hirsch (2004), and Tavakoli-Targhi (2001:19–20). It is worth noting that Said (1976a) was not alone in criticizing Lewis's role in coediting the *Cambridge History of Islam*; see Hourani (1972a; 1976:125).

208   Lewis (1998:39). Lewis (2002:6) also refers to Chinese civilization as encompassing "one racial group." Similar facile statements can be found throughout most of Lewis's writings. In his popular *The Middle East and the West*, he assumes that the Middle East has "an unmistakeable character and identity" and then finds the "most striking" characteristic to be the geographical "aridity" of the region; Middle East history is exemplified in Toynbeean style as "conquest from the desert" (Lewis 1964:10).

209   Lewis (1993b:362).

210   The quoted phrase is from Lewis (2002b:3). In the same book, Lewis concludes with the observation that "the suicide bomber may become a metaphor for the whole region" (159). Perhaps, if enough people believe Lewis.

211   Lewis continually speaks of the "infidel West," "the barbarian infidels," "the outer infidels and barbarians," "infidel allies," and "the previously despised infidel" (2002b:12, 13, 21, 22, 25).

212   Lewis (1973:12). My other quotes here come from the succeeding pages of this essay.

213   Richard Fox (1992:145) is right to characterize the kind of scholarship practiced by Lewis as "unreflective opposition." Thierry Hentsch (1992:192) also notes that Lewis refuses to address "the heart" of Said's argument.

214   Lewis (1982a). This was reprinted with minor changes in Lewis (1993a).

215   Lewis (1993a:99). As Phiroze Vasunia (2003:91) observes, this appeal to the Greeks only reinforces Lewis's own blindness to the inevitable politics of knowledge. Unfortunately for Lewis, whose reprint did not involve any rethinking, such a scenario need

not be imagined, for it is precisely the thesis of Martin Bernal (1987). Bernal, dubbed in one review as the Edward Said of ancient history, was influenced by *Orientalism* and has subsequently been approvingly cited by Said (1993:110). In a response to his critics, Bernal (2001:33) notes that he has "important differences" from the approach of Said: "In the first place, his work is literary and allusive, whereas mine is historical and pedestrian. More important, I do not accept his view that Orientalism, or, for that matter, ancient history, is almost entirely self-referential." For an insightful comparison of Bernal and Said, see Berlinerblau (1999:200n28).

216 For example, consider the loaded retort in Lewis's book review (1993a:101): "What, then, is Orientalism? What did the word mean before it was poisoned by the kind of intellectual pollution that in our time has made so many previously useful words unfit for use in rational discourse?"

217 Cole (1995: 510).

218 Hart (2000:5). Bruce Robbins (1994:26), however, suggests that Said opposes the secular to nationalism rather than to religion.

219 Butterworth (1980:176).

220 Ansell-Pearson et al. (1997:9).

221 Bové (2000:1). Such totemic rendering of a literary critic who mainly taught the Western canon into a virtual factotum for all fields borders on the facetious.

222 Frykenberg (1996:286), an evangelical Christian with a sharp ax to grind on anything "postmodern," comments: "But Said's rhetoric is an angry rhetoric. For those who remain attached to the norms of conventional scholarship and its methodologies, it is a polemic blinded by its own rage." Yes, but I would counter that Said writes with a remarkably controlled rage, which is why his polemic has received such a wide audience. However, it is also not hard to find an element of self-pity in Said (see Gordon 1982:111).

223 Said (1979:323–324).

224 Said, in a 1992 interview recorded in Viswanathan (2001:381).

225 In publicly asking for permission to narrate, Said emphasizes with justification that there have been numerous attempts to silence his voice because of his support for Palestine (Said 1994b:x). His extensive corpus, recognized public persona, and secure position as a tenured professor suggest that Said has been able to narrate more than most intellectuals without needing to ask a prejudicial society for permission.

226 Said (1994b:82). Sympathetic readers accept this ideal with admiration; e.g., Merod (2000:115) writes: "It is, in truth, the reach of an amateur, which is to say it is the informed, unimpeded labor of one who cares greatly about his work."

227 Said (1994b:109). In this regard Said is often contrasted with Noam Chomsky, an outspoken public advocate for many of the same controversial stands but whose scholarly work ironically defines a very specific theoretical dogma about language.

228 Said (1983:29). Whereas the abstract is unassailable in a civil society, the concrete poses a problem. Other amateurs can sincerely disagree on who is being the tyrant and who is being abused.

229 Said (1994b:76, 80).

230 Said (1994b:77).

231 Although he is recognized as the most powerful American voice for Palestinians, Said

(quoted in Viswanathan 2001:55) insists that he never accepted "an official role of any sort." He adds: "Sometimes I worry whether that's a kind of irresponsibility that I can afford, thanks to the freedom guaranteed by a professorship at Columbia." Elsewhere, Said (1994b:107–108) insists, quite rightly, that his role in the Palestine National Congress was minimal and never taken by him to be formal.

232 Said (1983:221).

233 David Gordon (1982:108) takes Said to task for assuming that any Middle East expert who acts as a government consultant "necessarily forfeits his credibility."

234 Said (1979:53).

235 Said (1979:4–5; 1994a:331); see also Said (1983:111–118). I note, with irony, that Vico was also the inspiration for the French scholar Renan. Said clings Vico-cariously to the laurels of the earlier Italian humanist to validate his critique of a certain kind of humanity.

236 Said (1983:32).

237 Said (1994b:76).

238 Said (1979:326).

239 Said (1979:326).

240 Said (1979:327). This term is Said's idiosyncratic conflating of the social sciences and the humanities.

241 Geertz's (1968) *Islam Observed* would have been the main anthropological study of Islam at the time of Said's writing. For a critical assessment of this seminal text, see Varisco (2005).

242 Geertz (1983:20).

243 Said (1982:44–46).

244 Rodinson (1987:130). A similar point is made by Carl Steenstrup (1985–86:237), who notes that the Saidian controversy "created the opportunity to haul onto the surface submerged prejudices."

245 Manzalaoui (1980:838) argues that Said does not see the "neophiliac fatuities" in his own work.

246 Ashcroft and Ahluwalia (1999:21–22, 48).

247 Owen (1979:61). Josef van Ess (1980:51) has made the same argument for the scholars Said criticizes: "It is distance which makes the task of a Western Orientalist easier; it permits him to see things more sharply, providing that his being aware of otherness blends with that indispensable sympathy, without which understanding is not possible."

248 In his BBC Reith Lectures, Said (1994b:47) calls exile "one of the saddest fates," implying that it is most often a course determined rather than chosen.

249 Said (1994b:60).

250 Said (1979:25).

251 Said (1993a:xxvi).

252 There is a substantial literature on Said as a Palestinian. His detractors at times deny that he has authentic Palestinian roots, while his admirers praise him as an activist "who has always nurtured his ties to Palestine, returning to his people and land as often and as long as possible" (Alam 2000:33). Valerie Kennedy (2000:5) observes that Said returned to Palestine only a few times after his family left in 1947.

253 Said, in a 1986 interview quoted in Viswanathan (2001:57).

254 Said (1993a:xxvii).

255 See JanMohammed (1992) for a discussion of Said as "specular border intellectual." In the words of Leela Gandhi (1998:132) Said "submits all too easily to an over-valorisation of the unhoused, exilic intellectual," which does not stop Shelley Walia (2001:11) from asking "And what better example of a migrant than Said?" Anouar Majid (2000:28) remains unconvinced of Said's valorization of exile for the intellectual as critic. Paul Armstrong (2003:118–119) also criticizes Said's privileging of his exile status. In an otherwise sympathetic review, Martha Hildreth (1995:71) faults Said for not addressing the implications of his "subject position" as an intellectual situated in the United States. In his selection of America's public intellectuals, Richard Posner (2001:32n34) singles out Said, a tenured Columbia University professor, as an unconvincing "outsider." Richard Armstrong (2005:144), after examining Said's identification with Jewish intellectuals, warns: "But the Jews whose work forms the foundation of his later humanism were *refugees*, and for that reason Said's humanism will have to be defended in the future from accusations of being merely a salaried alienation."

256 Said (1983:7). This quote is well traveled, with Said acknowledging it from Auerbach's *Mimesis*. For example, Fred Dallmayr (1996) uses it as an epigraph.

257 See Said (1983:5–9). Stuart Burrows (1999:50) views *Orientalism* as "both corollary and antidote" to Auerbach's *Mimesis*. Aamir Mufti (2000:256) discusses the impact of Auerbach on Said, arguing that both ask the same fundamental question: "How is it possible that a conception of culture meant to embody the dignity of the victims of fascism could be at the same time ethnocentric and, in fact, fearful of the coming challenge to European cultural supremacy?" In validating Said's insistence that his own Palestinian diaspora mirrors the Jewish diaspora, exemplified here by Auerbach's temporary sojourn in Istanbul, Mufti ignores a critical but haunting similarity: neither man recognizes a viable home for himself outside the Western academy. H. D. Harootunian (2005:433) argues that "Said's lifelong identification with Auerbach often worked against his best impulses." For further critique of Said's interpretation of Auerbach, see Bové (1986:189).

258 Said (1983:8).

259 Von Grunebaum (1962:472); he then quotes, on the same page, a statement by Hisham Sharabi on the need of Arab intellectuals to escape the "'other's' understanding." Sharabi, an Arab scholar writing about Arab intellectuals well before *Orientalism*, is not cited by Said in any of his major texts.

260 The phrase is from Said (2004:2).

261 Said (1994b:36).

262 Said (1994c:38).

263 Said (2002:4).

264 Said (2002:11).

265 P. Williams (2001:xxv).

266 Said (1985:1).

267 Said (1994a:344). I invite the reader to examine the thorough reviews by Daniel (1982), Kerr (1980), Malti-Douglas (1979), Musallam (1979), Owen (1979), and Winder (1981) to see if all is banal. I believe Joseph Massad (2004:8) is wrong in assuming that the

negative reaction to *Orientalism* was due to readers' perception of "the presumed inso-lence of subjecting white Europeans to an Oriental gaze." It is rather Said's misread-ing of history that infuriated many who knew that history firsthand.

268   Said (2003:xx). In this preface Said appears content to remember his book primarily as "a source of amazement" (xv).

269   Huggan (2005:128).

270   The first is in reference to Bernard Lewis (Said 1994a:342), the second responding to Robert Griffin (Said 1989a:643).

271   Said (1994a:330). None of the numerous misreadings, such as the mistranslation of a passage by Goethe, are admitted or addressed in the afterword.

272   Said (1983:26; 1994a:329).

273   Marrouchi (2004:55) .

274   Shulevitz (2001:39).

275   Gandhi (1998:73). Given that "there is no theory capable of covering, closing off, pre-dicting all the situations in which it might be useful" (Said 1983:241), then it is the critic's job "to provide resistance to theory" (Said 1983:242). The one thing Said rules out for theory—and misses out on in methodology—is that it might just be probable enough to go beyond the roving amateur stage.

276   Said, quoted in Scott (1998).

277   Rubin (2003:863).

278   Woodcock (1980:303).

279   Docherty (1990:210).

280   Hussein (2002:210). Hussein also praises *Orientalism*'s "theoretical rigor and sophis-tication" (230), which he argues has been largely ignored by critics.

281   Testimonies to Said's role as teacher and mentor include that of Mustapha Marrouchi (2004:56–57). As relentless as Said could be as a critic, he also greatly encouraged many younger scholars to be as critical as he was, no matter what the consequences. Anthropologist Diane King (2003:9) notes that Said once told her to allow her Kurdish friends' voices to be heard even though they supported the American war in Iraq that he personally did not.

282   Chandra Mohanty's critique of a Foucaldian notion of oppression is applicable to Said's essentialist reduction of Orientalism to a homogenized West vs. East. "The major prob-lem with such a definition of power is that it locks all revolutionary struggles into binary structures—possessing power versus being powerless" (Mohanty 1994:213).

283   Van Nieuwenhuijze (1979:11).

284   Dennis Porter (1991:5) notes that Said offers only a pious wish for alternatives to Ori-entalism. Thomas Greene (1979:581) criticizes Said's failure to provide a "theory of cross-cultural understanding." For similar criticisms, see Amin (1989:102), Butterworth (1980:175), Gare (1995:310), Halbfass (1997:7), Majeed (1992:198), Rassam (1980:508), Sardar (1999:74), Weeks (1998:46–47), and Young (2001:391). Joseph Massoud (2004:11) is correct to note that the legacy of *Orientalism* has not been Said's method, but this is because of its faults rather than being misunderstood in Middle East studies.

285   Joseph (1980:948).

286   Lindholm (1996:6).

287   Ahmed (1992:185). Catherine Gimelli Martin (1990:526) makes a similar point: "Since

he [Said] consistently refuses to supply the means or even postulate the possibility of transcultural translation, his project is in its own terms doomed from the start." What is doomed, however, is not the project itself—if that be the needed criticism of the excesses of establishment representation—but Said's ability to do it only as an accusatory polemic.

288 Gran (1980:330).

289 Chow (2002:104). As JanMohamed (1992:105) notes, the missing ingredient in *Orientalism* is an "alternative positivity."

290 R. King (1999:3).

291 Berkhofer (1995:198). As Meyda Yegenoglu (1998:18) comments, "Said's attempt to understand the constitutive power of Orientalist discourse is not very convincing at times, for his analysis poses a set of theoretical problems that he does not fully engage with."

292 Ashcroft and Ahluwalia (1999:78). Ernest Wilson (1981:64) also notes that it is "perfectly legitimate" for Said to focus on the oppressors, but that this "leaves the reader with little vision of a reconstructed future vision of a truly liberated society."

293 Makdisi (1998:216n64).

294 Brennan (2001:95).

295 Said (1983:172).

296 Said (1983:172).

297 Laroui (1976:ix–x).

298 Huntington (1993:25).

299 Huntington (1993:31).

300 Huntington (1993:40).

301 Ajami (1993:3).

302 Kilpatrick (1993:22).

303 Said (2001a). For other critical accounts of Huntington's thesis, see Bulliet (2004:1–5), Lockman (2004:142–143) and several of the articles in Qureshi and Sells (2003). Sadiq Jalal al-'Azm (2005:15) offers a more nuanced approach in noting that there is already a weak sense of the "clash" in place since Islamic extremists buy into the same logic. It is worth noting that Huntington had earlier in 1968 used *Foreign Affairs* to justify the large-scale American bombing of Vietnam.

304 Bulliet (2004:9).

305 Said provides a wider list, including imperialism, positivism, utopianism, historicism, and Marxism, later in *Orientalism* (Said 1979:43).

306 Fischer (1970:151) critiques earlier historians such as Spengler and Arnold Toynbee for succumbing to the fallacy of archetypes, which "consists in conceptualizing change in terms of the re-enactment of primordial archetypes which exist outside of time." Much of what Said finds faulty in Orientalist reconstructions of history had already been discussed and dismissed in historiography.

307 Said (1979:206) implies that Cuvier's and Gobineau's racial formulations fit with what he calls a "second-order Darwinism," but in fact Darwin wrote against such classifications.

308 Said (1979:16). Said (1979:263) cautions that no scholar is a perfect representative of a national type, but then proceeds to argue that "in so relatively insulated and specialized a tradition as Orientalism, I think there is in each scholar some awareness, partly conscious and partly non-conscious, of national tradition, if not of national ideology."

309   Said (1979:16).

310   Said (1979:263).

311   It is tempting to ask if the subaltern can speak without speaking of Spivak's "Can the subaltern speak?" Leela Gandhi (1998:2) comments: "Utterly unanswerable, half-serious and half parodic, this question circulates around the self-conscious scene of postcolonial texts, theory, conferences and conversation." Also relevant is Bruce Robbins's (1992a:50) brilliant paradox: "The critic who accuses another of speaking for the subaltern by denying that subalterns can speak for themselves, for example, is of course also claiming to speak for them." A further paradoxical question is whether subalterns are no longer "sub" when they do speak. And what happens to those who might now be called snub-alterns, as they have tenured positions in Ivy League institutions rather than Third-World salaries? "To put it crudely," as Russell Jacoby (1995:33–34) does so well, "as professors at Western universities, do the post-colonial theorists live off the colonies they decry?" Subaltern studies has been praised by Said (1988a), despite the implicit critique that its emergence poses for Said's muted-Orient thesis. Scholars in Middle East studies, observes Sabra Webber (1997:11) have largely ignored the field.

312   Berlinerblau (1999:195).

313   Young (2001:392).

Bibliography

Abaza, Mona, and Georg Stauth

    1988   Occidental Reason, Orientalism, Islamic Fundamentalism: A Critique. *International Sociology* 3:343–364.

Abdel Malek, Anouar

    1963   Orientalism in Crisis. *Diogenes* 44:104–112.

    1981   *Civilisations and Social Theory. Volume 1 of Social Dialectics.* Albany: State University of New York Press.

Abu El-Haj, Nadia

    2001   *Facts on the Ground: Archaeological Practice and Territorial Self-Fashioning in Israeli Society.* Chicago: University of Chicago Press.

    2005   Edward Said and the Political Present. *American Ethnologist* 32(4):538–555.

AbuKhalil, Asʿad

    2001   Orientalism in the Arab Context. In Aruri and Shuraydi 2001, 100–117.

Abu-Laban, Yasmeen

    2001   Humanizing the Oriental: Edward Said and Western Scholarly Discourse. In Aruri and Shuraydi 2001, 74–85.

Abu-Lughod, Ibrahim

    1982   In Memoriam: A. L. Tibawi (1910–1981). *Arab Studies Quarterly* 4:i–ii, v–viii.

Abu-Lughod, Lila

    1990   Anthropology's Orient: The Boundaries of Theory on the Arab World. In Sharabi, editor, 1990, 81–131.

    2001   Orientalism and the Middle East in Middle East Studies. *Feminist Studies* 27:101–113.

    2005   About Politics, Palestine, and Friendship: A Letter to Edward Said from Egypt. *Critical Inquiry* 31:381–388.

Adams, Robert M.

    1971   The Sense of Verification: Pragmatic Commonplaces about Literary Criticism. In Clifford Geertz, editor, *Myth, Symbol, and Culture*, 203–214. New York: W. W. Norton.

Adnan-Adivar, Abdülhak

    1953   A Turkish Account of Orientalism. *The Muslim World* 43:261–282.

Adonis

    1974   *Al-Thabit wa-al-mutahawwil.* Beirut: Dar al-ʿAwda.

    1990   *An Introduction to Arab Poetics.* Translated by Catherine Cobham. Austin: University of Texas Press.

Ahiska, Meltem

2003   Occidentalism: The Historical Fantasy of the Modern. *The South Atlantic Quarterly* 102(2/3):351–379.

Ahmad, Aijaz

1992   *In Theory: Classes, Nations, Literatures*. London: Verso.

1993   A Response. *Public Culture* 6:143–191.

2000   The Future of English Studies in South Asia. In Niaz Zaman, Firdous Azim, and Shawkat Hussein, editors, *Colonial and Post-Colonial Encounters*, 36–55. New Delhi: Manohar.

Ahmad, Jalal Al-i

1984   *Occidentosis: A Plague from the West*. Translated by R. Campbell. Berkeley: Mizan.

Ahmed, Akbar

1992   *Postmodernism and Islam*. London: Routledge.

Ajami, Fouad

1993   The Summoning. *Foreign Affairs* 72(4):2–9.

Akbari, Suzanne Conklin

2000   From Due East to True North: Orientalism and Orientation. In Jeffrey Jerome Cohen, editor, *The Postcolonial Middle Ages*, 19–34. New York: St. Martin's.

Alam, Fakrul

2000   Edward Said and the Counter-Discourse of Post-Colonial Intellectuals. In Niaz Zaman, Firdous Azim, and Shawkat Hussein, editors, *Colonial and Post-Colonial Encounters*, 15–35. New Delhi: Manohar.

Alatas, Syed Hussein

1977   *The Myth of the Lazy Native*. London: Cass.

Alexander, Boyd, editor

1954   *The Journal of William Beckford in Portugal and Spain 1787–1788*. London: Rupert Hart-Davies.

Alexander, Edmund

1989   Professor of Terror. *Commentary* 88 (August):49–50.

Algar, Hamid

1971   The Problem of Orientalists. *Islamic Literature* 17(2):95–106.

1984   Introduction. In Ahmad 1984, 9–21.

Alleaume, Ghislaine

1982   L'Orientalisme dans le miroir de la littérature Arabe. *British Journal of Middle Eastern Studies* 9:5–13.

Allen, Brian T.

2000   "The Garments of Instruction from the Wardrobe of Pleasure": American Orientalist Painting in the 1870s and 1880s. In Holly Edwards, editor, *Noble Dreams, Wicked Pleasures: Orientalism in America, 1870–1930*, 59–75. Princeton, NJ: Princeton University Press.

Almond, Philip C.

1988   *The British Discovery of Buddhism*. Cambridge: Cambridge University Press.

American Oriental Society

> 1843   Constitution of the American Oriental Society. *Journal of the American Oriental Society* 1(1):vi–viii.

ʿAmil, Mahdi

> 1985   *Marks fi istishraq Adward Saʿid.* Beirut: Dar al-Farabi.

Amin, Samir

> 1978   *Arab Nation.* London: Zed.

> 1989[1988]   *Eurocentrism.* Translated by Russell Moore. New York: Monthly Review Press.

Amir, Javed

> 1998   Intolerance of Islam. *Hamdard Islamicus* 21(1):1–5.

Amireh, Amal

> 2002   Framing Nawal El Saadawi: Arab Feminism in a Transnational World. In Theresa Saliba, Carolyn Allen, and Judith A. Howard, editors, *Gender, Politics, and Islam*, 269–303. Chicago: University of Chicago Press.

Anawati, George C.

> 1970   La civilisation musulmane dans l'oeuvre du professor Gustav von Grunebaum. *Mélanges de l'Institut Dominicain d'Études Orientales* 10:37–82.

Anderson, Benedict

> 1991   *Imagined Communities: Reflections on the Origin and Spread of Nationalism.* Revised Edition. London: Verso.

Ansari, Humayun

> 2004   *"The Infidel Within": Muslims in Britain since 1800.* London: Hurst.

Ansell-Pearson, Keith, Benita Parry, and Judith Squires, editors

> 1997   *Cultural Readings of Imperialism: Edward Said and the Gravity of History.* New York: St. Martin's.

Antoun, Richard

> 1976   Anthropology. In Leonard Binder, editor, *The Study of the Middle East*, 137–213. New York: John Wiley and Sons.

Appiah, Kwame Anthony

> 1991   Is the Post- in Postmodernism the Post- in Postcolonial? *Critical Inquiry* 17:336–357.

Apter, Emily

> 1994   Acting Out Orientalism: Sapphic Theatricality in Turn-of-the-Century Paris. *L'Esprit Créateur* 34(2):102–116.

Arac, Jonathan

> 1980   Review of *Orientalism*. *Clio* 9(3):465–468.

> 2000   Criticism between Opposition and Counterpoint. In Bové, editor, 2000, 66–77.

Arberry, Arthur John

> 1943   *British Orientalists.* London: William Collins.

> 1960   *Oriental Essays: Portraits of Seven Scholars.* London: George Allen and Unwin.

Argyrou, Vassos

> 1999   Sameness and the Ethnological Will to Meaning. *Current Anthropology* 40[supplement]:29–41.

Aristotle

    1971   *Aristotle: On Man in the Universe*. New York: Gramercy Books.

    1991   *The Art of Rhetoric*. Translated by H. C. Lawson-Tancred. London: Penguin.

Arkoun, Mohammed

    1964   L'Islam moderne vu par le professeur G. E. von Grunebaum. *Arabica* 11: 113–126.

    1984   *Pour une critique de la raison islamique*. Paris: Édition Maisonneuve et Larose.

    1985–86   Discours islamiques, discours Orientalistes et pensée scientifique. *Comparative Civilizations Review* 13–14:90–110.

    1994   *Rethinking Islam: Common Questions, Uncommon Answers*. Boulder: Westview.

Armitage, David

    1998   Literature and Empire. In Nicholas Canny, editor, *The Oxford History of the British Empire. Volume I. The Origins of Empire: British Overseas Enterprise to the Close of the Seventeenth Century*, 99–123. Oxford: Oxford University Press.

Armstrong, Karen

    1992   *Holy War: The Crusades and Their Impact on Today's World*. New York: Anchor Books.

Armstrong, Nancy

    1990   The Occidental Alice. *differences: A Journal of Feminist Cultural Studies* 2(2):3–40.

Armstrong, Paul B.

    1991   Play and Cultural Difference. *Kenyon Review* 13(1):157–171.

    2003   Being "Out of Place": Edward W. Said and the Contradictions of Cultural Differences. *Modern Language Quarterly* 64(1):97–121.

Armstrong, Richard

    2005   Last Words: Said, Freud, and Traveling Theory. *Alif* 25:120–148.

Aruri, Naseer, and M. A. Shuraydi, editors

    2001   *Revising Culture, Reinventing Peace: The Influence of Edward Said*. New York: Olive Branch.

Asad, Muhammad

    1954   *The Road to Mecca*. New York: Simon and Schuster.

Asad, Talal

    1980   Review of *Orientalism. English Historical Review* 95:648–649.

Ashcroft, Bill, Gareth Griffiths, and Helen Tiffin

    1989   *The Empire Writes Back: Theory and Practice in Post-colonial Literature*. London: Routledge.

    1998   *Key Concepts in Post-Colonial Studies*. London: Routledge.

Ashcroft, Bill, and Pal Ahluwalia

    1999   *Edward Said: The Paradox of Identity*. London: Routledge.

Asín Palacios, Miguel

    1919   *La Escatología Musulmana en la Divina Comedia*. Madrid: E. Maestre.

    1926   *Islam and the Divine Comedy*. Translated by Harold Sunderland. London: Murray.

Assad, Thomas J.

    1964   *Three Victorian Travellers: Burton, Blunt, Doughty*. London: Routledge and Kegan Paul.

Atiyah, Edward

    1955   *The Arabs*. Baltimore: Penguin.

Atkinson, Paul, and Amanda Coffey

    1995   Realism and Its Discontents: On the Crisis of Cultural Representation in Ethnographic Texts. In Barbara Adam and Stuart Allan, editors, *Theorizing Culture: An Interdisciplinary Critique after Postmodernism*, 41–57. New York: New York University Press.

Austen, Jane

    1933   *The Complete Novels of Jane Austen*. New York: Modern Library.

Ayalon, David

    1965   Al-Djabarti. *The Encyclopaedia of Islam*, New Edition. II:355–357. Leiden: Brill.

al-ʿAzm, Sadiq Jalal

    1984   Orientalism and Orientalism in Reverse. In Jon Rothschild, editor, *Forbidden Agendas: Intolerance and Defiance in the Middle East*, 349–376. London: Al Saqi.

    2005   Islam, Terrorism, and the West. *Comparative Studies of South Asia, Africa and the Middle East* 25(1):6–15.

Al-Azmeh, Aziz

    1984   The Articulation of Orientalism. In Afaf Hussain, Robert Olson, and Jamil Qureshi, editors, *Orientalism, Islam, and Islamists*, 89–124. Brattleboro, VT: Amana.

Baderoon, Gadeba

    2002   Shooting the East / Veils and Masks: Uncovering Orientalism in South African Media. *African and Asian Studies* 1(4):367–384.

Bakshi, Parminder Kaur

    1990   Homosexuality and Orientalism: Edward Carpenter's Journey to the East. *Prose Studies* 13(1):151–177.

Baldick, Chris

    1996   *Criticism and Literary Theory 1890 to the Present*. London: Longman.

Barakat, Halim

    1990   Beyond the Always and Never: A Critique of Social Psychological Interpretations of Arab Society and Culture. In Sharabi, editor, 1990, 132–159.

Baratta, Giorgio

    1999   The Individual and the World: From Marx to Gramsci to Said. *Socialism and Democracy* 13(1):31–44.

Barenboim, Daniel

    2003   Remembering Edward Said. *The Electronic Intifada*, September 26. Electronic document, www.danielbarenboim.com/journal_remembering.htm, accessed July 2006.

Barfoot, C. C.

    1998   English Romantic Poets and the "Free-Floating Orient." In Barfoot and D'haen 1998, 65–96.

Barfoot, C. C., and Theo D'haen, editors

    1998   *Oriental Prospects: Western Literature and the Lure of the East*. Amsterdam: Rodopi.

Barthes, Roland

    1972[1957]   *Mythologies*. Translated by A. Lavers. London: Cape.

    1982[1970]   *Empire of Signs*. Translated by Richard Howard. New York: Hill and Wang.

Bates, Daniel, and Amal Rassam

    2001   *Peoples and Cultures of the Middle East*. Second Edition. Upper Saddle River, NJ: Prentice-Hall.

Bauerlein, Mark

    1997   *Literary Criticism, an Autopsy*. Philadelphia: University of Pennsylvania Press.

Bawer, Bruce

    2002   Edward W. Said, Intellectual. *The Hudson Review* 54(4):620–634.

Bayat, Asef

    2001   Studying Middle Eastern Societies: Imperatives and Modalities of Thinking Comparatively. *The Middle East Studies Association Bulletin* 35(2):151–158.

Bayoumi, Moustafa

    2005   Reconciliation without Duress: Said, Adorno, and the Autonomous Intellectual. *Alif* 25:46–64.

Bayoumi, Moustafa, and Andrew Rubin, editors

    2000   *The Edward Said Reader*. New York: Vintage.

Beard, James

    1959   Critical Problems in the Orientalism of Western Poetry. In Horst Frenz, editor, *Asia and the Humanities: Papers Presented at the Second Conference on Oriental-Western Literary and Cultural Relations Held at Indiana University*, 38–57. Comparative Literature Committee, Indiana University. Danville, IL: Interstate Printers and Publishers.

Beard, Michael

    1979   Between West and World. *Diacritics* 9(4):2–12.

    1980   Review of *Orientalism*. *World Literature* 54(1):177.

Beatty, Bernard

    1999   Calvin in Islam: A Reading of *Lara* and *The Giaour*. *Romanticism* 5(1):70–86.

Beaulieu, Jill, and Mary Roberts, editors

    2002   *Orientalism's Interlocutors: Painting, Architecture, Photography*. Durham, NC: Duke University Press.

Beckford, William

    1971   *Vathek*. New York: Ballantine.

Beckingham, Charles F.

    1976   Misconceptions of Islam: Medieval and Modern. *Journal of the Royal Society of Arts* 124:606–611.

    1979   Review of *Orientalism*. *Bulletin of the School of Oriental and African Studies* 42(3):562–564.

    1985–86   Some Examples of Myopia. *Comparative Civilizations Review* 13–14:56–61.

Behdad, Ali

    1994a   *Belated Travelers: Orientalism in the Age of Colonial Dissolution*. Durham, NC: Duke University Press.

    1994b   Orientalism after *Orientalism*. *L'Esprit Créateur* 34(2):3–11.

2005   Edward Said: The Founder of Postcolonial Discursivity. *Amerasia Journal* 35(1):10–16.

Beidelman, Thomas O.

1974   *W. Robertson Smith and the Sociological Study of Religion*. Chicago: University of Chicago Press.

Beit-Hallahmi, Benjamin

1980   Review of *Orientalism*. *Journal for the Scientific Study of Religion* 19:69–70.

Ben Jelloun, Mohammed

2002   Agonistic Islam. *Jouvert: A Journal of Postcolonial Studies* 6(3). Electronic document, http://152.1.96.5/jouvert/v613/agon.htm, accessed April 2003.

Benjamin, Roger

1997   The Oriental Mirage. In Benjamin, editor, 1997, 7–31.

2003   *Orientalist Aesthetics: Art, Colonialism, and French Africa, 1880–1930*. Berkeley: University of California Press.

Benjamin, Roger, editor

1997   *Orientalism: Delacroix to Klee*. Sydney: Art Gallery of New South Wales.

Berger, Morroe

1964   *The Arab World Today*. Garden City, NY: Anchor.

1976   Letter to the Editor, *Orientalism*. *New York Times Book Review*, October 16, 36.

Berkhofer, Robert F.

1995   *Beyond the Great Story: History as Text and Discourse*. Cambridge, MA: Belknap.

Berlin, Isaiah

1976   *Vico and Herder: Two Studies in the History of Ideas*. New York: Viking.

Berlinerblau, Jacques

1999   *Heresy in the University: The* Black Athena *Controversy and the Responsibilities of American Intellectuals*. New Brunswick, NJ: Rutgers University Press.

Berman, Nina

1997   *Orientalismus, Kolonialismus und Moderne: Zum Bild des Orients in der deutschensprachigen Kultur um 1900*. Stuttgart: M & P.

2005   Ottoman Shock-and-Awe and the Rise of Protestantism: Luther's Reactions to the Ottoman Invasions of the Early Sixteenth Century. *Seminar—A Journal of Germanic Studies* 41(3):226–245.

Bernal, Martin

1987   *Black Athena: The Afroasiatic Roots of Classical Civilization. Volume 1, The Fabrication of Ancient Greece, 1785–1985*. New Brunswick, NJ: Rutgers University Press.

2001   *Black Athena Writes Back*. Durham, NC: Duke University Press.

Bernstein, Matthew, and Gaylyn Studlar, editors

1997   *Visions of the East: Orientalism in Film*. New Brunswick, NJ: Rutgers University Press.

Bernstein, Richard

2003   Edward W. Said, Literary Critic and Advocate for Palestinian Independence, Dies at 67. *New York Times*, September 26, A23.

Bhabha, Homi

    1986   The Other Question: Difference, Discrimination and the Discourse of Colonialism. In Francis Barker, Peter Hulme, Margaret Iversen, and Diana Loxley, editors, *Literature, Politics and Theory*, 148–172. London: Methuen.

    1994   *The Location of Culture*. London: Routledge.

Bhatnagar, Rashmi

    1986   Uses and Limits of Foucault: A Study of the Theme of Origins in Edward Said's *Orientalism*. *Social Scientist* (Delhi) 16(7):3–22.

Biddick, Kathleen

    1994   Bede's Blush: Postcards from Bali, Bombay, Palo Alto. In John Van Engen, editor, *The Past and Future of Medieval Studies*, 16–44. Notre Dame, IN: University of Notre Dame Press.

    2000a   Coming Out of Exile: Dante on the Orient Express. In Jeffrey Jerome Cohen, editor, *The Postcolonial Middle Ages*, 35–52. New York: St. Martin's.

    2000b   Coming Out of Exile: Dante on the Orient(alism) Express. *The American Historical Review* 105:1234–1249.

Biddiss, Michael D.

    1981   Review of *Orientalism*. *French Studies* 35:372–373.

Bill, James, and Carl Leiden

    1974   *The Middle East: Politics and Power*. Boston: Allyn and Bacon.

Binder, Leonard

    1988   *Islamic Liberalism: A Critique of Development Ideologies*. Chicago: University of Chicago Press.

Binder, Leonard, editor

    1976   *The Study of the Middle East: Research and Scholarship in the Humanities and Social Sciences*. New York: John Wiley and Sons.

al-Bitar, Nadim

    1982   *Hudud al-huwiyya al-qawmiya*. Beirut: Dar al-Wahda.

Blank, Jonah

    2001   *Mullahs on the Mainframe: Islam and Modernity among the Daudi Bohras*. Chicago: University of Chicago Press.

Blanks, David R., and Michael Frassetto, editors

    1999   *Western Views of Islam in Medieval and Early Modern Europe*. New York: St. Martin's.

Bloch, Marc

    1953   *The Historian's Craft*. New York: Vintage.

Blunt, Anne, and Wilfrid Scawen Blunt

    1879   *Bedouin Tribes of the Euphrates*. 2 volumes. London: John Murray.

    1881   *A Pilgrimage to Nejd*. London: John Murray.

    1903   *The Seven Golden Odes of Pagan Arabia, Known also as the Moallakat*. London: Chiswick Press.

Blunt, Wilfrid Scawen

    1882   *The Future of Islam*. London: Kegan Paul, Trench.

    1922[1907]   *Secret History of the English Occupation of Egypt*. New York: Knopf.

    1923   *My Diaries, 1888–1914*. 2 volumes. New York: Knopf.

Blythe, Martin
>1993 "What's in a Name?" Film Culture and the Self/Other Question. In Hamid Naficy and Teshome H. Gabriel, editors, *Otherness and the Media: The Ethnography of the Imagined and the Imaged*, 221–231. Chur, Switzerland: Harwood Academic.

Boehmer, Elleke
>1995 *Colonial and Postcolonial Literature: Migrant Metaphors*. Oxford: Oxford University Press.

Bohrer, Frederick N.
>1988 Review of Lynne Thornton, *Women as Portrayed in Orientalist Painting*. *Art Journal* 47(1):50–51.
>2003 *Orientalism and Visual Culture: Imagining Mesopotamia in Nineteenth-Century Europe*. Cambridge: Cambridge University Press.

Boon, James A.
>1982 *Other Tribes, Other Scribes: Symbolic Anthropology in the Comparative Study of Cultures, Histories, Religions, and Texts*. Cambridge: Cambridge University Press.

Boone, Joseph A.
>1995 Vacation Cruises; or, the Homoerotics of Orientalism. *Publications of the Modern Language Association of America* 110(1):89–107.

Bosworth, C. E.
>1977 Orientalism and Orientalists. In Diana Grimwood-Jones, Derek Hopwood, and J. D. Pearson, editors, *Arab Islamic Bibliography: The Middle East Library Committee Guide*, 148–156. Atlantic Highlands, NJ: Humanities Press.

Boulainvilliers, Henri de
>1731 *The Life of Mahomet*. London: W. Hinchliffe.

Boullata, Issa J.
>1990 *Trends and Issues in Contemporary Arab Thought*. Albany: SUNY Press.

Bové, Paul A.
>1986 *Intellectuals in Power*. New York: Columbia University Press.
>2000 Introduction. In Bové, editor, 2000, 1–8. Durham, NC: Duke University Press.

Bové, Paul A., editor
>2000 *Edward Said and the Work of the Critic: Speaking Truth to Power*. Durham, NC: Duke University Press.

Boyne, Roy, and Ali Rattansi
>1990 The Theory and Politics of Postmodernism: By Way of an Introduction. In Roy Boyne and Ali Rattansi, editors, *Postmodernism and Society*, 1–45. New York: St. Martin's.

Bracken, Christopher
>1998 Postcolonialism. In Paul Bouissac, editor, *Encyclopedia of Semiotics*, 505–506. Oxford: Oxford University Press.

Brahimi, Denise
>1982 *Arabes des lumières et bédouins romantiques*. Paris: Le Sycomore.

Brandabur, Clare

    2003   Hitchens Smears Edward Said: Responding to the Words of a Weasel. *CounterPunch*, September 19. Electronic document, www.counterpunch.org/brandabur09192003.html, accessed March 2004.

Brantlinger, Patrick

    1990   *Rule of Darkness: British Literature and Imperialism, 1830–1914.* Ithaca, NY: Cornell University Press.

    1992   Nations and Novels: Disraeli, George Eliot and Orientalism. *Victorian Studies* 35(3):255–275.

Braude, Benjamin

    1997   The Sons of Noah and the Construction of Ethnic and Geographic Identities in the Medieval and Early Modern Periods. *The William and Mary Quarterly* 3rd Series 54(1):103–142.

Breasted, James Henry

    1919   The Place of the Near Orient in the Career of Man and the Task of the American Orientalist. *Journal of the American Oriental Society* 39:159–184.

Breckenridge, Carol A., and Peter van der Veer

    1993   Orientalism and the Postcolonial Predicament. In Breckenridge and van der Veer, editors, 1993, 1–19.

Breckenridge, Carol A., and Peter van der Veer, editors

    1993   *Orientalism and the Postcolonial Predicament: Perspectives on South Asia.* Philadelphia: University of Pennsylvania Press.

Breisach, Ernst

    2003   *On the Future of History: The Postmodernist Challenge and its Aftermath.* Chicago: University of Chicago Press.

Brennan, Timothy

    1992   Places of Mind, Occupied Lands: Edward Said and Philology. In Sprinker, editor, 1992, 74–95. Oxford: Blackwell.

    2000   The Illusion of a Future: Orientalism as Traveling Theory. *Critical Inquiry* 26(3):558–583.

    2001   Angry Beauty and Literary Love: An Orientalism for All Time. In Aruri and Shuraydi 2001, 86–99.

    2004   Edward Said and Comparative Literature. *Journal of Palestine Studies* 33(3):23–37.

    2005   Resolution. *Critical Inquiry* 31:406–418.

Brockman, Harold A. N.

    1956   *The Caliph of Fonthill.* London: Werner Laurie.

Brodie, Fawn M.

    1971   *The Devil Drives: A Life of Sir Richard Burton.* Harmondsworth, UK: Penguin.

Brogan, Terry V. F.

    1996   PRE(*Till We have Faces*)Face: Culture, Poetry, the Other, "Sexy Ideas," "Clerical Work," and Genuine Savagery. In T. V. F. Brogan, editor, *The Princeton Handbook of Multicultural Poetries*, v–xiii. Princeton, NJ: Princeton University Press.

Brombert, Victor

    1979   Orientalism and the Scandals of Scholarship. *The American Scholar* 48: 532–542. [review]

Brower, D. R., and E. J. Lazzerini, editors

    1997   *Russia's Orient: Imperial Borderlands and Peoples, 1700–1917.* Bloomington: Indiana University Press.

Brown, James

    1999   The Solitude of Edward Said: The Fate of Gibb, Lane and Massignon in *Orientalism. Economy and Society* 28:550–569.

Brown, Keith, and Dimitrios Theodossopoulos

    2004   Others' Others: Talking about Stereotypes and Constructions of Otherness in Southeast Europe. *History and Anthropology* 15(1):3–14.

Brown, L. Carl

    1985–86   Movies and the Middle East. *Comparative Civilizations Review* 13–14:17–35.

Browne, Edward G.

    1956[1902–1924]   *A Literary History of Persia.* 4 volumes. Cambridge: Cambridge University Press.

Buaben, Jabal Muhammad

    1996   *Image of the Prophet Muhammad in the West: A Study of Muir, Margoliouth and Watt.* Leicester: Islamic Foundation.

Bulliet, Richard W.

    1994   Orientalism and Medieval Islamic Studies. In John Van Engen, editor, *The Past and Future of Medieval Studies*, 94–104. Notre Dame, IN: University of Notre Dame Press.

    1996   Historiography. In Reeva S. Simon, Philip Mattar, and Richard W. Bulliet, editors, *Encyclopedia of the Modern Middle East*, 2:809–810. New York: Macmillan Reference.

    2004   *The Case for Islamo-Christian Civilization.* New York: Columbia University Press.

Bullock, Katherine

    2002   *Rethinking Muslim Women and the Veil: Challenging Historical and Modern Stereotypes.* Herndon, VA: International Institute of Islamic Thought.

Buonaventura, Wendy

    1998   *Serpent of the Nile: Women and Dance in the Arab World.* New York: Interlink.

Burke, Edmund, III

    1993   Introduction: Marshall G. S. Hodgson and World History. In Marshall Hodgson, *Rethinking World History: Essays on Islam, Europe and World History*, ix–xxi. Cambridge: Cambridge University Press.

    1998a   Orientalism and World History: Representing Middle Eastern Nationalism and Islamism in the Twentieth Century. *Theory and Society* 27:489–507.

    1998b   Theorizing the Histories of Colonialism and Nationalism in the Arab Maghrib. *Arab Studies Quarterly* 20(2):5–19.

Burkert, Walter

    1992   *The Orientalizing Revolution: Near Eastern Influence on Greek Culture in the Early Archaic Age.* Cambridge, MA: Harvard University Press.

Burrows, Stuart
    1999   Books of the Century. *New Statesman* 12(536):50.

Burton, Antoinette
    1998   *At the Heart of Empire: Indians and the Colonial Encounter in Late-Victorian Britain.* Berkeley: University of California Press.

Burton, Lady Isabel
    1897   *The Romance of Isabel, Lady Burton.* 2 volumes. New York: Dodd, Mead.

Burton, Jonathan
    2000   Anglo-Ottoman Relations and the Image of the Turk in Tamburlaine. *Journal of Medieval and Early Modern Studies* 30(1):125–156.

Burton, Richard Francis
    1885   *The Book of the Thousand Nights and a Night.* 10 volumes. The Burton Club.

    1886–1888   *Supplemental Nights to the Book of the Thousand and One Nights with Notes Anthropological and Explanatory.* 6 volumes. The Burton Club.

Buruma, Ian, and Avishai Margalit
    2002   Occidentalism. *New York Review of Books* 49(January 17): 4–7.

    2004   *Occidentalism: The West in the Eyes of Its Enemies.* New York: Penguin Press.

Butterfield, Herbert
    1931   *The Whig Interpretation of History.* London: G. Bell and Sons.

Butterworth, Charles E.
    1980   Review of *Orientalism* by Edward Said. *American Political Science Review* 74: 174–176.

Buzard, James
    1993   *The Beaten Track: European Tourism, Literature, and the Ways to "Culture" 1800–1918.* Oxford: Clarendon.

    2005   *Disorienting Fiction: The Autoethnographic Work of Nineteenth-Century British Novels.* Princeton, NJ: Princeton University Press.

Cahen, Claude, and Charles Pellat
    1973   Les études arabes et islamiques. *Journal Asiatique* 261:89–107.

Cain, William E.
    1984   *The Crisis in Criticism: Theory, Literature, and Reform in English Studies.* Baltimore, MD: Johns Hopkins Press.

Calder, Angus
    2000   Does "Post-Coloniality" Mean Anything? In Niaz Zaman, Firdous Azim, and Shawkat Hussain, editors, *Colonial and Post-Colonial Encounters*, 1–14. New Delhi: Manohar.

Cannadine, David
    2001   *Ornamentalism: How the British Saw their Empire.* Oxford: Oxford University Press.

Cannon, Garland
    1964   *Oriental Jones: A Biography of Sir William Jones, 1746–94.* London: Asia Publishing House.

1990   *The Life and Mind of Oriental Jones: Sir William Jones, the Father of Modern Linguistics*. Cambridge: Cambridge University Press.

1998   Sir William Jones and Literary Orientalism. In Barfoot and D'haen 1998, 27–41.

Cantor, Paul A.

1996   The Uncanonical Dante: The Divine Comedy and Islamic Philosophy. *Philosophy and Literature* 20(1):138–153.

Cardini, Franco

1999   *Europe and Islam*. Translated by Caroline Beamish. Oxford: Blackwell.

Carlyle, Thomas

1993[1840]   *On Heroes, Hero-Worship, and the Heroic in History*. Berkeley: University of California Press.

Carrier, James G.

1992   Occidentalism: The World Turned Upside Down. *American Ethnologist* 19:195–212.

1995   Introduction. In James G. Carrier, editor *Occidentalism: Images of the West*, 1–32. Oxford: Clarendon.

Casada, James A.

1990   *Sir Richard F. Burton: A Biobibliographic Study*. Boston: G. K. Hall.

Castronovo, Russ

1995   Who Wants Interdisciplinary Turf Anyway? *Nineteenth-Century Contexts* 19:85–88.

Caton, Steven C.

1999   *Lawrence of Arabia: A Film's Anthropology*. Berkeley: University of California Press.

Celik, Zeynep

2000   Speaking Back to Orientalist Discourse at the World's Columbian Exposition. In Holly Edwards, editor, *Noble Dreams, Wicked Pleasures: Orientalism in America, 1870–1930*, 77–97. Princeton, NJ: Princeton University Press.

2002   Speaking Back to Orientalist Discourse. In Beaulieu and Roberts 2002, 19–41.

Chalala, Elie

2004   Rethinking Edward Said's *Orientalism*: An Interview with Charbal Dagher. *Al-Jadid* 10(48):2, 4.

Chambers, Ross

1980   Representation and Authority. *Comparative Studies in Society and History* 22:509–512.

1994   Pointless Stories, Storyless Points: Roland Barthes between *Soirées de Paris* and *Incidents*. *L'Esprit Créateur* 34(2):12–30.

Charles-Roux, Jules

1925   *L'Angleterre et l'expédition française en Égypte*. Cairo: I.F.A.O.

Chatterjee, Partha

1992   Their Own Words? An Essay for Edward Said. In Sprinker 1992, 194–220.

Chaudhuri, Nirad C.

1974   *Scholar Extraordinary: The Life of Professor the Rt. Hon. Friedrich Max Müller*. New York: Oxford University Press.

Chaudhury, Ajit

1994   On Colonial Hegemony: Toward a Critique of Brown Orientalism. *Rethinking Marxism* 7(4):44–58.

Chen, Xiaomei

1995   *Occidentalism: A Theory of Counter-Discourse in Post-Mao China.* Oxford: Oxford University Press.

Chew, Samuel C.

1937   *The Crescent and the Rose: Islam and England during the Renaissance.* New York: Oxford University Press.

Chow, Rey

1993   *Writing Diaspora: Tactics of Intervention in Contemporary Cultural Studies.* Bloomington: Indiana University Press.

2002   Theory, Area Studies, Cultural Studies: Issues of Pedagogy in Multiculturalism. In Masao Miyoshi and H. D. Harootunian, editors, *Learning Places: The Afterlife of Area Studies,* 103–118. Durham, NC: Duke University Press.

2005   "Have You Eaten?"—Inspired by an Exhibit. *Amerasia Journal* 35(1):19–22.

Chuaqui, Rubén

2005   Notes on Edward Said's View of Michel Foucault. *Alif* 25:89–119.

Chun, Allen

1995   An Oriental Orientalism: The Paradox of Tradition and Modernity in Nationalist Taiwan. *History and Anthropology* 9:27–56.

Çirakman, Aslı

2002   *From the "Terror of the World" to the "Sick Man of Europe": European Images of Ottoman Empire and Society from the Sixteenth Century to the Nineteenth.* New York: Peter Lang.

Clark, Robert L. A.

1999   Queering Orientalism: The East as Closet in Said, Ackerley, and the Medieval Christian West. *Medieval Encounters* 5(3):336–349.

Clarke, J. J.

1997   *Oriental Enlightenment: The Encounter Between Asian and Western Thought.* London: Routledge.

Clayson, Hollis

2002   Henri Regnaut's Wartime Orientalism. In Beaulieu and Roberts 2002, 131–178.

Clifford, James

1988   *The Predicament of Culture: Twentieth-Century Ethnography, Literature, and Art.* Cambridge, MA: Harvard University Press.

Cockburn, Alexander

2003   Edward Said, Dead at 67: A Mighty and Passionate Heart. *CounterPunch,* September 25, 2003. Electronic document, www.counterpunch.org/cockburn0925 2003.html, accessed March 2004.

Cocks, Joan

1989   *The Oppositional Imagination: Feminism, Critique, and Political Theory.* London: Routledge.

Codell, Julie F.

　　1998　Resistance and Performance: Native Informant Discourse in the Biographies of Maharaja Sayaji Rao III (1863–1939). In Codell and MacLeod, editors, 1998, 13–45.

Codell, Julie F., and Dianne Sachko MacLeod

　　1998　Introduction: Orientalism Transposed: The "Easternization" of Britain and Interventions of Colonial Discourse. In Codell and MacLeod, editors, 1998, 1–10.

Codell, Julie F., and Dianne Sachko MacLeod, editors

　　1998　*Orientalism Transposed: The Impact of the Colonies on British Culture.* Aldershot, UK: Ashgate.

Cole, Juan

　　1995　Power, Knowledge, and Orientalism. *Diplomatic History* 19:507–513.

Colwell, Danny

　　1996　"I Am Your Mother and Your Father": Paul Scott's *Raj Quartet* and the Dissolution of Imperial Identity. In Bart Moore-Gilbert, editor, *Writing India 1757–1990: The Literature of British India*, 213–235. Manchester, NY: Manchester University Press.

Comaroff, Jean, and John Comaroff

　　1992　*Ethnography and the Historical Imagination.* Boulder, CO: Westview.

Combs-Schilling, M. Elaine

　　1989　*Sacred Performances: Islam, Sexuality, and Sacrifice.* New York: Columbia University Press.

Conant, Martha Pike

　　1908　*The Oriental Tale in England in the Eighteenth Century.* New York: Columbia University Press.

Confino, Alon

　　2000　Remembering Talbiyah: On Edward Said's *Out of Place. Israel Studies* 5(2):182–198.

Connor, Steven

　　1989　*Postmodernist Culture: An Introduction to Theories of the Contemporary.* Oxford: Basil Blackwell.

Conrad, Lawrence I.

　　1999　Ignaz Goldziher on Ernest Renan: From Orientalist Philology to the Study of Islam. In Martin Kramer, editor, *The Jewish Discovery of Islam: Studies in Honor of Bernard Lewis*, 137–180. Tel Aviv: Moshe Dayan Center for Middle Eastern and African Studies.

Constable, E. L.

　　1996　Critical Departures: *Salammbô*'s Orientalism. *MLN* 111:625–646.

Coronil, Fernando

　　1996　Beyond Occidentalism: Toward Nonimperial Geohistorical Categories. *Cultural Anthropology* 11(1):51–87.

Crinson, Mark

　　1996　*Empire Building: Orientalism and Victorian Architecture.* London: Routledge.

Crush, Jonathan
    1994   Post-colonialism, De-colonization, and Geography. In Anne Godlewska and Neil Smith, editors, *Geography and Empire*, 333–350. Oxford: Blackwell.

Cruz, Jo Ann Hoeppner Moran
    1999   Popular Attitudes towards Islam in Medieval Europe. In Blanks and Frassetto 1999, 55–81.

Curzon, George Nathaniel
    1915   *Subjects of the Day: Being a Selection of Speeches and Writings*. London: George Allen and Unwin.

Dalby, Michael
    1980   Nocturnal Labors in the Light of Day. *The Journal of Asian Studies* 39:485–493.

Dallal, Ahmad
    1994   Kanan Makiya, Cruelty and Silence. *Social Text* 12:85–90.

Dallmayr, Fred
    1996   *Beyond Orientalism: Essays on Cross-Cultural Encounter*. Albany: SUNY Press.
    1997   The Politics of Nonidentity: Adorno, Postmodernism—and Edward Said. *Political Theory* 25:33–56.

Al-Daʿmi, Muhammad A.
    1998   Orientalism and Arab-Islamic History: An Inquiry into the Orientalists' Motives and Compulsions. *Arab Studies Quarterly* 20(4):1–11.

Daniel, Norman
    1960   *Islam and the West: The Making of an Image*. Edinburgh: Edinburgh University Press.
    1966   *Islam, Europe and Empire*. Edinburgh: Edinburgh University Press.
    1982   Edward Said and the Orientalists. *Mélanges de l' Institut Dominicain d'Études Orientales* 15:211–222.
    1990   Orientalism Again. In Derek Hopwood, editor, *Studies in Arab History: The Antonius Lectures, 1978–87*, 175–189. New York: St. Martin's.
    1997   The Image of Islam in the Medieval and in the Early Modern Period. In Nanji, editor, 1997, 128–148.

Dante Alighieri
    1954   *The Inferno*. Translated by John Ciardi. New York: Mentor.

Davidson, John
    1901   Introduction. In John Davidson, translator, *Persian and Chinese Letters*, 1–24. Washington, DC: M. Walter Dunne.

Davis, Eric
    2002   Representations of the Middle East at American World Fairs 1876–1904. In Abbas Amanat and Magnus T. Bernhardsson, editors, *The United States and the Middle East: Cultural Encounters*, 342–381. New Haven, CT: The Yale Center for International and Area Studies.

Davis, Kathleen
    2000   Time Behind the Veil: The Media, the Middle Ages, and Orientalism Now. In Jeffrey Jerome Cohen, editor, *The Postcolonial Middle Ages*, 105–122. New York: St. Martin's.

Davis, Lennard J.

    2001   Nationality, Disability, and Deafness. In Aruri and Shuraydi 2001, 2–28.

Dawn, C. Ernest

    1979   Review of Edward W. Said, *Orientalism*. *The American Historical Review* 84:1334.

Dawood, N. J., translator

    1990   *The Koran with a Parallel Arabic Text*. New York: Penguin.

Dawson, Raymond

    1967   *The Chinese Chameleon: An Analysis of European Conceptions of Chinese Civilization*. London: Oxford University Press.

De Groot, Rokus

    2005   Perspectives of Polyphony in Edward Said's Writings. *Alif* 25:219–240.

De Jong, Frederick

    1986   Middle Eastern Studies in the Netherlands. *MESA Bulletin* 20(2):171–186.

De la Jonquière, Clement

    1899–1907   *L'Expédition d'Égypte, 1798–1801*. 5 volumes. Paris: M. Charles-Lavauzelle.

Delaney, Sheila

    1994   *The Naked Text: Chaucer's Legend of Good Women*. Berkeley: University of California Press.

Deny, Jean

    1936   Les Pseudo-Prophétes concernant les Turcs au XVIe siècle. *Revue des études islamiques* 10:201–205.

Deutsch, Nathaniel

    2001   "The Asiatic Black Man": An African American Orientalism? *Journal of Asian American Studies* 4(3):193–208.

DeVries, Kelly

    1999   The Lack of a Western European Military Response to the Ottoman Invasions of Eastern Europe from Nicopolis (1396) to Mohacs (1526). *Journal of Military History* 63(3):539–559.

Dibble, R. F.

    1926   *Mohammed*. New York: Viking.

Dickinson, Goldsworthy Lowes

    1904   *Letters from a Chinese Official Being an Eastern View of Western Civilization*. New York: McClure, Phillips.

di Leonardo, Micaela

    1998   *Exotics at Home: Anthropologies, Others, American Modernity*. Chicago: University of Chicago Press.

Dimmock, Matthew

    2005   *New Turkes: Dramatizing Islam and the Ottomans in Early Modern England*. Aldershot, UK: Ashgate.

Dirks, Nicholas B.

    1992a   Castes of Mind. *Representations* 37:56–78.

    1992b   Introduction: Colonialism and Culture. In Nicholas B. Dirks, editor, *Colonialism and Culture*, 1–25. Ann Arbor: University of Michigan Press.

1993   Colonial Histories and Native Informants: Biography of an Archive. In Breck-
        enridge and van der Veer, editors, 1993, 279–313.

2004   Edward Said and Anthropology. *Journal of Palestine Studies* 33(3):38–54.

Dirlik, Arif

1996   Chinese History and the Question of Orientalism. *History and Theory* 35(5):
        96–118.

1997   *The Postcolonial Aura: Third World Criticism in the Age of Global Capitalism.*
        Boulder, CO: Westview.

Disraeli, Benjamin

1877   *Tancred, or The New Crusade.* New York: G. Routledge.

Djait, Hichem

1985[1978]   *Europe and Islam.* Translated by Peter Heinegg. Berkeley: University
        of California Press.

Dobie, Madeleine

2001   *Foreign Bodies: Gender, Language, and Culture in French Orientalism.* Stanford,
        CA: Stanford University Press.

Docherty, Thomas

1990   *After Theory: Postmodernism/postmarxism.* London: Routledge.

Dodge, Bayard, editor and translator

1970   *The Fihrist of al-Nadim: A Tenth-Century Survey of Muslim Culture.* New York:
        Columbia University Press.

Doniger, Wendy

1999   Presidential Address: "I Have Scinde": Flogging a Dead (White Male Orien-
        talist) Horse. *The Journal of Asian Studies* 58(4):940–960.

Donner, Fred

1996   Philip K. Hitti. *Al-ʿUsur al-Wusta* 8(2):48–52.

2001   Modern Nationalism and Medieval Islamic History. *Al-ʿUsur al-Wusta* 13(1):
        21–22.

Doughty, Charles M.

1936[1888]   *Travels in Arabia Deserta.* Third Edition. 2 volumes. London: Jonathan
        Cape.

Drews, Robert

1973   *The Greek Accounts of Eastern History.* Publications of the Center for Hellenic
        Studies. Cambridge, MA: Harvard University Press.

Driss, Hager Ben

2001   Women Writing/Women Written: The Case of Oriental Women in English Colo-
        nial Fiction. *MESA Bulletin* 35(2):159–174.

D'Souza, Dinesh

2002   Two Cheers for Colonialism. *The Chronicle Review* 48(35):B7–B9.

Dugat, Gustave

1868–70   *Histoire des orientalistes de l'Europe du XIIe au XIXe siècle.* 2 volumes. Paris:
        Maisonneuve.

Duncanson, Dennis

1980   Review of *Orientalism. Asian Affairs* 67:200–201.

Dunn, Allen

    1995   The Ethics of *Mansfield Park*: MacIntyre, Said, and Social Context. *Soundings* 78:483–500.

Durkheim, Emile

    1965[1912]   *The Elementary Forms of the Religious Life.* New York: Free Press.

Dutton, Michael, and Peter Williams

    1993   Transplanting Theories: Edward Said on Orientalism, Imperialism and Alterity. *Southern Humanities Review* 26(3):314–357.

Eagleton, Terry

    1991   *Ideology: An Introduction.* London: Verso.

    1996   *Literary Theory: An Introduction.* Second Edition. Oxford: Blackwell.

Easthope, Antony

    1991   *Literary into Cultural Studies.* London: Routledge.

    1998   Bhabha, Hybridity and Identity. *Textual Practice* 12:341–348.

Easthope, Antony, and Kate McGowan, editors

    1992   *A Critical and Cultural Theory Reader.* Toronto: University of Toronto Press.

Eaton, Richard M.

    2000   (Re)imag(in)ing Other²ness: A Postmortem for the Postmodern in India. *Journal of World History* 11(1):57–78.

Edwards, Holly

    2000   A Million and One Nights: Orientalism in America, 1870–1930. In Holly Edwards, editor, *Noble Dreams, Wicked Pleasures: Orientalism in America, 1870–1930*, 11–57. Princeton, NJ: Princeton University Press.

Eickelman, Dale

    2002   *The Middle East and Central Asia: An Anthropological Approach.* Fourth Edition. Upper Saddle River: Prentice-Hall.

El Kasri, Mustapha

    1999   Voltaire face à l'Islam et à son Prophète. *Le Temps du Maroc*, 171, February 5–11.

Ellingson, Ter

    2001   *The Myth of the Noble Savage.* Berkeley: University of California Press.

El Zein, Abdul Hamid

    1977   Beyond Ideology and Theology: The Search for the Anthropology of Islam. *Annual Review of Anthropology* 6:227–254.

Ephal, I.

    1976   "Ishmael" and "Arab(s)": A Transformation of Ethnological Terms. *Journal of Near Eastern Studies* 35(4):225–235.

Esposito, John L.

    1990   Presidential Address 1989. The Study of Islam: Challenges and Prospects. *MESA Bulletin* 24(1):1–11.

Esposito, John L., and John O. Voll

    2001   *Makers of Contemporary Islam.* Oxford: Oxford University Press.

Ess, Josef van

    1980   From Wellhausen to Becker: The Emergence of *Kulturgeschichte* in Islamic

Studies. In Malcom H. Kerr, editor, *Islamic Studies: A Tradition and Its Problems*, 27–52. Malibu, CA: Undena Publications.

Ettinghausen, Richard

    1976   Letter to the Editor, *Orientalism*. *New York Times Book Review*, December 16:37.

Evans, Richard

    2001   *In Defence of History*. Second Edition. London: Granta.

Fabian, Johannes

    1999   Comments. *Current Anthropology* 40[supplement]:S38.

Fähndrich, Hartmut

    1988   Orientalismus und *Orientalismus*: Überlegungen zu Edward Said, Michel Foucault und westlichen "Islamstudien." *Die Welt des Islams* 28:178–186.

Falk, Richard

    2001   Empowering Inquiry: Our Debt to Edward W. Said. In Aruri and Shuraydi 2001, x–xvi.

Fathy, Ibrahim

    2005   Al-'Itiradat 'ala Sa'id bayn al-tahafut wa-al-tahazzub wa-al-tahlil [Objections to Said between Incoherence, Partisanship, and Analysis]. *Alif* 25:157–171.

Ferguson, Russell, Martha Gever, Trin T. Minh-Ha, and Cornel West, editors

    1990   *Out There: Marginalization and Contemporary Cultures*. Cambridge, MA: M.I.T. Press.

Fernea, Elizabeth W., and Basima Qattan Bezirgan, editors

    1977   *Middle Eastern Women Speak*. Austin: University of Texas Press.

Fieldhouse, D. K.

    1980   Review of *Orientalism*. *History* 65(213):85–86.

Figueira, Dorothy

    1994   *The Exotic: A Decadent Quest*. Albany: SUNY Press.

Findlay, Carter Vaughn

    1998   An Ottoman Occidentalist in Europe: Ahmed Midhat Meets Madame Gulnar. *The American Historical Review* 103(1):15–49.

Fink, Karl J.

    1982   Goethe's *West Östlicher Divan*: Orientalism Restructured. *International Journal of Middle East Studies* 14:315–328.

Fischer, David Hackett

    1970   *Historians' Fallacies: Toward a Logic of Historical Thought*. New York: Harper Torchbacks.

Flanagan, Patrick

    1986   Review of *Orientalism*. *Journal of Contemporary Asia* 16:382–383.

Flaubert, Gustave

    1926   *Oeuvres Complètes de Gustave Flaubert. Correspondance. Nouvelle Édition Augmentée. Deuxième Série (1847–1852)*. Paris: Louis Conard.

    1991   *Voyage en Égypte*. Edited by Pierre-Marc de Biasi. Paris: Grasset.

Fleming, K. E.

    1999   *The Muslim Bonaparte: Diplomacy and Orientalism in Ali Pasha's Greece*. Princeton, NJ: Princeton University Press.

2000   *Orientalism*, the Balkans, and Balkan Historiography. *The American Hsitorical Review* 105:1218–1233.

Florenne, Yves

1980   L'orientalisme ou l'Orient absent. *Le Monde Diplomatique* 27(321):38. [review of *Orientalism*]

Fokkema, Douwe

1996   Orientalism, Occidentalism and the Notion of Discourse: Arguments for a New Cosmopolitanism. *Comparative Criticism* 18:227–241.

Foster, Benjamin R.

2002   Yale and the Study of Near Eastern Languages in America, 1770–1930. In Abbas Amanat and Magnus T. Bernhardsson, editors, *The United States and the Middle East: Cultural Encounters*, 1–56. New Haven: Yale Center for International and Area Studies.

Foucault, Michel

1972[1969]   *The Archaeology of Knowledge*. Translated by A. M. Sheridan Smith. London: Tavistock.

1984   What Is an Author? In Paul Rabinow, editor, *The Foucault Reader*, 101–120. New York: Pantheon.

Fox, Richard G.

1992   East of Said. In Sprinker1992, 144–155.

Fraiman, Susan

1995   Jane Austen and Edward Said: Gender, Culture, and Imperialism. *Critical Inquiry* 21:805–821.

Franklin, Michael J.

1998   Accessing India: Orientalism, Anti-"Indianism," and the Rhetoric of Jones and Burke. In Tim Fulford and Peter J. Kitson, editors, *Romanticism and Colonialism: Writing and Empire, 1780–1830*, 48–66. Cambridge: Cambridge University Press.

Franklin, Michael J., editor

1995   *Sir William Jones: Selected Poetical and Prose Works*. Cardiff: University of Wales Press.

Frantzen, Allen J.

1990   *Desire for Origins: New Languages, Old English and Teaching the Tradition*. New Brunswick, NJ: Rutgers University Press.

Frassetto, Michael

1999   The Image of the Saracen as Heretic in the Sermons of Ademar of Chabannes. In Blanks and Frassetto 1999, 83–96.

Freeman, Kathryn S.

1998   "Beyond the Stretch of Labouring Thought Sublime": Romanticism, Postcolonial Theory and the Transmission of Sanskrit Texts. In Codell and MacLeod, editors, 1998, 140–157.

Freitag, Ulrike

1997   The Critique of Orientalism. In Michael Bentley, editor, *Companion to Historiography*, 620–638. London: Routledge.

Freund, Charles
  2001   2001 Nights. The End of the Orientalist Critique. *Reasononline*. Electronic document, www.reason.com/0112/cr.cf.2001.shtml, accessed June 2002.
Friedman, John Block
  1981   *The Monstrous Races in Medieval Art and Thought*. Cambridge, MA: Harvard University Press.
Frykenberg, Robert Eric
  1996   *History and Belief: The Foundations of Historical Understanding*. Grand Rapids, MI: Eerdmans.
Fuchs, Stephan
  2001   *Against Essentialism: A Theory of Culture and Society*. Cambridge, MA: Harvard University Press.
Fuchs-Sumiyoshi, Andrea
  1984   *Orientalismus in der deutschen Literatur: Untersuchungen zu Werken des 19. und 20. Jahrhunderts, von Goethes* West-östlichem Divan *bis Thomas Manns* Joseph-*Tetralogie*. Germanistische Texte und Studien, 20. Hildesheim, Germany: Georg Olms Verlag.
Fück, Johann
  1955   *Die Arabischen Studien in Europa bis in den Anfang des 20. Jahrhunderts*. Leipzig: Harrassowitz.
  1962   Islam as an Historical Problem in European Historiography since 1800. In Lewis and Holt, editors, 1962, 303–314.
Fuller, Robert
  1995   *Naming the AntiChrist: The History of an American Obsession*. Cambridge: Cambridge University Press.
Gabrieli, Francesco
  1965   Apology for Orientalism. *Diogenes* 50:128–136.
Gaeffke, Peter
  1990   A Rock in the Tides of Time: Oriental Studies Then and Now. *Academic Questions* 3(2):67–74.
Gafurov, B. G., and Y. V. Gankovsky, editors
  1967   *Fifty Years of Soviet Oriental Studies (Brief Reviews)*. Moscow: "Nauka" Publishing House.
Gallagher, Catherine
  1985   Politics, the Profession, and the Critic. *Diacritics* 15:37–43.
Gandhi, Leela
  1998   *Postcolonial Theory: A Critical Introduction*. New York: Columbia University Press.
Garber, Marjorie
  1992   The Chic of Araby: Transvestism and the Erotics of Appropriation. In Marjorie Garber, *Vested Interests: Cross-Dressing and Cultural Anxiety*, 304–352. New York: Routledge.
Gare, Arran E.
  1995   Understanding Oriental Cultures. *Philosophy East and West* 45:309–328.

Gates, Henry Louis Jr.

    1991   Critical Fanonism. *Critical Inquiry* 17:457–470.

Geertz, Clifford

    1968   *Islam Observed*. Chicago: University of Chicago Press.

    1982   Conjuring with Islam. *New York Review of Books* 29(May 27):25–28.

    1983   *Local Knowledge: Further Essays in Interpretive Anthropology*. New York: Basic.

Gellner, Ernest

    1994   *Encounters with Nationalism*. Oxford: Blackwell.

Gemmett, Robert J.

    1975   Introduction. In William Beckford, *The Episodes of Vathek*, ix–l. Cranbury, NJ: Association of University Presses.

Gerard, René

    1963   *L'Orient et la pensée romantique allemande*. Paris: Marcel Didier.

Ghazanfar, S. J.

    2001   Medieval Islamic Studies: The Intellectual "Gaps." *Al-ʿUsur al-Wusta* 13(1): 19–21.

Ghazoul, Ferial J.

    1992   The Resonance of the Arab-Islamic Heritage in the Work of Edward Said. In Sprinker 1992, 157–172.

Gibb, Hamilton A. R.

    1953   *Mohammedanism*. Second edition. Oxford: Oxford University Press.

Gilbert, Helen, and Joanne Tompkins

    1996   *Post-Colonial Drama: Theory, Practice, Politics*. London: Routledge.

Gilliot, Claude

    1991   Review of Katharina Mommsen, *Goethe und die Arabische Welt*. *Arabica* 38:389–391.

Gilmour, David

    1995   Empire and the East: The Orientalism of Lord Curzon. *Asian Affairs* 26:270–277.

Gilsenan, Michael

    2000   The Education of Edward Said. *New Left Review* Second Series 4:152–158.

Goldammer, Kurt

    1962   *Der Mythus von Ost und West: Eine kultur- und religionsgeschichtliche Betrachtung*. Basel: Ernst Reinhardt.

Goldsmith, Oliver

    1901   *The Citizen of the World*. In John Davidson, translator, *Persian and Chinese Letters*, 291–427. Washington, DC: M. Walter Dunne.

Goldziher, Ignaz, and J. Jomier

    1965   Djamal al-Din al-Afghani. In *The Encyclopaedia of Islam*. New Edition. II:416–419. Leiden: Brill.

Goodman, Dena

    1989   *Criticism in Action: Enlightenment Experiments in Political Writing*. Ithaca, NY: Cornell University Press.

Goody, Jack

    2000   Experience and Expectations of the East. In Wil Arts, editor, *Through a Glass, Darkly: Blurred Images of Cultural Tradition and Modernity over Distance and Time*, 30–39. Leiden: Brill.

Goonatilake, Susantha

    2001   *Anthropologizing Sri Lanka: A Eurocentric Misadventure*. Bloomington: Indiana University Press.

Gordon, David C.

    1982   Review of *Orientalism*. *Antioch Review* 40(1):104–112.

    1989   *Images of the West: Third World Perspectives*. Totowa, NJ: Rowman and Littlefield Publishers.

Gossett, Thomas F.

    1965   *Race: The History of an Idea in America*. New York: Schocken.

Gossman, Lionel

    1990   *Between History and Literature*. Cambridge, MA: Harvard University Press.

Grabar, Oleg

    1982   Orientalism: An Exchange. *New York Review of Books* 29(August 12):46.

    2000   Roots and Others. In Holly Edwards, *Noble Dreams, Wicked Pleasures: Orientalism in America, 1870–1930*, 3–9. Princeton, NJ: Princeton University Press.

Graf, E. C.

    1999   When an Arab Laughs in Toledo: Cervantes's Interpellation of Early Modern Spanish Orientalism. *Diacritics* 29(2):68–85.

Gran, Peter

    1980   Review of *Orientalism*. *JAOS* 100(3):328–331.

Green, Anne

    1982   *Flaubert and the Historical Novel: Salammbô Reassessed*. Cambridge: Cambridge University Press.

Greenblatt, Stephen

    1997   What is the History of Literature? *Critical Inquiry* 23:460–481.

Greene, Thomas M.

    1979   One World, Divisible. *The Yale Review* 68:577–581. [review of *Orientalism*]

Gregory, Derek

    1997   Orientalism Re-Viewed. *History Workshop Journal* 44:268–278.

Grewgious

    1994   Used Books: *Orientalism* by Edward Said. *Critical Quarterly* 36:87–98.

Grimm, Jacob, and Wilhelm Grimm

    1889   *Deutsches Wörterbuch*. 16 volumes. Leipzig: S. Hirzel.

Grose, Frances

    1811   *Lexicon Balatronicum: A Dictionary of Buckish Slang, University Wit and Pickpocket Eloquence*. London: C. Chappel.

Grosrichard, Alain

    1979   *Structure du sérail: La fiction du despotisme asiatique dans l'occident classique*. Paris: Seuil.

1998   *The Sultan's Court: European Fantasies of the East*. Translated by Liz Heron. London: Verso.

Grunebaum, Gustave E. von

1961[1946]   *Medieval Islam: A Study in Cultural Orientation*. Chicago: University of Chicago Press.

1962   Self-Image and Approach to History. In Lewis and Holt, editors, 1962, 457–483.

1964   *Modern Islam: the Search for Cultural Identiy*. New York: Vintage.

Guérin Dalle Mese, Jeannine

1991   *Égypte: la mémoire et le rêve: itinéraires d'un voyage, 1320–1601*. Biblioteca dell' "Archivum Romanicum" Ser. I, Vol. 237. Florence: Leo S. Olschki.

Gutting, Gary

1994   Introduction. Michel Foucault: A User's Manual. In Gary Gutting, editor, *The Cambridge Companion to Foucault*, 1–27. Cambridge: Cambridge University Press.

Haddad, Emily A.

2002   *Orientalist Poetics: The Islamic Middle East in Ninetenth-century English and French Poetry*. Aldershot, UK: Ashgate.

Haddad, Yvonne Y.

1991   Presidential Address 1990. Middle East Area Studies: Current Concerns and Future Directions. *MESA Bulletin* 25(1):1–13.

Hafez, Sabry

2004   Edward Said's Intellectual Legacy in the Arab World. *Journal of Palestine Studies* 33(3):76–90.

Haim, Sylvia

1964   Introduction. In Sylvia Haim, editor, *Arab Nationalism: An Anthology*, 3–72. Berkeley: University of California Press.

Halbfass, Wilhelm

1985   Review of *The Oriental Renaissance: Europe's Rediscovery of India and the East, 1680–1880*. *Journal of Asian Studies* 44:799–800.

1988   *India and Europe: An Essay in Understanding*. Albany: SUNY Press.

1991   *Traditions and Reflections: Explorations in Indian Thought*. Albany: SUNY Press.

1997   Research and Reflections: Responses to My Respondents. In Eli Franco and Karin Preisendanz, editors, *Beyond Orientalism: The Work of Wilhelm Halbfass and Its Impact on Indian and Cross-Cultural Studies*, 1–25. Poznan Studies in the Philosophy of the Sciences and Humanities, 59. Amsterdam: Rodopi.

Hale, Sondra

2005   Edward Said—Accidental Feminist. *Amerasia Journal* 31(1):1–5.

Hall, Josef Washington

1929   *Eminent Asians: Six Great Personalities of the New East*. New York: D. Appleton.

Halliday, Fred

1999   *Islam and the Myth of Confrontation: Religion and Politics in the Middle East*. London: I. B. Tauris.

Hamady, Sania

1960   *Temperament and Character of the Arabs*. New York: Twayne.

Hamalian, Leo, and John D. Yohannan, editors

    1978   *New Writing from the Middle East*. New York: New American Library.

Hamilton, Edith

    1942[1930]   *The Greek Way*. New York: W. W. Norton.

Hammoudi, Abdellah

    1997   *Master and Disciple: The Cultural Foundations of Moroccan Authoritarianism*. Chicago: University of Chicago Press.

Hanafi, Hasan

    1990   De l'Orientalisme a l'occidentalisme. *Peuples méditerranéens* 50:115–119.

    1991   *Muqaddima fi ʿilm al-istighrab*. Cairo: Al-Dar al-Fanniyya li-al-Nashr wa-al-Tawziʿ.

Handlin, Oscar

    1979   *Truth in History*. Cambridge, MA: Belknap.

Hansen, Peter H.

    2002   Ornamentalism and Orientalism: Virtual Empires and the Politics of Knowledge. *Journal of Colonialism and Colonial History* 3(1):1–18.

Harootunian, H. D.

    2002   Postcoloniality's Unconscious / Area Studies' Desire. In Masao Miyoshi and H. D. Harootunian, editors, *Learning Places: The Afterlife of Area Studies*, 150–174. Durham. NC: Duke University Press.

    2005   Conjunctural Traces: Said's "Inventory." *Critical Inquiry* 31:431–442.

Harris, Marvin

    1968   *The Rise of Anthropological Theory*. New York: Thomas Y. Crowell.

Hart, William D.

    2000   *Edward Said and the Religious Effects of Culture*. Cambridge Studies in Religion and Critical Thought 8. Cambridge: Cambridge University Press.

Hartog, François

    2001[1980]   *Le miroir d'Hérodote: Essai sur la représentation de l'autre*. Paris: Gallimard.

Hassan, Ihab

    1986   Pluralism in Postmodern Perspective. *Critical Inquiry* 12:503–520.

Hay, Denys

    1957   *Europe: The Emergence of an Idea*. Edinburgh: Edinburgh University Press.

Hay, Stephen N.

    1970   *Asian Ideas of East and West: Tagore and His Critics in Japan, China, and India*. Cambridge, MA: Harvard University Press.

Haykel, Muhammad

    1976[1935]   *The Life of Muhammad*. Translated by I. Al Faruqi. Plainfield, IN: American Trust Publications.

Heehs, Peter

    2003   Shades of Orientalism: Paradoxes and Problems in Indian Historiography. *History and Theory* 42:169–195.

Heffernan, Teresa

    2000   Feminism against the East/West Divide: Lady Mary's Turkish Embassy Letters. *Eighteenth-Century Studies* 33:201–215.

Hefner, Robert W.

    2000   *Civil Islam: Muslims and Democratization in Indonesia.* Princeton, NJ: Princeton University Press.

Hegel, Georg Wilhelm Friedrich

    1954   *The Philosophy of Hegel.* Edited by Carl J. Friedrich. New York: Modern Library.

    1975   *Lectures on the Philosophy of History.* Cambridge: Cambridge University Press.

Hentsch, Thierry

    1992   *Imagining the Middle East.* Translated by Fred A. Reed. Montreal: Black Rose.

Herder, Johann Gottfried von

    1968[1784–91]   *Reflections of the Philosophy of the History of Mankind.* Translated by T. O. Churchill; abridged by Frank E. Manuel. Chicago: University of Chicago Press.

Hersh, Seymour

    2004   The Gray Zone: How a Secret Pentagon Program Came to Abu Ghraib, *The New Yorker* May 24:38–44.

Herzfeld, Michael

    1987   *Anthropology through the Looking Glass: Critical Ethnography in the Margins of Europe.* Cambridge: Cambridge University Press.

Hess, Jonathan M.

    2000   Johann David Michaelis and the Colonial Imaginary: Orientalism and the Emergence of Racial Antisemitism in Eighteenth-Century Germany. *Jewish Social Studies* 6(2):56–101.

Higgins, Iain MacLeod

    1997   *Writing East: The "Travels" of Sir John Mandeville.* Philadelphia: University of Pennsylvania Press.

Hildebrandt, Thomas

    1998   *Emanzipation oder Isolation vom westlichen Lehrer? Die Debatte um Hasan Hanafis "Einführung in die Wissenschaft der Okzidentalistik."* Islamkundliche Untersuchungen, 212. Berlin: Klaus Schwarz.

Hildreth, Martha L.

    1995   Lamentations on Reality: A Response to John M. Mackenzie's "Edward Said and the Historians." *Nineteenth-Century Contexts* 19:65–73.

Hirsch, Michael

    2004   Bernard Lewis Revisited. *Washington Monthly,* November. Electronic document, www.washingtonmonthly.com/features/2004/0411.hirsh.html, accessed April 2005.

Hitchens, Christopher

    2003   Where the Twain Should Have Met. *Atlantic Monthly* 292(2):153–159.

Hodgson, Marshall G. S.

    1974   *The Venture of Islam.* Volume 1. *The Classical Age of Islam.* Chicago: University of Chicago Press.

    1993   *Rethinking World History: Essays on Europe, Islam, and World History.* Cambridge: Cambridge University Press.

Hoenselaars, Ton
    1998   The Elizabethans and the Turk at Constantinople. In Barfoot and D'haen 1998,
            9–26.
Hogarth, David G.
    1925   *The Wandering Scholar*. London: Oxford University Press.
Holmlund, Christine Anne
    1993   Displacing Limits of Difference: Gender, Race, and Colonialism in Edward Said
            and Homi Bhabha's Theoretical Models and Marguerite Duras's Experimen-
            tal Films. In Hamid Naficy and Teshome H. Gabriel, editors, *Otherness and
            the Media: The Ethnography of the Imagined and the Imaged*, 1–22. Chur,
            Switzerland: Harwood Academic.
Holt, P. M.
    1962   The Treatment of Arab History by Prideaux, Ockley and Sale. In Lewis and
            Holt, editors, 1962, 290–302.
Holub, Renate
    1992   *Antonio Gramsci: Beyond Marxism and Postmodernism*. London: Routledge.
Hoogvelt, Ankie
    2001   *Globalization and the Post-colonial World: The New Political Economy of Devel-
            opment*. Baltimore: Johns Hopkins University Press.
Hopwood, Derek, and Diana Grimwood-Jones, editors
    1972   *Middle East and Islam: A Bibliographic Introduction*. Bibliotheca Asiatica, 9.
            Zug, Switzerland: Inter Documentation Company.
Horsley, Richard A.
    2003   Religion and Other Products of Empire. *Journal of the American Academy of
            Religion* 71(1):13–44.
Hourani, Albert
    1962   Introductory Remarks. In Lewis and Holt, editors, 1962, 451–456.
    1970   *Arabic Thought in the Liberal Age, 1798–1939*. Oxford: Oxford University Press.
    1972a   Review of *The Cambridge History of Islam*. *The English Historical Review*
            87:348–357.
    1972b   Revolution in the Arab Middle East. In Vatikiotis 1972, 65–72.
    1976   History. In Leonard Binder, editor, *The Study of the Middle East: Research and
            Scholarship in the Humanities and Social Sciences*, 97–135. New York: John
            Wiley and Sons.
    1980a   *Europe and the Middle East*. London: Macmillan.
    1980b   Islamic History, Middle Eastern History, Modern History. In Malcom H. Kerr,
            editor, *Islamic Studies: A Tradition and Its Problems*, 5–26. Malibu, CA: Undena.
    1991   *Islam in European Thought*. Cambridge: Cambridge University Press.
Hudson, Brian
    1977   The New Geography and the New Imperialism: 1870–1918. *Antipode* 9(2):12–19.
Huggan, Graham
    2005   (Not) Reading Orientalism. *Research in African Literatures* 36(3):124–136.
Humbert, Jean-Marcel, Michael Pantazzi, and Christiane Ziegler
    1994   *Egyptomania: Egypt in Western Art, 1730–1930*. Ottawa: National Gallery of
            Canada.

Humphries, R. Stephen
> 1991 *Islamic History: A Framework for Inquiry*. Princeton, NJ: Princeton University Press.

Huntington, Samuel P.
> 1993 The Clash of Civilizations? *Foreign Affairs* 72(3):22–49.

Hussein, Abdirahman A.
> 2002 *Edward Said: Criticism and Society*. London: Verso.

Ibn Tufayl, Abu Bakr Muhammad
> 1982 *The Journey of the Soul*. Translated by Riad Kocache. London: Octagon.

Ibn Warraq
> 2002 Debunking Edward Said: Edward Said and the Saidists: or Third World Intellectual Terrorism. Institute for the Secularisation of Islamic Society website. Electronic document, www.secularislam.org/articles/debunking.htm, accessed April 2004.
> 2003[1995] *Why I Am Not a Muslim*. Amherst: Prometheus.

Iggers, Georg G.
> 1997 *Historiography in the Twentieth Century: From Scientific Objectivity to the Postmodern Challenge*. Hanover, NH: Wesleyan University Press.

Inden, Ronald
> 1986 Orientalist Constructions of India. *Modern Asian Studies* 20(3):401–446.
> 1990 *Imagining India*. Oxford: Basil Blackwell.

Insoll, Timothy
> 1999 *The Archaeology of Islam*. Oxford: Blackwell.

Iqbal, Muhammad
> 1955 *Poems from Iqbal*. Translated by V. G. Kiernan. London: John Murray.

Iron Sheik
> 2004 Orientalism. *Mizna* 6(1):47–49).

Irwin, Robert
> 1981–82 Writing about Islam and the Arabs. *Ideology & Culture* 9:102–112. [review of *Orientalism*]
> 2004 *The Arabian Nights: A Companion*. Second Edition. London: Tauris Parke.
> 2006 *For Lust of Knowing*. London: Allen Lane.

Isotalo, Riina
> 1995 Edward Westermarck and Hilma Granqvist in the Field of Orientalist Discourse in Finland. *Third Nordic Conference on Middle Eastern Studies: Ethnic Encounter and Culture Change, Joensuu, Finland, 19–22 June 1995*. Electronic document, www.hf.uib.no/smi/paj/Isotalo.html, accessed August 2006.

Itzkowtiz, Norman
> 1958 Eighteenth Century Ottoman Realities. *Studia Islamica* 16:73–94.

al-Jabarti, ʿAbd al-Rahman
> 1993 *Napoleon in Egypt. Al-Jabarti's Chronicle of the French Occupation, 1798*. Translated by Shmuel Moreh. Princeton, NJ: Markus Wiener.

Jacoby, Russell
> 1995 Marginal Returns: The Trouble with Post-Colonial Theory. *Lingua Franca* 5(6):30–37.

Jameelah, Maryam

    1966   *Islam and Modernism*. Lahore: Mohammad Yusuf Khan.

    1981   *Islam and Orientalism*. Second Edition. Lahore: Mohammad Yusuf Khan and Sons.

JanMohamed, Abdul R.

    1992   Worldliness-without-World, Homelessness-as-Home: Toward a Definition of the Specular Border Intellectual. In Sprinker 1992, 96–120.

Jarah, Nouri

    1999   Edward Said Discusses *Orientalism*, Arab Intellectuals, Reviving Marxism, and Myth in Palestinian History. *Al Jadid Magazine* 5(28):4ff. Electronic document, www.aljadid.com/EdwardSaidDiscussesOrientalismArabIntellectualsReviv ingMarxism.html, accessed January 2004.

Jenks, Gregory C.

    1991   *The Origins and Early Development of the Antichrist Myth*. New York: Walter de Gruyter.

Johansen, Baber

    1990   Politics and Scholarship: The Development of Islamic Studies in the Federal Republic of Germany. In Tareq Y. Ismael, editor, *Middle East Studies: International Perspectives on the State of the Art*, 71–130. New York: Praeger.

Johnson, Samuel

    1773   *A Dictionary of the English Language*. Fourth Edition. London: W. Strahan.
    [1755]

Joseph, Roger

    1980   Review of *Orientalism*. *American Anthropologist* 82:948.

Joubin, Rebecca

    2000   Islam and Arabs through the Eyes of the *Encyclopédie*: The "Other" as a Case of French Cultural Self-Criticism. *International Journal of Middle East Studies* 32:197–217.

Kabbani, Rana

    1986   *Europe's Myth of Orient: Devise and Rule*. London: MacMillan.

Kabir, Ananya Jahanara

    2005   Becoming Minor: On Some Significant Encounters with Edward Said. *Alif* 25:18–20.

Kahf, Mohja

    1999   *Western Representations of the Muslim Woman: From Termagant to Odalisque*. Austin: University of Texas Press.

Kaiwar, Vasant, and Sucheta Mazumdar

    2003   Race, Orient, Nation in the Time-Space of Modernity. In Vasant Kaiwar and Sucheta Mazumdar, editors, *Antimonies of Modernity: Essays on Race, Orient, Nation*, 261–298. Durham, NC: Duke University Press.

Kalinowski, Izabela

    2004   *Between East and West: Polish and Russian Nineteenth-Century Travel to the Orient*. Rochester, NY: University of Rochester Press.

Kamps, Ivo, and Jyotsna G. Singh
    2001   Introduction. In Kamps and Singh, editors, 2001, 1–16.

Kamps, Ivo, and Jyotsna G. Singh, editors
    2001   *Travel Knowledge: European "Discoveries" in the Early Modern Period*. New York: Palgrave.

Kandiyoti, Deniz
    1996   Contemporary Feminist Scholarship and Middle East Studies. In Deniz Kandiyoti, editor, *Gendering the Middle East: Emerging Perspectives*, 1–27. Syracuse, NY: Syracuse University Press.
    2002   Post-Colonialism Compared: Potentials and Limitations in the Middle East and Central Asia. *International Journal of Middle East Studies* 34:279–297.

Karayanni, Stavros Starou
    2005   Dismissing Veiling Desire: Kuchuk Hanem and Imperial Masculinity. In Anthony Shay and Barbara Sellers-Young, editors, *Belly Dance: Orientalism, Transnationalism, and Harem Fantasy*, 114–143. Costa Mesa, CA: Mazda.

Katrak, Ketu H.
    2005   Exilic Homes: The Legacy of Edward Said. *Amerasia Journal* 35(1):34–38.

Kayali, Hasan
    1997   *Arabs and Young Turks: Ottomanism, Arabism, and Islamism in the Ottoman Empire, 1908–1918*. Berkeley: University of California Press.

Kazim, Nasir
    2001   Idward Saʿid wa-nassuh bayn taʿ addud al-siyaqat wa-al-taʿwilat al-maghluta. *al-Bahrayn al-Thaqafiyya* 28:108–124.

Keddie, Nikki R.
    1968   *An Islamic Response to Imperialism: Political and Religious Writings of Sayyid Jamal ad-Din "al-Afghani."* Berkeley: University of California Press.
    2002   Women in the Limelight: Some Recent Books on Middle Eastern Women's History. *International Journal of Middle East Studies* 34:553–573.

Kedourie, Elie
    1956   Islam and the Orientalists: Some Recent Discussions. *British Journal of Sociology* 7:217–225.
    1980   *Islam and the Modern World*. New York: Holt, Rinehart, and Winston.

Kejariwal, O. P.
    1988   *The Asiatic Society of Bengal and the Discovery of India's Past, 1784–1838*. Delhi: Oxford University Press.

Kelsall, Malcolm
    1998   "Once Did She Hold the Gorgeous East in Fee...": Byron's Venice and Oriental Empire. In Tim Fulford and Peter J. Kitson, editors, *Romanticism and Colonialism: Writing and Empire, 1780–1830*, 243–260. Cambridge: Cambridge University Press.

Kemp, Percy
    1980   Orientalistes éconduits, Orientalisme reconduit. *Arabica* 27:154–179. [review of *Orientalism*]
    1984   Désapprendre l'orientalisme. *Arabica* 31:1–35.

Kennedy, Dane

1996   Imperial History and Post-Colonial Theory. *Journal of the Imperial and Commonwealth History* 24:345–363.

2000   "Captain Burton's Oriental Muck Heap": The Book of the Thousand Nights and the Uses of Orientalism. *Journal of British Studies* 39:317–339.

Kennedy, Dane, and Burke Casari

1997   Burnt Offerings: Isabel Burton and the "Scented Garden" Manuscript. *Journal of Victorian Culture* 2:229–244.

Kennedy, Valerie

2000   *Edward Said: A Critical Introduction.* Cambridge: Polity.

Kerr, Malcolm H.

1966   *Islamic Reform: The Political and Legal Theories of Muhammad 'Abduh and Rashid Rida.* Berkeley: University of California Press.

1980   Review of *Orientalism. International Journal of Middle East Studies* 12:544–547.

Khalidi, Rashid

2004   *Resurrecting Empire: Western Footprints and America's Perilous Path in the Middle East.* Boston: Beacon.

Khan, Mirza Abul Hassan

1988   *A Persian at the Court of King George 1809–10. The Journal of Mirza Abul Hassan Khan.* Translated by Margaret M. Cloake. London: Barrie and Jenkins.

al-Kharbutli, 'Ali Husni

1976   *Al-Istishraq fi al-ta'rikh al-Islami.* Cairo: Jam'at al-Dirasat al-Islamiyya.

al-Khatibi, 'Abd al-Kabir

1980   *Al-Naqd al-muzdawij.* Beirut: Dar al-'Awda.

Khosrokhavar, Farhad

1990   Du neo-orientalisme de Badie: Enjeux et methods. *Peuples méditerranéens* 50:121–148.

Kiernan, Victor Gordon

1969   *The Lords of Human Kind: Black Man, Yellow Man, and White Man in an Age of Empire.* Boston: Little, Brown.

1979   Review of *Orientalism. Journal of Contemporary Asia* 9(3):345–348.

Kietzman, Mary Jo

1998   Montagu's *Turkish Embassy Letters* and Cultural Dislocation. *Studies in English Literature* 38(3):537–551.

Killingley, Dermot

1993   *Rammohun Roy in Hindu and Christian Tradition: The Teape Lectures 1990.* Newcastle upon Tyne, UK: Grevatt and Grevatt.

Kirkpatrick, Jeane J.

1993   The Modernizing Imperative: Tradition and Change. *Foreign Affairs* 72(4):22–26.

King, Diane

2003   The Doubly Bound World of Kurdish Women. *Voices* 6(1):1, 8–10.

King, Richard

1999   *Orientalism and Religion: Postcolonial Theory, India and "The Mystic East."* London: Routledge.

Kirschbaum, Leo, editor

    1962   *The Plays of Christopher Marlowe*. Cleveland: World Publishing.

Knight, Diana

    1993   Barthes and Orientalism. *New Literary History* 24:617–633.

Koebner, R.

    1951   Despot and Despotism: Vicissitudes of a Political Term. *Journal of the Warburg and Courtault Institutes* 14:275–302.

Koetzle, Michael

    2005   *1000 Nudes: A History of Erotic Photography from 1839–1939*. Cologne: Taschen.

Kohl, Philip L.

    1995   The Material Culture of the Modern Era in the Ancient Orient: Suggestions for Future Work. In Daniel Miller, Michael Rowlands, and Christopher Tilley, editors, *Domination and Resistance*, 240–245. London: Routledge.

Kontje, Todd Curtis

    2004   *German Orientalisms*. Ann Arbor: University of Michigan Press.

Kopf, David

    1969   *British Orientalism and the Bengal Renaissance: The Dynamics of Indian Modernization 1773–1835*. Berkeley: University of California Press.

    1980   Hermeneutics versus History. *Journal of Asian Studies* 39:495–506. [review of *Orientalism*]

    1995   The Historiography of British Orientalism, 1772–1992. In Garland Cannon and Kevin R. Brine, editors, *Objects of Enquiry: The Life, Contributions and Influence of Sir William Jones (1746–1794)*, 141–160. New York: New York University Press.

Koppes, Clayton R.

    1976   Captain Mahan, General Gordon, and the Origin of the Term "Middle East." *Middle East Studies* 12(1):95–98.

Koptiuch, Kristin

    1999   *A Poetics of Political Economy in Egypt*. Minneapolis: University of Minnesota Press.

Kramer, Martin

    2001   *Ivory Towers on Sand: The Failure of Middle Eastern Studies in America*. Washington, DC: Washington Institute for Near East Policy.

Krupat, Arnold

    1992   *Ethnocriticism: Ethnography, History, Literature*. Berkeley: University of California Press.

Kurzman, Charles, editor

    2002   *Modernist Islam, 1840–1940: A Sourcebook*. Oxford: Oxford University Press.

Kushigian, Julia A.

    1991   *Orientalism in the Hispanic Literary Tradition: In Dialogue with Borges, Paz, and Sarduy*. Albuquerque: University of New Mexico Press.

Laissus, Yves

    1998   *L'Égypte, un aventure savante: Avec Bonaparte, Kléber, Menou 1798–1801*. Paris: Fayard.

Lal, Vinay

    2005   The Intellectual as Exemplar: Identity, Oppositional Politics, and the Ambivalent Legacy of Edward Said. *Amerasia Journal* 35(1):39–42.

Lamoreaux, John C.

    1996   Early Christian Responses to Islam. In J. V. Tolan, editor, *Medieval Perceptions of Islam*, 3–31. New York: Garland.

Landberg, Carlo

    1883   *Proverbes et dictons de la province de Syrie*. Leiden: Brill.

Landolt, Hermann

    1999   Henry Corbin, 1903–1978: Between Philosophy and Orientalism. *Journal of the American Oriental Society* 119(3):484–490.

Landry, Donna

    2001   Horsy and Persistently Queer: Imperialism, Feminism and Bestiality. *Textual Practice* 15(3):467–485.

Lane, Edward

    1863–93   *An Arabic-English Lexicon*. London: Williams and Norgate.

    1973[1860]   *An Account of the Manners and Customs of the Modern Egyptians*. New York: Dover. [facsimile of the 1860 edition]

Langland, William

    1966   *Piers the Ploughman*. Translated by Frank Goodridge. New York: Penguin.

Lanman, Charles Rockwell

    1920   India and the West with a Plea for Team-work among Scholars. *Journal of the American Oriental Society* 40:225–247.

Lapidus, Ira

    1995   H. A. R. Gibb. *al-ʿUsur al-Wusta* 7(2):42–43.

Laroui, Abdallah

    1974   *La crise des intellectueles arabes: Traditionalisme ou historicisme?* Paris: François Maspero.

    1976   *The Crisis of the Arab Intellectual: Traditionalism or Historicism?* Translated by Diarmid Cammell. Berkeley: University of California Press.

    1997   Western Orientalism and Liberal Islam: Mutual Distrust? *MESA Bulletin* 31(1):3–10.

Larsen, Mogens Trolle

    1995   Orientalism and Near Eastern Archaeology. In Daniel Miller, Michael Rowlands, and Christopher Tilley, editors, *Domination and Resistance*, 229–239. London: Routledge.

Lassner, Jacob

    2000   *The Middle East Remembered: Forged Identities, Competing Narratives, Contested Spaces*. Ann Arbor: University of Michigan Press.

Latham, J. Derek

    1972   Classical Arabic Literature. In Hopwood and Grimwood-Jones 1972, 291–309.

Laurens, Henry

    1997   *L'Expédition d'Égypte: 1798–1801*. Paris: Editions du Seuil.

Lawrence, T. E.

    1962   *Seven Pillars of Wisdom*. Middlesex: Penguin.

Layton, Susan

    1997   Nineteenth-Century Russian Mythologies of Caucasian Savagery. In Brower and Lazzerini 1997, 80–99.

Lazarus, Neil

    2005   Representations of the Intellectual in Representations of the Intellectual. *Research in African Literatures* 36(3):112–123.

Leaman, Oliver

    1996   Orientalism and Islamic Philosophy. In Seyyed Hossein Nasr and Oliver Leaman, editors, *History of Islamic Philosophy*, II:1143–1148. London: Routledge.

Leask, Nigel

    1992   *British Romantic Writers and the East: Anxieties of Empire*. Cambridge: Cambridge University Press.

Le Bon, Gustave

    1884   *La Civilisation des Arabes*. Paris: Firmin-Didot.

Leerssen, Joep

    1998   Irish Studies and *Orientalism*: Ireland and the Orient. In Barfoot and D'haen 1998, 161–173.

van Leeuwen, Richard

    2000   Translation and Referentiality: The European Translations of the Thousand and One Nights. In Gonzalo Fernández Parrilla and Manuel C. Feria García, editors, *Orientalismo, Exotismo y Traducción*, 191–207. Cuenca: Ediciones de la Universidad de Castilla-La Mancha.

Leitch, Vincent B.

    1992   *Cultural Criticism, Literary Theory, Poststructuralism*. New York: Columbia University Press.

Lele, Jayant

    1993   Orientalism and the Social Sciences. In Breckenridge and van der Veer, editors, 1993, 45–75.

Lenning, Joseph

    2004   *Irish Orientalism: A Literary and Intellectual History*. Syracuse, NY: Syracuse University Press.

Leonard, Major Arthur Glyn

    1909   *Islam. Her Moral and Spiritual Value*. London: Luzac.

Lesch, David W.

    2001   *1979: The Year that Shaped the Modern Middle East*. Boulder, CO: Westview.

Levine, Mark

    1999   An Interview with Edward Said. *Tikkun* 14(2):11–15.

Levinson, Marjorie

    1993   News from Nowhere: The Discontents of Aijaz Ahmad. *Public Culture* 6:97–131.

Lévi-Strauss, Claude

    1967[1961]   *Tristes Tropiques*. Translated by John Russell. New York: Atheneum.

Lew, Joseph W.

    1991a   The Deceptive Other: Mary Shelley's Critique of Orientalism in *Frankenstein*. *Studies in Romanticism* 30(2):255–283.

    1991b   Lady Mary's Portable Seraglio. *Eighteenth-Century Studies* 24(4):432–450.

Lewis, Bernard

    1961   *The Emergence of Modern Turkey*. Oxford: Oxford University Press.

    1964   *The Middle East and the West*. New York: Harper Torchbacks.

    1966   *The Arabs in History*. New York: Harper Torchbacks.

    1970[1954]   Islam. In Denis Sinor, editor, *Orientalism and History*, Second Edition, 16–34. Bloomington: Indiana University Press.

    1972   Islamic Concepts of Revolution. In Vatikiotis 1972, 30–40.

    1973   *Islam in History: Ideas, Men and Events in the Middle East*. New York: Library Press.

    1976   Letter to the Editor, "Orientalism." *New York Times Book Review*, December 16, 36–37.

    1979   The State of Middle Eastern Studies. *The American Scholar* 48:365–381.

    1982a   The Question of Orientalism. *New York Review of Books* 29(June 24):49–56. [review of *Orientalism*]

    1982b   Orientalism: An Exchange. *New York Review of Books* 29(August 12):46–47.

    1990   The Roots of Muslim Rage. *Atlantic Monthly* 266(3):47–60.

    1993a   *Islam and the West*. Oxford: Oxford University Press.

    1993b   *Islam in History: Ideas, Men and Events in the Middle East*. Second Edition. Chicago: Open Court.

    1995   *Cultures in Conflict: Christian, Muslims, and Jews in the Age of Discovery*. Oxford: Oxford University Press.

    1998   *The Multiple Identities of the Middle East*. London: Weidenfeld and Nicolson.

    2002a   In the Finger Zone. *New York Review of Books* 49(May 23):61–63.

    2002b   *What Went Wrong? Western Impact and Middle Eastern Response*. Oxford: Oxford University Press.

Lewis, Bernard and P. M. Holt

    1962   Introduction. In Lewis and Holt, editors, 1962, 1–19.

Lewis, Bernard and P. M. Holt, editors

    1962   *Historians of the Middle East*, 1–19. London: Oxford University Press.

Lewis, Reina

    1996   *Gendering Orientalism: Race, Femininity and Representation*. London: Routledge.

Leys, Simon

    1985   *The Burning Forest: Essays on Chinese Culture and Politics*. New York: Holt, Rinehart, and Winston.

Lezcano, Víctor Morales

    1988   *Africanismo y Orientalismo español en el Siglo XIX*. Madrid: Universidad Nacional de Educación a Distancia.

Lincoln, Bruce

    1999   *Theorizing Myth: Narrative, Ideology, and Scholarship*. Chicago: University of Chicago Press.

Lindenberger, Herbert

    1996   On the Reception of *Mimeses*. In Seth Lerer, editor, *Literary History and the Challenge of Philology: The Legacy of Erich Auerbach*, 195–213. Stanford, CA: Stanford University Press.

Lindholm, Charles

    1996   *The Islamic Middle East: An Historical Anthropology*. Oxford: Blackwell.

Lindsay, Hal

    1973   *The Late Great Planet Earth*. New York: Bantam.

Lindstrom, Lamont

    1995   Cargoism and Occidentalism. In James G. Carrier, editor, *Occidentalism: Images of the West*, 33–60. Oxford: Clarendon.

Lippman, Thomas W.

    1981   Review of *Covering Islam. Middle East Journal* 35:646–647.

Little, Donald P.

    1979   Three Arab Critiques of Orientalism. *The Muslim World* 69:110–31.

Little, Douglas

    2003   *American Orientalism: The United States and the Middle East since 1945*. Charlotte: University of North Carolina Press.

Lloyd, Christopher

    1973   *The Nile Campaign*. New York: Barnes and Noble.

Lloyd, Trevor

    1999   Myths of the Indies: Jane Austen and the British Empire. *Comparative Criticism* 21:59–78.

Lockman, Zachary

    2004   *Contending Visions of the Middle East: The History and Politics of Orientalism*. Cambridge: Cambridge University Press.

Longino, Michèle

    2002   *Orientalism in French Classical Drama*. Cambridge: Cambridge University Press.

Lopez, Donald Jr.

    1995   Introduction. In Donald Lopez Jr., editor, *Curators of the Buddha: The Study of Buddhism under Colonialism*. Chicago: University of Chicago Press.

Lörinsky, Ikdikó

    2002   *L'Orient de Flaubert. Des écrits de jeunesse à Salammbô: la construction d'un imaginaire mythique*. Paris: L'Harmattan.

Loshitzky, Yosefa

    2000   Orientalist Representations: Palestinians and Arabs in some Postcolonial Film and Literature. In Elizabeth Hallam and Brian V. Street, editors, *Cultural Encounters: Representing "Otherness,"* 51–71. London: Routledge.

Lowe, Lisa

    1991   *Critical Terrains: French and British Orientalists*. Ithaca, NY: Cornell University Press.

    1995   Nationalism and Exoticism: Nineteenth-Century Others in Flaubert's *Salammbô* and *L'Education sentimentale*. In Jonathan Arac and Harriet Ritvo, editors, *Macropolitics of Nineteenth-Century Literature*, 213–242. Durham, NC: Duke University Press.

Luckett, Richard
    1982   On Inhumane Discourse. *Cambridge Quarterly* 10(3):271–281. [review of *Orientalism*]

Ludden, David
    1993   Orientalist Empiricism: Transformations of Colonial Knowledge. In Breckenridge and van der Veer, editors, 1993, 250–278.

Lyall, Alfred C.
    1882   *Asiatic Studies: Religious and Social*. London: Murray.

Lytton, Noel Anthony Scawen
    1961   *Wilfrid Scawen Blunt*. London: MacDonald.

Mabro, Judy
    1991   *Veiled Half-truths: Western Travellers' Perceptions of Middle Eastern Women*. London: I. B. Tauris.

Macfie, A. L.
    2000   Preface, Introduction. In A. L. Macfie, editor, *Orientalism: A Reader*, ix–x, 1–8. New York: New York University Press.

MacKenzie, John M.
    1994   Edward Said and the Historians. *Nineteenth-Century Contexts* 18:1–18.
    1995a *Orientalism: History, Theory and the Arts*. Manchester, UK: Manchester University Press.
    1995b A Reply to My Critics. *Nineteenth-Century Contexts* 19:91–100.

MacKerras, Colin
    1989   *Western Images of China*. Hong Kong: Oxford University Press.

MacLean, Gerald
    2001   Ottomanism before Orientalism? Bishop King praises Henry Blount, Passenger in the Levant. In Kamps and Singh, editors, 2001, 85–96.

Mahdi, Muhsin
    1997   The Study of Islam, Orientalism and America. In Nanji, editor, 1997, 149–180.

Mailloux, Steven
    1985   Truth or Consequences: On Being Against Theory. In W. J. T. Mitchell, editor, *Against Theory: Literary Studies and the New Pragmatism*, 65–71. Chicago: University of Chicago Press.

Majeed, Javed
    1992   *Ungoverned Imaginings: James Mill's* The History of British India *and Orientalism*. Oxford: Clarendon Press.

Majid, Anouar
    1998   The Politics of Feminism in Islam. *Signs* 23:321–361.
    2000   *Unveiling Traditions: Postcolonial Islam in a Polycentric World*. Durham, NC: Duke University Press.
    2004   *Freedom and Orthodoxy: Islam and Difference in the Post-Andalusian Age*. Stanford, CA: Stanford University Press.

Makari, George J.

 1985 On Seeing Arabs. *Arab Studies Quarterly* 7(1):58–66.

Makdisi, Saree S.

 1992 The Empire Renarrated: *Season of Migration to the North* and the Reinvention of the Present. *Critical Inquiry* 18:804–820.

 1998 *Romantic Imperialism: Universal Empire and the Culture of Modernity.* Cambridge: Cambridge University Press.

Makiya, Kanan

 1993 *Cruelty and Silence: War, Tyranny, Uprising, and the Arab World.* New York: W. W. Norton.

Malak, Amin

 2005 *Muslim Narratives and the Discourse of English.* Albany: SUNY Press.

Malik, Charles

 1964 The Near East: The Search for Truth. In Sylvia Haim, editor, *Arab Nationalism: An Anthology*, 189–224. Berkeley: University of California Press.

Malroux, André

 1992[1926] *The Temptation of the West.* Translated by Robert Hollander. Chicago: The University of Chicago Press.

Malti-Douglas, Fedwa

 1979 Re-Orienting Orientalism. *The Virginia Quarterly Review* 55:724–733. [review of *Orientalism*]

 1985–86 The Middle Eastern Response and Reaction to Western Scholarship. *Comparative Civilizations Review* 13–14:36–55.

 1991 *Woman's Body, Woman's Word: Gender and Discourse in Arabo-Islamic Writing.* Princeton, NJ: Princeton University Press.

Mani, Lata, and Ruth Frankenberg

 1985 The Challenge of Orientalism. *Economy and Society* 14:174–192.

Manzalaoui, Mahoud

 1965 English Analogues to the Liber Scalae. *Medium Aevum* 34:21–35.

 1980 Review of *Orientalism. Modern Language Review* 75:4:837–839.

Marcus, George E., and Michael M. J. Fischer

 1986 *Anthropology as Cultural Critique: An Experimental Moment in the Human Sciences.* Chicago: University of Chicago Press.

Marrouchi, Mustapha

 1991 The Critic as Dis/Placed Intelligence: The Case of Edward Said. *Diacritics* 21(1):63–74.

 1997 Rootprints. *Dalhousie Review* 77(1):67–95.

 2000 Counternarratives, Recoveries, Refusals. In Bové, editor, 2000, 187–228.

 2003 The New/Old Idiot: Re-reading Said's Contributions to Post-Colonial Studies. *Philosophia Africana* 6(2):37–60.

 2004 *Edward Said at the Limits.* Albany: SUNY Press.

Marshall, Peter

 1968 *Problems of Empire: Britain and India 1757–1813.* London: Allen and Unwin.

Martin, Catherine Gimelli
    1990   Orientalism and the Ethnographer: Said, Herodotus, and the Discourse of Alterity. *Criticism* 32:511–529.

Martin, Richard C.
    1985   Islam and Religious Studies: An Introductory Essay. In Richard C. Martin, editor, *Approaches to Islam in Religious Studies*, 1–21. Tucson: University of Arizona Press.

Martin, Richard C., Mark R. Woodward, and Dwi S. Atmaja
    1997   *Defenders of Reason in Islam: Muʿtazilism from Medieval School to Modern Symbol*. Oxford: Oneworld.

Marx, Karl
    1963[1852]   *The Eighteenth Brumaire of Louis Bonaparte*. Translated by Daniel De Leon. New York: International Publishers.

Massad, Joseph
    2004   The Intellectual Life of Edward Said. *Journal of Palestine Studies* 33(3):7–22.

Matar, Nabil
    1998   *Islam in Britain 1558–1685*. Cambridge: Cambridge University Press.
    2003   *In the Lands of the Christians: Arabic Travel Writing in the Seventeenth Century*. New York: Routledge.

Mazrui, Ali A.
    1999   Black Orientalism: Further Reflections on "Wonders of the African World" by Henry Louis Gates Jr. Institute of Global Cultural Studies. Electronic document, http://igcs.binghamton.edu/igcs_site/dirton2.htm, accessed June 2002.

McAlister, Melani
    2001   *Epic Encounters: Culture, Media, and U.S. Interests in the Middle East, 1945–2000*. Berkeley: University of California Press.

McClintock, Anne
    1994   The Angel of Progress: Pitfalls of the Term "Post-colonialism." In Williams and Chrisman 1994, 291–304.
    1995   *Imperial Leather: Race, Gender, and Sexuality in the Colonial Contest*. London: Routledge.

McCormack, W. J.
    1985   *Ascendancy and Tradition in Anglo-Irish Literary History from 1789 to 1939*. Oxford: Clarendon.

McGowan, John
    1991   *Postmodernism and its Critics*. Ithaca, NY: Cornell University Press.

McIntyre, Kevin
    1996   Geography as Destiny: Cities, Villages and Khmer Rouge Orientalism. *Comparative Studies in Society and History* 38:730–758.

McLean, Adrienne L.
    1997   The Thousand Ways There Are to Move: Camp and Oriental Dance in the Hollywood Musicals of Jack Cole. In Bernstein and Studlar 1997, 130–157.

Mee, Jon
    2000   Austen's Treacherous Ivory: Female Patriotism, Domestic Ideology, and

Empire. In You-Me Park and Rajeswari Sunder Rajan, editors, *The Postcolonial Jane Austen*, 74–92. London: Routledge.

Meeks, John

    2003   In the Wake of Edward Said. *Journal for Cultural and Religious Theory* 5(1):130–138.

Mehdid, Malika

    1993   A Western Invention of Arab Womanhood: The "Oriental Female." In Haleh Afshar, editor, *Women in the Middle East: Perceptions, Realities and Struggles for Liberation*, 18–58. New York: St. Martin's.

Melman, Billie

    1992   *Women's Orients: English Women and the Middle East, 1718–1918: Sexuality, Religion and Work*. Ann Arbor: The University of Michigan Press.

Melville, Lewis

    1910   *The Life and Letters of William Beckford of Fonthill (Author of "Vathek")*. New York: Duffield.

Memmi, Albert

    1991[1957]   *The Colonizer and the Colonized*. Translated by Howard Greenfeld. Boston: Beacon.

Menocal, María Rosa

    1987   *The Arabic Role in Medieval Literary History: A Forgotten Heritage*. Philadelphia: University of Pennsylvania Press.

Mernissi, Fatema

    2001   *Scheherazade Goes West: Different Cultures, Different Harems*. New York: Washington Square Press.

Merod, Jim

    2000   The Sublime Lyrical Abstractions of Edward W. Said. In Bové, editor, 2000, 114–138.

Metlitzki, Dorothee

    1977   *The Matter of Araby in Medieval England*. New Haven, CT: Yale University Press.

Meyer, Eric

    1991   "I Know Thee Not, I Loathe Thy Race": Romantic Orientalism in the Eye of the Other. *ELH* 58:657–699.

Michael, John

    2003   Beyond Us and Them: Identity and Terror from an Arab American's Perspective. *South Atlantic Quarterly* 102(4):701–728.

Michalak, Laurence O.

    1985   Popular French Perspectives on the Maghreb: Orientalist Painting of the Late 19th and Early 20th Centuries. In Jean-Claude Vatin, editor, *Connaissances du Maghreb: Sciences Sociales et Colonisation*, 47–63. Paris: Centre National de la Recherche Scientifique.

Mikoulski, Dimitri

    1997   The Study of Islam in Russia and the Former Soviet Union: An Overview. In Nanji, editor, 1997, 95–107.

Miller, B. D. H.

    1982   Review of *Orientalism*. *Oriental Art* 28(3):284.

Miller, Christopher L.

    1985   *Black Darkness: Africanist Discourse in French*. Chicago: University of Chicago Press.

Miller, Jane

    1990   *Seductions: Studies in Reading and Culture*. Cambridge, MA: Harvard University Press.

Milligan, Spike

    1976   *"Rommel?" "Gunner Who?": A Confrontation in the Desert*. New York: Penguin.

Mills, Sara

    1991   *Discourses of Differences: An Analysis of Women's Travel Writing and Colonialism*. New York: Routledge.

    1997   *Discourse*. London: Routledge.

Millward, James A.

    1994   A Uyghur Muslim in Qianlong's Court: The Meaning of the Fragrant Concubine. *Journal of Asian Studies* 53(2):427–458.

Milner, Anthony, and C. Andrew Gerstle

    1994   Recovering the Exotic: Debating Said. In C. Andrew Gerstle and Anthony Milner, editors, *Recovering the Orient: Artists, Scholars, Appropriations*, 1–6. Chur, Switzerland: Harwood Academic.

Minear, Richard H.

    1980   Orientalism and the Study of Japan. *The Journal of Asian Studies* 39:507–517. [review of *Orientalism*]

Mitchell, Timothy

    1991   *Colonising Egypt*. Berkeley: University of California Press.

    1992   Orientalism and the Exhibitionary Other. In Nicholas B. Dirks, editor, *Colonialism and Culture*, 289–317. Ann Arbor: University of Michigan Press.

Mitchell, W. J. T.

    2005a   Edward Said: Continuing the Conversation. *Critical Inquiry* 31:365–370.

    2005b   Secular Divination: Edward Said's Humanism. *Critical Inquiry* 31:462–471.

Miyoshi, Masao

    1994[1979]   *As We Saw Them: The First Japanese Embassy to the United States*. New York: Kodansha.

Moghith, Anwar

    2005   Saʿid wa-Marks wa-al-istishraq [Said, Marx, and Orientalism]. *Alif* 25:105–120.

Mohanty, Chandra Talpade

    1994   Under Western Eyes: Feminist Scholarship and Colonial Discourse. In Williams and Chrisman 1994, 196–220.

Mommsen, Katharina

    1988   *Goethe und die Arabische Welt*. Frankfurt am Main: Insel.

Moncrif, François Augustin-Paradis de

    1971[1929]   *The Adventures of Zeloide and Amanzarifdine*. Translated by C. K. Scott Moncrieff. New York: Benjamin Blom.

Montagu, Ashley

    1942   *Man's Most Dangerous Myth: The Fallacy of Race*. New York: Columbia University Press.

Montagu, Lady Mary Wortley

    2001   Letter XXIX. In Kamps and Singh, editors, 2001, 100–103.

Montesquieu, Charles Louis, Baron de

    1901   *Persian Letters*. In John Davidson, translator, *Persian and Chinese Letters*, 25–289. Washington, DC: M. Walter Dunne.

Moore, Thomas

    1861   *Lalla Rookh: An Oriental Romance*. London: Longman.

    1915   *The Poetical Works of Thomas Moore*. Edited by A. D. Godley. London: Oxford University Press.

Moore-Gilbert, Bart

    1986   *Kipling and Orientalism*. New York: St. Martin's.

    1996a   "The Bhabal of Tongues": Reading Kipling, Reading Bhabha. In Bart Moore-Gilbert, editor, *Writing India 1757–1990: The Literature of British India*, 111–138. Manchester, UK: Manchester University Press.

    1996b   Introduction: Writing India, Reorienting Colonial Discourse Analysis. In Bart Moore-Gilbert, editor, *Writing India 1757–1990: The Literature of British India*, 1–29. Manchester: Manchester University Press.

    1997   Introduction. In Moore-Gilbert et al. 1997, 1–72.

Moore-Gilbert, Bart, Gareth Stanton, and Willy Maley, editors

    1997   *Postcolonial Criticism*. London: Longman.

Morier, James

    1976[1824]   *The Adventures of Hajji Baba of Ispahan*. New York: Hart.

Morton, Timothy

    1998   Blood Sugar. In Tim Fulford and Peter J. Kitson, editors, *Romanticism and Colonialism: Writing and Empire, 1780–1830*, 87–106. Cambridge: Cambridge University Press.

Moseley, C. W. R. D.

    1983   *The Travels of Sir John Mandeville*. New York: Penguin.

Motabbagani, Mazin S.

    1994   *The Methodology of Bernard Lewis in his Approach to the Intellectual Aspects of Islamic History*. Imam Muhammad ibn Saud University, College of Dawa at Madinah, Department of Orientalism. [in Arabic]

Moughrabi, Fouad

    1978   The Arab Basic Personality: A Critical Study of the Literature. *International Journal of Middle East Studies* 7:99–112.

Mudimbe, V. Y.

    1988   *The Invention of Africa: Gnosis, Philosophy, and the Order of Knowledge*. Bloomington: Indiana University Press.

Mufti, Aamir R.

    2000   Auerbach in Istanbul: Edward Said, Secular Criticism, and the Question of Minority Culture. In Bové, editor, 2000, 229–256.

    2005   Global Comparativism. *Critical Inquiry* 31:472–489.

Muir, William

    1898   *The Caliphate, Its Rise, Decline, and Fall: From Original Sources*. Third Edition. London: Smith, Elder.

Mukherjee, S. N.

    1996   *Citizen Historian: Explorations in Historiography*. New Delhi: Manohar.

Mullen, Bill V.

    2004   *Afro-Orientalism*. Minneapolis: University of Minnesota Press.

Müller, August

    1885–1887   *Der Islam im Morgen- und Abendland*. 2 volumes. Berlin: G. Grote.

Musallam, Basim

    1979   Review Essay: Power and Knowledge. *Middle East Report* 79(July–August): 19–26. [review of *Orientalism*]

Mutman, Mahmut

    1993   Under the Sign of Orientalism: The West vs. Islam. *Cultural Critique* 23:165–197.

Myers, Jeffrey

    1980   Under Western Eyes. *The Sewanee Review* 88:xlv–xlviii. [review of *Orientalism*]

Naff, William E.

    1985–86   Reflections on the Question of "East" and "West" from the Point of View of Japan. *Comparative Civilizations Review* 13–14:215–232.

Nanji, Azim

    1997   Introduction. In Nanji, editor, 1997, xi–xxi.

Nanji, Azim, editor

    1997   *Mapping Islamic Studies: Genealogy, Continuity and Change*. Berlin: Mouton de Gruyter.

Nash, Geoffrey P.

    2005   Revisiting Pro-Muslim British Orientalists. *ISIM Review* 16:47.

Nasir, Sari J.

    1976   *The Arabs and the English*. London: Longman.

Nasr, Seyyid Hossein

    1972[1966]   *Ideas and Realities of Islam*. Boston: Beacon.

Nawwab, Ismail Ibrahim

    2002   Berlin to Makkah: Muhammad Asad's Journey into Islam. *Saudi Aramco World* 53(1):6–32.

Needham, Gerald

    1982   Orientalism in France. *Art Journal* 42(4):338–341.

Nelson, Cynthia

    1998   Feminist Expressions as Self-identity and Cultural Critique: The Discourse of Doria Shafik. In John C. Hawley, editor, *The Postcolonial Crescent: Islam's Impact on Contemporary Literature*, 95–120. New York: Peter Lang.

Newman, John Henry

    1908[1865]   *Apologia Pro Vita Sua*. London: Longmans, Green.

Nietzsche, Friedrich

    1974[1882]   *The Gay Science*. Translated by Walter Kaufmann. New York: Vintage.

Ning, Wang

    1997   Orientalism versus Occidentalism? *New Literary History* 28:57–67.

Nishihara, Daisuke

    2005   Said, Orientalism, and Japan. *Alif* 25:241–253.

Nochlin, Linda

    1983   The Imaginary Orient. *Art in America* 71(May):118–31, 186–91.

    1989   *The Politics of Vision: Essays on Nineteenth-Century Art and Society.* New York: Harper and Row.

Northrop, F. S. C.

    1966   *The Meeting of East and West.* New York: Collier.

Nyang, Sulayman S. Nyang, and Samir Abed-Rabbo

    1984   Bernard Lewis and Islamic Studies: An Assessment. In Afaf Hussain, Robert Olson, and Jamil Qureshi, editors, *Orientalism, Islam, and Islamists*, 259–286. Brattleboro, VT: Amana.

Nygren, Scott

    1993   Doubleness and Idiosyncrasy in Cross-Cultural Analysis. In Hamid Naficy and Teshome H. Gabriel, editors, *Otherness and the Media: The Ethnography of the Imagined and the Imaged*, 173–187. Chur, Switzerland: Harwood Academic.

    1994   *Unthinking Eurocentrism: Multiculturalism and the Media.* London: Routledge.

Obeidat, Marwan

    1998   *American Literature and Orientalism.* Islamkundliche Untersuchungen, 219. Berlin: Klaus Schwarz.

Obenzinger, Hilton

    1999   *American Palestine: Melville, Twain, and the Holy Land Mania.* Princeton, NJ: Princeton University Press.

Ockman, Carol

    1995   *Ingres's Eroticized Bodies: Retracing the Serpentine Line.* New Haven, CT: Yale University Press.

Odell, Dawn

    1999   Is This the Orient? *Medieval Encounters* 5(3):322–335.

O'Hanlon, Rosalind, and David Washbrook

    1992   After Orientalism: Culture, Criticism, and Politics in the Third World. *Comparative Studies in Society and History* 34:141–167.

O'Hara, Daniel T.

    1980   The Romance of Interpretation: A "Postmodern" Critical Style. *Boundary 2* 8(3):259–283.

Ohlmeyer, Jane H.

    1998   "Civilizinge of those Rude Partes": Colonization within Britain and Ireland, 1580s–1640s. In Nicholas Canny, editor, *The Oxford History of the British Empire. Volume I. The Origins of Empire: British Overseas Enterprise to the Close of the Seventeenth Century*, 124–147. Oxford: Oxford University Press.

Olender, Maurice

    1987   The Indo-European Mirror: Monotheism and Polytheism. *History and Anthropology* 3:327–374.

Orr, Mary

 1998 Flaubert's Egypt: Crucible and Crux for Textual Identity. In Paul Starkey and Janet Starkey, editors, *Travellers in Egypt*, 189–200. London: I. B. Tauris.

Otterspeer, Willem

 1998 The Vulnerabilities of an Honest Broker: Edward Said and the Problem of Theory. In Barfoot and D'haen 1998, 189–198.

Owen, Alex

 1997 The Sorcerer and His Apprentice: Aleister Crowley and the Magical Exploration of Edwardian Subjectivity. *Journal of British Studies* 36:99–133.

Owen, Roger

 1973 Studying Islamic History. *Journal of Interdisciplinary History* 4(2):287–298.

 1979 The Mysterious Orient. *Monthly Review* 31(4):58–63. [review of *Orientalism*]

 2005 Conversation with Edward Said. *Critical Inquiry* 31:490–497.

Oxtoby, Willard G., editor

 1976 *Religious Diversity. Essays by Wilfred Cantwell Smith*. New York: Harper and Row.

Padoux, André

 1979 Un procès de l'orientalisme. *Critique* 35(391):1103–1105. [review of *Orientalism*]

Palgrave, Francis Turner

 1994 *The Golden Treasury of the Best Songs and Lyrical Poems in the English Language*. Sixth Edition. Oxford: Oxford University Press.

Palmer, Bryan D.

 1990 *Descent into Discourse: The Reification of Language and the Writing of Social History*. Philadelphia: Temple University Press.

Paret, R.

 1960 Ashab al-Kahf. In *The Encyclopaedia of Islam*, New Edition, 1:691. Leiden: Brill.

Parker, J. S. F.

 1980 From Aeschylus to Kissinger. *Gazelle Review of Literature on the Middle East* 7:4–18. [review of *Orientalism*]

Parker, Kenneth, editor

 1999 *Early Modern Tales of Orient: A Critical Anthology*. London: Routledge.

Parry, Benita

 1992 Overlapping Territories and Intertwined Histories: Edward Said's Postcolonial Cosmopolitanism. In Sprinker, editor, 1992, 19–47.

 2002 Directions and Dead Ends in Postcolonial Studies. In David Theo Goldberg and Ato Quayson, editors, *Relocating Postcolonialism*, 66–81. Oxford: Blackwell.

Parry, V. J.

 1962 Renaissance Historical Literature in Relation to the Near and Middle East (with Special Reference to Paolo Giovio). In Lewis and Holt, editors, 1962, 277–289.

Patai, Raphael

 1977 *The Jewish Mind*. New York: Scribners.

 1979 The Orientalist Conspiracy. *Midstream* 25(9):62–66. [review of *Orientalism*]

 1983 *The Arab Mind*. Revised Edition. New York: Scribner's Sons.

1987   *Ignaz Goldziher and His Oriental Diary. A Translation and Psychological Portrait*. Detroit: Wayne State University Press.

1988   *Apprentice in Budapest: Memories of a World that Is No More*. Salt Lake City: University of Utah Press.

Pelckmans, Paul

1998   Walter Scott's Orient: *The Talisman*. In Barfoot and D'haen 1998, 97–109.

Peltre, Christine

1998   *Orientalism in Art*. Translated by John Goodman. New York: Abbeville.

Peters, Emyrs

1967   Preface. In W. Robertson Smith, *Kinship and Marriage in Early Arabia*, xxx–xiii. Boston: Beacon.

Phillips, William

1989   Intellectuals, Academics and Politics. *Partisan Review* 56:342–347.

Pick, Lucy K.

1999   Edward Said, Orientalism and the Middle Ages. *Medieval Encounters* 5(3): 265–271.

Pickering, John

1843   Address to the First Annual Meeting. *Journal of the American Oriental Society* 1(1):1–78.

Plumb, John Harold

1979   Looking East in Error. *New York Times Book Review*, February 18, 23, 28 [review of *Orientalism*].

Polk, William R.

1975   Islam and the West: 1) Sir Hamilton Gibb between Orientalism and History. *International Journal of Middle Eastern Studies* 6(2):131–139.

Pollock, Sheldon

1993   Deep Orientalism? Notes on Sanskrit and Power beyond the Raj. In Breckenridge and van der Veer, editors, 1993, 76–133.

Poole, Sophia

2003   *The Englishwoman in Egypt. Letters from Cairo, Written During a Residence There in 1842–46*. Cairo: American University in Cairo Press.

Porter, Dennis

1991   *Haunted Journeys: Desire and Transgression in European Travel Writing*. Princeton, NJ: Princeton University Press.

1994   Orientalism and Its Problems. In Williams and Chrisman 1994, 150–161.

Posner, Richard A.

2001   *Public Intellectuals: A Study of Decline*. Cambridge, MA: Harvard University Press.

Pouillon, François

1990   Legs colonials, patrimonie national: Nasreddine Dinet, peintre de l'indigène algérien. *Cahiers d'études africaines* 30(3):329–63.

Prakash, Gyan

1992a   Can the "Subaltern" Ride? A Reply to O'Hanlon and Washbrook. *Comparative Studies in Society and History* 34:168–184.

1992b   Writing Post-Orientalist Histories of the Third World: Indian Historiography is Good to Think." In Nicholas B. Dirks, editor, *Colonialism and Culture*, 353–388. Ann Arbor: University of Michigan Press.

1994   Subaltern Studies as Postcolonial Criticism. *The American Historical Review* 99(5):1475–1490.

1995   *Orientalism* Now. *History and Theory* 34:199–212.

Prasch, Thomas J.

1995   Orientalism's Other, Other Orientalisms: Women in the Scheme of Empire. *Journal of Women's History* 7(4):174–188.

Pratt, Mary Louise

1992   *Imperial Eyes: Travel Writing and Transculturation*. London: Routledge.

Prochaska, David

1994   Art of Colonialism, Colonialism of Art: The *Description de l'Égypte* (1809–1828). *L'Esprit Créateur* 34(2):69–91.

1996   History as Literature, Literature as History: Cagayous of Algiers. *American Historical Review* 101(3):671–711.

Pruett, Gordon E.

1980   The Escape from the Seraglio: Anti-Orientalist Trends in Modern Religious Studies. *Arab Studies Quarterly* 2(4):291–317.

1984   "Islam" and Orientalism. In Afaf Hussain, Robert Olson, and Jamil Qureshi, editors, *Orientalism, Islam, and Islamists*, 43–87. Brattleboro, VT: Amana.

Prutz, Hans

1883   *Kulturgeschichte der Kreuzzüge*. Berlin: E. S. Mittler und Sohn.

Quandt, William

1997   Review of *Orientalism*, by Edward Said. *Foreign Affairs* 76(5):232–233.

Quayson, Ato

2000   *Postcolonialism: Theory, Practice or Process?* Cambridge: Polity.

Qureshi, Emran, and Michael Sells, editors

2003   *The New Crusades: Constructing the Muslim Enemy*. New York: Columbia University Press.

Racevskis, Karlis

2005   Edward Said and Michel Foucault: Affinities and Dissonances. *Research in African Literatures* 36(3):83–97.

Rafael, Vincent L.

1999   Regionalism, Area Studies, and the Accident of Agency. *American Historical Review* 104(4):1208–1220.

Ragan, John David

1998   French Women Travellers in Egypt: A Discourse Marginal to Orientalism? In Paul Starkey and Janet Starkey, editors, *Travellers in Egypt*, 222–230. London: I. B. Tauris.

Rahimieh, Nasrin

1990   *Oriental Responses to the West: Comparative Essays in Select Writers from the Muslim World*. Leiden: Brill.

Rajan, Rajeswari Sunder
    2000   Austen in the World: Postcolonial Mappings. In You-Me Park and Rajeswari Sunder Rajan, editors, *The Postcolonial Jane Austen*, 3–25. London: Routledge.

Ramadan, Yasmine
    2005   A Bibliographic Guide to Edward Said. *Alif* 25:270–287.

Rao, P. Kodonda
    1939   *East versus West: A Denial of Contrasts*. London: Allen and Unwin.

Rassam, Amal
    1980   Representation and Aggression. *Comparative Studies in Society and History* 22:505–508. [review of *Orientalism*]

Raymond, Andre
    1994   Islamic City, Arab City: Orientalist Myths and Recent Views. *British Journal of Middle Eastern Studies* 21(1):3–18.

Reig, Daniel
    1988   *Homo orientaliste: Le langue arabe en France depuis le XIXe siècle*. Paris: Editions Maisonneuve et Larose.

Rendall, Jane
    1982   Scottish Orientalism: From Robertson to James Mill. *The Historical Review* 25(1):43–69.

Rey, Alain, editor
    1992   *Dictionnaire historique de la langue français*. 2 volumes. Paris: Dictionnaires le Robert.

Rice, James P.
    2002   In the Wake of Orientalism. *Comparative Literature Studies* 37(2):223–238.

Richardson, Michael
    1990   Enough Said: Reflections on Orientalism. *Anthropology Today* 6(4):16–19.

Riedel, Dagmar A.
    1999   Medieval Arabic Literature between History and Psychology: Gustave von Grunebaum's Approach to Literary Criticism. In K. Dévényi and T. Iványi, editors, *Proceedings of the Arabic and Islamic Sections of the 35th International Congress of Asian and North African Studies*, Budapest Studies in Arabic, 19–20, 111–122.

Robbins, Bruce
    1992a   The East Is a Career: Edward Said and the Logics of Professionalism. In Sprinker 1992, 48–73.
    1992b   Colonial Discourse: A Paradigm and Its Discontents. *Victorian Studies* 35(2):209–214.
    1994   Secularism, Elitism, Progress, and other Transgressions: On Edward Said's "Voyage In." *Social Text* 12:25–37.
    1995   The Seduction of the Unexpected: On Imperalism and History. *Nineteenth-Century Contexts* 19:73–79.

Roche-Mahdi, Sarah
    1997   The Cultural and Intellectual Background of German Orientalism. In Nanji, editor, 1997, 108–127.

Rocher, Ludo, editor

  1984   *Ezourvedam: A French Veda of the Eighteenth Century*. University of Pennsyl-
         vania Studies on South Asia, 1. Philadelphia: John Benjamins.

Rocher, Rosane

  1993   British Orientalism in the Eighteenth Century: The Dialectics of Knowledge
         and Government. In Breckenridge and van der Veer, editors, 1993, 215–249.

Rodenbeck, John

  1998   Edward Said and Edward William Lane. In Paul Starkey and Janet Starkey,
         editors, *Travellers in Egypt*, 233–243. London: I. B. Tauris.

Rodinson, Maxime

  1963   Bilan des études mohammediennes. *Revue historique* 229:169–220.

  1974   The Western Image and Western Studies of Islam. In Joseph Schacht and
         C. E. Bosworth, editors, *The Legacy of Islam*, 9–62. Oxford: Oxford University
         Press.

  1991   *Europe and the Mystique of Islam*. Translated by Roger Veinus. Seattle: Uni-
         versity of Washington Press.

Rogers, Katherine M.

  1986   Subversion of Patriarchy in *Les Lettres Persanes*. *Philological Quarterly*
         65:61–78.

Rogers, Mary Eliza

  1862   *Domestic Life in Palestine*. London: Bell and Daldy.

Roman, James S.

  1992   *The Edges of the Earth in Ancient Thought*. Princeton, NJ: Princeton Univer-
         sity Press.

Romm, James

  1998   *Herodotus*. New Haven, CT: Yale University Press.

Roosbroeck, Gustave Leopold

  1972[1932]   *Persian Letters before Montesquieu*. New York: Burt Franklin.

Roper, Geoffrey

  1998   Texts from Nineteenth-Century Egypt: The Role of E. W. Lane. In Paul Starkey
         and Janet Starkey, editors, *Travellers in Egypt*, 244–254. London: I. B. Tauris.

Rorty, Richard

  1991   *Essays on Heidegger and Others: Philosophical Papers*. Volume 2. Cambridge:
         Cambridge University Press.

Rose, Jacqueline

  2000   Edward Said Talks to Jacqueline Rose. In Bové, editor, 2000, 9–30.

Rosellini, M., and S. Said

  1978   Usages de femmes et autres nomoi chez les "sauvages" d'Hérodote: Essai de
         lecture structurale. *Annali della Scuola Normale Superiore di Pisa. Classe di
         Lettre e Filosofia*. Ser. 3, 8(3):949–1005.

Rosenberg, Warren

  1979   The Dark Side of Knowledge: Edward Said's *Orientalism*. *Denver Quarterly*
         14(3):108–112. [review]

Rosengarten, Frank
  1998 Homo Siculus: Essentialism in the Writing of Giovanni Verga, Giuseppe Tomasi Di Lampedusa, and Leonardo Sciascia. In Jane Schneider, editor, *Italy's "Southern Question": Orientalism in One Country*, 117–131. Oxford: Berg.

Rotter, Andrew J.
  2000 Saidism without Said: *Orientalism* and U.S. Diplomatic History. *American Historical Review* 105:1205–1217.

Rousillon, Alain
  1990 Le debat sur l'Orientalisme dans le champ intellectual arabe: l'aporie des sciences sociales. *Peuples méditerranéens* 50:7–39.

Roy, Anindyo
  1995 Postcoloniality and the Politics of Identity in the Diaspora: Figuring "Home," Locating Histories. In Gita Rajan and Radhika Mohanran, editors, *Postcolonial Discourse and Changing Cultural Contexts*, 101–115. Westport, CT: Greenwood.

Rubenstein, Murray
  1998 *Missionary Orientalism and the Missionary Lens: Using Saidian Mode of Analysis to Read the Western Missionaries' Accounts of the Development of the Protestant Presence in Taiwan*. Cambridge: Currents in World Christianity Project.

Rubin, Andrew N.
  2003 Techniques of Trouble: Edward Said and the Dialectics of Cultural Philology. *South Atlantic Quarterly* 102(4):861–876.

Rudolph, Ekkehard
  1991 *Westliche Islamwissenschaft im Spiegel muslimischer Kritik: Grundzüge und aktuelle Merkmale einer innerislamischen Diskussion*. Islamkundliche Untersuchungen, 137. Berlin: Klaus Schwarz.

Rushdie, Salman
  1991 On Palestinian Identity: A Conversation with Edward Said. In Salman Rushdie, *Imaginary Homelands: Essays and Criticism, 1981–1991*, 166–184. London: Granta Books.

Russell, John
  1992 Race and Reflexivity: The Black Other in Contemporary Japanese Mass Culture. In George E. Marcus, editor, *Rereading Cultural Anthropology*, 296–318. Durham, NC: Duke University Press.

Ryckmans, Pierre
  1980 Orientalism and Sinology. *Asian Studies Association of Australia Review* 7(3):18–21. [review of *Orientalism*]

al-Saffar, Muhammad
  1991 *Disorienting Encounters: Travels of a Moroccan Scholar in France in 1845–1846: The Voyage of Muhammad al-Saffar*. Translated and edited by Susan Gilson Miller. Berkeley: University of California Press.

Saghiyya, Hazim
  1995 *Thaqafat al-Khumayniyya: Mawqif min al-istishraq am harb 'ala tayf*. Beirut: Dar al-Jadid.

Saglia, Diego
>   2002   William Beckford's "Sparks of Orientalism" and the Material-Discourse Ori-
>   ent of British Romanticism. *Textual Practice* 16(1):75–92.

Sahas, Daniel J.
>   1972   *John of Damascus on Islam: The "Heresy of the Ishmaelites."* Leiden: Brill.

Sahlins, Marshall
>   2002   *Waiting for Foucault.* Chicago: Prickly Paradigm.

Said, Edward
>   1975a   *Beginnings: Intention and Method.* New York: Basic.
>   1975b   Orientalism and the October War: The Shattered Myths. In Baha Abu-Laban
>   and Faith T. Zeadey, editors, *Arabs in America: Myths and Realities*, 83–112.
>   Wilmette, IL: Medina University Press International.
>   1976a   Arabs, Islam and the Dogmas of the West. *New York Times Book Review*,
>   October 31, 4–5, 35–37. [review of several titles]
>   1976b   Letter to the Editor, "Orientalism." *New York Times Book Review*, Decem-
>   ber 16, 37–38.
>   1979   *Orientalism.* New York: Vintage.
>   1980a   Review of Albert Hourani, *Europe and the Middle East. Arab Studies Quar-
>   terly* 2(iv):386–393.
>   1980b   Islam, the Philological Vocation, and French Culture: Renan and Mas-
>   signon. In Malcom H. Kerr, editor, *Islamic Studies: A Tradition and Its Prob-
>   lems*, 53–72. Malibu, CA: Undena.
>   1982   Orientalism: An Exchange. *New York Review of Books* 29(August 12):44–46.
>   1983   *The World, the Text, and the Critic.* Cambridge, MA: Harvard University Press.
>   1984   Foreword. In Raymond Schwab, *The Oriental Renaissance: Europe's Redis-
>   covery of India and the East, 1680–1880*, vii–xxiv. New York: Columbia Uni-
>   versity Press.
>   1985   Orientalism Reconsidered. *Race & Class* 27(2):1–15.
>   1986a   Foucault and the Imagination of Power. In David C. Hoy, editor, *Foucault: A
>   Critical Reader*, 149–155. Oxford: Blackwell.
>   1986b   Orientalism Reconsidered. In Francis Barker et al., editors, *Literature, Pol-
>   itics and Theory*, 210–229. London: Methuen.
>   1988a   Foreword. In Ranajit Guha and Gayatri Chakravorty Spivak, editors, *Selected
>   Subaltern Studies*, v–x. Oxford: Oxford University Press.
>   1988b   Orientalism Revisited: An Interview with Edward W. Said. *Middle East
>   Report* 18(1):32–36.
>   1989   Representing the Colonized: Anthropology's Interlocutors. *Critical Inquiry*
>   15:205–225.
>   1993a   *Culture and Imperialism.* New York: Knopf.
>   1993b   The Phony Islamic Threat. *New York Times Magazine*, November 21, 63–65.
>   1994a   Afterword. In Edward Said, *Orientalism*, 329–352. New York: Vintage.
>   1994b   *Representations of the Intellectual.* New York: Pantheon.
>   1994c   Secular Interpretation, the Geographical Element, and the Methodology of
>   Imperialism. In Gyan Prakash, editor, *After Colonialism: Imperial Histories and
>   Postcolonial Displacements*, 21–39. Princeton, NJ: Princeton University Press.

1997   *Covering Islam*. Revised Edition. New York: Vintage.

1998   Gulliver in the Middle East. Electronic document, www.geocities.com/Col-legePark/Library/9803/edward_said/gulliver.html, accessed May 2002.

1999   *Out of Place: A Memoir*. New York: Knopf

2000   *Reflections on Exile and Other Essays*. Cambridge, MA: Harvard University Press.

2001a   The Clash of Ignorance. *The Nation* 273(12)[October 22]:11.

2001b   Tatawwur Fukaw li-al-sulta. *al-Bahrayn al-Thaqafiyya* 28:84–88. [Translation of Said 1986a by ʿAlaʾ al-Din Husayn]

2002   In Conversation with Neeladri Bhattacharya, Suvir Kaul, and Ania Loomba. In David Theo Goldberg and Ato Quayson, editors, *Relocating Postcolonialism*, 1–14. Oxford: Blackwell.

2003   Preface to the Twenty-Fifth Anniversary Edition. In Edward Said, *Orientalism*, xv–xxx. New York: Vintage.

2004   *Humanism and Democratic Criticism*. New York: Columbia University Press.

2005   On the University. *Alif* 25:26–36.

Said, Edward, and David Barsamian

1994   *The Pen and the Sword*. Monroe, ME: Common Courage.

Said, Khalidah

1979   *Harakiyat al-ibdaʿ*. Beirut: Dar al-ʿAwda.

Salamandra, Christa

2004   *A New Old Damascus: Authenticity and Distinction in Urban Syria*. Bloomington: Indiana University Press.

Salamini, Leonardo

1981   *The Sociology of Praxis: An Introduction to Gramsci's Theory*. London: Routledge and Kegan Paul.

Saleh, Tayeb

1989   *Season of Migration to the North*. Translated by Denys Johnson-Davies. New York: Michael Kesend.

Sale-Harrrison, L.

1934   *The Remarkable Jew: His Wonderful Future*. Harrisburg: Evangelical Press.

Salem, Elie

1958   Form and Substance: A Critical Examination of the Arabic Language. *Middle East Forum* 33(7):17–19.

Salem, Lori Anne

2001   Race, Sexuality, and Arabs in American Entertainment, 1850–1900. In Sherifa Zuhur, editor, *Colors of Enchantment: Theater, Dance, Music, and the Visual Arts of the Middle East*, 211–232. Cairo: American University in Cairo Press.

Salisbury, Edward E.

1860–63   Contributions from Original Sources to Our Knowledge of the Sciences of Muslim Tradition. *Journal of the American Oriental Society* 7:60–142.

Samarrai, Alauddin

1999   Arabs and Latins in the Middle Ages: Enemies, Partners, and Scholars. In Blanks and Frassetto 1999, 137–145.

San Juan, E.

    2005   Edward Said's Use-Value for Asian American Cultural Projects. *Amerasia Journal* 35(1):61–64.

Sanders, Paula

    2003   The Victorian Invention of Medieval Cairo: A Case Study of Medievalism and the Construction of the East. *MESA Bulletin* 37(2):179–198.

Sangren, P. Steven

    1995   "Power" against Ideology: A Critique of Foucaultian Usage. *Cultural Anthropology* 10(1): 3–40.

Sardar, Ziauddin

    1999   *Orientalism*. Philadelphia: Open University Press.

Sarkar, Sumit

    1994   Orientalism Revisted: Saidian Framework in the Writing of Modern Indian History. *Oxford Literary Review* 10(1–2):205–224.

    1997   *Writing Social History*. Delhi: Oxford University Press.

Sartre, Jean-Paul

    1981–94[1971–72]   *The Family Idiot: Gustave Flaubert, 1821–1857*. Translated by Carol Cosman. 5 volumes. Chicago: University of Chicago Press.

Sauvaget, Jean

    1965[1943]   *Introduction to the History of the Muslim East: A Bibliographical Guide*. Berkeley: University of California Press.

Sayyid, Bobby S.

    1997   *A Fundamental Fear: Eurocentrism and the Emergence of Islamism*. London: Zed.

al-Sayyid, Radwan

    2001   Al-Istishraq wa-al-anthrubulujiyya. *Al-Ijtihad* 12(49):5–9.

Sax, William S.

    1998   The Hall of Mirrors: Orientalism, Anthropology, and the Other. *American Anthropologist* 100(2):292–301.

Schaar, Stuart

    1979   Orientalism at the Service of Imperialism. *Race & Class* 21(1):67–79. [review of *Orientalism*]

Schacker-Mill, Jennifer

    2000   Otherness and Otherworldliness: Edward W. Lane's Ethnographic Treatment of the Arabian Nights. *Journal of American Folklore* 113:164–184.

Schaub, Diana

    1995   *Erotic Liberalism: Women and Revolution in Montesquieu's* Persian Letters. London: Rowman and Littlefield.

Schaub, Uta Liebmann

    1989   Foucault's Oriental Subtext. *Publications of the Modern Language Association of America* 104:306–316.

Schick, Irvin Cemil

    1990   Representing Middle Eastern Women: Feminism and Colonial Discourse. *Feminist Studies* 16:345–380.

    1999   *The Erotic Margin: Sexuality and Spatiality in Alterist Discourse*. London: Verso.

Schimmel, Annemarie

    1980   Review of Edward W. Said, *Orientalism. Journal of Ecumenical Studies* 17(4):149–150.

    1985   *And Muhammad Is His Messenger: The Veneration of the Prophet in Islamic Piety*. Chapel Hill: University of North Carolina Press.

    1993   *The Mystery of Numbers*. Oxford: Oxford University Press.

Schneider, Jane

    1998   Introduction: The Dynamics of Neo-orientalism in Italy (1848–1995). In Jane Schneider, editor, *Italy's "Southern Question": Orientalism in One Country*, 1–23. Oxford: Berg.

Schueller, Malini Johar

    1998   *U.S. Orientalisms: Race, Nation, and Gender in Literature, 1790–1890*. Ann Arbor: University of Michigan Press.

Schwab, Raymond

    1934   *Vie d'Anquetil-Duperron*. Paris: E. Leroux.

    1984[1950]   *The Oriental Renaissance: Europe's Rediscovery of India and the East, 1680–1880*. Translated by Gene Patterson-Black and Victor Reinking. New York: Columbia University Press.

Schwartz, Benjamin I.

    1980   Area Studies as a Critical Discipline. *Journal of Asian Studies* 40:15–25.

Schwoebel, Robert

    1967   *The Shadow of the Crescent: The Renaissance Image of the Turk*. Nieuwkoop, Netherlands: B. de Graaf.

Scott, Janny

    1998   A Palestinian Literary Critic Confronts Time. *New York Times*, September 19:A17, A19.

Scott, Sir Walter

    1997   *Ivanhoe: A Romance*. New York: Modern Library.

    [1819]

Searight, Sarah

    1969   *The British in the Middle East*. New York: Atheneum.

Senghor, Léopold Sédar

    1994[1970]   Negritude: A Humanism of the Twentieth Century. In Patrick Williams and L. Chrisman, editors, *Colonial Discourse and Post-Colonial Theory: A Reader*, 27–35. New York: Columbia University Press.

Serghini, El Habib Benrahhal

    1998   William Beckford's Symbolic Appropriation of the Oriental Context. In Barfoot and D'haen 1998, 43–64.

Setton, Kenneth Meyer

    1992   *Western Hostility to Islam and Prophecies of Islam*. Memoirs of the American Philosophical Society, 201. Philadelphia: American Philosophical Society.

Shaffer, E. S.

    1975   *"Kubla Khan" and* The Fall of Jerusalem: *The Mythological School in Biblical Criticism and Secular Literature 1700–1880*. Cambridge: Cambridge University Press.

Shah, Idries

    1987   *Darkest England*. London: Octagon.

Shaheen, Jack G.

    2001   *Reel Bad Arabs: How Hollywood Vilifies a People*. New York: Olive Branch.

Shahid, Irfan

    1984   *Rome and the Arabs: A Prolegomenon to the Study of Byzantium and the Arabs*. Washington, DC: Dumbarton Oaks Research Library and Collection.

Shalev, Zur

    2002   Measurer of All Things: John Greaves (1602–1652), the Great Pyramid and Early Modern Metrology. *Journal of the History of Ideas* 63(4):555–575.

Sharabi, Hisham

    1970   *Arab Intellectuals and the West: The Formative Years, 1875–1914*. Baltimore: Johns Hopkins Press.

    1990   The Scholarly Point of View: Politics, Perspective, Paradigm. In Sharabi, 1990, 1–51.

Sharabi, Hisham, editor

    1990   *Theory, Politics and the Arab World: Critical Responses*. London: Routledge.

Sharafuddin, Mohammed

    1996   *Islam and Romantic Orientalism: Literary Encounters with the Orient*. New York: I. B. Tauris.

Shay, Anthony, and Barbara Sellers-Young

    2003   Belly Dance: Orientalism—Exoticism—Self-Exoticism. *Dance Research Journal* 35(1):13–37.

Shelley, Mary

    1981[1818]   *Frankenstein*. New York: Bantam.

Shohat, Ella

    1992   Antinomies of Exile: Said at the Frontiers of National Narrations. In Sprinker 1992, 121–143.

    1993   Gender and Culture of Empire: Toward a Feminist Ethnography of the Cinema. In Hamid Naficy and Teshome H. Gabriel, editors, *Otherness and the Media: The Ethnography of the Imagined and the Imaged*, 45–84. Chur, Switzerland: Harwood Academic.

    2004   The "Postcolonial" in Translation: Reading Said in Hebrew. *Journal of Palestine Studies* 33(3):55–75.

Shohat, Ella, and Robert Stam

    1994   *Unthinking Eurocentrism: Multiculturalism and the Media*. London: Routledge.

Shulevitz, Judith

    2001   At War with the World. *New York Times Book Review*, October 21, 39.

Sim, Stuart, editor

    2002   *The Routledge Companion to Postmodernism*. London: Routledge.

Simmons, Claire A.

    1995   Thoughts on "Said and the Historians." *Nineteenth-Century Contexts* 19:89–90.

Simon, Reeva

    1989   *The Middle East in Crime Fiction: Mysteries, Spy Novels and Thrillers from 1916 to the 1980's*. New York: Lilian Barber.

Singh, Amardeep

    2004   An Introduction to Edward Said, Orientalism, and Postcolonial Literary Studies. Electronic document, www.lehigh.edu/~amsp/2004/09/introduction-to-edward-said.html, accessed January 2006.

Singh, Amritjit, and Bruce G. Johnson, editors

    2004   *Interviews with Edward W. Said.* Jackson: University Press of Mississippi.

Singh, Amritjit, and Peter Schmidt

    2000   On the Borders between U.S. Studies and Postcolonial Theory. In Amritjit Singh and Peter Schmidt, editors, *Postcolonial Theory and the United States: Race, Ethnicity, and Literature*, 3–69. Jackson: University Press of Mississippi.

Singh, Michael Garbutcheon, and James Greenlaw

    1998   Postcolonial Theory in the Literature Classroom: Contrapuntal Readings. *Theory into Practice* 37:193–202.

Sinha, Mrinalini

    1995   *Colonial Masculinity: The "Manly Englishman" and the "Effeminate Bengali" in the Late Nineteenth Century.* Manchester, NY: Manchester University Press.

Sivan, Emmanuel

    1985   *Interpretations of Islam: Past and Present.* Princeton, NJ: Darwin Press.

Slater, Robert L.

    1963   *World Religions and World Community.* New York: Columbia University Press.

Smith, Byron Porter

    1977[1939]   *Islam in English Literature.* Delmar, NY: Caravan Books.

Smith, Janet, editor

    1962   *Mark Twain on the Damned Human Race.* New York: Hill and Wang.

Smith, Neil, and Anne Godlewska, editors

    1994   *Geography and Empire.* Oxford: Blackwell.

Smith, Wilfred Cantwell

    1957   *Islam in Modern History.* New York: New American Library.

Smith, William Robertson

    1912   *Lectures and Essays of William Robertson Smith.* London: Adam and Charles Black.

    1967[1885]   *Kinship and Marriage in Early Arabia.* Boston: Beacon.

    1972[1889]   *Lectures on the Religion of the Semites.* New York: Schocken.

Sokal, Alan D.

    1996   Transgressing the Boundaries: Toward a Transformative Hermeneutics of Quantum Gravity. *Social Text* 46/47:217–252.

    1998   What the Social Text Affair Does and Does Not Prove. In Noretta Koertge, editor, *A House Built on Sand: Exposing Postmodernist Myths about Science*, 9–22. Oxford: Oxford University Press.

Sonn, Tamara

    1996   *Interpreting Islam: Bandali Jawzi's Islamic Intellectual History.* Oxford: Oxford University Press.

Southern, Richard

    1962   *Western Views of Islam in the Middle Ages.* Cambridge, MA: Harvard University Press.

Spence, Jonathan D.

    1992a   *Chinese Roundabout*. New York: Norton.

    1992b   Preface. In Malroux 1992, i–xvii.

Spencer, Jonathan

    1989   Orientalism without Orientals. *Anthropology Today* 5(2):18–19.

    1997   Post-Colonialism and the Political Imagination. *Journal of the Royal Anthropological Institute* 3(1):1–19.

Spiegel, Gabrielle M.

    1997   *The Past as Text: The Theory and Practice of Medieval Historiography*. Baltimore, MD: Johns Hopkins University Press.

Spivak, Gayatri C.

    1993   *Outside in the Teaching Machine*. London: Routledge.

    1999   *A Critique of Postcolonial Reason: Toward a History of the Vanishing Present*. Cambridge, MA: Harvard University Press.

    2000   Race Before Racism: The Disappearance of the American. In Bové, editor, 2000, 51–65.

    2005   Thinking about Edward Said: Pages from a Memoir. *Critical Inquiry* 31:519–525.

Sprinker, Michael

    1993   The National Question: Said, Ahmad, Jameson. *Public Culture* 6:3–29.

Sprinker, Michael, editor

    1992   *Edward Said: A Critical Reader*. Oxford: Blackwell.

Starn, Orin

    1992   Missing the Revolution: Anthropologists and the War in Peru. In George E. Marcus, editor, *Rereading Cultural Anthropology*, 152–180. Durham, NC: Duke University Press.

Steadman, John M.

    1969   *The Myth of Asia*. New York: Simon and Schuster.

Steegmuller, Francis

    1972   *Flaubert in Egypt: A Sensibility on Tour*. Boston: Little, Brown.

Steele, Meili

    1997   *Critical Confrontations: Literary Theories in Dialogue*. Columbia: University of South Carolina Press.

Steenstrup, Carl

    1985–86   Reflections on "Orientalism" from the Angle of Japan-related Research. *Comparative Civilizations Review* 13–14:233–252.

Stewart, Robert Wilson

    1975   *Disraeli's Novels Reviewed, 1826–1968*. Metuchen, NJ: Scarecrow Press.

Stone, Lawrence

    1981   *The Past and the Present*. London: Routledge and Kegan Paul.

Studlar, Gaylyn

    1997   "Out-Salomeing Salome": Dance, the New Woman, and Fan Magazine Orientalism. In Matthew Bernstein and Gaylyn Studlar, editors, *Visions of the East: Orientalism in Film*, 99–129. New Brunswick, NJ: Rutgers University Press.

Suleri, Sara

 1992 *The Rhetoric of English India*. Chicago: University of Chicago Press.

Sweetman, John

 1988 *The Oriental Obsession: Islamic Inspiration in British and American Art and Architecture 1500–1920*. Cambridge: Cambridge University Press.

Tahan, Malba

 1993[1972] *The Man Who Counted: A Collection of Mathematical Adventures*. Translated by Leslie Clark and Alastair Reid. New York: W. W. Norton.

al-Tahtawi, Rifaʿa Rafiʿ

 2002 The Extraction of Gold, or an Overview of Paris *and* the Honest Guide for Boys and Girls. In Charles Kurzman, editor, *Modernist Islam, 1850–1940: A Sourcebook*, 31–39. Oxford: Oxford University Press.

Tanaka, Stefan

 1993 *Japan's Orient: Rendering Pasts into History*. Berkeley: University of California Press.

Tavakoli-Targhi, Mohamad

 2001 *Refashioning Iran: Orientalism, Occidentalism, and Historiography*. New York: Palgrave.

Taylor, Patrick

 1995 Rereading Fanon, Rewriting Caribbean History. In Gita Rajan and Radhika Mohanran, editors, *Postcolonial Discourse and Changing Cultural Contexts*, 17–31. Westport, CT: Greenwood Press.

Tehranian, Majid

 1982 Review of *Covering Islam*. *Journal of International Affairs* 35(2):261–263.

Teltscher, Kate

 1995 *India Inscribed: European and British Writing on India 1600–1800*. Delhi: Oxford University Press.

Tessler, Mark, Jodi Nachtwey, and Anne Banda, editors

 1999 *Area Studies and Social Science: Strategies for Understanding Middle East Politics*. Bloomington: Indiana University Press.

Thieck, Jean-Pierre

 1980 Un Autre Orientalisme. *Annales Économies Sociétés Civilisations* 35(3–4):512–516. [review of *Orientalism*]

Thiry, Jean

 1973 *Bonaparte en Égypte décembre 1797–24 août 1799*. Paris: Berger-Levrault.

Thomas, Nicholas

 1991 Anthropology and Orientalism. *Anthropology Today* 7(2):4–7.

 1994 *Colonialism's Culture: Anthropology, Travel and Government*. Princeton, NJ: Princeton University Press.

Thompson, Jason

 2000 Editor's Introduction. In Edward William Lane, *Description of Egypt*, ix–xxv. Cairo: American University in Cairo Press.

Thornton, Lynne

 1985 *Women as Portrayed in Orientalist Painting*. Paris: ACR Editions.

Tibawi, Abdul Latif

    1961   *British Interests in Palestine, 1800–1901*. Oxford: Oxford University Press.

    1963   English-speaking Orientalists: A Critique of Their Approach to Islam and Arab Nationalism. *The Muslim World* 53:185–204, 298–313.

    1964   English-speaking Orientalists: A Critique of Their Approach to Islam and Arab Nationalism. *Islamic Quarterly* 8(1–2):25–44; 8(3–4):73–88.

    1979   Second Critique of English-speaking Orientalists and Their Approach to Islam and Arabs. *Islamic Quarterly* 23(1):3–54.

Tibi, Bassam

    2001   *Islam Between Culture and Politics*. New York: Palgrave.

Tizini, Tayyib

    1978   *Min al-turath ila al-thawra*. Beirut: Dar Ibn Khaldun.

Todorov, Tzvetan

    1980   Preface. In Edward Said, *L'Orientalisme. L'Orient créé par l'Occident*, 8–9. Paris: Éditions du Seuil.

    1984   *The Conquest of America: The Question of the Other*. New York: Harper and Row.

    1993   *On Human Diversity: Nationalism, Racism and Exoticism in French Thought.* Cambridge: Cambridge University Press.

Tolan, John V.

    1999   Muslims as Pagan Idolaters in Chronicles of the First Crusade. In Blanks and Frassetto 1999, 97–117.

    2002   *Saracens: Islam in the Medieval European Imagination*. New York: Columbia University Press.

Tolmacheva, Marina

    1995   The Medieval Arabic Geographers and the Beginnings of Modern Orientalism. *International Journal of Middle East Studies* 27(2):141–156.

Tønnesson, Stein

    1994   Orientalism, Occidentalism and Knowing about Others. *Nordic Newsletter of Asian Studies* 2:14–18.

Toynbee, Arnold J.

    1935   *A Study of History. I*. London: Oxford University Press.

    1961   *A Study of History. XII. Reconsiderations*. London: Oxford University Press.

Trafton, Scott

    2004   *Egypt Land: Race and Nineteenth-Century American Egyptomania*. Durham, NC: Duke University Press.

Triveldi, Harish

    1995   *Colonial Transactions: English Literature and India*. Manchester, UK: Manchester University Press.

Trumpener, Katie

    1987   Rewriting Roxane: Orientalism and Intertextuality in Montesquieu's *Lettres Persanes* and Defoe's *The Fortunate Mistress*. *Stanford French Review* 11:177–191.

Tsuda, Sokichi

    1955   *What is the Oriental Culture?* Translated by Y. Mori. Tokyo: Hokuseido.

Tucker, Judith

    1990   Taming the West: Trends in the Writing of Modern Arab Social History in Anglophone Academia. In Sharabi, editor, 1990, 198–227.

Turner, Bryan S.

    1974   *Weber and Islam: A Critical Study*. London: Routledge and Kegan Paul.

    1978   *Marx and the End of Orientalism*. London: George Allen and Unwin.

    1981   Review of *Orientalism*. *Iranian Studies* 14:107–112.

    1984   Orientalism and the Problem of Civil Society in Islam. In Asaf Hussain, Robert Olson, and Jamil Qureshi, editors, *Orientalism, Islam, and Islamists*, 23–43. Brattleboro, VT: Amana.

    1994   *Orientalism, Postmodernism, and Globalism*. London: Routledge.

    2000   Outline of a Theory of Orientalism. In Bryan S. Turner, *Orientalism: Early Sources. Volume I. Readings in Orientalism*, 1–31. London: Routledge.

Twain, Mark [Samuel Clemens]

    1894   *Tom Sawyer Abroad*. New York: Charles L. Webster.

    1966[1869]   *The Innocents Abroad, or, The New Pilgrim's Progress*. New York: Signet.

Ueckmann, Natasche

    2001   *Frauen und Orientalismus*. Stuttgart: J. B. Metzler.

Uraybi, Muhammad Yasin

    1991   *al-Istishraq wa-taghrib al-ʿaql al-ta'rikhi al-ʿArabi*. 2 volumes. Rabat: al-Majlis al-Qawmi li-al-Thaqafa al-ʿArabiyya.

Urbinati, Nadia

    1998   The Souths of Antonio Gramsci and the Concept of Hegemony. In Jane Schneider, editor, *Italy's "Southern Question": Orientalism in One Country*, 135–156. Oxford: Berg.

Valensi, Lucette

    1993   *The Birth of the Despot: Venice and the Sublime Porte*. Translated by Arthur Denner. Ithaca, NY: Cornell University Press.

van der Veer, Peter

    1993   The Foreign Hand: Orientalist Discourse in Sociology and Communalism. In Breckenridge and van der Veer, editors, 1993, 23–44.

    2001   *Imperial Encounters: Religion and Modernity in India and Britain*. Princeton, NJ: Princeton University Press.

    2003   Edward Said in the Netherlands. *ISIM Newsletter* 13:33.

Van Keuren, D. K.

    1980   Review of Edward W. Said, *Orientalism*. *Isis* 71(258):502.

van Nieuwenhuijze, C. A. O.

    1979   Palestinian Politician-Scholar Hits Back Hard. *Bibliotheca Orientalis* 36(1–2): 10–16. [review of *Orientalism*]

Varadharajan, Asha

    1995   *Exotic Parodies: Subjectivity in Adorno, Said, and Spivak*. Minneapolis: University of Minnesota Press.

Varisco, Daniel Martin

    1982a   "The Adaptive Dynamics of Water Allocation in al-Ahjur, Yemen Arab

Republic." Ph.D. dissertation, Department of Anthropology, University of Pennsylvania.

1982b   Despotic Orientalism and Anthropological Discourse. *MERA Forum* 5(4):8–10.

1994   *Medieval Agriculture and Islamic Science: The Almanac of a Yemeni Sultan.* Seattle: University of Washington Press.

1995   Metaphors and Sacred History: The Genealogy of Muhammad and the Arab "Tribe." *Anthropological Quarterly* 68(3):139–156.

2001   Slamming Islam: Participant Webservation with a Web of Meanings to Boot. *Working Papers from the MES.* Electronic document, www.aaanet.org/mes/lectvar1.htm, accessed June 2002.

2002   The Archaeologist's Spade and the Apologist's Stacked Deck: The Near East through Conservative Christian Bibliolatry. In Abbas Amanat and Magnus T. Bernhardsson, editors, *The United States and the Middle East: Cultural Encounters,* 57–113. New Haven, CT: Yale Center for International and Area Studies.

2004   Reading Against Culture in Edward Said's *Culture and Imperialism. Culture, Theory and Critique* 45(2):93–112.

2005   *Islam Obscured: The Rhetoric of Anthropological Representation.* New York: Palgrave.

Vasunia, Phiroze

2001   *The Gift of the Nile: Hellenizing Egypt from Aeschylus to Alexander.* Berkeley: University of California Press.

2003   Hellenism and Empire: Reading Edward Said. *Parallax* 9/4:88–97.

Vatikiotis, P. J., editor

1972   *Revolution in the Middle East, and Other Case Studies.* Totowa, NJ: Rowman and Littlefield.

Vaughan, Dorothy

1954   *Europe and the Turk: A Pattern of Alliances, 1350–1700.* Liverpool: Liverpool University Press.

Veit, Walter

2002   Goethe's Fantasies about the Orient. *Eighteenth-Century Life* 26(3):164–180.

Venn, Couze

2000   *Occidentalism: Modernity and Subjectivity.* London: Sage.

Vercellin, Giorgio

1991   Fine della storia, storia orientale e orientalistica. *Studi Storici: Rivista trimestrale dell'Istituto Gramsci* 32(1):97–110.

Vincent, John

1990   *Disraeli.* Oxford: Oxford University Press.

Viswanathan, Gauri, editor

2001   *Power, Politics, and Culture: Interviews with Edward Said.* New York: Pantheon.

Vitkus, Daniel J.

2001   Trafficking with the Turk: English Travelers in the Ottoman Empire During the Early Seventeenth Century. In Kamps and Singh, editors, 2001, 35–52.

Voltaire

    1964   *Mahomet the Prophet or Fanaticism*. Translated by Robert L. Myers. New York:

    [1740] Frederick Ungar.

    1971   *Philosophical Dictionary*. Edited and translated by Theodore Besterman. Bal-

    [1764] timore, MD: Penguin.

    1991   *Candide*. New York: Dover.

    [1759]

von Däniken, Erich

    1971   *Chariots of the Gods?* New York: Bantam.

Waardenburg, Jacques

    1963   *L'Islam dans le miroir de l'Occident*. The Hague: Mouton.

    1973   Changes of Perspective in Islamic Studies over the Last Decade. *Humaniora Islamica* 1:247–60.

    1992   Mustashrikun. In *The Encyclopaedia of Islam*, New Edition, 7:735–753. Leiden: Brill.

    1997a The Study of Islam in Dutch Scholarship. In Nanji, editor, 1997, 68–94.

    1997b The Study of Islam in German Scholarship. In Nanji, editor, 1997, 1–32.

Wahba, Magdi

    1989   An Anger Observed. *Journal of Arabic Literature* 20:187–199.

Wahi, Tripta

    1996   Orientalism: A Critique. *Revolutionary Democracy* 2:1, April. Electronic document, http://revolutionarydemocracy.org/rdv2n1/orient.htm, accessed February 2006.

Walia, Shelley

    2001   *Edward Said and the Writing of History*. Cambridge: Icon.

Wall, Geoffrey

    2002   *Flaubert, a Life*. New York: Farrar, Straus, and Giroux.

Walpole, Horace

    1982[1785]   *Hieroglyphic Tales*. Los Angeles: University of California, Los Angeles.

Walzer, Michael

    1985   *Exodus and Revolution*. New York: Basic.

Wassil, Gregory

    2000   Keat's Orientalism. *Studies in Romanticism* 39:419–447.

Watkins, Daniel P.

    1987   *Social Relations in Byron's Eastern Tales*. Rutherford, NJ: Fairleigh Dickinson University Press.

Watson, William E.

    2003   *Tricolor and Crescent: France and the Islamic World*. Westport, CT: Prager.

Watt, Katherine

    2002   Thomas Walker Arnold and the Re-evaluation of Islam, 1864–1930. *Modern Asian Studies* 36:1:1–98.

Watt, W. Montgomery

    1972   *The Influence of Islam on Medieval Europe*. Edinburgh: Edinburgh University Press.

Webber, Sabra J.

    1997   Middle East Studies and Subaltern Studies. *MESA Bulletin* 31(1):11–16.

Weeks, Emily M.

    1998   About Face: Sir David Wilkie's Portrait of Mehemet Ali, Pasha of Egypt. In Codell and Macleod, editors, 1998, 46–62.

Weiner, Justus Reid

    1999   "My Beautiful Old House" and Other Fabrications by Edward Said. *Commentary* 108(2):23–31.

Weiss, Harold

    1989   The Genealogy of Justice and the Justice of Genealogy: Chomsky and Said vs. Foucault and Bové. *Philosophy Today* 33:73–94.

Wells, H. G.

    1931[1920]   *The New and Revised Outline of History.* Garden City, NY: Garden City Publishing.

Whalen-Bridge, John

    2001   Orientalism, Politics and Literature. *The Asian Journal of Social Sciences* 129(2):193–204.

Whately, Richard

    1958[1819]   Historic Doubts Relative to Napoleon Buonaparte. In Houston Peterson, editor, *Essays in Philosophy*, 143–171. New York: Washington Square Press.

White, Hayden

    1987   *The Content of the Form: Narrative Discourse and Historical Representation.* Baltimore, MD: Johns Hopkins University Press.

White, Jon Manchip

    1973   Introduction to the Dover Edition. In Lane 1973, v–xiv.

Wicke, Jennifer, and Michael Sprinker

    1992   Interview with Edward Said. In Sprinker 1992, 221–264.

Wickens, G. M.

    1971   *Lalla Rookh* and the Romantic Tradition of Islamic Literature in English. *Yearbook of Comparative and General Literature* 20:61–66.

    1985–86   Western Scholarship on the Middle East. *Comparative Civilizations Review* 13–14:62–72.

Wielandt, Rotraud

    1980   *Das Bild der Europäer in der Modernen Arabischen Erzähl- und Theaterliteratur.* Beiruter Texte und Studien, 23. Wiesbaden: Franz Steiner.

Wilde, Oscar

    1907   *Intensions.* New York: Brentano's.

Williams, Patrick, editor

    2001   *Edward Said.* 4 volumes. London: Sage.

Williams, Patrick, and Laura Chrisman, editors

    1994   *Colonial Discourse and Postcolonial Theory: A Reader.* New York: Columbia University Press.

Williams, Raymond
    1976   *Keywords*. New York: Oxford University Press.
Wilson, A. Leslie
    1964   *A Mythical Image: The Ideal of India in German Romanticism*. Durham, NC:
            Duke University Press.
Wilson, Ernest J. III
    1981   Orientalism: A Black Perspective. *Journal of Palestine Studies* 10(2):59–69.
            [review of *Orientalism*]
Wilson, George M.
    1994   Edward Said on Contrapuntal Reading. *Philosophy and Literature* 18:265–273.
Winder, Richard Bayly
    1981   Review of *Orientalism*. *Middle East Journal* 35(4):615–619.
Windschuttle, Keith
    1999   Review of *Orientalism*. *The New Criterion* 17(5):30–38.
Winters, Christopher, editor
    1991   *International Dictionary of Anthropologists*. New York: Garland.
Wittfogel, Karl
    1957   *Oriental Despotism*. New Haven, CT: Yale University Press.
Wolf, Margery
    1992   *A Thrice-Told Tale: Feminism, Postmodernism, and Ethnographic Responsibil-
            ity*. Stanford, CA: Stanford University Press.
Wolf, Mary Ellen
    1994   Rethinking the Radical West: Khatibi and Deconstruction. *L'Esprit Créateur*
            34(2):58–68.
Wolfe, Patrick
    1997   History and Imperialism: A Century of Theory, from Marx to Postcolonial-
            ism. *American Historical Review* 102(2):388–420.
Woodcock, George
    1980   The Challenge of the Other. *Queen's Quarterly* 87(2):298–304. [review of *Ori-
            entalism*]
Woodward, Mark
    1996   Introduction. Talking across Paradigms: Indonesia, Islam, and Orientalism.
            In Mark R. Woodward, editor, *Toward a New Paradigm: Recent Developments
            in Indonesian Islamic Thought*, 1–45. Tempe: Arizona State University, Pro-
            gram for Southeast Asian Studies.
Worcester, Joseph E.
    1874   *A Comprehensive Dictionary of the English Language*. Boston: Brewer and
            Tileston.
Worrell, William H.
    1919   An Account of Schools for Living Oriental Languages Established in Europe.
            Journal of the American Oriental Society 39:189–195.
Xenophon
    1998   *Anabasis*. Translated by C. L. Brownson and John Dillery. Cambridge, MA:
            Harvard University Press.

Yacoubi, Youssef
> 2005   Edward Said, Eqbal Ahmad, and Salman Rushdie: Resisting the Ambivalence of Postcolonial Theory. *Alif* 25:193–218.

Yeats, William Butler
> 1956   *The Collected Poems of W. B. Yeats*. New York: Macmillan.

Yeazell, Ruth Bernard
> 2000   *Harems of the Mind: Passages of Western Art and Literature*. New Haven, CT: Yale University Press.

Yegenoglu, Meyda
> 1998   *Colonial Fantasies: Towards a Feminist Reading of Orientalism*. Cambridge: Cambridge University Press.

Yeghiayan, Eddie, compiler
> 2001   Edward W. Said: A Bibliography. Electronic document, http://sun3.lib.uci.edu/~scctr/Wellek/said/index.html, accessed June 2002.

Yoshihara, Mari
> 2003   *Embracing the East. White Women and American Orientalism*. Oxford: Oxford University Press.

Young, Robert
> 1990   *White Mythologies: Writing History and the West*. London: Routledge.
> 1995   *Colonial Desire: Hybridity in Theory, Culture and Race*. London: Routledge.
> 2001   *Postcolonialism: An Historical Introduction*. Oxford: Blackwell.

Yusuf-Ali, Abdullah
> 1912   Goethe's Orientalism. *Publications of the English Goethe Society* 15:30–48.

Zammito, John H.
> 2002   *Kant, Herder, and the Birth of Anthropology*. Chicago: University of Chicago Press.

Zayur, ʿAli
> 1977   *At-Tahlil al-nafsi li-al-dhat al-ʿArabiya*. Beirut: Dar al-Taliʿa.

Zonana, Joyce
> 1993   The Sultan and the Slave: Feminist Orientalism and the Structure of *Jane Eyre*. *Signs* 18(3):592–617.

Index

Arnold, Thomas, 106, 352*n*76

art, 23–27, 81, 125, 165–67, 172, 175,
223, 316*n*95, 324*nn*225–26, 361*n*193,
379–80*n*447, 380*n*448, 380*nn*450–51,
380*nn*454–56. *See also* odalisque

Aryan Myth, 130, 245, 395*n*682

Asad, Mohammed, 230

Asad, Talal, 43, 144, 279, 286, 369*n*298

Asia, 52–53, 56, 61, 63–64, 69, 98, 108,
137

Asiatic Society of Bengal, 88, 363*n*214

Asín Palacios, Miguel, 346*n*329

Auerbach, Erich, 37, 41, 284–85, 327*n*33,
365*n*241, 392*n*637, 419*n*257

Austen, Jane, 153–54, 203–6, 314*n*59,
375*n*378, 393*n*649, 393*nn*654–56

Averroes, 118, 218, 357*n*147

Azhar, al-, 43, 124, 373*n*348

'Azm, Sadiq Jalal al-, 62, 64, 174, 235,
384*n*508, 385*n*517

Bakhtin, Mikhail, 20, 321*n*196

Balfour, Lord Arthur James, 101, 132,
350*n*41, 375*n*384

Balzac, Honoré de, 197, 245, 355*n*113

Barenboim, Daniel, 38, 327*n*36

Barthes, Roland, 18, 43, 199–200, 243,
391*n*631, 391*n*634

Baudelaire, Charles, 161, 197

Beauvoir, Simone de, 16, 327*n*33

Beckford, William, 81, 170–72, 382*n*485,
383*n*487, 393*n*652, 396*n*705

Bedouin, 27, 70, 72, 108, 117, 131, 194,
217, 228, 251, 391*n*616, 400*n*760

Bedwell, William, 343*n*294, 360*n*186

Beirut, xii, xiv, 216, 285, 308*n*16

Bell, Gertrude, 106, 156, 162, 376*n*393

Berger, Morroe, 32, 101

Berlin, Sir Isaiah, 130–31, 350*n*48,
364*n*230

Bernal, Martin, x, 356*n*132, 378*n*421,
417*n*215

Bernard of Clairvaux, 84

Bernhardt, Sarah, 381*n*469

Berque, Jacques, 43, 280–82, 370*n*312,
385*n*520

Bhabha, Homi Jehangir, 9–10, 14, 82,
96, 256–58, 286, 312*n*37, 312*n*39,
317*n*133, 379*n*442, 409*n*103

Bible, 186, 390*n*611, 396*n*708; bibliolatry, 66, 226, 244; King James Version, 73, 75, 297; Latin, 77; literary
criticism, 114–15, 182, 221

Bibliothèque orientale (d'Herbelot), 80,
171, 340*n*248

Bin Laden, Osama, 274, 308*n*17

binary, 47–48, 50–52, 116, 133–34,
147, 160, 195, 250, 257, 290, 302–3,
331*n*97, 359*n*166

Bitar, Nadim al-, 90, 252, 352*n*66,
384*n*509

Blount, Sir Henry, 180, 224, 386*n*544

Blunt, Lady Anne, 228, 293, 373*nn*342–43,
400*n*760

Blunt, Wilfrid Scawen, 228–29, 293,
395*n*688, 400*n*757

Boulainvillier, Henri de, 180, 387*n*546

Brockelmann, Carl, 89, 109, 329*n*59

Brombert, Victor, 96, 262, 388*n*569

Browne, Edward G., 106–8, 232, 352*n*76,
353*n*82, 388*n*568

Browne, Henriette, 166

Buddhism, 79, 371*n*327, 391*n*626

Bulliet, Richard, 42, 296, 318*n*140

Burckhardt, John Louis, 179, 225,
326*n*18

Burton, Lady Isabel, 161, 378*n*426,
381*n*464, 394*n*679

Burton, Sir Richard Francis, 33,
102, 126, 129, 138, 162–64, 167,
196, 225, 229, 283, 293, 350*n*48,
354*n*103, 360*n*186, 379*n*432,
379*n*434, 379*n*436, 381*n*464, 390*n*611,
394*n*663

Butterfield, Herbert, 119–20

Byron, Lord George Gordon, 80, 102,
218, 220–21, 229, 311*n*28, 382*n*485,
394*n*663, 397*n*720, 397*n*722

Caetani, Leone, 91, 229–30, 346n332

Cahen, Claude, 32, 43, 120, 347n344, 348n8

Cairo, 35, 37–38, 53, 117, 124, 152, 228, 230, 285, 326n20, 359n166, 360n185, 368n283, 373n348

Cambridge History of Islam, 120, 357n141, 369n298, 416n207

camel, 27, 270–71, 412n159

Camus, Albert, 415n191

Candide (Voltaire), 23–24, 323n222

Carioca, Tahia, 207

Carlyle, Thomas, 192, 362n205

Carpenter, Edward, 164, 381n465

Carthage, 160–61, 377n408, 382n482

Cartwright, John, 75, 174

catachresis, 103, 351n55, 362n206

Cervantes, Miguel de, 23, 174, 346n329

Césaire, Aimé, 144–45, 228, 369n298, 369n301

Chanson de Roland, 74, 203, 338n217

Chariots of the Gods (von Däniken), 44

charmeur des serpentes, Le (Gérôme), 24–25, 171

charmeur de vipères, Le (Dinet), 26

Chateaubriand, François-René, Vis-comte de, 126, 159, 361n195, 392n634

Chaucer, 122

China, 53, 55, 66, 68, 70, 87, 148, 189, 197–98, 229, 272, 328n50

Christ, Jesus, 27, 31, 66, 73, 76, 103, 194, 227, 244, 338n221, 390n613, 412n160

Christianity: antichrist, 74–76, 85, 337n203, 338n225, 339nn226–27; apocalypse, 73, 75, 339n228, 359n170, 390n613, 412n160; Arab, 16, 70–71, 74, 215; Catholicism, 16, 83, 123, 185–86, 190–91, 195, 266, 359n171, 386n544, 389n594; "civi-lization," 295, 382n485; Council of Vienna, 83; Eucharist, 192; Jesuits, 70, 88, 151, 180–81, 185, 192; mission-aries, 56, 130, 148, 226, 363n215,

399n748; Orthodox, 52, 81, 337n208, 364n231; pilgrimage, 31, 66, 211–13, 227; Protestants, 37, 77, 123, 190, 193, 195, 224, 226, 266; Quaker, 86, 190, 393n651; theology, 48, 284. *See also* Crusades; Islam: bias against, conversion to

"clash of civilizations," 295–96, 421n303

class, 48, 136–37, 170, 172–74, 281, 332n125, 383n493, 385n511

Clifford, James, 10, 45, 92, 96, 256

Colebrook, Henry Thomas, 129

Coleridge, Samuel Taylor, 218, 221–22, 393n651

colonialism, 5, 9, 19, 21, 56, 60–61, 79, 81, 92, 104, 132, 134, 144, 147, 150, 176, 203, 208, 229, 258, 365n236, 367n280, 369n298, 373n342, 384n502, 384n507, 385n523

Columbian Exposition (1893), 157, 167

communism, 5, 53, 132, 154, 176, 260, 266, 272, 346n334

Conrad, Joseph, 39, 119, 154, 206, 230

contrapuntal reading, 26, 117, 126, 160, 163, 203–7, 211, 271, 314n59, 360n186, 393nn645–46, 393n649, 394n661

Covering Islam (Said), xiv, 241, 308n16, 348n13

Creighton, Colonel, 102

Cromer, Lord Evelyn Baring, 101–2, 132, 228, 350n42

Crusades, 67, 72, 74–76, 84–85, 122, 183, 208, 337n208, 338n219, 383n498, 412n159

Culture and Imperialism (Said), 16, 51, 129, 132, 139–40, 145, 153, 175, 202–3, 207–8, 255, 283, 287, 292, 314n58, 353n95, 360n182, 362n206, 368n294, 369n301, 370n312, 371n318, 373n342, 375n377, 383n493

Curzon, Lord George Nathaniel, 68, 102, 173, 223, 230, 276, 350n45

376nn405–6, 377nn408–9, 377n411,
377nn414–15, 378n420, 381n463,
382n484, 390n611, 391n634, 394n663,
399n744
Foucault, Michel, 7, 18–21, 41, 45,
49–50, 54, 57, 98, 103, 112–13, 119,
122, 152, 169, 231, 239, 242, 252–59,
262–63, 266, 286, 311n26, 322n207,
333n129, 351n54, 372n337, 385n515,
392n635, 406n68, 407n81, 407n87,
409n107
Frankenstein (Shelley), 210
Freud, Sigmund, 17, 257, 297, 356n123,
408n101
Fromentin, Eugène, 166, 380n458

Gabrieli, Francesco, 43, 176
Gadamer, Hans-Georg, 20, 321n195
Gates, Henry Louis, Jr., 9–10, 258,
314n59, 341n268
Gautier, Théophile, 218, 392n634
Geertz, Clifford, 280, 282, 329n56,
418n241
Gellner, Ernest, 43, 329n56, 384n502,
385n511, 392n638
Gérôme, Jean-Léon, 24–25, 167, 172–73,
380n454
Gibb, Sir Hamilton A. R., 45, 77, 153,
170, 298–99, 325n8, 348n12, 350n48,
354n103
Gibbon, Edward, 171
Gide, André, 154
Gilsenan, Michael, 43, 267, 273, 309n29,
311n22, 329n56, 384n509
Gladstone, William Ewart, 228, 395n695
Gobineau, Joseph-Arthur, Comte de, 43,
106, 136, 347n344, 388n566, 421n307
Goethe, Johann Wolfgang von, 80,
175, 197, 218–20, 232, 249, 332n114,
394n663, 396nn708–9, 397n712,
397n715, 397n717–18
Goldziher, Ignaz, 43, 89, 91, 109, 182–
83, 328n53, 355n115
Gramsci, Antonio, 41, 54, 57, 103,

145–46, 169, 176, 255, 260–61,
266, 357n152, 385n515, 385n518,
410nn120–23
Greece: ancient, 63–65, 69, 81, 114, 130,
207, 275, 334n157, 334n162, 362n204,
377n409; resistance to Ottomans,
221
Grunebaum, Gustave von, 145, 285,
369n303, 371n325

Halliday, Fred, xiii, 22, 81, 137, 231
Hamady, Sania, 44, 108–11, 156, 231
Hamdi Bey, Osman, 167
Hamilton, Edith, 47, 65
Hammer-Purgstall, Josef von, 88, 220,
396nn708–9
Hanafi, Hasan, 152, 265, 374n369
Handbuch der Orientalistik, 121,
357n148
harem, 33–34, 154, 156–57, 160, 165–69,
184, 186–89, 193, 210, 221, 358n161,
376n397, 380n450, 383n488, 388n577,
389n579, 398n727
Haykel, Muhammad, 107, 150, 375n372
Hayy ibn Yaqzan (Ibn Tufayl), 86
Hebrew language, 42, 114, 355n112,
356n126
Hegel, Georg Wilhelm Friedrich, 68–69,
87, 120, 297
hegemony, 7, 21, 55, 57, 119, 146, 149,
153, 169, 181, 229, 255, 260–61, 264,
268, 291, 301, 357n152, 410n120,
411n126, 411n128
Herbelot, Barthélemy d', 80, 171, 222
Herder, Johann Gottfried von, 67,
88, 130–31, 297, 363n224, 364n225,
364nn229–31, 396n709, 397n715,
397n718
Herodotus, 64–65, 121, 243, 301, 334n151
Hinduism, 79, 162, 181, 222, 231, 295,
297, 362n204, 372n330
historiography, 8, 54, 119–23, 140, 145,
205, 220, 237, 277, 282, 322n211,
325n9

Jones, Sir William, 88, 127–28, 130, 146, 148, 152, 182, 204, 221–22, 246, 297, 350n48, 361n202, 362–63n214, 363n219, 363n222

Judaism: biblical history, 70; conversion from, 191, 214; England, 208–9, 214–15; female body, 166; and Islam, 75; Kurdish, 109; Orthodox, 266. *See also* anti-Semitism; Zionism

Keats, John, 218, 221

Kemal, Mustapha (Ataturk), 68, 133, 335n173

Kerr, Malcolm, xiv, 43, 149, 251

Khan, Mirza Abul Hassan, 164

Khan, Sayyed Ahmad, 371n330

Kharbutli, ʿAli Husni, al-, 151

Khatami, President Mohammad, 220

Khatibi, ʿAbd al-Kabir al-, 144, 368n295, 406n68

Khomeini, Ayatollah, 265, 320n179, 338n225

Kim (Kipling), 208–9, 231

Kinglake, Alexander, 225–26, 399n745

Kipling, Rudyard, 53, 102, 107, 154, 156, 208, 219, 231, 334n147, 350n50, 375n378

Kitchener, Lord Horatio Herbert, 102, 229

Kopf, David, 16, 88, 121, 127, 139, 152, 253, 315n65, 358n156

Kramer, Martin, xiii–xiv

Kuchuk Hanem, 155, 158–59, 161, 167, 333n130, 377n416

Lacan, Jacques, 57, 286, 233n129

Lalla Rookh (Moore), 183, 222–24, 398nn732–33

Lamartine, Alphonse de, 103, 194, 351n52, 376n393

Lammens, Henri, 151, 374n356

Lane, Edward, 33–36, 111, 114, 126–27, 138–39, 151–53, 163, 225, 231, 246, 293, 325n14, 325n17, 326n20, 354n103,

366n250, 373n347, 375n373, 376n397, 379n435, 394n663

Langland, William, 190

Laroui, Abdallah, 144–46, 260, 279, 294, 369n299, 369n302

Latin, 64, 73, 76–77, 83–86, 130, 277–78, 340n249, 363n219

Lawrence, Thomas Edward, 106, 117, 156, 201, 326n28, 350n46, 354n103, 356n126, 381n462

Le Bon, Gustave, 183, 373n347, 388n566

Lebanon, xiv, xvi, 18, 60, 109, 216, 310n12

Lettres persanes (Montesquieu), 183–89, 389n580

Lévi, Sylvain, 198, 591n626

Levi della Vida, Giorgio, 43, 346n332

Lewis, Bernard, 4, 6, 9, 19, 21–22, 32, 45, 96, 105, 108, 119, 173, 176, 199, 230–31, 267–77, 279, 287, 291, 295, 323n216, 324n3, 328n46, 328n52, 348n12, 354n103, 413n179, 413n181, 414n185, 414n188, 415n204, 416nn205–8, 416nn210–15

Lewis, John Frederick, 166, 380n451

literary criticism, 4, 7, 8, 11–12, 121–22, 158, 201, 240, 247, 249, 263, 268, 279, 281–82, 300, 310n10, 311n30

Loti, Pierre, 198

Luther, Martin, 123, 174, 337n203, 343n283, 359n170, 403n34

Lyall, Sir Alfred Comyn, 129, 350n48

Lyall, Sir Charles James, 106, 232, 350n48

Lyotard, François, 18, 286, 313n41, 326n22

Macaulay, Lord Thomas Babington, 81, 127–30, 361–62nn204–6, 362n211, 366n260

Machiavelli, Niccolo, 190, 288, 388n572

"Mahomet," 74, 77

Mahomet, ou le fanatisme (Voltaire), 191–92, 203, 323n222

Makdisi, George, 43, 322n211, 328n54

Orient: absence, 55, 141, 149, 290, 367n274, 372n341; despotism, 186, 216–18, 340n247, 388n572, 408n99; etymology, 64–65; Far East, 42, 53, 60; feminine, 27, 58, 158, 160, 381n471, 401n780; imaginary, xii, xvi, 5, 81, 89, 103, 125, 142, 148, 172, 199, 222, 258, 334n154, 392n635, 396n707; invention of, 31, 61, 65, 85, 302, 304; myth of, 52, 98, 180; "Near Orient," 53, 61, 65, 148, 220; real, xvi, 17, 60, 69, 122, 132, 141, 178, 202, 215, 231, 238, 241–42, 281, 290–91, 294, 300, 302–3, 359n163; romantic, 67, 219, 232; surrogate, 54

Orientalism: academic, 5, 8, 44, 57, 59, 83, 87, 201, 222, 273, 290–91, 324n3; 342n279, 342n286, 344n313; American, 48–49, 145, 347n337; "Black Orientalism," 81, 341–42n268; Congress of Orientalists, 32, 43, 88; definition, 10, 41–62, 79–83, 275, 324n2; 325n6, 327n42, 328n48; discourse, 7, 47, 50–51, 59, 92, 99, 112, 133, 139, 156, 174, 182, 231, 241, 243, 252–59, 263–64, 268, 272, 288, 290–91, 294, 297, 381n470, 406n80, 407n88, 407n91; dogma, 51, 58, 119, 181; Dutch, 90–91, 346n328; fan magazine, 381n469; film, 5, 336n194, 393n649; French, 92, 111–12, 347n344; German, 89–90, 100, 311n29, 328n53, 340n253, 345n317, 346n327; ghosts of, 303; guild, 99, 104, 145, 156, 179, 249, 278, 298, 301; istishraq, 150–51, 341n258, 373n346; Irish, 398n739; Italian, 91, 346n332, 354n105; latent and manifest, 56–59, 136, 172, 257–58, 333n133, 356n136, 386n535; "neo-Orientalism," 81; photography, 161, 167, 336n194; Russian, 346n334, 349n17; self-critique, 22, 27, 46, 128, 167, 178–98, 228–29, 252, 395n692, 397n717; Spanish, 91, 183,

346nn329–30; style, 54; termination of term, 32, 415n198, 417n216. See also art

Orientalism (Said): Arab critique, xv, 153, 252, 263, 319n172, 319n173; essentialist, 216, 251–52, 263, 266, 281, 292–93, 404n40–41; feminist critique, 156–58, 168–69, 375n385, 382n477, 382n482; intended readers, 7–8; methodology, 7, 10, 12, 54, 247–49, 254, 279, 288, 298, 357n151, 412n162, 420n284; Muslim critique, 16, 263–64, 292; origin, 7; polemic, xv, 6, 12, 15, 20, 22–23, 39, 56, 62, 91, 97, 139, 151, 200, 231, 262, 268, 271, 273, 280, 282, 291, 300, 302, 311n16; "provocative," 12; readability, 10; representation, 21, 31, 55, 59, 142, 232, 237–43, 247, 290, 297, 358n163, 403n20; reviews of, 5, 12–16, 20–21, 23, 96–97, 139, 314n55, 315n66, 321n192, 358n155, 367n276, 404n39; rhetoric, 21, 49–50, 56–61, 96–104, 159, 233, 248, 266, 268, 331n93, 347n2, 349n27, 349n32; Said's response to critics, 15, 39, 44, 95–96, 106, 153, 266, 273, 277, 287, 358n155, 382n477, 415n200; translations, 11, 220, 314n62, 319n171; 384n509, 396n710–11; women in, 155–56

other, 21, 33, 48, 57, 91, 142, 152, 160, 168–69, 185, 190, 210, 281, 292, 299, 302, 304, 365n248, 374n363

Ottomans, 24, 55, 65, 68, 72–73, 90, 117, 123–25, 133, 157, 167, 174, 180, 189–90, 192, 217, 221, 265, 270, 274, 337n203, 340n248, 344n314, 359nn169–70, 365nn40–42, 365n248, 372n331, 386n544, 388n572, 390n604, 416n207

Owen, Roger, 21, 272, 282, 349n30, 357n142, 369n298, 370n312

"Ozymandias" (Shelley), 160, 218, 377n415

subaltern, 9, 14, 141, 149, 301, 367*nn*273–74, 422n311

Suez Canal, 89, 150, 364*n*235, 373*n*344

Syria, 148, 191, 212, 215–16, 228, 356*n*125

Tacitus, 334*n*148, 362*n*204

Tagore, Rabindranath, 369*n*299, 371*n*330, 391*n*626

Tahtawi, Rifa'a Rafi' al-, 149, 372*n*338

Talisman, The (Scott), 203, 218, 394*n*664

Tamar, 27

Tamburlaine (Marlowe), 190

Tancred (Disraeli), 203, 210–17, 299, 366*n*261

Taverner, Richard, 187

Temperament and Character of the Arabs (Hamady), 44, 108, 231

Tenniel, John, 223

Tennyson, Alfred Lord, 218

"tent and tribe," 98, 114, 348*n*16

tentation de l'Occident, La (Malroux), 178, 197

"Terminal Essay" (Burton), 162, 379*n*434

terrorism, xii, 9, 18, 38, 76, 269, 295, 308*n*16

Thackeray, William Makepeace, 193–94, 390*n*609

Thapar, Romila, 144, 369*n*298

Thévenot, Jean de, 231, 400*n*7, 401*n*777

Thomas, Nicholas, 7, 20, 23, 104

Thompson, William, 226

Thucydides, 362*n*204

Tibawi, Abdul-Latif, 119, 144, 153, 369*n*298, 369*n*299, 374*n*372, 374*n*374

Tizini, Tayyib, 144

Tolstoy, Leo, 197

Tom Sawyer Abroad (Twain), 196

Tours, Battle of, 295

Toynbee, Arnold, 18, 120, 180, 295, 297, 357*n*140

travel literature, 34, 156, 158, 162, 194,

225–28, 233, 368*n*296, 375*nn*387–88, 378*n*430, 383*n*500

Travels in Arabia Deserta (Doughty), 224

Travels of Sir John Mandeville, The, 75, 122, 226, 336*n*185

"troubadour," 388*n*567

True Nature of Imposture, The (Prideaux), 389*n*596

truth, xvi, 21, 45, 98, 205, 243, 254, 292–93, 302, 349*n*22, 402*n*14

"truth to power," xiii, 121, 163, 241, 279, 293

"Turk," 72–73, 190, 337*n*198, 365*n*240

Turkey, 24, 68, 123, 133, 272, 376*n*399

Turner, Bryan S., xvi, 7, 19, 104, 235, 259

Twain, Mark (Samuel Clemens), 24, 193–96, 225–26, 390*n*611, 391*n*617, 391*n*620

Umm Kulthum, 207, 394*n*659

Unigenitus, 186

Vanity Fair (Thackeray), 390*n*609, 393*n*649

Vathek (Beckford), 170–71, 382*n*485

Vatikiotis, P. J., 271–72

Venerable Bede, 73

Verdi, Giuseppe, 207

Vernet, Emile-Jean-Horace, 27

Vico, Giambattista, 16, 18, 41, 130, 160, 266, 279, 286, 288, 297, 327*n*33, 418*n*235

Virgil, 74, 334*n*148, 341*n*258

Voltaire, François Marie Arouet, 23–24, 105, 130, 171, 180, 185, 191–92, 363*n*215

Waardenburg, Jacques, 106, 182

Walpole, Horace, 189, 388*n*577

Walzer, Michael, 276–77

Watt, W. Montgomery, 43, 112, 329*n*59, 340*n*243, 385*n*513

Weber, Max, 17, 19

Wellhausen, Julius, 43, 91, 136, 373*n*347

Wells, H. G., 76

Wesley, John, 344*n*301

West, 49, 52, 60–61, 82, 143, 148, 153, 198, 224, 226, 228, 241, 265–66, 272, 284, 290, 295–96, 335*n*162, 356*n*129, 372*n*339, 374*n*362, 376*n*402

Westermarck, Edward, 346*n*336

Westöstlicher Diwan (Goethe), 203, 219–20, 396*n*708

White, Hayden, 18

Wieseltier, Leon, 269, 309*n*5

Wilberforce, William, 363*n*215

Wilde, Oscar, 354*n*108, 392*n*635

Wilkens, Charles, 87

Wilkie, Sir David, 361*n*193

Williams, Raymond, 18, 41, 176

Wittfogel, Karl, 340*n*247

"wog," xiii, 5, 72, 280, 337*n*197

women: European, 34, 164–65, 186, 192, 388–89*n*578; Muslim, 144, 157, 168, 186–87, 190, 381*n*472, 389*n*579; travelers, 156–57

Wordsworth, William, 217–18, 221

World, the Text, and the Critic, The (Said), 254–55, 280, 286, 318*n*143, 320*n*183, 330*n*70, 402*n*8

World Trade Center, xii, 76, 264

World War I, 90, 133, 299, 365*nn*241–42, 376*n*393

World War II, 5, 53, 56, 68, 72, 77, 134–35, 150, 274, 283, 299, 352*n*74, 376*n*401

Wycliffe, John, 77

Yeats, William Butler, 350*n*50

Yemen, 22, 305, 322*n*210, 334*n*156, 360*n*181

Young, Robert, 5, 14, 304, 313*n*47

Zionism, 9, 105–6, 110, 122, 138, 266, 269, 274, 276–77, 284, 350*n*45, 366*n*264, 391*n*626